Practical Arduino

Cool Projects for Open Source Hardware

Jonathan Oxer
Hugh Blemings

Apress®

Practical Arduino: Cool Projects for Open Source Hardware

ISBN-13 (pbk): 978-1-4302-2477-8

ISBN-13 (electronic): 978-1-4302-2478-5

Printed and bound in the United States of America 9 8 7 6 5 4

Cover picture of Arduino Duemilanove used with permission of SparkFun Electronics.

Distributed to the book trade worldwide by Springer+Business Media, LLC, 233 Spring Street, 6th Floor, New York, NY 10013. Phone 1-800-SPRINGER, fax (201) 348-4505, e-mail `orders-ny@springer-sbm.com`, or visit `www.springeronline.com`.

For information on translations, please e-mail `rights@apress.com`, or visit `www.apress.com`.

Apress and friends of ED books may be purchased in bulk for academic, corporate, or promotional use. eBook versions and licenses are also available for most titles. For more information, reference our Special Bulk Sales–eBook Licensing web page at `www.apress.com/info/bulksales`.

The source code for this book is available to readers at `www.apress.com`.

For everyone who looks at the everyday objects around them and sees the potential of what they could become...

For all those in the Free & Open Source Software/Hardware Communities that create the tools to help realise those potentials.

Contents at a Glance

Contents

About the Authors

Jonathan Oxer, who has been labeled "Australia's Geekiest Man," has been hacking on both hardware and software since he was a little child. He is a former President of Linux Australia, and founder and technical director of Internet Vision Technologies. He is author of a number of books including *How to Build a Website and Stay Sane, Ubuntu Hacks,* and *Quickstart Guide to Google AdWords.*

Oxer is set to host an upcoming TV show called *SuperHouse* (`www.superhouse.tv`), which features high-tech home renovations, open source automation systems, and domestic hardware hacking. He has appeared on top-rating TV shows and been interviewed on dozens of radio stations about his home-automation system. He was technical supervisor for the first season of the reality TV show *The Phone,* has connected his car to the Internet for `www.geekmyride.org`, and has even been surgically implanted with an RFID chip. Oxer is also a member of the core team of Lunar Numbat (`www.lunarnumbat.org`), an Australian group working with the European team White Label Space (`www.whitelabelspace.com`) on an unmanned moon mission for the Google Lunar X-Prize.

Hugh Blemings took a radio apart when he was about eight years old and never recovered. From this start and an interest in ham radio, an early career in hardware and embedded software development easily followed, back when 68HC11s were the latest and greatest. Blemings has been working on Free Software since the mid 1990s for fun, and in a (still fun!) professional capacity since 1999. He was co-author of the gnokii project and developed kernel device drivers for the Keyspan USB-serial adaptors.

Blemings worked at IBM's Linux Technology Centre as a open source hacker in the Canberra-based OzLabs team for just shy of eight years doing everything from first-line management to Linux kernel porting for embedded PowerPC platforms.

He now works on Ubuntu Linux at Canonical in the kernel team, but remains firmly of the view that any day that involves a soldering iron, a 'scope, and emacs is a good day.

About the Technical Reviewers

■ **Nathan Seidle** is the founder of SparkFun Electronics based in Boulder, Colorado. When he's not building large blinky things for BurningMan, Nathan designs development tools to enable users to build their wild imaginations.

■ **Andy Gelme** is a distributed systems designer, currently working for Geekscape in Melbourne, Australia. Throughout his career, he has enjoyed playing at the extremes of the computing landscape, from networks of embedded microprocessors to supercomputers. His current focus is on software and hardware development based around the Internet of Things, in particular the Aiko platform. He is also a co-founder of the Connected Community HackerSpace (Melbourne).

■ **Thomas Sprinkmeier** graduated from the University of South Australia in 1992 with a degree in electronics engineering. It was there that he was seduced by PCs early in his first year. He was intrigued by "free as in beer" about a decade ago, and subverted by "free as in speech" soon after. Thomas is a recovering sysadmin.

■ **Trent Lloyd** lives in Perth, Australia, and works as MySQL Technical Support Engineer for Sun Microsystems. He is also the director and lead developer for Web in a Box. In addition, he is co-author of the Avahi project, an amateur poker player, and a *Star Trek* fan.

■ **Scott Penrose** is a full-time developer in Linux. He is the principal architect at myinternet Limited and the owner of Digital Dimensions. He lives with his wife Amanda and his beautiful daughter Teha in Melbourne, Australia.

■ **Marc Alexander** is an embedded electronics engineer, programmer, and gadget-head. He has worked on projects from the Apple Newton as well as another favorite area—real-time control and engine-management systems, including the Wolf3D and Bike Interceptor. Alexander does automotive and consumer electronics design and loves devices that "just work," hiding the thorough development underneath.

■ **Philip Lindsay** has a particular interest in the intersection of software, hardware, craft, and art. He has integrated network and USB technologies into the Arduino ecosystem. Occasionally, he can be heard mumbling how a prominent industry figure once called him a "troublemaker" for his Google Maps reverse engineering.

Acknowledgments

From the Authors, our thanks to:
The tech reviewers who provided us the benefit of their expertise and years of experience: Andy Gelme, Marc Alexander, Nathan Seidle, Trent Lloyd, Scott Penrose, Thomas Sprinkmeier, and Philip J Lindsay.

The core Arduino team whose vision conjured the whole Arduino ecosystem into existence: Massimo Banzi, David Cuartielles, Tom Igoe, Gianluca Martino, David Mellis, and Nicholas Zambetti.

The parts suppliers who were so helpful when it came to sourcing the random assortment of bits needed for developing these projects: SparkFun, AsyncLabs, and NKC Electronics.

Arduino developers everywhere. The amazing success of Arduino is due to the strong community that has blossomed around it. It's a beautiful thing when imaginative people have new tools placed in their hands, and the results have been inspirational to us both.

Michelle Lowman and James Markham, our editors at Apress who had to turn out of bed early to catch us in a totally different timezone on our weekly update call.

From Jon:

More thanks than I can express to Ann, Amelia, and Thomas. Their patience during this project has been amazing.

Thankyou to my parents, Michael and Jenny, who never imposed restrictions on my wild ideas and taught me that no dream is too big to pursue. And for buying me a subscription to an electronics magazine when I was just a little tacker with a burning curiosity about the way things work.

And to Hugh Blemings, my partner in crime whose patient discussions during many late-night phone calls helped me understand far more about Arduino.

From Hugh:

A profound thankyou to Lucy and Rachael for their love and support, for tolerating the smell of solder from the end room and for making the greater journey so worthwhile.

My thanks also to my parents, Brian and Rosemary Blemings, who raised Kay and I to have enquiring minds and happily answered innumerable "Why..?" questions during the formative years. My father also helped me take that first alarm clock apart :)

Thank you Jon for inviting me to be a part of this project and for kind words during some tricky periods in the writing process.

CHAPTER 1

■ ■ ■

Introduction

Phenomenon is an overused and overloaded term, but somehow it seems appropriate for Arduino—an endeavor that has caught the attention of an astonishingly wide range of people and provided opportunities for those who might otherwise have never picked up a soldering iron or written a single line of code. From dyed-in-the-wool hardware hackers to web page developers, robotics enthusiasts to installation artists, textile students to musicians: all can be found in the Arduino community. The versatility of the platform encompassing both hardware and software, combined with its inherent openness, has captured the imagination of tens of thousands of developers.

One of Arduino's many strengths is the sheer volume of information available in both printed form and on the web. Getting started is really pretty easy, as the core Arduino team intended. There are plenty of excellent introductory works already available both online and in print, so we didn't want to waste your time by providing yet another "blinking LED" tutorial. We figure that if you've gotten as far as picking up a 400+ page book about Arduino it's a good sign that you're ready for something a bit more substantial and wanting to learn more about the *why* rather than just the *how*.

We don't want you to be just a color-by-numbers painter, only able to assemble other peoples' designs by dutifully plugging in wires according to a position overlay without really understanding the meaning behind it. We want you to become a true artist, able to conceptualize, design, and assemble your own creations.

We would be terribly disappointed if all our readers just reproduced our projects exactly as presented in the book, never deviating from the script. We want you to take these projects as inspiration and examples of how to apply a variety of handy techniques and then adapt them to suit your own requirements, coming up with new ideas that put ours to shame. We also hope that you'll share your creations with us and with the world, inspiring others in turn.

So we haven't included assembly overlays, and we don't expect you to slavishly follow a series of steps to exactly reproduce what we've prototyped. Instead we've included circuit diagrams, parts lists, photos, and in-depth explanations. That may seem a little scary and the idea of learning how to read a schematic may feel overwhelming, but a little effort invested to learn this fundamental skill will pay off many times over as you progress to designing and debugging your own projects.

Thus we have consciously left material out of *Practical Arduino*. We do not, for example, cover how to set up basic software tools such as the Arduino IDE. This is for two reasons—firstly because it is described very well on the http://arduino.cc web site itself, and secondly because anything that we provide in written form here will be out of date in a few short months! Instead we focused on providing the sort of information and background explanation that you will continue to draw on for years to come.

We hope that by following through the projects in this book, assembling some for yourself and reading through the others, you will gain a number of insights into the flexibility of Arduino as a platform for taking software and hardware and linking them to the physical world around us.

Fundamentals

Arduino is a fusion of three critical elements: hardware, software, and community. To get the most out of it you need to have a basic understanding of all three elements, and for most people the biggest challenge of the three will be hardware. Before you jump into any of the projects please take the time to read through this chapter. Not only will it provide background information that the projects require, but it could save your life!

Sharing Your Work

One of the key aspects of the success of Arduino has been the community that has sprung up around it due to the open nature of the Arduino software and hardware. The software used on Arduino is entirely open source and the hardware design information (schematics, PCB layouts, etc.) have been made available under Creative Commons licenses.

In practice, this means it is easy to adapt both the software and the hardware to your needs, and then contribute what you do back into the Arduino project as a whole.

The authors are unashamed proponents of this model and would encourage you to consider making your own work available back to the Arduino community in a similar way. For software source code, please provide explicit copyright and/or licensing information in the source files. Doing so makes it possible for others to reuse your code in their own work and know that they are doing so with your permission. For that reason, wherever possible we've licensed *Practical Arduino* code under the GNU General Public License (GPL).

Similarly for hardware details, even if it's a simple schematic on a web page, it never hurts to be explicit about if/how it can be reused.

Practical Electronics for Software Developers

One of the beauties of designing projects around Arduino is that much of the low-level electronic detail is taken care of for you. For all but the most simple of projects, having some basic skill in electronics will serve you well and allow you to understand what is going on behind the scenes. To that end, we've gathered together some basic and not-so-basic things you will find helpful in the remainder of this chapter. The reference material in Chapter 16 covers some more advanced topics that may be of use as you develop more complex projects of your own. We also introduce some topics within the different project chapters. We encourage you to read through the projects for this reason, even if you're not planning on trying it out yourself.

Current, Voltage, and Power

Current, voltage, and power are interrelated and worth understanding if you're to avoid inadvertently cooking your hardware.

Voltage is measured in units of volts (V). With the symbol V, it is the measure of potential in a circuit. The oft used analogy is water - voltage then becomes the height from which the water is flowing or falling. Greater height, more potential energy from the water flow, similarly greater voltage, more potential energy.

Current is measured in units of amperes (A), usually abbreviated to amps, and is the rate of flow of electric charge past a point. The symbol used for current is I. To continue the water analogy, current might be considered the width/depth of the water flow.

Power is the amount of energy in a system, and is measured in units of watts (W). With the symbol P, in quantitative terms for an electrical circuit, it is equal to current × voltage. Hence, P = I × V. To round out the water analogy, there is a lot more power in Niagara Falls than the downpipe on the side of your house.

Bringing these three quantities into an Arduino context, the typical voltage supply rail on an Arduino board is 5V, or 3.3V on some designs. The output pin of an ATMega168 can provide a maximum of 20mA (0.02A). The total current you can pass through the output circuitry of the 168 as a whole is 100mA, which at 5V is 0.5W.

We'll have more to say about maximum currents and current limiting in the next section.

Units of Measure

Unsurprisingly, electronics makes extensive use of SI Units and SI Prefixes.

When it comes to smaller quantities, you will see **m** for milli, **µ** for micro, and **n** for nano. These equate to 10^{-3}, 10^{-6} and 10^{-9}, respectively; thus, 20mA is 0.02A, 45µs is 0.000045 seconds, etc.

For larger figures, you'll come across **k** for kilo (10^{3}) and **M** for mega (10^{6}), most often when dealing with frequencies (8MHz–8,000,000Hz) or resistances (10kΩ–10,000Ω).

While not part of the SI system, a convention you'll see used is decimal points being replaced with the unit of measure; thus 3.3V becomes 3V3, 1.5kΩ becomes 1k5, etc. This alternative approach is common in Europe and Australia, but less so in North America.

Mains Is Nasty

No discussion of electronics would be complete without discussing issues around mains voltages—that which comes out of the socket in your home—early in the piece.

As a first approximation, any voltage over 40V or so has the potential to give you a tingle or mild shock. Not far above this, sufficient current can flow through your body, your heart in particular, and really ruin your day. While it varies with individual physiology, anything over 20mA flowing through your heart will be fatal.

In practice, this means that you should take extreme care if you have to deal with mains voltages. We strongly encourage you to avoid them if possible, but if you must interact with mains, some precautions you must take include the following:

- Don't work on mains-based projects solo. Have someone around who knows where to turn off the power and provide first aid if things go wrong.
- Don't work on the hardware when tired.
- Wear insulated footwear, such as rubber sole shoes.
- Only touch the hardware with one hand at a time. This, combined with insulated shoes, lessens the chance of your heart being in the current path.
- Isolate (i.e., unplug) the hardware whenever possible. Only work on equipment live as a last resort.
- Assume equipment is live unless you are absolutely sure it isn't.
- Ensure any metalwork is securely earthed.
- Ensure any wiring carrying mains voltage is of a suitable gauge (thickness) and insulation rating.
- Ensure any mains connections are well insulated and, as far as possible, hard to touch accidentally.
- If you are at all unsure of any aspect, consult an expert. Mains voltages don't provide much in the way of second chances.
- Don't be discouraged. If you're just using regular low-voltage Arduino applications, it's pretty hard to hurt yourself!

Reading Schematics

A schematic or circuit diagram is a diagram that describes the interconnections in an electrical or electronic device. In the projects presented in *Practical Arduino*, we've taken the approach of providing both a photograph and/or line drawing of the completed device along with a schematic. While learning to read schematics takes a modest investment of your time, it will prove useful time and time again as you develop your projects. With that in mind, we present a quick how-to in this section.

Figure 1-1 is a photo of the hardware equivalent of "hello world!"—a battery, a switch, an LED, and a resistor. Figure 1-2 is the corresponding schematic diagram with some additional annotations to make clear what corresponds to what.

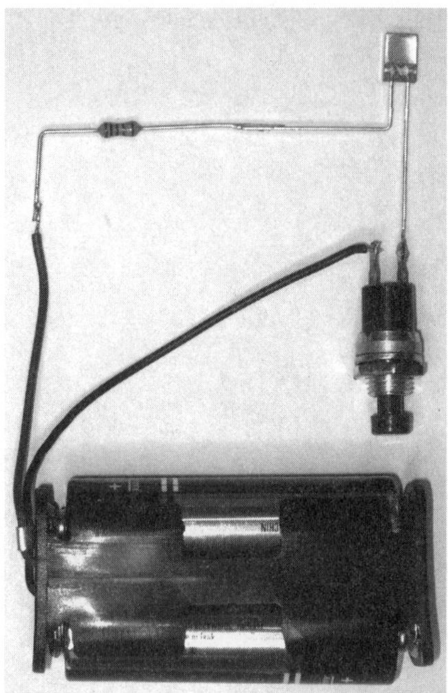

Figure 1-1. *A battery, resistor, LED and switch – the hardware version of "hello world!"*

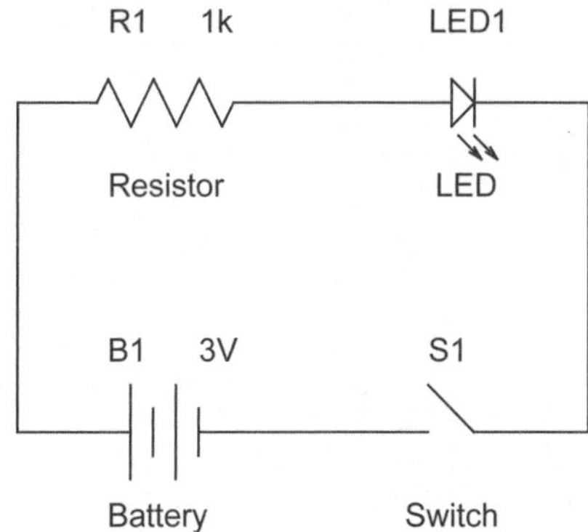

Figure 1-2. *Schematic representation of the circuit shown in Figure 1-1*

You'll note that the lines on the schematic closely follow the physical layout of the circuit. This isn't always the case, but a well drawn schematic will strive to have some correspondence to the physical layout as well where possible.

The component symbols used in schematics vary a little depending on the age of the diagram (valves anyone?) and where it was drawn—European schematics often use slightly different symbols than ones from North America or Australia. We won't try to cover all the differences here, as there are excellent references on the Internet that do so.

Figure 1-3 shows how we represent two wires passing each other, but not electrically connected, and two wires that are electrically connected.

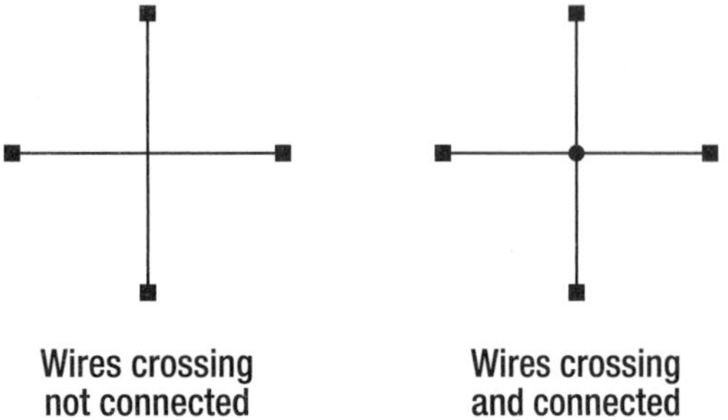

Figure 1-3. *Crossed wires where there is no connection (left) and connected (right)*

Schematics also make use of symbols to show implied interconnections. Figure 1-4 is an admittedly rather contrived example of how power and ground signals are used to simplify larger diagrams. They are an example of a "net"—a connection in a circuit diagram that is inferred by a label or name rather than a physical line on the schematic. You'll see examples of this power/ground and "net" shorthand throughout *Practical Arduino.*

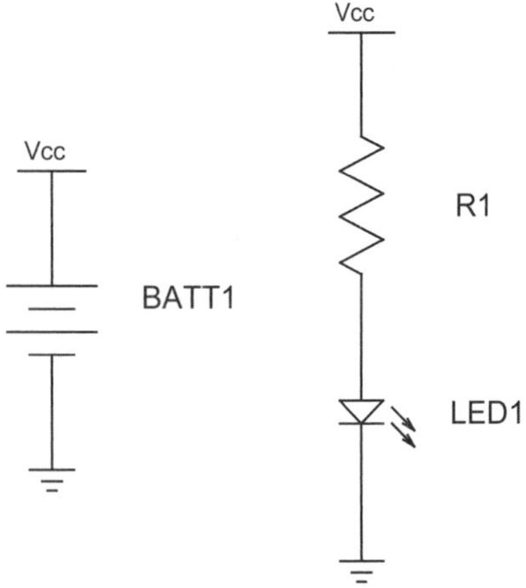

Figure 1-4. *Example of the usage of "nets" in a schematic*

Resistance and Resistors

Resistance, as the name suggests, is the restriction of current flow in a circuit. The most common example of a circuit element that does this is a resistor, a component specifically designed to resist the flow of current in the circuit. The other situation where resistance is encountered (sorry...) is when using long lengths of wire, which we discuss further in the following section.

Resistance is measured in units of ohms (Ω or R) and uses the symbol R. If you connect resistors in series (see Figure 1-5) the total resistance is the sum of the resistors—in the example shown, a 1k resistor is connected in series with a 500 Ω resistor yielding a total of 1.5k Ω.

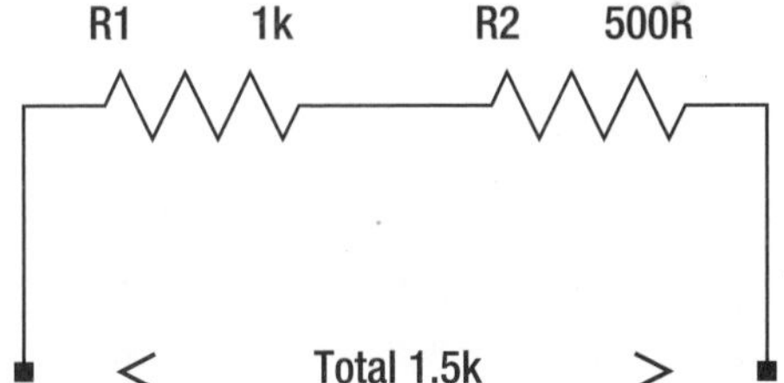

***Figure 1-5.** Two resistors connected in series*

Resistors connected in series can be used to create a "voltage divider" circuit, which can be useful for reducing an input voltage by a known fixed ratio before being measured. We discuss this further in the section "Input Conditioning" in Chapter 5.

Resistors connected in parallel (see Figure 1-6) are more or less the opposite of resistors in series. The total resistance is given by

R = R1 × R2 / (R1 + R2)

In the example shown, the parallel 10k resistors result in a resistance of 5k.

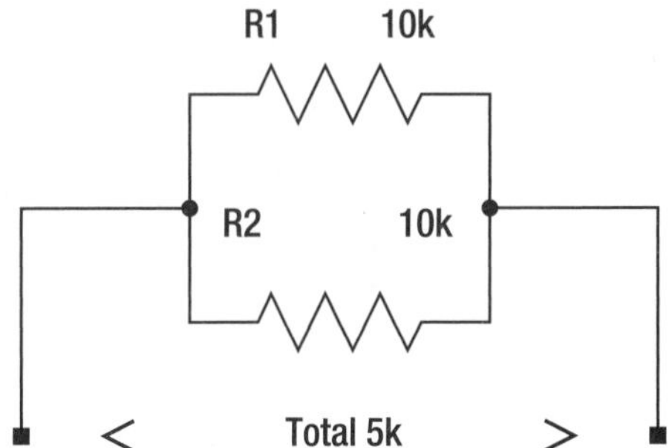

***Figure 1-6.** Resistors in parallel*

Two rules of thumb: (1)resistors in series give a total equal to the sum of the resistances, and (2)resistors in parallel give a resistance lower than the lowest value resistor.

Ohm's Law and Current Limiting

Ohm's Law is a simple formula that ties voltage, current, and resistance together. It can be expressed in three ways.

R= V / I
I = V / R

$$V = I \times R$$

Thus, if an output pin on the Arduino is supplying five volts and is connected to a 250 Ω resistor in turn connecting to ground, the resistor will reduce the current flow to 20mA. This resistor is said to be acting as a current-limiting resistor.

■ The resistor "soaks up" this current by converting it into heat, so it is conventional to have a power rating for a resistor— this denotes the maximum power the resistor can dissipate at room temperature assuming a free flow of air around it. Typical low power resistors have a rating of 1/4W or 1/2W— when driving LEDs and other low-power devices from 5V supplies, you can usually ignore the power rating as you're well within it. Another analogy for a resistor power rating is a household water pipe— put too much pressure (power) through the pipe and the pipe bursts, or the resistor smokes!

As noted above, the ATMega168 can supply a maximum of 20mA per output pin and a total of 100mA per device. Although there is internal current-limiting circuitry (a resistor!) on the chip itself, it is considered good engineering practice to use external current-limiting resistors if at all possible; otherwise, you run the risk of damaging the chip.

To understand current limiting a little further, we take the example of driving a red LED (see Figure 1-7).

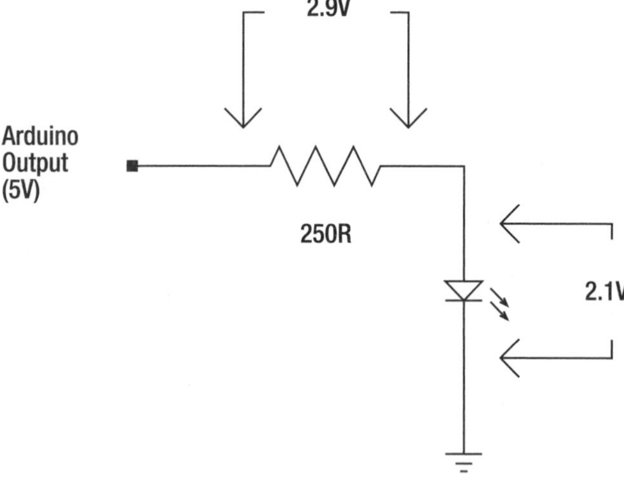

Figure 1-7. Example of current limiting for a LED

As seen in Figure 1-7, the Arduino's I/O pin connects to a resistor to the LED to ground. Note that the meter across the LED is measuring 2.1V. This is known as the "forward voltage drop" or V_f and varies with the color of the LED and the model of LED itself. The meter across the resistor is measuring 2.9V, which is the difference between the supply rail (5V) and the forward voltage drop of the LED (2.1V).

Using Ohm's law, we can calculate the current through the 250 Ω resistor as I = V / R = 2.1 / 250 Ω = 11.6mA. This is a reasonable figure for a modern red LED.

It should be apparent that by changing the value of the resistor, we can increase or decrease the current through the LED as required. While we've used an LED in this example, it could be replaced by any other device.

Choosing Wire

A final aspect of resistance that is worth mentioning is so-called IR (internal resistance) loss— losing power in the wires that interconnect your circuit. In the majority of applications, this can be safely ignored, but if you are constructing circuits that use higher currents and/or long cabling runs, IR losses should be considered.

The problem stems from the fact that any conventional wire conductor has resistance, the exception being superconductors which remain a little out of reach.

Common stranded "hookup wire" with a diameter of 1.25mm (AWG16) has a resistance of around 0.014 ohms/meter. By way of example, say you use two 1m lengths of this wire to supply 5V to your Arduino board consuming 100mA. The voltage drop in each conductor can be calculated using Ohm's law as being V = IR = 0.1 × 0.014 or 0.0014V (1.4mV). There are two conductors (supply and ground) so the total drop becomes 2.8mV— not a large enough drop to give a second thought.

However, consider if you were using a longer run of cable— maybe down the other end of the house (say, 15m)—and drawing higher current (perhaps a few high-wattage LEDs or a solenoid) to arrive at 500mA. The voltage drop now increases to 7mV per meter or 0.21V over the 30m combined up and back length. In practice, an Arduino would probably cope with this, but other devices being used may not. In any case, good engineering practice suggests you ought to opt for thicker wire.

As another reference point, most of us have some Cat5 network cabling lying around, which is rated at 0.094 ohm/meter (worse than the hookup wire mentioned previously). While it's okay for short distances/low currents, do some math before you use it for longer runs/higher currents. On the plus side, you get eight conductors (four pairs) so you can parallel them up to increase the current handling capability through lower IR loss.

Another way to work around cable IR loss is to increase the voltage in use—so rather than supplying 5V from the near end, use 12V and have a voltage regulator at the far end to drop this back to 5V. This is arguably a better engineered solution, as the supply seen by the Arduino will be cleaner as the regulation is closer to the board.

As an aside, this same principle of raising the operating voltage is applied in the mains power supply where the main grid supply runs at tens of thousands of volts to reduce the cable loss.

Diodes

A signal or rectifier diode is a component that allows current to flow (essentially) unimpeded in one direction, when "forward biased," but blocks it all but completely in the opposite direction when "reverse biased"—a one-way gate for electrons, if you will. We use diodes extensively in the various projects in *Practical Arduino*, so we dig into them a little here.

There are at least three parameters that you need to consider when selecting diodes for use in your projects, these are:

- *Current-handling capability:* Diodes can only pass a certain amount of current without damage. Small "signal" diodes like the venerable 1N4148/1N914 can cope with about 200mA, Rectifier diodes like the 1N4004 are good for an amp or so; for higher ratings, you'll find plenty of options at your favorite supplier.
- *Maximum reverse voltage:* Diodes can only cope with a certain amount of reverse bias (voltage) before they are damaged. Again, looking at our two usual suspects of the 1N4148 and 1N4004, the maximum reverse voltage is 100V and 400V, respectively.
- *Forward voltage drop:* Nothing comes for free! When conducing (forward biased), the diode drops a certain amount of voltage across its terminals. This, of course, ends up as heat and so diodes have power limitations as well. The 1N4148 and 1N4004 have similar forward voltage drops of 1V.

A common use of a diode is to avoid damage to a piece of circuitry if the power is connected back to front. When using diodes in this manner, you need to consider all three of the previously mentioned parameters, particularly the current-handling capability—is it high enough; and the forward voltage drop —are you going to end up with a marginal supply voltage because of it? An alternative approach is to use a diode connected *across* the power supply input such that it only conducts if the power is connected back to front. A quick blow fuse must also be used so that the diode doesn't stay conducting all this power for too long. The advantage of this approach is that you don't get the forward voltage drop, the drawback being you blow a fuse—and if your design is marginal, you may blow the diode, negating the protection circuit entirely. Some subtlety is called for with this one.

Power Supplies

There are many different ways of powering your Arduino project. Low-power Arduino projects can be powered from either the host PCs USB port or batteries. Projects that make use of devices with higher power demands—solenoids, servos, motors, lots of LEDs and the like—are best powered off a mains-powered supply (transformer or plugpack/wallwart) or larger capacity battery. This section discusses some of the options available to the Arduino experimenter.

USB Power

The regular USB port on a PC provides 5V at a maximum of 500mA or so—about 2.5W. This is ample for many projects that just contain a few LEDs, an LCD, or an Arduino shield, but that's about it. Anything that involves motors, solenoids, or servos will likely have peak current demands higher than the port can provide, meaning it shouldn't be used.

On the plus side, USB ports on most PCs are pretty well protected. If you draw too much current, they *usually* will just shut down gracefully before anything melts. With this in mind, using a $30 mains-powered USB hub while experimenting may be prudent insurance for your $1,500 laptop.

USB ports have power control; that is to say, in most cases, they start out with a lower maximum current then switch up when the device is identified by the host as a high-power device. In practice, this means that if you simply tap into the USB supply, you can draw a maximum of 100mA, not 500mA, though this varies among computers.

The FTDI chip commonly used to provide a serial interface to Arduino boards can either identify itself as low or high power according to an EEPROM setting. If you are going down this route and need the higher power, you'll need to do some homework into how the FTDI has been programmed in your case.

Two more caveats if using USB to power your project: (1) USB has a specific lower power or sleep state—if your device continues to draw power when the system powering it expects to go to sleep, strange things may happen and/or you'll flatten the battery of your host device; and (2) never feed power back into the USB port of the host system!

Batteries

Batteries can either be rechargeable (secondary cells) or non-rechargeable (primary cells). Within each category there is a vast array of different battery chemistries and capacities. Key figures for batteries are the terminal voltage (V) and capacity, typically measured in ampere-hours (Ah), which give an indication of how long they can provide power before being discharged.

The standard 9V "PP3" battery is really only a good choice for very low-current applications, perhaps a project that drives one or two LEDs and/or an LCD.

Three or four 1.5V AAA, AA, C, or D cells provide a great deal more capacity at the expense of size, particularly for C or D cells. But, if you're driving motors, servos, or solenoids, you'll want to aim for C or D cells as a minimum to get any reasonable battery life.

■ A crude but effective trick when powering 5V circuitry from a 6V battery is to put one or two diodes in series with the supply. The typical forward voltage drop of 0.4V per diode brings the 6V down to a more ideal 5.2V and you get reverse polarity protection for "free."

For these readily available cells, there are also rechargeable equivalents which we'd encourage you to consider to reduce landfill. Bear in mind that the base cell voltage is lower for nickel-cadmium (NiCd) or nickel-metal hydride (NiMH) cells at 1.25V per cell, so an AA NiCd will provide around 1.3V when fully charged versus 1.5–1.6V for an alkaline.

Sealed lead acid (SLA) batteries are an attractive option. While heavier, they have, depending on size, the ability to supply several amps for a few hours or more—good if you're building a robot, for example. The strength of SLA batteries can be a weakness if things go wrong— that same ability to provide high currents can result in melted wires or circuit boards if things go amiss. Accordingly, we strongly encourage you to put a fuse in the circuit, as near the battery as practicable, if you use an SLA.

Constructing your own charger circuit is beyond the scope of this book, but good resources are available on the Internet. For most applications, it's likely to be simpler to just swap the batteries out into a commercial charger.

What About LiPo?

Lithium polymer (LiPo) and similar "exotic" batteries are very attractive from a weight/capacity standpoint, but require specific circuitry to ensure they work correctly and, when being charged, don't overheat or catch fire. The per cell voltage for a LiPo battery is around 3.7V, but being sensitive to over discharge, steps must be taken to disconnect the battery when its terminal voltage drops below around 3.2V. LiPo cells can be permanently damaged if the terminal voltage drops below 3V or so.

If your application needs the power density or the light weight of LiPo, a little Googling will yield some ready-made packs that have built-in charge/discharge controllers. We provide links to some examples on the *Practical Arduino* web site.

Wall Warts/Plugpacks

Wall warts (or plugpacks as they tend to be called in Australia) are an ideal way of powering all but the most power-hungry Arduino projects. Most plugpacks output a DC voltage, and this voltage can be regulated or unregulated (more on this in a moment).

Some plugpacks output AC only, so are just a transformer in a safe-to-use box. These can be useful for some applications (such as referencing a clock to the mains as we touch on in Chapter 16) or when you otherwise want to do your own rectification and filtering. We won't go into AC plugpacks in more detail here.

DC plugpacks supply a DC voltage. "Regulated" plugpacks have built-in voltage-regulation circuitry, so they will provide a specific voltage (say, 5V) for any output current up to their rated maximum. By contrast, unregulated plugpacks have limited, if any, regulation and instead provide the nominated voltage only under the expected load. So if the plugpack is rated at 12V at 500mA, it may actually output 15V or more if only 200mA is being drawn. This explains why when you measure some supplies with a multimeter they show a much higher output voltage than what is written on the label.

For Arduino projects, we generally recommend you stick with regulated supplies, as it reduces the chances of exceeding maximum voltages for any connected circuitry. Experience suggests that if the supply is rated at 5V or 3V3, then it's probably regulated; by contrast, 12V supplies often aren't. Regulated supplies use a transformer, rectifier, filter capacitor, and regulator or may be a more sophisticated switchmode supply. Switchmode supplies are often much smaller and lighter, more energy efficient, have good stable outputs, and tend to have better over-current protection.

You can often pick up plugpacks cheaply at surplus sales, new from your local electronics store, or for lower-power projects from mobile phone chargers. Nokia in particular seem to have standardized on 5.2V for some years now, which is ideal for 5V-based projects.

Capacitance and Capacitors

Capacitors are electronic components that store charge. From an Arduino perspective, we most commonly encounter them when they are used to ensure stable power supply for our circuits.

Fundamentals

Capacitance (C) is measured in farads (F), though most devices we will encounter will be considerably smaller than a Farad— µF or nF, for microfarad and nanofarad, respectively.

Capacitors can be connected in series or parallel to yield a circuit element that has a total capacitance lower or higher than the individual components.

When capacitors are connected in series as in Figure 1-8 the total is given by

$$C = C1 \times C2 / (C1 + C2)$$

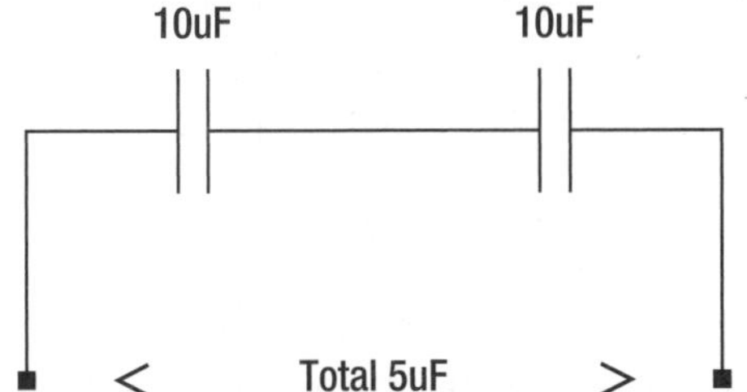

Figure 1-8. *Two capacitors connected in series.*

As shown in Figure 1-9, the total capacitance of two capacitors in parallel is the sum of their values.

Note that capacitance values work in the "opposite" way to resistance values when multiple components are connected together.

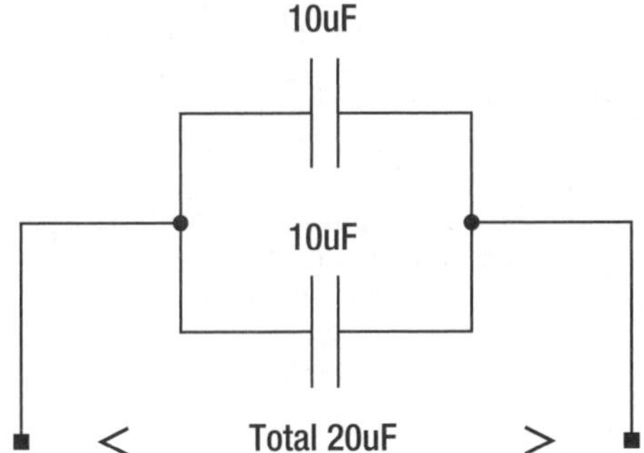

Figure 1-9. *Two capacitors connected in parallel*

Capacitor Types

There are many different types of capacitors, but the main differentiator is polarized vs. nonpolarized or unipolar. Polarised capacitors are most common for capacitances over 1µF or so and will be clearly marked with a + symbol or stripe to show the lead that should be connected to the most positive part of the circuit.

Nonpolarized capacitors are typically used for filter circuits or directly adjacent to digital ICs to provide supply bypassing (see the section "Power Supply Bypass" for more information).

All capacitors have a maximum, or safe-working, voltage. These are particularly important for high-capacitance values where the capacitor is physically small. The maximum working voltage will be printed on the capacitor body.

There are many different capacitor chemistries/construction methods. Wherever we make use of capacitors in *Practical Arduino* projects, we'll call out what types are suitable.

Power Supply Bypass

Cutting a rather long and complex story short, digital circuits like the Arduino have quite low constant current requirements, but relatively higher peak or transient current when internal circuits change state. Supply bypass capacitors give a means to supply these transients in a circuit and ensure reliable operation. The Arduino boards themselves have these built in, but when prototyping or building your own external circuits, it's good practice to add in these parts.

For each digital IC, a 0.1µF-chip ceramic capacitor across the power supply pins and physically adjacent to the part is good practice. Each group of digital ICs or board is well served to have 10–100µF of electrolytic or tantalum capacitors where the supply enters the board.

ESD Precautions

Electrostatic discharge (ESD) is a phenomenon familiar to everyone—the spark or small shock you get when you touch a metal door handle after walking on synthetic carpet, for example.

While the shock we experience is a mere irritation, it can be very problematic for electronic circuitry. The design and handling considerations necessary to avoid ESD-related problems are taken care of in well designed electronics, but when we are dealing with hardware of our own making, we need to do this ourselves.

When constructing or prototyping circuitry, it is good to get in the habit of grounding yourself to an earthed piece of equipment before picking up any bare components or circuit boards. Keep static-sensitive components or assemblies in antistatic bags when not in use and consider getting an antistatic mat and wrist strap for your work area.

The I/O lines of the standard Arduino boards connect directly to the ATMega chip itself without any filtering or protection. This is appropriate given the myriad of ways the board may end up being used, but does mean the chip is prone to damage if seriously mishandled.

If your project needs signals to be brought into the Arduino board from the outside world, take a few minutes to review the section on Input Conditioning in Chapter 16 for design considerations.

That said, we've heard the ATMega chips described as tanks—pretty hard to damage in practice—but good ESD habits will serve you well nonetheless!

Tools

Figure 1-10 shows a selection of tools that will be invaluable in your Arduino endeavors. A selection of small screwdrivers, diagonal cutters, long-nose pliers , tweezers, soldering iron, soldering iron tip cleaner, solder, desoldering braid, anti-static wrist strap, and a multimeter will well equip you to begin with. Adafruit and SparkFun are among a number of Arduino suppliers that have kits of these basic tools to help you get started.

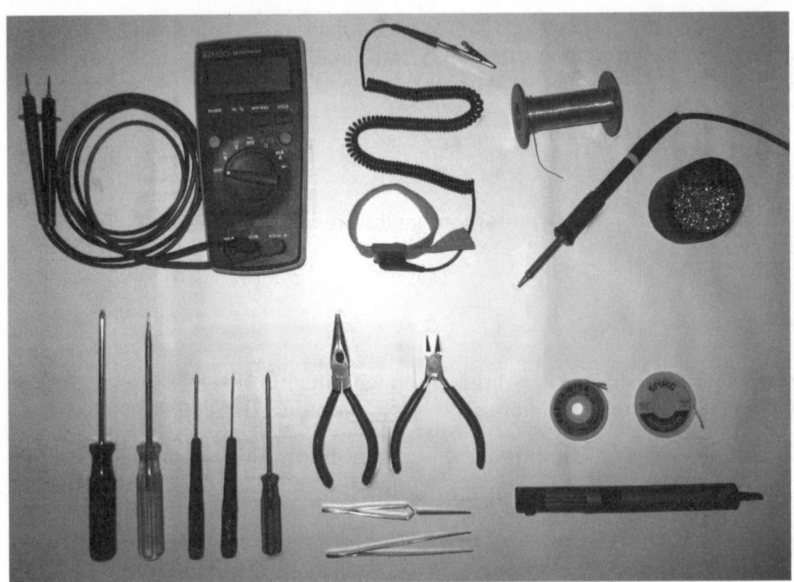

Figure 1-10. *A recommended starter set of tools*

Soldering is a whole topic in itself—we provide a few pointers in the projects that involve soldered shields, and the *Practical Arduino* web site has some links to more resources. Don't be daunted by soldering. As long as you take the obvious precautions (the handle is the "cool" end), it's pretty easy to get the hang of it.

More "exotic" tools become a matter of personal choice, necessity, or budget and often are only needed for more involved projects. Thus an illuminated magnifier, stereo microscope and oscilloscope are all nice to have, but only if you're doing fine work, surface mount soldering, or sophisticated electronics development, respectively.

Start off small, buy as good a quality as you can afford, and in no time you'll have a nice range of tools.

Parts

A selection of parts—what the hobbyists of yore would call their "junk box"—can be tremendously useful, particularly when inspiration strikes late at night.

Consider having on hand at least the following:

- *A good assortment of 1/4W resistors:* you can usually pick up mixed bulk packs for a few dollars from your local electronics component shop or online. Consider adding some extras of popular values—the authors tend to have lots of 270R (for LEDs), 1k, and 10k resistors on hand, for example.
- *A handful of LEDs:* obviously, you'll need more if your project is specifically using them, but even if not, they're handy to have on hand for debugging purposes.

- *Some signal and rectifier diodes:* 1N4148 and 1N4004 (or equivalents), the former for logic level applications, the latter for protection circuits, back EMF protection when using relays etc.
- *A few capacitors:* 100nF, 1uF, 10uF.
- *An assortment of bipolar transistors:* 2N3904, BC548, etc.
- *Some momentary buttons:* for, say, reset or interacting with the circuit and some breadboard friendly switches.

Further Reading

Clearly, electronics engineering is a whole field in its own right, and we can give only a limited treatment within a few chapters. We have found these two titles to be a good companion when tinkering:

- Williams, Tim. The Circuit Designer's Companion, Second Edition. Newnes, 2005.
- Horowitz, Paul, and Winfield Hill. The Art of Electronics, Second Edition. Cambridge Univeristy Press, 1989.

CHAPTER 2

■ ■ ■

Appliance Remote Control

One of the basic tasks in many home automation systems is controlling power to appliances. These could be lights, a heater, an exhaust fan, or just about anything else that runs on mains power. The problem, of course, is that it's dangerous to mess with mains-level power directly and you may even be in violation of your local building code if you don't have the necessary qualifications. This project uses a general-purpose appliance remote control that can be obtained from a local hardware store. It can be easily modified to link it to an Arduino for software control of devices around your house, without having to touch any mains-level wiring.

This technique isn't limited to just controlling appliances, though, and is a great way to modify just about any device with a remote control so that it can be linked to an Arduino. Any device with push-button control can be modified so that an Arduino can simulate button presses and have the device respond as if you'd pressed the buttons yourself. You could do the same thing with a TV remote control or a garage door opener. One of the authors has even done it with the temperature preset buttons on a gas-powered continuous hot-water service and on the control panel for his electric curtain tracks. You can see the parts needed in Figure 2-1 and the complete schematic in Figure 2-2.

Parts Required

1 x Arduino Duemilanove, Arduino Pro, Seeeduino, or equivalent

1 x RF appliance remote control

1 x Prototyping shield

4 x 5V reed relays

4 x 1N4001 power diodes or similar

4 x PCB-mount male connectors

4 x line-mount female connectors

10cm ribbon cable

Source code available from

`www.practicalarduino.com/projects/appliance-remote-control`

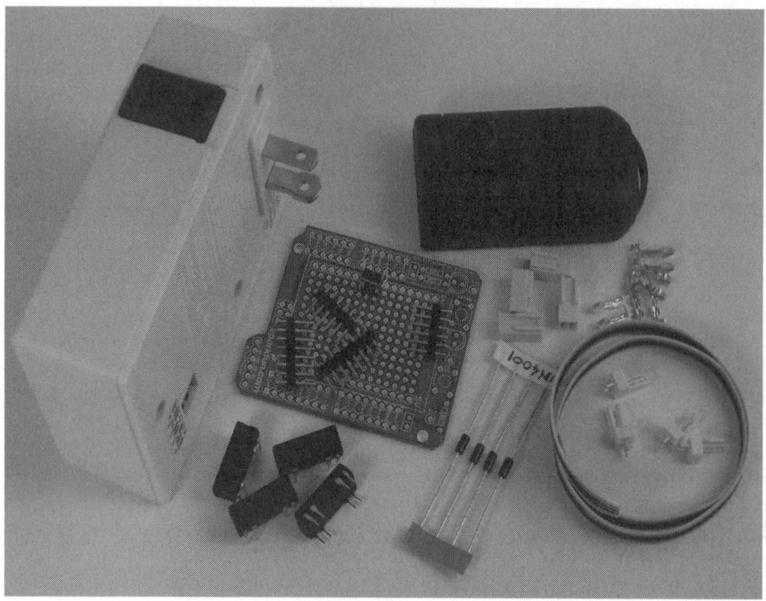

Figure 2-1. Parts required for Applicance Remote Control

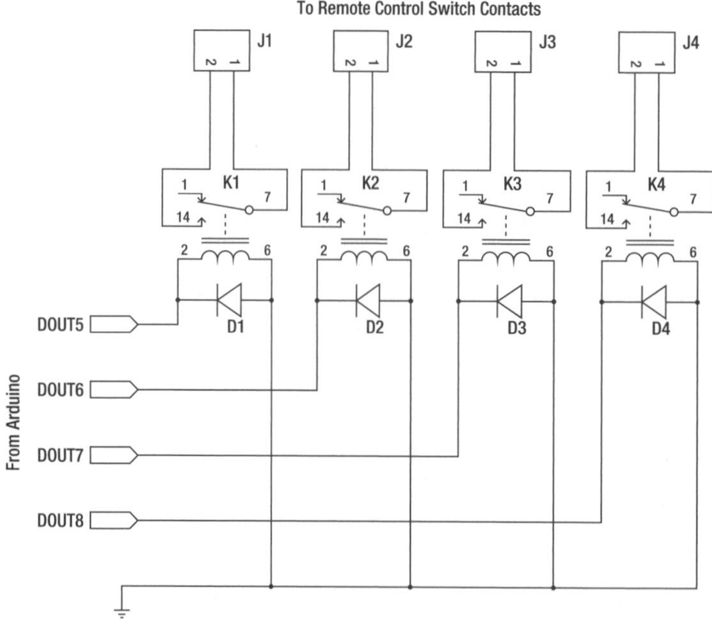

Figure 2-2. Complete schematic for Appliance Remote Control

Instructions

Test and Investigate Appliance Remote

Plug the appliance remote control receiver into a handy power outlet and then plug an appliance (a small lamp is ideal when testing) into the socket on the receiver. Test that the unit works correctly in factory form by using the remote control to turn the appliance on and off. There's no point doing a lot of work modifying something if it doesn't work as intended in the first place!

Also pay attention to how long you need to hold the button down for the transmitter to operate correctly. Some systems require you to hold the button for half a second or so, and others will operate if you stab at it very briefly. You may find you need to adjust the button press time variable in the example programs that follow if your remote control has unusual characteristics.

Some remotes also perform different functions depending on whether you hold the button down or not, such as toggling a lamp on a brief press or fading it up/down on a long press.

The photo in Figure 2-3 shows two different appliance remote control sets. The set on the left is designed for Australian power sockets running at 240V and has four sets of on/off buttons, and can switch between four different ranges to control a total of 16 devices from one remote control. The receiver unit has a visual indication of status and is designed to be plugged into a wall socket, then an appliance plugged into it. It also supports a ground connection so it's suitable for many types of appliances.

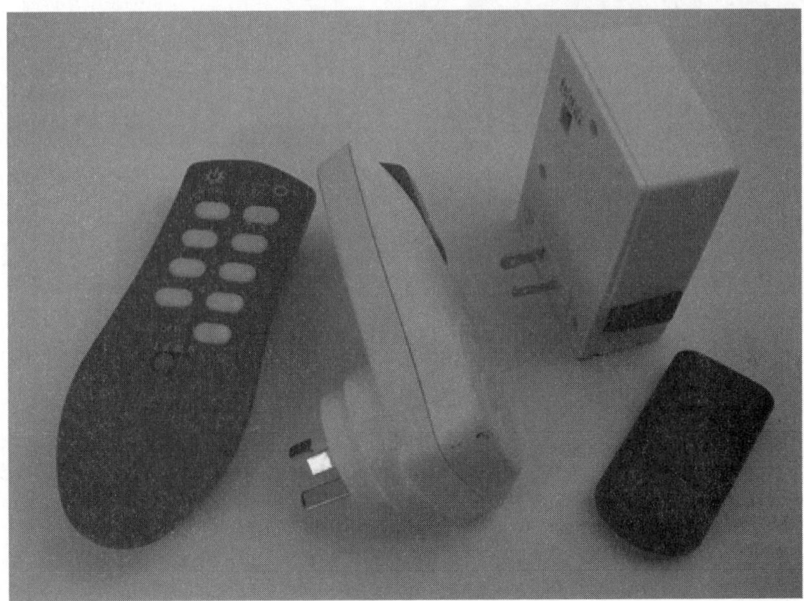

Figure 2-3. *Appliance remote controls*

The set on the right is designed for U.S. power sockets running at 110V, and has a much smaller transmitter, but it can only turn one appliance on or off. This particular model doesn't have a ground connection, so it's suitable only for double-insulated appliances that don't require a ground pin, such as most lamps.

There are many other types of appliance remote controls available and you can often pick up sets containing one remote control and three receivers for $30 to $50.

Once you've tested your remote control on an appliance such as a desk lamp, take the battery out of the transmitter module and open it up by either removing the screws or (if it clips together) forcing the shell apart with a screwdriver to gain access to the circuit inside. You will probably find everything on a single PCB with a wire antenna connected at one end and the battery clip connected at the other. The buttons on the front of the remote control are usually just plastic or rubber covers that mount over the top of the actual buttons mounted on the circuit board, so locate the relevant "appliance on" and "appliance off" buttons on the circuit board and then turn it over to find the soldered connections to the back of the buttons.

Figure 2-4 shows the location of the solder pads on the back of the buttons for a typical remote control.

Figure 2-4. *PCB of appliance remote control transmitter*

If each button has only two connections as in the particular remote control shown in Figure 2-4, you're on easy street, but many PCB-mount buttons have four pins to provide them with a strong mechanical mount even though they only have two actual connections so it's not always obvious which ones you need to use. The four pins are usually arranged in two pairs that are joined together internally so that when the button is pressed the pairs are shorted together. What you need to do is find a pair of pins that are normally open but then short together when the button is pressed.

There are several ways of doing this: you could use a multimeter to measure the resistance between pairs of pins and see if it changes from very high to very low when the button is pressed, or you could even just put the battery back in the transmitter and then touch a short piece of wire across a pair of pins and see what happens. It doesn't matter if you get it wrong because the matching pins are joined together inside the switch anyway. If you get it right, the remote control will act as if you pressed the button and send a signal to the receiver and turn your test appliance on or off depending on which button you shorted out.

Every four-pin pushbutton we have ever seen joins connections together internally along two opposite sides, so if you pick two diagonally opposite pins it will almost certainly work no matter what the orientation of the button may be.

Once you've found an operational pair of pins behind each button, use a felt-tip marker to put a dot next to each one to make things easier for yourself when it comes time to connect to the Arduino.

Assemble Reed Relay Shield

To link your Arduino to the appliance remote control you need to make sure the two devices are electrically isolated. The simplest way to do this is with one 5V reed relay for each button you want to control. A reed relay is a very low-power electromechanical switch that allows a low current to control a higher current. Modern 5V reed relays require only about 20mA to operate. That's low enough that you can drive it directly from an Arduino output without requiring any other buffer circuitry at all, so the next step is to mount some reed relays on a prototyping shield and connect them to Arduino outputs.

A regular Arduino prototyping shield will comfortably fit four reed relays plus connectors. If you only want to operate a single device, you probably only need two relays (one to connect to the "on" button, one for "off") but it can be handy having more outputs so I installed four.

Start by fitting the relays and male PCB-mount headers to the shield as shown in Figure 2-5.

Figure 2-5. *Reed relays and male headers fitted to PCB*

The reed relays have their inputs (coil connections) on the bottom center pair of pins when aligned with the notch to the left, as in Figure 2-5, and their outputs on the outer pairs of pins.

Turn the shield over and solder the relays and connectors in place. You only need to solder the pins that will actually be used, but you can solder all the pins if you prefer (see Figure 2-6).

Figure 2-6. Reed relay connections soldered to shield

The particular prototyping shield shown in Figure 2-6 has a strip of ground connections down one side and +5V down the other. Use some short lengths of wire to join a coil connection from each relay together and then to ground. Also connect the PCB-mount plug pins to the adjacent outer connections (outputs) on the reed relays and fit the breakaway headers that allow the shield to plug into an Arduino.

You'll notice in the photo shown in Figure 2-7 that we only fitted three of the four breakaway headers. This may seem odd, but we didn't need to make a connection to any of the analog input pins so there's no need to put that connector on the board. The shield will still mount very firmly with three connectors and having the fourth connector installed would just make it a little bit harder to align and insert into an Arduino for no benefit.

Turn the board back over and install jumper leads from the other coil connection on each relay to the matching Arduino digital output. In this project we started with digital output 5 for the first relay, 6 for the second, and so on (see Figure 2-8).

Figure 2-7. Connections to +5V and ground

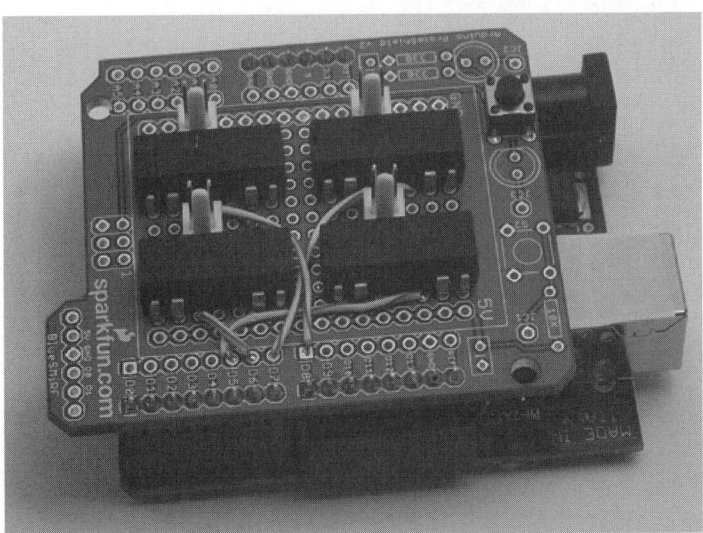

Figure 2-8. Connections from digital outputs to relay inputs

Electro-mechanical relays operate by running current through a coil to generate a magnetic field and pull output contacts together, thus completing a circuit. When power to the relay is turned off, the magnetic field collapses and the contacts release, but while it is collapsing the field generates a "reverse spike" or "back-EMF"—a brief high voltage of opposite polarity to the original voltage. What this means is that the Arduino output that was previously supplying +5V to hold the relay on is temporarily subjected to a big blast of negative voltage, and if the spike is big enough the output can actually be damaged or destroyed.

The simple solution is to fit a "reverse biased" diode across the relay coil so that as soon as the reverse spike begins it will be shorted out by the diode and the Arduino output will be protected. Diodes only pass current in one direction, so by fitting it backward across the relay, it won't do anything in normal operation and will appear as an open circuit, but will easily conduct the reverse-voltage spike while the relay's magnetic field collapses. This will protect your Arduino from the reverse voltage.

Given the extremely low power involved in a small reed relay it's highly unlikely that it will blow an I/O pin right away, so it can be tempting to leave off the protection diode and hope everything will be all right. However, damage to I/O pins can be subtle and cumulative and putting a diode in now is much cheaper than replacing an Arduino later so it's better to play it safe.Because the voltages and currents involved are very small, you can use just about any power diode or signal diode you may have available. We used 1N4004 diodes, which are commonly available for only a few cents each—we buy them by the hundred so that we always have plenty around when we need them.

Fit a diode across each relay coil with the "anode" lead going to the pin connected to ground, and the "cathode" lead (the end with the stripe) going to the relay pin connected to the Arduino output as shown in Figure 2-9.

Figure 2-9. *Protection diodes connected across relay coils*

That's the shield all done, so next you need to assemble a couple of small wiring harnesses.

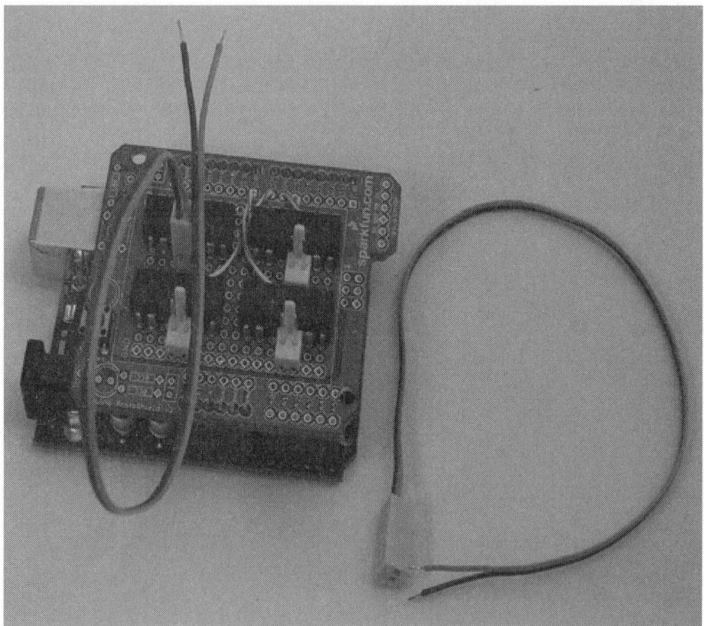

Figure 2-10. Connections to link shield with remote control

Separate pairs of wires from the ribbon cable by nipping between the ends and pulling it apart with your fingers, then solder one end of each pair of wires to a female line connector and assemble the connector to make a wiring harness that you can plug into the shield as shown in Figure 2-10.

You now have a useful general-purpose relay shield that you can connect to any low-voltage device that you want to control simply by soldering the ends of the wiring harnesses into place.

Connect Reed Relay Shield to Remote Control

Solder the pair of wires from each wiring harness across the back of the buttons in the remote control using the connections you marked on the PCB earlier, as shown in Figure 2-11.

Mount the reed relay shield on your Arduino and plug each wiring harness into the connectors on the reed relay shield, as shown in Figure 2-12.

If your appliance remote control runs on 3V you can optionally remove the battery from the remote control and solder a pair of wires across the (+) and (–) battery terminals, then connect them to +3.3V and GND, respectively, on your Arduino. The remote control will then draw its power from the Arduino and you never need to worry about its battery going flat. In our case, though, the remote control uses a little "A23" type 12V battery so we left it in place in the transmitter.

Now all the hardware is done, so on to the software!

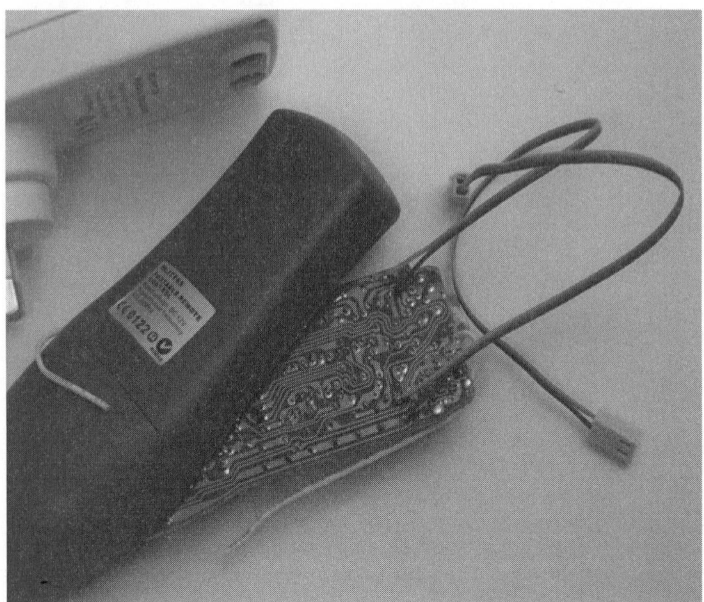

Figure 2-11. *Remote control transmitter with connections in place*

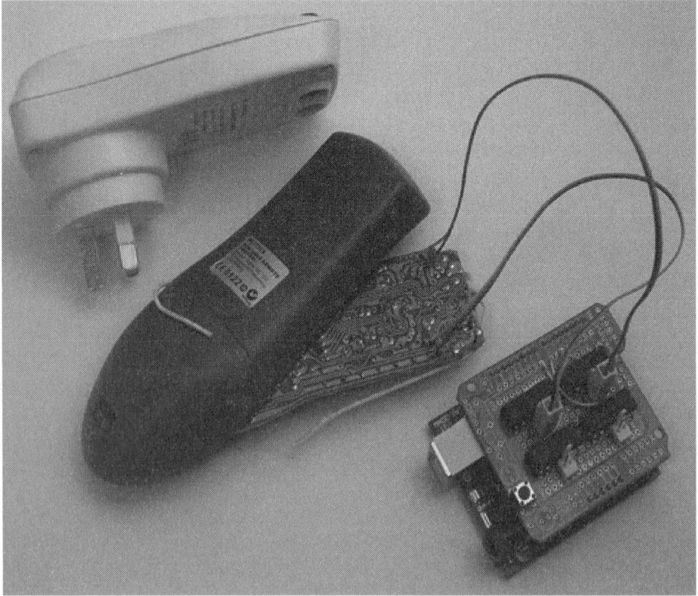

Figure 2-12. *Remote control linked to shield*

Create Reed Relay Control Program

When you use the appliance remote control manually you only press the buttons momentarily and don't hold them down indefinitely, so to simulate a button press we'll pulse a reed relay on for 250ms (1/4 of a second) and then turn it off again. That should be plenty of time for the appliance remote to detect the virtual "button press" and then send the appropriate signal to the receiver.

There are two versions of the code available for download from the *Practical Arduino* web site. The first version, called ApplianceRemoteControl, is designed to be as conceptually simple as possible to make it easy for a beginner to follow what it does. The second version, called ApplianceRemoteControlCompact, is functionally identical but uses some more advanced concepts to make the code smaller. The second version is harder for a beginner to understand, but comparing the two programs is a great way to see how more advanced concepts (such as arrays) can make your code much smaller. Since the Arduino has very limited memory capacity it is important to know how to minimize your code size.

When you compile ("Verify") a program in the Arduino IDE, the size of the resulting program is shown in bytes in the bottom left of the window. It's good to get into the habit of looking at the size of the programs you create to get a feel for how much memory your software will take up. With larger programs it can become quite a juggling act to squeeze all the features you want into the few kilobytes of available space.

We'll start by working through the longer, but conceptually simpler, ApplianceRemoteControl program.

ApplianceRemoteControl

The code starts by defining some basic values such as which digital I/O lines need to be used as outputs and how long to hold each "button press" on for.

```
// Use pins 5 through 12 as the digital outputs
int output1 = 5;
int output2 = 6;
int output3 = 7;
int output4 = 8;
int output5 = 9;
int output6 = 10;
int output7 = 11;
int output8 = 12;
int buttonPressTime = 250;    // Number of milliseconds to hold outputs on
```

You'll notice that it defines eight outputs, not just the two or four we use in this project. The extra outputs don't matter if we don't use them, but by defining them now you can plug in a shield with up to eight relays or even an eight-way opto-isolator later on and use exactly the same program with no modification required. This would come in very handy if you want to connect up all eight on/off buttons on an eight-way appliance remote control.

However, keep in mind that the ATMega CPU in an Arduino can only supply a limited amount of current from each pin and that the total output current is also limited. If you try turning on eight reed relays at once on eight outputs you'd probably exceed the chip's current supply rating. With the example programs shown here it's not a problem because they only ever allow one output to be turned on at a time, but if you use different code to turn outputs on and off independently you need to be careful of the total current draw.

The program then runs the setup function that tells the CPU to switch each of those digital pins into output mode, then forces them to an initial low state so all the relays are turned off when the program starts running. It also opens the serial port (USB on a Duemilanove) for communication with the host computer at a speed of 38400bps.

```
void setup()
{
  // Open the serial connection to listen for commands from the host
  Serial.begin(38400);

  // Set up the pins as outputs
  pinMode(output1, OUTPUT);
  pinMode(output2, OUTPUT);
  pinMode(output3, OUTPUT);
  pinMode(output4, OUTPUT);
  pinMode(output5, OUTPUT);
  pinMode(output6, OUTPUT);
  pinMode(output7, OUTPUT);
  pinMode(output8, OUTPUT);
  // Make sure the outputs are all set LOW initally
  digitalWrite(output1, LOW);
  digitalWrite(output2, LOW);
  digitalWrite(output3, LOW);
  digitalWrite(output4, LOW);
  digitalWrite(output5, LOW);
  digitalWrite(output6, LOW);
  digitalWrite(output7, LOW);
  digitalWrite(output8, LOW);
}
```

The program then enters the main loop, which is where the real action happens.

The main loop watches the serial port for data being sent to it and examines any characters to see if they match the ID of a known output. If there is a match it pushes that output high to turn on the relay connected to it, waits 250ms, and then takes it low again to turn off the relay before going back to the start of the loop to listen for the next command. The outputs are labelled "1" through "8," corresponding to the eight output pins defined previously.

```
void loop()
{
  byte val;
  // Check if a value has been sent by the host
  if(Serial.available()) {
    val = Serial.read();

    if(val == '1') {
      // Pulse the 1st button
      Serial.println("Output 1 ON");
      digitalWrite(output1, HIGH);
      delay(buttonPressTime);
      digitalWrite(output1, LOW);
      Serial.println("Output 1 OFF");
```

```
    } else if(val == '2') {
      // Pulse the 2nd button
      Serial.println("Output 2 ON");
      digitalWrite(output2, HIGH);
      delay(buttonPressTime);
      digitalWrite(output2, LOW);
      Serial.println("Output 2 OFF");
    } else if(val == '3') {
      // Pulse the 3rd button
      Serial.println("Output 3 ON");
      digitalWrite(output3, HIGH);
      delay(buttonPressTime);
      digitalWrite(output3, LOW);
      Serial.println("Output 3 OFF");
    } else if(val == '4') {
      // Pulse the 4th button
      Serial.println("Output 4 ON");
      digitalWrite(output4, HIGH);
      delay(buttonPressTime);
      digitalWrite(output4, LOW);
      Serial.println("Output 4 OFF");
    } else if(val == '5') {
      // Pulse the 5th button
      Serial.println("Output 5 ON");
      digitalWrite(output5, HIGH);
      delay(buttonPressTime);
      digitalWrite(output5, LOW);
      Serial.println("Output 5 OFF");
    } else if(val == '6') {
      // Pulse the 6th button
      Serial.println("Output 6 ON");
      digitalWrite(output6, HIGH);
      delay(buttonPressTime);
      digitalWrite(output6, LOW);
      Serial.println("Output 6 OFF");
    } else if(val == '7') {
      // Pulse the 7th button
      Serial.println("Output 7 ON");
      digitalWrite(output7, HIGH);
      delay(buttonPressTime);
      digitalWrite(output7, LOW);
      Serial.println("Output 7 OFF");
    } else if(val == '8') {
      // Pulse the 8th button
      Serial.println("Output 8 ON");
      digitalWrite(output8, HIGH);
      delay(buttonPressTime);
      digitalWrite(output8, LOW);
      Serial.println("Output 8 OFF");
    }
  }
}
```

One subtlety that may not be apparent on first inspection of the code above is what sort of data is being examined in the series of "if" comparisons. You'll notice that the variable that holds the data from the serial port is of type "byte," which is not a numeric type: it could actually be any character at all. Each "if" condition is comparing the data in the variable "val" with a string in quotes, such as `'1'`, or `'2'`, not with the actual number 1 or 2.

If that's beyond you right now, don't worry about it. Things like variable types will become second nature as you spend more time working with Arduino.

Once you've loaded the sketch in the Arduino IDE, plug your Arduino into the USB port, select the port from Tools ➤ Serial Port, select your Arduino board type from Tools ➤ Boards, click "verify" to compile the sketch, and if there were no errors, click "upload" to push it across to the Arduino.

ApplianceRemoteControlCompact

One thing you'll notice from the preceding version of the program is that although it is conceptually quite simple there is a lot of repetition in it. There are eight nearly identical lines defining output pins, and eight nearly identical lines forcing them low. There are also eight nearly identical blocks of code in the main loop, which makes it very long for such a simple program.

The compact version of the program uses a number of techniques to reduce the repetition in the code.

The button press definition doesn't change, but the definition of the output pins is much shorter because it lists them in an array rather than defining each of them as a separate variable. We also need to know how many outputs are listed in the array. We could have done that manually by simply counting them ourselves and assigning that value to a variable, but then we would have to remember to change the value if we changed the array. To avoid that problem we do a little trick that gets the total size of the array and then divides it by the size of a single element to get the number of elements. It doesn't actually matter which element we use as the divisor, because every element takes up the same number of bytes in memory. We'll just use the first element (element 0) in this case.

```
// Use pins 5 through 12 as the digital outputs
int pinMap[] = {5, 6, 7, 8, 9, 10, 11, 12};
byte pinCount = sizeof(pinMap) / sizeof(pinMap[0];
```

As before ,we also set a variable to specify how long to pulse each button for.

```
//Number of milliseconds to hold the outputs on
int buttonPressTime = 250;
```

An array is a list of values with the positions in the array numbered from 0. What that means is that the first entry is position 0 and has value 5, the second entry is position 1 and has value 6, the third entry is position 2 and has value 7, and so on.

What this allows us to do is simplify the setup function because instead of listing every single pin and setting it as an output and forcing it low, we can loop through the elements in the array and use each one in turn.

```
void setup()
{
  // Open the serial connection to listen for commands from the host Serial.begin(38400);

  int count = 0;  // Variable to store current array position
```

```
  // Set up the pins as outputs and force them LOW
  for(count; count < pinCount; count++) {
    pinMode(outputArray[count], OUTPUT);
    digitalWrite(outputArray[count], LOW);
  }
}
```

The for loop uses a simple counter that starts at 0 to read the first position in the array, then increments up through the positions to read each in turn.

The biggest change is in the main program loop which no longer has to check for every possible value explicitly, but can just check that it falls within an acceptable range.

```
void loop()
{
  byte val;     // The raw character read from the serial port
  int channel;  // Integer version of channel ID
  // Check if a value has been sent by the host
  if(Serial.available()) {
    val = Serial.read();

    channel = (int)val - 48; // Convert ASCII value to digit
    if(channel > 0 && channel <= pinCount) {
      pulseOutput(channel);  // Pulse the appropriate button
    }
  }
}
```

That's certainly a much shorter function than in the first version! There are a few things to pay careful attention to in the new version of the loop, though.

You'll notice that we have a new variable called "channel," which is an integer. While reading the serial port there is a cryptic line that sets the value of "channel" by taking the integer value of the "val" variable and subtracting 48 from it.

What's going on here? The byte received from the serial port is not actually a number, as you would generally expect. It's an ASCII value that represents a character, and that character may (or may not) be a number. The ASCII code for the character "1" is 49, and the ASCII code for the character "2" is 50, and so on. So when we receive a value of "1" from the serial port, the ASCII code that is transmitted (and loaded into the variable "val") is "49."What that line does is "cast" (convert) the value of "val" into an integer using the (int) prefix, then subtract 48 from it to convert it to the equivalent number. If the value sent via the serial port is "1" it will come through as ASCII code 49, then have 48 subtracted from it, and end up as the integer 1. The end result of all this trickery is that you send "1" at one end and get "1" out at the other end, but unfortunately it's not as simple as you might expect it to be!

After converting the received value, "val," to an integer value, "channel," it is then tested to see if it falls inside the acceptable range from 1 to "pinCount," which is the number of pins defined in the array.

Finally, if that test is met, the loop calls another function called pulseOutput(channel) which is where the actual work of firing the relay takes place.

```
void pulseOutput(int channel)
{
  Serial.print("Output ");
  Serial.print(channel);
```

```
  Serial.println(" ON");
  digitalWrite(outputArray[channel - 1], HIGH); // Channel number is 1 higher than array
position
  delay(buttonPressTime);
  digitalWrite(outputArray[channel - 1], LOW);
  Serial.print("Output ");
  Serial.print(channel);
  Serial.println(" OFF");
}
```

The pulseOutput function accepts a single integer value passed to it from the main program loop, and then sends notification via the serial port that it is about to turn on that channel. It then looks up the array listing the output pins (outputArray) to find the pin number that corresponds to the requested output. Because arrays are numbered starting from 0, while our output channels are numbered starting from 1, we have to subtract 1 from the requested channel to access the correct position in the array: output channel 1 is array position 0, and so on.

The function then pauses briefly, turns the appropriate relay back off, and sends notification that it's all done.

As you can see the compact version of the program is much shorter than the original. Once you're used to the way things such as arrays and functions work, you'll find it much less clumsy working with programs structured to remove repetition using techniques such as these.

Test Reed Relay Shield and Sketch

Your Arduino should now be connected to the appliance remote control transmitter using the reed relay shield, the transmitter should have its battery in place, and your Arduino will be listening on the serial port for an instruction to "press" a button.

Click the "monitor" button in the IDE to switch to serial-monitor mode where you can see values being sent to you by the Arduino and also send values to it. Select 38400 from the baud rate drop-down box (see Figure 2-13) to match the value we set the Arduino to in the setup function.

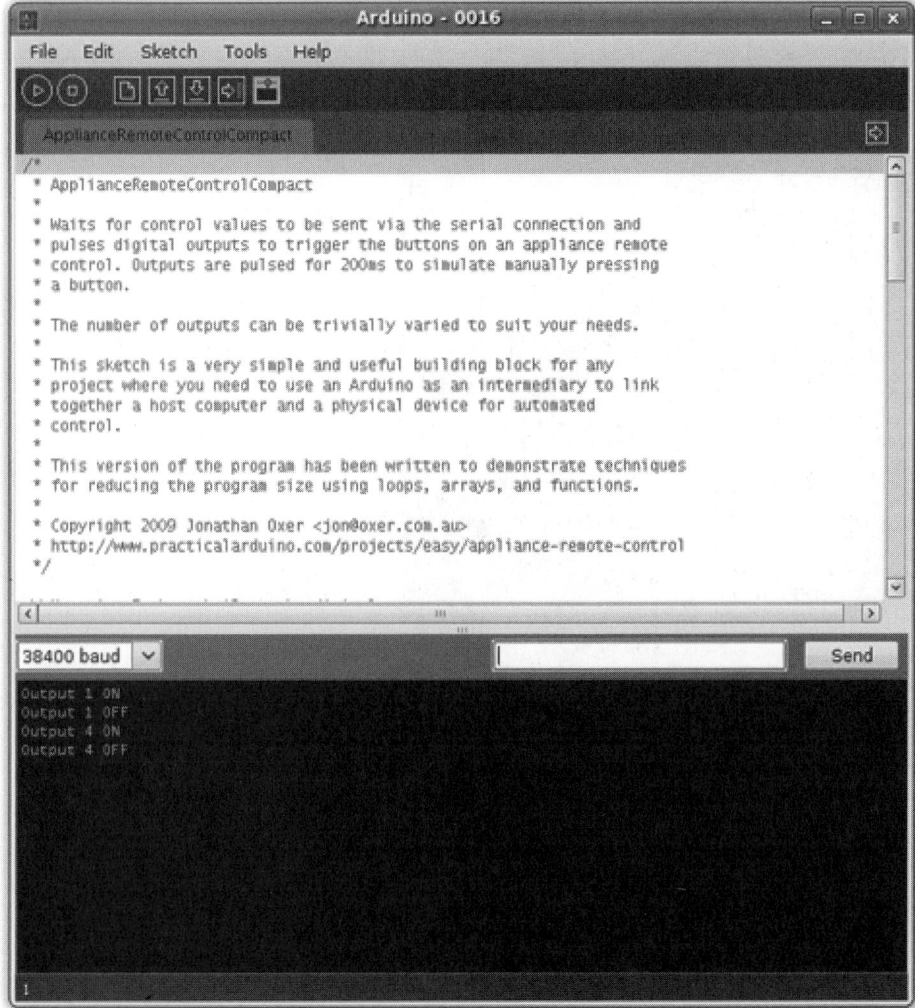

Figure 2-13. *Serial monitor in Arduino IDE*

Now for the moment of truth! Enter the value 1 into the text input area on the right and click Send or press Enter, and you should immediately see your Arduino send you a response saying that it received the command and is activating output 1, followed almost immediately by notification that it is turning the output off again. If everything is working as expected your appliance should turn on, and sending a value of 2 to the Arduino should turn it off again. You can see this at work in Figure 2-14.

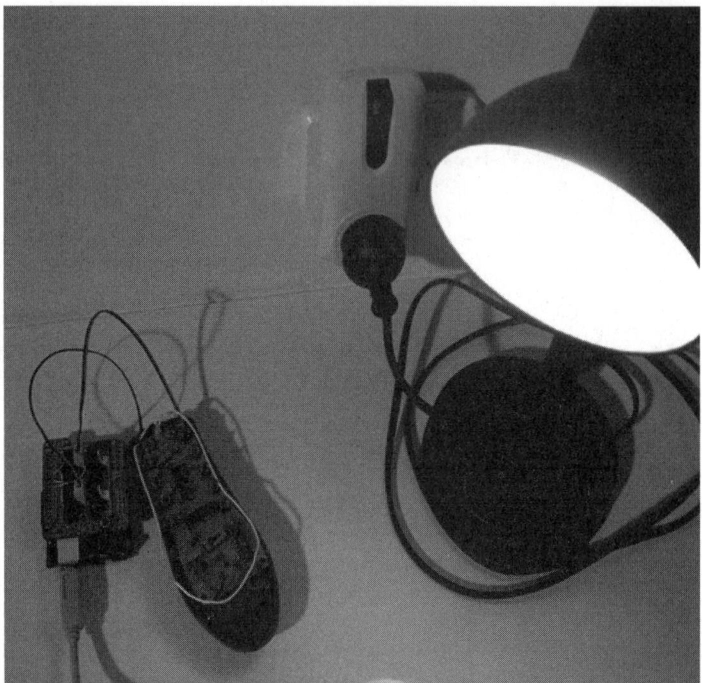

Figure 2-14. Arduino and shield using an appliance remote control to activate a lamp

Variations

Wireless Link

Rather than having the Arduino tethered to a computer, you could replace the USB connection with a wireless link such as an XBee or 433MHz wireless module or even with an Ethernet shield to provide you with a web-services interface to your appliances. WiFi and Ethernet connectivity are discussed in later projects.

Automatic Trigger

The example programs rely on messages being sent to the Arduino via a serial connection. By connecting an Arduino I/O line as an input and checking the status of a device, such as a motion detector, it could instead trigger outputs based on events such as a motion detector being triggered, a shop door-minder beam being broken, or a window being opened. Connecting to various devices including security sensors is covered later in the book.

Socket Connections

Using the serial monitor in the Arduino IDE is fine for testing, but to make this project useful you probably want to be able to control devices from a scripting language such as Python, Perl, or PHP so that events can be triggered automatically rather than manually through the IDE. A utility such as ser2net (on Linux) or serproxy (on MacOS and Windows) will take a serial connection and expose it as a network socket so that it can be accessed over a network. This is also a huge help when working with scripts running on the computer directly connected to the Arduino because most scripting languages are great at making socket connections but terrible at connecting to serial ports. Using a serial-to-network proxy allows you to use any scripting language that can open a network socket and have it talk to your Arduino via the USB connection as easily as if it were a network service.

There is more information on serial-to-network proxies on the Arduino web site at `www.arduino.cc/playground/Interfacing/Flash`.

CHAPTER 3

■ ■ ■

Time-Lapse Camera Controller

Simple digital cameras can produce remarkably good quality photos and are now cheap enough that it doesn't hurt the wallet too much to buy one with the intention of modifying it for use in a project. You may even have an old digital camera lying around that you don't mind sacrificing for a good cause!

Modifying a camera to control it from an Arduino opens up a world of possibilities. This project lets your Arduino take control of the camera to take photos at regular intervals so they can be reconstructed as a time-lapse movie. Set your frame interval to suit your subject and you could make a movie of plants growing, or a house being painted, or a house being built, or flowers blooming. Time lapse movies can be spectacular and this project will give you the tools to let your imagination run wild.

Parts Required

1 x Digital camera

1 x Arduino Duemilanove, Arduino Pro, Seeeduino, or equivalent

1 x Prototyping shield

2 x Reed relay

2 x 1N4001 diode or equivalent

1 x 3.5mm stereo socket

1 x Light-dependent resistor (optional)

1 x 10K resistor (optional)

Camera connection for Canon:

2 x 3.5mm stereo line plug

50cm shielded stereo cable

Camera connection for Panasonic:

1 x 3.5mm stereo line plug

1 x 2.5mm 4-connection line plug

1 x 1K8 resistor

1 x 27K resistor

1 x 33K resistor

50cm shielded mono cable

Camera connection via infrared:

1 x IR LED

Source code available from
`www.practicalarduino.com/projects/time-lapse-camera-controller`

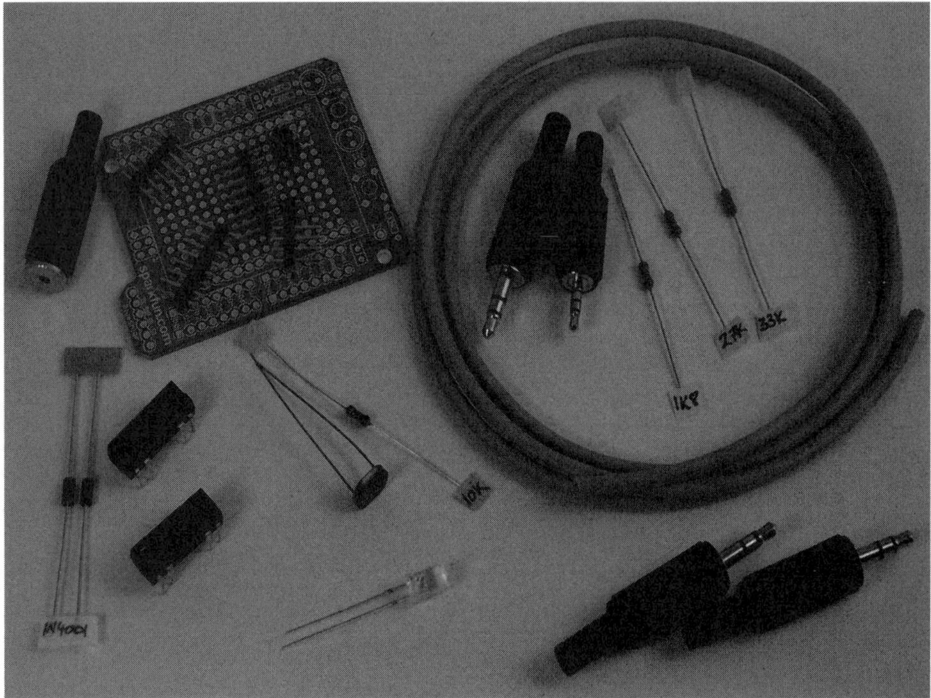

Figure 3-1. *Parts required for Time-Lapse Camera Controller*

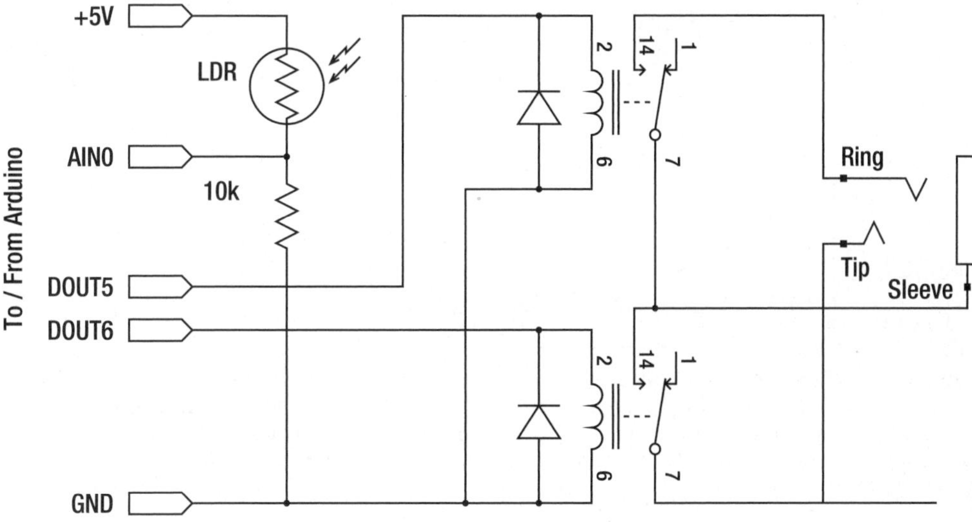

Figure 3-2. Schematic for non-camera-specific portion of the circuit

Instructions

Assemble Prototyping Shield

Control connections to the camera are made using a pair of reed relays that provide complete electrical isolation between your Arduino and the camera itself. In fact, this project has been designed to use the same pins as the first two outputs on the relay board used in the very first project, Appliance Remote Control, so that if you've already built that project, you can use the same board without modification. That's exactly what we did, and the only difference is that rather than wiring the 3.5mm stereo socket directly to the relay outputs, we needed to connect it to a pair of headers to plug into the relay outputs.If you're building a shield specifically for this project you can start by following the instructions for the Appliance Remote Control project in Chapter 2, but only fit the first two relays that are connected to Arduino digital I/O lines 5 and 6 along with their matching reverse-biased diodes.

Then wire up the 3.5mm stereo socket so that the outer (shield) connection goes to one terminal on both relays, the center (ring) connection for the focus trigger goes to the other terminal of the relay on digital pin 5, and the tip connection for the shutter trigger goes to the other terminal of the relay on digital pin 6.

The result is a 3.5mm stereo socket with one common connection and a pair of independently switched connections that have one link in common. The two relays will then be connected to "focus" and "shutter release," respectively, in the camera.

Connect Camera Shutter Release

There are several different methods shown here for controlling the shutter release of your camera, and which one you use will depend on the camera itself.

Remote Shutter Release Connector

If you are exceptionally lucky, your camera will have a remote shutter release connector. If this is the case, your job is made easy and you can assemble a cable that links your Arduino directly to your camera. Many Canon, Olympus, and Panasonic cameras, in particular, have a shutter release connector. Because there's no standardization among manufacturers, you may have to do a bit of research for your particular camera to figure out what the connections are.

Most remote shutter release connections have provision for both focus and shutter ("shoot") control. This allows you to tell the camera whether to activate auto-focus when taking the photo, which is usually what you want.

Panasonic Cable Connection

Panasonic cameras, such as the FZ series, use a 4-conductor 2.5mm connector that can be a bit hard to find. It looks like a smaller version of the 3.5mm connector used on earbuds and some headphones, but with four connections rather than three. Despite requiring a 4-conductor jack, they only use two of the connections, and also require a set of external resistors to indicate to the camera what command you want to send to it (see Figure 3-3).

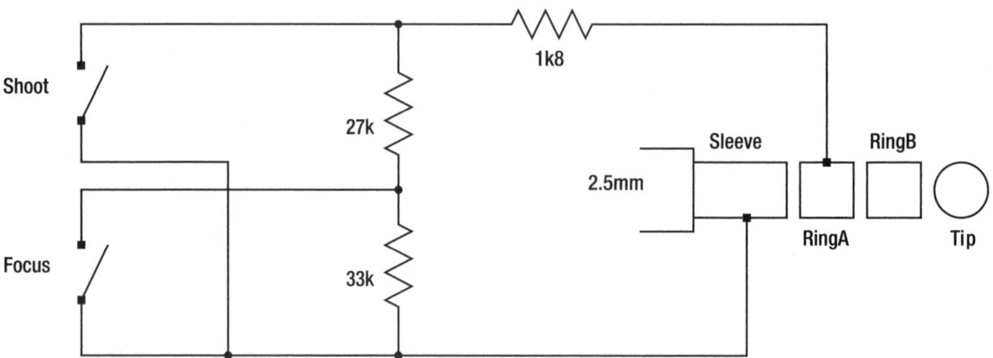

Figure 3-3. *Manual control connection for Panasonic cameras*

The Panasonic connection puts a resistance of around 62K across the connections when plugged in so that the camera can detect it. When the "focus" switch is activated, the resistance falls to around 29K, and when the "shoot" switch is activated the resistance falls to 1K8.

To make a cable to connect a Panasonic camera to your time-lapse controller, start by stripping back one end of the shielded cable and soldering the shield to the ring connection on a 2.5mm 4-connection plug. Then solder the cable's internal conductor to the first ring, the one adjacent to the sleeve.

The other end of the cable is a bit tricky to assemble. Start by soldering the shield to the sleeve connection on a 3.5mm stereo line plug, then fit a 33K resistor so that it goes from the sleeve connection to the ring connection. Next, connect the 27K resistor from the ring connection to the tip connection. Finally, connect the internal conductor in the cable to one end of the 1K8 resistor, and the other end of the resistor to the tip connection (see Figure 3-4). If you keep all the connections neat and tight and use some heat-shrink tubing as insulation at appropriate points, you should be able to make the whole assembly small enough to fit within the plastic cover for the plug.

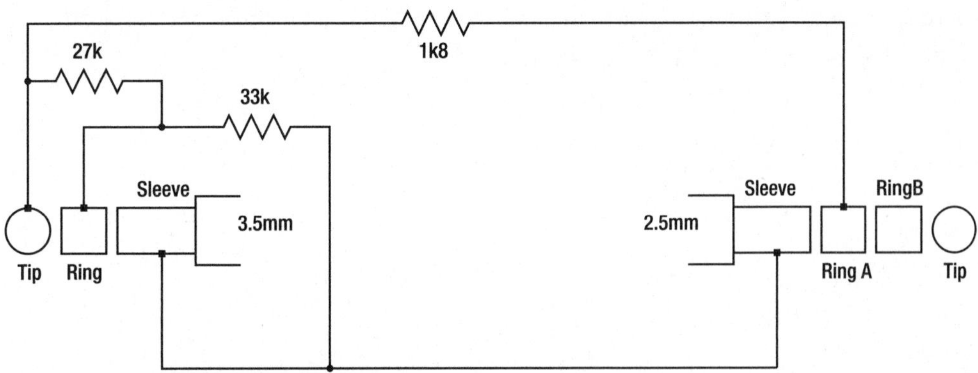

Figure 3-4. Automatic control cable for Panasonic cameras

Canon Connection

Many Canon cameras use a similar system to the Panasonic remote shutter release, but with a commonly available stereo 3.5mm connector instead. The Canon system uses all three connections in the plug—one for ground and the other two for the "focus" and "shoot" switches—making it even simpler to assemble (see Figure 3-5). In fact, all you need to build your own Canon external shutter release is a 3.5mm plug, two push buttons, and some wire. In this project, we'll use the same circuit, but rather than using manual switches, we'll make a cable that connects the camera to the reed relay outputs to control focus and shoot.

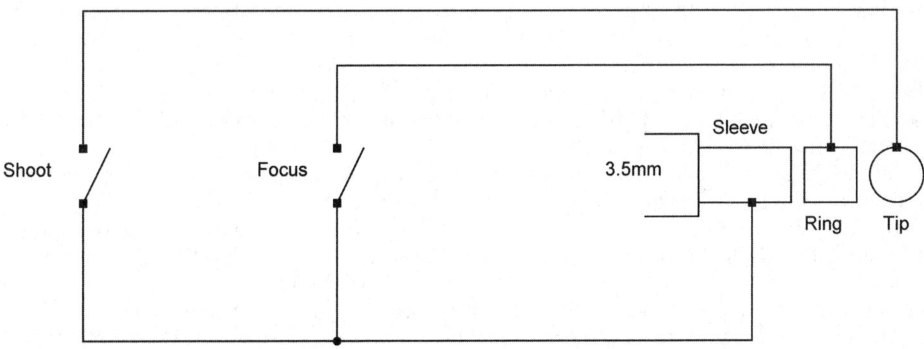

Figure 3-5. Manual control cable for Canon cameras

Strip back one end of the shielded cable and solder it onto a 3.5mm stereo line plug, using the shield for the sleeve connection and one of the internal conductors for the ring next to it. Connect the other conductor to the tip. Our personal preference is to be consistent with the audio color codes typically used in 3.5mm plugs and connect the red conductor to the ring (the "focus" connection), and white to the tip (the "shoot" connection).

Then strip back the other end of the shielded cable and solder on another 3.5mm stereo line plug using the exact some connections, forming a "straight through" cable that connects the sleeve on one plug to the sleeve on the other, the ring on one to the ring on the other, and the tip on one to the tip on the other (see Figure 3-6).

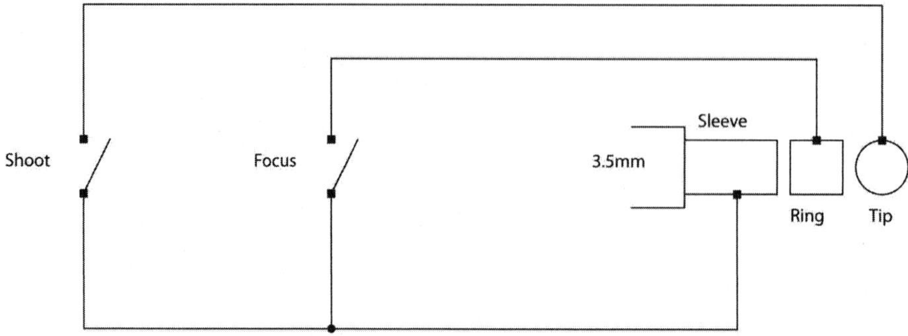

Figure 3-6. *Automatic control cable for Canon cameras*

In both Panasonic and Canon cables, the remote shutter release mechanism uses two outputs from the time-lapse controller, and as far as the software is concerned, they behave in exactly the same way. The only difference is the cable you need to assemble to connect the Arduino to the camera.

Infrared Remote Control

If you're a bit lucky, your camera will have an infrared remote control intended to allow you to control it from a distance, such as when it's sitting on a tripod and you want to take a group photo while you're in the group. Even if your camera didn't ship with a remote control, it may have an IR receiver intended for use with an optional remote that can be purchased separately.

Many digital video cameras come with an IR remote control and are capable of taking good quality still photos onto an SD memory card, so you might find that a digital video camera is a good alternative to using a regular digital camera.

If your camera came with a remote control, you can open it up and connect the "shutter" reed relay output on the shield across the terminals of the appropriate button in a similar way to the Appliance Remote Control project. A simple cable made using a 3.5mm stereo line plug and a mono shielded cable is all you need (see Figure 3-7). This could allow you to trigger the shutter without modifying the camera at all.

An alternative approach is to connect an IR LED to your Arduino and have it emulate a remote control by sending the same code as a factory control. For Nikon cameras, the easiest way to do this is using the nikonIrControl library that you can download from `www.vonroth.com/Arduino/NikonIrControl`.

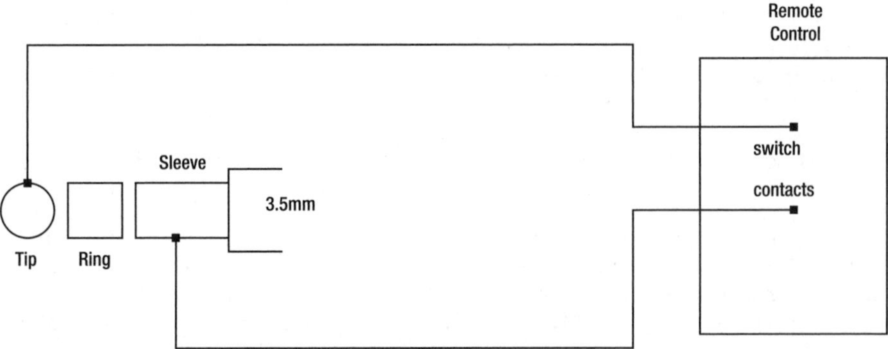

Figure 3-7. Automatic control cable for I/R remotes

Extract the library and install it into your Arduino environment by placing it into the hardware/libraries directory in your Arduino directory and then clicking Sketch > Import Library and choosing the library (see the section "Writing an Arduino Library" in Chapter 16 for more details). Then plug the anode lead (the longer lead) of an IR LED into pin 13, and the cathode (shorter lead) into ground. You can then trigger a Nikon camera with a very simple program, like the on that follows, which takes one photo per second.

```
#include <nikonIrControl.h>      // Use the nikonIrControl library
int CameraIrPin = 13;            // IR LED connected to digital pin 13
void setup()
{
  pinMode(CameraIrPin, OUTPUT); // Sets the digital pin as output
}
void loop()
{
  cameraSnap(CameraIrPin);       // Send the IR code to take a photo
  delay(1000);                   // Wait 1 second
}
```

Other brands handle IR control in different ways, so if you have a different type of camera you might need to do a bit of research to see if there is a similar library for your camera.

Modify Camera

If you're not at all lucky, your camera has no built-in method for triggering it externally and no IR remote control, so you'll need to open it up and find the connections to the shutter release button so you can solder wires onto them. Most cameras have a multistage shutter-release button that activates auto-focus when pressed half way, then takes a photo when fully depressed.

Make up a cable similar to the one described previously for connection to an IR remote control, and open up your camera to find the connections to the shutter release button. Obviously every camera is different in this respect, so you're pretty much on your own in terms of finding the appropriate connections. A bit of careful investigation with a multimeter and some tests with a short length of wire to bridge the button connections should help you quickly find the correct connections.

Solder the end of the cable to the button connections and you should be ready to go.

Configure Camera

To keep your camera running for days, weeks, or even months, you will need to provide an external power source and disable the camera's power-saving mode so it doesn't turn itself off.

Many cameras have an external power socket, so it may be as simple as finding an appropriate wall wart power supply and plugging it in. Alternatively, you might be able to solder leads to the battery connectors inside the camera and connect a socket to match a power supply that runs at the same voltage as the batteries. For example, most digital cameras use two AA batteries in series to provide 3V, so a 3V wall wart with the plug cut off might be just what you need. If you can't get a soldering iron onto the battery terminals, you can even use some old batteries and put tape over the ends so you can use them to physically jam wires against the battery terminals while bypassing the batteries themselves.

Go into the settings for your camera and disable power-saving mode so that it doesn't turn off after a period of inactivity. If your camera doesn't allow you to do that, set it to the longest setting possible and make sure that you take photos more often than that interval to prevent it from going to sleep.

And while you're adjusting the camera settings, remember to disable the audible feedback that the camera makes when it takes a photo. Otherwise it will probably drive you insane after the first ten minutes!

Calculate Photo Interval

It's quite straightforward to calculate how often the camera needs to take a photo. Start by deciding how long your final movie is likely to be and what framerate it will run at: a 2 minute movie running at 25 frames/second, for example, will require a total of 2 × 60 × 25 = 3000 frames. Then consider how long the sequence you're filming is likely to take and convert it to seconds: a tree losing its leaves over the space of a week takes 7 × 24 × 60 × 60 = 604800 seconds. Divide the second number by the first to get the image interval, which in this example is 604800 / 3000 = 201 seconds. That's how often you need the camera to take a photo to end up with a movie of the right length.

Keep in mind there might be periods you'll need to cut out of your sequence, such as photos taken at night, so remember to factor that into your calculation.

Configure and Load Sketch

The sketch for this project is incredibly simple. All it does is set up digital I/O lines 5 and 6 as outputs for the "focus" and "shutter" reed relays, respectively, and make sure they are set low. It then does the same for digital I/O line 13 to use the onboard LED as an activity indicator, and then goes into an infinite loop that triggers both outputs for half a second at a configurable interval.

The only tunable parameter is the delay interval that needs to be set in seconds at the top of the sketch.

```
int frameInterval = 300;          // Delay between pictures (in seconds)
int focusPin = 5;                 // Reed relay on digital pin 5

int shutterPin = 6;               // Reed relay on digital pin 6

int ledPin = 13;                  // LED connected to digital pin 13

void setup()
{
```

```
  pinMode(focusPin, OUTPUT);        // Set the focus pin as an output
  digitalWrite(focusPin, LOW);
  pinMode(shutterPin, OUTPUT);      // Set the shutter pin as an output
  digitalWrite(shutterPin, LOW);
  pinMode(ledPin, OUTPUT);          // Set the LED pin as an output
  digitalWrite(ledPin, LOW);
}
void loop()
{
  digitalWrite(ledPin, HIGH);       // Turn on activity LED
  digitalWrite(focusPin, HIGH);     // Turn on focus relay
  digitalWrite(shutterPin, HIGH);   // Turn on shutter relay
  delay(500);                       // Hold the button for 1/2 second
  digitalWrite(ledPin, LOW);        // Turn off activity LED
  digitalWrite(shutterPin, LOW);    // Turn off shutter relay
  digitalWrite(focusPin, LOW);      // Turn off focus relay
  delay(1000 * frameInterval);      // Wait the required interval before repeating
}
```

While this simple delay-loop approach works perfectly well for simple projects like this, it can become a problem if you want to add a bit of intelligence to the system later. Whenever the Arduino is waiting for the delay() function at the end of the loop to finish, it is effectively locked: it can't process other commands even though the CPU isn't doing anything useful at the time.

It's good practice to avoid unnecessary delay loops in your sketches if possible, so we've also included another version of the same sketch that has been written using the Aiko application framework. Aiko is an Arduino library that is designed to make it easy to write "event-driven" sketches consisting of many subsections that may either run independently or interact with each other in a complex way. Although it's overkill for this little project, it's a good exercise to compare the simple delay-loop approach shown previously to a version of the same sketch written using Aiko.

To use Aiko in your sketches, you need to download and install it using the instructions shown at the development repository at `github.com/geekscape/Aiko`.

Once it's installed you'll be able to compile the following "Aiko-ised" version of the sketch.

```
#include <AikoEvents.h>
using namespace Aiko;
int frameInterval = 300;            // Delay between pictures (in seconds)
int focusPin = 5;                   // Reed relay on digital pin 5

int shutterPin = 6;                 // Reed relay on digital pin 6
int ledPin = 13;                    // LED connected to digital pin 13
void setup()
{

  pinMode(focusPin, OUTPUT);        // Set the focus pin as an output
  digitalWrite(focusPin, LOW);
  pinMode(shutterPin, OUTPUT);      // Set the shutter pin as an output
  digitalWrite(shutterPin, LOW);
  pinMode(ledPin, OUTPUT);          // Set the LED pin as an output
  digitalWrite(ledPin, LOW);

  Events.addHandler(takePhoto, frameInterval * 1000); // Every 'frameInterval' seconds
```

```
}
void loop()
{
  Events.loop();
}
void takePhoto()
{
  digitalWrite(ledPin, HIGH);      // Turn on activity LED
  digitalWrite(focusPin, HIGH);    // Turn on focus relay
  digitalWrite(shutterPin, HIGH); // Turn on shutter relay
  delay(500);                      // Hold the button for 1/2 second
  digitalWrite(ledPin, LOW);       // Turn off activity LED
  digitalWrite(shutterPin, LOW);  // Turn off shutter relay
  digitalWrite(focusPin, LOW);    // Turn off focus relay
}
```

All programs using the Aiko framework start by including the Aiko library itself and declaring the Aiko namespace. This step allows the rest of the program to use the features provided by Aiko.

The program then uses the same configuration values as the original sketch, and also sets up the digital outputs in the same way.

The differences begin on the last line of the setup() function where the program calls Aiko's Events.addHandler() function to define an event handler that needs to be called at a regular interval. In this case, the event handler is the takePhoto() function and we declare that we need it to be executed every "frameInterval" seconds. Because Aiko's time-based event handler needs the delay to be defined in milliseconds, we multiply the frameInterval value by 1000 so it will be set correctly.

You'll notice that the loop() function in the Aiko version is dramatically simplified: instead of performing the delay and controlling the digital outputs inside the main program loop, all we need to do is have a call to Events.loop(), another Aiko function that ensures any event handlers due to be executed are processed as required.

Finally, you can see that we have defined a new function called takePhoto(), which is the function declared as the event handler earlier in the program using Events.addHandler(). Every time the event handler comes due for execution (every 300 seconds, in this case) it will be invoked automatically by the Events.loop() line inside the main loop.

This approach sounds more complicated, but it gains us a very important advantage: whenever the Arduino is not actually executing the takePhoto() function it is free to do other things. The CPU is not bound in a delay() function for the entire time between taking photos, so you can easily extend the program to add other functionality independently of clicking the shutter on your camera.

The following trivial extension to the Aiko version of the program shows how easy this is.

```
#include <AikoEvents.h>
using namespace Aiko;
int frameInterval = 300;          // Delay between pictures (in seconds)
int focusPin = 5;                 // Reed relay on digital pin 5

int shutterPin = 6;               // Reed relay on digital pin 6
int ledPin = 13;                  // LED connected to digital pin 13
void setup()
{

  pinMode(focusPin, OUTPUT);      // Set the focus pin as an output
  digitalWrite(focusPin, LOW);
```

```
  pinMode(shutterPin, OUTPUT);     // Set the shutter pin as an output
  digitalWrite(shutterPin, LOW);
  pinMode(ledPin, OUTPUT);         // Set the LED pin as an output
  digitalWrite(ledPin, LOW);
  Events.addHandler(takePhoto, frameInterval * 1000); // Every 'frameInterval' seconds
  Events.addHandler(blinkLed, 5000); // Blink status LED every 5 seconds
}
void loop()
{
  Events.loop();
}
void takePhoto()
{
  digitalWrite(ledPin, HIGH);      // Turn on activity LED
  digitalWrite(focusPin, HIGH);    // Turn on focus relay
  digitalWrite(shutterPin, HIGH); // Turn on shutter relay
  delay(500);                      // Hold the button for 1/2 second
  digitalWrite(ledPin, LOW);       // Turn off activity LED
  digitalWrite(shutterPin, LOW);  // Turn off shutter relay
  digitalWrite(focusPin, LOW);     // Turn off focus relay
}

void blinkLed()
{
  digitalWrite(ledPin, HIGH);
  delay(100);
  digitalWrite(ledPin, LOW);
}
```

All we've done in this example is add another event handler called blinkLed() that flickers the status LED on for 1/10th of a second, and used another call to Events.addHandler() to set that handler to be invoked every five seconds. With this sketch your Arduino time-lapse controller will now flicker its status LED to show an "I'm alive" heartbeat every five seconds, no matter what your photo frequency is set to: the two event handlers are totally independent and will be called automatically at the correct intervals by Aiko—much neater than trying to manage the timing of two independent events within a single large delay loop!

Another advantage which may not be so obvious at first glance is that it makes the photo interval more consistent: it won't "drift" due to time used to take the photo itself. If you go back to the first version of the sketch, you will notice that it won't actually take a photo every 300 seconds as intended because there is a small amount of time spent taking the photo itself. What it actually does is take a photo, wait 300 seconds, take another photo (which itself takes 1/2 a second), wait 300 seconds, and so on. Each cycle will therefore take just over 300.5 seconds because the program doesn't subtract the time spent taking a photo from the delay between photos. The result is that photos will tend to drift over time until they're no longer on neat intervals of 300 seconds, 600 seconds, 900 seconds, and so on.

Sure, in this example you don't really care about a 1/2 second drift, and even if you did care you could just code around the inaccuracy by figuring out how long each photo takes and then have the program subtract that value from the frameInterval period, but with the Aiko version this problem simply doesn't exist. If you set an Aiko event to be executed every 300 seconds, then it will be executed every 300 seconds, even if the event itself takes some time to complete.

Check Memory Capacity

Check that the memory in your camera is large enough to handle the number of photos you need to take based on the previous calculation. SD memory cards are very cheap these days, so a 2GB or 4GB card should give you enough storage for thousands of photos for just a few dollars. Try adjusting the image quality/resolution setting to a medium level to dramatically increase the number of frames the camera can store compared to a typical high-resolution setting, which is probably overkill anyway since the resolution of the final movie will be much less than a typical still photo.

Set Up Your Shoot

When taking a series of photos over a long period of time, it's critical that the camera remain as still as possible. Even slight movement can ruin the effect, so mount the camera very firmly using a tripod or other solid mount.

Process the Images

When it's all over, transfer all the images from your camera to a computer either using the cable supplied with the camera or by removing the memory card and connecting it to your computer using a card reader. Once you have the images in a folder on your computer, you need some software to process them all and convert them into a movie, but of course the exact process will depend on what operating system you run and what end result you're trying to achieve.

Once you're done and have a cool time-lapse movie, make sure you share it with the world! Upload it to a video-sharing web site like YouTube or Vimeo and tag it with "practicalarduino," and then let us know about it so we can link to it from the *Practical Arduino* site.

Linux

Most Linux distributions have a command-line image-processing suite called "convert" available, so the simplest approach for creating a movie is to open a terminal, go into the folder containing your images, and type the following:

```
convert *.jpg timelapse.mpg
```

This will take all images with a lowercase .jpg extension (adjust the command as necessary to suit the naming scheme used by your camera) and create an MPEG movie called "timelapse." You can then play the movie with whatever media player is provided, such as Kino, MPlayer, Xine, or VLC.

Windows

A free program called PhotoLapse can take a sequence of JPEG image files and convert them into an AVI movie file. You can download PhotoLapse free from the author's web site at `home.hccnet.nl/s.vd.palen`.For more information about how to use it and what codecs to install, see the brief tutorial on the AddictiveTips site at `www.addictivetips.com/windows-tips/make-time-lapse-video-from-sequence-photos`. Another option is to use Windows Movie Maker, included with many versions of Windows. However, Windows Movie Maker has a limitation that it can only create time-lapse movies up to 8 frames per second, which may make your movie look a bit jerky.

Macintosh

The free version of QuickTime included with MacOS X can create time-lapse movies, but has the limitation that it can't resize the end result, It also doesn't apply any compression. If you have QuickTime Pro (or, better still, Apple Final Cut) they have more options, but for a basic movie the regular version of QuickTime, included with Leopard and earlier releases of MacOS X, will do.

Be careful if you have Snow Leopard, though: you'll need to do a little bit more preparation because it ships with a dumbed-down version of QuickTime called QuickTime X and doesn't include this functionality. You'll need to insert your Snow Leopard disk, select Customize, and install the 7.x version of QuickTime. It will then be available under Applications ➤ Utilities ➤ QuickTime Player 7. More information on this process is available at `support.apple.com/kb/HT3678`.

Once you have QuickTime installed, launch it and go to the File menu, select Open File..., then choose the last image in your sequence. You'll then see a new movie player containing the image. Then select all the other images in the Finder in the correct order (excluding the last image) and drag them on top of the open movie window. The additional images will be added as frames in order before the already opened image, which is why we started by selecting the last image first. Confusing, but it works.

At this point you can't save the movie directly through the menu so you have to click the Close button in the window. Rather than immediately closing, QuickTime will then ask if you want to save the unsaved movie.

Select the "Save as a self-contained movie" option, give the movie a name, and save it.

The result will be a fairly large, uncompressed movie that runs at 15fps. If you want to put it online, you'll probably need to process it with a movie editor to compress it.

Variations

Adding a light-level sensor to the Arduino allows it to skip taking photos when it's too dark, which can be very handy if you're making a movie outside that you can't light artificially at night.

Light-dependent resistors (LDRs) vary their resistance inversely to the amount of light that is falling on them: in other words, in bright light they have very low resistance and allow a current to flow, while in darkness they have very high resistance and prevent current from flowing. The schematic shows how to add an LDR so that it can be read using an analog input to detect the current light level.

Connect an LDR so that one lead is connected to analog input 0 on the Arduino and the other lead is connected to the VCC (+5V) pin. Then connect a 10k resistor so that one pin connects to the analog input 0 and the other end goes to GND. What this will do is create a variable voltage divider that will present a low voltage to the analog input when it's dark and a high voltage when it's light. The voltage will also vary between those two extremes in partial lighting. You can then run the alternative example sketch, available from the *Practical Arduino* site, to have your Arduino only take photos when it is light.

The takePhoto() function can then be extended to wrap its functionality inside an analog read so that if the voltage divider is above a certain level it will operate, but otherwise it will do nothing.

```
void takePhoto()
{
  if(analogRead(0) > 300)
  {
    digitalWrite(ledPin, HIGH);     // Turn on activity LED
    digitalWrite(focusPin, HIGH);   // Turn on focus relay
    digitalWrite(shutterPin, HIGH); // Turn on shutter relay
    delay(500);                     // Hold the button for 1/2 second
    digitalWrite(ledPin, LOW);      // Turn off activity LED
    digitalWrite(shutterPin, LOW);  // Turn off shutter relay
    digitalWrite(focusPin, LOW);    // Turn off focus relay
  }
}
```

You might need to experiment with the comparison value for the analogRead to have the sketch disable the shutter output at the correct light level.

CHAPTER 4

■ ■ ■

Virtual USB Keyboard

Giving your Arduino the ability to pretend to be a keyboard, mouse, or joystick opens up a whole world of possibilities because it means your Arduino can now interact with software that was never intended for automated control by a smart device. This could be desktop software, such as a game or a web browser. For example, your Arduino could "type" into a web form and submit it on your behalf, or act as a custom controller for a game.

You could also use an Arduino to connect a custom input device to your computer so that it is seen as a regular keyboard or joystick. The custom input device could be a chording keyboard, for example, or even something such as a virtual-reality glove or head tracking system that controls the cursor location in joystick mode. The required parts are shown in Figure 4-1, and the complete schematic is in Figure 4-2.

Parts Required

1 x Arduino Duemilanove, Arduino Pro, Seeeduino, or equivalent

1 x Prototyping shield

1 x PCB-mount female USB "B" connector

1 x USB A-to-B cable (commonly used as a printer cable)

2 x 3.6V Zener diodes (must be rated at 0.5W or less, 1W won't work)

1 x 2.2K 0.25W or 0.5W resistor

2 x 68R 0.25W or 0.5W resistor

4 x SPST push buttons (optional)

Source code available from
`www.practicalarduino.com/projects/virtual-usb-keyboard`

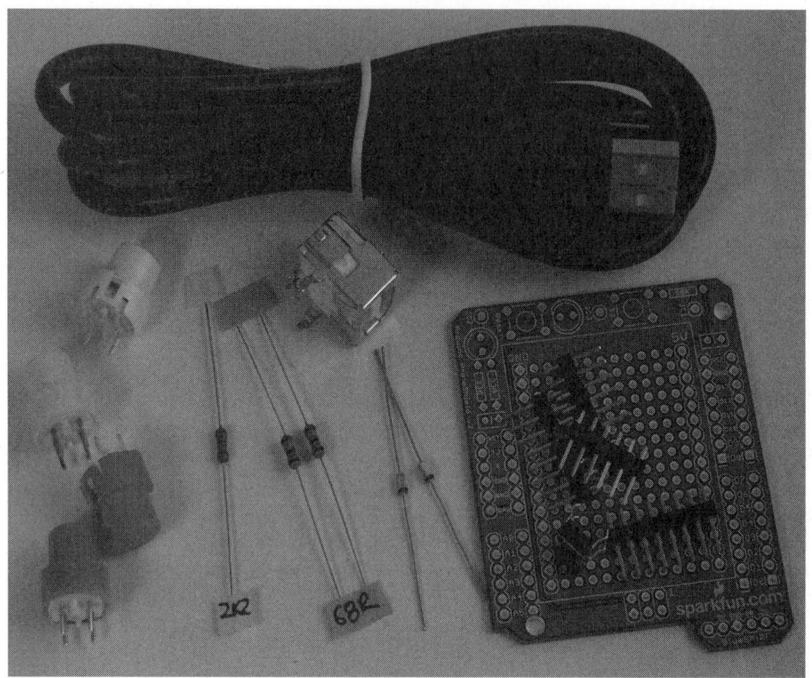

Figure 4-1. Parts required for the Virtual USB Keyboard

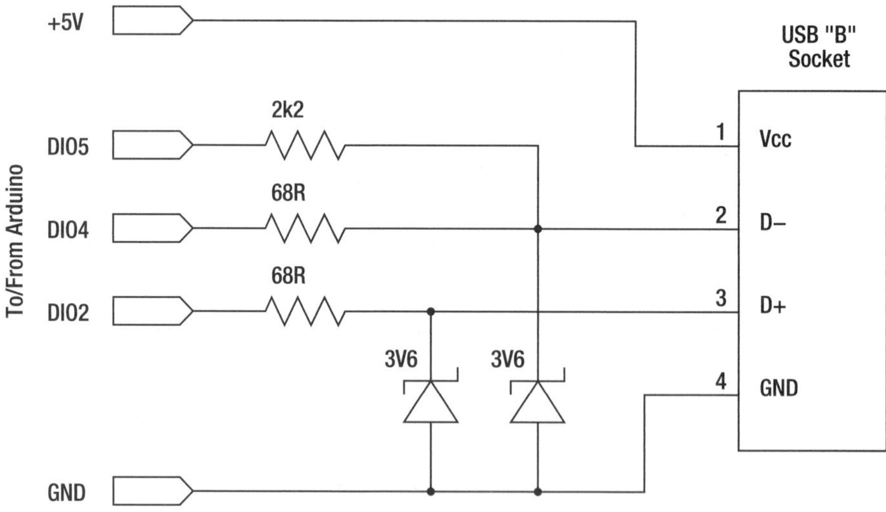

Figure 4-2. Schematic for the Virtual USB Keyboard

Instructions

Populate Prototyping Shield

While there's not much that can go drastically wrong, before beginning construction you should consider using a USB hub to connect your virtual USB keyboard shield to your computer the first few times. Even though they have excellent internal protection already, we wouldn't want a fault in the shield to fry a USB port in your expensive computer—much better to sacrifice a cheap USB hub.

There aren't many parts in this project so the layout isn't particularly critical. You can rearrange components to suit yourself if you have particular requirements for fitting it inside a case and still getting access to the USB connector.

Start by mounting the USB connector on one edge of the prototyping shield. It's important to mount it in such a way that you will be able to plug the USB lead into the connector while it is mounted on the board without any other components getting in the way. PCB-mount USB connectors have two tabs sticking out of the body to provide physical stability since the force of plugging and unplugging a cable can be quite large, so it's important to use the tabs to hold the socket in place rather than rely on the four tiny pins used for electrical connections. As a general principle it's not a good idea to have mechanical support ("strain relief") provided by signal-carrying electrical connections if you can avoid it, and many parts designed to be subjected to physical force provide mechanical mounts separate from the pins.

The tabs on the bottom of the USB socket are kinked so they can clip into appropriately sized holes, but that provides very weak support and we certainly wouldn't rely on it. Instead we used a pair of pliers to straighten the tabs and then drilled two holes through the prototyping shield so they could slide down neatly with the four pins aligned with existing holes in the shield. Then, with the socket pushed hard against the shield, we bent the tabs inward and soldered them onto pads on the shield to give it a very strong physical mount that won't budge when a USB cable is inserted or removed. Make sure you keep the tabs away from the pads used to connect the pins to prevent any short circuits.

Before adding any more parts to the shield it's a good idea to use the USB cable to connect it to the computer and use a multimeter to verify the 0V and +5V connections on the socket pins. Then disconnect the USB lead and fit the 2K2 resistor linking the D– line (pin 2) to Arduino digital I/O pin 5. This allows the UsbKeyboard library to reset the USB connection under software control.

If you're curious about how USB works, it can be interesting at this point to temporarily connect digital I/O pin 5 to the +5V pin and plug the shield back into the cable connected to your computer. If you watch the system log on your computer while you do it, you'll discover that even the basic shield with nothing on it but the connector and one resistor will be identified by the computer as a low-speed USB device! Obviously it can't actually send or receive data because there's no intelligence in it yet, but it demonstrates that device presence detection is an electrical operation and has nothing to do with data flowing on the bus.

Disconnect the temporary connection between digital I/O pin 5 and +5V if you performed the previous experiment and proceed to fitting the 68R resistors that connect the D– and D+ USB data lines to the Arduino digital I/O lines. D– (USB pin 2) connects via one resistor to Arduino digital I/O pin 4, while D+ (USB pin 3) connects via the other resistor to digital I/O pin 2 (see Figure 4-3).

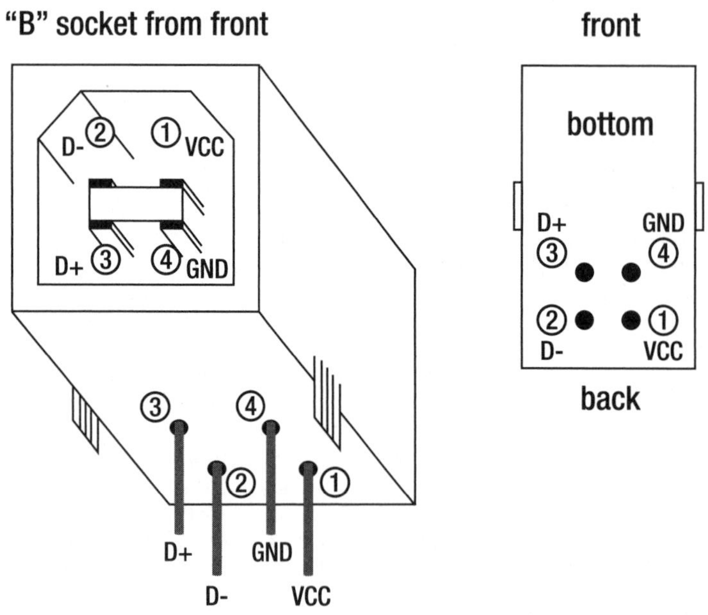

Figure 4-3. Physical pinout of USB "B" socket

Table 4-1. Pin assignment of USB "B" socket

Pin	Name	Cable Color	Description
1	VCC	Red	+5 VDC
2	D–	White	Data –
3	D+	Green	Data +

Note that the use of Arduino digital I/O pins 2 and 4 is hard-coded into the UsbKeyboard library itself and can't be changed in your program. The use of digital I/O pin 2, in particular, is critical because the library relies on the "interrupt" associated with that pin to detect events on the USB connection.

Fit the 3.6V Zener diodes that link the D– (USB pin 2) and D+ (USB pin 3) USB data lines to ground, being careful with orientation of the diodes: the ends with the bands connect to the data lines with the other ends connected to ground.

The purpose of the Zener diodes may seem a bit cryptic at first, but they are absolutely critical to the operation of the circuit. The USB standard specifies that even though the power supply line is +5V, the communication lines themselves run at a nominal voltage of 3.3V. It's also a little different to what you may have seen on other serial connections, such as RS232, which have "TX" (transmit) and "RX" (receive) lines. The D– and D+ lines are not independent TX/RX lines, as you may expect, but are actually what is known as a "half-duplex differential signalling pair." This approach helps USB run at very high data rates by reducing the effect of electrical noise.

A Zener diode has a special property in that it "clamps" a voltage to around the same voltage level as the diode is specified for. In the forward direction it acts just like a normal diode, conducting with the common 0.6V drop. However, in the reverse direction, unlike a normal diode which is basically open circuit until it breaks down, the Zener diode will start conducting at its specified voltage. This is commonly called "clamping."This makes them very useful for regulating and setting voltage levels in low-power circuits, and also invaluable as voltage reduction and protection devices.

In this circuit the Zener diodes clip the 5V supplied by the Arduino I/O pins down to the 3.3V USB standard.

But wait. Why use a 3.6V Zener to achieve a 3.3V limit?

That's because, in this particular application, the electrical characteristics of the circuit mean that the voltage actually achieved will be a little below the rating on the Zener. Using a 3.6V Zener results in the voltage on the data lines ending up clipped to approximately the correct 3.3V level. Since the USB standard specifies that the voltage must be in the range of 2.8 to 3.6V, it doesn't matter if we exceed 3.3V a little and it all works out just nicely.

One final word about the Zener diodes: power rating is critical, but not in the way you might expect. Power rating on components is based on how much energy they can safely dissipate before the magic smoke comes out, so most of the time it's perfectly safe to overrate your parts and use a component with a higher rating than required for the particular circuit. However, in this case that approach can actually prevent the circuit from working because the trade-off in Zener diode design is that as its power rating increases it also exhibits more capacitance—not only will it behave like a Zener, but it will also behave like a tiny capacitor! For simple power-regulation requirements that's just fine. However, in this case, the data lines need to change state very fast and any capacitance added to the line will effectively "damp" the data lines and prevent them from moving between low and high values fast enough. Capacitance on a high-speed data line is very bad and needs to be avoided or the circuit simply won't work. In practice, a 1/4W Zener diode should work fine; a 1/2W Zener should work, but is a bit on the borderline; and a 1W Zener almost certainly won't work—it will simply have too much capacitance.

Finding stock of through-hole (leaded) Zeners below 1W can be quite tricky now because many electronics shops only stock the 1W versions, but if you're lucky you may find a shop with old stock of 1/4W or 1/2W diodes. If not, you may need to resort to using surface-mount diodes: SMD Zeners are commonly available in low power ratings. With a steady hand and a small soldering iron tip you should be able to solder them between adjacent pads on a prototyping shield without too much difficulty, particularly if you can find them in a larger package size such as 1206 or 0805.

Zener diodes are truly bizarre components with some very unusual characteristics. If you want to find out more about them, read the Wikipedia article at `en.wikipedia.org/wiki/Zener_diode`.

Finally, install jumper leads from the GND pin on the USB connector (pin 4) to the Arduino's ground connection on the shield, and VCC (USB connector pin 1) to the Arduino's +5V on the shield. This can't be seen in the photograph of our prototype (see Figure 4-4) because the connection was made directly underneath the shield from one pad to another. The connection from USB VCC to Arduino +5V is optional, and if you are going to power your Arduino from some other power source you should leave it off. However, with that connection in place the Arduino can draw its power from the USB port on the host and doesn't need any other connections at all. It allows you to just plug your USB shield/Arduino combination into a host using the socket on the shield and the Arduino will power up automatically.

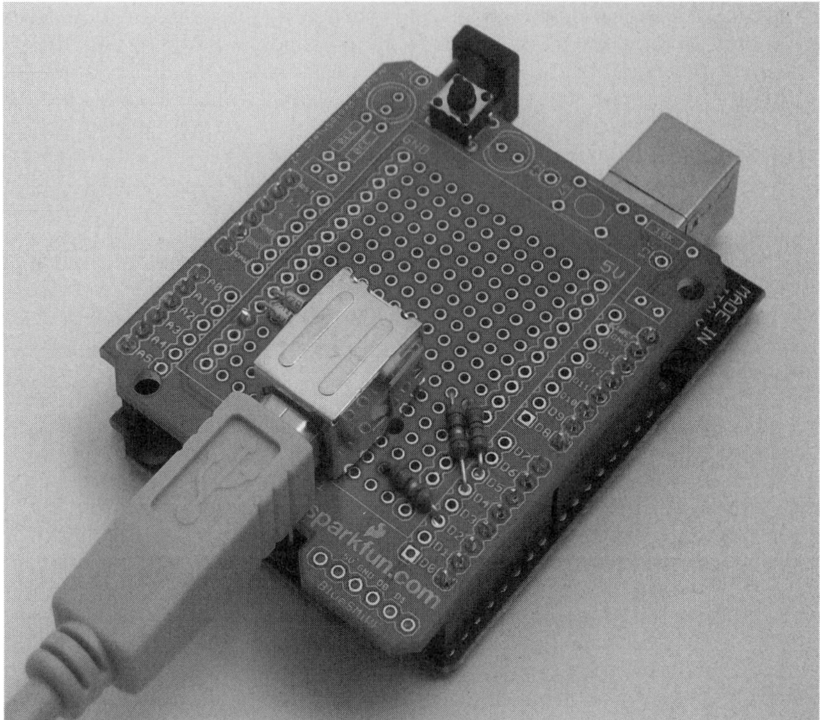

Figure 4-4. *USB "B" connector, Zener diodes, and resistors assembled on shield*

Prepare the UsbKeyboard Library

The example sketch simply emulates a USB keyboard and reads the value of four digital input lines and sends characters to the host computer whenever one of the inputs is pulled low. On our shield we installed four PCB-mount push buttons that connect Arduino inputs 8, 9, 10, and 11 to ground when pressed, but you could just as easily use an external sensor such as the output from a motion detector to pull one of the inputs low and trigger transmission of characters.

The program relies on the UsbKeyboard Arduino library, created by Philip Lindsay, that incorporates a generic USB library created by Objective Development (`www.obdev.at`). The UsbKeyboard library is available for download from Lindsay's site at `code.rancidbacon.com/ProjectLogArduinoUSB`.

Unfortunately, at the time of writing the library won't compile under Arduino 0017 or 0018. You'll need to download and install version 0016 (still available from the Arduino web site) for this project.

The library download is a compressed tarball called arduinousb_release_002.tar.gz. Download and extract it. Inside you'll find a directory called libraries/UsbKeyboard. With Arduino 0017 and later you can install libraries inside the libraries directory inside your sketchbook, but that location doesn't work with Arduino 0016 so instead you'll need to move the UsbKeyboard directory into the libraries directory inside your actual Arduino 0016 installation.

Compile and Upload Sketch

The very first thing the sketch does is include the UsbKeyboard library.

```
#include "UsbKeyboard.h"
```

It then specifies which digital inputs to use for the four buttons. Note that the labels for the buttons could have been anything you like and doesn't have any correlation to what characters might be sent when that button is pushed: we just used those names so it would be easy to remember what each one represents. The sketch also specifies a pin for a status LED at this point.

```
#define BUTTON_A 8
#define BUTTON_B 9
#define BUTTON_MSG 10
#define BUTTON_ENTER 11
byte ledPin = 13;
```

The setup function has to do a few different things, starting with setting up the status LED and setting the pins for the button connections to inputs, as follows.

```
void setup()
{
  pinMode (ledPin, OUTPUT);
  digitalWrite (ledPin, HIGH);
  pinMode (BUTTON_A, INPUT);
  pinMode (BUTTON_B, INPUT);
  pinMode (BUTTON_MSG, INPUT);
  pinMode (BUTTON_ENTER, INPUT);
```

To save some external components, it then enables the CPU's internal pull-up resistors on the pins being used for the buttons. By doing this, we don't need to connect external pull-up resistors, just the buttons themselves.

```
  digitalWrite (BUTTON_A, HIGH);
  digitalWrite (BUTTON_B, HIGH);
  digitalWrite (BUTTON_MSG, HIGH);
  digitalWrite (BUTTON_ENTER, HIGH);
```

Now for the USB setup. Because USB is extremely time-critical we need to mess with the interrupts a bit to ensure the Arduino will enumerate itself properly with the host computer. Notice that while forcing re-enumeration there is a 250 millisecond delay using a function called delayMs(), which is not a built-in Arduino function. Because timer0 has been disabled at that point in the code we can't use functions like delay() and must define our own.

```
  TIMSK0&=!(1<<TOIE0);
```

The sketch then clears the interrupt flags before it performs time-critical operations.

```
  cli();
```

To make the host detect that the Arduino is present, the program uses functions in the UsbKeyboard library to disconnect and then reconnect. This forces it to be re-enumerated by the host.

```
  usbDeviceDisconnect();
  delayMs(250);
  usbDeviceConnect();
```

The interrupts then need to be enabled again.

```
  sei();
}
```

The main program loop is very simple and repetitive. It just loops as fast as possible and calls the update() function in the UsbKeyboard library each time through, then checks each of the digital inputs to see if any of them have been pulled low by a push button or other device connecting it to ground. If they have, it calls sendKeyStroke() to send an appropriate keypress event to the host.

```
void loop()
{
  UsbKeyboard.update();
  if (digitalRead(BUTTON_A) == LOW) {
    UsbKeyboard.sendKeyStroke(KEY_A);
    digitalWrite(ledPin, !digitalRead(ledPin)); // Toggle status LED
  }

  if (digitalRead(BUTTON_B) == LOW) {
    UsbKeyboard.sendKeyStroke(KEY_B);
    digitalWrite(ledPin, !digitalRead(ledPin)); // Toggle status LED
  }

  if (digitalRead(BUTTON_MSG) == LOW) {
    UsbKeyboard.sendKeyStroke(KEY_H, MOD_SHIFT_LEFT);
    UsbKeyboard.sendKeyStroke(KEY_E);
    UsbKeyboard.sendKeyStroke(KEY_L);
    UsbKeyboard.sendKeyStroke(KEY_L);
    UsbKeyboard.sendKeyStroke(KEY_O);
    UsbKeyboard.sendKeyStroke(KEY_SPACE);
    UsbKeyboard.sendKeyStroke(KEY_W, MOD_SHIFT_LEFT);
    UsbKeyboard.sendKeyStroke(KEY_O);
    UsbKeyboard.sendKeyStroke(KEY_R);
    UsbKeyboard.sendKeyStroke(KEY_L);
    UsbKeyboard.sendKeyStroke(KEY_D);
    UsbKeyboard.sendKeyStroke(KEY_ENTER);
    digitalWrite(ledPin, !digitalRead(ledPin)); // Toggle status LED
  }

  if (digitalRead(BUTTON_ENTER) == LOW) {
    UsbKeyboard.sendKeyStroke(KEY_ENTER);
    digitalWrite(ledPin, !digitalRead(ledPin)); // Toggle status LED
  }
}
```

As you can see from the sequence sent when BUTTON_MSG is asserted you aren't limited to sending one keypress event per input: you can also send sequences of characters.

Finally, the sketch defines its own delay function that can be used inside setup() while timer0 is disabled.

```
void delayMs(unsigned int ms)
{
  for (int i = 0; i < ms; i++) {
    delayMicroseconds(1000);
  }
}
```

One thing to note about the example sketch is that it doesn't introduce any delays inside the main program loop. It's critical that the loop executes quickly so just about the only thing you can do inside the loop is read digital inputs: if you try to do anything that will slow down the program, the host computer may fail to get a response at a critical time and decide the device is misbehaving. If that happens the host will de-enumerate the device and your fake keyboard will stop working.

Once you've compiled the sketch and uploaded it to your Arduino, open a new document in a text editor or word processor on the host computer so it's all ready for your Arduino to begin typing into it.

Then disconnect the USB lead from the normal USB socket on the Arduino board and plug it instead into the additional USB socket on the prototyping shield. This will cause the Arduino to power down and then power up again using power from the USB connection coming in via the shield. It will also attempt to enumerate itself with the host computer as a Human Interface Device (HID) so if you're curious about what happens you could open the system log on your computer and watch it while plugging the USB cable into the shield.

If all goes well your Arduino will now behave like an extra keyboard plugged into your computer, so try pressing one of the buttons or connecting one of the inputs to ground to trigger a keypress event. You should see corresponding characters appear in the text document on your computer—and, as far as it knows, that's just you typing the letters on a regular keyboard!

For a more complete list of available characters supported by the library, have a look in the library header file (hardware/libraries/UsbKeyboard/UsbKeyboard.h) using a text editor.

For even more information have a look at the USB HID to PS/2 scan code translation table document published by Microsoft at `download.microsoft.com/download/1/6/1/161ba512-40e2-4cc9-843a-923143f3456c/translate.pdf`. Note that although the letters are defined using uppercase names such as KEY_J for the letter j, the character sent through will actually be the lowercase version unless you apply a modifier to the key. The modifier is sent through as a second parameter to the sendKeyStroke() function, so to send an uppercase J you would call the following:

```
sendKeyStroke(KEY_J, MOD_SHIFT_LEFT);
```

The example program includes a couple of modifiers so you can see it in action.

Just for fun, we mapped the four buttons to characters used to control the game Frozen Bubble (left, right, fire, and centre) so we could use an Arduino as a custom game controller (see Figure 4-5).

Figure 4-5. Using the virtual USB keyboard as a custom game controller

We also connected a Nintendo DS touch screen to another Arduino as described in the Touch Control Panel project in Chapter 8 and ran a program that defined different regions on the screen for left, right, and fire. We then linked the two Arduinos together with the digital outputs from the touch screen Arduino connected to digital inputs on the USB keyboard Arduino to give touch screen control of Frozen Bubble. There are videos of both systems in action on the *Practical Arduino* site.

Variations

Chording Keyboard

A chording keyboard is a special type of input device that has a very small number of buttons compared to the number of characters it can send: rather than having one button for each letter of the alphabet like a normal keyboard, a chording keyboard allows you to press a combination ("chord") of keys at once to select the letter you want. A five-button chording keyboard can be comfortably held in a one-handed grip and allow the operator to type a huge number of different characters by simultaneously pressing several keys, with the added advantage that it doesn't need to be placed on a surface to be used: you can even walk around with a chording keyboard in one hand and type while on the move.

CHAPTER 5

■ ■ ■

PS/2 Keyboard or Mouse Input

Arduino isn't limited to taking input from sensors: you can even connect a full-size PS/2 keyboard just as if it were a "real" computer and type away! Connecting a keyboard to an Arduino may sound a bit odd (after all, it's just a little microcontroller), but keep in mind that an Arduino actually has more processing power and memory than a complete desktop machine of not-so-many years ago. Adding some peripherals that you would normally associate with a full-size computer opens up some interesting possibilities.

Perhaps PS/2 seems a bit dated and you'd rather use a modern USB keyboard with your Arduino. After all, even finding a PS/2 keyboard can be difficult these days, and you might have to go dumpster diving or hunting through that pile of crusty old hardware in the company storeroom to find one. Using a USB keyboard might sound like the obvious solution, but unfortunately an Arduino just isn't up to the job of acting as a USB host natively—it's simply not fast enough. All is not lost, however, because many USB keyboards are designed for backward compatibility and come with a little purple USB-to-PS/2 adapter that allows them to be plugged into a PS/2 port. Keyboards that come with those adapters are designed to detect when they are plugged into a PS/2 port rather than a USB port and automatically switch modes to become a PS/2 device, so this project should work just as well with a modern USB keyboard connected via an adapter as it would with a genuine antique PS/2 keyboard.

Or if you want to go even more retro you can use this same circuit with an old-style AT keyboard, because even though they use a different connector, they have the same electrical interface as a PS/2 keyboard.

Connecting a keyboard or mouse to an Arduino opens up a wide range of possibilities in terms of non-human input, too. A hacked keyboard can provide you with 100+ digital inputs using only a few Arduino I/O pins, and the X/Y encoders in a mouse are perfect for tracking movement of a robot.

The required parts are pictured in Figure 5-1, and the schematic is in Figure 5-2.

Parts Required

1 x Arduino Duemilanove, Arduino Pro, Seeeduino, or equivalent

1 x Prototyping shield

1 x PS/2 extension cable or 6-pin mini-DIN socket

1 x PS/2 keyboard or 1 PS/2 mouse

Hookup wire

Source code available from
`www.practicalarduino.com/projects/ps2-keyboard-or-mouse`

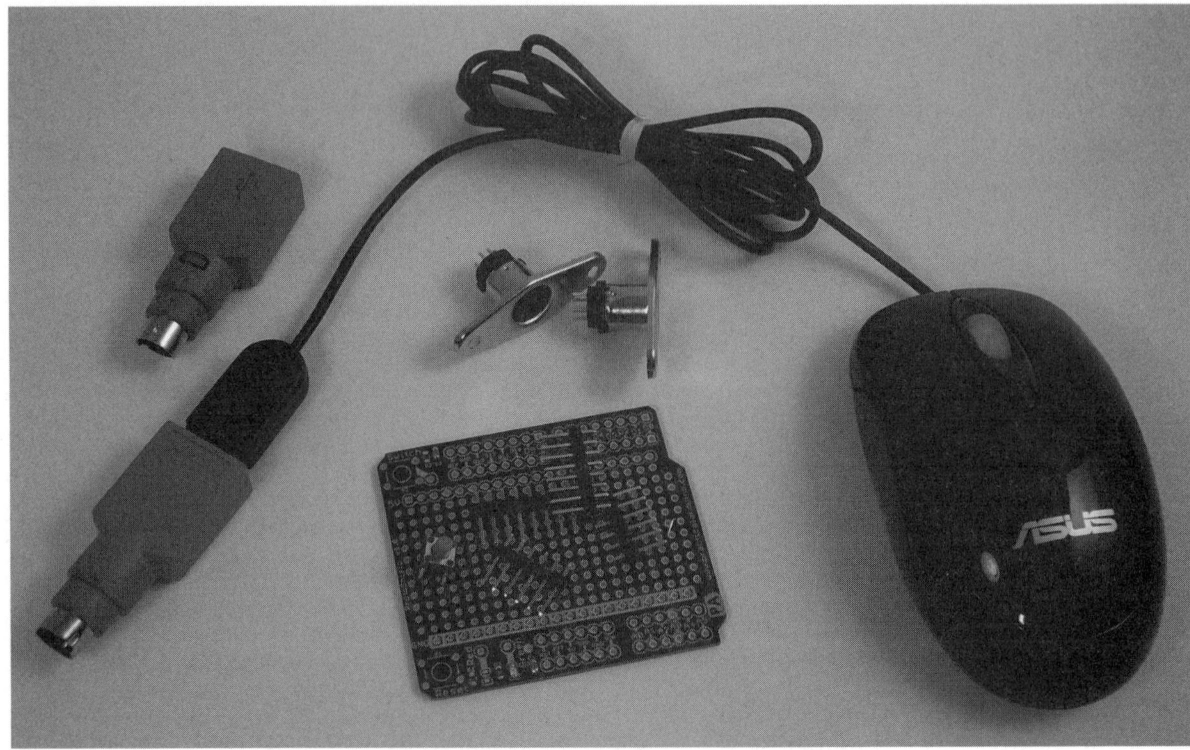

Figure 5-1. Parts required for PS/2 keyboard or mouse connection to Arduino

Instructions

This project can be built to provide connections for just a keyboard, just a mouse, or both. We'll step you through the process of assembling connections for both but if you want to only fit the parts for one or the other, that's perfectly fine.

There are two options for providing the connections: either fitting a PS/2-style socket (generally referred to as a "6-pin mini-DIN") to the prototyping shield, or using a PS/2 extension cable and cutting off one end so you can attach it to the shield as a fly-lead.

Note that if you want to go really retro you can even use an early AT-style keyboard fitted with a 5-pin DIN connector. The difference between AT and PS/2 connectors is purely mechanical: both types of keyboard use the exact same electrical specifications, so if you happen to have an old AT keyboard lying around it should work just as well provided you use the correct socket or extension cable. You might find they pull more current, though, so stick to a more modern PS/2 keyboard or a USB keyboard with a PS/2 adapter if possible.

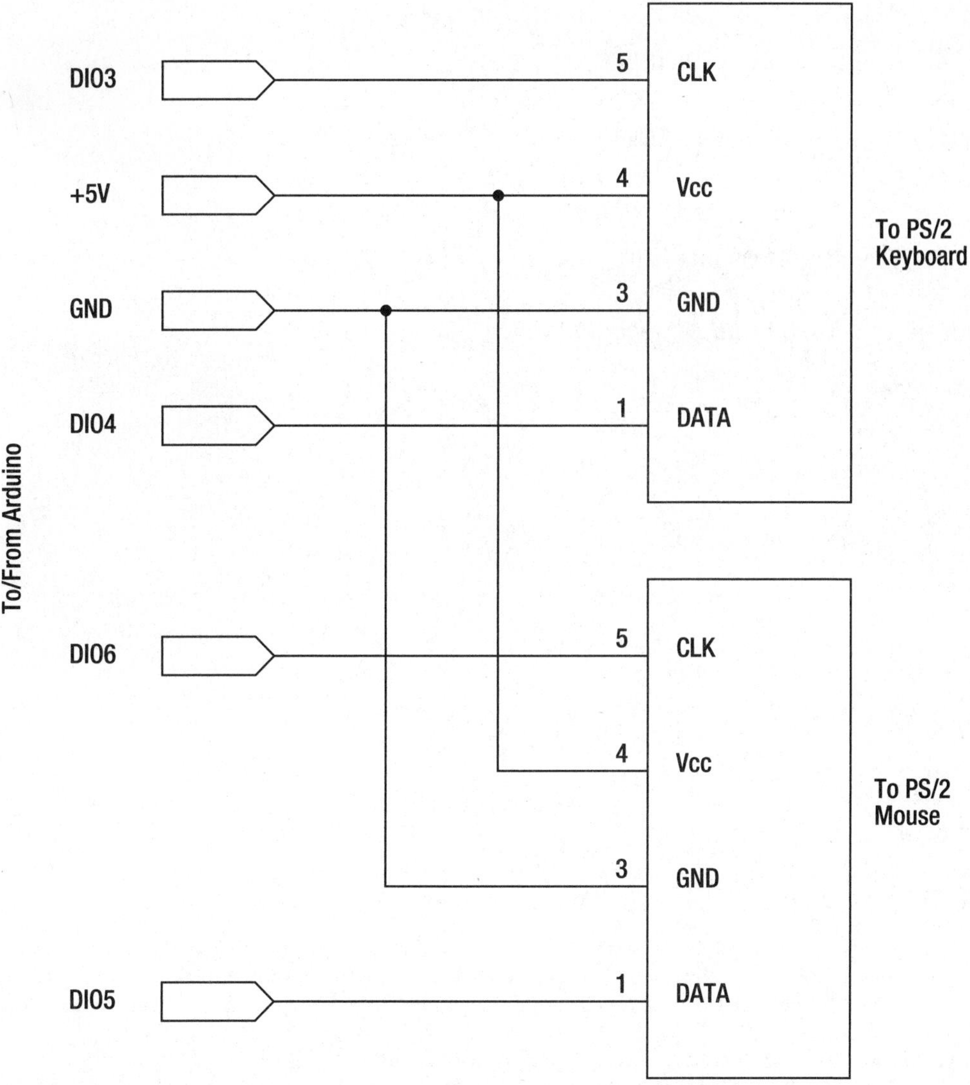

Figure 5-2. *Schematic of PS/2 keyboard or mouse connection to Arduino*

PS/2 Connections

PS/2 devices need connections for +5V power, ground, data, and clock, as shown in Figure 5-3. Table 5-1 gives the specifications.

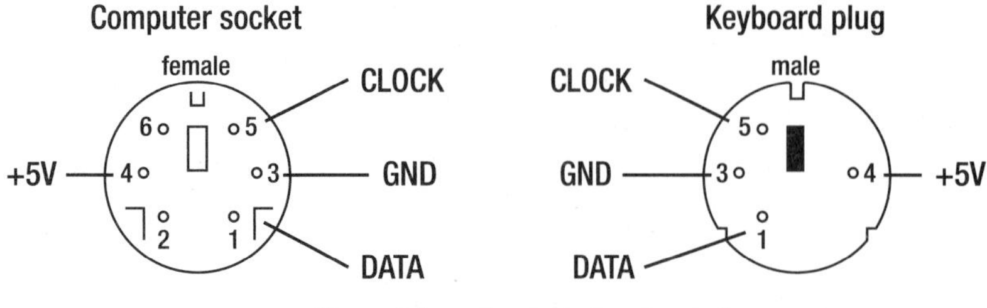

Figure 5-3. *PS/2 pinout in 6-pin mini-DIN plug and socket*

Table 5-1. *PS/2 pinout*

Pin	Purpose
1	DATA
2	unused
3	Ground
4	+5V
5	CLOCK
6	unused

Recycled 6-Pin Mini-DIN Sockets

Using a PCB-mount 6-pin mini-DIN socket will make your shield neater, but they have become surprisingly hard to find. Some suppliers, such as SparkFun, have them available along with breakout boards, but if you're not averse to a bit of scavenging you might also be able to obtain them from an old computer.

If you have an old computer motherboard lying around and some luck, patience, a hacksaw, and a solder sucker, you might be able to remove the combination keyboard/mouse socket and repurpose it. The shield shown in Figure 5-4 uses a double connector cut from a motherboard using a hacksaw. The section of PCB attached to the socket was trimmed tightly against the edges of the socket case and left in place, with the edges cleaned up so there are no slivers of metal to short things out. Removing the PCB entirely would be very difficult and there's not much reason to do so anyway, since all of the socket connections are isolated from each other. It also conveniently links pin 3 (ground) on each socket to the socket case, which is then attached to the shield's ground connection on the other side, out of sight.

Figure 5-4. *Recycled PS/2 keyboard and mouse connector mounted on a prototyping shield*

A small rectangle of PCB material was glued to the prototyping shield with two-part epoxy glue as a spacer, and the socket assembly was then glued on top of that. The result is an extremely strong mechanical mount for the socket that was then linked to the shield using short jumper leads.

6-Pin Mini-DIN Panel Sockets

If you don't want to sacrifice a motherboard it may be necessary to use panel-mount sockets instead, which unfortunately can be quite tricky to mount on a shield.

The only new 6-pin mini-DIN sockets we could get locally were panel-mount sockets with long mounting tabs on the sides, so we cut the tabs cut off and placed the sockets sideways on the shield with the edges overlapping the PCB. Make sure you mount the socket right near one edge of the shield so there's plenty of clearance for the lead to plug in without fouling the shield or the Arduino, and keep them far enough apart that if you want to plug in both a keyboard and a mouse at the same time the plugs won't foul each other. That's even more of an issue if you use USB-PS/2 adapters, of course, and you may need to mount them on opposite ends of the board or mount them sideways so the wide part of the adapters sit vertically.

We then inserted some bare single-core hookup wire (stripped from a bit of leftover Ethernet cable) beside one of the sockets, soldered it to the shield, and threaded it over the socket and down the other side. We pulled it tight using pliers and looped it around a couple of times before soldering it all in place, then put dobs of two-part epoxy on top to provide lots of mechanical support. The result is very strongly mounted sockets that definitely won't be ripped off the shield.

On our board we fitted two sockets: one for a keyboard, one for a mouse. If you can get sockets that are color-coded green for a mouse and purple for a keyboard, that's perfect, but if not just use whatever is available and mark them so you know which is which. We used plain sockets and put colored markers on the shield using pieces cut from a sticker intended to go on the back of a computer case.

The photograph in Figure 5-5 shows our board with two sockets glued in place. On this particular board the sockets are mounted at the same end as the USB port (the left end when looking at an Arduino with the labeling oriented correctly) and wouldn't clear the large USB socket on a typical Arduino. In this case, though, it's being assembled to fit an Arduino Pro from SparkFun, so there'll be plenty of room to clear the 6-pin USB header.

Figure 5-5. *Panel mount 6-pin mini-DIN sockets attached to a shield with looped wire and epoxy*

Each socket needs to be connected to ground, +5V, and a pair of Arduino digital I/O lines. Start by using short lengths of hookup wire to connect the power lines.

At this point you should fit the shield on your Arduino, power it up, and use a multimeter to measure that you have ground and +5V on the appropriate holes in the socket. Most keyboards are pretty robust but it's better not to feed them power the wrong way if you can help it.

The keyboard socket needs to be wired up with the CLOCK pin connected to digital I/O line 3, and the DATA pin connected to digital I/O pin 4. You can actually change the DATA pin to something other than 4 if you prefer, but the CLOCK pin absolutely must be connected to line 3 because the software we'll be using in a moment needs to use the interrupt on that pin to manage communications with the keyboard.

Likewise, use short lengths of hookup wire from the mouse socket to connect the CLOCK pin to digital I/O line 6, and the DATA pin to digital I/O line 5. The mouse driver library is less fussy, so both these pins can be remapped to something else if you need those particular pins for another device in your project.

With both sockets connected up the end result should look something like Figure 5-6.

Figure 5-6. *PS/2 sockets wired to power and data on the shield*

That's it. The shield is done. Mount it on your Arduino, plug in a keyboard or mouse as appropriate, and proceed to the software section.

PS/2 Extension Cable

A simple alternative to mounting sockets on the shield is to cut one end off a PS/2 extension cable and attach it.

Before you do any cutting, plug your PS/2 extension cable into your keyboard or mouse just to make sure you chop off the correct end. With the cable plugged in, cut off the connector at the other end to leave you with a nice long lead with a PS/2 socket attached. Then strip back about three or four centimeters of the outer insulation and you should be left with a set of four or possibly six color-coded wires plus a foil or braid shield. Even if there are more wires inside the cable, there are actually only four that you need to care about: ground, +5V, DATA, and CLOCK. You can ignore the others because we won't be using them.

Don't be fooled by the color-coding on the wires, though, because the colors might not be what you expect them to be. For example, in the PS/2 extension cable we used for this project the red wire is the ground connection—quite deceiving if you're the trusting type who assumes red always means positive! In our case, the color codes were as shown in Table 5-2.

Table 5-2. *Typical color codes in PS/2 extension cable. Varies between manufacturers.*

Pin	Purpose	Color
3	Ground	Red
4	+5V	Green
1	DATA	Orange
5	CLOCK	Brown

To identify which wire is which you can use a multimeter as a continuity tester by setting it to a low Ohms range, with one multimeter probe connected to one of the wires and the other inserted into each of the socket connections in turn to find which pin that wire connects to. If your multimeter probe won't fit into the tiny holes in the PS/2 connector, you can use a resistor leg or other piece of thin wire held against the multimeter probe and pushed inside the socket to make contact as shown in Figure 5-7.

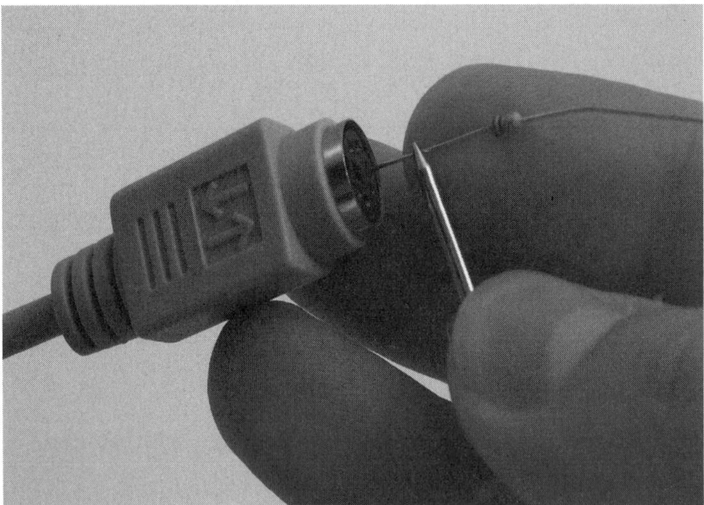

Figure 5-7. *Using a thin resistor leg to reach inside a socket*

Once you've identified the four important connections make sure you write down the color codes for reference so you don't lose track of which is which.

Other than those four connections there is one more you need to care about: the foil or braid "shield" connection that wraps around the central conductors to minimize electrical noise that might be induced by nearby electromagnetic fields. The shield needs to be connected to ground as well.

Strip back about 3mm of insulation from each of the four important wires, then twist the bare end of each wire between your fingers so the conductors make a tight little spiral before "tinning" them with a small amount of solder as shown in Figure 5-8 so they are all ready to connect to Arduino pins.

You should also tin the end of the shield connection.

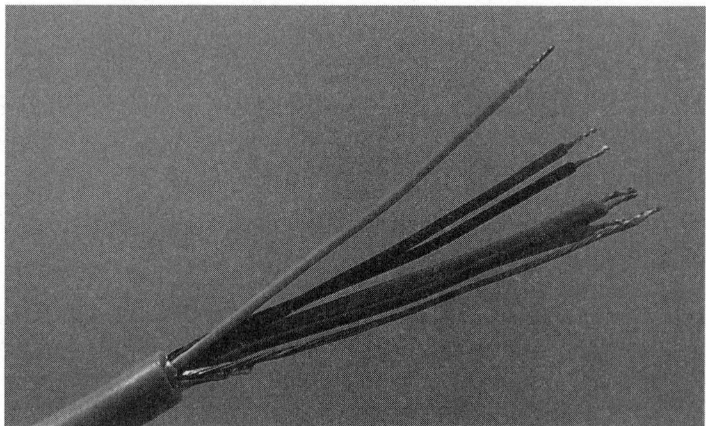

Figure 5-8. *Wire ends "tinned" and ready to connect*

Since there are only four connections to be made, and they're all directly to Arduino pins, you might not even need to use a prototyping shield. The connections could be made just as easily to two pairs of breakaway male header pins (one pair for power/ground and another pair for clock/data), and the headers inserted directly into your Arduino. However, we assembled ours on a prototyping shield because it allowed us to add more mechanical support to the cable and reduce the likelihood of the connections being ripped off the Arduino if the keyboard or mouse is moved.

Lay the end of the PS/2 cable over the prototyping shield and anchor it in place with cable ties so it is firmly fixed to the shield as shown in Figure 5-9. The prototyping shield we used for this version of the project came from Little Bird Electronics and has a couple of handy oversize holes that are perfect for threading small cable ties through, but if your prototyping shield doesn't have holes in the right place you might need to use a small drill bit to expand a couple of the tiny component lead holes so you can fit a cable tie through them.

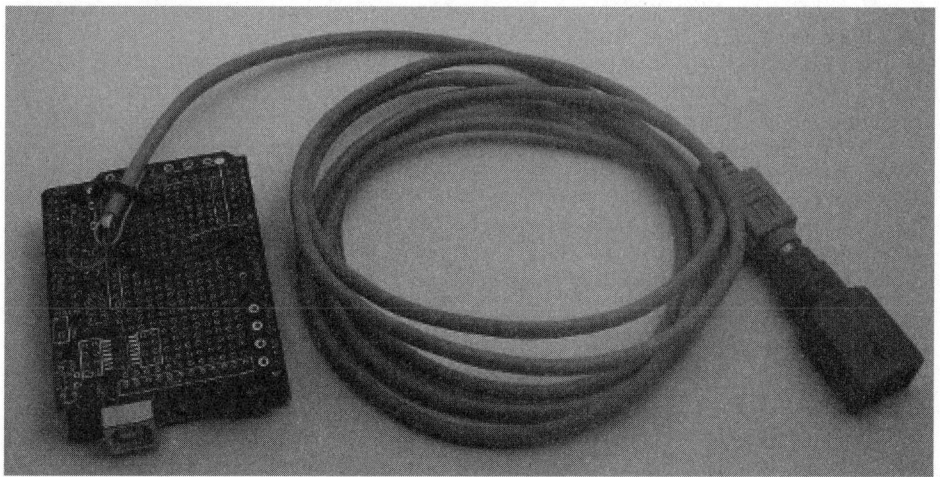

Figure 5-9. *PS/2 extension cable attached to shield*

Bend the ground and +5V leads around to the matching power rails on the prototyping shield and solder them in place. Also take the shield lead over to the same area and solder it onto a ground connection.

Next, bend the CLOCK and DATA leads across in the opposite direction toward the digital I/O lines.

For a keyboard connection solder the CLOCK lead onto digital I/O pin 3, and the DATA lead onto digital I/O pin 4.

For a mouse connection solder the CLOCK lead onto digital I/O pin 6, and the DATA lead onto digital I/O pin 5. These specifications are given in Table 5-3.

Table 5-3. *Arduino pin assignments for PS/2 connections*

Lead	Digital I/O Line
Keyboard CLOCK	3
Keyboard DATA	4
Mouse CLOCK	6
Mouse DATA	5

If your extension cable has more conductors in it that you aren't using, you can either bend them back out of the way and tuck them inside a cable tie to keep them neat or cut them off short near where the insulation is stripped back.

If you prefer to save a few dollars you can make a very simple DIY shield using some breakaway male headers and a piece of prototyping board. Techniques for building DIY shields discussed in Chapter 16 are perfect for projects like this where you have a small number of parts and a professionally produced prototyping shield would be overkill. In this project it's preferable to have some kind of shield, even if it is a DIY shield, because mechanically anchoring the cable is very important.

Figure 5-10 shows a version we made on a cheap DIY shield with just a keyboard connector and no mouse input.

Make sure you clearly label which socket is which. Nothing will be damaged if you plug a keyboard into a mouse socket or vice versa, but you can save yourself some annoyance by marking each socket.

That's it. You're done. Mount the shield on your Arduino, plug in a keyboard or mouse, and proceed to the software.

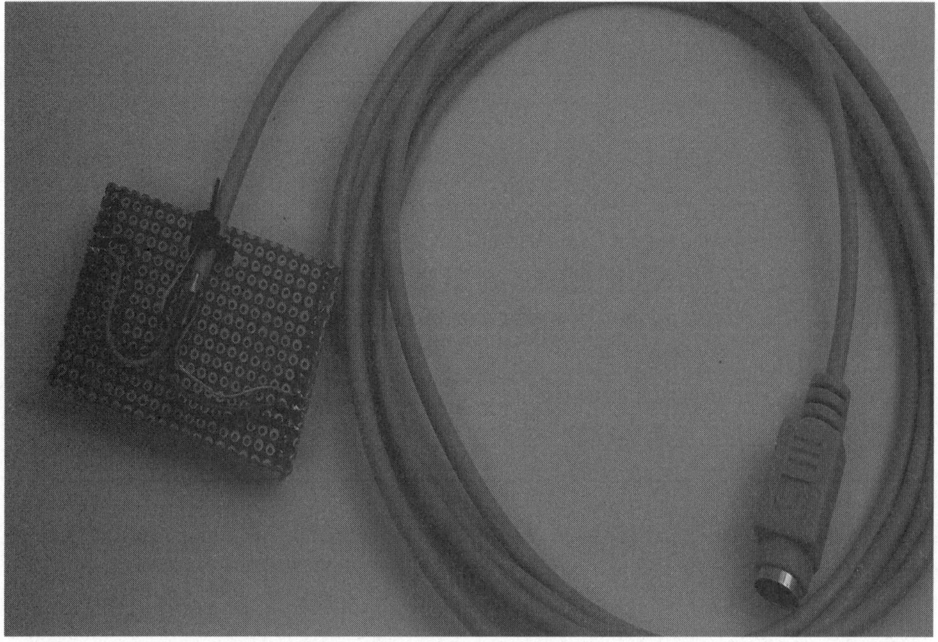

Figure 5-10. *PS/2 keyboard interface assembled on a DIY shield*

Keyboard Software

All the hard work of understanding the PS/2 communications protocol for reading keypresses from a keyboard is taken care of by an Arduino library called PS2Keyboard. The latest version of the library is linked to from the project page on the *Practical Arduino* web site, or you can download it directly from `www.arduino.cc/playground/Main/PS2Keyboard`.

Make sure you download the latest version (called PS2Keyboard014 at the time of writing) because that page also contains links to other variants of the library. If in doubt use the link from the *Practical Arduino* web site which goes to the correct version.

Once you have downloaded PS2Keyboard.zip to your computer, it needs to be decompressed and installed. Note, however, that the folder inside the archive has the wrong name: the folder in the archive is called "zip and submit as PS2Keyboard014," so you need to rename it to "PS2Keyboard" when installing it into your Arduino environment. Make a directory called "libraries" inside your sketchbook directory if it doesn't already exist, move the PS2Keyboard directory inside it, and restart the Arduino IDE to activate the new library. The basic PS2Keyboard library handles the low-level PS/2 communications, but it doesn't contain all the mappings to convert every possible raw PS/2 scancode to useful ASCII characters and it also doesn't take care of detecting whether SHIFT is being held down and changing to upper-case automatically. In fact it even maps all the letter keys to their uppercase equivalent all the time, even when you're not holding down SHIFT.

That's because a scancode sent by the keyboard is not quite as simple as an indication of a single keypress, as you might expect. PS/2 keyboards are remarkably dumb and offload a lot of the work of interpreting user action onto the host computer, rather than processing it internally. For example, they don't send a different scancode for a press of a key based on whether SHIFT is currently held down. They leave it up to the host computer to figure out that SHIFT has been depressed, but not yet released, at the time the next character is pressed.

For example, consider the sequence of typing a lowercase letter a followed by an uppercase letter A. It's not just two codes sent from the keyboard, but is rather more complex and goes something like this:

1. You press the A key. The keyboard sends scancode 0x1C, which represents a "make" (keydown) event on the A key.
2. You release the A key. The keyboard sends scancode 0xF01C, which represents a "break" (keyup) event on the A key.
3. You depress the SHIFT key. The keyboard sends scancode 0x12 (if it's the left SHIFT key) or 0x59 (if it's the right SHIFT key) to represent a make event on SHIFT.
4. You depress the A key. The keyboard sends scancode 0x1C (make on A).
5. You release the A key. The keyboard sends scancode 0xF01C (break on A).
6. You release the SHIFT key. They keyboard sends scancode 0xF012 (break on SHIFT).

What this means is that the host computer can't simply receive one code that represents a lowercase letter a and another that represents an uppercase letter A. The scancode for the keypress is exactly the same in both cases. What's different is that the SHIFT key was depressed prior to the A key being depressed, and not previously released.

Supporting modifier keys, such as SHIFT, therefore requires the host computer to implement a state-machine that switches to different states based on modifier-key events. The state of each modifier key must be maintained independently and then the current state combined to determine the action to take on a keypress: for example, SHIFT-A may need to cause an uppercase A to be sent, but CONTROL-SHIFT-A may need to cause a "select all" event.

This all sounds unnecessarily complicated, but there is a good reason for it. By taking this approach the host computer has far more control over what each key represents, and allows it to control things such as auto-repeat rate rather than having the keyboard determine when auto-repeat needs to begin and sending a stream of identical characters. Once you get your head around it you can understand why it was done this way, but it may not be intuitive first time you come across it.

If you're not intending to use the keyboard for character input, and don't care about mapping scancodes to specific characters, then the PS2Keyboard library will do everything you need and you can do your own interpretation of the codes it sends through. That might sound a bit strange, but a keyboard can be very handy in situations other than as a text-input device. For example, home automation hacker Scott Penrose uses a modified PS/2 keyboard as an input multiplexer. He connects the outputs of devices, including motion detectors and reed switches, across the contacts for individual keys inside a gutted PS/2 keyboard, so that events around the house cause scancodes to be sent to an Arduino which then processes them to determine the state of each device. Very clever, because it means he can connect about a hundred sensors to an Arduino using only two digital I/O lines and an old spare keyboard! You can find out more about Penroses's home automation work at his web site, linux.dd.com.au/wiki/Rainbow_House.The basic example sketch provided on the *Practical Arduino* web site simply watches for keypresses and sends them straight on to the serial connection so you can see them using the Serial Monitor mode in the Arduino IDE.

It starts by including the PS2Keyboard library, then defines which pin to use for the DATA pin connection. We don't have to define the CLOCK pin connection because it's hard-coded inside the library to use Arduino digital I/O pin 3 so it can trigger an interrupt defined by the library.

```
#include <PS2Keyboard.h>
#define DATA_PIN 4
```

Next, it creates a PS2Keyboard object simply called "keyboard." This is the object that our sketch will use to interact with the PS/2 keyboard.

```
PS2Keyboard keyboard;
```

The setup function configures the keyboard object by telling it which Arduino digital I/O pin to use for the PS/2 DATA connection. It then sets up a serial connection to the host and announces that it's alive.

```
void setup()
{
  keyboard.begin(DATA_PIN);
  Serial.begin(38400);
  Serial.println("Initialised PS/2 reader");
  delay(1000);
}
```

The main program loop checks the event buffer in the keyboard object to see if there are any keypress events queued up for processing. If there are, it calls the keyboard.read() method to fetch the next keypress and stores it in a single-byte variable called "data."

```
void loop()
{
  if(keyboard.available()) {
    byte data = keyboard.read();
```

The keyboard can send either normal alphanumeric keys or special keys such as SHIFT and BACKSPACE. The PS2Keyboard library defines a list of mappings from raw scancodes to these special keys so you can simply refer to the name rather than the scancode. As of version .14 of the library, the special key codes it supports are as follows:

```
PS2_KC_BREAK
PS2_KC_ENTER
PS2_KC_ESC
PS2_KC_KPLUS
PS2_KC_KMINUS
PS2_KC_KMULTI
PS2_KC_NUM
PS2_KC_BKSP
```

The example sketch checks the key value for matches against each of these special keys and displays appropriate output.

```
    if(data == PS2_KC_BREAK) {
      Serial.print("[BREAK]");
    } else if(data == PS2_KC_ENTER) {
      Serial.println("");
    } else if(data == PS2_KC_ESC) {
      Serial.print("[ESC]");
```

```
    } else if(data == PS2_KC_KPLUS) {
      Serial.print("+");
    } else if(data == PS2_KC_KMINUS) {
      Serial.print("-");
    } else if(data == PS2_KC_KMULTI) {
      Serial.print("*");
    } else if(data == PS2_KC_NUM) {
      Serial.print("[NUMLOCK]");
    } else if(data == PS2_KC_BKSP) {
      Serial.print("[BACKSPACE]");
    } else {
```

If the check makes it through to this point it means the keycode hasn't matched any of the known special keys, so the sketch then prints it directly to the host.

```
      Serial.println(data, HEX);
    }
  }
}
```

Load up the sketch, compile it, upload it to your Arduino, make sure your keyboard is plugged in, and activate the serial monitor in the IDE at 38400bps. Pressing keys on the keyboard should then cause the matching value to be sent through to your computer and displayed in the IDE.

Mouse Software

Just as with the keyboard example, our mouse example uses a library to do most of the heavy lifting so that the sketch itself can be very small and simple. The PS2Mouse library needs to be downloaded and installed into your Arduino environment. A link to the latest version of the library is included on the project page on the *Practical Arduino* web site, so grab a copy and make sure the library folder is named "PS2Mouse" (rename it if necessary) and is placed inside the libraries folder in your sketchbook directory where your Arduino environment can see it.

The example sketch first includes the PS2Mouse library, then defines which pins will be used for the CLOCK and DATA connections as per the wiring on your shield.

```
#include <PS2Mouse.h>
#define MOUSE_DATA 5
#define MOUSE_CLOCK 6
```

Next the sketch creates a PS2Mouse object simply called "mouse," and passes in the defined CLOCK and DATA pin values as the first and second arguments.

The third argument sets the mouse mode to STREAM, which tells the mouse to send updates to the host whenever there are values to send. The other mode supported by the PS2Mouse library is REMOTE, in which the mouse only sends updates in response to requests from the hosts. PS/2 mice also support a third mode called ECHO in which it simply echoes back any values sent to it, but that mode isn't very useful unless you're testing the mouse so the PS2Mouse library doesn't implement it.

```
PS2Mouse mouse(MOUSE_CLOCK, MOUSE_DATA, STREAM);
```

The setup function is trivial. It just opens a serial connection to the host to report the X and Y values from the mouse, and calls a special method called "initialize()" on the mouse object. Calling initialize() forces the library to set up the I/O lines appropriately and then send a reset command to the actual physical mouse so it will start sending data.

```
void setup()
{
  Serial.begin(38400);
  mouse.initialize();
}
```

The main program loop is also quite simple. It starts by defining a three-element array to hold the mouse status and X/Y movement data, then calls the report() function and passes in the array. The report() function then performs some magic within the library to talk to the mouse and populates the array so the values can be accessed by the program.

```
void loop()
{
  int data[2];
  mouse.report(data);
```

Next the sketch sends the status value to the host, followed by the X and then the Y movement values.

```
  Serial.print(data[0]);
  Serial.print(":")
  Serial.print(data[1]);
  Serial.print(",");
  Serial.print(data[2]);
  Serial.println();
  delay(200);
}
```

Connect a mouse to your shield, load up the sketch in the Arduino IDE, compile and upload it, and open the serial monitor with the baud rate set to 38400bps. You should then see a stream of values that change as you move the mouse around.

The X and Y values should be fairly obvious, but the status value can be very useful as well. It's a bitwise representation of the state of various things in the mouse including the sign bits for the X and Y values and the state of the three buttons, so by processing the status value it's possible to detect mouse button presses.

Each bit in the status byte represents something specific. Bit 3 is always set high so the status value will always be at least 8, or a binary value of b00001000. The left mouse button asserts bit 0, the right mouse button asserts bit 1, and the middle button asserts bit 3. This should be fairly obvious if you hold the mouse still and click the left mouse button while running the previous sketch and watching the serial console, because the status value will increase from 8 to 9. Clicking the right mouse button sets the status value at 10, and the middle mouse button puts it at 12. Clicking the left and right buttons together sets it to 11, and so on.

The meaning of each of the bits in the status byte is given in Table 5-4.

Table 5-4. Status byte values

Bit	7	6	5	4	3	2	1	0
Value	128	64	32	16	8	4	2	1
Purpose	Y overflow	X overflow	Y sign bit	X sign bit	Always high	Middle button	Right button	Left button

A bitwise comparison of the status byte can, therefore, tell you whether any of the buttons are currently being pressed. Checking for a specific bit can be done using the logical "&" bit comparison operator and an appropriate mask value that sets only the bit you want to check. For example, to modify the previous example sketch to report when buttons are pressed you could add the following lines right before the delay(200) at the end of the main loop.

```
if(data[0] & 1) {
  Serial.println("Left");
}
if(data[0] & 2) {
  Serial.println("Right");
}
if(data[0] & 4) {
  Serial.println("Middle");
}
```

You'll then see the effect of clicking the buttons reflected in the serial monitor. Using a mask value of 1 sets bit 0, a mask value of 2 sets bit 1, and a mask value of 4 sets bit 2, all neatly matching up with the status byte valuess shown in Table 5-4.

Most of the time you won't care about the other bits in the status byte, but something to be careful of is getting updates from the mouse quickly enough to prevent the X and Y values from overflowing the buffer. The previous example sketch has a delay(200) at the end of the main loop so that as you're watching the serial monitor you get a chance to see what the numbers are, but if the mouse is moved very fast you might find it overflows one of the axis values and sets the matching overflow bit. You can check for this situation by adding the following lines just before the delay(200) and watching the serial monitor while you zip the mouse around really fast.

```
if(data[0] & 64) {
  Serial.println("X OVERFLOW");
}
if(data[0] & 128) {
  Serial.println("Y OVERFLOW");
}
```

If you're using the mouse to sense motion on something like a robot it's unlikely that it would move fast enough to overflow, but if your sketch spends a lot of time busy doing other things and doesn't process the mouse data very often you might need to pay attention to the overflow bits and restructure things to decrease the time between samples.

Variations

Barcode Reader for a Stock Control System

A number of seemingly "exotic" peripherals, such as barcode scanners as shown in Figure 5-11, actually present themselves as keyboards to a host computer. That's very handy because it means you don't need any special drivers or hardware to talk to them. A typical barcode scanner reads the code and then immediately sends it to the host as a series of keypresses, so as far as the computer is concerned scanning a barcode is exactly the same as if you simply typed in the barcode string on a keyboard.

Most barcode scanners have a number of options that can be set, such as whether they should automatically append a carriage return at the end of each scan. This means you should be able to connect any PS/2 barcode scanner to your Arduino using the shield and sketch shown in this project and have any barcode you scan sent through to the Arduino as a series of characters followed by a carriage return. Very neat.

By adding an Ethernet shield to your Arduino and creating a simple web client in your sketch, you can have it call a web service and submit the barcode value whenever you scan a barcode. The web service could be anything from a home inventory management system (scan groceries when you bring them home from the shops to add them to a stock list, or scan wrappers as you thrown items out so they can be added to a shopping list) to a CD collection manager or stock-take system. Or if you add a battery pack and use an XBee module or WiShield instead of a regular Ethernet shield you can create a network-enabled, fully wireless intelligent barcode scanner!

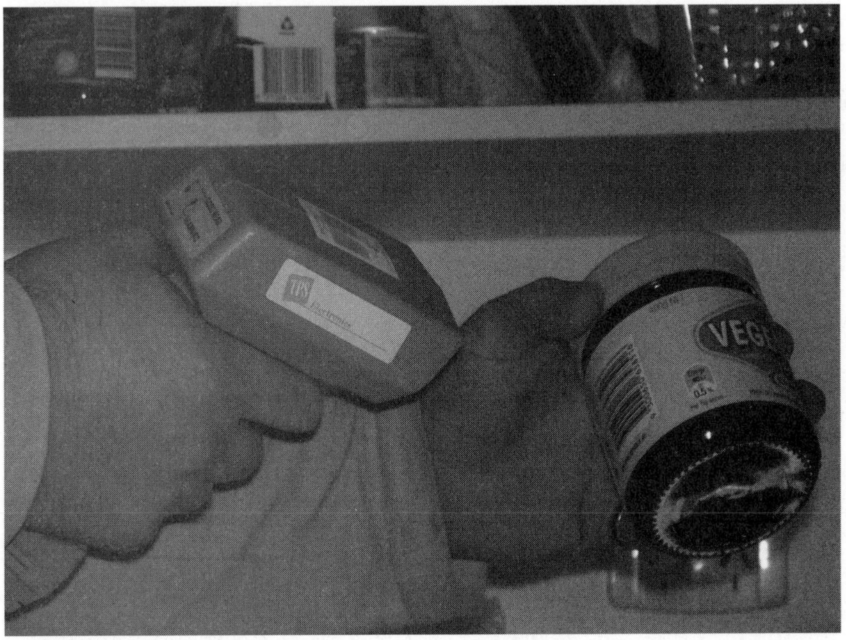

Figure 5-11. *PS/2 barcode scanner*

Resources

For more detailed information about how the PS/2 protocol works, as well as the electrical and mechanical standards, there are some very good guides on both `Computer-Engineering.org` and Wikipedia:

```
www.computer-engineering.org/ps2keyboard/
www.computer-engineering.org/ps2mouse/
en.wikipedia.org/wiki/PS/2_connector
```

CHAPTER 6

■ ■ ■

Security/Automation Sensors

Security system sensors such as motion detectors, reed switches, pressure mats, glass-break detectors, infrared beams, and conductive film, can be very handy for all sorts of things including home automation systems, interactive art installations, and even security systems!. Almost all security system sensors provide a simple switched output that changes state based on whether the sensor has been tripped, which means that, when connected up in a circuit, they behave just like a switch that is activated automatically. That makes them extremely easy to connect to an Arduino to read their status.

However, things are not quite as simple as they may first appear.

Most security sensors provide a "normally closed" (or N.C.) output: that is, when they have not been tripped their output is closed-circuit, and when it has been tripped it goes open-circuit. This is the exact opposite behavior of something like a simple push button switch, which is normally open-circuit and then goes closed-circuit when you press it.

The reasoning behind using normally closed outputs is that it allows an alarm panel to verify the integrity of the connection to the sensor. If an intruder cuts the wire going to a motion detector, the central alarm panel sees this action as the same as the detector being triggered, and will sound the alarm even though the detector itself has been totally removed from the circuit and can't send back a signal to the panel.

That inverted logic is easily handled in software. If you want to use a security sensor for a non-security application, such as triggering a kinetic sculpture when people walk up to it or automatically triggering lights to turn on and off as you walk around your house, then you can treat a sensor as a simple switch and connect it to a digital input. Just remember that it will behave in the opposite way to a normal switch, and you'll be all set.

However, any professional alarm installer will tell you that such a simple approach is totally inadequate for sensors that are security critical. Having a sensor that will trigger the alarm if the wire is cut is a good start, but it doesn't go nearly far enough. What happens if an intruder climbs in through the roof, finds your motion detector wires inside the ceiling, strips back the insulation, and short-circuits them? It doesn't matter what the sensor does then because the alarm panel will think the sensor circuit is good. The intruder can walk around inside your house with the alarm fully activated and it won't even notice. Or what happens if someone gets underneath a motion detector without triggering it, such as by coming in through a doorway underneath it, and then removes its cover to mess with it? Or even more insidiously, what if someone was in your premises when the security system was disarmed (such as a customer in a store during regular business hours) and took the opportunity to take the cover off a motion detector and bypass it so they could return later when the store is closed and the security system has been armed?

To guard against these sorts of attacks, a security system needs to detect far more than a simple open or closed circuit. It needs to be able to detect if the wire to a sensor has been cut, or a wire short-circuited, or the sensor has been tripped. It also needs to detect if the sensor is being tampered with, even when the alarm system itself is in a disarmed state. Well designed security systems treat all parts of the system as untrusted and can detect tampering in nearly any cable or sensor at any time, whether it is currently armed or disarmed.

In this project we'll use the flexibility of the Arduino's analog inputs to build sensor circuits that are as fully featured as any professional system, and will allow you to detect any of those possible failure, tamper, or trigger conditions automatically. You can then use your Arduino as a security system controller, or as part of a home automation system to turn lights on and off as you enter and leave rooms, or to control an art installation based on viewer activity. The required parts are shown in Figure 6-1, and the complete schematic is in Figure 6-2

Parts Required[1]

1 x Arduino Duemilanove, Arduino Pro, Seeeduino, or equivalent

1 x Prototyping shield

1 x 2-connection PCB-mount screw terminals (for 12V power)

8 x 2-connection PCB-mount screw terminals (2 per channel, total 4 channels)

1 x Green or blue LED

1 x 1K5 resistor

4 x Red LEDs (1 per channel)

4 x 680R resistors (1 per channel)

4 x 1K resistors (1 per channel)

12 x 4K7 resistors (3 per channel)

4 x Passive infrared (PIR) motion detectors (simple switched output, not a "smart" PIR)

1 x 12V power supply rated to at least 500mA

4-core security cable (long enough to connect to sensors)

20cm hookup wire or ribbon cable

Source code available from

`www.practicalarduino.com/projects/security-sensors`

[1] Note: parts specified are to build a 4-channel board supporting one sensor per channel. For a different number of channels, adjust the quantity of "per channel" parts as appropriate.

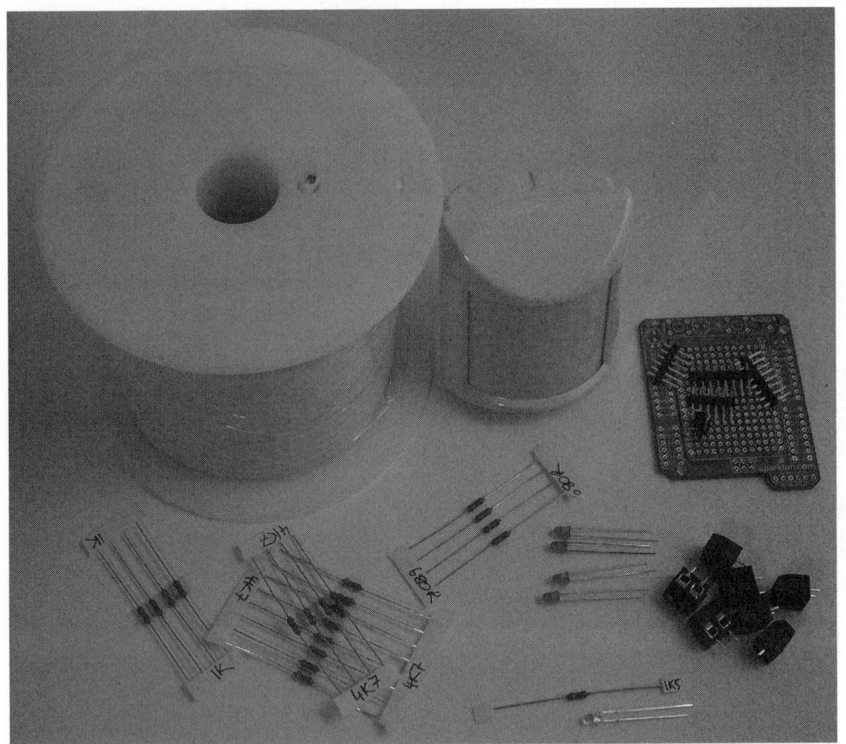

Figure 6-1. Parts required for security sensor inputs

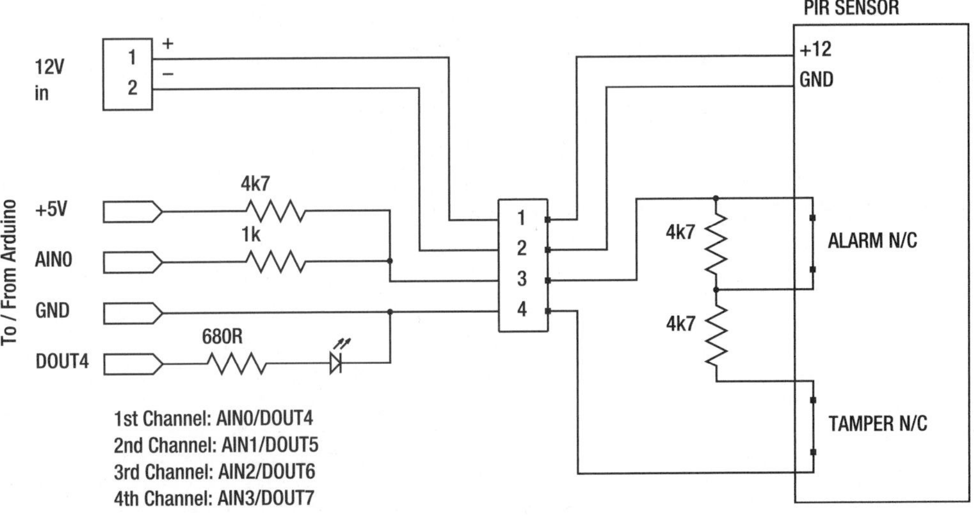

Figure 6-2. Schematic for security sensor inputs

EOL resistors can also be used with "normally open" (N.O.) sensors simply by putting the resistor in parallel with the sensor output instead of in series with it (see Figure 6-4). In this scenario the line will go into a low-resistance state if the sensor is triggered, but otherwise operates in a similar way to an N.C. sensor.

Instructions

Security Sensor Basics

Security systems most commonly detect line tampering using end-of-line (EOL) resistors. By putting a resistor inside the sensor case and fitting it in series with the sensor circuit, the alarm panel can continuously measure the resistance and detect if the line has been either cut or short-circuited (see Figure 6-3). If the line is cut, the resistance will go high; if it's short-circuited, it will go low. And because the sensor itself has a normally closed (N.C.) output, if it is triggered it will cause an open-circuit which will also trigger the alarm.

The advantage of a simple approach like this is that all it requires is a resistor added inside each sensor, and at the alarm panel end a voltage comparator circuit consisting of an op-amp and a couple of diodes provides a "good/bad" output depending on whether the overall resistance is within the desired range.

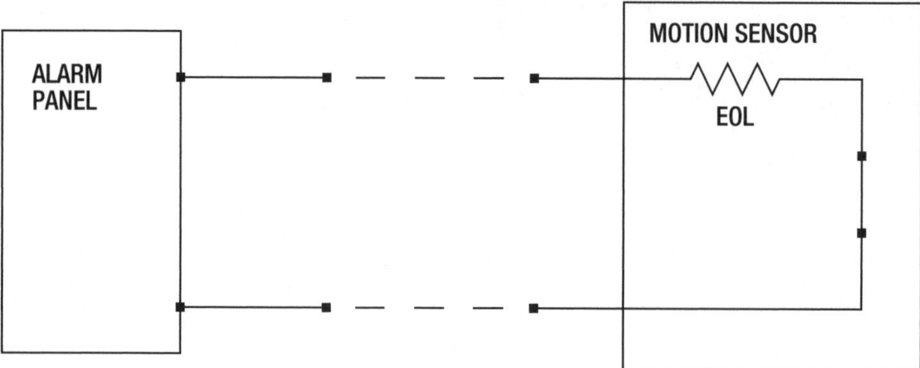

Figure 6-3. *Simple End-Of-Line resistor with normally-closed contacts*

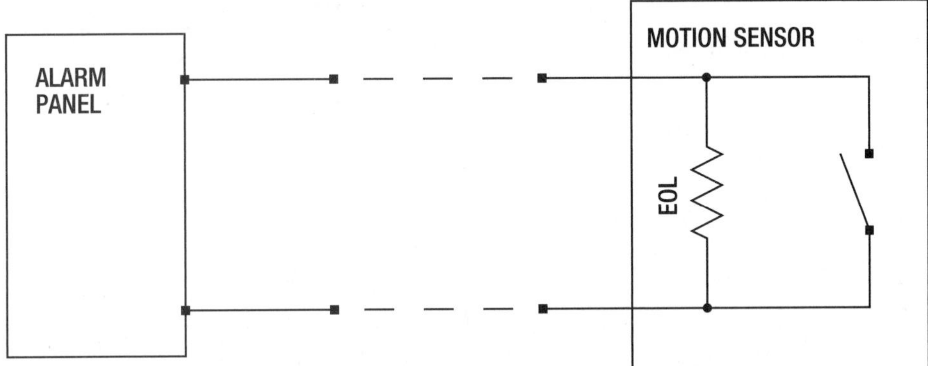

Figure 6-4. *Simple End-Of-Line resistor with normally-open contacts*

Many sensors such as passive infrared (PIR) motion detectors include internal tamper switches that detect if the case is open. Once again, these are typically N.C. connections that go open-circuit if the case is opened. A simple way to incorporate a tamper switch is to wire it in series with the line, so that if either the sensor is triggered normally or the case is opened, the line will go open-circuit and the alarm will be tripped.

This is a bit of a naive approach, though, because it can't detect tampering while the alarm system is disarmed. In a situation such as a retail shop a motion detector will be regularly tripped as customers walk around, and the alarm panel will ignore those events because it's in a disarmed state. If a customer starts taking a PIR apart while nobody is looking, the alarm system won't be able to tell because, as far as it knows, it's simply motion being reported by the sensor, which of course it ignores. The customer could then bypass the sensor within a few seconds just by shorting across the N.C. output terminals, putting the cover back on, and walking away. The sensor will appear to still be functioning normally, but later when the shop is closed and the security system is armed, the PIR will fail to report movement.

The most common way to avoid this particular type of attack is to wire the tamper switch separately and run it on a special input to the alarm panel that is active all the time, even when the system is disarmed. Each sensor then has two output pairs: one for the regular sensor output that is only acted on when the system is armed, and one for the tamper detection output that is acted on at any time of day or night. The only exception is when the system is not only disarmed but also put into a special "maintenance mode" so that technicians can work on sensors without tamper switches setting off an alert.

The downside, of course, is that you've just increased your cabling requirements and, unless you wire all the tamper circuits together and therefore lose the ability to determine which sensor is being tampered with, you've also doubled the number of input channels required in the panel—a very expensive proposition in many cases.

But there is a cheap and easy solution that gives you the best of both worlds, and it's the system we'll use in this project. It's called "double end-of-line" resistors, and it allows you to detect four possible circuit states with just one pair of wires.

With this approach, the N.C. alarm output is wired with an end-of-line resistor in parallel across its terminals, and the N.C. tamper switch is wired with another EOL resistor in series with it. They are then both wired together in series to create a circuit that will produce a different resistance for each of four possible states: cable shorted, normal, sensor tripped, and cable cut or tamper activated.

In this project we'll use a pair of 4K7 EOL resistors, and combine them with another 4K7 pull-up resistor at the Arduino and a 1K resistor in series with the sensor line at the Arduino end (see Figure 6-5).

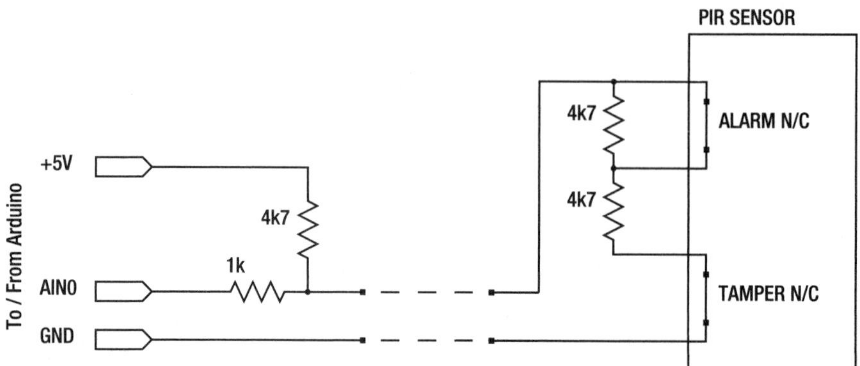

Figure 6-5. Double End-Of-Line resistors connected to an analog input

Looking only at the right half of the circuit for now, you can see that the resistance across the sensor output wires can be one of the four different values shown in Table 6-1.

Table 6-1 Sensor resistance in various states

Resistance	Meaning
0R	Wire shorted. Alarm to be activated unless in maintenance mode.
4K7	Normal.
9K4	Sensor tripped. Alarm to be activated if armed.
Infinite	Wire cut or tamper detected. Alarm to be activated unless in maintenance mode.

Looking now at the left half of the circuit, you can see how we use an analog input on an Arduino to detect these different states. The 1K resistor in series with the sensor line provides some protection for the input pin against unexpected current flow. The 4K7 pull-up resistor, when combined with the resistance provided by the sensor, acts as a voltage divider, exposing the analog input to a different voltage depending on the state of the sensor.

- If the sensor wire has been short-circuited the analog input will be pulled down to 0V.
- When the sensor is in a normal state it will have an overall resistance of 4K7, so the voltage divider will split the 5V supply in half and pull the analog input to 2.5V.
- If the sensor has been triggered the overall resistance of the sensor circuit will rise to 9K4, which will combine with the 4K7 pull-up resistor to form a voltage divider that pulls the input to (9400 / (9400 + 4700)) × 5V, for a total of about 3.3V.
- If the sensor wire has been cut or the tamper switch has been activated the input will be pulled up hard to 5V through the 4K7 and 1K resistors in series.

This gives us four possible voltage levels applied to the Arduino analog input depending on the state of the sensor, so we can expand the Table 6-1 to add in those values and give us an overall picture of what levels the Arduino needs to detect and what each level represents. See Table 6-2.

Table 6-2. *Sensor resistance and voltage in various states*

Resistance	Voltage	Meaning
0R	0V	Wire shorted. Alarm to be activated unless in maintenance mode.
4K7	2.5V	Normal.
9K4	3.3V	Sensor tripped. Alarm to be activated if armed.
Infinite	5V	Wire cut or tamper detected. Alarm to be activated unless in maintenance mode.

With a single analog input we can therefore read the voltage level on a sensor channel and detect any of those four possible states with just one pair of wires to the sensor.

Assemble Four-Channel Alarm Sensor Shield

Start assembly by fitting the screw terminal connections onto the prototyping shield. Many types of sensors, including PIRs, require a 12V power supply so we'll actually be running a 4-core cable to each sensor with one pair for power and one pair for the sensor output.

Snap the screw terminals together into pairs to form four sets of four connections each plus one separate pair for the connection from the 12V power supply.

In this system, the power for the sensors will be kept totally separate from the Arduino and will have no connection to it at all—it doesn't even need a common ground. The output from a PIR is typically a tiny reed relay that provides total electrical isolation from the device itself, and the tamper switch is likewise a simple switch output. By keeping the power supply for sensors totally separated from the Arduino, we avoid possible problems with noise induced in the supply, and also protect the system against possible attack methods such as shorting the power supply going to a sensor to disable the entire security system. If that particular attack was attempted with this system, the sensors would go offline and their outputs would drop open, but the Arduino would continue running and could trigger an alarm.

Many commercial security systems scrimp on power connections and provide only one pair of connections for all sensors connected to the system. If you wanted to save space on the shield, you could do that here as well, but the downside is that you then have to twist all the sensor positive leads together and all the negative leads together and jam them into a single pair of screw terminals. That approach can be awkward and frustrating and some of the power leads may tend to fall out, so we prefer to provide dedicated power supply connections for every sensor channel.

Using this approach we can comfortably fit connections for four PIRs, plus the input from a 12V power supply, on one shield (see Figure 6-6). Of course, most Arduino models have a total of six ADC inputs and we're wasting two in this project, so if you can find smaller screw terminals or choose to switch to plugs/sockets instead you could probably fit connections for six PIRs on a single shield.

Figure 6-6. Screw terminals mounted on shield

Once you have soldered the screw terminals in place, the next step is to connect all the (+) connections together and then to the +12V input; and, likewise, connect all the (–) connections together and then to the 0V input. On our prototype we oriented the connectors so that when it as aligned vertically, the top connection on each channel is (+), the next connection down is (–), and the following two connections are for the sensor connections. (See Figure 6-7.) Use some hookup wire to link the (+) and (–) connections together as appropriate.

Figure 6-7. Connections for _12V and 0V for sensor terminals

Because the 12V supply for the sensors is totally separate to the Arduino supply, we also added a power LED across the (+) and (–) inputs to provide visual feedback that it's on. Insert a green or blue LED through the shield just behind the pair of +12V terminals so that the anode (long) lead is nearer the (+) input, and the cathode (short) lead is near the (–) input. Solder the legs in place, then use a wire link and the 1K5 resistor to join them to the appropriate power connections. In Figure 6-8, the left-hand link to the (+) connection looks like a black component, but it's actually a short length of heat-shrink tubing threaded over the LED leg before it was bent over and soldered directly onto the (+) connection. The 1K5 resistor then joins the cathode lead to the (–) connection.

***Figure 6-8.** Common ground connections for sensor outputs*

1K5 is a fairly high value to use as a current limiting resistor on a 12V supply, but because the LED is just a status indicator there's no need to run it at full brightness. Using a high resistance value is also a bit of extra protection that may be helpful because plugpack power supplies are notorious for not providing a clean and consistent output, and their voltages can vary significantly depending on how much load they are under.

Next, use short lengths of jumper wire to connect one of the sensor connections from each set to the Arduino's GND on the shield. Because this particular prototyping shield provides GND and +5V rails down the sides, it's a simple matter of bridging across between the screw terminals and then to the GND rail.

The SparkFun prototyping shield has a handy spot for a reset button to make it easy to reset the Arduino when the shield is in place, so insert and solder the reset button.

The other sensor connection needs to be pulled to +5V using 4K7 pull-up resistors, so insert one resistor for each channel and bring them together near the middle so they can be bridged to +5V on the shield. In Figure 6-9, you can also see the blue LED mounted toward the top of the board just behind the +12V input terminals.

Figure 6-9. *4K7 pull-up resistors linked to sensor inputs*

One end of each pull-up resistor connects to a sensor channel, and the other ends all join together and are then jumpered to the +5V rail.

Each sensor channel then needs to be linked to its matching analog input using a 1K resistor. Because the resistors bridge across other connections, we slipped short lengths of heatshrink tubing over them to prevent any short circuits from occuring. Channel A connects to analog input 0, channel B to 1, channel C to 2, and channel D to 3. (See Figure 6-10.)

At this point the shield is fully functional in terms of being ready to connect to motion detectors, but after the system has been installed it can be handy to have a quick visual indication of the status of each

Figure 6-10. Connections to analog inputs from screw terminals

channel so we also added four LEDs connected to four digital output pins. The software on the Arduino can then activate the LEDs to show the status of the matching sensor channel, giving you an immediate visual indication that the software is operating correctly and detecting changes in the sensors.

Insert the four red LEDs with one near each sensor channel, oriented so that the short (cathode) lead is closer to the screw terminal. That lead is then bent across under the shield and soldered to the nearby Arduino GND connection where it has already attached to another screw terminal.

Each LED also needs a current-limiting resistor, so insert the four 680R resistors directly beside the LEDs and join the longer (anode) LED lead to the adjacent resistor lead (see Figure 6-11).

Figure 6-11. Status LEDs and their current-limiting resistors

After making those soldered joints, each channel should have a connection from GND to an LED, then through the LED to the current-limiting resistor. The other side of the resistor will not yet be attached to anything. Each resistor needs to be connected to a digital output pin, so use short lengths of hookup wire to link them up. The LED near sensor channel A connects to digital pin 4, channel B to pin 5, channel C to pin 6, and channel D to pin 7 (see Figure 6-12).

Figure 6-12. *Digital pin connections to status LEDs*

Install End-of-Line Resistors on Sensor

Your board is now all ready to go, so the next step is to prepare a motion detector with the correct EOL resistors. In Figure 6-13, you can see the connections to a typical PIR with the tamper, power supply, and output (N.C.) connections clearly marked. As previously discussed the PIR needs one 4K7 resistor directly across the N.C. outputs, and another 4K7 resistor in series with the tamper output. The easiest way to achieve this is to simply insert one resistor into the N.C. terminals, use the other one to link one N.C. terminal to one of the tamper terminals, and then connect up a pair of wires to the two outer connections as shown in Figure 6-12.

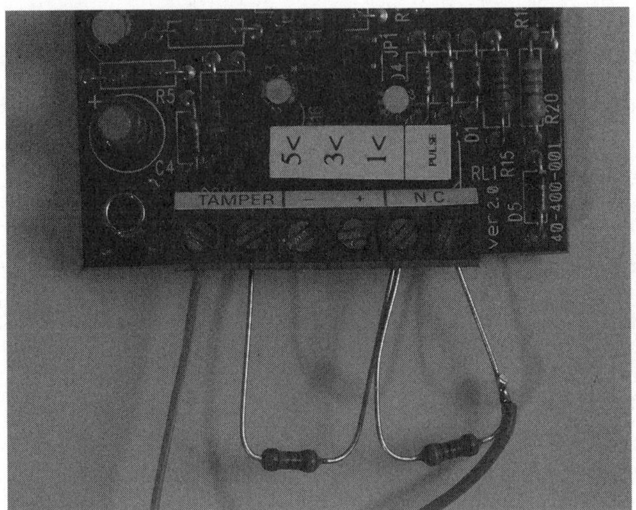

Figure 6-13. Temporary connection of End-Of-Line resistors to sensor terminals

One thing you'll notice in Figure 6-14 is a large label with markings for 5, 3, and 1. Just above that label is a set of three pairs of male PCB headers with a female jumper bridging the middle pair. Those numbers refer to the "pulse count" setting, which is an option to control the sensitivity of the detector to spurious inputs. The pulse count is the number of movements that must be detected within a certain moving time window before the sensor will trigger the alarm output. With the setting on 1 the output will be triggered immediately as soon as any motion is detected, while with the setting on 3 it will require three detection events within a rolling four-second period before the output will the triggered. Likewise, the 5 setting requires five detection events within a rolling four-second period.

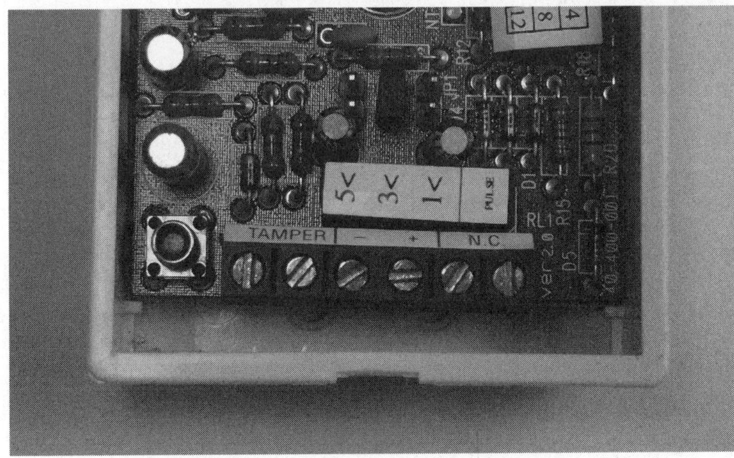

Figure 6-14. PIR mounted in case leaves little room for connections

The reason for this is that PIR sensors can be prone to triggering on transitory events such as a bright flash of light coming through a window when a car drives by and reflects the sun momentarily. With a setting of 1, even a brief event like this can be enough to trigger an alarm. Increasing the pulse count makes the sensor more immune to random events, while still allowing it to detect actual movement if a person is within its operational field of view. A high pulse-count setting will decrease its ability to detect very slow movement which is why the setting should generally be left low. Setting it to about 3 is usually a good compromise and is often how PIR sensors are shipped by default.

If you look elsewhere on the PIR circuit board, you will probably find another pair of jumper pins labelled "LED" or similar with a bridge over them. This jumper is to enable the red LED that you see on many PIRs when you walk past them, and the idea is that alarm installers are meant to leave it in place while they do a "walk test" to make sure the sensor is working, then remove it when all testing is complete. The reasoning is that if the LED is left active after installation, it gives random people who may walk past it an opportunity to test the sensitivity and coverage of the PIR by giving them immediate visual feedback when it has detected them. If the LED is disabled it's harder for a prospective burglar to test the security system in premises such as a store during business hours prior to returning after it has closed. If you see a PIR with an LED that blinks as you walk past it, you know the installer didn't remove the bridge after doing their final walk test.

Something else you'll notice in Figure 6-14 is there is usually very little space near the screw terminals to fit the EOL resistors, and even if there was room it's very awkward trying to fit resistors to the terminals while balanced up a ladder and trying to hold onto everything at once. Soldering the EOL resistors to the end of the cable is difficult because you'll need to hold a hot soldering iron while climbing up and down a ladder, and if you just push them into the terminals and screw them down tight they're liable to pull out if pressure is put on the cable.

Our preferred solution is to permanently solder the EOL resistors in place on the underside of the PIR sensor's circuit board while it is out of its case and conveniently sitting on a workbench. No need to carry your soldering iron up a ladder! See Figure 6-15.

***Figure 6-15.** End-Of-Line resistors soldered in place on the PIR circuit board make installation much easier*

By soldering the EOL resistors onto the PIR in advance the job of installing the unit is made far easier, because once you are balancing up on the top of that ladder all you need to do is strip back the four conductors in the security cable and make the two connections for power to (+) and (–), and two connections for the output. See Figure 6-16.

With the EOL resistors in place, as shown in Figure 6-16, you can connect the pair of wires for the output onto one tamper terminal and one N.C. terminal. It will look like the unit has been miswired, but the EOL resistors that are out of sight behind the PCB will make sure everything works the way it should even though it appears to be missing a pair of wires.

Figure 6-16. Simplified power and sensor connections made possible with EOL resistors pre-soldered under the PCB

Load Test Program

You're now ready to load a test program and read the status of a sensor. Note that this source code is available for download from the project page on the *Practical Arduino* web site to save you some typing. The program assumes that you have connected the four channels to the same analog and digital pins as we used on the prototype (see Figure 6-17).

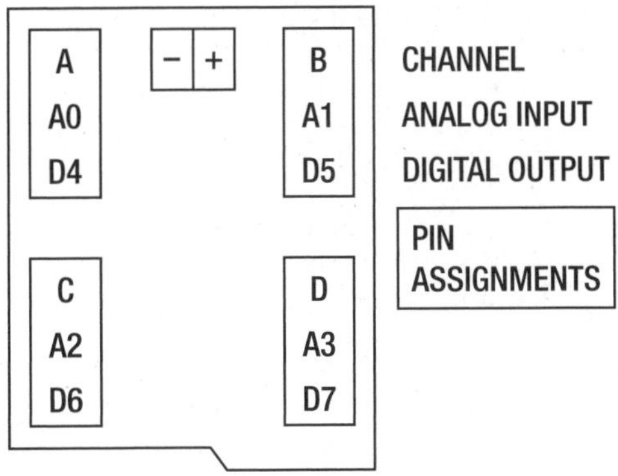

Figure 6-17. Connections to shield

First the program specifies which analog inputs to use for each sensor channel, as follows:

```
byte channelAInput = 0;
byte channelBInput = 1;
byte channelCInput = 2;
byte channelDInput = 3;
```

Then it does the same for the digital outputs to use for the matching status LEDs, as follows:

```
byte channelALed = 4;
byte channelBLed = 5;
byte channelCLed = 6;
byte channelDLed = 7;
```

The setup function configures a serial connection to your computer so the Arduino can report the current readings coming back from the sensors, and then sets up all the digital output lines for the status LEDs and sets them to a low (off) state, as follows:

```
void setup() {
  Serial.begin(38400);   // Use the serial port to report back readings

  pinMode(channelALed, OUTPUT);    // Set up channel A
  digitalWrite(channelALed, LOW);

  pinMode(channelBLed, OUTPUT);    // Set up channel B
  digitalWrite(channelBLed, LOW);

  pinMode(channelCLed, OUTPUT);    // Set up channel C
  digitalWrite(channelCLed, LOW);

  pinMode(channelDLed, OUTPUT);    // Set up channel D
  digitalWrite(channelDLed, LOW);
}
```

The main program loop is very simple. All it does is call the checkSensor() function to read each sensor in turn. Each call to checkSensor() results in a status value being returned, but we don't use the status value in this simple test program. It's included so that you can expand the program simply by applying some logic to make decisions on the basis of the status value. The main loop ends by printing a carriage return to the host to terminate the values sent by checkSensor(), then pauses for half a second before repeating the process.

It may seem that the system is vulnerable to missing brief triggers on PIRs because the program only checks the status of each input every half second. In practice this isn't a problem because PIRs themselves have an internal trigger-and-hold function that causes them to hold their output state for a few seconds, even if they were only tripped briefly. The 500ms delay is only included so that the output comes out slowly enough for you to read it, so if you were fitting this into an automated system and using the state of the sensors to control other devices rather than send the value to the serial port, you could remove the delay and make it run through the loop at full speed so it would trip immediately.

```
void loop() {
  byte sensorStatus;
  sensorStatus = checkSensor(channelAInput, channelALed);
  sensorStatus = checkSensor(channelBInput, channelBLed);
  sensorStatus = checkSensor(channelCInput, channelCLed);
```

```
  sensorStatus = checkSensor(channelDInput, channelDLed);

  Serial.println("");
  delay(500);   // Wait half a second before reading all channels again
}
```

The main program loop is so simple because the hard work of checking each sensor is done within the checkSensor() function. This function accepts two arguments: the first is which analog input line to read from, and the second is the digital output line to write to for the status display.

The analog reading from the sensor returns a result between 0 and 1023 corresponding to the voltage level currently applied to that pin. The voltage on the pin is determined by the state of the voltage divider circuit controlled by the sensor as discussed previously. A reading of 0 corresponds to 0V, and a reading of 1023 corresponds to a 5V level. A reading of about 511 corresponds to 2.5V, and a reading of about 680 corresponds to 3.3V.

This function therefore checks whether the reading falls within certain ranges and sets the output state appropriately. The four possible output state values that it can return are as follows:

- 0: Wire shorted. Possible tampering.
- 1: Normal, sensor not triggered.
- 2: Sensor triggered.
- 3: Open circuit. Wire cut or tamper switch triggered.

It then sends the analog pin number, the reading, and the state to the host via the serial connection.

```
boolean checkSensor( byte sensorInput, byte statusOutput )
{
  byte state;

  int sensorReading = analogRead(sensorInput);

  if( sensorReading < 400 ) {
    state = 0;                        // Wire shorted. Possible tampering.
    digitalWrite(statusOutput, HIGH); // Turn the associated status LED on
  } else if ( sensorReading >= 400 && sensorReading < 590 ) {
    state = 1;                        // Normal state, sensor not triggered
    digitalWrite(statusOutput, LOW);  // Turn the associated status LED off
  } else if ( sensorReading >= 590 && sensorReading < 800 ) {
    state = 2;                        // Sensor triggered.
    digitalWrite(statusOutput, HIGH); // turn the associated status LED on
  } else {
    state = 3;                        // Open circuit. Cut or tamper triggered.
    digitalWrite(statusOutput, HIGH); // Turn the associated status LED on
  }
  // Output the current reading to the host via the serial connection
  Serial.print(sensorInput, DEC);
  Serial.print(": ");
  Serial.print(sensorReading, DEC);
  Serial.print(" (");
  Serial.print(state, DEC);
  Serial.print(")  ");
```

```
  // Pass the current state back to the calling function
  return state;
}
```

Load the program in the Arduino IDE, compile it, and upload it to your Arduino. Then click the "serial monitor" button to watch the values being sent back by the unit. Make sure the baud rate is set to 38400 to match the value in the program.

Make sure you have a PIR connected to one of the channels on your shield and apply the 12V power supply to start it up. Note that PIRs take a little while to warm up and stabilize before they can detect movement, so it may appear to not be working at all or perhaps be frozen in a triggered state when you first apply power. Wait a minute or two and it should spring to life.

PIR Placement

When placing PIR motion sensors, there are a few tricks to watch out for.

The most important is to have the sensor pointed away from windows or other openings through which they may be able to detect movement. You don't want your alarm triggered just because someone came to your front door to deliver a package while you were out and the loungeroom motion sensor picked them up through the front window! Likewise, you need to be careful of anything that can move of its own accord when there is nobody present such as curtains that can move when blown by a central heating system or a fan.

Finally, think about your pets: you may want to be able to leave your cat inside, yet still turn the security system on when you go out. There are special motion detector lenses specifically designed for this purpose called "pet-alley lenses," and they give the motion detector a deliberately induced blind spot so an animal can walk underneath the sensor's active area without setting it off. If a person walks through, however, they are tall enough that they will enter the active area covered by the sensor and trigger the alarm.

Even if you get the placement exact, there can still be long-term problems with PIRs. The classic problem is that because they are slightly warm and provide a nice protected space, they often become home to creepy crawlies such as spiders, which can even cause the PIR to trip. Many alarm technicians carry a can of insecticide with them and spray carefully around every PIR they work on as a preventative measure.

Variations

Visual Display Written in Processing

The Processing programming language (www.processing.org) that is used elsewhere in this book including the Oscilloscope / Logic Analyzer project in Chapter 11 could be used to create a visual front-end for your sensors, reading values sent via the serial port and updating a plan of your house to show which sensors have been tripped. The Touch Control Panel project in Chapter 8 uses a very similar system to indicate which hot zones on a touch screen have been touched, and the Processing code for that project could be easily adapted to show current sensor status.

Home Security System

We have presented this system as simply a way to read security sensors, but it could be extended to build a complete home alarm system controlled by an Arduino. Alarm systems consist of several subsystems including the alarm panel, which is the cental control system that runs the show. The alarm panel needs to be securely locked away inside the house and innaccessible. It is often fitted inside a metal case that is mounted inside a cupboard or inside the ceiling. To build your own alarm panel, you could mount the Arduino inside a box and hide it.

An alarm system also needs a mechanism for arming and disarming it. This is often done using a numeric keypad mounted in an easily accessible location, and containing no critical functionality that could disable the alarm panel. Intruders should be able to smash or tamper with the keypad without preventing the alarm panel from being activated. Another mechanism to arm or disarm the system could be the RFID reader project in Chapter 14. Rather than trigger a strike plate, you could have the RFID reader deactivate the security system.

Of course, an alarm system also needs a way to get attention, so you could wire up a relay using the transistor circuit used in the RFID Access Control System project so that it activates a siren and a flashing light. You could even use your Arduino to control a phone dialler or send an SMS.Battery backup is also an important part of a security system. By combining a sealed lead acid battery, a plugpack, and a battery charger, you can ensure your security system will run for many hours or days even if the power to your house is cut.

Multiple Buttons on One Input

Using an analog input to read the value on a multistate voltage divider is a very handy trick that can also let you connect multiple buttons to a single analog input. If you're running low on digital I/O lines and want to connect more buttons to an Arduino, you can set them up as a resistor ladder that will allow any one of them to close a circuit and apply a different resistance to one side of a voltage divider. In the example shown in Figure 6-18, the pull-down resistor to ground could be 100K and all the resistors in the ladder 10K. With no buttons pushed the analog input will be pulled down hard to 0V.

However, if the first button is pushed, a voltage divider will be created with 10K pulling the pin up and 100K pulling it down, so the voltage applied to the input will be (100 / (10 + 100) × 5V, or about 4.55V.

If the second button is pushed, a voltage divider will be created with 20K pulling the pin up and 100K pulling it down, so the voltage applied to the input will be (100 / (20 + 100) × 5, or about 4.17V.

The third button sets up a voltage of about 3.84V, the fourth about 3.57V, and so on.

You might notice that for each subsequent button the voltage difference between it and the previous switch decreases, making it increasingly difficult to distinguish between them on the analog input. To increase the voltage separation as you move further down the chain, it's necessary to progressively decrease the resistance, so in practise you might find it works well to use, say, 33K for the first two resistors, then 18K, then 10K, then 4K7. With a bit of judicious calculation you can string quite a number of buttons onto a single analog input pin and distinguish between them by checking the value returned by analogRead().

If you look at the resistor ladder schematic in Figure 6-18 you may wonder why the first 10K resistor has been included at all. After all, if that resistor wasn't included you could simply detect the first button being pressed by measuring a voltage of +5V being applied to the input for an analog reading of 1023 or very close to it.

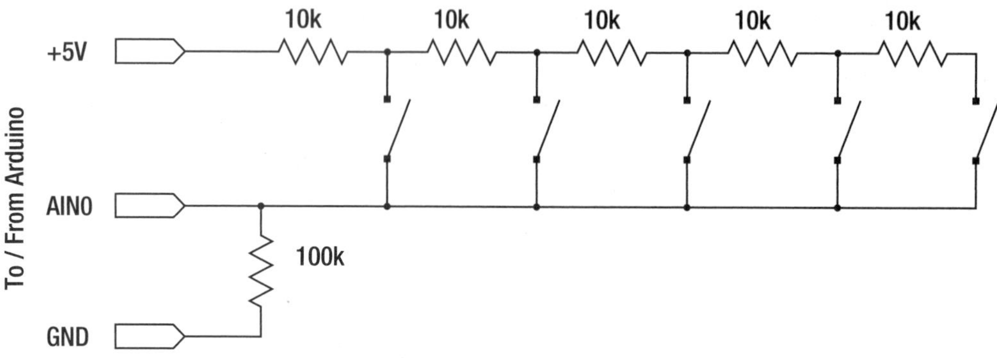

Figure 6-18. Resistor ladder connected to analog input

The reason for including that resistor is to allow detection of simultaneous presses of multiple buttons. Without the first resistor, pressing the first button will pull the analog input hard to +5V no matter what any of the other buttons do. With the resistor in place, however, combinations of buttons will produce different voltages and it's possible to detect which combination is being pressed at any one moment. One common real-world application of this technique is the buttons often found on car steering wheels to control the sound system, cruise control, and other vehicle functions. Because a steering wheel has to be able to turn, it's quite tricky getting connections from the static wiring loom under the dash to buttons mounted on the wheel itself, and car designers often use tricks like spring-loaded pads mounted on the steering assembly that slide around conductive rings that go around the steering column. The more connections that have to be made to the steering wheel, the harder it is to engineer the coupling, so most steering wheel controls use resistor ladders to allow up to a dozen buttons to be placed on the steering wheel, while using only one or two connections in addition to the ground connection back through the metal structure of the steering shaft.

If you want to modify your car by adding something such as a PC-based onboard entertainment system to replace the existing sound system, it's therefore possible to use an Arduino connected to the original steering column wiring to read the button presses on the steering wheel and pass button press events on to another device.

CHAPTER 7

■ ■ ■

Online Thermometer

Arduino makes a great building block for data acquisition and logging systems, including sensors commonly used in home automation such as temperature sensors. By combining an Arduino and a few DS18B20 temperature sensors, you can install sensors around your home or office and access an up-to-the-moment report using a web browser.

Readings can also be logged and graphed over time, showing trends or measuring the effectiveness of your home heating or cooling systems. By placing sensors outside the house, inside your ceiling cavity, and inside every room, you can plot how well your home maintains its temperature when climate conditions change.

The information can also be used as part of the feedback loop for a control system, such as to control active heating or cooling, or to trigger servos or linear actuators to open and close windows and passive ventilation systems. The required parts are shown in Figure 7-1, and the complete schematic is in Figure 7-2.

Parts Required

1 x Arduino Duemilanove, Arduino Pro, Seeeduino, or equivalent

1 x Seeed Studio Ethernet Shield or nuElectronics Ethernet Shield with prototyping shield

6 x DS18B20 Dallas 1-wire temperature sensors (Note: not DS18S20)

6 x 4K7 1/4W resistors

6 x PCB-mount 3-pin male connectors

6 x Lead-mount 3-pin female connectors

Twisted-pair cable or alarm cable (minimum 3 conductors)

Source code available from
`www.practicalarduino.com/projects/online-thermometer`

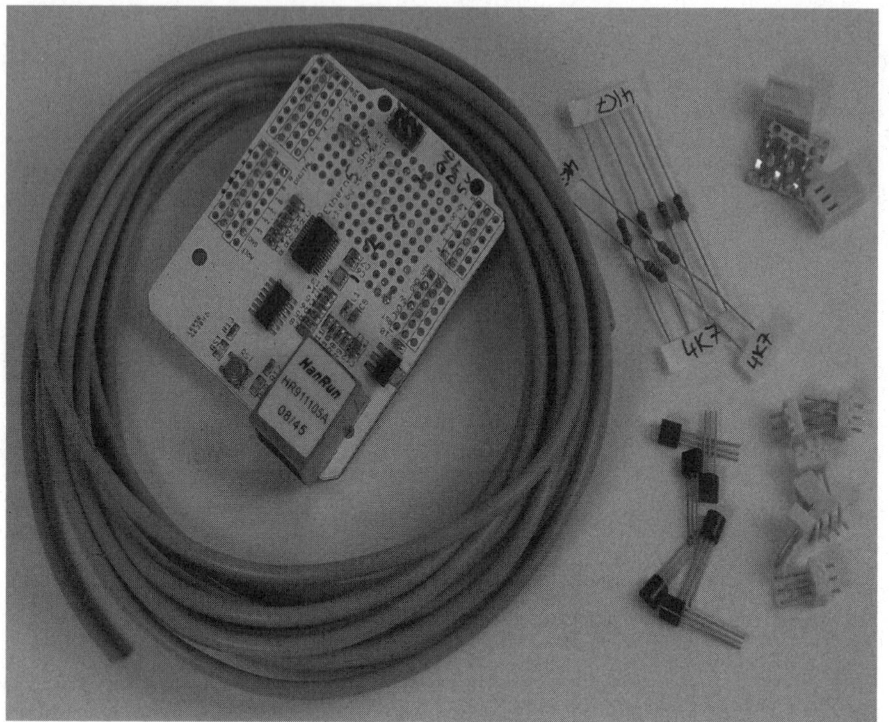

Figure 7-1. Parts required for online temperature sensor

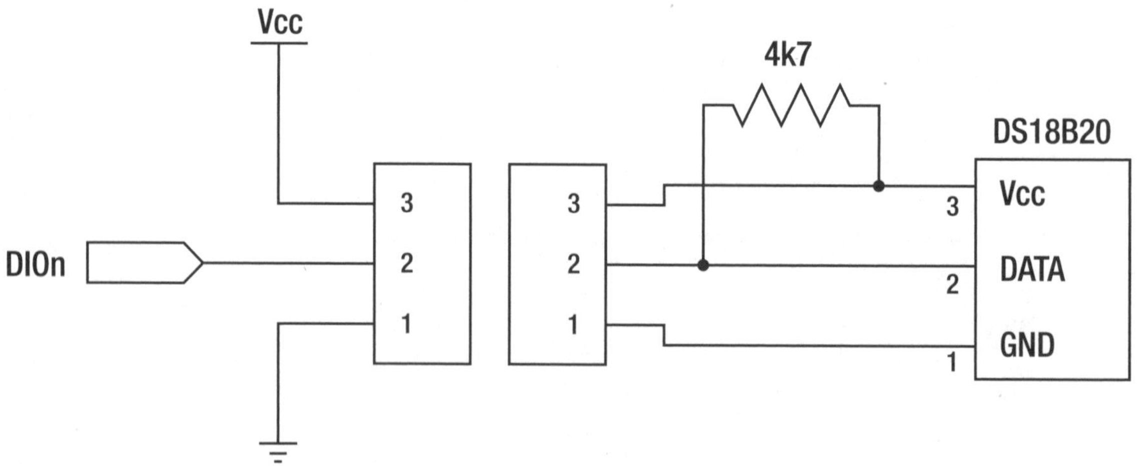

Figure 7-2. Circuit diagram of one channel

Instructions

There are a variety of Ethernet adapters for Arduino, but for this project we chose a Seeed Studio Ethernet Shield because the designers at Seeed Studio were clever enough to realize something very important: most people who add Ethernet to an Arduino also want to add other custom parts as well. It's not very often that you'd plug an Ethernet shield into an Arduino, connect up power and network, and let it run just like that. Most of the time you want to add other devices to the spare Arduino inputs or outputs so it can do something useful, but every other Ethernet shield we've seen wastes a large part of the shield area with blank PCB—not very useful. What Seeed Studio did is cram all the Ethernet circuitry up toward one end of the board and then use the remaining space to provide a prototyping area with all the Arduino I/O pins helpfully brought out on pads at the edge. Hallelujah!

But it's not all cookies and cream. The Seeed Studio Ethernet Shield is based on the design of the NuElectronics Ethernet Shield and requires use of the NuElectronics etherShield library. Unlike the official Arduino Ethernet library, which hides the gory details of TCP/IP and lets you create a simple network client or server with only a few lines of code, the etherShield library exposes a lot of the nastiness you shouldn't have to care about, and it can make your Arduino program quite hard to understand. The version of the etherShield library commonly available for download (v1.0) also has a bug that prevents it from operating correctly on computers with a case-sensitive filesystem, such as most Linux machines, so an updated release (v1.1) is available for download from the *Practical Arduino* web site.

The result is that the example code in this project will only work as-is with the Seeed Studio and NuElectronics shields, and not with Ethernet shields based on the "official" design. However, a version of the code modified to operate on an official shield is also available for download from the *Practical Arduino* web site. If you use a shield other than the Seeed Studio design, though, you will probably have to assemble the project using a prototyping shield that plugs on top of the Ethernet shield rather than have everything on one board.

Mount PCB Plugs on Shield

To make the shield easy to test, it's a good idea to use plugs and sockets to connect external devices, such as the DS18B20 temperature sensors. That way, you can easily plug and unplug things while you're working with it on your bench and also while you're installing it in a more permanent location.

We used 3-pin PCB-mount headers on our prototype because they're inexpensive, don't take up much space on the shield, and only allow you to fit the connectors one way around so it's almost impossible to plug in a sensor backward.

The Seeed Studio Ethernet Shield has plenty of space to easily fit six connectors. In fact, if you fitted another three across the top prototyping area and a third connector just to the left of the one marked "E," you could fit up to 10 on the shield. That won't leave you with enough digital I/O lines on the two digital connectors at the top of the shield (considering that the Ethernet shield itself uses pins 3, 10, 11, and 12 to communicate with the Arduino). However, something that many people don't realize is that the analog inputs on the bottom of the Arduino can also be used as digital I/O pins.

The Arduino's analog pins can also be addressed as digital pins 14 through 19, as follows:

```
analog 0 = digital 14
analog 1 = digital 15
analog 2 = digital 16
analog 3 = digital 17
analog 4 = digital 18
analog 5 = digital 19
```

For example, to use analog pin 3 as a digital input you could simply do the following:

```
pinMode(17, INPUT);
```

This is something very handy to keep in mind if you run out of digital pins and don't need all the analog inputs.

The example sketch provided for this project only addresses six temperature sensors, but it could easily be extended to read 10 if you really wanted to pack as much on the board as possible.

Connect +5V and GNDAfter you have soldered the connectors in place on the shield, strip off a short length of single-core cable (conductors out of Ethernet cable offcuts work great!) and link all the +5V connections together and then to the +5V connection on the shield.

Likewise, link all the ground connections together and then to the GND connection on the shield. That way, each connector will have its own GND (left) and +5V (right) leads, as shown in Figure 7-3 and Figure 7-4.

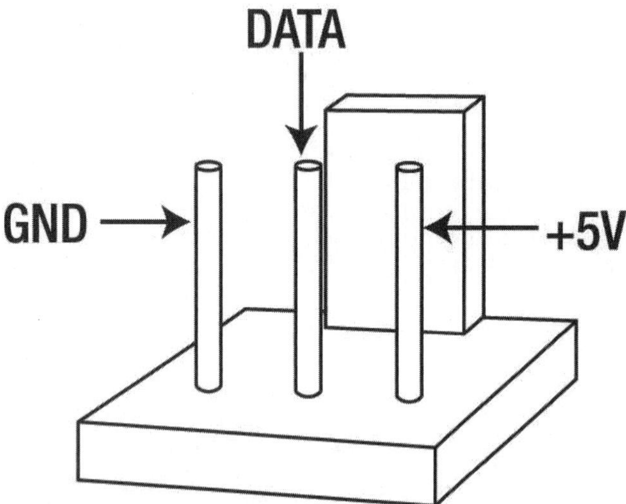

Figure 7-3. *Pin assignments for male header connections to sensors*

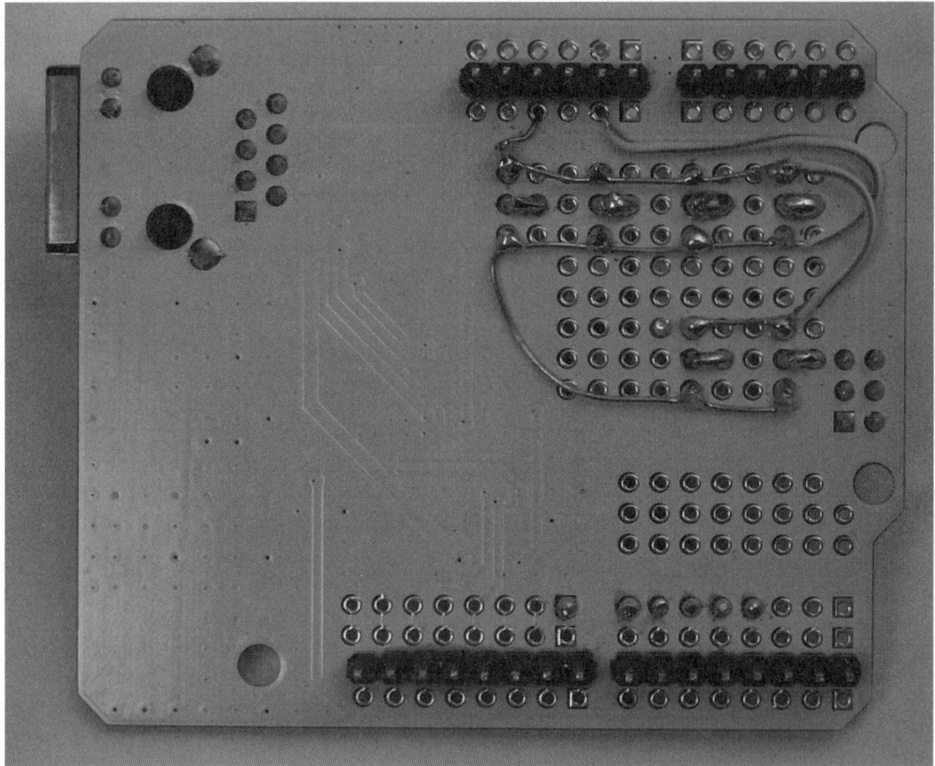

Figure 7-4. Connections for +5V and GND to headers on shield

Connect Data Lines

Trim off a few short pieces of single-core cable and use it to link the center (data) pin of each connector to the matching digital I/O line. The assignments we used are as follows:

```
sensor A = digital 3
sensor B = digital 4
sensor C = digital 5
sensor D = digital 6
sensor E = digital 7
sensor F = digital 8
```

Notice that we skipped the first few pins and started at digital pin 3. Pins 0 and 1 are used for the serial connection (USB) to the host, and pin 2 is used by the Ethernet shield itself to communicate with the Arduino. Many shields use pin 2 because it's a special pin associated with an interrupt on the Arduino.

We installed each wire, in turn, by inserting it from the top of the shield into the center hole behind the connector and bending the end across to join with the connector pin, then guiding the rest of the wire to the appropriate digital connection, and finally soldering both ends from underneath the shield. The result is shown in Figure 7-5.

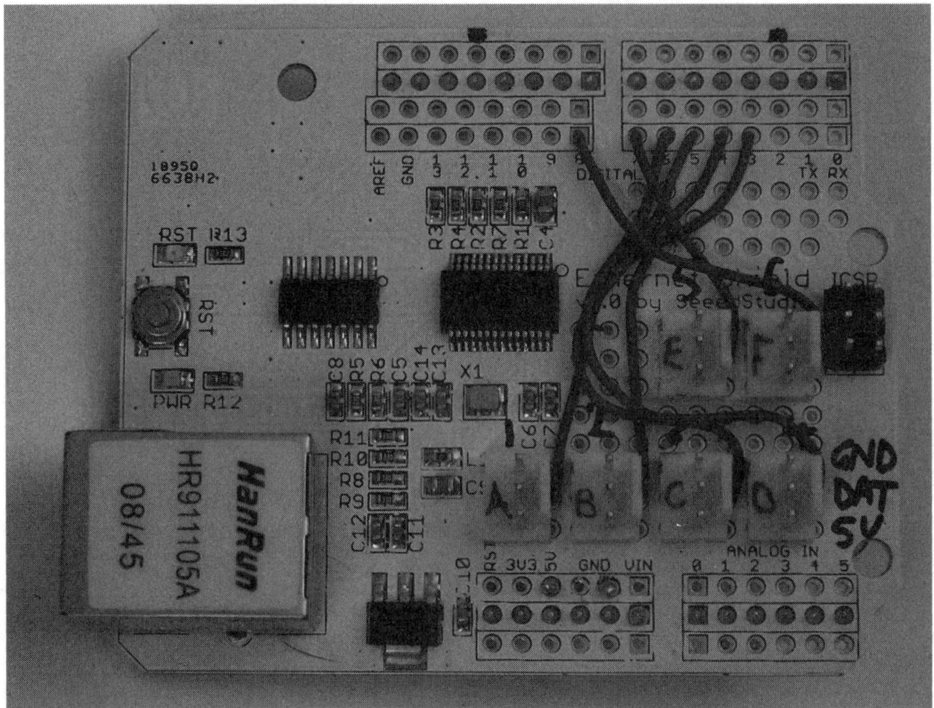

Figure 7-5. Connections to digital I/O lines from center pin of each connector

That's it for the shield setup. Notice that nothing we've done so far is actually specific to the DS18B20 sensors: in fact, all we've done is create an Ethernet shield with connectors that each provide power, ground, and access to one digital I/O line each. That makes this shield quite useful for a range of things, such as plugging in other types of sensors or controlling devices if you provide appropriate external buffering. By modifying the code, you could even have a mix of DS18B20s and other devices all connected at once.

Assemble Sensors

Most of your sensors will be on long leads so they can be placed in interesting spots, but to test the system on the bench we'll fit a DS18B20 directly to a connector so it can be plugged straight into the shield.

Each DS18B20 needs a 4k7 resistor between the data and +5V pins, so for the first sensor that will be plugged directly into the board we'll fit the sensor to the connector and solder the resistor to the sensor leads.

It's important to solder on the contacts the right way around because they only fit into the connector body one way, and it has to align with the pin assignments on the shield. Lay the sensor facedown on your workbench and fit the contacts so that the open side is up. Be careful to fit each one at the same position on the pin because they need to line up when they slide into the connector body.

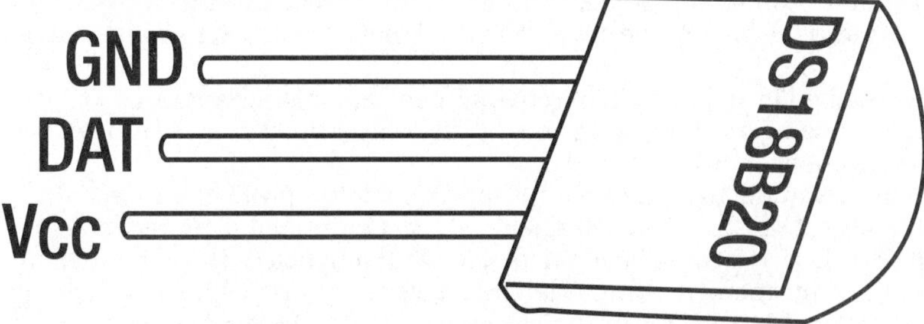

Figure 7-6. Pinout for DS18B20 temperature sensor

Bend one leg of a 4k7 resistor back around so it's parallel to the other leg, then cut them off about 5mm from the resistor body and bend them slightly sideways.

Solder the resistor across the data and +5V leads on the temperature sensor using the pinout in Figure 7-6 as a guide, and finally slide the contacts into the connector body to have a fully assembled sensor as shown in Figure 7-7.

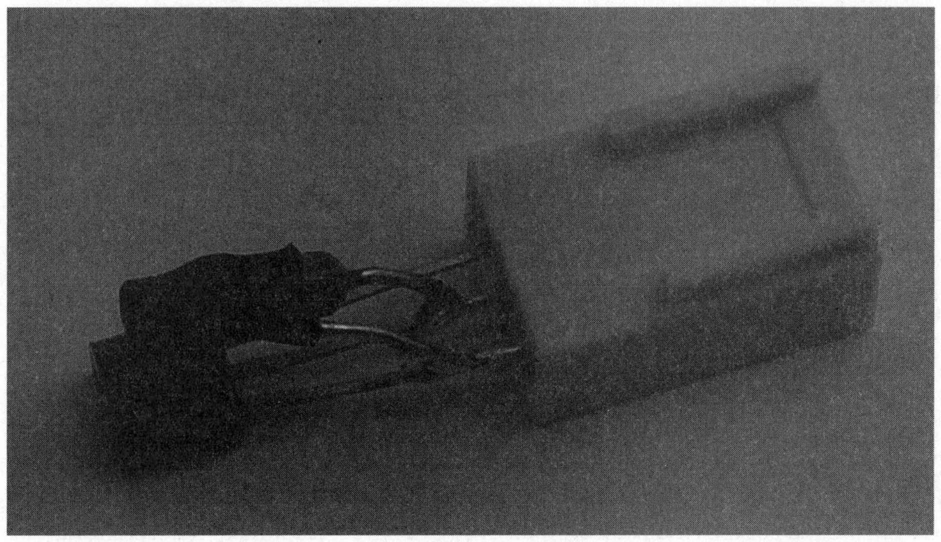

Figure 7-7. Sensor and resistor soldered to female connector

Plug the sensor into the shield and you're ready to load the example program and test that it works.

To assemble other sensors on longer leads you can use pretty much any wire you want. Twisted pair cable such as Ethernet cable works very well, and for shorter runs stereo shielded cable with the shield connected to ground and the two internal conductors connected up with to data and +5V should work well. Just be careful of very long runs with shielded cable because the shield can produce capacitance on the line that interferes with digital data transmission. That shouldn't be a problem for typical cable runs within a house at a low data rate but it's something to keep in mind for future reference.

We also fitted the 4k7 resistors into the back of the connector so all that's needed at the other end is the sensor itself.

If your sensor is going to be installed in an inhospitable environment you might want to smear silicon on the leads and connections, being careful to leave most of the sensor body exposed so it will pick up environmental temperature changes quickly.

For our particular application we wanted to fit the Arduino and shield into a protective case and still be able to easily connect and disconnect sensors. We used a heavy-duty environmental protection case and fitted it with DIN-rail mounting clips so it could be fitted in place with other electrical equipment in a home automation system, and fitted inexpensive 3.5mm stereo sockets to the case with a small wiring loom linking them to the PCB-mount connectors. We cut holes in the side of the case and fitted the Arduino and shield into it so that the USB, power, and Ethernet sockets are accessible on one side, and used DIY Power over Ethernet (PoE) to supply power to the system through the Ethernet cable.

More information about this particular home automation system and how Arduino is being used in it is available at www.superhouse.tv.

Load Program

The example program for this project runs your Arduino as a simple web server that responds to web requests with a page containing the current sensor readings. The program can be modified to change the format of the web page that is sent, but before getting into the details of the code there are a few limitations you should be aware of.

Because this program is based on the etherShield library for nuElectronics and Seeed Studio Ethernet Shields, it doesn't implement a full TCP/IP stack. One of the major limitations is that the etherShield library doesn't support packet fragmentation, which means the size of the response that can be sent is strictly limited. A full TCP/IP implementation breaks up large messages into packets, each of which is transmitted independently across the network and reassembled at the other end to reconstruct the complete message. Packets are, as a major generalization, limited to between 64 and 1518 bytes in size including all the headers. Because the TCP/IP header and the checksum eat into that you actually end up with somewhat less than 1518 bytes as the upper size.

The upshot of this is that the entire web page that you send back has to fit within a single packet or things simply won't work, but what exactly is meant by "a single packet" depends a little on how your local network is set up so we can't give a definitive answer as to how many bytes it has to be. The example program limits the TCP buffer to 500 bytes, but you can experiment with other values if you like.

The other limitation is that the etherShield library doesn't have any provision for specifying a gateway or netmask, so it has no concept of routing. You can't configure a gateway address in your program and have it initiate a TCP/IP connection to a host outside your network because it simply won't understand where to send the packet. Note, however, that you can have it respond to requests from outside your network if your gateway does source-NAT (network address translation), because as far as the Arduino is concerned the request came from the gateway, which it thinks is just another host on your network. It will reply to it on the LAN, and the gateway can then forward the response packet back to the actual requesting client out on the Internet. TCP/IP networking is a huge topic, though, so we can't go into it in detail here.

So, on to the example program. It's quite long for an Arduino program because so much of the TCP/IP detail is exposed in the program itself.

First, it includes the etherShield library, then sets some variables to define the networking configuration.

```
#include "etherShield.h"
// Modify the following two lines to suit your local network
// configuration. The MAC and IP address have to be unique on your LAN:
static uint8_t myMac[6] = {0x54,0x55,0x58,0x10,0x00,0x24};
static uint8_t myIp[4]  = {192,168,1,15};
static char baseurl[]   = "http://192.168.1.15/";
static uint16_t myPort = 80; // Listen port for tcp/www (range 1-254)
```

It's essential that the MAC address setting be unique on your network, so if you have multiple Arduinos connected you could decrement the last value (0x24) for each subsequent device. Make sure you keep track of what value you've assigned to each one.

Likewise, the IP address needs to be unique on your network, and you need to enter it twice: once as the four elements in the myIp array and then as a string in baseurl. These values are different because the TCP/IP stack needs to use the actual local IP address in the headers, but the web page that is created also needs to display a form that submits to itself, and the address used in your browser may be different to the actual IP address if your device is behind a NAT (network address translation) device such as as firewall. If you want to expose your device externally you should set the actual local IP address in the myIp variable, and set the external address in the baseurl variable.

The myPort value can be changed if you want your device to listen on a port other than the default port 80. However, if you change it make sure you also change the baseurl variable to include the port number or the form won't work. For example, if you wanted to listen on port 81, you could change those lines to the following:

```
static char baseurl[]   = "http://192.168.1.15:81/";
static uint16_t myPort = 81; // Listen port for tcp/www (range 1-254)
```

The program then creates two buffers used in creating the TCP/IP packet, and creates an instance of the EtherShield object called "es" as follows:

```
// Set up variables for the TCP/IP buffer
#define BUFFER_SIZE 500
static uint8_t buf[BUFFER_SIZE+1];
#define STR_BUFFER_SIZE 22
static char strbuf[STR_BUFFER_SIZE+1];
// Create an instance of the EtherShield object named "es"
EtherShield es=EtherShield();
// Prepare the web page by writing the data to the TCP send buffer
uint16_t print_webpage(uint8_t *buf);
int8_t analyse_cmd(char *str);
```

We've set up our shield with six connectors for temperature sensors, so the program defines which digital I/O lines to use for sensors A through F as follows:

```
// Specify data pins for connected DS18B20 temperature sensors
#define SENSOR_A  3
#define SENSOR_B  4
#define SENSOR_C  5
#define SENSOR_D  6
```

```
#define SENSOR_E  7
#define SENSOR_F  8
```

The setup function does some setup of the Ethernet connection, and then sets all the sensor data pins to be inputs as follows:

```
void setup()
{
  /*initialize enc28j60*/
  es.ES_enc28j60Init(myMac);
  // Change clkout from 6.25MHz to 12.5MHz
  es.ES_enc28j60clkout(2);
  delay(10);
  /* Magjack leds configuration, see enc28j60 datasheet, page 11 */
  // LEDA=green LEDB=yellow
  // 0x880 is PHLCON LEDB=on, LEDA=on
  es.ES_enc28j60PhyWrite(PHLCON, 0x880);
  delay(500);
  // 0x990 is PHLCON LEDB=off, LEDA=off
  es.ES_enc28j60PhyWrite(PHLCON, 0x990);
  delay(500);
  // 0x880 is PHLCON LEDB=on, LEDA=on
  es.ES_enc28j60PhyWrite(PHLCON, 0x880);
  delay(500);
  // 0x990 is PHLCON LEDB=off, LEDA=off
  es.ES_enc28j60PhyWrite(PHLCON, 0x990);
  delay(500);
  // 0x476 is PHLCON LEDA=links status, LEDB=receive/transmit
  es.ES_enc28j60PhyWrite(PHLCON, 0x476);
  delay(100);
  //init the ethernet/ip layer:
  es.ES_init_ip_arp_udp_tcp(myMac, myIp, myPort);
  // Set up the data pins for communication with DS18B20 sensors
  digitalWrite(SENSOR_A, LOW);
  pinMode(SENSOR_A, INPUT);
  digitalWrite(SENSOR_B, LOW);
  pinMode(SENSOR_B, INPUT);
  digitalWrite(SENSOR_C, LOW);
  pinMode(SENSOR_C, INPUT);
  digitalWrite(SENSOR_D, LOW);
  pinMode(SENSOR_D, INPUT);
  digitalWrite(SENSOR_E, LOW);
  pinMode(SENSOR_E, INPUT);
  digitalWrite(SENSOR_F, LOW);
  pinMode(SENSOR_F, INPUT);
}
```

The main program loop is quite complex because it checks the Ethernet receive buffer each time through and manages the appropriate responses.

The interesting part is toward the end where it performs three checks on the request to determine if it needs to respond with the web page. The first check is for a request to the base URL, and if that matches it calls print_webpage() to generate the default page containing sensor data.

The second and third checks are both done using a call to analyse_cmd(), which processes the request header to find the value of the cmd variable passed through in the request. If the value is 1 it responds with the default page once again. This check is not strictly necessary because if you only ever wanted your program to return the page with the sensor data on it, you won't care what arguments are passed through: you want your Arduino to always just respond with the same page. However, we've included it in this example because it demonstrates how you can create a crude navigation system and have your Arduino return different pages depending on what argument has been sent through. In the example it does this by checking for a cmd value of 2, in which case it knows the user is specifically requesting the About page rather than the page with sensor data and makes a call to print_webpage_about() instead of print_webpage().

You could define a whole bunch of pages and store them in your program, then use identifiers to load different pages on demand.

Or alternatively you could modify the print_webpage() function so that it only returns the value from one sensor, and have it use a value submitted by the user to determine which sensor to process. That way, you could connect to a URL such as http://192.168.1.15/?cmd=4, to access the data for sensor 4.

Just remember the restriction on page size and don't try to create the next big CMS (content management system) on your Arduino!

```
void loop(){
  uint16_t plen, dat_p;
  int8_t cmd;
  plen = es.ES_enc28j60PacketReceive(BUFFER_SIZE, buf);
  /*plen will ne unequal to zero if there is a valid packet (without crc error) */
  if(plen!=0) {
    // arp is broadcast if unknown but a host may also verify the mac address by sending it to
a unicast address.
    if (es.ES_eth_type_is_arp_and_my_ip (buf,plen)) {
      es.ES_make_arp_answer_from_request (buf);
      return;
    }
    // check if ip packets are for us:
    if (es.ES_eth_type_is_ip_and_my_ip (buf,plen) == 0) {
      return;
    }
    if (buf[IP_PROTO_P]==IP_PROTO_ICMP_V && buf[ICMP_TYPE_P]==ICMP_TYPE_ECHOREQUEST_V) {
      es.ES_make_echo_reply_from_request (buf,plen);
      return;
    }
    // tcp port www start, compare only the lower byte
    if (buf[IP_PROTO_P] == IP_PROTO_TCP_V && buf[TCP_DST_PORT_H_P] == 0 &&
buf[TCP_DST_PORT_L_P] == myPort) {
      if (buf[TCP_FLAGS_P] & TCP_FLAGS_SYN_V) {
        es.ES_make_tcp_synack_from_syn (buf); // make_tcp_synack_from_syn does already send
the syn,ack
        return;
      }
      if (buf[TCP_FLAGS_P] & TCP_FLAGS_ACK_V) {
        es.ES_init_len_info (buf); // init some data structures
        dat_p = es.ES_get_tcp_data_pointer();
        if (dat_p==0) { // we can possibly have no data, just ack:
          if (buf[TCP_FLAGS_P] & TCP_FLAGS_FIN_V) {
```

```
            es.ES_make_tcp_ack_from_any (buf);
          }
          return;
        }
        if (strncmp ("GET ", (char *) & (buf[dat_p]), 4) != 0) {
          // head, post, and other methods for possible status codes see:
          // http://www.w3.org/Protocols/rfc2616/rfc2616-sec10.html          plen =
es.ES_fill_tcp_data_p (buf,0,PSTR ("HTTP/1.0 200 OK\r\nContent-Type: text/html\r\n\r\n<h1>200
OK</h1>"));
          goto SENDTCP;
        }
        if (strncmp("/ ", (char *) & (buf[dat_p+4]), 2) == 0){
          plen = print_webpage (buf);
          goto SENDTCP;
        }
        cmd = analyse_cmd ((char *) & (buf[dat_p+5]));
        if (cmd == 1){
          plen = print_webpage (buf);       // Send the "Data" page
        }
        if (cmd == 2){
          plen = print_webpage_about (buf); // Send the "About" page
        }
SENDTCP:  es.ES_make_tcp_ack_from_any(buf); // send ack for http get
          es.ES_make_tcp_ack_with_data(buf,plen); // send data
      }
    }
  }
}
```

The next function is for doing what C does worst—text processing. It's a utility function called a little later in the program to process the arguments passed through in the HTTP request, as follows:

```
// The returned value is stored in the global var strbuf
uint8_t find_key_val (char *str,char *key)
{
  uint8_t found = 0;
  uint8_t i = 0;
  char *kp;
  kp = key;
  while (*str &&  *str!=' ' && found==0) {
    if (*str == *kp) {
      kp++;
      if (*kp == '\0') {
        str++;
        kp=key;
        if (*str == '=') {
          found = 1;
        }
      }
    } else {
      kp = key;
    }
```

```
    str++;
  }
  if (found == 1) {
    // copy the value to a buffer and terminate it with '\0'
    while (*str &&  *str!=' ' && *str!='&' && i<STR_BUFFER_SIZE) {
      strbuf[i]=*str;
      i++;
      str++;
    }
    strbuf[i]='\0';
  }
  return(found);
}
```

Next is the function that calls it. The analyse_cmd() function looks specifically for a request argument called "cmd," and returns the value if it's a number. If you wanted to pass another argument through to your device and have it process them both (such as one argument for the page and the other argument for the device ID), you could make another version of this function to process the other argument:

```
int8_t analyse_cmd (char *str)
{
  int8_t r = -1;
  if (find_key_val (str,"cmd")) {
    if (*strbuf < 0x3a && *strbuf > 0x2f) {
      // is a ASCII number, return it
      r = (*strbuf-0x30);
    }
  }
  return r;
}
```

The function to print the web page with the sensor data is long, but that's only because it's very repetitive; the structure of the function is quite simple. Before any HTML purists look at what is being returned and start complaining about things such as lack of a doctype declaration or even basic things such as HTML body tags, we should point out that the page defined in this function is designed to be absolutely minimal in size rather than technically correct. The reality is that in 500 or so bytes it's simply not possible to return a fully formed HTML page including all the headers and the content required, so we've taken more than a few shortcuts that would have us on trial for crimes against RFCs if we tried to pass this off as a valid web page. It gets the job done, though, which is what matters.

The function first defines a set of arrays to hold the values returned by each sensor, as well as variables for a counter (to be used a little later in the function) and for the packet length. If you want to expand this project to support more sensors you would need to define more arrays to suit.

```
uint16_t print_webpage (uint8_t *buf)
{
  // Arrays to hold the temperature reading from each sensor
  char temp_string_a[10];
  char temp_string_b[10];
  char temp_string_c[10];
  char temp_string_d[10];
```

```
char temp_string_e[10];
char temp_string_f[10];
int i;                  // Counter used while iterating over reading arrays
uint16_t plen;          // Length of response packet
```

It then reads all the temperature sensors. This can safely be done even if you don't have six sensors connected because it will simply return 0.0 degrees for any unconnected channels.

```
// Read all the temperature sensors
getCurrentTemp(SENSOR_A, temp_string_a);
getCurrentTemp(SENSOR_B, temp_string_b);
getCurrentTemp(SENSOR_C, temp_string_c);
getCurrentTemp(SENSOR_D, temp_string_d);
getCurrentTemp(SENSOR_E, temp_string_e);
getCurrentTemp(SENSOR_F, temp_string_f);
```

Then the function pushes the HTTP response header into the packet buffer as follows:

```
// Send HTTP content-type header
plen = es.ES_fill_tcp_data_p (buf, 0, PSTR ("HTTP/1.0 200 OK\r\nContent-Type:
text/html\r\n\r\n"));
```

Now for the bit that actually sends you the value you're interested in. The packet buffer has the string "Sensor A:" pushed into it, then the counter that was defined earlier is used to loop through the value array for this particular sensor and push each element into the buffer. While that is happening the packet length variable, plen, is incremented so it will correctly reflect the number of characters in the buffer. Finally, an HTML <br /> tag is appended so each row of data will appear on a separate line, and the whole shebang is repeated for each of the six sensor channels.

```
// Read sensor A
plen = es.ES_fill_tcp_data_p (buf, plen, PSTR ("Sensor A:"));
i=0;
while (temp_string_a[i]) {
  buf[TCP_CHECKSUM_L_P+3+plen]=temp_string_a[i++];
  plen++;
}
plen = es.ES_fill_tcp_data_p (buf, plen, PSTR ("<br />"));

// Read sensor B
plen = es.ES_fill_tcp_data_p (buf, plen, PSTR ("Sensor B:"));
i=0;
while (temp_string_b[i]) {
  buf[TCP_CHECKSUM_L_P+3+plen]=temp_string_b[i++];
  plen++;
}
plen = es.ES_fill_tcp_data_p (buf, plen, PSTR ("<br />"));

// Read sensor C
plen = es.ES_fill_tcp_data_p (buf, plen, PSTR ("Sensor C:"));
i=0;
while (temp_string_c[i]) {
  buf[TCP_CHECKSUM_L_P+3+plen]=temp_string_c[i++];
```

```
    plen++;
  }
  plen = es.ES_fill_tcp_data_p (buf, plen, PSTR ("<br />"));

  // Read sensor D
  plen = es.ES_fill_tcp_data_p (buf, plen, PSTR ("Sensor D:"));
  i=0;
  while (temp_string_d[i]) {
    buf[TCP_CHECKSUM_L_P+3+plen]=temp_string_d[i++];
    plen++;
  }
  plen = es.ES_fill_tcp_data_p (buf, plen, PSTR ("<br />"));

  // Read sensor E
  plen = es.ES_fill_tcp_data_p (buf, plen, PSTR ("Sensor E:"));
  i=0;
  while (temp_string_e[i]) {
    buf[TCP_CHECKSUM_L_P+3+plen]=temp_string_e[i++];
    plen++;
  }
  plen = es.ES_fill_tcp_data_p (buf, plen, PSTR ("<br />"));

  // Read sensor F
  plen = es.ES_fill_tcp_data_p (buf, plen, PSTR ("Sensor F:"));
  i=0;
  while (temp_string_f[i]) {
    buf[TCP_CHECKSUM_L_P+3+plen]=temp_string_f[i++];
    plen++;
  }
  plen = es.ES_fill_tcp_data_p (buf, plen, PSTR ("<br />"));
```

At the end of the page we append two HTML forms to display navigation buttons. The first form causes a hidden input field, cmd, to be submitted with a value of 1, while the second does almost the exact same thing but submits a value of 2.

```
  // Display a form button to update the display
  plen = es.ES_fill_tcp_data_p (buf, plen, PSTR ("<form METHOD=get action=\""));
  plen = es.ES_fill_tcp_data (buf, plen, baseurl);
  plen = es.ES_fill_tcp_data_p (buf, plen, PSTR ("\">"));
  plen = es.ES_fill_tcp_data_p (buf, plen, PSTR("<input type=hidden name=cmd value=1>"));
  plen = es.ES_fill_tcp_data_p (buf, plen, PSTR("<input type=submit value=\"Data\">"));
  plen = es.ES_fill_tcp_data_p (buf, plen, PSTR("</form>"));

  // Display a form button to access the "About" page
  plen = es.ES_fill_tcp_data_p (buf, plen, PSTR ("<form METHOD=get action=\""));
  plen = es.ES_fill_tcp_data (buf, plen, baseurl);
  plen = es.ES_fill_tcp_data_p (buf, plen, PSTR ("\">"));
  plen = es.ES_fill_tcp_data_p (buf, plen, PSTR("<input type=hidden name=cmd value=2>"));
  plen = es.ES_fill_tcp_data_p (buf, plen, PSTR("<input type=submit value=\"About\">"));
  plen = es.ES_fill_tcp_data_p (buf, plen, PSTR("</form>"));

  return (plen);
```

```
}
```

The function to generate the About page is similarto the previous function but is much simpler. Rather than reading the temperature sensors, it simply sends back some static text followed by the navigation links.

```
/**
 * Generate a web page containing the "About" text
 */
uint16_t print_webpage_about (uint8_t *buf)
{
  uint16_t plen;          // Length of response packet
  // Send HTTP content-type header
  plen = es.ES_fill_tcp_data_p (buf, 0, PSTR ("HTTP/1.0 200 OK\r\nContent-Type:
text/html\r\n\r\n"));
  // Display the text for the "About" page
  plen = es.ES_fill_tcp_data_p (buf, plen, PSTR ("<h1>Online Thermometer v1.0</h1>"));
  plen = es.ES_fill_tcp_data_p (buf, plen, PSTR ("As featured in Practical Arduino.<br />"));
  plen = es.ES_fill_tcp_data_p (buf, plen, PSTR ("See <a
href=\"http://practicalarduino.com\">practicalarduino.com</a> for more info."));
  // Display a form button to update the display
  plen = es.ES_fill_tcp_data_p (buf, plen, PSTR ("<form METHOD=get action=\""));
  plen = es.ES_fill_tcp_data (buf, plen, baseurl);
  plen = es.ES_fill_tcp_data_p (buf, plen, PSTR ("\">"));
  plen = es.ES_fill_tcp_data_p (buf, plen, PSTR("<input type=hidden name=cmd value=1>"));
  plen = es.ES_fill_tcp_data_p (buf, plen, PSTR("<input type=submit value=\"Data\">"));
  plen = es.ES_fill_tcp_data_p (buf, plen, PSTR("</form>"));

  // Display a form button to access the "About" page
  plen = es.ES_fill_tcp_data_p (buf, plen, PSTR ("<form METHOD=get action=\""));
  plen = es.ES_fill_tcp_data (buf, plen, baseurl);
  plen = es.ES_fill_tcp_data_p (buf, plen, PSTR ("\">"));
  plen = es.ES_fill_tcp_data_p (buf, plen, PSTR("<input type=hidden name=cmd value=2>"));
  plen = es.ES_fill_tcp_data_p (buf, plen, PSTR("<input type=submit value=\"About\">"));
  plen = es.ES_fill_tcp_data_p (buf, plen, PSTR("</form>"));

  return (plen);
}
```

The next few functions are utility functions for managing the communications with the DS18B20 sensors using the Dallas 1-wire bus. These functions use a technique called "bit-banging" to send data to the communications pin or read data from it.

Bit-banging requires the main processor to use software timing to literally send and receive every individual bit directly on a serial port, which is obviously quite inefficient compared to handing the job off to dedicated hardware. Serial communications is usually offloaded from the main processor to dedicated hardware, such as a USART (universal synchronous/asynchronous receiver/transmitter), that handles all the timing issues and buffers data transparently so the main processor can just send it bytes to be transmitted and then get on with other things, or read data from the USART's buffer even if it arrived while the processor was busy. A USART acts as a messaging service for the main processor, sending out messages on request and holding incoming messages until the CPU is ready to deal with them.

Arduino boards do have at least one USART but it's tied up managing serial communications via the USB connection on pins 0 and 1, and even the Arduino Mega only has a total of four USARTs including the one used for the USB connection. It is possible to add more USARTs externally but that can be expensive and complicated, and since we're only dealing with low-volume, low-speed communications, it makes sense to resort to bit-banging instead in this case.

The big benefit of bit-banging in this project is that it allows us to use any digital I/O pin we like as a serial communications port simply by switching it high and low with the correct timing.

If you're curious about the details of how bit-banging works you can find out a lot more in the SoftSerial Arduino library, which uses bit-banging to let you turn any digital pin into a communications port. There's also more information about bit-banging on Wikipedia at en.wikipedia.org/wiki/Bit-banging.

```
/**
 */
void OneWireReset(int Pin) // reset.  Should improve to act as a presence pulse
{
  digitalWrite(Pin, LOW);
  pinMode(Pin, OUTPUT);        // bring low for 500 us
  delayMicroseconds(500);
  pinMode(Pin, INPUT);
  delayMicroseconds(500);
}
/**
 */
void OneWireOutByte(int Pin, byte d) // output byte d (least sig bit first).
{
  byte n;
  for (n=8; n!=0; n--)
  {
    if ((d & 0x01) == 1)  // test least sig bit
    {
      digitalWrite(Pin, LOW);
      pinMode(Pin, OUTPUT);
      delayMicroseconds(5);
      pinMode(Pin, INPUT);
      delayMicroseconds(60);
    }
    else
    {
      digitalWrite(Pin, LOW);
      pinMode(Pin, OUTPUT);
      delayMicroseconds(60);
      pinMode(Pin, INPUT);
    }

    d = d>>1; // now the next bit is in the least sig bit position.
  }
}

/**
 */
byte OneWireInByte(int Pin) // read byte, least sig byte first
```

```
{
  byte d, n, b;
  for (n=0; n<8; n++)
  {
    digitalWrite (Pin, LOW);
    pinMode (Pin, OUTPUT);
    delayMicroseconds (5);
    pinMode (Pin, INPUT);
    delayMicroseconds (5);
    b = digitalRead (Pin);
    delayMicroseconds (50);
    d = (d >> 1) | (b<<7); // shift d to right and insert b in most sig bit position
  }
  return (d);
}
```

The function to actually read a value from one of the temperature sensors uses the previous utility functions to send commands out the appropriate pin and receive the response. This function works by populating the received value into an array passed in by the calling function, which is a sneaky way of getting around the problem that a function can't simply return an array directly.

```
/**
 * Read temperature from a DS18B20.
 * int sensorPin: Arduino digital I/O pin connected to sensor
 * char *temp: global array to be populated with current reading
 */
void getCurrentTemp (int sensorPin, char *temp)
{
  int HighByte, LowByte, TReading, Tc_100, sign, whole, fract;
  OneWireReset (sensorPin);
  OneWireOutByte (sensorPin, 0xcc);
  OneWireOutByte (sensorPin, 0x44); // Perform temperature conversion, strong pullup for one
sec
  OneWireReset (sensorPin);
  OneWireOutByte (sensorPin, 0xcc);
  OneWireOutByte (sensorPin, 0xbe);
  LowByte = OneWireInByte (sensorPin);
  HighByte = OneWireInByte (sensorPin);
  TReading = (HighByte << 8) + LowByte;
  sign = TReading & 0x8000;  // test most sig bit
  if (sign) // negative
  {
    TReading = (TReading ^ 0xffff) + 1; // 2's complement
  }
  Tc_100 = (6 * TReading) + TReading / 4;    // multiply by (100 * 0.0625) or 6.25
  whole = Tc_100 / 100;  // separate off the whole and fractional portions
  fract = Tc_100 % 100;
  if (sign) {
    temp[0] = '-';
  } else {
    temp[0] = '+';
  }
```

```
  if (whole/100 == 0) {
    temp[1] = ' ';
  } else {
    temp[1] = whole/100+'0';
  }
  temp[2] = (whole-(whole/100)*100)/10 +'0' ;
  temp[3] = whole-(whole/10)*10 +'0';
  temp[4] = '.';
  temp[5] = fract/10 +'0';
  temp[6] = fract-(fract/10)*10 +'0';
  temp[7] = '\0';
}
```

It looks like a large, complicated program, but most of that is because of the TCP/IP details included in the program rather than concealed by the library. The actual logical structure of the program is relatively simple.

After you've compiled and uploaded the program to your Arduino, plug it into a spare Ethernet connection on your network, open up a web browser, and open the address you configured in the baseurl variable (http://192.168.1.15/).

If all went well, you'll see a web page containing readings taken from each of the connected temperature sensors.

Sometimes DS18B20 temperature sensors return bogus values the first time they are accessed after powering up, so if the numbers look wildly wrong just hit refresh and you should see proper values come back.

Variations

The project as described runs a web server on the Arduino so you can poll it to access the current temperature readings. Alternatively, you could run a web client on the Arduino in a loop so that every few minutes it reads from the temperature sensors, connects to a web server, and submits the values through as arguments in the URL to be stored or processed by a script on the server. Just remember that because of the lack of routing information available in the etherShield library, the server would need to be on your local network. Alternatively, you could run a local reverse proxy as a gateway so the Arduino thinks it's connecting to a local host but the request is actually being forwarded on to an external machine. That way you could use a third-party service such as Pachube (`www.pachube.com`) or Watch My Thing (`www.watchmything.com`) to store and graph the data.

CHAPTER 8

■ ■ ■

Touch Control Panel

Small four-wire resistive touch screens are now amazingly inexpensive: they are produced in such enormous quantities for mobile phones, PDAs, and particularly handheld games such as the Nintendo DS that they can be bought brand new for under US $10.

Larger touch screens are also rapidly falling in price. The popularity of netbooks with screens between 7 and 10 inches in size has resulted in a healthy market for touch screens that can be retrofitted to them and plugged into an internal USB port. Despite the fact that they come with control electronics and a USB interface, those screens are also predominantly four-wire resistive devices, so if you dump the control module that comes with them and interface to the screen directly you can have a 10-inch touch screen on your Arduino! And if you want to go even bigger, there are often 15-inch, 17-inch, and 19-inch touch screen kits available on eBay for under $150.

Note, however, that what is advertised as a "touch screen" is not actually a complete screen including an LCD. It's just the transparent glass and plastic panel that fits onto the front of an appropriately sized LCD so the CPU can detect the coordinates at which the screen is being touched. If you want your Arduino to display information on a screen and let you select or control it by touch, you'll have to do a bit more work to set up the LCD that goes behind the touch screen overlay.

Even on its own, though, a touch screen is a very handy device. They're very thin and can be mounted over the top of any flat surface, not just an LCD, so they're great for creating little custom control panels with the "buttons" printed on a sheet that goes behind the touch screen. All you have to do is map the buttons to X/Y coordinates and your Arduino can figure out which button is being pressed by matching the coordinates. Of course, your control panel could represent anything, not just buttons. You could have a slider on it to select volume or temperature level by touching somewhere along a scale, or it could be a plan of a house so you can control lights in different rooms by touching the correct part of the floor plan.

In this project, we mount a Nintendo DS touch screen on a blank electrical wall plate to create a touch-sensitive control panel that can link to a home automation system. The techniques we describe here should work with pretty much any four-wire resistive touch screen available, but note that some touch screens are also made using other technologies, such as capacitive and infrared, so make sure the screen you buy is definitely a resistive model. The required parts are shown in Figure 8-1, and the schematic is in Figure 8-2.

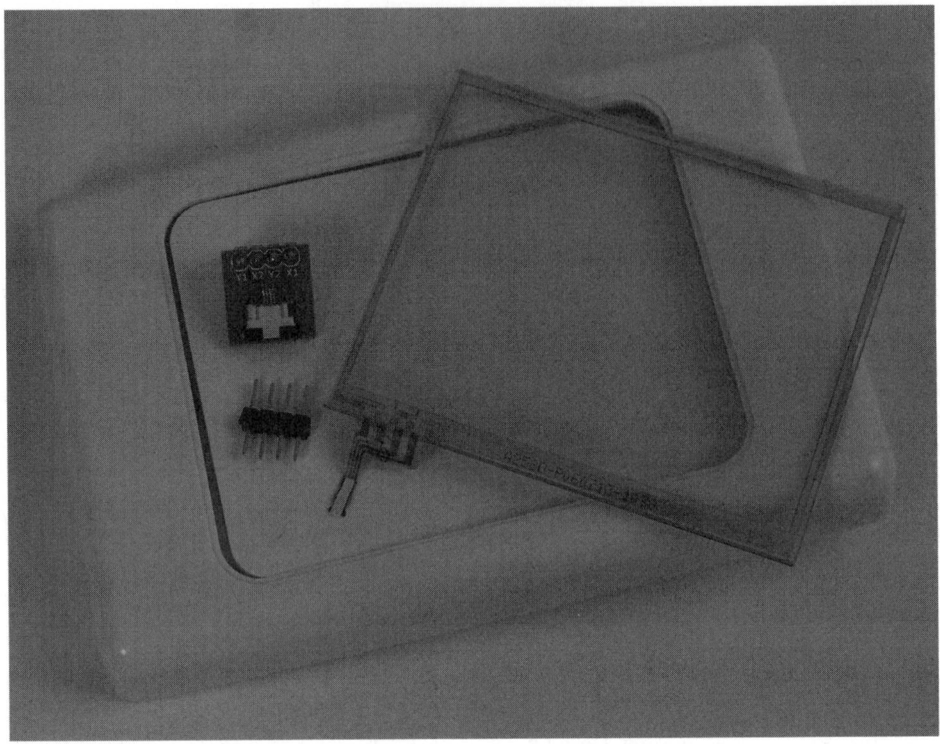

Figure 8-1. Parts required for connecting a resistive touch screen

Parts Required

1 x Arduino Duemilanove, Mini, Pro Mini, or equivalent

1 x Nintendo DS touch screen

1 x Nintendo DS touch screen breakout board

1 x Blank electrical wall plate

1 x 4-pin male breakaway header

Source code available from
`www.practicalarduino.com/projects/touch-control-panel`

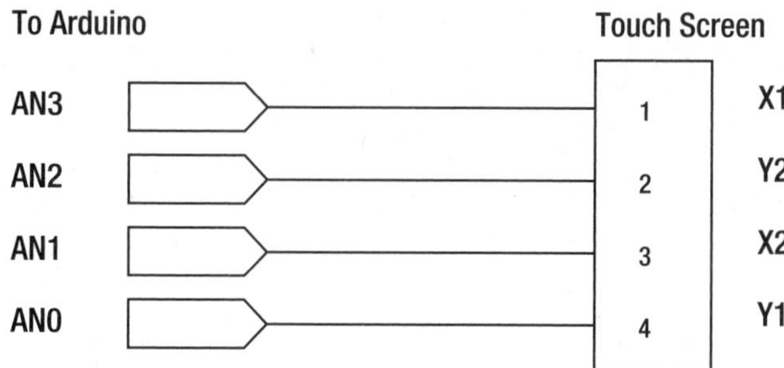

Figure 8-2. *Schematic for connection of resistive touch screen*

Instructions

Reading a resistive touch screen accurately is not quite as straightforward as it first sounds because, despite what you may have read online in various Arduino forums and blogs, they don't have specific output connections for X and Y values. You can't read both the X and Y axis simultaneously: you have to set up the pins in one configuration to read the X value, and change them to another configuration to read the Y value. In practice, this can be done so fast that there is no way the user can tell you're not reading both the X and the Y value at the same time.

Once you understand the physical structure of a touch screen you'll realize why they don't have simple connections for power, ground, X, and Y, as many people claim.

How Resistive Touch Screens Work

A resistive touch screen consists of several plastic layers built on a glass substrate that provides rigidity to the whole structure. In front of this substrate is a thin plastic layer coated with a resistive material. In some touch screens the resistive material is applied directly to the glass substrate to achieve the same end result. In front of this is a layer of microdots, which are tiny spacers laid over the surface to support a second thin plastic layer, also coated with resistive material (see Figure 8-3).

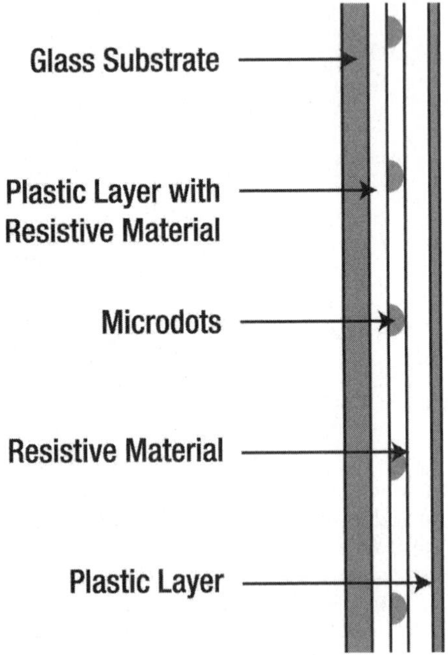

Figure 8-3. Layers in a resistive touch screen

When the screen is not being touched, the microdots hold the two resistive layers apart to cause it to be an open circuit. When the front layer is touched, it distorts and makes contact with the back layer, allowing electricity to conduct from one layer to the other.

Each of the four sides of the touch screen contains a conductive electrode that runs the whole length of the edge and connects to the resistive surface on either the top or bottom layer matched up by axis. For example, the left and right edges may connect to the front layer, while the top and bottom edges connect to the back layer (see Figure 8-4).

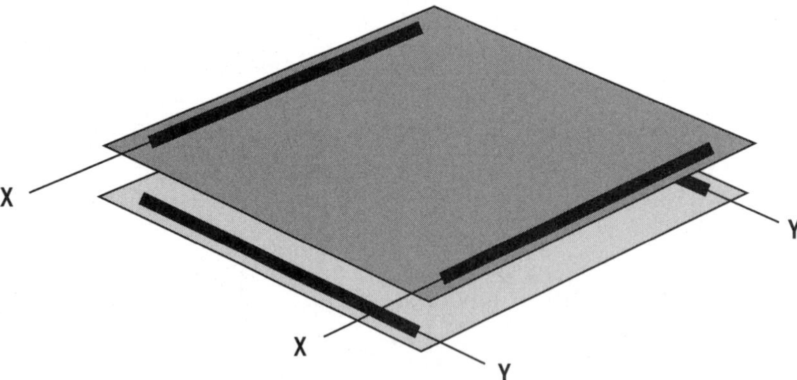

Figure 8-4. X and Y axis electrodes inside a resistive touch screen

Those four edges are then brought out onto the touch screen connector as X1, X2, Y1, and Y2, although the order on the connector may vary depending on the particular brand and model of touch screen. If you have a touch screen with no datasheet available for it, you can figure out the pairs of connections by measuring the resistance between them with a multimeter while the screen is not being touched. Each matching pair will have a resistance between them of somewhere around 1K or lower, while nonmatching electrodes will be open-circuit.

To read one axis of contact with the screen, one of the layers is connected to GND on one edge and +5V on the other edge to provide a continuously varying voltage across the surface of that layer. One of the edges on the other layer is then read using an analog input to determine the relative position of the contact between the two edges: if it's closer to the GND edge, the reading will be a lower voltage; and if it's closer to the +5V edge, the reading will be a higher voltage. When doing this the pins connected to one layer need to be configured as digital outputs and driven to GND and +5V to power up that layer, while one of the pins connected to the other layer needs to be configured as an analog input to read the touch value.

Reading the other axis then requires switching around the connections so that the layer previously being used for analog input now has GND and +5V applied across it, and one edge of the layer previously providing power is switched to being an analog input so the value can be read from it.

This is all pretty easy on an Arduino because the analog input pins are actually also general-purpose digital I/O pins, and their mode can be switched in software as required. We don't need to waste time and I/O lines externally switching the touch screen connections between an analog input and GND or +5V. By connecting the X1, X2, Y1, and Y2 lines of a touch screen directly to four analog input pins, we can then use software to switch pin modes between readings and use them as digital outputs to provide GND and +5V to whichever layer needs it at the time.

On a Nintendo DS touch screen, the connector brings out the edges in order as Y1, X2, Y2, and X1. To keep the physical connections as simple as possible, we'll maintain that physical order and connect those to analog inputs A0 through A3, respectively, as follows:

```
Y1 to A0
X2 to A1
Y2 to A2
X1 to A3
```

A minimal Arduino program that just reads and returns the values is fairly simple and helps explain how the touch screen works. Before getting into the details of the project, we'll look at a sketch that reads values from the touch screen five times per second and reports the values to a computer via the USB connection.

We start by defining variables to hold the values as read from the screen, as follows:

```
int xVal = 0;
int yVal = 0;
```

Next, we set up the serial connection to the host computer so we can report the X and Y values, as follows:

```
void setup()
{
  Serial.begin(38400);
  Serial.println("Starting up touch screen reader");
}
```

The main program loop reads the X and then the Y value each time through. Reading the X value involves setting up the Y-axis analog input pins as digital outputs and then doing an analog read. One optional step we're doing here is waiting for 2ms after setting up the outputs so the voltages have time to settle. The Arduino's analog inputs are very sensitive to eddy currents and induced voltages nearby, and switching outputs immediately adjacent to an analog input can cause it to give spurious readings. Adding a delay of a couple of milliseconds allows the input to settle down and returns a more consistent reading.

```
void loop()
{
  pinMode( 15, INPUT );       // Analog pin 1
  pinMode( 17, INPUT );       // Analog pin 3
  pinMode( 14, OUTPUT );      // Analog pin 0
  digitalWrite( 14, LOW );    // Use analog pin 0 as a GND connection
  pinMode( 16, OUTPUT );      // Analog pin 2
  digitalWrite( 16, HIGH );   // Use analog pin 2 as a +5V connection
  delay(2);                   // Wait for voltage to settle
  xVal = analogRead( 1 );     // Read the X value
```

At this point we have the X-axis value, but not yet the Y-axis value. Next we need to switch around the pin modes to do the same thing for the Y axis.

```
  pinMode( 14, INPUT );       // Analog pin 0
  pinMode( 16, INPUT );       // Analog pin 2
  pinMode( 15, OUTPUT );      // Analog pin 1
  digitalWrite( 15, LOW );    // Use analog pin 1 as a GND connection
  pinMode( 17, OUTPUT );      // Analog pin 3
  digitalWrite( 17, HIGH );   // Use analog pin 3 as a +5V connection
  delay(2);                   // Wait for voltage to settle
  yVal = analogRead( 0 );     // Read the Y value
```

We now have both the X- and Y-axis values, so finally we report them back to the host computer via the USB connection and then wait a little while before doing it all over again, as follows:

```
  Serial.print(xVal);

  Serial.print(",");
  Serial.println(yVal);

  delay (200);
}
```

That's it! Not so hard really when you understand what's going on.

The complete source code for this sketch is available from the project page on the *Practical Arduino* web site, and is called TouchscreenCoordinates.

Basic Touch Screen Connection Test

Touch screen connections are generally a very thin plastic ribbon with flexible metal strips attached to it. By far the easiest way to connect to them is to use a breakout board with a connector mounted on it to clip the ribbon into place. The example in Figure 8-5 is from SparkFun, and has a retention clip to lock the ribbon into the connector. Before the ribbon can be inserted, the locking clip needs to be released by sliding it toward the direction of the ribbon, which you can then insert before sliding the clip back again. It's a very delicate operation, though, and the locking clip is small and easily broken, so be careful when sliding the clip in and out.

Another thing to watch is the thickness of the ribbon on the touch screen. The connector is designed to firmly grasp a ribbon of 0.3mm thickness, but a bare touch screen ribbon is only about 0.1mm thick and will pull straight out of the connecter unless it has a shim of some kind to make it thicker. For some reason, touch screens seem to be supplied either with or without a shim attached and you never know what you're going to get. One of the touch screens we used for our prototypes had a tiny mylar shim attached to the back of the ribbon, while the other one didn't and needed a little piece of electrical tape applied to the back to make the ribbon thick enough to lock into the clip.

You can solder hookup wire or ribbon cable to the breakout board if you like, or you can solder a 4-pin male header to it so you can plug it straight into a breadboard or an Arduino.

The SparkFun breakout board brings the touch screen pins out in the same order as the touch screen ribbon, which is Y1, X2, Y2, and X1. The example code previously shown also uses this order, so for a basic connection test you can plug it straight into analog inputs 0 through 3.

Figure 8-5 shows a Nintendo DS touch screen connected to an Arduino Pro using a SparkFun breakout board. Note that in this picture the touch screen is upside down, To access the touch surface, it would be folded back over the top of the Arduino.

Figure 8-5. *Nintendo DS touch screen connected to Arduino Pro via a SparkFun breakout board with male headers soldered on*

Plugging directly into the Arduino probably isn't very convenient, so a short extension cable consisting of a four-core strip of ribbon cable with a male header on one end and a female header on the other can be a handy thing to have on hand.

To test out the touch screen, connect it to your Arduino, then load the previous example sketch in the Arduino IDE, compile it, and upload it to the Arduino. Then activate the serial monitor in the IDE and make sure it's set to 38400bps so you can see the values being reported by the Arduino as you touch different parts of the touch screen. Try moving your finger or a stylus around on the screen to see how one value changes if you move along one axis, and the other value changes with the other axis.

If it seems like the touch screen isn't working, make sure you're using the correct side—it can be hard to tell sometimes! The back has a feel like hard glass, while the front (sensitive) side is coated with a plastic film that will feel softer.

Arduino TouchScreen Library

The previous sketch is a great way to understand how touch screens work and how to interface with them, but the sections of code that twiddle the analog pins are a bit painful and repetitive. To make it even easier to write programs that use touch screens, we've created an Arduino library that abstracts all the details away for you. The library is called TouchScreen, and you can find a link to it on the project page on the *Practical Arduino* web site.

Once you've downloaded and installed the TouchScreen library, you can access the screen with an even simpler sketch that is included in the library as an example. In the Arduino IDE, go to File -> Sketchbook -> Libraries -> TouchScreen -> ReadTouchscreen to load it up. That example provides the exact same functionality as the program we just looked at, but is far more concise.

```
#include <TouchScreen.h>
TouchScreen ts(3, 1, 0, 2);
void setup()
{
  Serial.begin(38400);
}
void loop()
{
  int coords[2];
  ts.read(coords);
  Serial.print(coords[0]);
  Serial.print(",");
  Serial.println(coords[1]);
  delay (200);
}
```

Much neater!

A full explanation of how the TouchScreen library was written is included in the section "Writing an Arduino Library" in Chapter 16.

Controlling a "Processing" Program

Seeing raw numbers come back to you on the screen is only interesting for about 20 seconds, so to do something more visual, we've written a simple demonstration program in Processing to use those coordinates to control a 3D cube visualization. Processing is the sister project to Arduino: while Arduino is all about controlling physical events, Processing is all about visualization, image processing, and representing events graphically. In fact the Arduino IDE is based on the Processing IDE, so if you're familiar with one, you'll feel right at home with the other.

To run the 3D cube program you'll need to download the latest version of Processing from www.processing.org and install it on your computer. You can then download the sketch called TouchCube from the project page on the *Practical Arduino* web site.

Processing programs follow a very similar structure to Arduino programs. They have a setup() function at the start that is called first, just as in Arduino, but rather than having a main program loop called loop(), it's called draw() in Processing.

The first thing the TouchCube program does is include the serial port class and create an instance called myPort.

```
import processing.serial.*;
Serial myPort;
```

Then we set up variables for storing values from the Arduino and the current camera position.

```
int touchX;          // The X coordinate value received from the serial port
int touchY;          // The Y coordinate value received from the serial port
float xPos = 512;    // Current camera X-axis position
float yPos = 512;    // Current camera Y-axis position
```

The setup function determines how big the window should be for the visualization using the size() function, sets the background fill color, and then opens the serial port to wait for values sent by the Arduino.

One critical part of this setup function is the line right at the end that tells the serial port object to buffer (store) all values it receives until it gets a newline. We'll get back to that in just a moment.

```
void setup()
{
  size( 800, 600, P3D );
  fill( 204, 104, 0 );
  myPort = new Serial(this, Serial.list()[0], 38400);
  myPort.bufferUntil('\n');
}
```

The main program loop, called draw(), doesn't need to do anything in this case because everything is done in an event handler. We still need to declare it though.

```
void draw() {
  // Nothing to do here!
}
```

This next section might seem a little bit like magic because we declare a function that isn't called from anywhere else in the code. However, the serial object uses this function as an event handler that is automatically invoked when a certain thing happens. In this case, it's called when the serial port has buffered some input and then received a newline character as specified in the setup() function using bufferUntil('\n'). When that occurs, the serialEvent() function is called and the serial port object (called myPort) is passed into it so the event handler can process it.

Very cool, because it means the program can totally ignore the serial port until there is a value waiting to be processed.

The first thing the event handler does is pull the characters currently in the serial buffer into a variable called inString.

```
void serialEvent( Serial myPort )
{
  String inString = myPort.readStringUntil( '\n' );
```

Then, if we're happy that we were given a value and not just a lonesome newline character with no other characters, we continue processing it. We also have to chop off any whitespace so we have just the alphanumeric characters using the trim() function, as follows:

```
  if( inString != null )
  {
    inString = trim( inString );
```

At this point we have a value that probably looks something like "32,874" stored in the variable, so we need to split it apart on the comma delimiter and put the two resulting chunks into an array.

```
    int[] coordinates = int( split( inString, ',' ) );
```

Finally, we have the X and Y coordinates separated out so we can do something with them.

Because a touch screen that is not being touched will return a very high or very low value on the 0–1023 range, we chop off the ends of the range. That way we only update the value if the screen is being touched, and leave it at its previous value if not.

```
    touchX = coordinates[0];
    if( touchX > 20 && touchX < 1000 ) {
```

When updating the coordinate, we apply some trickery to scale it out based on the size of the window we created earlier. The map function takes an input variable and then two ranges: the first is the acceptable range for the input, and the second is the required range for the output. What we're doing here is taking the touchX value and saying that it currently falls onto a scale between 0 and 1023, but what we want to do is adjust it onto a scale between 0 and the width of the screen.

What that means is that if the touchX value is halfway along the 0–1023 scale (at, say, 511), the result will be a value halfway along the 0–width scale. If width is 900, the result will, therefore, be 450.

```
      xPos = map( touchX, 0, 1023, 0, width );
    }
```

Then we do the exact same thing for the Y coordinate.

```
    touchY = int( coordinates[1] );
    if( touchY > 20 && touchY < 900 ) {
      yPos = map( touchY, 0, 1023, 0, height );
    }
```

We're almost ready to draw the cube! The next section activates lighting on the window and sets the background.

```
    lights();
    background( 51 );
```

Finally, we set the camera position based on the coordinates we extracted and then draw the actual 3D cube.

```
    camera( xPos, yPos, 100.0, // eyeX, eyeY, eyeZ
         0.0, 0.0, 0.0,        // centerX, centerY, centerZ
         0.0, 1.0, 0.0 );      // upX, upY, upZ
    noStroke();
    box( 150 );
    stroke( 255 );
    line( -100, 0, 0, 100, 0, 0 );
    line( 0, -100, 0, 0, 100, 0 );
    line( 0, 0, -100, 0, 0, 100 );
  }
}
```

With your Arduino connected and running either the TouchscreenCoordinates or the ReadTouchscreen sketches previously described to feed values through the serial port, and the TouchCube program running on your computer to read them, you should be able to move your finger around the Nintendo touch screen and see the view of the 3D cube change.

One little catch though: make sure you turn off the serial monitor in your Arduino IDE first. Otherwise, Processing might not be able to open the port to receive the coordinates.

You might find the display jumps around a bit because it updates immediately every time it receives a new coordinate. One approach to minimize this effect would be to use a small «FIFO» (First In, First Out) buffer that holds perhaps the last three sets of coordinates and then average the values to set the camera position.

Construct Hardware for Home Automation Control Panel

This project is quite straightforward in terms of both the software and the electronics. The tricky part is entirely in the physical construction of the panel itself so that you end up with a professional end result. Of course, the exact process will vary depending on what you will use as a mounting location so we can't give precise steps that will work for you, but the following principles should apply in most cases and will help give you some inspiration for your own designs.

For our prototype we wanted to fit the touch panel into a standard blank electrical wall plate with a printed background. The Nintendo DS touch screen just barely fits within the plate dimensions, so we sat the touch screen on top, marked around the edges with a fine felt-tip pen, then carefully cut out the center with a hacksaw to provide a neat clearance area just barely larger than the touch screen (see Figure 8-6).

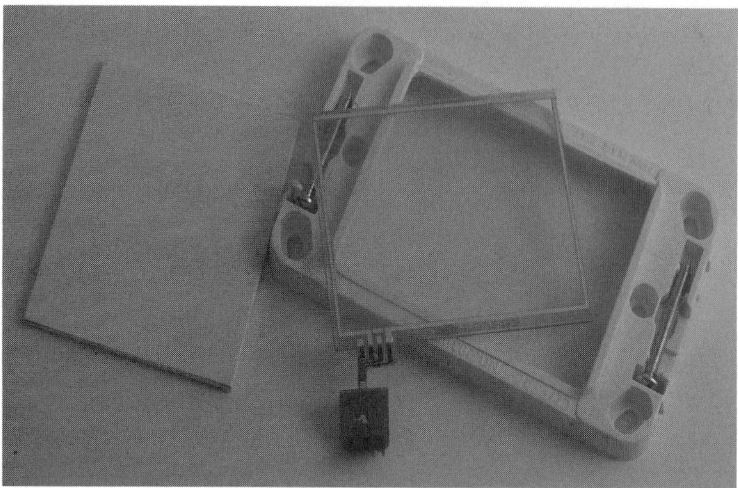

Figure 8-6. *Wall plate with hole cut for touch screen*

The offcut piece was then trimmed to fit snugly into the resulting hole and a slot was cut to allow the touch screen connection tab to pass through. The pieces were then assembled upside down by placing the touch screen facedown on a smooth surface, sitting the plastic insert on top of it, fitting the modified faceplate over the whole lot, and pushing it down flush with the front of the touch screen.

This caused the plastic insert to be recessed several millimeters into the faceplate, just perfectly aligned to hold the touch screen in place. Two-part epoxy glue was then run in a bead along two of the edges to attach the insert to the faceplate, and it was left to sit undisturbed while the glue cured.

The result is a faceplate with the front panel recessed just enough for the touch screen to be set in front of it, plus a slot for the connection tab to pass through to the rear of the panel (see Figure 8-7).

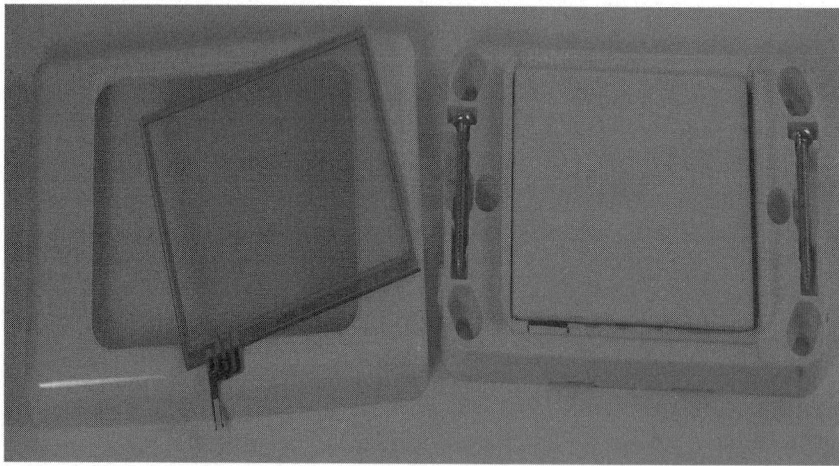

Figure 8-7. *Wall plate with removed piece glued back in place behind its original location*

Next you need to decide what "buttons" you will display behind the touch screen, if any. For a really sleek look you can leave the touch screen totally blank and just use it as a large "touch on, touch off" button. You can even combine this with gesture recognition, such as sliding your finger up/down to increase/decrease volume or brightness of something you're controlling. If you have electrically operated drapes you could use slide detection to control them: slide up to open the drapes, slide down to close them.

With a bit of work you can even implement detection of things such as a circular motion similar to the scroll wheel on an iPod: clockwise to increase volume or brightness, counterclockwise to decrease.

We created a simple graphic to go behind the touch screen to show the location of "hot zones," which act as virtual buttons. This is placed on the wall plate and the touch screen is then laid on top. The graphic can be printed on a self-adhesive sheet and stuck in place to prevent it moving if you prefer.

The areas designated on our prototype were on/off for an exhaust fan, open/closed for electrically operated drapes, and a slide bar for controlling lighting intensity (see Figure 8-8).

Figure 8-8. *Touch control panel with button graphics mounted behind the touch surface*

The background isn't limited to just static elements, either. You could drill holes through the back panel and mount LEDs to display the current status of the item being controlled, or cut a rectangular hole and mount 7-segment LED or even LCD modules inside the panel.

If you don't expect to ever change the graphic overlay you could glue the touch screen in place with epoxy resin or similar, using a toothpick to apply a tiny amount along the edges where it won't be seen.

An alternative is to use a piece of self-adhesive vinyl. Cut a rectangle out of the center, slightly smaller than the touch screen, and stick it over the top so that it overlaps the panel. Then trim it around the edges so it forms a neat border.

Calibrate Hot Zones

Connect your newly constructed touch control panel to your Arduino, plug in the USB connection to your computer, and run the example code previously described. Open the serial monitor so you can see the X and Y values being reported by the Arduino.

Draw a sketch of the layout of your buttons for reference, then use a stylus to touch the diagonally opposite corners of each button in turn. Write down the X,Y values on your sketch. For our prototype we printed an enlarged (150 percent) version of the background graphic and wrote the coordinates directly on it (see Figure 8-9).

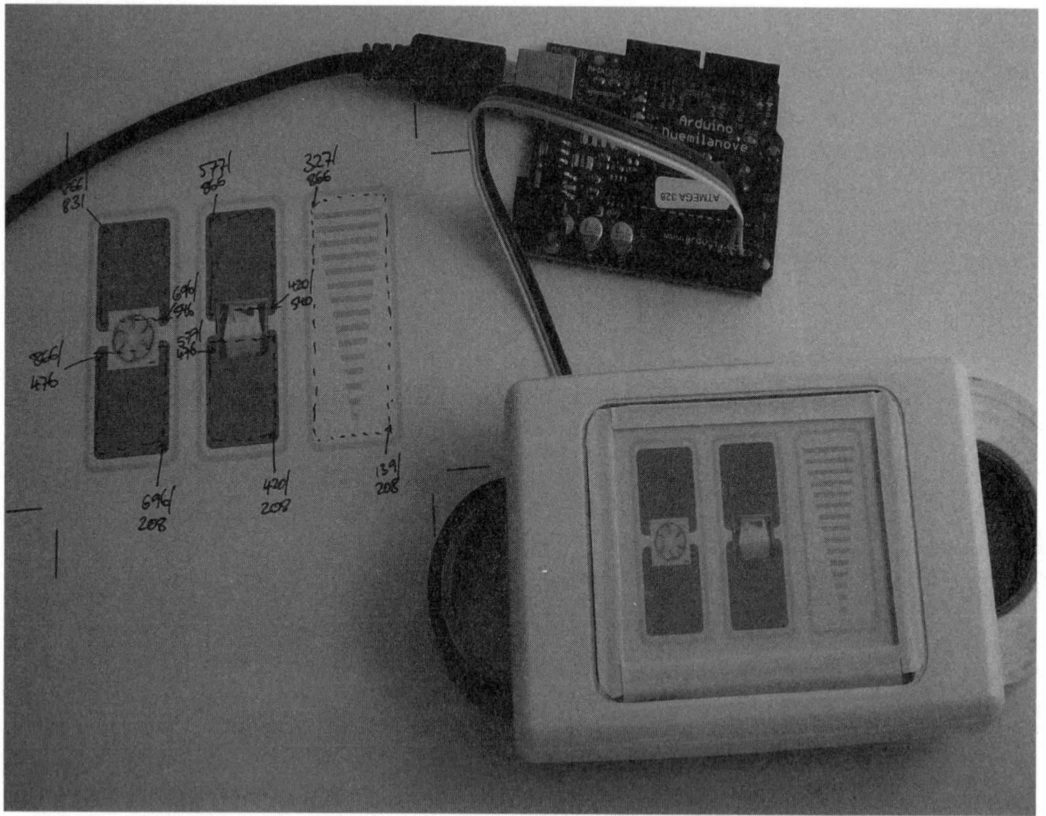

Figure 8-9. Calibrating touch control panel by noting X and Y coordinates for button regions

What you'll end up with is a set of coordinates that define the bounds of each button. If you're using simple rectangular areas it's pretty easy to then plot them into a table that shows the range of X and Y values for each button (see Table 8-1).

Table 8-1. Example X and Y coordinates for button regions

Button	Xmin	Xmax	Ymin	Ymax
Fan on	696	866	546	831
Fan off	696	866	208	476
Drapes open	420	577	540	866
Drapes close	420	577	208	476

You'll notice that on our prototype the X and Y values don't start from either the bottom left or top left corner as you might expect: they start from the bottom right corner. This really doesn't matter and is easy to compensate for in software, and can also be adjusted by changing the connections to the touch screen pins if necessary. In this case we could have changed the orientation by physically rotating the whole wall plate by 180 degrees to put 0,0 at the top left. Regardless, it works perfectly well in any orientation.

Having defined the button corner coordinates it should be fairly obvious what needs to be done in software for the button hot zones: check the X and Y values and compare them to each defined range, and if a match is found that button is considered to have been pressed. The slide control isn't much harder, and simply adds a response value proportional to the Y-axis position within the button.

The ReadTouchscreen example sketch included with the TouchScreen library is a good starting point for a system to read button presses. All we have to do is extend the program by plugging the values from the coordinate table into a series of comparisons to determine which button is being pressed.

```
#include <TouchScreen.h>

TouchScreen ts(3, 1, 0, 2);

void setup()
{
  Serial.begin(38400);
}

void loop()
{
  int coords[2];
  ts.read(coords);
  Serial.print(coords[0]);
  Serial.print(",");
  Serial.print(coords[1]);

  if((coords[0] > 696) && (coords[0] < 866)
  && (coords[1] > 546) && (coords[1] < 831)) {
    Serial.print(" Fan ON");
  }
  if((coords[0] > 696) && (coords[0] < 866)
```

```
    && (coords[1] > 208) && (coords[1] < 476)) {
      Serial.print(" Fan OFF");
    }
    if((coords[0] > 420) && (coords[0] < 577)
    && (coords[1] > 540) && (coords[1] < 866)) {
      Serial.print(" Drapes OPEN");
    }
    if((coords[0] > 420) && (coords[0] < 577)
    && (coords[1] > 208) && (coords[1] < 476)) {
      Serial.print(" Drapes CLOSE");
    }
    if((coords[0] > 139) && (coords[0] < 327)
    && (coords[1] > 208) && (coords[1] < 866)) {
      Serial.print(" Illumination:");
      Serial.print(map(coords[1], 208, 866, 0, 100));
      Serial.print("%");
    }

    Serial.println();
    delay (1000);
}
```

As you can see the illumination slider reports not just that it is being pressed, but it also maps the Y coordinate from the range of the slide area onto a range of 0 to 100 to determine the percentage illumination to apply based on the position of the contact. Touching high on the slide scale will set the illumination high, and touching it low will set it low.

There's another improvement we can still make, which is to tweak the handling of the illumination slider to provide larger areas at the top and bottom of the range for full-on and full-off. With the current arrangement it would be very hard to turn the lights off entirely because if you touch near the bottom of the slider it will still probably be at 4 or 5 percent illumination, while undershooting the contact area will do nothing at all.

There are two ways to fix this problem. The first, and probably the most obvious, is to divide the illumination slider into three separate zones so that it is treated as if it were three separate buttons. The top section could map to a "lights on" response, the bottom to a "lights off" response, and the middle remain as a variable illumination level.

We can also do it in a slightly more subtle way by making use of an obscure property of the map() function to fudge the values at the top and bottom of the range. If you pass an input value to map() that is outside the origin range—either lower than the bottom of the range or higher than the top of the range—it returns a value that will exceed the destination range. We can, therefore, change the illumination slider section of the previous code by increasing the bottom value and decreasing the top value to shrink the range away from the ends of the hot zone, as follows:

```
    if((coords[0] > 139) && (coords[0] < 327)
    && (coords[1] > 208) && (coords[1] < 866)) {
      Serial.print(" Illumination:");
      Serial.print(map(coords[1], 318, 756, 0, 100));
      Serial.print("%");
    }
```

It will then return negative values for contact right near the bottom of the range, and values greater than 100 percent for contact right near the top of the range.

Negative values and readings greater than 100 percent obviously don't make much sense, so next the result needs to be constrained so it will be truncated to fit the desired range of 0 to 100. This is done with the constrain() function that we can wrap around the map() function, as follows:

```
if((coords[0] > 139) && (coords[0] < 327)
&& (coords[1] > 208) && (coords[1] < 866)) {
  Serial.print(" Illumination:");
  Serial.print(constrain(map(coords[1], 318, 756, 0, 100), 0, 100));
  Serial.print("%");
}
```

The complete version of this sketch, TouchControlPanel, is available for download from the project page on the *Practical Arduino* web site.

It's then a matter of deciding what you want the various buttons to do. You could control devices directly using outputs on the Arduino, or you could attach an Ethernet or WiFi shield and have it send commands to a home automation system using web services..

Just for fun we've also created a matching program written in Processing called TouchControlPanelDisplay, also available for download from the project page. If you run TouchControlPanel on your Arduino and TouchControlPanelDisplay on your computer you will see a visual representation on your computer of the current state of the hot zones on the touch screen.

Mount Arduino

Because wall plates have very little clearance and you only need four analog inputs to read the touch screen, this project works well with one of the small form-factor Arduino models such as the Pro Mini or the Arduino Nano. Make sure the breakout board connecting to the touch screen is securely mounted to prevent the connection ribbon from coming loose, and use short lengths of hookup wire to connect the pads to the analog inputs on the Arduino. The rest of the installation we'll have to leave to your ingenuity because you'll almost certainly have a different mounting location and requirements to us.

CHAPTER 9

■ ■ ■

Speech Synthesizer

Synthesized speech was, for a long time, the Holy Grail of computing. Back in the 1980s, when a 4MHz CPU made your computer the fastest machine in the neighborhood, it just wasn't practical for software to create intelligible speech. In those days, the only sensible way to generate speech was to offload the task to dedicated hardware because the CPU simply couldn't keep up. The most widely used speech chip through the 1980s and early 1990s was the famous General Instrument SPO256A-AL2 Allophone Speech Processor. It was used in toys, external speech synthesizer peripherals for desktop computers, industrial control systems, and all sorts of other unexpected places. Then, as CPU power continued to increase rapidly, speech synthesis was moved to being a software function. Nowadays, of course, it is almost always done entirely with software in the main CPU, using only a tiny fraction of the available processing power. As a result the SPO256 became unnecessary, dropped out of production, and became a footnote in the history of technology.

This leaves Arduino developers in a quandary, because in terms of processing power the ATMega chips put us back into the realm of 1980s desktop performance again. An ATMega could possibly produce intelligible speech directly, but it would use every available CPU cycle to do it and the Arduino itself would be pretty much useless at doing anything else at the same time—not much good if you just want to add voice feedback to an existing project. And the demise of the SPO256 means you can't just link one up to your Arduino and offload speech generation to it.

With old stock of the SPO256 drying up Magnevation decided to do something about it, and designed their own speech chip that works on the same principles as its predecessor but has a much smaller physical package and offers a handy serial interface rather than a clunky parallel interface. The result is the SpeakJet, an 18-pin DIP device that can do everything the old SPO256 did plus more.

In this project we'll assemble a speech synthesizer shield that combines a SpeakJet chip with a simple audio amplifier to let you add speech output to a new or existing Arduino project. The required parts are pictured in Figure 9-1, and the complete schematic is in Figure 9-2. (The schematic might be a bit difficult to see, but you can also find it on the Practical Arduino web site.)

Parts Required

Main parts:

1 x Arduino Duemilanove or equivalent

1 x Prototyping shield

1 x SpeakJet speech synthesizer chip (www.magnevation.com)

1 x 18-pin DIP IC socket

3 x 1K resistors

2 x 10K resistors

2 x 27K resistors

2 x 10nF monolithic ceramic capacitors (may be marked "103")

1 x 100nF monolithic ceramic capacitors (may be marked "104")

1 x 10uF electrolytic capacitor (6.3V or greater)

1 x 3mm Ggreen LED

1 x 3mm red LED

1 x 3mm blue LED

1 x 2-pin, 0.1-inch pitch pin header (for line output option cable)

On-board audio amplifier:

1 x LM386 audio amplifier IC, DIP8 package

1 x 8-pin DIP IC socket

1 x 220uF electrolytic capacitor (6.3V or greater)

2 x 10uF electrolytic capacitors (6.3V or greater)

1 x 100uF electrolytic capacitor (6.3V or greater)

1 x 1nF (1000pF) ceramic capacitor (may be marked "102")

1 x 100nF monolithic ceramic capacitor (may be marked "104")

1 x 10K trimpot

1 x 2-pin PCB-mount screw terminal

1 x Audio speaker (usually 8 ohms)

Line-level output cable:

1 x 2-pin, 0.1-inch pitch socket

1 x 3.5mm stereo line socket[1]

1 x Length of single-core shielded cable

---

[1] If you prefer an RCA output, simply swap out the 3.5mm socket for an RCA socket, and use a male-to-male RCA connection cable to reach your connected device.

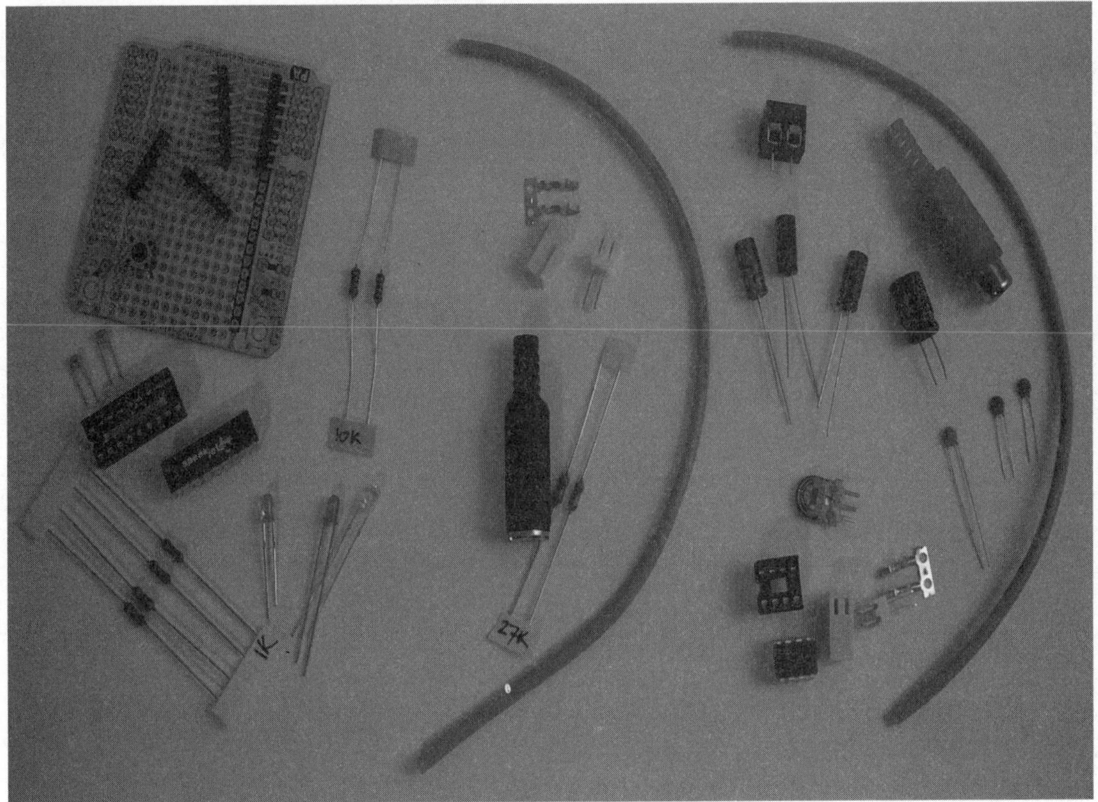

Figure 9-1. Parts required for SpeakJet-based speech synthesizer

If you prefer an RCA output simply swap out the 3.5mm socket for an RCA socket, and use a male-to-male RCA connection cable to reach your connected device.

Source code available from `www.practicalarduino.com/projects/speech-synthesizer`.

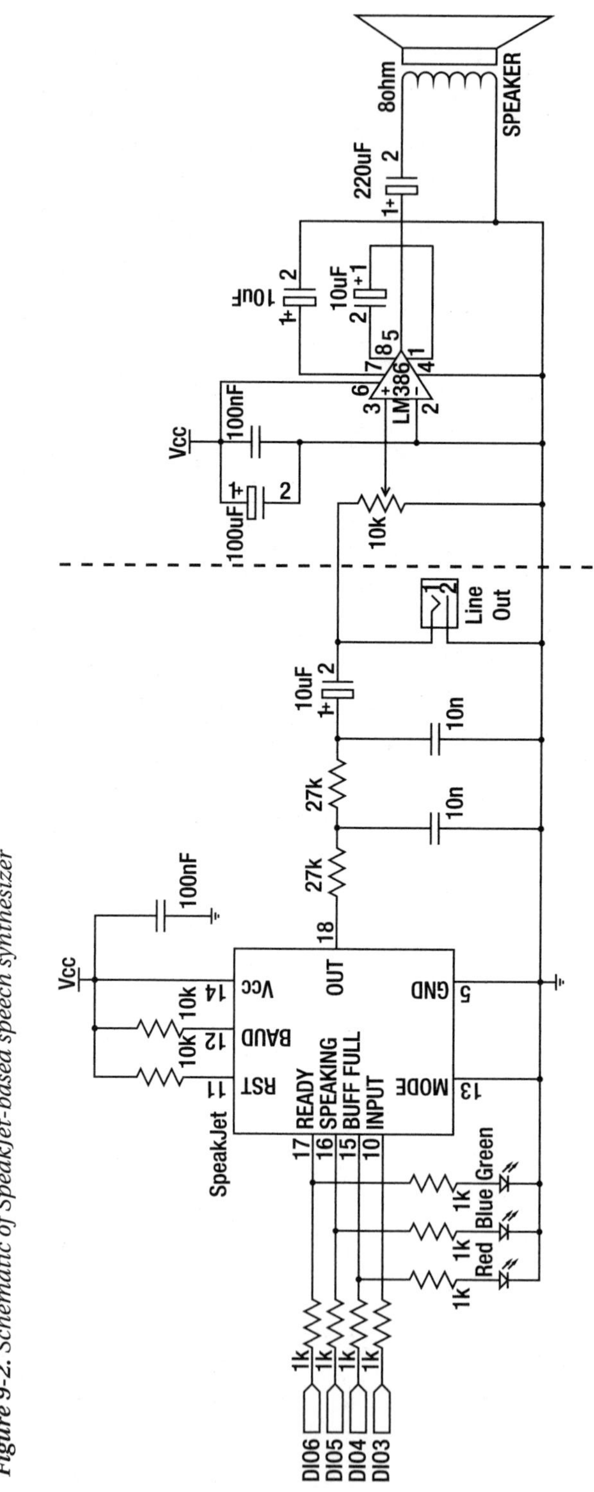

Figure 9-2. Schematic of SpeakJet-based speech synthesizer

Instructions

The SpeakJet chip used in this project uses a technique called "allophone-based speech synthesis" to create the necessary sounds that we interpret as intelligible speech. It's very important to understand how it works if you want to get good results from it.

You can't simply send the SpeakJet a string of letters spelled out literally such as "hello world," because the way we write words down and the way we say them is often quite different. We don't speak phonetically, so the original spelling of a word cannot be trivially converted to intelligible sounds. Instead we subconsciously apply dozens of conventions that alter the sound represented by any particular letter based on its context within a word or sentence, and even on factors such as emotion being conveyed or whether a sentence is a question or a statement. Accents come into play as well just to make things really complicated.

The result is that it's not possible to take a specific letter, such as "e," and define a sound for that letter that will apply in all contexts. The letter "e" may be short, as in "set," or it can be long, as in the first e in "concrete." It can even be silent, but have an effect on the pronunciation of other letters within the word, as in the last e in "concrete." Letters can also combine to form dipthongs, sometimes known as gliding vowels, such as the "oy" in "boy," where the "o" sound slides smoothly into the "y" sound.

Disregard the spelling of words for a moment and think only about the sounds we actually make when we speak those words. The smallest meaningful unit of sound in human speech is called a "phoneme." Written text consists of a series of letters, but spoken text consists of a series of phonemes.

Phonemes, in turn, are represented by allophones, which are the smallest audible units of sound. A phoneme can be represented by a variety of allophones, depending on context, accent, and other factors. Variation in allophones is what gives people different accents while still being intelligible: a speaker with one accent may use a particular allophone to represent a phoneme, and a speaker with a different accent may use a different allophone to represent that same phoneme. The result is that we can hear that the sound (allophone) is different, but our brain still maps it conceptually to the same phoneme: the word sounds odd when someone has a different accent, but we can usually still understand what the speaker means.

It's critical to understand the difference between letters and allophones if you want to be able to generate intelligible speech from an allophone-based speech synthesizer such as the SpeakJet. Stop thinking about words visually as a series of letters and start thinking about them audibly as a series of sounds or allophones. There are only 26 basic letters in the English alphabet, but there are hundreds of different allophones. You don't send letters representing words to the speech synthesizer, instead you send allophones that represent the sounds you want it to make. By stringing together a sequence of allophones you can make it say pretty much anything.

Speech Output Signal

There are a few different ways you could incorporate a speech synthesizer into a larger project, so we've provided different output options in the design. You can install all the parts, including a nice on-board audio amplifier with speaker, or stop at just the line output if you're connecting to amplified speakers or another device.

The circuit diagram follows a direct signal path from left to right, with the commands from the Arduino coming in from digital pin 3 on the left and ending at the loudspeaker output on the right. There is a dashed line drawn vertically through the circuit, so you can stop at that point if you just want a line-level output and don't want an on-board amplifier and speaker.

Conversion of commands to an analog audio signal is performed within the SpeakJet chip, which listens on pin 10 for serial communications from the Arduino. Several pins on the SpeakJet need to be connected either to low (GND) or high (VCC) levels to put it into the correct mode as will be explained later.

A line-level output can be brought out to a 3.5mm stereo jack or RCA connector, as shown in the schematic. RCA connectors are commonly used to connect audio and video inputs and outputs together in home entertainment systems, so if you want to really give your Arduino a voice to rock the neighborhood you can use the line-level output to drive an amplifier or send the speech to the audio input of your TV.

For a self-contained speaking device the audio amplifier components in the project are capable of driving a speaker directly to a fairly respectable volume. With this output you can connect a regular speaker from a sound system to the screw terminals on the shield and get both good volume and decent audio quality. If you're building a device that has to operate stand-alone and still provide voice feedback this is probably the best route to take.

The best sound will come from a larger speaker, or a system without sensitive high-frequency response, as they won't let the high-frequency digital switching noise of the SpeakJet's underlying PWM (pulse-width modulation) carrier through.

Beginning Assembly

No matter which output method you choose you'll definitely need the SpeakJet chip and a few other supporting parts, so begin by fitting those to the shield. Because the SpeakJet itself is quite expensive we fitted an 18-pin IC socket to the shield rather than solder the chip in directly. Using a socket protects the chip from possible thermal damage during soldering and also allows you to remove it to use in other projects later if you want to.

The SpeakJet GND connection is on pin 5, and VCC is on pin 14. Link them directly to the appropriate supply connections on the prototyping shield. A 100nF bypass capacitor between every IC's VCC pin and GND is always good practice, so connect the 100nF capacitor from pin 14 to GND. In our case we took advantage of the prototyping shield's built-in 100nF capacitor mounting points.

Apart from the power supply pins, the SpeakJet has several other pins that need to be tied to either GND or VCC to force it to run in a mode that can be controlled externally by the Arduino.

Pin 11 is the active-low reset pin, so use a 10K resistor to pull it up to VCC to allow the SpeakJet to run.

Pin 12 is M1, the "Baud Configure" pin, which is also active-low. We don't want the chip to enter automatic baud-rate configuration mode so use another 10K resistor to disable it by pulling it up to VCC as well.

Pin 13 is M0, the "Demo Mode" pin. This one is active-high, so you can tie it straight to GND by putting a jumper wire on the underside of the board to connect pin 13 diagonally across to pin 5, the GND pin on the IC.

The only other SpeakJet pin that absolutely must be connected is pin 10, the RCX (serial input) pin. That's the pin the Arduino will use to send data to the SpeakJet chip. In this project we use a software serial communications library to connect the SpeakJet to one of the general-purpose digital I/O lines rather than tie up the hardware USART on digital pins 0/1, so use a short jumper lead and a 1K resistor to connect from Arduino digital pin 3 to SpeakJet pin 10 (see Figure 9-3).

Figure 9-3. SpeakJet chip mounted on shield with basic connections in place

The prototyping shield we used has mounting points for surface-mount parts including two 100nF bypass capacitors mentioned previously (C1 and C2 on the shield) and active-low (GND-to-illuminate) status LEDs. We fitted surface-mount bypass capacitors and linked the green surface-mount LED to GND, providing a handy power-on indicator.

At this point the SpeakJet is ready to receive instructions from the Arduino, but in order to hear the result you need to connect something to the output.

SpeakJet PWM "Audio" Output

The SpeakJet works by varying the duty cycle of a fixed 32KHz frequency pulse-width–modulated (PWM) "carrier" from pin 18 into an external two-pole low-pass filter, successfully converting the PWM digital signal into an analog voltage waveform suitable for line output or audio amplifiers.

Done fast enough, what this means is that the duty cycle percentage of the PWM signal converts to the same percentage of DC voltage output from the filter, so a 50% 0 to 5V PWM duty cycle will convert to about 2.5 volts DC out of the filter.

This is a great, inexpensive way to generate analog voltages and waveforms from any microcontroller PWM output, and is used in many projects to get a DAC voltage (Digital-Analog-Conversion) output without special hardware.

The raw PWM from SpeakJet output pin 18 is digital and sounds somewhat noisy, but intelligible speech can still be heard. There is a 120-ohm minimum load and 25mA maximum current specified for this pin; be careful not to connect anything that may load the output pin more than this and risk damage to the IC.

Quick Test

A simple way to test that everything is working up to this point is to connect a pair of powered computer speakers directly to the SpeakJet output pin 18. We placed a header on pin 18 just for this purpose, though this quick test and the header can be skipped if you'd like to move straight on to the more useful filtered audio line output. It's only a few more parts, and the same cable can be used.

For the quick test, connect a 3.5mm stereo headphone socket to the pin header as shown in Figure 9-4. The SpeakJet is a single mono output, so we connect it to both the left and right channels on the socket.

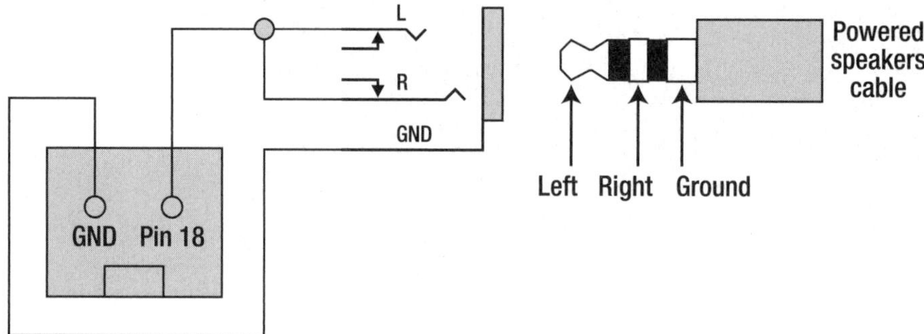

Figure 9-4. *Connection from header to powered computer speakers*

At this point you could mount the shield on your Arduino, plug in some powered speakers or earbuds, and proceed to the software section to test that it works.

Fit Status Indicators

You certainly don't need status indicators for the speech synthesizer to operate, but it can be handy to have visual feedback of what the chip is doing. Pins 15, 16, and 17 operate as status outputs when the SpeakJet is in normal operation, so by connecting three LEDs with matching dropper resistors we can see exactly what it's up to. These pins can also be connected to the Arduino so that the software can monitor the SpeakJet speech operation.

The status pins, as shown from left to right in Figure 9-5, are described in Table 9-1.

Table 9-1. SpeakJet status outputs

Pin	Name	Function
17	D0	Ready
16	D1	Speaking
15	D2	Buffer Half Full

We use a 1K resistor and an LED connected from each output to GND as you can see in Figure 9-5. Green indicates the SpeakJet is ready, blue indicates that it is currently speaking, and red indicates that its input buffer more than half full.

Figure 9-5. SpeakJet status outputs connected to LEDs

Because the SpeakJet has a 64-byte input buffer and the command size is one byte per allophone, it doesn't take many words to fill up the input buffer on the SpeakJet. Of course it also takes more time for the SpeakJet to sound out the allophones than it takes for the Arduino to send them to it, so using appropriate delay times or waiting for the Buffer Half Full signal to clear before sending more allophones to it is important.

Once the SpeakJet buffer is full any additional bytes sent to it are simply ignored. If you try to send a large sequence of allophones to it very fast you may find the buffer fills up quite quickly. The red LED on D2 (pin 15) can be handy to give you a quick visual indicator that you're sending data to the SpeakJet faster than it can keep up with speaking it.

At the end of the project we'll discuss use of this output to provide feedback to the Arduino so the software can automatically detect when to stop sending data and wait a little while before sending any more.

You can also see in Figure 9-5 a small 100nF power supply decoupling capacitor near the top center, mounted between the +5V rail and the GND connection used by the LEDs. Once again that's optional, but there's no harm in having additional decoupling capacitors. They can help prevent unexplained glitches and noise caused by supply fluctuations, so it's always good practice to fit them when possible.Line-Level Output

A "line-level" signal is generally a larger signal than you would get from a device such as a microphone, but a lower level than would be used to directly drive a speaker or headphones. Line level is the connection that is typically fed into a mixer, amplifier, powered computer speakers, or other pieces of audio equipment. Without going into all the technicalities of unusual units such as decibel volts (dBV), as a general rule of thumb a line-level signal in consumer-grade audio equipment has a nominal amplitude of about 0.5V.

By creating a simple two-pole low-pass filter we can generate a clean output from the SpeakJet that can be fed straight to other audio equipment. A "low-pass" filter is a circuit that allows signals below a certain nominated frequency to pass through, but attenuates (decreases the level) of signals above that frequency. Simple filters don't have a hard cutoff frequency but instead tend to roll off gradually around the cutoff point, with signals below that frequency passing through the filter more easily than those above it.

The two-pole filter consists of a pair of 27K resistors in series with the SpeakJet's output along with a pair of 10nF capacitors, each connected between ground and the output side of one of the resistors. The resulting circuit filters the SpeakJet's digital PWM output into a smooth voltage waveform, removing the carrier and induced noise.

Fit the pairs of resistors and capacitors as shown in Figure 9-6. You can do this even with the pin 18 direct connection still in place.

The output from the second 27K resistor then connects to the positive side of a 10uF electrolytic capacitor (not yet fitted in Figure 9-6) with the negative side of the electro going to the signal (non-ground) pin of the Line Out connector.

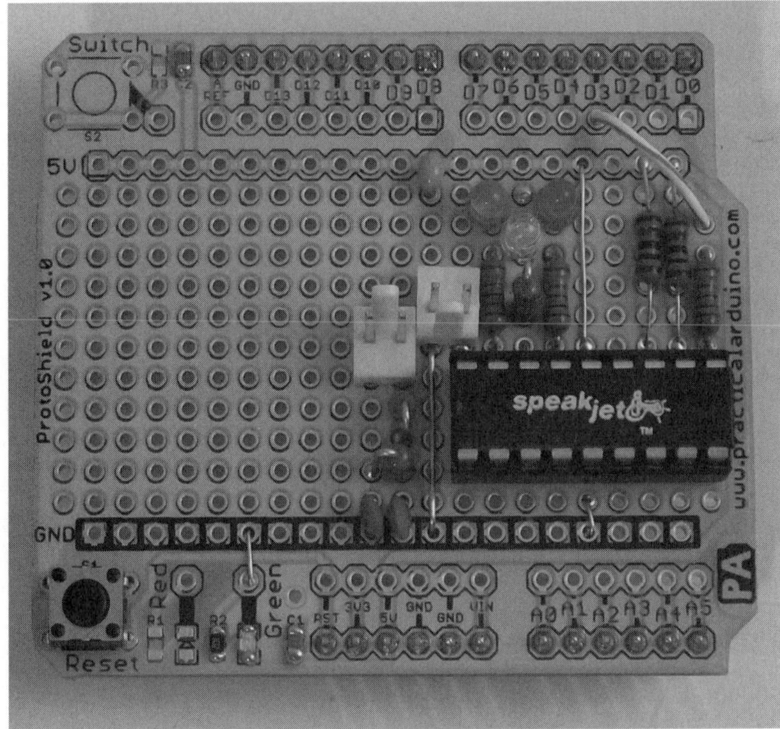

Figure 9-6. Shield with two-pole output filter in place

Making a Line-Level Output Cable

Solder a short length of shielded cable to your chosen line plug or socket. If you'd like to use a 3.5mm stereo socket for powered computer speakers the Quick Test cable described previously is perfect.

For RCA, the braid (shield) conductor connects to the outer shell, and the inner conductor connects to the center pin. Choose a male or female RCA connector to suit your needs.

If you use a male RCA plug you have the convenience of being able to plug your speech synthesizer shield directly into a piece of audio equipment, such as an amplifier or TV. Using a female RCA socket as shown in Figure 9-7 allows you to use a common male-to-male RCA extension cable to do the same thing. Which gender you decide to use depends on what you want to connect your speech synthesizer to and how far away it is. Keep in mind that line-level signals should be kept as short as possible, so if you connect a 10-foot length of cable to your shield and put an RCA plug on the other end, the sound quality might not be very good. Shorter is always better when it comes to maintaining audio signal quality.

Figure 9-7. Shielded cable connected to female RCA line plug

Once your shield is fitted to an Arduino and plugged into an amplifier you can go to the following section "Speech Synthesizer Software" to test it out.

On-Board Amplifier

Adding a small amplifier to the shield so you can drive a speaker directly is quite easy with the LM386 audio amplifier IC. LM386 chips are very common in small audio devices, such as compact portable radios, because they're very easy to use and produce reasonable quality sound at a good volume level. They certainly won't compete with the amp in your stereo system, but for simple voice-level output in a portable device they're perfect.

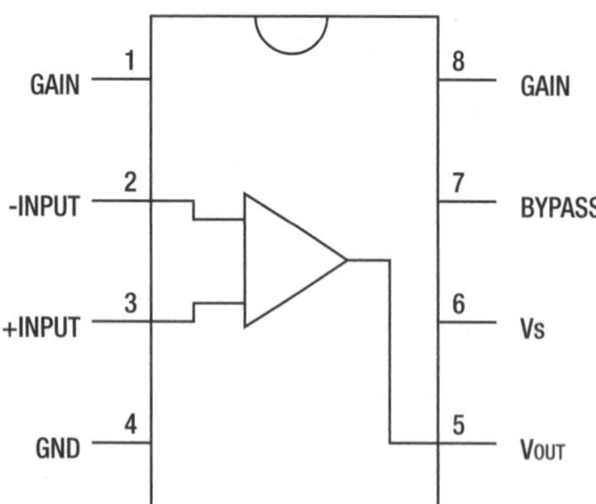

Figure 9-8. Pinout of LM386 audio amplifier

To build a simple audio amplifier with a gain of about 20 you can use the LM386 on its own with pretty much nothing else required. However, with a few extra parts it can be configured to deliver a gain of about 50. If necessary it can be configured for a gain of up to 200, but that's pushing the limits of what it can do and since we're powering the amplifier circuit from the Arduino's 5V supply the current drain and noise on the supply rails could become a problem. Audio amplifiers pull a lot more power than the typical digital circuits you might be used to dealing with on an Arduino: since amps equals watts divided by volts, even a tiny 1/4W amplifier running on a 5V supply can suck down 50mA of current, assuming it runs at an unrealistic 100% efficiency. Even worse than the current drain, though, are the fluctuations that can be induced on the supply rails, since the current consumption isn't consistent but rather jumps around all over the place depending on the input signal.

A gain of 50 gives a reasonable balance between a high output volume and low power consumption, and won't strain the Arduino's power supply. If you want more volume you'll probably need to use a more substantial external amplifier and feed it with the line-level output connection, and also make sure the supply rails are adequately filtered.

The LM386 needs to be fed with a filtered version of the output from the SpeakJet, so it uses the same low-pass filter as the line-level output and then adds the LM386 to provide an amplified version of the signal. Add the LM386 to the shield along with its associated parts, the 10K trimpot and the various resistors and capacitors, as shown in Figure 9-9. Finally, solder on the PCB-mount two-pin screw terminal to provide a handy connection for a speaker.

***Figure 9-9.** Shield with LM386-based audio amplifier in place and speaker connected*

If you have an old speaker from a stereo system you can connect a pair of wires to it and attach them to the screw terminals. Otherwise, use a small speaker from an electronics parts shop, an old computer speaker, or even a speaker out of a car stereo system, and solder two wires to the speaker. Then insert the other ends into the screw terminals on the shield.

Turn the trimpot to about halfway as a starting point so it has a reasonable volume level. Mount the shield on your Arduino, and install the software to test it.

Speech Synthesizer Software

To test the speech synthesizer, start with a minimal program that sends a series of allophones to the SpeakJet to sound out a simple sentence.

Because the Arduino communicates with the SpeakJet using serial communications at 9600bps we first need to include the SoftwareSerial library, then specify which pins will be used for RX and TX. We don't actually care about the SoftwareSerial RX (receive) pin, because all we'll be doing is sending values to the SpeakJet and not reading anything back. However, SoftwareSerial needs both to be defined so we'll set it anyway and then ignore it.

```
#include <SoftwareSerial.h>


#define rxPin 2
#define txPin 3
```

Then create a new software serial port object called "speakJet."

```
SoftwareSerial speakJet =  SoftwareSerial(rxPin, txPin);
```

Words are stored as a series of allophones in an array, so to make it easier to read the array we'll define a memorable token for the "Word Pause" value that is appended after each word. The SpeakJet has six different pauses available, but the most commonly used pause between words is allophone 6 which has a duration of 90 milliseconds. By defining WP as the value 6 we can simply put WP into the word array as if it's a single byte, and not have to remember that allophone 6 is a magic value.

```
#define WP 6
```

Next, we'll set up an array called "message" to hold the allophones for the words we want to speak. By breaking it up visually and embedding comments within each line we can make the array much easier to read. Finally, tacking a WP value onto the end of each word inserts allophone 6, the word pause.

Working with the message array this way makes it relatively simple to copy and paste different words into place to make up your own sentences, as follows:

```
byte message[] = {
  /* hello   */  183, 007, 159, 146, 164, WP, WP,
  /* my      */  140, 155, WP,
  /* name    */  141, 154, 140, WP,
  /* is      */  8,   129, 167, WP,
  /* arduino */  152, 148, 175, 147, 128, 141, 164, WP
};
```

Later the program will need to know the length of the message array, so rather than count the values manually and have to update it every time the message is changed we'll instead have the program count the array elements and store it for future reference.

```
int messageSize = sizeof(message);
```

The setup function is called once when the program starts, and configures the software serial connection to the SpeakJet. Since the SpeakJet runs by default at 9600bps we set up the software serial port to match.

```
void setup()
{
  pinMode(rxPin, INPUT);
  pinMode(txPin, OUTPUT);
  speakJet.begin(9600);
```

It then sends some initialization values to the SpeakJet. Some bytes are treated as a special case by the SpeakJet, including 20 (which sets the volume) and 21 (which sets the speaking rate). When the SpeakJet sees either of these bytes it interprets the next byte as the value for that parameter and updates its internal settings. These settings are stored in nonvolatile memory inside the SpeakJet.

So, to set the volume to a value of 96 (on a scale of 0 through 127), we first send byte 20 (volume command) followed by a value of 96, as follows:

```
  speakJet.print(20, BYTE);
  speakJet.print(96, BYTE);
```

Setting the speech rate is done in a similar way. First we send byte 21 (speed command), followed by a value of 114 to set the speaking rate to 114 (on a scale of 0 to 127), as follows:

```
  speakJet.print( 21, BYTE);
  speakJet.print(114, BYTE);
```

Both those settings are actually the default values, but by putting these lines into the setup function, it makes it easy to experiment with different volumes and speech rates. The setup function then pauses for one second to give the SpeakJet time to receive and process the values.

```
  delay(1000);
}
```

After all that preparation the main program loop is incredibly simple. It steps through the message array using a counter, i, and sends each value it finds to the SpeakJet via the serial connection defined earlier. It then pauses for five seconds before repeating.

```
void loop()
{
  int i;
  for (i=0; i<messageSize; i++)
  {
    speakJet.print(message[i], BYTE);
  }
  delay (5000);
}
```

With a short sentence repeated at five second intervals there is plenty of time for the SpeakJet to say the whole the sentence before it is sent through again, so we are not checking for the Buffer Half Full state.

When you power up your Arduino and speech synthesizer shield it will immediately say "ready," even if you haven't sent any values to the SpeakJet yet. That's just the SpeakJet's internal self-test indicating that it has finished and is ready to receive commands.

Create Your Own Messages

The allophones and commands listed below allow you to create any word you want your Arduino to say by breaking it up into sounds and then creating a list of the bytes that represent those sounds.

The SpeakJet accepts one-byte values from 0 to 255, with some values treated as commands and others as allophones to sound out.

Low values are used for commands sent to the SpeakJet. Because the SpeakJet chip can also function as a multichannel sound synthesizer it has a number of commands other than the ones listed in Table 9-2. Just the ones that are relevant to speech synthesis are shown here. Full details of all available commands are included in the SpeakJet datasheet.

Table 9-2. *SpeakJet commands*

Byte	Command
0	Pause 0 (0ms)
1	Pause 1 (100ms)
2	Pause 2 (200ms)
3	Pause 3 (700ms)
4	Pause 4 (30ms)
5	Pause 5 (60ms)
6	Pause 6 (90ms)
7	Play next sound fast
8	Play next sound slow
14	Stress next phoneme
15	Relax next phoneme
20	Volume X (range 0–127, default 96)
21	Speed X (range 0–127, default 114)
22	Pitch X (range 0–255, default 88)
23	Bend X (range 0–15, default 5)
30	Delay X (range 0–255 times 10ms increments)

Five of the commands listed in Table 9-2 are two-byte commands. The first byte sent is the command itself, and the second X byte is the value for that parameter. Sending a pair of bytes, such as 20 and then 56, would set the volume to a value of 56.

Values 128 and above are the allophones themselves. Spoken sounds that are used to form words are values 128 through 199, and are listed in Table 9-3 with the letter representation of the associated phoneme, sample words to show the pronunciation, the duration of the sound in milliseconds, and the type of sound.

Table 9-3. *SpeakJet allophones*

Byte	Phoneme	Sample Words	Duration	Type
128	IY	See, Even, Feed	70	Voiced Long Vowel
129	IH	Sit, Fix, Pin	70	Voiced Short Vowel
130	EY	Hair, Gate, Beige	70	Voiced Long Vowel
131	EH	Met, Check, Red	70	Voiced Short Vowel
132	AY	Hat, Fast, Fan	70	Voiced Short Vowel
133	AX	Cotten	70	Voiced Short Vowel
134	UX	Luck, Up, Uncle	70	Voiced Short Vowel
135	OH	Hot, Clock, Fox	70	Voiced Short Vowel
136	AW	Father, Fall	70	Voiced Short Vowel
137	OW	Comb, Over, Hold	70	Voiced Long Vowel
138	UH	Book, Could, Should	70	Voiced Short Vowel
139	UW	Food, June	70	Voiced Long Vowel
140	MM	Milk, Famous	70	Voiced Nasal
141	NE	Nip, Danger, Thin	70	Voiced Nasal
142	NO	No, Snow, On	70	Voiced Nasal
143	NGE	Think, Ping	70	Voiced Nasal
144	NGO	Hung, Song	70	Voiced Nasal
145	LE	Lake, Alarm, Lapel	70	Voiced Resonate

146	LO	Clock, Plus, Hello	70	Voiced Resonate
147	WW	Wool, Sweat	70	Voiced Resonate
148	RR	Ray, Brain, Over	70	Voiced Resonate
149	IYRR	Clear, Hear, Year	200	Voiced R Color Vowel
150	EYRR	Hair, Stair, Repair	200	Voiced R Color Vowel
151	AXRR	Fir, Bird, Burn	190	Voiced R Color Vowel
152	AWRR	Part, Farm, Yarn	200	Voiced R Color Vowel
153	OWRR	Corn, Four, Your	185	Voiced R Color Vowel
154	EYIY	Gate, Ate, Ray	165	Voiced Diphthong
155	OHIY	Mice, Fight, White	200	Voiced Diphthong
156	OWIY	Boy, Toy, Voice	225	Voiced Diphthong
157	OHIH	Sky, Five, I	185	Voiced Diphthong
158	IYEH	Yes, Yarn, Million	170	Voiced Diphthong
159	EHLL	Saddle, Angle, Spell	140	Voiced Diphthong
160	IYUW	Cute, Few	180	Voiced Diphthong
161	AXUW	Brown, Clown, Thousand	170	Voiced Diphthong
162	IHWW	Two, New, Zoo	170	Voiced Diphthong
163	AYWW	Our, Ouch, Owl	200	Voiced Diphthong
164	OWWW	Go, Hello, Snow	131	Voiced Diphthong
165	JH	Dodge, Jet, Savage	70	Voiced Affricate
166	VV	Vest, Even	70	Voiced Fictive
167	ZZ	Zoo, Zap	70	Voiced Fictive
168	ZH	Azure, Treasure	70	Voiced Fictive

169	DH	There, That, This	70	Voiced Fictive
170	BE	Bear, Bird, Beed	45	Voiced Stop
171	BO	Bone, Book, Brown	45	Voiced Stop
172	EB	Cab, Crib, Web	10	Voiced Stop
173	OB	Bob, Sub, Tub	10	Voiced Stop
174	DE	Deep, Date, Divide	45	Voiced Stop
175	DO	Do, Dust, Dog	45	Voiced Stop
176	ED	Could, Bird	10	Voiced Stop
177	OD	Bud, Food	10	Voiced Stop
178	GE	Get, Gate, Guest	55	Voiced Stop
179	GO	Got, Glue, Goo	55	Voiced Stop
180	EG	Peg, Wig	55	Voiced Stop
181	OG	Dog, Peg	55	Voiced Stop
182	CH	Church, Feature, March	70	Voiceless Affricate
183	HE	Help, Hand, Hair	70	Voiceless Fricative
184	HO	Hoe, Hot, Hug	70	Voiceless Fricative
185	WH	Who, Whale, White	70	Voiceless Fricative
186	FF	Food, Effort, Off	70	Voiceless Fricative
187	SE	See, Vest, Plus	40	Voiceless Fricative
188	SO	So, Sweat	40	Voiceless Fricative
189	SH	Ship, Fiction, Leash	50	Voiceless Fricative
190	TH	Thin, Month	40	Voiceless Fricative
191	TT	Part, Little, Sit	50	Voiceless Stop

192	TU	To, Talk, Ten	70	Voiceless Stop
193	TS	Parts, Costs, Robots	170	Voiceless Stop
194	KE	Can't, Clown, Key	55	Voiceless Stop
195	KO	Comb, Quick, Fox	55	Voiceless Stop
196	EK	Speak, Task	55	Voiceless Stop
197	OK	Book, Took, October	45	Voiceless Stop
198	PE	People, Computer	99	Voiceless Stop

Values 200 and above are special purpose sounds such as sound effects and DTMF tones. These are listed in Table 9-4.

Table 9-4. *SpeakJet sound effects and tones*

Byte	Phoneme	Sample Words	Duration	Type
200	R0	80	Robot	
201	R1	80	Robot	
202	R2	80	Robot	
203	R3	80	Robot	
204	R4	80	Robot	
205	R5	80	Robot	
206	R6	80	Robot	
207	R7	80	Robot	
208	R8	80	Robot	
209	R9	80	Robot	
210	A0		300	Alarm
211	A1		101	Alarm

212	A2		102	Alarm
213	A3		540	Alarm
214	A4		530	Alarm
215	A5		500	Alarm
216	A6		135	Alarm
217	A7		600	Alarm
218	A8		300	Alarm
219	A9		250	Alarm
220	B0		200	Beeps
221	B1		270	Beeps
222	B2		280	Beeps
223	B3		260	Beeps
224	B4		300	Beeps
225	B5		100	Beeps
226	B6		104	Beeps
227	B7		100	Beeps
228	B8		270	Beeps
229	B9		262	Beeps
230	C0	160	Biological	
231	C1	300	Biological	
232	C2	182	Biological	
233	C3	120	Biological	
234	C4	175	Biological	

235	C5	350	Biological	
236	C6	160	Biological	
237	C7	260	Biological	
238	C8	95	Biological	
239	C9	75	Biological	
240	D0	0	95	DTMF
241	D1	1	95	DTMF
242	D2	2	95	DTMF
243	D3	3	95	DTMF
244	D4	4	95	DTMF
245	D5	5	95	DTMF
246	D6	6	95	DTMF
247	D7	7	95	DTMF
248	D8	8	95	DTMF
249	D9	9	95	DTMF
250	D10	*	95	DTMF
251	D11	#	95	DTMF
252	M0	Sonar Ping	125	Miscellaneous
253	M1	Pistol Shot	250	Miscellaneous

Creating easily understood words using allophones can be a painstaking process. Even a short sentence can take quite a while to put together if you have to sound out every single word individually. To save you some time, the speech synthesizer project page on the *Practical Arduino* web site has a link to a file of nearly 2,000 words and their equivalent phonemes. All you have to do is look up the word you want on the list and copy the associated codes into your software.

Variations

Read SpeakJet Status

Because the SpeakJet has a small 64-byte input buffer it doesn't take many commands to fill it up. Remember that the input buffer stores a sequence of allophones, each of which is one byte in size and represents a sound within a word or a pause between words. Although it varies depending on the word, the number of allophones required to represent the sounds in a word is similar to the number of letters within it. However, be aware that commands such as changes to pitch, volume, and rate take up two bytes in the buffer: one to indicate the parameter, and one to indicate the value.

With just 64 bytes available a single sentence can easily fill the buffer and leave you with a sentence that's chopped off at the end.

One simple way around the problem is to send a few values together as a block and insert a delay before sending the next block, but that approach is fraught with danger. If the delay is too long you will hear a pause while the SpeakJet is waiting for the next batch of allophones, and if the delay is too short the text will be chopped up with pieces missing where the buffer overflowed. With some experimentation you can probably make it work fairly reliably, but it's certainly not ideal.By connecting status pins from the SpeakJet to digital inputs on the Arduino it's possible to have your software automatically detect whether the SpeakJet is ready to receive more data, and then drip-feed the commands to it at a rate that can be spoken without overflowing the buffer.

The shield for this project uses LEDs connected to D0, D1, and D2 to visually indicate Ready, Speaking, and Buffer Half Full, respectively. Use three additional 1K resistors to link the SpeakJet pins to Arduino digital pins, as listed in Table 9-5.

***Table 9-5.** SpeakJet status pin connections to Arduino inputs*

SpeakJet Pin	Name	Function	Arduino Pin
17	D0	Ready	Digital I/O 6
16	D1	Speaking	Digital I/O 5

Because the top of the prototyping shield has the LEDs and their dropper resistors in place it's probably easiest to put the 1K resistors underneath the board to link directly from the IC pin connections to the Arduino pin connections as shown in Figure 9-10. Make sure the bare resistor leads are kept well clear of any other joints, and use the resistor bodies across the bottom of the connections for the LEDs and their dropper resistors to minimize the risk of shorting them. If you're really worried about the possibility of the leads touching something they shouldn't you could put the resistors inside short lengths of heat-shrink tubing. Generally that shouldn't be necessary.

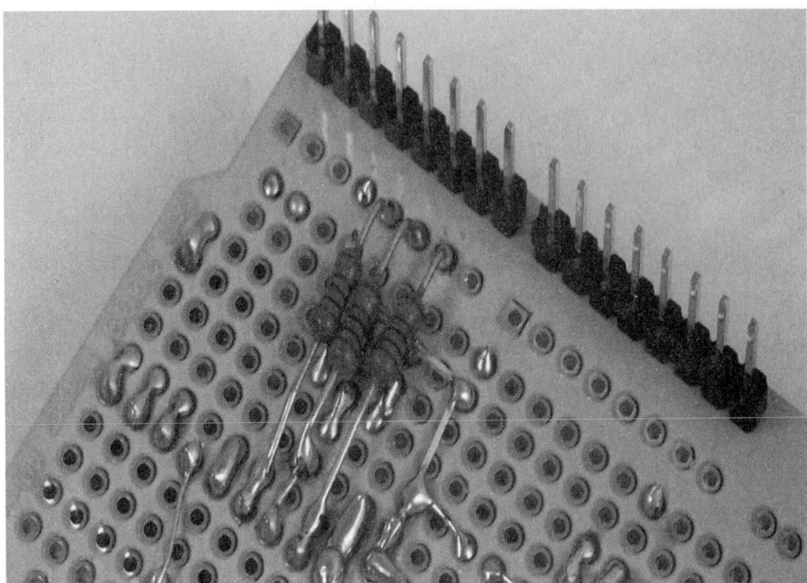

Figure 9-10. Resistors connecting SpeakJet outputs to Arduino inputs

By reading digital pins 4, 5, and 6 using the Arduino, you can now check whether the SpeakJet is ready to accept more values before sending them through. If pin 6 (Ready) is high the SpeakJet has passed its internal self-test and is ready to receive values. Pin 5 will go high only while the SpeakJet is actually speaking, and then immediately go low again. Pin 4 is the important one as far as knowing when it is safe to send through more data: once the input buffer exceeds half full this line will go high, indicating to the host that it should stop sending values for a while. By checking for pin 4 to go low again your Arduino will know when the SpeakJet has enough room in its buffer to accept at least another 32 values.

Example code that uses the Buffer Half Full signal to regulate the rate of data transmission to the speech synthesizer shield is available on the project page on the *Practical Arduino* web site.

Resources

The Magnevation web site, at www.magnevation.com, has an excellent SpeakJet user manual available for download as a PDF. The user manual explains the background behind allophone-based speech synthesis and the various options available on the SpeakJet, and includes details of all the command codes that can be sent to it as well as a reference guide for allophones.

CHAPTER 10

■ ■ ■

Water Flow Gauge

Determining the consumption of a resource that is measured in units of volume can be more tricky than it sounds. Use of resources such as water, gas, and even electricity is typically measured by gauges that determine either instantaneous flow rate or cumulative volume over time. Both techniques have problems. Measuring flow rate at frequent intervals allows you to do time-based reporting and generate a graph of how the flow rate varied over time, but to determine the total consumption by volume across a specific time period, you then have to integrate the data. This means there is the danger of underreporting usage if your sample rate is slow and usage rapidly fluctuates or spikes. Measuring cumulative volume makes it easy to determine total consumption across a period and is accurate in terms of total usage, but to generate a flow-rate graph, you then need to calculate the difference between each sample. If your recording interval isn't brief enough, any short-term spikes in usage will be averaged across the recording interval and might not show clearly on the graph.

Flow gauges typically output a series of pulses proportional to the instantaneous flow rate, which means that to interpret them it's necessary to implement a simple frequency counter. This is actually the same way many car speedometers work: a wheel sensor outputs a pulse for each rotation of a wheel, which means the pulse frequency varies proportionally to the vehicle speed. The speedometer then displays a scaled version of the current pulse frequency to show instantaneous speed, while the odometer displays a scaled cumulative pulse count to show distance traveled. Both pieces of information are based on the same underlying data, but they are recorded and displayed in different ways.

This project uses a flow-rate gauge containing a Hall-effect sensor that outputs a pulse rate proportional to flow rate. Not only is it a useful project in its own right, but it also demonstrates a very useful technique that you can use in a wide range of projects that need to measure the rate at which something happens. We've also included an LCD module so that the unit can report flow rate and volume both via the serial connection to a host computer and also directly via the LCD.

The example program calculates and displays current flow rate, and also maintains two cumulative counters of the volume that has flowed through the sensor. Two pushbuttons allow you to reset the counters independently. This allows you to leave one counter running as a long-term accumulator, and reset the other one occasionally prior to measuring short-term events such as the water consumed by filling a bath, running an irrigation system, or running a washing machine. The required parts are shown in Figure 10-1, and the complete schematic is in Figure 10-2.

Parts Required

1 x Arduino Duemilanove, Arduino Pro, Seeeduino, or equivalent

1 x Prototyping shield

1 x Flow-rate gauge, such as a ZD1200 or ZD1202

1 x 16x2 LCD module, HD44780-compatible

3 x 1K resistor

1 x 10R resistor

1 x 680R resistor

1 x LED

2 x Momentary-action pushbuttons

Ribbon cable

Three-core cable

Three-way line plug and socket

Source code available from
`www.practicalarduino.com/projects/water-flow-gauge`

Figure 10-1. *Parts required for water flow gauge*

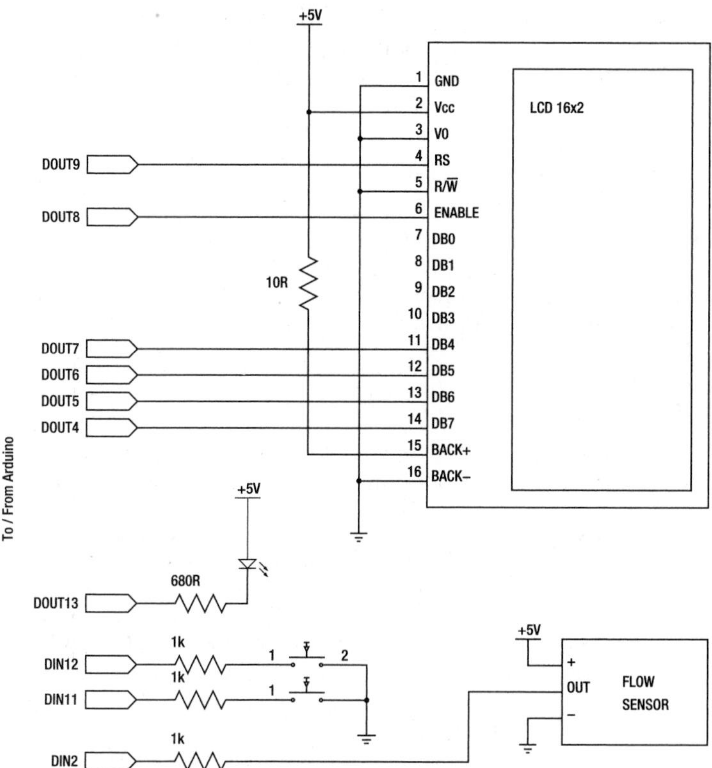

Figure 10-2. Schematic of water flow gauge

Instructions

If you don't care about including an LCD or counter reset buttons, the basic circuit for this project is so trivially simple that you don't even need the prototyping shield. In fact, all you need is the Arduino, the Hall-effect flow sensor, one 1K resistor, and three male breakaway header pins. Just connect the positive and ground lines from the sensor to Arduino 5V and ground, respectively. Then connect the sensor output line to Arduino digital I/O line 2 via the 1K resistor, and you're done. The example code that follows will run perfectly fine and you'll still get values reported via the serial port, but adding an LCD and counter reset buttons makes this project much more useful as a stand-alone device.

Replace Sensor Connector

The flow sensor we used came fitted with a 3-pin plug for which we could not find a matching socket. The simplest solution is to cut off the existing connector and replace it with a new 3-pin line plug. We used a matching pair of automotive-style nylon connectors that are commonly available in many electronics parts stores for only a few dollars.

The Hall-effect flow sensor we used has three connections: black (ground), red (power), and brown (signal). Cut off the existing plug, then strip about 5mm of insulation from the leads and solder them to the pins in your new connector. We laid them out in the same order as the original connector so ground is at one end, signal is in the middle, and power is at the other end.

Strip back the end of your three-core cable in a similar way and solder the matching connector onto the end, taking note of the color codes so you know which colors in your cable represent the ground, power, and signal leads on the sensor. To save confusion, it's best to match up the colors if possible, but if your cable has different colors in it just match them as best you can and write yourself a note about what connection each color represents. This will save you from crawling around under your house later, after the sensor has been installed and you've forgotten which color is which!

The ZD-series sensors are very flexible and can operate on any voltage from 2.4 to 26V. They also consume less than 6mA of power so they can easily be run directly from the 5V line of an Arduino.

Prepare Prototyping Shield

The two counter reset buttons connect to Arduino digital I/O lines 11 and 12, so fit a pair of 1K resistors with one end of each connected to those lines. In a moment we'll connect the other ends of the resistors to wires running to the buttons.

Also install a 1K resistor with one end connected to digital I/O line 2. The other end of this resistor will ultimately be connected to the sensor output so that the Arduino can read it. You can actually dispense with the 1K resistor and connect the sensor directly to the input if you prefer, but it's good to get into the habit of using a low-value resistor in series with inputs to provide a bit of extra protection for the ATMega's pins just in case something nasty happens on the wire running to the sensor. It's not so important with connections within a device, but in this case the wire to the input could run some distance to the location where the sensor is installed. Long wire runs have more tendency to pick up electrical noise so it's best to play it safe.

What you don't see in the schematic is that I/O line 2 will be biased toward 5V using a 20K "pull-up" resistor that's inside the ATMega CPU itself, and can be activated by software. That resistor pulls pin 2 toward +5V but still allows it to be explicitly pulled down if an external device, such as the flow sensor used in this project, shorts it to ground. This is a common technique when working with digital inputs because it puts the input into a known default "HIGH" state, which can then be changed by forcing the input to ground to assert a "LOW" state. In this scenario the resistor is referred to as a "pull-up" resistor because it will tend to pull up the voltage on the pin, and a device can override the high value by shorting it to ground.

The alternative arrangement is to use a "pull-down" resistor, with one end connect to the input and the other end connected to ground. A pull-down resistor holds the voltage on the input down at 0V unless a device overrides the low value by shorting it to +5V and taking it high. So there are two basic approaches we could take: a pull-up resistor combined with an active-low input, or a pull-down resistor combined with an active-high input. At first it might sound more logical to use a pull-down resistor and an active-high input because we're accustomed to thinking in terms of LOW being off and HIGH being on. However, that won't work in this case because the flow sensor used for this project has what is known as an "open-collector" output. This means the output is generally left as an open circuit (unconnected, or floating value with high resistance), and that output pulses are generated by shorting it to ground. By connecting an open-collector device to an input fitted with a pull-up resistor, the value on the input will tend to be +5V except when the device is sending an output pulse, at which time it will drop to 0V courtesy of the short to ground through the sensor.

The schematic in Figure 10-3 shows how this works in practice. The 20K pull-up resistor biases the ATMega input HIGH, but when the sensor sends a pulse it momentarily connects the input to ground via the 1K protection resistor. We don't need to actually install the pull-up resistor because this is such a common method of connecting inputs that it's provided inside the ATMega itself, but it's shown on the schematic to demonstrate what happens behind the scenes.

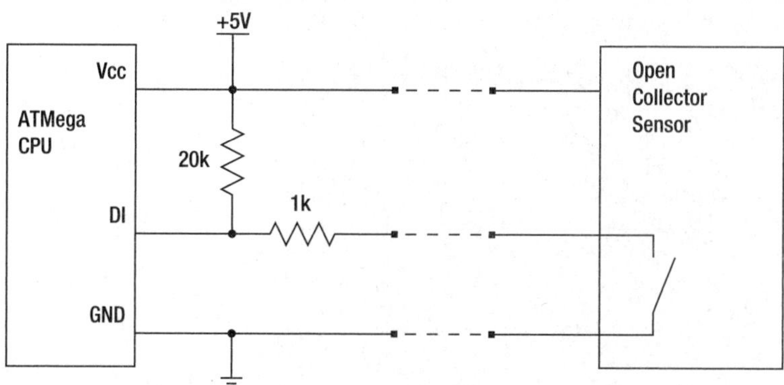

Figure 10-3. *Open-collector sensor connected to an Arduino*

This may all sound confusing at first because the logic is doing the opposite of what you might expect, but it all works out nicely in the end! Use of a pull-up resistor that is overridden by a device using 0V to indicate an event is an important concept to understand because many devices use open-collector outputs, and interfacing with them is a common requirement in Arduino projects. In fact, it's such a common arrangement that all ATMega digital inputs have internal pull-up resistors fitted to them, but the CPU designers didn't even bother including corresponding pull-down resistors.

At this point you could also fit the status LED, with the anode (long) lead connected to +5V. The cathode (short) lead connects to a 680R resistor, which in turn connects to Arduino digital I/O line 13. The result is that the LED will be off if Arduino output 13 is HIGH, and on if it's LOW. Many Arduino models already have an LED connected to pin 13 so you can leave that one off if you like. However, if you're using the shield, the LED on the Arduino will be hidden from view. It will also have the opposite logic (LOW to turn off, HIGH to turn on), so the Arduino LED will be off whenever the additional LED is on, and vice versa (see Figure 10-4).

It may be hard to see in Figure 10-4 because they're so tiny, but this particular prototyping shield comes with a pair of red and green surface-mount LEDs and matching dropper resistors fitted on the bottom left of the board so we didn't need to add the LED ourselves. We just used one of the LEDs already on the shield and connected it to line 13, and connected the other one as a power-on indicator by linking it between ground and 5V via the prefitted dropper resistor.

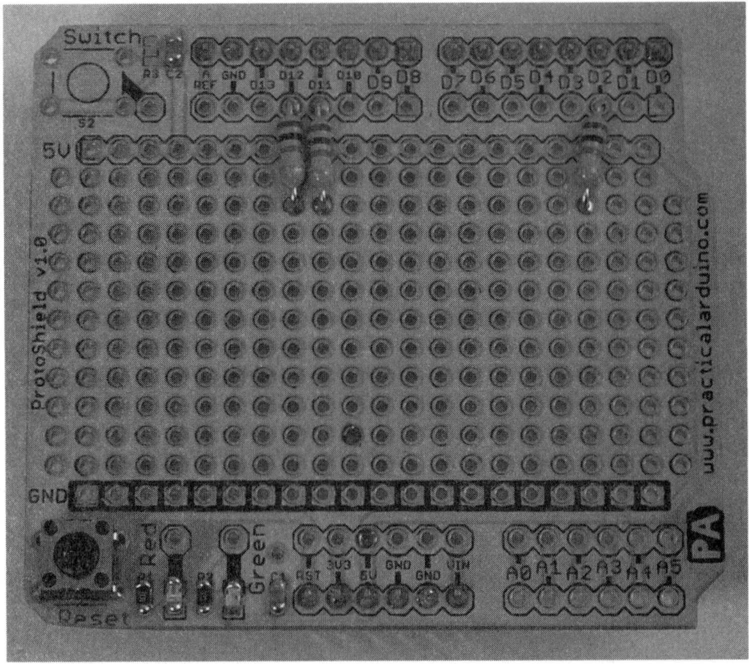

Figure 10-4. 1K resistors in place for button inputs and sensor input

Prepare LCD Module

For this project we picked quite possibly the most common LCD type ever made: the venerable HD44780-compatible 16-character by 2-line (16x2) display. The HD44780 display controller chip was originally developed by Hitachi and has since been copied by so many manufacturers that it has become a de facto industry standard, and you can buy displays with a compatible interface just about anywhere.

HD44780-compatible displays are commonly available in 8x1, 8x2, 16x1, 16x2, 20x2, 20x4, and even 40x4 sizes. The larger formats sometimes combine several driver chips within the module, but from the microcontroller's point of view they still behave in the same way with the same interface format. They simply let you address more lines and write more characters before running off the end of the screen.

The HD44780 uses a "parallel" interface so there are a lot of pins to connect. Parallel interfaces work by presenting a complete byte (8 bits) of data to a set of 8 data lines all at once, then pulsing an "Enable" pin to indicate to the module that the byte is ready to read. This allows the microcontroller to take whatever time it needs to set each of the data lines to the correct state, and while that is happening the module will totally ignore the state of those pins. Then when they're all set to the correct state a short pulse on Enable causes them to be read in all at once.

Like many parallel interfaces, the HD44780 interface is bidirectional. That means it can be used both to send data to the LCD module and also to read data back from the module if required by changing the state of the "R/W" (Read/Write) pin. Some LCD modules come with control buttons mounted as part of the same assembly and setting the mode to "Read" allows the state of the buttons to be accessed, but we're not doing that in this project so we'll just hard-wire the R/W pin to ground to force it into "Read" mode. That saves us one data line when connecting it to the Arduino.By hard-wiring the R/W pin to ground on the module we're down to a total of 12 connections to the LCD module, 10 of which are using up the limited number of I/O lines available on the Arduino: eight data bits, Enable, RS, Ground, and 5V. It's still a bit of a rat's nest, and uses up almost all of the limited number of I/O lines available on the Arduino.

The RS connection is the "Register Select" line, and it's used to switch between command and data modes in the LCD. We can't tie it permanently HIGH or LOW like the Enable connection because the LCD drivers use it to initialize the module and then send data to it.

Luckily the HD44780 can also operate in 4-bit mode, a strange mode that's something like a cross between a parallel and a serial interface. In 8-bit mode an entire byte is presented at once to the data lines. In 4-bit mode half a byte (called a "nibble") is presented to four of the data lines and read into the LCD controller, then the other half of the byte is presented and read in the same way. The LCD controller then reassembles the two nibbles into a complete byte internally, just as if it had all been transmitted at once. Using 4-bit mode saves us another four connections to the controller, bringing it down to a total of eight wires including power and ground. That's six data lines on the Arduino taken up just driving the LCD, which isn't ideal, but does leave enough I/O lines available for us to connect the buttons and Hall-effect flow sensor.

If you're really running short of I/O lines in a project and need to reduce the number of connections to an LCD module even further, you can use a device called a "shift register" such as a 74HC4094. A shift register acts as a serial-to-parallel converter, allowing you to use just three data lines to send a sequence of bits in series that are then exposed in parallel on the shift register outputs. Using a 74HC4094 to connect an HD44780 to an Arduino is more complicated than connecting it up directly, but it drops the I/O line requirement to just three—saving you even more lines. It's not necessary in this project because we're not that short of I/O lines, but if you want to give it a go there is a good explanation on the Arduino web site: `www.arduino.cc/playground/Code/LCD3wires`.

Since we're going to use 4-bit mode we need a total of eight connections from the LCD module to the Arduino, so cut off a short length of ribbon cable and strip it down to eight wires. Strip back both ends of each wire and "tin" it with solder, then connect one end to the LCD module using the connections shown in the schematic in Figure 10-2. The result is shown in Figure 10-5.It's also necessary to make several connections between pads on the LCD module itself since we won't be controlling them from the Arduino. Use short lengths of hookup wire to jumper pins 1 (ground), 3 (contrast), 5 (R/W), and 16 (backlight ground) together.

In most HD44780 displays you can simply tie pin 3 (contrast) to ground and the module will supply maximum contrast, with the text very crisp and easily visible. Some displays, though, can require a bit more fiddling with the contrast to make them visible. If shorting the contrast pin to ground doesn't produce visible text on your display it may be necessary to use a 10K variable resistor or trimpot to provide it with a voltage somewhere between 0V and 5V. If you connect the center (wiper) pin of a trimpot to pin 3, one side of the trimpot to ground, and the other side of the trimpot to 5V, you can then use it to adjust the contrast setting. The three-wire LCD page on the Arduino web site includes a contrast adjustment trimpot in the schematic in case you find it's necessary for your particular LCD.

Also use the 10R resistor to connect pin 2 (+5V) to pin 15 (backlight power) if you want to illuminate the backlight. In most cases 10R is a reasonable value to try as a starting point and should work fine on a typical 16x2 display with LED backlighting. However, the current required by displays of different sizes can vary and some displays even use different backlight technology entirely, so it's a good idea to check the datasheet for your specific display if you're not sure what it requires.

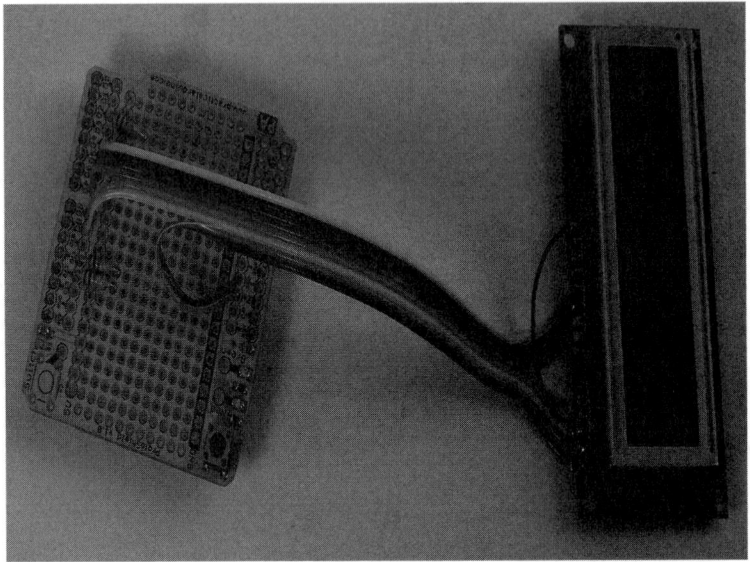

Figure 10-5. LCD module connected to shield using ribbon cable

The other end of the ribbon cable needs to be connected to the prototyping shield. Working from left to right on the LCD module, the ground and 5V lines obviously need to connect to GND and 5V on the shield. RS and Enable then connect to digital I/O lines 9 and 8, respectively. Data bits 4 through 7 connect to I/O lines 7 through 4, respectively. See Table 10-1.

Table 10-1. Connections between Arduino and LCD module

Arduino Pin	LCD Pin	Label	Name	Description
GND	1	GND	Ground	Display ground connection
+5V	2	VCC	Power	Display +5V connection
GND	3	Vo	Contrast	Contrast adjustment voltage
Digital OUT 9	4	RS	Register Select	Data input (HIGH) / Control input (LOW)

GND	5	R/W	Read / Write	Read (HIGH) / Write (LOW)
Digital OUT 8	6	E	Enable	Enable byte/nibble transfer
	7	D0	Data0	Data bit 0
	8	D1	Data1	Data bit 1
	9	D2	Data2	Data bit 2
	10	D3	Data3	Data bit 3
Digital OUT 7	11	D4	Data4	Data bit 4
Digital OUT 6	12	D5	Data5	Data bit 5
Digital OUT 5	13	D6	Data6	Data bit 6
Digital OUT 4	14	D7	Data7	Data bit 7
+5V via 10R	15	VB1	Backlight power	Backlight +5V connection
GND	16	VB0	Backlight ground	Backlight ground connection

Yes, the data bits are reversed between the Arduino and the LCD, but that really doesn't matter because we have to explicitly configure them in the program anyway and wiring them in this order makes the cabling neat and easy.

Fit LCD to Case

If you're measuring water flow you will probably have to place your Arduino in a location that is subject to dust and moisture. To keep it operating reliably over a long period of time it's a good idea to mount it inside a plastic case, preferably one designed for outdoor use that has a rubber gasket around the edge of the lid to ensure a watertight seal. We used a weatherproof PVC box with a transparent lid. It was perfect for mounting the LCD because you can see it right through the case, allowing the display to be kept safe and weatherproof.

The mounting holes in the corners of our particular LCD module were just a bit too small to fit standard M3 bolts through, but luckily there were no PCB tracks close to the holes so it was an easy job to enlarge them with a 3mm drill bit. We then drilled matching holes in the box lid and also drilled holes where the pair of reset buttons will be mounted, then bolted the LCD in place using 10mm plastic spacers and 20mm M3 bolts. Metal washers were used on the outside and plastic washers on the inside to ensure the nuts didn't short anything out on the LCD module's PCB.

The result is a very neatly mounted LCD with the face suspended just behind the transparent lid of the box (see Figure 10-6).

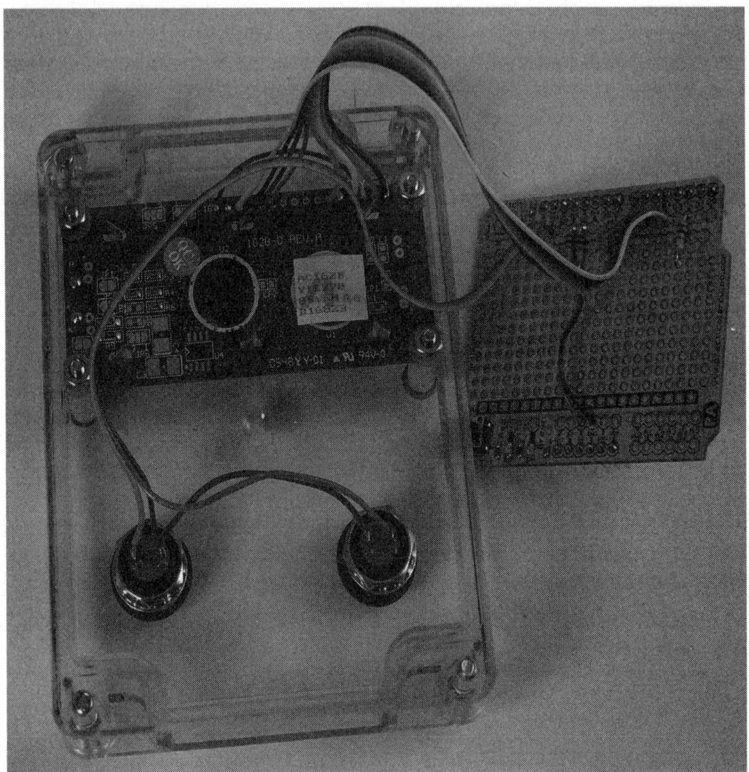

Figure 10-6. *LCD and pushbuttons mounted in case lid*

You can use just about any momentary-action pushbuttons, but we chose a couple of low-profile splash-proof buttons that came fitted with rubber seals to provide extra protection against wet hands.

Wiring up the buttons is easy. Connect one terminal of each button together as the common-ground connection, then link it to ground on the shield. The other terminals of each button then connect to the two 1K resistors fitted to the shield earlier and link to digital I/O lines 11 and 12. It doesn't even matter much which button you connect to which input. If you find that you got it wrong, it's trivial to swap the pin assignments in the software. We connected the left button (on the right when looking at the back of the case lid, remember!) to input 11 to reset counter A, and the right button to input 12 to reset counter B.

Fit Arduino in Case

The Arduino itself also needs to be mounted in the case. For convenience we cut a rectangular hole in the side of the box to allow the USB connector to protrude through. However, this prevents the box from being weathertight, so you may choose to mount it in a different way. Just like with the LCD module, we then used 20mm M3 bolts through the bottom of the case with plastic spacers (6mm this time) for the Arduino to sit on. Plastic washers on top of the Arduino PCB then protect it from the M3 nuts.

Once the Arduino is mounted in the bottom of the case you can test-fit the prototyping shield into it, joining the LCD and the front panel pushbuttons to the Arduino (see Figure 10-7). Even without the sensor fitted you can run tests on the hardware at this point; for example, by loading an example sketch from the LiquidCrystal library and altering to suit the pin assignments as explained in the following section "Configure, Compile, and Test Sketch."

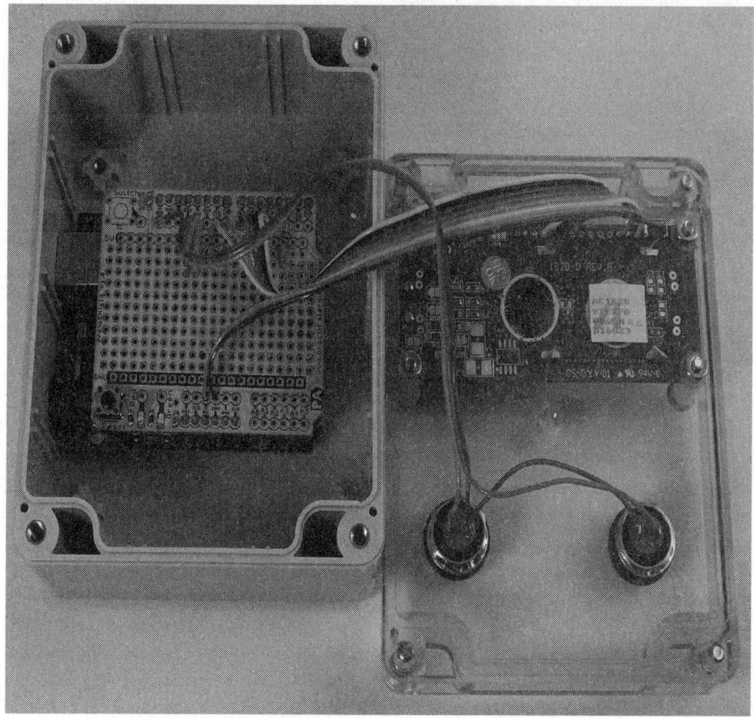

Figure 10-7. *Arduino, shield, LCD, and buttons all mounted inside weatherproof case*

The only hardware assembly left to do now is to connect the Hall-effect flow sensor. As shown on the circuit diagram in Figure 10-2, the sensor needs to be connected to ground, +5V, and to the end of the 1K resistor fitted previously to digital I/O line 2. You can either fit a line plug to the cable and mount a socket in the case, or just pass the cable through a hole in the box, tie a knot in it to prevent it from pulling back out, and solder it directly to the prototyping shield as shown in Figure 10-8.

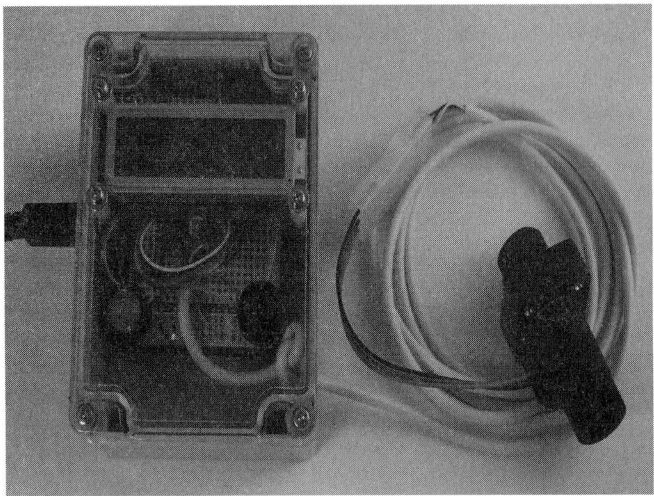

Figure 10-8. Assembled unit with sensor connected

With the sensor connections in place make sure the prototyping shield is firmly mounted, fit the lid, and move on to the software.

Determine Scaling Factor

Like almost all Hall-effect devices, water flow-rate sensors output a series of pulses at a rate that varies proportionally with the parameter being measured. All devices that output pulses need a scaling factor to convert the frequency into a meaningful value. For example, a car wheel rotation sensor might output one, two, four, or five pulses per rotation, but that information is useless on its own: you also need to know the circumference of the wheel so you can multiply the pulse count by the circumference to determine the distance traveled.

The sensor we used outputs approximately 4.5 pulses per second per liter of flow per minute. That sounds odd because we're using values measured in pulses per second to represent liters per minute. Consider the following examples:

- At 1 liter per minute, the sensor will output 4.5 pulses per second.
- At 5 liters per minute, the sensor will output 22.5 pulses per second.
- At 10 liters per minute, the sensor will output 45 pulses per second.
- At 20 liters per minute, the sensor will output 90 pulses per second.

This means our scaling factor to convert pulses per second into liters per minute is 1/4.5, or approximately 0.22. By measuring the pulse frequency and dividing by 4.5 (or multiplying by 0.22) we can determine the current flow rate in liters per minute.

The program for this project, therefore, acts as a simple frequency counter to determine how many pulses are being generated per second, and then applies that scaling factor to convert the measured frequency into a flow-rate value in liters per minute. It also outputs the value as the number of liters passed in that second, and as a cumulative total of the number of liters passed since the program began.

There is a slight complication though: most flow-rate sensors do not have a consistent scaling factor across their entire operational range.

At low flow rates the sensor might be impeded more by friction in the bearings, so its output frequency could actually be lower per liter than at higher flow rates. That variation could be corrected in software by applying a different scaling factor depending on the measured pulse rate. However, because the accuracy of inexpensive flow sensors is typically only +/– 10% anyway it doesn't really matter much in practice that the scaling factor deviates slightly at low flow rates.

Configure, Compile, and Test Sketch

The example sketch contains two things that are likely to be a bit puzzling if you haven't seen them before: hardware interrupts and volatile variables.

Hardware Interrupts

The first trick is the use of an interrupt to process pulses coming from the sensor.

An "interrupt" is a special signal sent to the CPU that does pretty much what it sounds like: it interrupts the current program flow and makes it jump off in a different direction temporarily, before returning to whatever it was doing previously. As far as the main program code is concerned, it doesn't even need to know that an interrupt has taken place. It will simply lose some time in the middle of whatever it was doing; other than that, everything will continue as if nothing happened.

Of course this can cause big problems if your main program code is doing something time-critical, and it's important to keep interrupts as short as possible.

Interrupts can come from a variety of sources, but in this case we're using a hardware interrupt that is triggered by a state change on one of the digital pins. Most Arduino designs have two hardware interrupts (referred to as "interrupt0" and "interrupt1") hard-wired to digital I/O pins 2 and 3, respectively. The Arduino Mega has a total of six hardware interrupts, with the additional interrupts ("interrupt2" through "interrupt5") on pins 21, 20, 19, and 18, respectively as shown in Table 10-2.

Table 10-2. *Hardware interrupt pin assignments*

Interrupt	Pin	Model
0	2	most Arduinos
1	3	most Arduinos
2	21	Arduino Mega
3	20	Arduino Mega
4	19	Arduino Mega
5	18	Arduino Mega

By defining a special function called an "Interrupt Service Routine" (usually simply called an "ISR") that you want executed whenever the interrupt is triggered, and then specifying the conditions under which that can happen (rising edge, falling edge, or both), it's possible to have that function executed automatically each time an event happens on an input pin. That way you don't have to keep checking the pin to see if it has changed state since the last time you checked it because your program can get on with doing something else and just be interrupted when necessary. It's like having a doorbell on your house: you don't have to keep checking if someone is at the front door because you know that if someone arrives they will ring the bell. Attaching an interrupt to a program is just like installing a doorbell and then getting on with doing other things until visitors arrive.

A common beginner's mistake is to put too much code into the ISR. It's important to remember that when an interrupt occurs and your ISR is being executed, your main program code is frozen and all other interrupts are automatically disabled so that one interrupt can't disrupt another while it is being processed. Disabling interrupts is, therefore, something that should be done for the briefest possible time so that no other events are missed, so always make your ISR code as short and fast as possible and then get straight back out again. A common approach, which is the technique we use here, is to have the ISR update a global variable and then immediately exit. That way the entire ISR can execute in only a few clock cycles and the interrupts are disabled for the shortest time possible. Then the main program loop just has to periodically check the global variable that was updated by the ISR and process it as appropriate in its own time.

Volatile Variables

The second trick is the use of the «volatile» keyword when declaring the pulseCount variable. The volatile keyword isn't technically part of the program itself: it's a flag that tells the compiler to treat that particular variable in a special way when it converts the source code you wrote into machine code for the Arduino's ATMega CPU to execute.

A "volatile" variable is one whose value may change at any time without any action taken by the code near it. Compilers are designed to optimize code to be as small and fast as possible, so they use techniques such as finding variables that are not modified within the code and then replacing all instances of that variable with a literal value. Normally that's exactly what you want, but sometimes the compiler optimizations trip up on situations that aren't quite what it's expecting. The volatile keyword is therefore a warning to the compiler that it shouldn't try to optimize that variable away, even when it thinks it's safe to do so.

In practice there are three general situations in which a variable can change its value without nearby code taking any action.

1. Memory-mapped peripheral registers. Some peripheral interfaces, including some digital I/O lines, map those lines directly into the CPU's memory space. A classic example is the parallel port on a PC: the pins on a parallel port map directly to three bytes of system memory starting at address 0x378. If the values in the memory locations for the output pins are changed by the CPU, the electrical state of the pins changes to match. If the electrical state of the input pins changes, the corresponding memory location values change and can be accessed by the CPU. In memory-mapped peripheral registers the interface is effectively a real-time physical representation of the current state of a chunk of system memory, and vice versa. In the case of memory-mapped input lines the value of that location in memory might never be changed by the running program and so the compiler could think it's valid to optimize it away with a static value, but the program will then never see changes caused by changing input levels from the connection to the peripheral.

2. Global variables within a multithreaded application. This doesn't really apply to Arduino programs, but it's worth remembering if you're working on larger systems. Threads are self-contained chunks of code that run in parallel to each other within the same memory space. From the point of view of each thread, a global variable is actually very similar to a memory-mapped peripheral register: it can change at any time due to the action of another thread. Threads, therefore, can't assume that a global variable has a static value, even if that particular thread never changes it explicitly.

3. Global variables modified by an ISR. Because an ISR appears to the compiler to be a separate chunk of code that is never called by the main program, it could decide that variables referenced by the main program can never change after initialization and so optimize them away by replacing them with literal values. This is obviously bad if the ISR changes the value because the main program will never see the change. The water flow sensor sketch uses an ISR to update the pulseCount variable, and because the main program loop accesses that variable but never modifies it the compiler could incorrectly decide that it can safely be optimized away and replaced with a literal value. In the example code we therefore need the volatile keyword to allow the main program loop to see changes to the pulseCount value caused by execution of the ISR.

Note that the example program disables interrupts while sending data to the host. This is important because otherwise it may end up in a situation where the next pulse arrives before the transmission has finished, and the interrupt could cause problems for the serial connection. While interrupts are disabled the CPU will still see additional interrupts at the hardware level and set an internal flag that says an interrupt has occurred, but it won't be allowed to disrupt the flow of the program because ISRs cannot be executed in a stacked or nested fashion. Only one can ever be in operation at a given time. Then, when the ISR finishes executing, the CPU could immediately trigger another ISR call if the interrupt flag has been set in the background. It's fairly common for interrupt-heavy systems to spend time processing an ISR, return, and be immediately shunted into another ISR without the main program code getting a chance to do any processing at all.

One thing to remember, however, is that the interrupt flag in the CPU is only a 1-bit flag. If you spend time with interrupts disabled and in that time an event occurs to set the flag, you have no way of knowing if it was only one event or one thousand. The CPU doesn't have an internal counter to keep track of how many times the interrupt was tripped. There is therefore the very real possibility of undercounting events such as input pulses if you spend too long with interrupts disabled.

In this project it's not a problem because the pulse rate is never particularly high. Handling 90 interrupts per second at the maximum rated flow for this sensor is trivial even for a relatively slow CPU such as those found in an Arduino. In fact, one thing that's slightly odd about the example program is that it spends most of its time with interrupts disabled: it disables them at the start of the main program loop, then enables them again at the end before it loops back to the start. Interrupts are therefore only enabled for a very brief period on each cycle, but because the CPU sets the interrupt flag even when interrupts are disabled it all works out nicely. Most pulses from the sensor will arrive while the program is in the main loop and interrupts are disabled, and will then be processed as soon as the main loop ends. Because the main loop executes in about 5ms and even at 90 pulses per second the interval between pulses is about 11ms we're fairly safe from missing any pulses.

Flow Gauge Sketch

First the sketch includes the LiquidCrystal library to take care of communicating with the LCD module for us. Then we create a LiquidCrystal object called "lcd" and configure it with the pins used for RS, Enable, and D4 through D7. Because of the way we wired the ribbon cable to the shield this corresponds directly to pins 9 through 4.

```
#include <LiquidCrystal.h>
LiquidCrystal lcd(9, 8, 7, 6, 5, 4);
```

We also need to specify the pins connected to the pair of counter reset buttons and the status LED. The LED is illuminated (pulled LOW) whenever a reset button is pressed.

```
byte resetButtonA = 11;
byte resetButtonB = 12;
byte statusLed    = 13;
```

The connection for the Hall-effect sensor also needs to be configured, and we need to specify two values: the interrupt number and the pin number. It would be nice if this could be done in a single command to avoid confusion but unfortunately there's no way to do that in an Arduino, because the interrupts are numbered from 0 up and they can correspond to different pins depending on what Arduino model you are using.

For our prototype we connected the sensor to pin 2, which corresponds to interrupt 0. Alternatively you could connect to pin 3 and use interrupt 1. A Mega gives you even more options.

```
byte sensorInterrupt = 0;
byte sensorPin       = 2;
```

We also need to set a scaling factor for the sensor in use as discussed previously. The Hall-effect flow sensor used in the prototype outputs approximately 4.5 pulses per second per liter/minute of flow.

```
float calibrationFactor = 4.5;
```

We also need a variable that will be incremented by the ISR every time a pulse is detected on the input pin, and as discussed previously this needs to be marked as volatile so the compiler won't optimize it away.

```
volatile byte pulseCount;
```

The measured values also need variables to store them in, and in this program we use three different types of numeric variables. The float type used for flowRate handles floating-point (decimal) numbers, since the flow rate at any one time will be something like 9.3 liters/minute. The unsigned int flowMilliLitres can store positive integer values up to 65,535, which is plenty for the number of milliliters that can pass through the sensor in a one-second interval. With a high-flow sensor that can measure more than 65 liters/second, it would be necessary to switch this to type unsigned long instead. The unsigned long variables, totalMilliLitresA and totalMilliLitresB, can store positive integer values up to 4,294,967,295, which is plenty for the cumulative counter of total milliliters that have passed through the sensor since the counter was reset. Eventually the counters will wrap around and start again at 0 after a bit more than 4 megaliters, but that should take quite a while in a typical domestic application!

```
float flowRate;
unsigned int flowMilliLitres;
unsigned long totalMilliLitresA;
unsigned long totalMilliLitresB;
```

The loop needs to know how long it has been since it was last executed, so we'll use a global variable to store the number of milliseconds since program execution began and update it each time the main loop runs. It needs to be of type long so that it can hold a large enough value for the program to run for a reasonable amount of time without the value exceeding the storage capacity of the variable and wrapping back around to 0.

```
unsigned long oldTime;
```

The setup routine is fairly straightforward except for the definition of the interrupt handler, which we'll get to in a moment.

First it makes some calls to methods in the lcd object. The begin call specifies the number of columns and rows in the attached LCD, then the cursor is set to character 0 on row 0 (the top row) before 16 spaces are printed. The cursor is then set to character 0 on row 1 (the second row) and another 16 spaces printed.

This ensures that the LCD starts off blank with no leftover characters visible on the display. Normally it's not a problem, but this just ensures that anything left from a previous program you may have run, such as an LCD test program, is erased.

```
void setup()
{
  lcd.begin(16, 2);
  lcd.setCursor(0, 0);
  lcd.print("                ");
  lcd.setCursor(0, 1);
  lcd.print("                ");
```

A serial connection is then opened to the host to report values back.

```
  Serial.begin(38400);
```

The pin to control the status LED is switched to an output and then set HIGH, which turns off the LED since we connected it via a dropper resistor to +5V.

```
  pinMode(statusLed, OUTPUT);
  digitalWrite(statusLed, HIGH);
```

The I/O lines connected to the counter reset buttons are set as inputs so we can read the button state, but then the program writes to them as if they're outputs. This has the effect of activating the ATMega CPU's internal 20K pull-up resistors on those inputs, biasing them high unless they are pulled low via the button and the 1K resistors.

```
  pinMode(resetButtonA, INPUT);
  digitalWrite(resetButtonA, HIGH);
  pinMode(resetButtonB, INPUT);
  digitalWrite(resetButtonB, HIGH);
```

The pin for connecting the Hall-effect sensor is then treated in the same way. We set it to be an input then write a HIGH value to it, activating the internal pull-up resistor so that it will be high unless the open-collector output of the sensor pulls it low.

```
  pinMode(sensorPin, INPUT);
  digitalWrite(sensorPin, HIGH);
A number of variables are initialised to starting values.
  pulseCount        = 0;
  flowMilliLitres   = 0;
  totalMilliLitresA = 0;
  totalMilliLitresB = 0;
  oldTime           = 0;
```

The attachInterrupt() function takes three arguments: the ID of the interrupt to configure, the name of the function to call when the interrupt is triggered, and the transition that will trigger the interrupt. In this case we're setting up interrupt0 so the first argument is simply 0. Our ISR function is going to be called pulse_counters passed in as the second argument. We only want to detect transitions from a high to a low state on the input, so the third argument is set to FALLING. Other possible values for the transition argument are RISING, to trigger on a transition from low to high; LOW, to trigger whenever the input is in a low state; and CHANGE, to trigger on both rising and falling transitions.

```
  attachInterrupt(sensorInterrupt, pulseCounter, FALLING);
}
```

The main program loop is where all the action is. The loop repeats very fast because there are no delays or other things happening to hold it up: it runs through each cycle quite quickly and goes straight back to the start. This simplifies a few things for us, particularly the way we manage the counter reset buttons. If the loop was slower we'd probably need to connect them to interrupts in a similar way to the flow gauge so that we wouldn't miss fast button presses. De-bouncing the buttons could also become an issue. Button de-bouncing is discussed in the Vehicle Telemetry Platform project in Chapter 15, but in this case we don't care about it because we're not toggling between states or counting button presses. We're simply checking whether either button is pressed on every pass through the loop, and if it is, we reset the associated counter. If the button is held down the associated counter will be reset on every pass through the loop but that really doesn't matter.Remember that the counter reset buttons are biased HIGH by the CPU and pulled LOW when the button is pressed, so we're checking for a LOW state to indicate that the counter needs to be reset.

When a counter is reset we don't just clear the associated variable. We also need to overprint that portion of the LCD with a zero value. Because of the way a character-based LCD works, any characters that are written to it are displayed continuously until they are replaced with something else. If counter A had incremented to, say, 123 liters, the first four characters on the bottom row of the display would read "123L." Resetting the counter without clearing the display would subsequently cause the value 0L to be written to the first two characters of the display, but the third and fourth characters wouldn't be altered. The result is that the display would end up reading "0L3L," which wouldn't make much sense. Overwriting those positions in the display with 0L followed by six spaces prevents this from happening.

The same thing is done for counter B, but of course we first set the cursor to position 8 (actually the ninth character on that row since it starts from 0) before writing it out.

```
void loop()
{
  if(digitalRead(resetButtonA) == LOW)
  {
```

```
    totalMilliLitresA = 0;
    lcd.setCursor(0, 1);
    lcd.print("0L      ");
  }
  if(digitalRead(resetButtonB) == LOW)
  {
    totalMilliLitresB = 0;
    lcd.setCursor(8, 1);
    lcd.print("0L      ");
  }
```

The status LED is illuminated if either of the counter reset buttons is pressed, so we then check if either button is pressed and set the status LED to LOW (on) or HIGH (off) appropriately.

```
  if( (digitalRead(resetButtonA) == LOW) || (digitalRead(resetButtonB) == LOW) )
  {
    digitalWrite(statusLed, LOW);
  } else {
    digitalWrite(statusLed, HIGH);
  }
```

The main loop spins through very fast and we don't want to do all the input processing every time through because we need to average the number of pulses across one second, so the rest of the main loop code is wrapped in a check to see if at least one second has passed since the last time it was executed. Only if the difference between the current time and the previous time is greater than 1,000 milliseconds is the rest of the code executed.

```
  if((millis() - oldTime) > 1000)
  {
```

We need to disable interrupts while executing this section of the loop, so the very first thing to do is call detachInterrupt() to disable the interrupt we set up previously. Otherwise, comms may fail if an interrupt arrives while the program is in the middle of sending data to the host. Note that this doesn't actually remove the configuration for the interrupt, and the CPU will still set the interrupt flag if it's triggered while in the main program loop as explained previously.

```
    detachInterrupt(sensorInterrupt);
```

The first step is to calculate the amount of flow that has occurred since last time. This is done by taking the pulse count and multiplying it by 1,000 to convert liters to milliliters, then dividing it by the product of the calibration factor and 60 to convert it from seconds to minutes.

```
    flowMilliLitres = pulseCount * (1000/(calibrationFactor*60));
```

All the calculations of flow rate (as opposed to volume) are based on time, so we could assume that this part of the loop executes once per second but that wouldn't necessarily be accurate. It will typically be slightly longer than one second and this error will be cumulative if we just assume that we reach this point every 1,000 milliseconds precisely. Instead, we calculate the actual number of milliseconds that have passed since the last execution and use that to scale the output. That leaves us with this somewhat complicated looking line that takes into consideration the amount of time that has passed and the flow volume in that period.

```
flowRate = (flowMilliLitres * (60000 / (millis() - oldTime))) / 1000;
```

This flow volume is then added to the pair of cumulative counters tracking the number of milliliters measured since the counters were reset.

```
totalMilliLitresA += flowMilliLitres;
totalMilliLitresB += flowMilliLitres;
```

During testing it can be useful to output the literal pulse count value so you can compare that and the calculated flow rate against the datasheets for the flow sensor. The next two lines display the raw pulse count value followed by a separator. You must uncomment them during testing if you want to make sure that the calculated values you're seeing actually make sense or you need to check the sensor calibration against a known flow rate.

```
//Serial.print(pulseCount, DEC);
//Serial.print("  ");
```

Now the program can write the calculated value to the serial port. Because we want to output a floating-point value and print() can't handle floats we have to do some trickery to output the whole number part, then a decimal point, then the fractional part. First, we define a variable that will be used to hold the part after the decimal point, i.e., the fractional part of the floating-point number.

```
unsigned int frac;
```

To print the previously calculated flow rate for this sample period in liters/minute we cast the flowRate variable to an integer value. This discards everything after the decimal point and sends only the whole number part to the host via the USB connection. Then we send a period to represent the decimal point.

```
Serial.print(int(flowRate));
Serial.print(".");
```

Now comes the trickery to determine the fractional part of the value. By subtracting the rounded (integer) value of the variable from the variable itself we're left with just the part after the decimal point. Then, multiplying this by 10 returns the number with the values after the decimal point shifted one digit to the left. A starting value of 13.5423 would, therefore, become 0.5423 after subtraction of the integer value. It is then shifted left to become 5.423, and then, because the result is being stored as an integer, it becomes 5. If you want more decimal places to be displayed you can change the multiplier to 100 for two decimal places, 1000 for three, 10000 for four, and so on. The resulting value is then simply sent to the serial port just like any other integer and appears to the host immediately after the decimal point sent previously.

```
frac = (flowRate - int(flowRate)) * 10;
Serial.print(frac, DEC);
```

Because the next three values to be displayed are simple integers we don't need to do any tricks. They're sent straight to the serial port as they are, with space separators in between. Note that the last output line uses Serial.println() instead of Serial.print() so that the display in the IDE will wrap to the next line ready for the next sample.

```
Serial.print(" ");
Serial.print(flowMilliLitres);
Serial.print(" ");
Serial.print(totalMilliLitresA);
Serial.print(" ");
Serial.println(totalMilliLitresB);
```

Having output the values to the host, we then need to update the LCD. First we clear the entire first row, then output the "Flow: " text that will appear in front of the flow-rate value.

```
lcd.setCursor(0, 0);
lcd.print("                ");
lcd.setCursor(0, 0);
lcd.print("Flow: ");
```

The sensor we used can output a flow rate from 0 up to about 20L/min, so sometimes the value to display will be a single digit and sometimes it will be two digits. Because the position is set from the left it can look a bit stupid if the decimal point jumps around, so we check whether the value is going to be less than 10 (i.e., a single digit), and pad it with a space if it is. That way the number will appear with the decimal place in the same location on the LCD no matter what value it displays.

```
if(int(flowRate) < 10)
{
  lcd.print(" ");
}
```

Just as before we then need to display the integer portion of the value, then a decimal point, and then the fraction. Then we output a space followed by the units.

```
lcd.print((int)flowRate);
lcd.print('.');
lcd.print(frac, DEC);
lcd.print(" L/min");
```

The two counters are displayed on the second line, with the first starting at position 0 and the second starting at position 8. Because the counters actually accumulate milliliters and we want to display liters we divide them by 1000 and convert the result to an integer before it is sent to the LCD.

```
lcd.setCursor(0, 1);
lcd.print(int(totalMilliLitresA / 1000));
lcd.print("L");
lcd.setCursor(8, 1);
lcd.print(int(totalMilliLitresB / 1000));
lcd.print("L");
```

Before finishing up the loop the pulse counter needs to be reset so that next time the ISR is called it will begin counting up from 0 again.

```
pulseCount = 0;
```

We're almost at the end now, so we need to update the oldTime variable to the current time so the main loop won't execute this chunk of code again for at least another 1,000 milliseconds. There's a little catch here, though, that doesn't cause us any problems in this project but is something to be very careful of in your own programs: technically, the millis() function is lying to us and returning an incorrect value. This is because millis() is updated behind the scenes by a time-triggered interrupt (as opposed to the input-triggered interrupt we used for the sensor) that fires approximately every millisecond and causes the time counter to increment. But while interrupts are disabled the millis() function won't actually be incrementing, and will simply return the value it was set to just before interrupts went away rather than what the current value should really be.

For us it doesn't matter so we just set the oldTime variable to the value returned by millis().

```
    oldTime = millis();
```

At this point, though, the interrupt is still disabled, so the ISR will never be called. Now that we're done with the main program loop we enable the interrupt again.

```
    attachInterrupt(sensorInterrupt, pulseCounter, FALLING);
  }
}
```

The last part of the sketch is the ISR itself. This function is never called by the main program, but is instead invoked by interrupt0 once per rotation of the Hall-effect sensor. The interrupt handler is kept extremely small so it returns quickly each time it executes. This is the ideal way to structure an ISR: a single instruction to increment a global variable and then immediately bail out. An ISR like this can execute in just a few microseconds.

```
void pulseCounter()
{
  pulseCount++;
}
```

Once you've uploaded the sketch to your Arduino and ensured your flow sensor is plugged in, click the "serial monitor" button near the top right of the Arduino IDE and make sure the port speed setting is set to 38400. You should see a series of values being displayed (hopefully 0.0) with one reading taken per second. The LCD will also display a flow rate of 0.0 and counter values of 0L.

Because the pickup on the flow-rate sensor spins quite easily, you can test that it is functioning by simply blowing through the sensor and watching the values displayed in your IDE or on the LCD. Note, however, that the sensor is directional. Look on the side of the body for an arrow that indicates the required liquid flow direction and blow through it in the direction of the arrow.

Try blowing gently through the sensor and watching the flow-rate value. After a few seconds the counters should click over to 1L and then continue incrementing as you keep blowing. Pressing either of the counter reset buttons should set that counter back to 0, leaving the other counter unaffected.

Install Flow Sensor

The flow sensor itself is manufactured from a very strong material consisting of a glass-fiber reinforced plastic resin and has a standard 1/2-inch BSP thread on each end so it can be screwed into standard plumbing fittings.

Find the lead-in pipe for the water source you want to measure and have a plumber fit the sensor into the pipe. In many jurisdictions it is illegal to perform plumbing work yourself without the necessary qualifications, but even if you are allowed to perform the work yourself it's best to seek expert assistance if you're at all unsure about working with pipes. However, if you have someone such as a plumber perform the installation for you, make sure you show them the direction marker on the sensor body so they know it needs to be installed so that the water flows through it in that direction.

Variations

Online Logging

By adding an Ethernet shield your flow gauge could connect to the Internet and upload readings to an online resource logging service such as Pachube (www.pachube.com) or Watch My Thing (www.watchmything.com).

However, something to be careful of in this particular project is possible contention for the pins used for interrupts. Interrupts are often used by shields that perform time-critical communications functions, including Ethernet shields, so if you want to combine this project with an Ethernet connection you need to be careful not to use any pins needed by the shield. Ethernet shields based on the official design published on the Arduino web site generally use interrupt1 on pin 3, while Ethernet shields based on the nuElectronics design, as well as the WiShield wifi shield, generally use interrupt0 on pin 2.

As discussed previously the input pin used for this project is determined by the sensorInterrupt variable: if the value is set to 0, it will use interrupt0 on pin 2; setting it to 1 causes it to use interrupt1 on pin 3. Check which interrupt your Ethernet shield uses and then configure the sensor to use the other one.

Multiple Sensors

We've only connected a single sensor in this example, but a standard Arduino has two interrupt pins, so you could connect one sensor to pin 2 and one to pin 3. You'd then need to modify the software to have two ISR functions and two sets of relevant variables such as pulseCount.

If you want to measure flow through even more sensors you could use an Arduino Mega to connect up to six flow gauges at once. Alternatively you may be able to use the port-level interrupt technique discussed in the Vehicle Telemetry Platform project in Chapter 15 to connect even more.

Resources

If you want to learn more about Hall-effect sensors there is an introductory article on Wikipedia explaining how they work:

```
en.wikipedia.org/wiki/Hall_effect_sensor
```

Wikipedia also has a basic article on the HD44780 display controller:

```
en.wikipedia.org/wiki/HD44780_Character_LCD
```

The datasheets for the ZD1200 and ZD1202 flow gauges also contain lots of helpful information:

```
www.jaycar.com.au/images_uploaded/ZD1200.pdf
www.jaycar.com.au/images_uploaded/ZD1202.pdf
```

CHAPTER 11

■ ■ ■

Oscilloscope/Logic Analyzer

One of the frustrating things about developing and debugging electronic circuits is that you can't look inside the circuit to see what is happening. Even with a circuit laid out before you on a workbench and powered up, it may seem like you're in the dark, unable to figure out why an input change or alteration in one part of the circuit isn't having the effect you expected. Sometimes it can feel like you're working with a blindfold on.

A multimeter lets you measure a constant or slowly changing voltage, such as checking whether ICs or other devices are being powered correctly, with 3.3V or 5V as appropriate. But they're no good at helping you visualize signals that change rapidly, such as a stream of data flowing through a serial port or an audio waveform coming out of an oscillator. The best you can hope for with a multimeter is a reading that represents the average voltage: a 5V bitstream with a random mix of 1s and 0s will read about 2.5V, since it spends half its time high and half low. If the multimeter tried to keep up with the changes, the display would flicker too fast for you to read it.

The solution is two different test instruments that started as totally separate devices, but over the years have progressively become more and more similar. Nowadays, their features often overlap so much that it can be hard classifying these two devices as strictly one or the other.

The first is an oscilloscope, an instrument most frequently used when working with analog circuits but also very handy for digital circuit analysis. An oscilloscope (or just "scope") has a screen to display a signal trace that is offset in the X and Y axis by measurements taken from two different inputs. The most common usage is with the Y (vertical) axis controlled by a probe connected to the system under test, and the X (horizontal) axis controlled by an internal timebase that can run at different frequencies. If the X input is left unconnected and the Y input is attached to a signal that oscillates rapidly between low and high values, the trace on the screen will flicker up and down rapidly and simply draw a vertical line. By applying the timebase on the X axis, the varying input signal is spread out horizontally so that it's possible to see how it varies with time.

The X input can alternatively be attached to another input probe, providing independent X and Y input to the oscilloscope and allowing two signals to be plotted against each other. The classic classroom example is to attach the X and Y probes to two sine waves of equal frequency and amplitude that are 90 degrees out of phase, with the result being that the oscilloscope plots a perfect circle on the screen (see Figure 11-1).

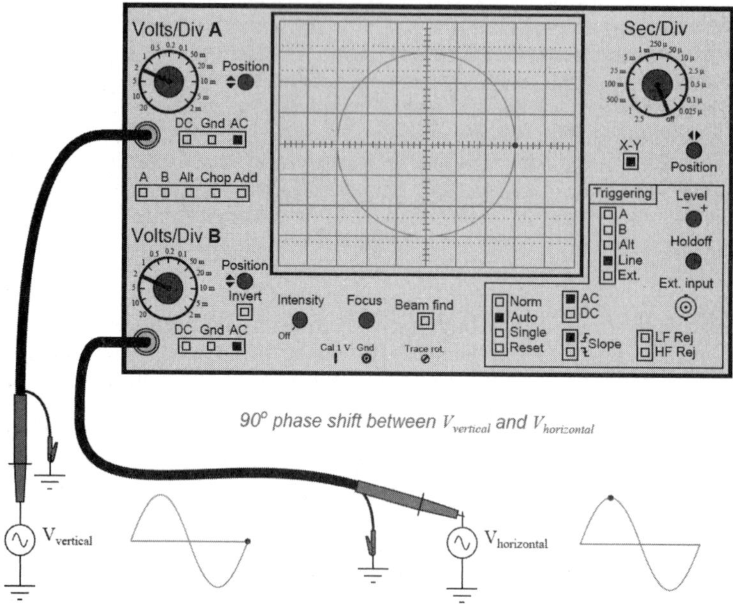

***Figure 11-1.** Oscilloscope displaying the combination of two equal sine waves 90 degrees out of phase*

Different amplitudes will cause the circle to be compressed around one of the axes, causing it to form an oval around either the horizontal or vertical axis. A 0 degree phase offset will cause a diagonal line to be plotted from bottom left to top right, a 180 degree offset will cause a diagonal line to be plotted from top left to bottom right, and other offsets will cause the shape to form an oval on a diagonal axis. Differences in frequency also alter the shape of the display, with a 1:2 frequency ratio creating a display that looks like a figure eight (8) and a 2:1 ratio looking like the infinity symbol, ∞

An experienced technician can look at a scope display and very quickly deduce a lot of information from it, such as the relative amplitudes, frequencies, and phase offset of two different waveforms.

Early oscilloscopes were called a "cathode-ray oscilloscope," or simply CRO, and many people still call them that. An old-style CRO is literally just a cathode-ray tube like the one found in an older television set but with no tuning circuit and two inputs connected to signal amplifiers that drive the X and Y deflection plates directly. It's even possible to convert an old TV into a basic CRO with some fairly simple alterations to the circuit, although you have to be careful of the high voltages required to run the electron gun and deflection circuitry.

Modern oscilloscopes no longer use cathode-ray tubes, and instead use high-speed analog-to-digital converters (ADCs) to sample an analog reading and process it digitally before displaying the result on an LCD. As a result, they can perform tricks such as recording a sequence of readings for future analysis rather than simply displaying it on-screen like older CROs, and they can also have multiple independent inputs so you can display different waveforms on-screen at the same time. Two, four, or eight individual input channels, each with their own timebase, are not uncommon.

The second instrument we need to discuss is a logic analyzer. Logic analyzers are a more recent development and came about from the need to track the digital status (high or low) of many connections in parallel, as well as a sequence of changes in series. With many digital devices using 8-, 16-, or 32-bit parallel buses internally, it can be handy to have a device that reads the logic level of each bus line independently and displays them all simultaneously, showing you what binary value was being transmitted at that point in time. Likewise, the transmission of a sequence of bits on a single serial data line can be captured and analyzed with a logic analyzer.

Advanced logic analyzers can deduce a tremendous amount of information about data that is passing through the circuit under test, and many also allow the operator to assign meaningful names to each input and to group inputs together. Some even apply heuristics to the data that has been acquired and process it to convert it into a meaningful form; for example, reading the raw electrical signals in an Ethernet connection and converting them into a bitstream before progressively decoding the layers of the network stack right up to, say, the HTTP packet level to display the message payload passing across the interface.

Once you start regularly using an oscilloscope or a logic analyzer, it's like your eyes have been opened to a vast amount of information and understanding that was previously locked away out of sight. Unfortunately, though, professional-quality oscilloscopes and logic analyzers don't come cheap and are out of the price range of most hobbyists.

But that doesn't mean you can't make do with a bit of ingenuity, and an Arduino makes a surprisingly good starting point for building your own basic test equipment. It has a decent number of digital inputs that can be used to sample the status of digital pins in a circuit under test, and even has analog inputs that can be used to build a crude oscilloscope so you can visualize analog waveforms using your PC monitor as the display.

In this project, we use an Arduino to capture multiple input values and pass them via the USB connection to a host computer running a program that deciphers the values and displays them on-screen. Because the Arduino itself is not providing any particular intelligence and simply passes on any values it reads, this project is very flexible and the behavior of the system can be changed simply by altering the software that runs on your computer. This opens up a wide range of possibilities for using the same basic hardware to process and visualize analog data, parallel digital data, and serial digital data.

The visualization program demonstrated in this project is written in Processing, a sister project to Arduino that is designed to allow rapid development of visual programs in the same way that Arduino allows rapid development of physical programs. Processing runs on Windows, Linux, and Mac OS X.

However, this simple approach has some major limitations in terms of both sample rate and resolution, so don't expect an Arduino-based system to rival a professional-grade oscilloscope or logic analyzer. The analog inputs on an Arduino operate by default at 10-bit resolution, which provides a scale of 0 to 1023. More advanced ADCs provide 12-bit resolution or higher. The Arduino analog inputs also take around 100 microseconds to take a reading in their default configuration, limiting the number of samples it can take per second and restricting it to much lower frequencies than a more advanced ADC.

The result is a system that will operate quite well at 10-bit resolution at up to around 5KHz, depending on how many channels you are monitoring. Not great specs, but certainly better than nothing if you can't afford a professional oscilloscope or logic analyzer. The required parts are shown in Figure 11-2, and the schematic is shown in Figure 11-3.

Parts Required

1 x Arduino Duemilanove, Arduino Pro, or equivalent

1 x Prototyping shield

1 x Panel-mount LED

1 x 470R resistor

1 x Black test clip or probe

8 x Yellow test clips or probes

1 x Black panel-mount socket

8 x Yellow panel-mount sockets

1 x Black line plug

8 x Yellow line plugs

5m shielded single-core cable

Metal project case

3 x 10mm plastic spacers

3 x 20mm M3 bolts with matching nuts

3 x Plastic insulating washers

4 x self-adhesive rubber feet

Source code available from
`www.practicalarduino.com/projects/scope-logic-analyzer`

***Figure 11-2.** Parts required for Arduino Oscilloscope / Logic Analyzer*

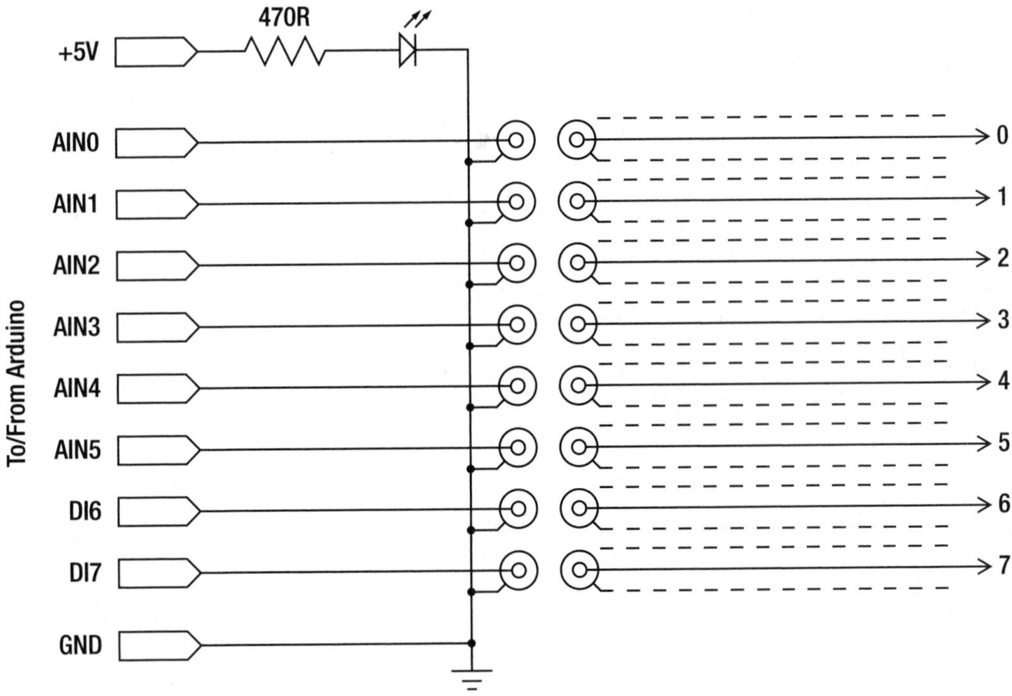

Figure 11-3. Schematic of Arduino Oscilloscope / Logic Analyzer

Instructions

The circuit for this project couldn't be much simpler. It's essentially just an Arduino with probes connected to a number of analog and/or digital inputs with all the hard work done in the software, plus a "power" LED to show when it's alive.

In our prototype, we fitted a total of eight input probes but because the Duemilanove and most other Arduino designs only have six analog inputs, we connected the first six probes to the analog inputs and the remaining two to digital inputs. This allows up to six analog waveforms to be sampled, which is plenty for most applications, but still allows up to eight digital lines to be analyzed in case we need to process an 8-bit parallel data bus.

Alternatively, you could use an Arduino Mega and take advantage of the fact that the Mega has 16 analog inputs. Just keep in mind that the more analog inputs you want to sample, the slower the program will run and the lower your sample frequency will be.

Or, if you only care about sampling one or two channels at a time, you could simplify things and leave the rest of the inputs off entirely. You could even use an Arduino Pro Mini and build the whole thing into a large probe body to create a single-channel, handheld device with a USB connection on the back. Bluetooth or ZigBee comms to the host computer would also be a possibility so that you could make it totally wireless. It's really up to you to decide how you want to configure it.

You'll note that we specified a metal project case and shielded cable for the probes. This is to reduce "cross talk" where a signal presented on one input influences the readings of other inputs by inducing tiny currents in them. You can certainly do without it but you may see a signal in one channel cause artifacts in the display for other channels.

You'll also note that we didn't bother including any form of input protection for the Arduino itself. The Arduino I/O lines are exposed directly on the front of the box as probe sockets, and the probes themselves connect those I/O lines straight to the circuit under test.

Initially, that may seem a little crazy. After all, what happens if you accidentally connect a probe to, say, a 24V circuit when the ATMega inputs are only rated to 5V?

The answer is that you'll probably blow at least that input on the ATMega CPU, if not the whole CPU itself, and will probably need to replace it. However, the fact is that buying a new ATMega328 is somewhere in the region of $8 at the time of writing, whereas fitting adequate input protection circuitry that would protect the CPU while not changing the characteristics of the inputs would be technically difficult and probably cost more than $8 in parts.

So we made a pragmatic decision to keep the circuit simple and acknowledge the fact that the ATMega CPU is inexpensive enough that we can simply pop it out and replace it if anything goes drastically wrong. Hopefully that won't be a common occurrence!

Assemble the Case

To make the end result look a bit more professional, we used a die-cast aluminum case that we lightly sanded with fine sandpaper before spraying it with gloss black paint. We also printed a front-panel overlay on self-adhesive paper with a color laser printer. The resulting front panel isn't especially durable, but does dress it up a little and helps make it clear which probe socket is which. The artwork for our panel is available for download from the project page on the *Practical Arduino* web site in case you'd like to use it.

Start by drilling the mounting holes for the Arduino. We mounted the case upside down with the lid on the bottom, allowing the Arduino and shield to be mounted on the inside of the lid on plastic standoffs with the probe sockets mounted on the side of the case. Because the sides of the case slope inward slightly, the Arduino had to be positioned a little back from the edge so that the power socket would clear the side while still keeping it as close as possible to the edge so the USB socket would protrude.

We used 10mm plastic spacers with 20mm M3 bolts passing up through the lid. The Arduino sits on the spacers with plastic washers on top to insulate the nuts from the circuit board. M3 nuts then hold it firmly in place and the result is that the Arduino is very securely mounted in the case. The USB cable can be inserted or removed with confidence that nothing will move around inside the box.

Turn the base over and stick a self-adhesive rubber foot in each corner so that it will sit nicely on a workbench without the bolt heads on the bottom making it rock around all over the place (see Figure 11-4).

The square USB socket needs to protrude through the side of the case but cutting square holes neatly can be very tricky. Depending on the material used in your project case you may be able to drill a single large hole in the middle of the area to be removed and then use a panel nibbler or Dremel tool to trim it to the correct dimensions. Otherwise, you might need to drill a series of small holes around the perimeter to remove the bulk of the material, then finish up with a file to neaten up the edges. The approach we took was to cut the hole as a slot from the edge of the case with a hacksaw and then breaking out the resulting tab. This leaves a little gap under the USB socket, but it's on the side of the box so it's not too unsightly and the result is that the cover can drop on easily over the Arduino.

Figure 11-4. *Arduino mounted on 10mm spacers using M3 bolts*

Next, mark the position for all the input probe sockets and the power LED.

To keep the paintwork and front label looking neat and unblemished, we also printed a disposable copy of the label on normal paper to use as a placement stencil. We taped the label to the box and used a center punch and a small hammer to tap a dimple into the center of each hole location, then removed the stencil and drilled pilot holes for the LED and probe socket holes. All this was done before the case was sprayed so the paint wouldn't be marred by the drilling process.

Once the paint was well and truly dry, we then stuck on the actual label and used a thin-blade craft knife to cut out all the holes (see Figure 11-5).

Insert the black panel-mount socket for the ground probe and the eight yellow sockets for the signal probes, and tighten up the nuts to hold them in place. We used RCA plugs and sockets in our prototype because they have a handy shield connection and are quite inexpensive. However, because they're not known for having the best quality electrical connection, and because electrical noise is important in a project like this, we used the best type we could get: gold-plated sockets and metal-body plugs. If you want to spend a bit more and use different connectors, you certainly can. The ones we used for our prototype worked fine for our purposes though.

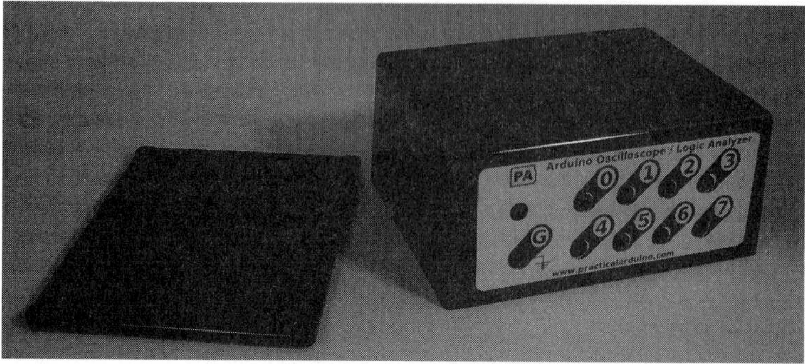

Figure 11-5. Front panel label in place with holes drilled

Alternatively, if you don't care about analog input and will only be measuring digital logic levels, you don't need to care about shielding and can go for cheaper plugs and sockets. Or you could do what many commercial logic analyzers do and combine all the inputs into a single multipin socket.

Next, mount the power LED. We used a relatively expensive panel-mount LED in a metal bezel, but you could just as easily use a regular LED and glue it into the hole or clip it into place with a plastic bezel if you prefer (see Figure 11-6).

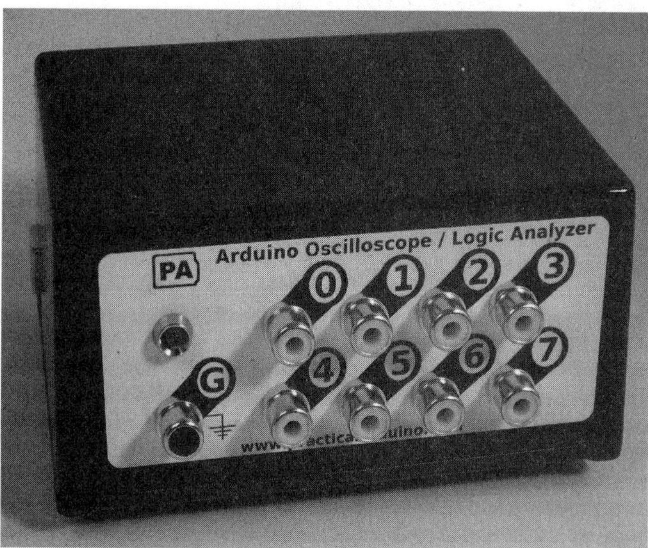

Figure 11-6. Connectors and LED mounted in front panel

At this point, the case looks like all the work is done, but it's still just a shell without the working internals in place.

Fit the Prototyping Shield

Cut eight short lengths of shielded single-core cable and strip back each end, then solder the center conductor of each cable between the panel-mount sockets and the prototyping shield. Inputs 0 through 5 connect to matching analog inputs 0 through 5, while inputs 6 and 7 connect to digital inputs 6 and 7, respectively. Also connect the shield braid to the GND power bar on the prototyping shield and to the outer terminals on the panel-mount sockets. By connecting the sockets this way, the entire case is connected to the Arduino ground and will be at 0V relative to the Arduino power supply, and each cable will be individually shielded between the socket and the prototyping shield. The signal will then have to travel down through the unshielded header pin to the Arduino and along the Arduino PCB to the input on the ATMega chip, of course, but by shielding as much of the signal path as practical, we improve the quality of the signal that will be sampled (see Figure 11-7).

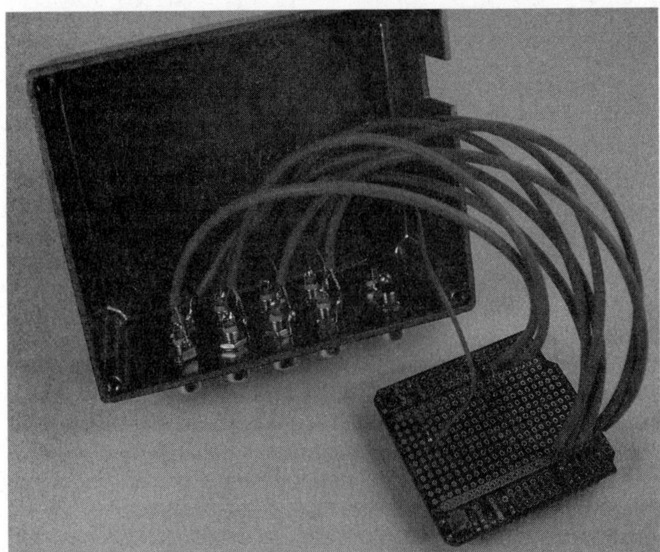

Figure 11-7. *Front panel connectors linked to prototyping shield using shielded cable*

Because the project case is well connected to ground via all the signal shields, we don't need a specific connection from the ground probe socket to the prototyping shield. We simply soldered a short piece of wire from the center pin on the socket to the tab for the shield connection, providing a good link from the case to the center pin through the body of the socket.

Next, fit the 680R resistor to the prototyping shield with one end connected to +5V and the other to a spare pad on the shield. Then run a length of hookup wire from the end of the resistor to the anode (long, or positive) lead of the panel-mount LED, and another short length of hookup wire from the cathode (short, or negative) lead of the LED to one of the panel-mount socket tabs so it connects to ground.

Make Test Probes

Depending on the types of circuits you test, you might find it handy to create a few different test probes for different purposes. Options include an alligator clip for attaching to bare wires or a metal case; a spring-loaded hook clip for linking to component pins; and a straight sharp probe for general-purpose use. Having a few different probe types handy can make things much easier.

We made a ground probe with a nickel-plated RCA plug, a black spring-loaded hook clip, and a length of unshielded hookup wire. We also made up test probes using shielded cable, connecting the center conductor to the test clip and the center pin of the RCA plug while the braided shield connects to the outer shield connection on the plug. A short length of heat-shrink tubing at the probe end of the cable keeps the trimmed end of the shield braid neat (see Figure 11-8).

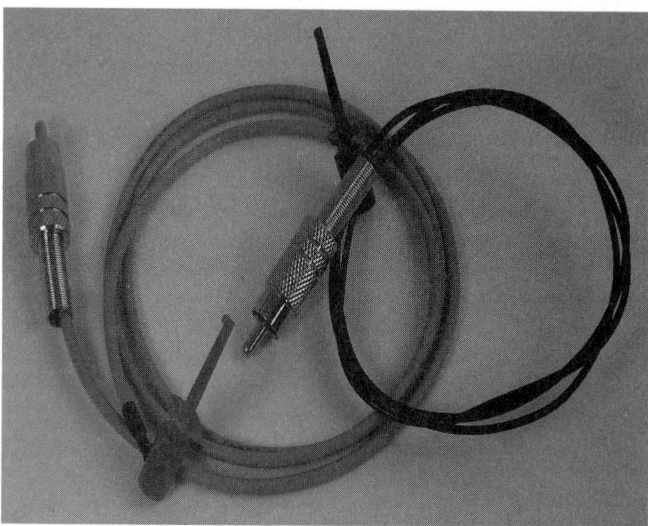

Figure 11-8. *Ground probe and test probe*

How Successive Approximation ADC Works

Converting an analog voltage level into its equivalent digital value (ADC) can be quite tricky, particularly if it needs to be done both quickly and accurately. The analog inputs on an ATMega CPU use a technique called "successive approximation ADC," which provides a decent trade-off between speed, accuracy, resolution, and complexity.

Successive approximation ADC uses a network of capacitors with exponentially scaled values that are first completely discharged to an offset voltage provided by a comparator, then charged to the voltage of the signal being sampled. The capacitors are then switched to the comparator input so that it is exposed to the same voltage as the original signal but with that voltage provided by the capacitors rather than by the circuit under test, which is completely isolated at that point. Each capacitor is then progressively switched to the reference voltage and the comparator compares the resulting voltage to the reference voltage to decide if it is higher or lower, and emit a 1 if it's higher or a 0 if it's lower. As each capacitor is switched, a new bit is emitted from the comparator.

The simplest way to conceptualize this is to imagine that the ADC starts with a very rough idea of the level of the input and progressively narrows it down to a more accurate value. The first reading, or bit, simply checks whether it's in the top or bottom half of the voltage range. If it's in the top half, it's 1; the lower half, it's 0. Then the second reading, or second bit, checks whether it's in the top or bottom half of that range. Every bit that is read doubles the resolution of the result by narrowing it down to a smaller part of the range (see Figure 11-9).

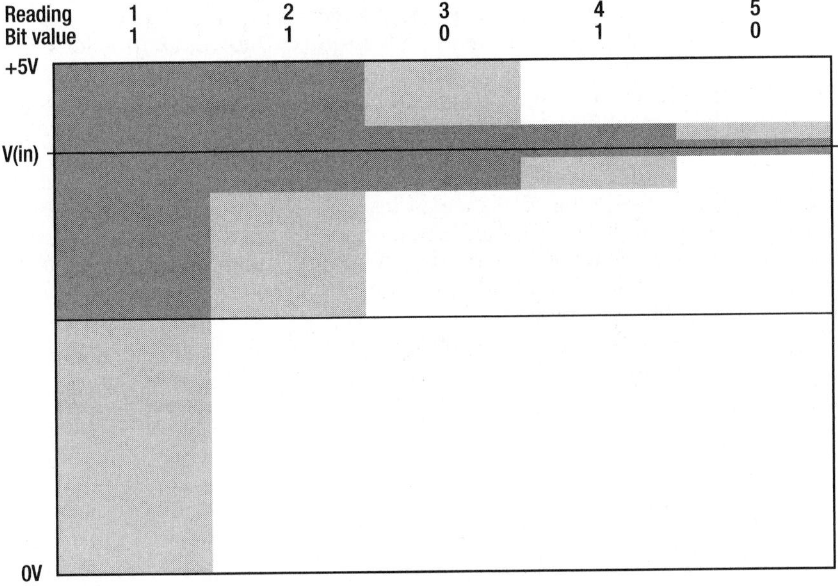

Figure 11-9. Successive-approximation ADC

This means that the number of capacitors in the array determines the number of successive readings and, therefore, the bits of resolution that the ADC can generate. In an ATMega each analog input uses a 10-capacitor array, so the highest resolution it can provide is a 10-bit value. This corresponds to a decimal number between 0 for a voltage at 0V, and 1023 for a voltage at the supply voltage of the system.

As you can imagine, it takes a little while for this process of discharging, switching, charging, switching, then stepping through each capacitor.

Adding more bits increases the resolution, but it also means more steps for the ADC circuit to perform while doing the conversion. Conversely, decreasing the number of bits also decreases the conversion time. A 10-bit sample on an ATMega used in an Arduino takes approximately 111 microseconds.

Compare this to reading a digital input, which is essentially just feeding the input signal straight to the comparator and returning a single bit immediately without going through all the steps with the capacitor array. That's why a digital read can take place in under one microsecond but an analog read takes more than one hundred times as long.

Note that the terms "accuracy" and "resolution" do not mean the same thing, even though many people use them interchangeably. Resolution tells us the number of intervals on a scale being used to measure something, while accuracy tells us how consistently the scale is applied. The resolution on an ATMega analog input is 10 bits, but it's not actually quite that accurate. By the time the ATMega gets to sampling the last two bits, there is a little bit of jitter in the voltage being tested and so they might fluctuate slightly even when reading a very consistent and accurately generated reference voltage. The resolution on the analog inputs may be 10 bits, but they don't actually provide quite that much accuracy.

If you want to do analog reads at the highest possible speed at the expense of a little accuracy it's possible to force the ATMega CPU to apply a custom prescaler value to the ADC clock. Because the ADC needs to perform a sequence of comparisons, the time it takes to complete an entire analog read is dependent on how quickly it can perform each individual step. The ATMega is rated to supply a clock rate of between 50KHz and 200KHz to its ADC depending on a combination of the overall CPU clock speed (16MHz on a typical Arduino) and the ADC prescaler factor. The Arduino environment sets the prescaler factor to a value of 128 in the file hardware/cores/arduino/wiring.c around line 231. This results in an ADC clock rate of 16MHz / 128 = 125KHz, which is well within the 50KHz to 200KHz range recommended by Atmel.

125KHz is a fairly conservative ADC clock rate, though, and you can get massive ADC speed gains by pushing it closer to its operational limit. The ATMega datasheet notes that ADC clock speeds up to 1MHz "do not reduce the ADC resolution significantly," which means that on a 16MHz Arduino you can push the prescaler value as low as 16 to increase the ADC clock speed right up to 1MHz (i.e., 16MHz / 16) and still get reasonably good accuracy. The result is analog reads that complete in around 16 microseconds—far faster than the 111 microseconds of a stock Arduino!

The settings can be altered by editing wiring.c so that it will apply to all programs you compile. The ATMega datasheet provides the data listed in Table 11-1 showing the effect of setting or clearing the three ADC prescaler select bits.

Table 11-1. *ADC prescaler bits and division factor*

ADPS2	ADPS1	ADPS0	Division Factor
0	0	0	2
0	0	1	2
0	1	0	4
0	1	1	8
1	0	0	16
1	0	1	32
1	1	0	64
1	1	1	128

Arduino sets all three bits to 1 in wiring.c with the following code:

```
sbi(ADCSRA, ADPS2);
sbi(ADCSRA, ADPS1);
sbi(ADCSRA, ADPS0);
```

The sbi call sets the bit, and a corresponding cbi call can also clear the bit. To set the prescaler value to 16 you would modify those lines to the following:

```
sbi(ADCSRA, ADPS2);
cbi(ADCSRA, ADPS1);
cbi(ADCSRA, ADPS0);
```

Rather than changing the Arduino environment, though, you can also do it directly within your Arduino program by using the previous code along with some macro definitions for sbi and cbi. For example, to change the prescaler value to 16 (first bit set, second and third bits cleared) you could start by adding the following macro definitions at the top of your program:

```
#ifndef cbi
#define cbi(sfr, bit) (_SFR_BYTE(sfr) &= ~_BV(bit))
#endif
#ifndef sbi
#define sbi(sfr, bit) (_SFR_BYTE(sfr) |= _BV(bit))
#endif
```

Then, inside the setup() function of your program, set and clear the appropriate bits using the sbi() and cbi() macros as follows:

```
sbi(ADCSRA,ADPS2);
cbi(ADCSRA,ADPS1);
cbi(ADCSRA,ADPS0);
```

Of course you could also set and clear different bits to achieve other prescaler values depending on your requirements.

Connection to Circuit under Test

Before testing a circuit the first thing to do is tie the Arduino oscilloscope's ground connection to the circuit ground using the black probe plugged into the GND socket. That provides the scope with a ground reference that's at the same voltage as the circuit ground, allowing the voltage of test points to be measured relative to it.

Figure 11-10 shows the ground lead connected to the ground of the circuit under test (an RFID reader shield on an Arduino Mega, in this case) with the test probe connected to the RX pin on the serial data connection to the RFID module.

If you need to frequently test ICs, you might find it worthwhile buying an IC test clip to suit the packages you use. An IC test clip is a spring-loaded device like a really wide clothes peg that fits over the top of an IC while it's in-circuit and exposes each pin as a test point on the top of the clip. This brings the electrical connections up high above the circuit to a convenient point for you to attach test probes.

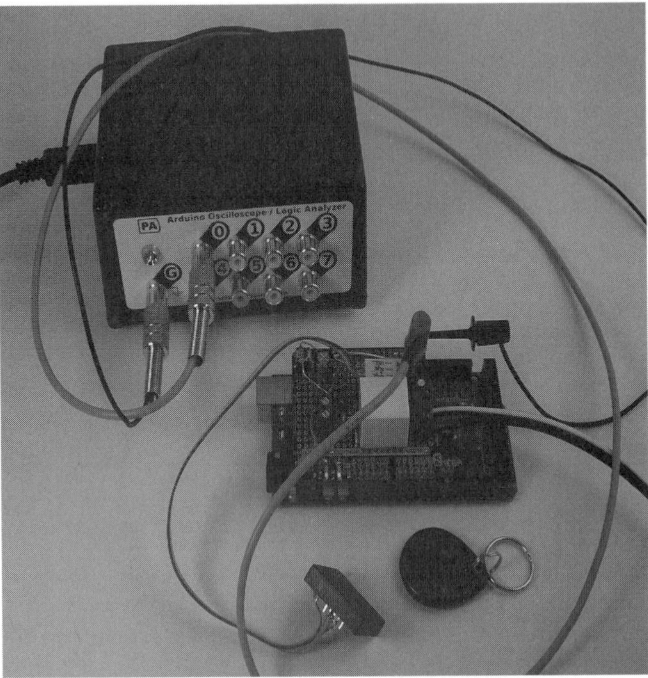

Figure 11-10. Connection to a circuit under test

Install Software in Arduino

Because all the hard work is done in the attached host, all the Arduino has to do is sample its inputs and send the values to the host as fast as possible. The Arduino program is, therefore, almost as simple as the circuit.

We've provided several different versions, though, because this project really pushes the limits of what the ATMega processor can do, and it's important to make the program run as fast as possible for the given test requirements. You can have different versions ready to go on your host computer and push them across to the Arduino as required for different tests.

Analog Read Version

The first version is the most flexible in terms of input values it can process but also the slowest, therefore providing the lowest sample rate. This is a good general-purpose sample program because it uses the first six inputs as analog inputs and returns a value from 0 to 1023 for each of those inputs, then reads the last two inputs as digital inputs and returns a value of either 0 for LOW or 1023 for HIGH.

However, this approach has performance limitations because reading an analog input takes over 100 microseconds, and the data stream returned to the host is quite verbose. For a typical reading the data stream sent to the host could look something like the following: `1023 1013 1001 992 981 972 0 0<CR><LF>`

To send a set of eight 10-bit values plus seven separator characters and a newline (CRLF) at the end requires between 17 and 41 bytes of data to be transmitted via the USB connection depending on the specific values. This limits it to sending to around 350 samples/second on average with the serial connection set to 115200bps.

Later examples attempt to overcome some of these limitations.

First, the program defines the cbi() and sbi() macros so we can use them to change the prescaler values.

```
#ifndef cbi
#define cbi(sfr, bit) (_SFR_BYTE(sfr) &= ~_BV(bit))
#endif
#ifndef sbi
#define sbi(sfr, bit) (_SFR_BYTE(sfr) |= _BV(bit))
#endif
```

Then the program defines a variable that will be used to store each reading as it is taken.

```
int val;
```

The setup() function sets the prescaler to 16 as described previously, then sets digital pins 6 and 7 to input mode and opens the connection to the host at 115200bps.

```
void setup() {
  sbi(ADCSRA,ADPS2);
  cbi(ADCSRA,ADPS1);
  cbi(ADCSRA,ADPS0);
  pinMode(6, INPUT);
  pinMode(7, INPUT);
  Serial.begin(115200);
}
```

The program loops as fast as possible, starting by taking a reading from each analog input starting at input 0 and counting up to analog input 5. The value from each input is sent straight to the host as soon as it is read, with a space character to separate them.

```
void loop() {
  for( int i=0; i<6; i++ ){
    Serial.print( analogRead(i) );
    Serial.print(" ");
  }
```

Because probes 6 and 7 are connected to digital inputs we have to fudge the values. If the reading is low, we return a value of 0; if it's high, we return a value of 1023. That way high and low values show the same range as the analog inputs, even though they'll never show an intermediate value like an analog input. Note that the values returned for input 6 have a space appended as a separator for the next value.

```
  if( digitalRead(6) == 1) {
    Serial.print(1023);
    Serial.print(' ');
  } else {
    Serial.print(0);
```

```
      Serial.print(' ');
    }

    if( digitalRead(7) == 1) {
      Serial.print(1023);
    } else {
      Serial.print(0);
    }
```

Once all the samples have been sent to the host the program sends a carriage return so the program running on the host knows it's reached the end of a line and needs to process it.

```
    Serial.println();
  }
```

Digital Read Version

A normal analog read takes over 100 microseconds and even our high-speed version takes about 16 microseconds, but a digital read can be accomplished in under 1 microsecond. It's therefore preferable to use digital reads if you don't care about the shape of the waveform and only want to know if a pin you are testing is high or low. This version of the program operates in the same basic manner as the previous version and returns data in the same space-separated format with one value per input probe so that it's compatible with the same host software, but it samples much faster by doing only digital reads rather than analog reads.

It's also optimized by using direct port manipulation rather than traditional Arduino-style calls to functions like digitalRead. The reason is that a simple function call like digitalRead(6) actually takes quite a few clock cycles to execute because what it does behind the scenes is:

1. Look up the Arduino pin number and convert it to the equivalent ATMega port number and pin number.
2. Disable any PWM (pulse-width modulation) functionality that might be running on that pin.
3. Read the pin.

Even after compilation this requires several dozen processor cycles just to do a simple digital read. There is work currently being performed to optimize digital read and write performance for a future release of Arduino, but at the time of writing they are fairly expensive operations in terms of processor time.

By addressing the appropriate ATMega port directly it's possible to perform a digital read in only a few cycles. This makes the code harder to read so it's not recommended for general Arduino projects, but in cases like this where we're squeezing every last bit of performance out of the processor it makes perfect sense.

As in the previous version the program starts by setting up the input pins, but because we're using analog inputs 0 through 5 in digital mode we address them using their alternative pin numbers as digital pins 14 through 19. Because the setup process isn't time critical we use the regular Arduino pinMode() function to configure the inputs rather than using direct port manipulation as in the main program loop.

Digital pins 6 and 7 are also set to input mode in the setup function and the connection to the host is opened at 115200bps.

```
void setup() {
  pinMode(14, INPUT);
  pinMode(15, INPUT);
  pinMode(16, INPUT);
  pinMode(17, INPUT);
  pinMode(18, INPUT);
  pinMode(19, INPUT);
  pinMode(6, INPUT);
  pinMode(7, INPUT);

  Serial.begin(115200);
}
```

The main program loop is where things get interesting. Rather than a series of lines something like "Serial.print(digitalRead(14));", it instead directly accesses the port registers and uses a bitmask to hide all the pins we're not interested in. The ATMega328P used in many Arduino models including the Duemilanove has three registers for each of the three ports exposed on an Arduino as I/O lines, with one register setting the direction (input or output) of each pin, one register storing the last value written to each pin, and one register returning the result of a digital read on each pin.

Port D is exposed as Arduino digital pins 0 through 7.

- DDRD: The port D Data Direction Register.
- PORTD: The port D Data Register.
- PIND: The port D Input Pins Register.

Port B is exposed as Arduino digital pins 8 through 13. The reason this isn't 8 through 15 is that the two high bits are used by the crystal that provides the Arduino with its clock source, so they're not available on the board as I/O lines.

- DDRB: The port B Data Direction Register.
- PORTB: The port B Data Register.
- PINB: The port B Input Pins Register.

Port C is exposed as Arduino analog pins 0 through 5. Once again the top two bits aren't usable in most Arduino designs because even though those pins exist on the CPU they simply aren't brought out on the Arduino's expansion headers.

- DDRC: The port C Data Direction Register.
- PORTC: The port C Data Register.
- PINC: The port C Input Pins Register

The loop takes the value of the appropriate input pins register (either PINC for the analog inputs or PIND for the digital inputs) and applies a bitmask before sending the result to the host. The & (logical AND) operator used to apply the bitmask takes two binary numbers and returns a number that only has bits set high where both the numbers have the corresponding bit set high. For example, the result of

```
B00001111 & B11000011
```

would be B00000011, because only the last two bits were set high in both numbers. By applying a sequence of bitmasks to the PINC and PIND values we can isolate the value of each pin and check whether it is low or high.

However, just applying the bitmask doesn't do everything we need because the value returned won't be just 0 for low or 1 for high except in the case of the very first pin. Reading the second pin would return 0 for low and 2 for high, while the third pin would return 0 or 4, the fourth 0 or 8, and so on. So after applying the bitmask we apply a bit shift right operator to move the bit we're interested in a certain number of positions to the right. That way, a value such as decimal 8 obtained by reading a high value on input 4 will be converted to a value of decimal 1, and the program will only ever return a 0 or a 1 value for any input pin depending on its state.

```
void loop() {
  Serial.print( PINC & B00000001 );
  Serial.print(" ");
  Serial.print( (PINC & B00000010) >> 1 );
  Serial.print(" ");
  Serial.print( (PINC & B00000100) >> 2 );
  Serial.print(" ");
  Serial.print( (PINC & B00001000) >> 3 );
  Serial.print(" ");
  Serial.print( (PINC & B00010000) >> 4 );
  Serial.print(" ");
  Serial.print( (PINC & B00100000) >> 5 );
  Serial.print(" ");
  Serial.print( (PIND & B01000000) >> 6 );
  Serial.print(" ");
  Serial.print( (PIND & B10000000) >> 7 );
```

Just as in the previous version, once all the samples have been sent to the host the program sends a carriage return so the program running on the host knows it's reached the end of a line and needs to process it.

```
  Serial.println();
}
```

Digital Read Sketch with Optimized Communications Format

The previous digital read sketch has a huge inefficiency in the way it communicates with the host, but it's one that was introduced deliberately to maintain compatibility with host-side software for processing the data and displaying it. There are several projects documented online to use an Arduino as an oscilloscope or logic analyzer and they generally use a data format consisting of individual readings from each pin transmitted as one or more bytes for each pin separated by spaces. That makes sense if you're dealing with analog values, but if all you care about is digital values it's a highly inefficient way of transferring data. Because the serial connection to the host is a major bottleneck that dramatically slows down the sample rate it's worth optimizing the data format to pump as much information through as possible in the smallest number of bytes.

If you want to represent the state of eight digital inputs simultaneously, the absolute minimum amount of data you can use is one byte, or eight bits. Each bit corresponds to the state of one of the inputs.

This version of the sketch is, therefore, designed to be incredibly fast and return just one byte of data per sample to represent the state of all eight inputs simultaneously. We even dispensed with the carriage return by making the host-side program assume that every byte received is one complete reading of eight inputs. That assumption only works because we're limiting ourselves to eight inputs, of course, but if you wanted to sample more inputs you could add a second data byte to represent inputs 8 through 15 and append a carriage return to signify the end of a sample to the host.

The program starts off just like the last one, setting up the pins and communications in the exact same way.

```
void setup() {
  pinMode(14, INPUT);
  pinMode(15, INPUT);
  pinMode(16, INPUT);
  pinMode(17, INPUT);
  pinMode(18, INPUT);
  pinMode(19, INPUT);
  pinMode(6, INPUT);
  pinMode(7, INPUT);

  Serial.begin(115200);
}
```

The difference is in the main program loop, which is actually simpler than the previous version because we don't have to muck around with sampling each bit individually and then bit-shifting the result.

Instead, we read the PINC and PIND registers just once each, apply a bitmask to each of them to ignore the top two bits on PINC and the bottom six bits on PIND, and use a bitwise "OR" operator (the | symbol) to combine them into a single byte before sending the result back to the host.

A bitwise OR operator combines two values by setting the resulting bit high if the corresponding bit is set high in either of the original values. For example, the result of

```
B11001100 | B00001111
```

would be B11001111 because the first two bits and the last four bits are all set to high in either or both of the original values.

Using the bitmask to select only the top two bits from PIND and the bottom six bits from PINC allows us to combine the two partial bytes into a single complete byte.

```
void loop() {
  Serial.print( (PIND & B11000000) | (PINC & B00111111) );
}
```

And that's it. All the magic is combined into that single optimized line, with the result that this version of the program will sample all eight digital inputs in under two microseconds and return the result as a single byte of data representing the current state of all eight inputs. It doesn't get much more optimized than that. Note, though, that this format won't work with the Arduinoscope program described next unless you modify the Arduinoscope data parser.

Install Processing and Run Visualization Program

In this project the Arduino does very little: it just samples its inputs and ships the values off to a host connected via USB as fast as possible. All the intelligence is in the program you run on the host.

There are several projects online for Arduino-based oscilloscopes, but one of the most well developed is Arduinoscope. All the code for Arduinoscope is published on Google Code for download. See code.google.com/p/arduinoscope/.We've also provided handy links on the project page at the *Practical Arduino* web site.

The Arduinoscope project consists of two parts: the sketch that runs on the Arduino, and the program that runs on the host. The first example sketch listed previously works in a very similar way to the sketch included in Arduinoscope, and returns its data in the same format with values separated by spaces and samples separated by newlines. The only difference is that we've added the ADC prescaler to make the conversion process run as fast as possible and tuned the pin selections to match the ones we wired up. If you prefer to run the Arduinoscope version of the program it will work just fine on the hardware we describe here, but depending on which inputs you wired up they may not match the channels in the program.

The project page on Google Code includes downloads for prepackaged versions for Windows, Linux, and Mac OS. The simplest approach is to just download a package and run it. There are also source downloads available if you're interested in modifying it to suit your requirements.

After downloading the appropriate version, open the folder and launch the program inside it to be presented with a display similar to the one shown in Figure 11-11.

Figure 11-11. *Arduinoscope program running on a host connected to an Arduino*

By default Arduinoscope is configured to display six input channels. With our hardware and the sampling program previously shown, the first six channels correspond to the analog inputs, so this is ideal if you want to read from analog circuits or see the shape of digital waveforms.

Arduinoscope supports a few different modes. The default mode simply shows the shape of the waveform being measured, but if you only care about the logical state (HIGH or LOW) of a line, you can click the LOGIC button in the top right for that channel. It will then highlight the entire channel in either red or green depending on whether the input is high or low, providing very quick visual feedback.

You can also pause individual channels and save the data to disk as a CSV file, so experiment with it a bit to learn about all the things it can do. And if you want to write your own variation you'll discover that the code has been neatly organized into a "scope" class that you can use in your own projects.

Note, though, that it won't work as-is with the "digital" version of the sampling program described previously because it expects values to be returned in the range 0 to 1023, while the digital sampler only ever returns values of 0 or 1. Arduinoscope will faithfully report either 0V or 0.005V (1/1023 of 5V) depending on the state of the input but the logic mode won't work because the input will never pass the threshold for a high value.

Variations

Input Voltage Prescaler

Arduino inputs can read values between 0V (ground) and the operating voltage of the CPU, which in the case of most Arduino designs is 5V. Some Arduinos run at 3.3V but they are the exception rather than the rule.

What this means for an Arduino-based oscilloscope or logic analyzer is that it can only be connected to circuits that run in that same voltage range. If you run in analog input mode and try plotting the waveform of an audio signal running through an amplifier at 36V, you'll probably blow the Arduino input if not the whole chip. Conversely, if you run in digital input mode and try to read the status of data lines on a 3.3V or 2.6V circuit, it might not be able to read a HIGH value because the voltage level of the system under test isn't high enough for the Arduino to read.

The solution to these problems is to apply a prescaler in the probe itself before the level is sent through to the Arduino for measurement.

Scaling down a high voltage to a safe level for the Arduino to read is quite simple using a voltage divider formed from two or more resistors. The principle of a voltage divider is that if you place a voltage across several resistors in series, the voltage at the points between the resistors will be a fraction of the total voltage.

This can be demonstrated by building a special input probe that uses a voltage divider connected between the probe input and the shield (ground) connection to bias one end of a divider network to 0V, with the other end of the network connected to the probe tip and the middle point connected to the probe input on the Arduino oscilloscope (see Figure 11-12).

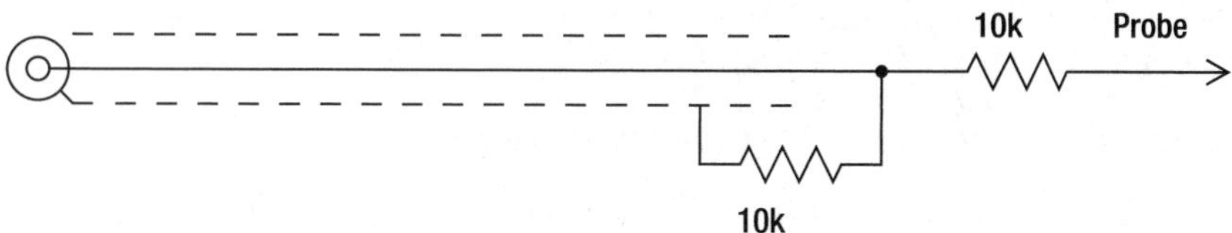

Figure 11-12. *2:1 Voltage divider probe*

If the probe is connected to a part of the circuit under test that happens to be at 10V, the full voltage will be seen at the start of the voltage divider, while 0V will be seen at the end thanks to the connection to ground. The matching pair of 10K resistors cause the voltage at the center point to be divided in half, presenting 5V to the Arduino input.

Using a pair of resistors of equal value gives a 2:1 voltage divider, but using different values allows you to change the division ratio. For example, a voltage divider with 40K at the top and 10K at the bottom would put the voltage at the division point at 1/5 of the total voltage.

This would allow you to connect the probe to circuits running at up to 25V while still only presenting up to 5V to the Arduino input.

Because of the way resistor ranges are scaled it's not actually possible to buy a 40K resistor, so one handy technique is to build a prescaler out of a resistor ladder consisting of multiples of the same value of resistor connected in series. You can even add a button or switch to let you select the prescale value, giving you a probe that can be altered depending on what you are trying to measure.

Scaling voltage up, on the other hand, is much trickier without altering the operation of the circuit under test. One of the basic principles of test equipment is not to alter the behavior of the circuit while you are measuring it, because otherwise your measurements could be invalid. An important concept in testing is input impedance, which is the effective resistance of the test equipment input as seen by the circuit under test. If the input has low impedance and is biased low, it will tend to pull the part of the circuit being measured down to a low voltage, and if it's biased high it will tend to pull it to a high voltage. Having a very high input impedance (typically in the region of several million ohms) is highly desirable because it minimizes the impact on the circuit under test.

Feeding the probe input to a transistor via a limiting resistor will allow the signal to be amplified, but could actually alter the characteristics of the circuit by presenting an input impedance that is too low and drawing too much current into the transistor. What is needed is an amplifier with a very linear response across its entire range and a very high input impedance. A circuit based around an op-amp might fit the bill, but since it's not a typical requirement for the sorts of circuits used with an Arduino it won't be covered here.

A simple, low-performance solution to the problem that would work with the hardware described in this project unchanged is to use analog inputs and apply a scaling factor to the readings. This would cause you to lose some resolution because only part of the input range would be exercised, but it may be acceptable in some situations.

It's also possible to change the ADC input range by changing the analog reference voltage. More information on this technique is available on the Arduino site at:

`www.arduino.cc/en/Reference/AnalogReference`

Resources

There are a number of different Arduino-based oscilloscope and logic analyzer projects, and they should all work with the hardware described in this project simply by changing the program on the Arduino and the program you run on the host. Experiment with a few and find the one that suits your needs best.

Poor Man's Oscilloscope: `accrochages.drone.ws/en/node/90`
Arduinoscope: `code.google.com/p/arduinoscope/`
Macduinoscope: `www.gabuku.com/scopeAVR`
Logic Analyzer: `www.uchobby.com/index.php/2008/09/09/avr-logic-analyzer/`

The Arduino site has some useful pages explaining how the analog inputs work as well as background on the direct port manipulation we used in the digital sampler program in this project.

```
www.arduino.cc/en/Tutorial/AnalogInputPins
www.arduino.cc/en/Reference/PortManipulation
```

If you want to learn a bit more about oscilloscopes and logic analyzers in general, there are good pages on Wikipedia about both topics.

```
en.wikipedia.org/wiki/Logic_analyzer
en.wikipedia.org/wiki/Oscilloscope
```

CHAPTER 12

■ ■ ■

Water Tank Depth Sensor

Water is a precious resource in many parts of the world and many people rely on water tanks to supplement their water supply by storing collected rainwater or water pumped from a well or bore. But how do you measure how full a tank is? Tanks are constructed of opaque material to prevent algae growth and are often kept closed up to prevent mosquito infestation or access by rodents, so it's inconvenient to physically look inside. And besides, having a way to measure tank depth electronically opens up a world of possibilities, such as automatic control of pumps to fill tanks when they get low or to disable irrigation systems when not enough water is available.

The obvious way to measure tank depth is by placing a series of conductive pickups at various heights inside the tank and measure the resistance between them. For example, you could attach ten exposed terminals at equal intervals on a length of material such as PVC tubing, and insert it into a tank vertically to measure the depth in 10 percent increments simply by reading the resistance between the bottom terminal and each of the terminals above it. The downside to this approach, though, is that you'll need to do a lot of wiring and you'll also need to read an analog input for every individual terminal. Also keep in mind that most Arduino designs have no more than six analog inputs. There are ways around this, such as using a resistor ladder, but it can still end up being quite time-consuming and still give very poor resolution.

This project works a little differently. It uses a device called a pressure transducer to measure the water pressure at the bottom of the tank, and from that measurement it calculates how full the tank is. Water pressure increases by about 9.8kPa per meter of depth (varying slightly depending on the purity of the water and other factors), so a full tank 1.5 meters tall will have a pressure at the bottom of about 14.7kPa above ambient atmospheric pressure. The "above ambient atmospheric pressure" part is important: it's not enough to simply measure the pressure at the bottom of the tank using a single-ended "absolute" pressure transducer because varying climate conditions will alter the reading as the air pressure changes. That's why this project uses a "differential" pressure transducer that has two inlets. By leaving one inlet open to the atmosphere and connecting the other to the bottom of the tank, the transducer will output the difference between the two. This approach provides automatic compensation for varying air pressure and giving a constant reading for constant depth even if the weather changes. The Arduino then reads the output of the transducer and reports the depth of the tank.

In this project we will use an Ethernet shield so the Arduino can connect to an online datalogging service called Pachube (`www.pachube.com`) to generate graphs of water depth over time, but you could also have it make decisions based on water depth to control items such as a water pump or irrigation system solenoid. You can see the required parts in Figure 12-1 and the complete schematic in Figure 12-2.

Parts Required

1 x Arduino Duemilanove, Arduino Pro, Seeeduino, or equivalent

1 x Ethernet shield or WiShield

1 x Prototyping shield

1 x MPX2010DP or MPX2053DP differential pressure transducer (see text)

1 x LM324 op-amp

1 x 14-pin IC socket

4 x 1K resistors

3 x 22K resistors

1 x 1K multiturn variable resistor

1 x 10K multiturn variable resistor

2 x 10nF MKT capacitors (typically marked "103")

1 x 100nF MKT capacitor (typically marked "104")

10cm of 4mm tubing (commonly used for aquarium air pumps)

3 x 4mm internal-diameter cable glands (typically sold as "3 to 6.5mm")

1 x small weatherproof PVC box (we used 64mm × 58mm × 35mm)

1 x medium weatherproof PVC box with O-ring seal (we used 115mm × 90mm × 55mm)

2 meters flexible four-conductor wire (such as security cable or telephone wire)

Source code available from
`www.practicalarduino.com/projects/water-tank-depth-sensor`

Figure 12-1. *Parts required for water tank depth sensor*

Instructions

If you come from a software background and haven't done much work with electronics before, this circuit can look a little intimidating, particularly as it deals with analog voltage levels rather than nice, neat, "on or off" digital levels.

The key to understanding the circuit is to temporarily ignore the section in the top right of the schematic shown in Figure 12-2 and just look at the overall symmetry of the central section, starting from the MPX2010DP differential pressure transducer on the left.

Before getting into the details, though, you need to consider the requirements for the pressure transducer. The MPX2010DP is fairly commonly available, but is only rated to 10kPa, equivalent to the pressure from just over a meter of water depth. In testing we've used it in tanks up to two meters deep and it's performed fine, but keep in mind that doing so is pushing the transducer beyond the manufacturer's specifications, and if you need to measure depth of a larger tank you may need to use a part with a higher pressure rating. For example, at the high end of the scale, the MPX2053DP is a similar part that is rated to 50kPa—equivalent to 5m of water depth.

The transducer has two ports protruding from it and will generate a tiny voltage differential between its outputs that is proportional to the difference in pressure between those ports. If the pressure applied to both ports is the same, the sensor will remain in equilibrium and the voltage on both outputs will be about half of the supply voltage, or about 2.5V in our case. The difference between them will, therefore, be zero. If the pressure applied to port 1 is higher than the pressure applied to port 2, the voltage on pin 2 will rise and the voltage on pin 4 will fall. The variation is tiny, though: a pressure differential of 10kPa will cause a voltage differential of only about 12.5mV.

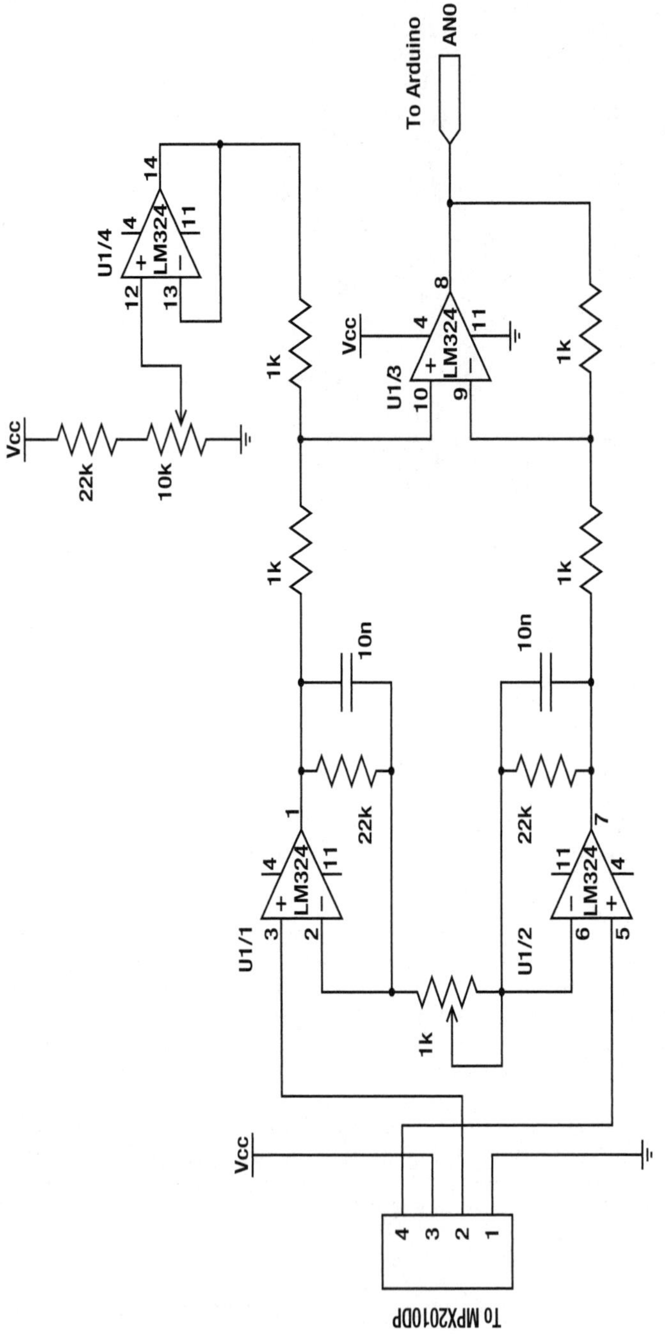

Figure 12-2. Schematic of water tank depth sensor

That's too small to be measured reliably by an analog input on an Arduino, so the rest of the circuit is dedicated to amplifying that voltage differential up to a higher level.

The two transducer outputs are fed into the inputs of "operational amplifiers," more commonly referred to simply as "op-amps." Op-amps are perhaps one of the most commonly manufactured nonpassive electronic devices ever, and they work by taking the difference between two inputs and outputting a signal that is an amplification of that difference. As such, we could have just used a single op-amp and fed both outputs from the transducer into it, but that wouldn't have provided enough gain to raise the signal to a level that the Arduino can read reliably. To overcome this we use a compound amplifier circuit that amplifies each of the outputs individually, driving the high signal further above the 2.5V reference point and the low signal further below 2.5V. The result is that the voltage difference between pins 1 and 7 on the outputs of op-amps 1 and 2 will be greater than the voltage difference between the transducer outputs.

The combination of the 22K resistors and 10nF capacitors linking the output of op-amps 1 and 2 back to their inputs provide "negative feedback," with a rise in output level decreasing the gain to maintain stability. It helps the amplifier maintain a steady state and may look counterintuitive, but this is a very common configuration for op-amps and you'll see it in many analog circuits. For more explanation of negative feedback op-amp circuits, see the Wikipedia page at en.wikipedia.org/wiki/Operational_amplifier.The 1K multiturn variable resistor joining the negative op-amp inputs together also controls the gain so that the overall effectiveness of the amplification circuit can be altered to best suit the characteristics of the transducer. Most variable resistors are single-turn, and adjust from 0R to their maximum rating through only about 270 degrees of rotation. That doesn't provide enough sensitivity when tuning an op-amp circuit, though, so we've specified multiturn variable resistors that are commonly available in either 10-turn or 20-turn versions. Multiturn variable resistors have a tiny threaded rod inside to gear down the turns you apply and provide very fine control of their resistance.

The outputs from the op-amps in the center of the schematic shown in Figure 12-2 then pass through a pair of 1K resistors and into the two inputs of op-amp 3, which once again amplifies the difference to drive an even greater variation on its output on pin 8. The result is that tiny variations in voltage across the transducer outputs on the extreme left of the circuit cause much larger voltage variations at the output on the far right where it will be connected to an Arduino analog input.

That's not quite the whole story, though. The section of the circuit we've been ignoring up in the top right also comes into play, biasing the input on pin 12 of op-amp 4, which in turn biases the input on pin 10 of op-amp 3. When tuning the circuit, the 10K variable resistor is adjusted until the output of op-amp 4 at pin 14 is about 1V when the pressure difference on the transducer is zero. This provides a base level of 1V to the Arduino input when the tank is empty.

Having set the bias for an empty reading, the 1K variable resistor controlling the gain on the first two op-amps is adjusted until the output to the Arduino is about 3V when port 1 of the transducer is exposed to the pressure at the bottom of a full tank. The circuit, therefore, has an output voltage that swings linearly between about 1V for an empty tank and 3V for a full tank, a variation of 2V.

So why bother with the bias to pull the "empty" value up to 1V and limit the gain to set the full value at 3V? Why not remove the "empty" bias and increase the amplification to provide a wider swing from 0V to 5V on the output and take advantage of the full input range of the Arduino's analog to digital converters?

The reason is that the performance characteristics of an op-amp typically don't allow it to provide a full rail-to-rail swing, and even if they could do so the linearity of the output could be compromised toward the edge of the range. Limiting it to a 1V-to-3V swing is well within the performance rating of the LM324 op-amp we're using, though, and avoids the non-linear regions toward the edges.

Looking at the schematic in Figure 12-2 you may be a little confused by the fact that it shows four op-amps, while looking at the photos there is only one integrated circuit. That's because the LM324 is a quad package with four op-amps inside one physical chip, all sharing common power and ground connections. Perfect for this application. What you see in the schematic is the logical representation of the four op-amps contained in the package because as far as the circuit is concerned they are separate devices. The fact that they're in the same physical package is just extra convenience for us when it comes to assembly.

Assemble the Shield

Begin by fitting the 14-pin IC socket, noting the direction of the orientation marker: the little notch in one end. That notch indicates which end of the chip is pin 1, which in the photo shown in Figure 12-3 is in the bottom right corner of the IC socket. The rest of the pins are numbered counterclockwise up the right side to 7 in the top right, 8 in the top left, and down to 14 in the bottom left with the socket oriented as shown in the photo. Note that this is rotated 180 degrees compared to most IC datasheets, which typically show the orientation marker at the top with pin 1 on the top left. In this case, though, it made sense to mount the chip upside down so the supporting parts are nearer the appropriate IC pins.

Next insert the resistors immediately adjacent to the socket, bending the leads underneath the shield to form jumpers to adjacent pads where necessary. The pair of 10nF MKT capacitors (probably marked "103K") just to the right of the socket go in next, and then the resistors are mounted vertically next to them. Then fit the 10K multiturn variable resistor on the left (marked "103"), and the 100nF MKT capacitor next to it (marked "104K") along with the jumpers that link them to ground and +5V. The 1K multiturn variable resistor and associated links go on the right.

For convenience when assembling and testing the system we fitted a 4-pin oriented male header for the cable to the pressure transducer. If you prefer, you can solder a lead for the transducer directly to the board.

Figure 12-3. *Parts assembled on shield ready for insertion of LM324 op-amp into the IC socket*

That's all the hard assembly work done. The only thing left to do on the prototyping shield is to install a jumper lead that connects pin 8 of the op-amp to analog input 0 on the Arduino. The 1K resistor mounted on the end connected between pins 8 and 9 provides a very convenient mounting point for one end of the jumper lead, which then stretches across the board to analog input 0. Connecting the op-amp output to the analog input with a jumper lead like this makes it easy later if you want to switch to a different input so you can stack multiple shields.

Finally, insert the LM324 op-amp into the socket. Inserting ICs can be tricky at first because the legs always spread out wider than the holes in the socket. You can buy special tools for inserting ICs into sockets but they're really not necessary on a small IC like an LM234: it's just as easy to bend the pins in a little until they align with the holes in the socket. Try putting the IC down on your workbench on one edge, grip it on the ends, and very carefully push down to bend the pins in. Turn the IC over and do the same to the other side so it will fit into the socket neatly. Be cautious in applying pressure to the pins, but don't be afraid. The worst that can happen is you bend them too far and have to bend them back.

You'll also notice a short link near the bottom left of the board to connect one of the LEDs provided on this particular prototyping shield to ground. The other end of the LED is connected to +5V via a 1K current-limiting resistor. That LED is included just to show when the shield is powered up and is entirely optional, so it doesn't appear in the circuit diagram.

Figure 12-4. *Fully assembled tank depth sensor shield*

Put the shield aside for a while and move on to assembling the sensor housing.

Determine Sensor Installation Method

Although the basic circuit will be the same regardless of how you mount it, this project has several options regarding how you expose the transducer to the pressure at the bottom of the tank while also exposing it to atmospheric pressure outside the tank. Before starting construction of the sensor assembly you need to think about how it will be connected.

There are four basic options for installation. The first, and most obvious, is to fit the Arduino and shield into a weatherproof case mounted just above the tank with one transducer hose exposed to the atmosphere and the other running down inside the tank with a weight attached to hold it on the bottom (see Figure 12-5). This can work in the short term but can cause problems over time due to diffusion of air in the tube into the water in the tank. Eventually, the water level will rise up the hose with the result that your Arduino will be reading the pressure from the height of the top of the water in the hose, not the pressure at the bottom of the hose. If left in long enough, a full tank will appear to be slowly draining until you get an "empty" reading. Of course, you can periodically pull the hose out of the tank and drain it to restore accuracy, but it's not really a good long-term solution.

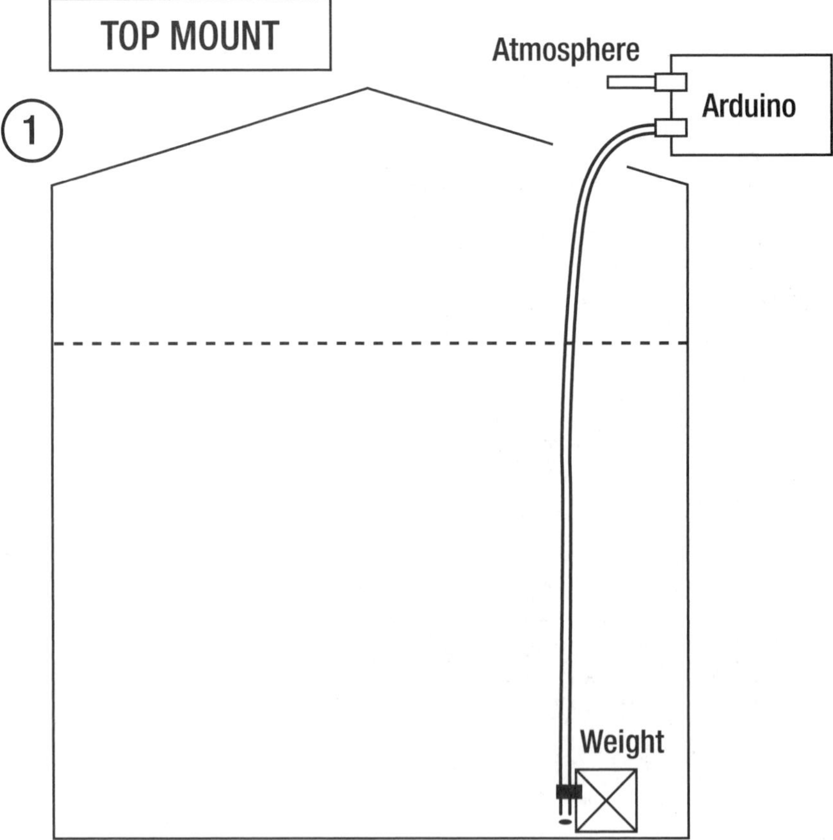

***Figure 12-5.** Pressure transducer mounted above tank*

The second option is to mount the entire Arduino and sensor inside a waterproof container submerged at the bottom of the tank with a short hose exposed to the water and a long hose running up and exiting the tank to provide an atmospheric pressure reference (see Figure 12-6). You'll also need to pass the power and data cabling up through the tank, and it goes without saying that electricity and water don't mix, so you need to be very careful to totally seal the assembly! Plastic project boxes with waterproof O-ring seals are fairly commonly available, and combined with waterproof cable glands and liberal doses of silicone sealant you should be able to build an assembly that can withstand long-term submersion without problems. Getting access to the Arduino for maintenance, though, could be quite tricky, and condensation in the atmospheric tube could build up over time.

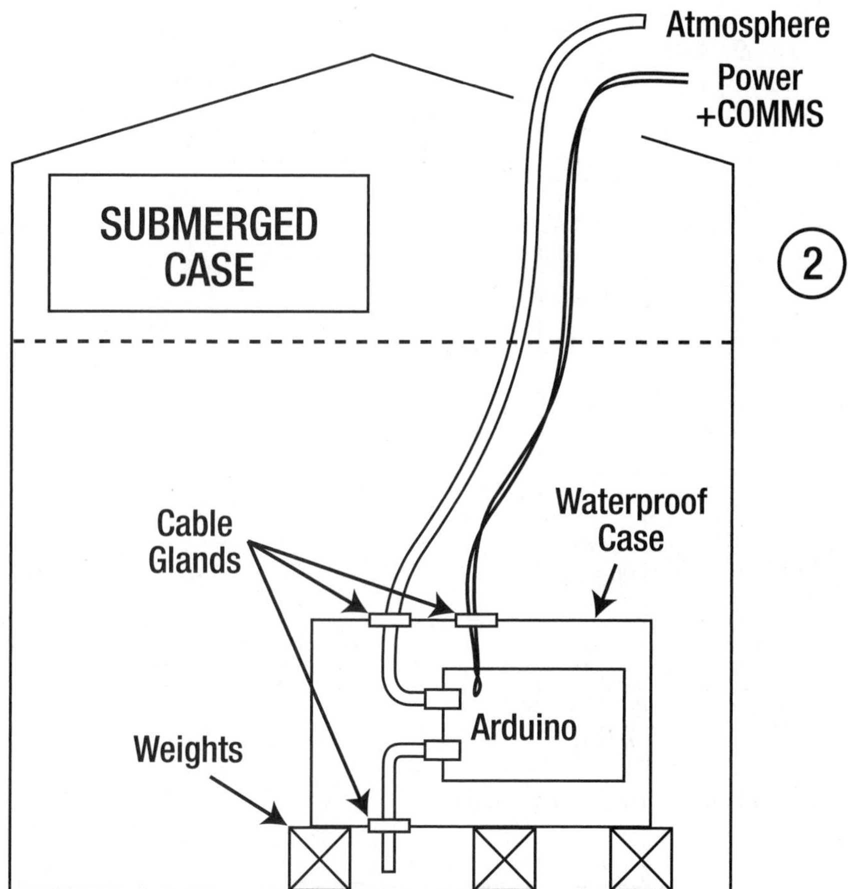

Figure 12-6. *Pressure transducer and Arduino mounted inside tank*

The third option is a clever variation on the previous approach that replaces the project box with a length of large-diameter pipe, sealed at one end and protruding from the bottom of the tank all the way up out of the water, or alternatively, a sealed box with a pipe attached. An Arduino with two shields stacked on top will slide easily into the end of a 75mm (3-inch) PVC pipe, and you can then pass a short length of hose out through a cable gland to sample the water pressure near the bottom of the tank. A 2m length of 75mm pipe can be inserted vertically into a tank with the top protruding, but be warned that it will displace a surprisingly large volume of water and will be extremely buoyant, so you will need to attach a significant weight to hold it down (see Figure 12-7).

You'll also need to make sure the top isn't directly exposed to the weather so the pipe fills up and drowns your Arduino first time it rains! And you'll be limited to using cabled Ethernet rather than WiFi for communications because a WiFi shield surrounded by several tons of water will have no range at all. Overall, though, this is a very practical way to do it and gives you reasonable access to the Arduino for future maintenance, but watch for corrosion over time since air can circulate so easily all the way down to the circuitry.

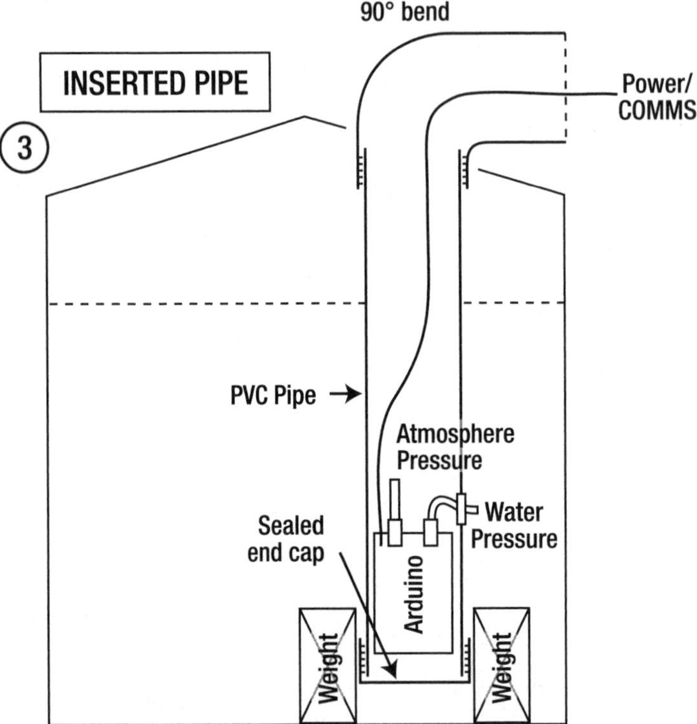

Figure 12-7. Pressure transducer and Arduino mounted in a pipe

The fourth option, and the one we recommend, is to mount the Arduino just outside the tank with a short hose from the pressure transducer entering an attached pipe, such as the outlet (see Figure 12-8). This is probably the safest way to go because you end up with no hose required at all to sample the outside air, a very short hose to sample water pressure, and much less chance of your Arduino suddenly turning into a submarine because you missed a spot with the silicone sealant. You retain excellent access to the Arduino for maintenance, it's not blocked by the mass of water so WiFi should still work well, and by placing it all in a weatherproof enclosure you can minimize corrosion and other bad things that happen to exposed electronics left outdoors.

The downside, though, is that this fitting method is much harder if your tank is already full of water. You'll need to drill a hole into the output pipe, and unless you do it on the outside of the stop valve you'll need to drain the tank first. Putting it on the outside of the valve isn't a perfect solution either, though, because you'll get an empty reading whenever the valve is closed. If your tank is full and there's no way to fit the pressure sensor without draining it, you might have to resort to one of the mounting methods described previously.

This is the mounting method we'll describe in this project, though, because it's definitely the safest for your Arduino.

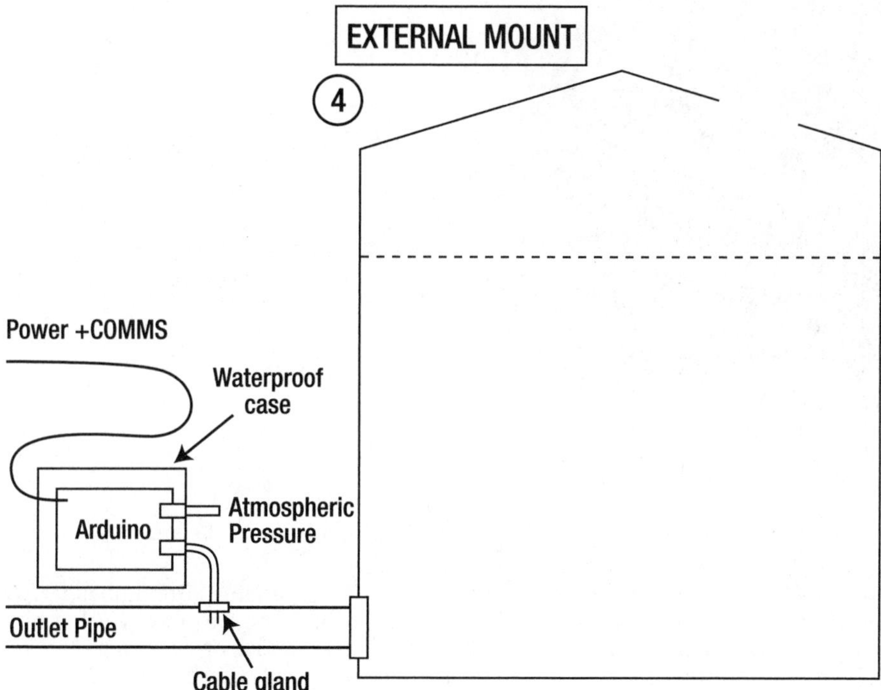

Figure 12-8. *Pressure transducer and Arduino mounted near outlet*

Assemble the Sensor Housing

If you intend to mount the sensor submerged inside the tank you will need to use your own creativity to determine a method to house and seal it. A good starting point would be to assemble the sensor box following our instructions and then add large quantities of silicone sealant and a long tube attached to transducer port 2 to exit the top of the tank.

For our prototype, we mounted the pressure transducer inside a small PVC project box by drilling holes in the back of the box and attaching the transducer using small bolts and plastic spacers to hold it 10mm clear of the back (see Figure 12-9). The box already had small spacers molded in place, but because they were in the wrong location and not quite long enough we didn't use them and added our own instead. Spacers are necessary to provide enough clearance for the sensor hose to be attached to the port on the transducer, and without them the transducer port won't have enough clearance from the back of the box.

After test-fitting the transducer in the box, measure the distance from the front edge of the box to the center of the port on the inside of the box and then use a felt-tip pen to transfer the measurement onto the outside.

***Figure 12-9.** Transducer mounted inside weatherproof box using plastic spacers and M3 bolts*

You can see in Figure 12-9 that the transducer is mounted upside down with the part number marking hidden on the other side of the case. This is to allow port 1 (the port opposite pin 4, which is on the top right in the picture) to be aligned vertically near the center of the box and provide enough clearance for the cable gland. Your physical mounting arrangement may vary, of course, so you'll need to plan how you will mount the transducer while retaining sufficient clearance for connections to it.

Measure sideways from one edge of the box and once again transfer that measurement to the outside, then remove the transducer and drill a small pilot hole through the box at the intersection of the markings. Drill a hole for a second cable gland on one of the other sides for the cable to the Arduino, keeping in mind the location in which the sensor box will be mounted. The cable can enter from the top, side, bottom, or even back of the box, whichever is most convenient.

Also drill a small hole of perhaps 2 or 3mm in the bottom of the box, well clear of the area that will be covered by the cable gland nut so that the inside air pressure will always be the same as atmospheric pressure. Alternatively, you could drill a hole just large enough for the tubing and fit a very short piece to port 2 on the transducer so that it just protrudes outside the box, keeping the inside of the box isolated from the atmosphere.

Switch to a drill bit large enough to allow the cable gland to be mounted (we used a 13mm spade bit) and enlarge the holes for the tubing and the cable. Use a hobby knife to clean up the edges of the large holes so there are no burrs to obstruct the cable glands or keep them from sitting flat against the box (see Figure 12-10).

Figure 12-10. Transducer mounting box with holes drilled for cable glands and pressure equalization

The purpose of the cable glands is not to provide a watertight seal, because the box needs to be open to the atmosphere anyway to sample ambient atmospheric pressure. Rather, the cable glands provide physical support for the tubing and cable and protect the transducer port from mechanical strain if the tubing or box are moved.

If you don't have any cable glands available you can make do without them, but you will need to make sure the tubing has good mechanical support as it enters the box. You could drill the hole out to the same size as the outside diameter of the tubing so that it fits through but is a snug fit. After everything is assembled and tested, you could then apply silicone sealant to the tube and cable to give them some mechanical support.

Before mounting the transducer back in the box it's a good idea to put a drop of mineral oil (commonly sold as baby oil) into each port. The mineral oil will help protect the transducer from water.

Fit one end of the tubing onto transducer port 1 while it's still out of the box. The tubing should be a very tight fit onto the transducer and you might have quite a bit of trouble getting it on. A handy trick is to boil some water and pour it into a mug, then hold the end of the tubing in the hot water for a minute to soften it up. Slide it onto the transducer while it's still hot and it should go on much more easily, then when it cools down it will shrink and form a tight seal. Just remember that if the tube isn't sealed properly onto the transducer port the water pressure from the tank may cause it to spray out inside the box, quickly flooding your expensive pressure transducer.

Slide the tubing through the cable gland mounted in the box until the transducer is in the correct place and is aligned with the spacers. Bolt it in again, and tighten up the cable gland around the tubing enough to give it good support without squashing it closed (see Figure 12-11).

Figure 12-11. *Transducer mounted with pressure hose fitted and cable gland for connection to Arduino in place*

To save you time later it's best to do a test-fit of the four-core cable at your actual tank, running it from the location in which you'll mount the sensor box to the location you'll mount the Arduino. Add a meter or so of extra length for safety and cut it to length so you can finish the assembly in the comfort of your workbench instead of trying to solder things together out in the yard.

Having cut it to length, insert one end of the four-core cable into the box through the other cable gland and strip back the ends, then solder them onto the pins of the pressure transducer. Make a note of which color connects to each pin for future reference. We used short lengths of heat-shrink tubing over each joint to help keep moisture off them.

Pin 1 on the transducer is marked with a tiny notch, with port 2 directly opposite pin 1, and port 1 directly opposite pin 4 (see Figure 12-12). The pin assignements are shown in Table 12-1.

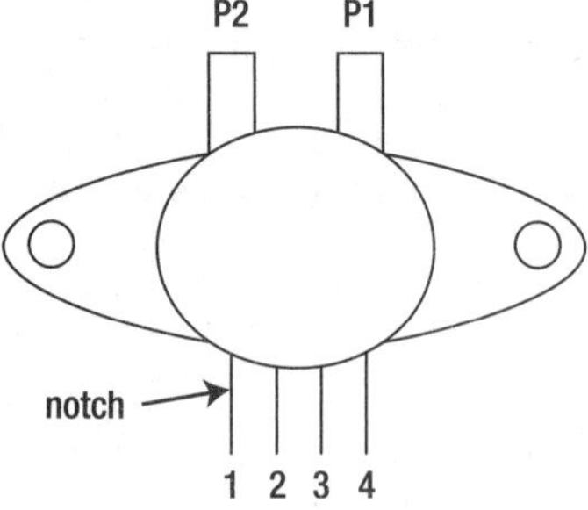

Figure 12-12. *Pin numbers and ports for pressure transducer*

Table 12-1. Pressure transducer pin assignments

Pin	Purpose
1	Ground
2	+Vout
3	Power
4	-Vout

Our cable had red, green, white, and yellow leads inside, so we connected black to pin 1 for ground, white to pin 2 for the +V output, red to pin 3 for +5V, and yellow to pin 4 for the -V output (see Figure 12-13).

***Figure 12-13.** Transducer box fully assembled and ready to be closed up*

The sensor assembly is all ready to go, so screw the lid on and put it aside.

Assemble the Arduino Housing

Mounting the Arduino along with the WiShield and the tank depth shield in a weatherproof box follows pretty much the same process as building the sensor assembly. Sit the Arduino in the bottom of the box and mark the location of the mounting holes. In our prototype we wanted to provide external access to the USB and power connections with everything mounted in place, so allowance had to be made for the distance the USB socket protrudes from the board. We marked the position of the mounting holes with the Arduino pushed up hard against the bottom of the box, then measured the distance that the USB socket protruded and offset all the markings by that same distance toward the bottom. This way, when the USB and power holes are cut, the Arduino will slide into them and the mounting holes will be in the correct location (see Figure 12-14).

Figure 12-14. *Determining the location of the mounting holes*

Cutting square holes is always awkward. We started by drilling a small hole in each corner, then drilled holes down each edge. The major section of the center of each hole was then clipped out with wire cutters before the edges were trimmed straight with a hobby knife.

Also drill a hole for a cable gland, once again keeping in mind where the cable will be mounted. We fitted the cable so it exits on the right-hand side of the box.

Fit M3 bolts up through the holes in the back of the box and sit 10mm spacers on top of them, then slide the Arduino down into the holes in the bottom and onto the bolts. This might take a bit of experimentation, but it shouldn't be too difficult if you let the bolts slide back down a little bit while you get the Arduino in position.

Put insulating washers over the bolts on top of the Arduino, followed by nuts, then tighten the bolts to hold everything firmly in place (see Figure 12-15).

With the Arduino mounted in the box plug the WiShield on top. One very neat thing about the WiShield is that it ships with long-lead female headers and all the parts on the board are kept low to make it stackable, so for this project it's perfect: after plugging the WiShield into your Arduino, just plug the prototyping shield on top to create a triple-decker assembly with the connector for the sensor cable easily accessible.

Slide the four-core sensor cable through the cable gland, strip back the insulation from the end of the cable and "tin" the ends with solder. Either solder the cable directly to the prototyping shield or, if you fitted a 4-pin female header to the shield, solder it to a 4-pin male header and plug it in.

Figure 12-15. *Arduino and cable gland mounted in box*

Adjust the cable length to leave a bit of slack looped around inside the box and tighten up the cable gland (see Figure 12-16). If the cable gland doesn't feel like it grips the cable properly, you can put a cable tie around the cable just inside the case and pull it tight so it stops the cable from sliding out.

Figure 12-16. *Transducer cable connected to shield and held in place by the cable gland*

That's the hardware assembly all done. Time to start playing with the software.

Install the WiShield Library and Driver

The WiShield supports 802.11b at 1 and 2Mbps (the Arduino couldn't keep up with anything faster anyway!) and even supports WEP and WPA/WPA2, in case you want to keep your top-secret water tank depth data secure from prying wardrivers. It communicates with the Arduino using SPI, which ties up digital I/O lines 10, 11, 12, and 13, along with line 2 for an interrupt connection and pin 9 for the shield's status LED, so it's important to keep those free in your project. Because we're only using one of the analog inputs, that's not a problem for us in this project.

The WiShield needs two software components to function correctly: the WiShield library from AsyncLabs, and the driver code from ZeroG Wireless. Unfortunately, the driver from ZeroG Wireless hasn't been released under a FOSS (Free / Open Source Software) license and therefore can't be distributed along with the library, so you need to install the library and then download and install the driver separately. More information is available from the AsyncLabs web site at `www.asynclabs.com`, or you can follow along the steps here.

Start by downloading the WiShield library using the WiShield Library link from the project page on the *Practical Arduino* web site. Extract it on your local computer and rename the directory to WiShield if necessary, and move it into your sketchbook/libraries directory so the Arduino environment can see it.

Next, go to the driver page using the WiShield Driver link from the project page. There you'll see the terms under which the driver has been made available. Click the WiShield Driver Download link at the bottom of the page to get an archive called wishield-g2100-driver.zip. Extract the ZIP file, and move the g2100.c and g2100.h source files into your sketchbook/libraries/WiShield/ directory.

The WiShield library supports several different modes. The default mode is the APP_WEBSERVER mode, which should run on most Arduinos but has limitations such as not being able to run as both a client and server simultaneously. An alternative mode called APP_WISERVER will run on any Arduino with an ATMega328P or better CPU, which includes the Duemilanove and most current third-party equivalents such as the Arduino Pro. Any reasonably modern Arduino should be able to run in APP_WISERVER mode so that's what we'll be using.

To switch the library into APP_WISERVER mode, open up the file sketchbook/libraries/WiShield/apps-conf.h and go to about line 39. Comment out the existing APP_WEBSERVER entry and uncomment the APP_WISERVER entry a few lines below it so that it looks like the following:

```
//#define APP_WEBSERVER
//#define APP_WEBCLIENT
//#define APP_SOCKAPP
//#define APP_UDPAPP
#define APP_WISERVER
```

With everything in place and those changes made to the library, you can now open up the Arduino IDE and have access to the WiShield library and example code. Note, though, that there are examples provided for several different modes: some examples only work in APP_WEBSERVER mode and some only work in APP_WISERVER mode. The ones that work in APP_WISERVER mode are all prefixed with "Simple."

To test that the WiShield is working correctly, open up the example at File Examples WiShield SimpleServer, adjust the network settings and WiFi encryption settings to suit your network, compile it, and upload it to your Arduino. If you're running on an open network it should associate pretty much immediately and the red status LED will illuminate to show it's joined the wireless network. If you're running WPA the process may take 30 seconds or so while the WiShield negotiates with your access point, but eventually the red LED will come to life to show that your Arduino is now on your network.

Open up a web browser, go to the IP address you set in the program, and you should see a "Hello World!" message from your Arduino.

The SimpleServer example implements logging via the serial connection, so if you're curious to see what the Arduino is doing you can open the serial monitor in the IDE and set the baud rate to 57600bps. Be warned, though, that with most modern Arduinos the act of opening the serial connection forces it to reset, and every time the Arduino boots up it may take another 30 seconds or so to reassociate with your wireless network. Lots of patience is required if you keep opening and closing the serial monitor.

Congratulations! Your Arduino is now connected to your WiFi network as a web server.

Load the Tank-Level Sketch

The tank-level reporting sketch is based on the SimpleServer example code with a simple addition to read an analog input and include the value in the web page sent back to the browser.

The sketch starts by including the WiShield library. Because we're using it in APP_WISERVER mode we include the WiServer.h header file instead of the WiShield.h header referenced in some of the other included examples. The sketch then defines a couple of tokens to make the code further down a bit more readable.

```
#include <WiServer.h>
#define WIRELESS_MODE_INFRA 1
#define WIRELESS_MODE_ADHOC 2
```

The sketch needs to know certain configuration values to connect to your WiFi network. These are set using a series of arrays and need to be changed to suit your requirements.

The basic network settings are the IP address of your Arduino (which must be unique on your network), the IP address of your router, and the subnet mask for your network. Note that most of the time you see an IP address it's represented in "dotted-quad" format, but in this case each quad is stored as a different element in an array so they have to be separated by commas instead of periods.

```
unsigned char local_ip[] = {10,0,1,200};
unsigned char gateway_ip[] = {10,0,1,1};
unsigned char subnet_mask[] = {255,255,255,0};
```

The wireless-specific settings start with the SSID (service set identifier) of your access point. This is the WiFi network name that you see on your computer when selecting a network. Maximum length for the SSID is 32 characters.

```
const prog_char ssid[] PROGMEM = {"YourSSID"};
```

You then need to specify the security type. The supported settings are shown in Table 12-2.

Table 12-2. *WiServer network security modes*

Value	Encryption
0	Open network
1	WEP
2	WPA
3	WPA2

On our prototype we connected to a WPA2-encrypted network, so we set it to 3.

```
unsigned char security_type = 3;
```

If you use WPA or WPA2 you also need to supply the passphrase to join the network. The value can be up to 64 characters long.

```
const prog_char security_passphrase[] PROGMEM = {"YourWifiPassphrase"};
```

If you are using WEP you need to define the 128-bit WEP key for your network. WEP supports multiple keys and so does the WiShield, so you can configure them by entering the appropriate hex values into the program.

```
prog_uchar wep_keys[] PROGMEM = {
  0x01, 0x02, 0x03, 0x04, 0x05, 0x06, 0x07, 0x08, 0x09, 0x0a, 0x0b, 0x0c, 0x0d, // Key 0
  0x00, 0x00, 0x00, 0x00, 0x00, 0x00, 0x00, 0x00, 0x00, 0x00, 0x00, 0x00, 0x00, // Key 1
  0x00, 0x00, 0x00, 0x00, 0x00, 0x00, 0x00, 0x00, 0x00, 0x00, 0x00, 0x00, 0x00, // Key 2
  0x00, 0x00, 0x00, 0x00, 0x00, 0x00, 0x00, 0x00, 0x00, 0x00, 0x00, 0x00, 0x00 // Key 3
};
```

WiFi supports two basic modes: infrastructure and ad-hoc. The most common is infrastructure with each mobile device connecting to a central access point, but it's also possible to run in ad-hoc mode where devices connect directly to their peers. We connected our Arduino to an access point so we set it to WIRELESS_MODE_INFRA, but you could alternatively set it to WIRELESS_MODE_ADHOC. Technically, all this is doing is setting the value of the variable to either 1 or 2, but that's not very self-explanatory so the defines that we set at the start of the sketch provide easily memorable tokens.

```
unsigned char wireless_mode = WIRELESS_MODE_INFRA;
```

The sketch then defines a couple of other variables for use by the WiShield.

```
unsigned char ssid_len;
unsigned char security_passphrase_len;
```

We also need to define some variables for processing the reading from the tank-level sensor. The sensorValue variable will hold the raw analog reading from the sensor and could have any value from 0 to 1023. The tankLevel variable will hold the tank level converted to a percentage so on first inspection it may look like we should be able to use a byte type rather than an int type to store the value, but as you'll see in a moment that wouldn't actually work. Finally, the TANK_SENSOR define is to specify which analog input the sensor is connected to. The shield design in this project uses analog input 0.

```
int sensorValue = 0;
int tankLevel   = 0;
#define TANK_SENSOR 0
```

The tank-level sensor won't provide a value that varies all the way from 0V when empty to +5V when full, so we need some calibration values that are used later in the program to adjust the lower and upper levels of the read range. These will need to be altered to suit your specific installation using a procedure that will be explained in a moment.

```
#define TANK_EMPTY 0
#define TANK_FULL 1023
```

The setup function is simple, but the WiServer.init() function is worth taking a look at. It accepts an argument that specifies the callback function to be executed in response to a connection request, and in this case we've told it to use the function sendWebPage(). This is a bit like setting up an interrupt because the sendWebPage() function is never called directly in the program, but by defining it and passing it to WiServer.init() it will be invoked automatically at the appropriate time.

```
void setup() {
  WiServer.init(sendWebPage);
```

Next, the sketch opens a serial connection to the host so it can send status messages back to you, and enables "verbose" mode so the server will send log messages via that connection.

```
  Serial.begin(38400);
  WiServer.enableVerboseMode(true);
}
```

The main program loop is trivial. All it does is repeatedly call the WiServer.server_task() method so that incoming data queued by the WiShield will be processed. Without this, a connection request from your browser will arrive at the WiShield and sit in the buffer without ever being acted on.

```
void loop(){
  WiServer.server_task();
  delay(10);
}
```

The last function generates the web page to send back to the browser. It's just a slightly extended version of the example included with the WiShield library with the addition of the reading from the tank-depth sensor connected to analog input pin 0.

```
boolean sendWebPage(char* URL) {
```

Before sending back the page the function makes a call to analogRead() to sample the sensor value. The theoretical range of the sensorValue variable is anywhere from 0 for a 0V reading on that input through to 1023 for a +5V reading, but because the reading will only swing from about 1V when empty to 3V when full the actual range is more limited. We wrap the analog reading in a call to the constrain()

function, which sets lower and upper limits on the value and prevents it from returning values outside that range. This way, if our TANK_EMPTY calibration value is set to, say, 123, and for some reason the system gets a reading of 119 at some point, the value will still be returned as 123 so it can't look like the tank has a negative depth.

```
sensorValue = constrain( analogRead( TANK_SENSOR ), TANK_EMPTY, TANK_FULL );
```

Because the reading will be between 1V and 3V it needs to be scaled using the TANK_EMPTY and TANK_FULL calibration factors defined earlier in the program. Otherwise you'll get readings showing the tank still contains water when it's bone dry, or partly empty when it's actually overflowing.

To make the value more human-readable we also want to convert it to a percentage rather than a 0 to 1023 scale, so we'll take care of both those problems at once using the map() function.

The map() function lets you take a value in one range and convert it to the equivalent value in a different range. For example, mapping a value of 255 from the range 0–1023 to the range 0–100 would return the value 25, because 255 is one-quarter of the way along the first range and 25 is one-quarter of the way along the second range. This is perfect for converting an analog sample to a percentage using a line such as the following:

```
tankLevel = map(sensorValue, TANK_EMPTY, TANK_FULL, 0, 100);
```

However, we also want to factor in the calibration values defined previously. The actual sensor value will only vary between the TANK_EMPTY and TANK_FULL values, not the full 0 to 1023 range, so we substitute those values for the first range in the mapping.

So far we haven't figured out what the TANK_EMPTY and TANK_FULL calibration values need to be, but we'll do that later. For now, just leave them at their default values.

```
tankLevel = map(sensorValue, TANK_EMPTY, TANK_FULL, 0, 100);
```

The function then checks the URL that has been requested to see if it's the default page using a global variable called "URL" that is set by the WiShield library. You could extend this function to check for other addresses and create subpages for your Arduino, but we only care about the default page with the address "/".

```
  if (strcmp(URL, "/") == 0) {
```

The WiServer object has special print() and println() functions that work just like the equivalent functions in the Serial library, but instead of sending the values to the serial port they're bundled into the response packet sent back via WiFi. This makes it extremely easy to send back a web page by simply printing the raw HTML.

To keep things simple and the response packet small, we don't send a full, standards-compliant web page. Instead, we just wrap the page content inside simple HTML tags and trust that browsers will be nice enough to render it anyway.

```
      WiServer.print("<html>");
      WiServer.print("Hello World!<br>");
```

It's also possible to print variable values, so we print the raw value of sensorValue, then a separator, then the mapped tankLevel value.

```
        WiServer.print(sensorVal);
        WiServer.print(" - ");
        WiServer.print(tankLevel);
```

Finally, we send a "%" symbol using the equivalent HTML entity, then close the HTML page.

```
        WiServer.print("&#37;</html>");
```

The function then returns true because we've just processed a recognized URL ("/").

```
        return true;
    }
```

If the program gets to this point the browser has requested a URL that isn't recognized, so the function returns false.

```
    return false;
}
```

Load the sketch in the Arduino IDE, compile it, and upload it. After the WiShield has joined the network and the status LED is illuminated you can try accessing it in a browser, and you should now see the "Hello World!" message followed by the literal sensor value and then the mapped value.

Prettier Web Interface

The web interface provided by the example program is functional, but not very pretty. With a little bit of work it's possible to create a web interface that is more visually appealing by replacing the contents of the sendWebPage() function.

Even without the use of images it's possible to fake a graphical display using colored table cells. For example, the alternative version of the sendWebPage() function shown next will display a visual representation of how much water is in the tank.

```
boolean sendWebPage(char* URL) {
  sensorValue = constrain( analogRead( TANK_SENSOR ), TANK_EMPTY, TANK_FULL );
  tankLevel = map(sensorValue, TANK_EMPTY, TANK_FULL, 0, 100);
    if (strcmp(URL, "/") == 0) {
        WiServer.print("<html><center>");
        WiServer.print("<h1>Tank Level</h1>");
        WiServer.print("<h2>");
        WiServer.print(tankLevel);
        WiServer.print("&#37;");
        WiServer.print("</h2>");
        WiServer.print("<table width=200 cellspacing=0 cellpadding=0 border=1>");
        WiServer.print("<tr><td bgcolor=#cccccc height=");
        WiServer.print(2 * (100 - tankLevel));
        WiServer.print("></td></tr>");
        WiServer.print("<tr><td bgcolor=#3333aa height=");
        WiServer.print(2 * tankLevel);
        WiServer.print("></td></tr>");
        WiServer.print("</table><br><br>");
```

```
        WiServer.print(sensorValue);
        WiServer.print("</center></html>");

        return true;
    }
    return false;
}
```

The result is a display that shows blue in the bottom section for the water depth and grey above it for the empty part of the tank, along with the percentage value at the top and the literal reading underneath for calibration purposes (see Figure 12-17).

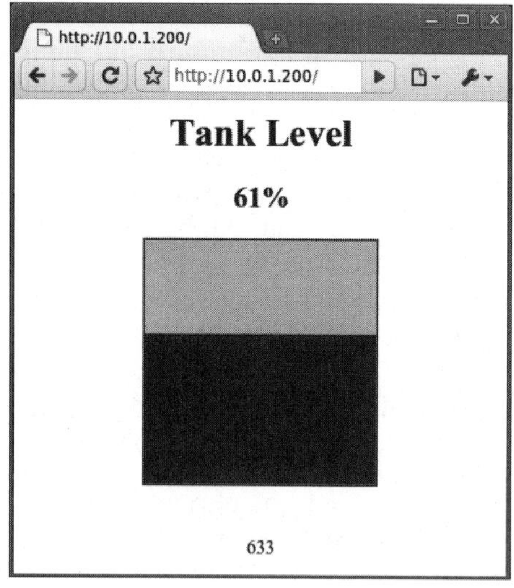

Figure 12-17. *Visual display of tank level using colored table cells*

Because you can't store separate files inside the Arduino on a traditional filesystem like you can with a typical web server it's a bit more difficult to create a page that is really graphical, but with a few little tricks it can still be done. One approach is to embed the HTML inside the program on the Arduino and have it reference images stored on a totally separate server located somewhere else. Once you've designed a graphical page that you want your Arduino to serve, you just upload all the images, CSS files, and other objects to a web host that you control and use absolute references in your HTML rather than relative references. All that means is that instead of referencing an image in your HTML like this:

```
<img src="myBigImage.jpg">
```

you do it like this:

```
<img src="http://www.example.com/myBigImage.jpg">
```

Using this technique you can even include Flash content, audio, video, and anything else you might want to put on a web page. Because the Arduino itself doesn't need to serve the files, you're only limited in terms of the size of the HTML you want to create and everything else comes from the external server.

The alternative version of the sendWebPage() function shown next looks even simpler than the previous one using tables, but this version uses an iframe pointing to a remote server that references a Flash movie that accepts the tank level as an argument and adjusts its display accordingly. The Flash movie has internal intelligence to process the tank-level value so the Arduino doesn't have to do anything except pass it along and let the user's browser fetch the Flash file, apply the level value, and display the result.

```
boolean sendWebPage(char* URL) {
  sensorValue = constrain( analogRead( TANK_SENSOR ), TANK_EMPTY, TANK_FULL );
  tankLevel = map(sensorValue, TANK_EMPTY, TANK_FULL, 0, 100);
    if (strcmp(URL, "/") == 0) {
        WiServer.print("<html><center>");
        WiServer.print("<iframe width=\"550\" height=\"400\" scrolling=\"no\" ");
        WiServer.print("src=\"http://www.example.com/tank.php?level=");
        WiSerevr.print(tankLevel);
        WiServer.print("\"></iframe>");

        WiServer.print("</center></html>");

        return true;
    }
    return false;
}
```

The result is a display that can include animation, visual and audible warnings of low tank level, or anything else you can do with Flash (see Figure 12-18).

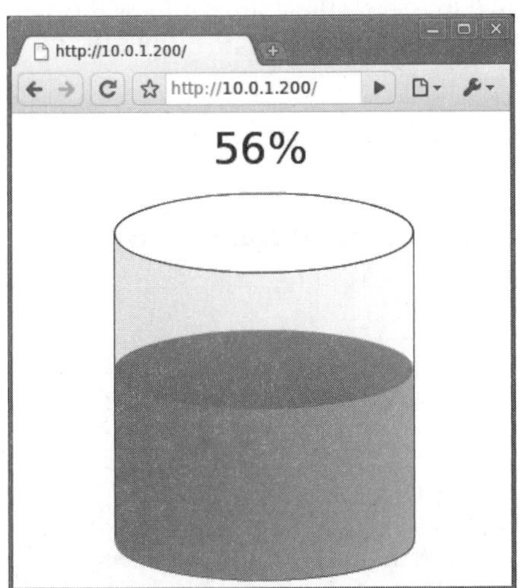

Figure 12-18. Animated visualization of tank level using an externally-referenced Flash file

For an even more wacky approach that will allow your Arduino to serve images without referencing an external server, it's possible to encode binary image data and embed it directly within the HTML itself. Normally image files are stored separately on a web server and the HTML includes a link to it, but by base-64 encoding a raw image to convert it to a text string it can then be placed within the HTML file itself. With this approach you can make a completely self-contained Arduino-based device that will serve graphical web pages without referencing any external resources.

Just keep in mind that this will rapidly bloat your sketch and the Arduino doesn't have much memory to begin with! You'll almost certainly need to use the PROGMEM directive to store the base-64–encoded objects inside program memory as explained on the Arduino site at `www.arduino.cc/en/Reference/PROGMEM`.

If you have an image that you want to base-64 encode it can be done on a Linux machine with a command such as the following:

```
base64 -w0 MyImage.jpeg > MyImage.b64
```

We use the "-w0" flag to disable line wrapping because when you include binary data inside a web page it won't work if you include line breaks. The result will be a text file named "MyImage.b64" containing an encoded version of your image.

If you don't have access to a Linux computer there are various services and scripts online that can do it for you if you upload an image to them. Just search for "base-64 encode image" to find a huge number of options.

Next, you need to include the encoded image in your HTML by placing it inside a specially formed image tag. Normally an image tag simply references the path to a separate image file, but by using an alternative format you can embed the literal encoded data straight into it and the browser will convert it back to an image when it loads the page.

```
<img src="data:image/jpeg;base64,R0lGODdhAQlqDRjow08CADs=" />
```

Something to remember, though, is that you can't put a double quote directly inside a call to print() because they are used to indicate the string boundaries. You'll need to escape the double quotes inside the HTML tag with a backslash when defining them in your program, so if you wanted to output the previous image data you would need to use a line such as this:

```
WiServer.print("<img src=\"data:image/jpeg;base64,R0lGODdhAQlqDRjow08CADs=\" />");
```

Note the backslashes before the double quotes in the HTML.

You can also use the same encoding technique to embed binary data inside CSS or XML. Wikipedia has more information about it in the "data URI scheme" article at en.wikipedia.org/wiki/Data_URI_scheme.

Calibrating the "Empty Tank" Level

Having loaded one of the previous example sketches into the Arduino and connected the sensor cable, switch your multimeter to low-voltage DC range and connect the negative probe to the ground connection on the shield and the positive probe to the jumper that links to analog input 0. This will let you read the voltage that will be supplied when the tank is empty and both ports of the transducer are exposed to the same pressure. Use a small screwdriver to adjust the 10k variable resistor until the voltage reads 1V.

Now open up a web browser and access the Arduino's IP address to see the output from the program, including the tank-level percentage and the raw analog reading value. Because the default value for TANK_EMPTY is 0 you will probably see a reading of 20 percent or so on the tank level even though the sensor is still sitting on your workbench and both ports are exposed to the air. The raw reading value therefore tells you the reading to expect when the tank is totally empty, so take that value and substitute it into the top of the program for TANK_EMPTY, then recompile the program and upload it again.

Try loading the web interface again after the WiShield has finished reassociating with the network and you should see that the tank level is now being reported as 0 percent, thanks to the offset provided by the TANK_EMPTY value.

The TANK_FULL calibration value still needs to be set, but that can't be done until the sensor has been installed and you can get a reading off a full tank.

Install the Sensor and Arduino

The easiest way to connect the sensor tube to the tank level is to fit a T-piece to the tank outlet and fit a blanking cap to the side pipe, with a cable gland fitted through it to allow the tube to enter the water (see Figure 12-19).

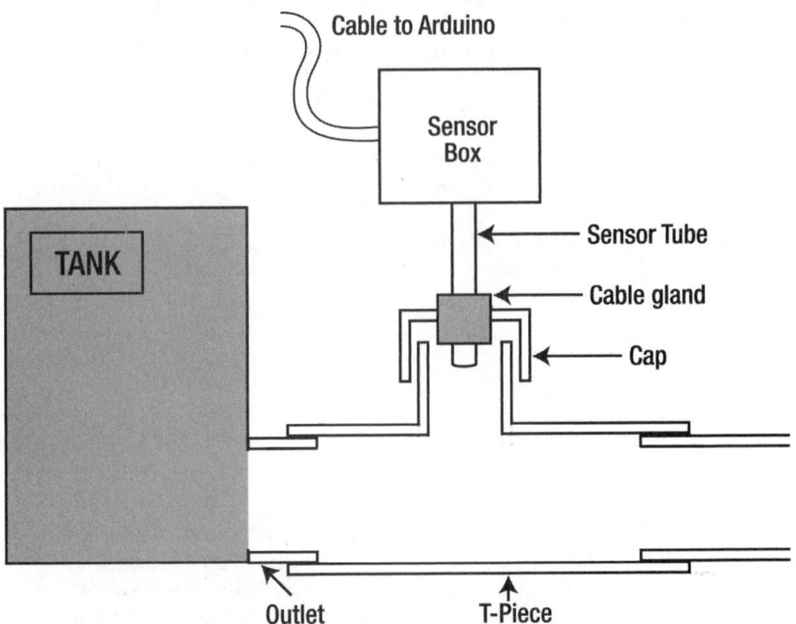

Figure 12-19. *Using a T-piece and cable gland to connect 4mm pipe to tank outlet*

Turn off the stop-valve on the tank outlet and disconnect the pipe that attaches to it, and install a T-piece between the two.

Then drill a hole through a blanking cap for a cable gland and screw the gland in place very firmly. Screw the blanking cap onto the T-piece, using plumbers teflon tape if necessary to get a perfect seal.

Due to the pressure that will be applied the cable gland will need to be sealed onto the sensor tubing very tightly. Because the tube will tend to be squashed by the cable gland when trying to get a really tight seal it's a good idea to insert a short length of metal pipe into the plastic tube first. A short section cut from an old telescopic antenna is perfect: cut out about 25mm from a section that fits snugly inside the tube and slide it in, then slide the tube into the cable gland. You can now tighten up the cable gland very tightly without the tubing being squashed closed, but air can still pass though the hollow metal tube to apply pressure to the transducer port.Rather than leaving the sensor box dangling loose on the top of the tube it's best to give it some form of mechanical mounting. A good solution is to attach the box to a piece of timber, hammered into the ground beside the tank outlet.

When everything is nice and tight, open the stop-valve again and watch carefully for leaks. If you've done a good job everything should stay nice and dry and the water should stay in the pipe where it belongs.

Mount the Arduino box in the location you previously selected and attach the sensor cable securely using cable ties or similar to keep it neatly out of the way.

Calibrating the "Full Tank" Level

To determine the TANK_FULL value you need the tank to actually be full and the sensor connected as previously described. If your tank isn't full at the moment you may need to fudge this value a bit based on an estimate of how full it currently is, and then adjust it later when the tank really is full.

With the tank stop-valve open so that the sensor is exposed to the full tank pressure, attach the negative probe of your multimeter to the ground connection on the shield and the positive probe to the jumper going to Arduino analog input 0. You'll get a reading somewhat higher than 1V, so using a small screwdriver adjust the 1K variable resistor until it reads 3V. This adjusts the gain on the amplifier for the TANK_FULL value.

Now use your computer to load the page again with the sensor exposed to the pressure from a full tank, and you'll see a tank-level reading probably somewhere around 60 percent and the literal sensor value below it. Take that literal sensor value and set it as the TANK_FULL value at the top of the program. Then recompile the program with those new values, upload it to your Arduino, and you're ready to go. The system should now report 0 percent when the tank is empty, 100 percent when it's full, and appropriate values in between.

Variations

Upload Data to Pachube

Pachube (pronounced "patch bay") is a web site that provides data collection and storage using web services and graphing/display using a web interface. It's primarily oriented around power data but it's extremely configurable so you can define any type of input you like, along with its units and various other parameters. At the time of writing Pachube is still in invitation-only mode, but plenty of people have spare invitations available so it shouldn't be too hard getting an account.

Visit the Pachube web site at `www.pachube.com` for more information.

Control Pumps or Irrigation

The example programs all report tank level via a web interface on-demand, but you could also run a program that checks the tank level and activates a pump or controls irrigation solenoids based on the current water level.

Local Level Display

The addition of an LCD or 7-segment LED module could allow the Arduino to directly display the tank level without requiring a network connection or web browser. The Water Flow Gauge project in Chapter 10 and the Vehicle Telemetry Platform project in Chapter 15 both include connection details for a 2-line, 16-character LCD module that can be easily added to this project to provide local display of tank level.

Reading Multiple Tanks

Each tank-depth sensor shield only needs connections for ground, +5V, and one analog input, so you could build several shields and connect each one to a different analog input. Then you could stack them together on top of each other by using long-leaded breakaway sockets that provide both a socket on top of the shield and long pins below, and alter the program to read from several inputs. However, note that if your multiturn trimpots are physically high you might need to lay them sideways.With multiple shields you could measure tanks of different sizes by applying a different scaling factor for each tank.

CHAPTER 13

■ ■ ■

Weather Station Receiver

The incredible popularity of home weather stations shows that it's not just farmers who are interested in the weather. Many people want to be able to track and record weather events within their local environment rather than relying on a state or national weather service that may not have adequate local details.

Home weather stations typically consist of two major parts: the sensors that sit outside your home and measure temperature, wind speed and direction, humidity, rainfall, and barometric pressure; and the display unit that lives inside your home so you can read the external temperature while sitting around the fire warming your feet and deciding whether it's too cold to go fishing. Generally, the external sensors connect together with cables, with one sensor also acting as a transmitter to send updates wirelessly to the display unit.

***Figure 13-1.** La Crosse weather station installed on a roof*

Many weather stations transmit their data at approximately 433MHz using a band reserved for low-power unlicensed use, which is ideal from a hacker's perspective because 433MHz receiver modules are commonly available for about $10 and can be easily interfaced with an Arduino to let you eavesdrop on the data feed. In fact, it's not just weather stations that use this approach: many short-range wireless devices work on the same 433Mhz band, so the techniques used in this project can be just as easily applied to intercepting data from other devices such as domestic power-consumption monitoring systems. Best of all, there's no modification required to the original device because it just transmits its data as usual, not even aware that it's being received and interpreted by another device. This project is essentially an exercise in listening to an unknown wireless data feed and converting the raw stream of data into values that make sense.

Figure 13-2. *Weather station sensors and transmitter being installed*

Once you can receive the data and process it in your Arduino, there are a wide range of things you can do with the information: you can simply display it as it updates, or you can log the readings and generate reports of trends over time, or you can even use it as the basis for making decisions such as sending rainfall data to an irrigation system to minimize water usage.

For this project we used a weather station from La Crosse, a popular brand that seems to be available in many parts of the world, but the same approach should work with other brands, as long as you can work out the data format.Many weather stations (including the La Crosse model we used) come with a serial interface on the display unit to feed data to a PC, but by doing the work directly in an Arduino with a receiver module, you don't even need the display unit at all and gain far more control over what you can do with the data. And because many weather station sensors are available individually, you might find you can buy just the sensors you want and save some money compared to buying a complete system while also gaining the flexibility of managing the data through an Arduino. You can see the required parts in Figure 13-3 and the schematic in Figure 13-4.

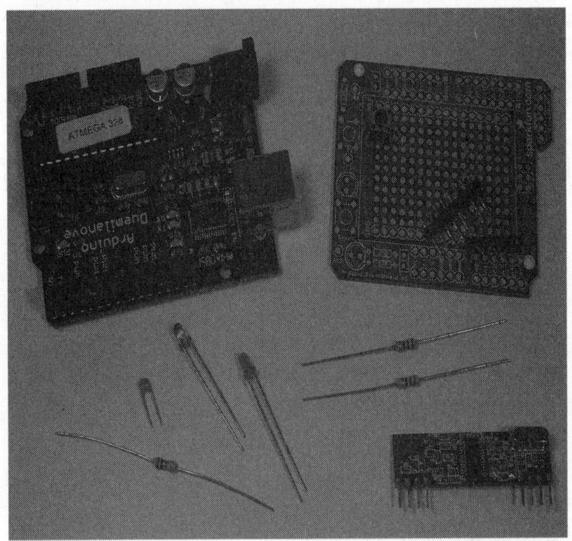

Figure 13-3. Parts required for Weather Station Receiver

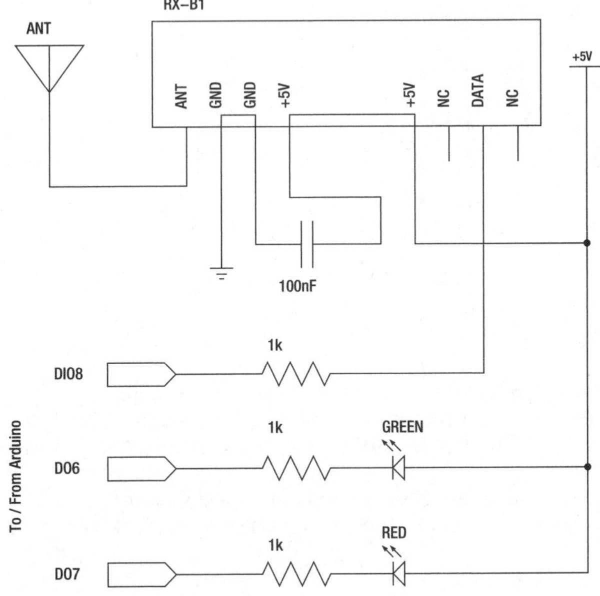

Figure 13-4. Schematic of Weather Station Receiver

Parts Required

1 x Arduino Duemilanove, Arduino Pro, Freeduino, Seeeduino, or equivalent

1 x Prototyping shield

1 x RXB1 433MHz receiver module (also known as ST-RX04-ASK)

2 x 680R resistors

1 x 1K resistor

1 x Red LED

1 x Green LED

1 x 100nF monolithic capacitor

1 x 33cm hookup wire

1 x Weather station
For our system we used a complete La Crosse (`www.lacrossetechnology.com`) WS-2355 Weather Station package, but you can also buy sensor modules individually including:

Integrated thermo/hygro/transmitter module, part number WS-2300-25S[1]

Rainfall sensor, part number WS-2300-16

Wind speed and direction sensor, part number TX20

Source code available from
`www.practicalarduino.com/projects/weather-station-receiver`

Instructions

Test and Install the Weather Station

Before you do anything else, you should start by assembling your weather station following the manufacturer's instructions and make sure it works with the original receiver/display module. You don't need to actually fit it to your roof yet, but at least plug it all together, put in the batteries, and check that the receiver sees values coming back from the sensors.

La Crosse systems start up in a "rapid-update" mode where they transmit sensor data very frequently for the first 15 minutes or so of operation to make it easy to test. After that, they drop back to a

---

[1]As an absolute minimum you will need a transmitter module either purchased individually or provided as part of a kit. The other sensors then use cables to connect to the transmitter module, which reads values from them and transmits the readings on their behalf.

power-saving mode where they only send updates about every five minutes, so if it looks like things are working initially and then the updates unexpectedly stop, don't panic. The system hasn't broken. It has probably just gone into low-power mode and you need to wait longer for each set of data to come through. You can switch it back to rapid-update mode by popping out a battery from the transmitter and putting it back in again, but each time you do that you then need to press the reset button behind the receiver/display module so it can reassociate with the transmitter. Each transmitter sends a station ID as part of every update. The ID changes randomly each time it powers up, so after it is reset the receiver watches for the first station ID it sees and latches onto it. It then only accepts updates containing that particular ID until the next time it is reset.

Understanding the Circuit

La Crosse systems transmit their updates on the unlicensed 433MHz band, so this project uses a shield with a 433MHz receiver module (shown in Figure 13-5) to feed the raw data stream to the Arduino where the bitstream is then processed and decoded in software. The shield is, therefore, quite simple and will work perfectly well with other 433MHz projects, while the software is relatively complex and does all the heavy lifting. You can use this exact same shield to process data from a wide variety of devices simply by changing the software on the Arduino.

***Figure 13-5.** RXB1 433MHz receiver module*

The schematic shows that, electrically, it's quite a simple system, but there are a few design decisions that might seem counterintuitive. Let's take a moment to follow through the circuit and understand how it works.

Most of the work is done by the RXB1 module, which only needs power, ground, and an antenna connected, and it will automatically start pumping a raw bitstream out the data pin for any transmissions it happens to pick up. It has two ground pins and two +5V pins that are connected internally on the module, so you can use whichever one happens to be more convenient for the physical layout of your device.

Notice that the receiver module has a 100nF capacitor (usually marked with a "104" on the body) connected directly across the ground and +5V pins. This is known as a "smoothing" or "decoupling" capacitor. It makes sure the receiver module has a clean source of power and minimizes the effect of variable current draw on other parts of the circuit. Decoupling capacitors are often not strictly necessary and the circuit might work perfectly well without one, but they fall into the "good design principle" category so it's worth understanding why we used one in this project.

The power drawn by active components can fluctuate very rapidly. The result of this fluctuation can be voltage "ripple" induced in the supply because the voltage will tend to drop slightly when higher current is drawn, and rise again when the current draw decreases. Putting a small capacitor across the supply rails helps to minimize this effect by storing power when the voltage is high and discharging it back into the circuit when the voltage falls, decreasing the overall fluctuation. To use a mechanical analogy, you can think of it as being a bit like adding mass to an object like a car: more mass gives it more inertia, which makes it tend to maintain its existing position or velocity and respond more slowly to forces attempting to push it in different directions. Decoupling capacitors likewise help stabilize the supply voltage and prevent it fluttering around at the slightest provocation, which can potentially decrease the performance of the circuit.

The actual value of a smoothing capacitor is usually not particularly critical so you can substitute a different part with a nearby value if that's what you happen to have handy, but don't fall into the trap of thinking that bigger is always better. Depending on the frequencies involved, a capacitor that is too large might not be able to follow the transients quickly enough and, therefore, give minimal benefit. A capacitor that is too small, on the other hand, will not store enough energy to ride out the low-voltage part of a ripple and will fully discharge its energy before the voltage begins to rise again. In some circuits it can be necessary to use several smoothing capacitors of different capacities connected in parallel to damp out ripple occurring at different frequencies.

It's a good principle to place decoupling capacitors as close as possible to the device they are protecting, and many circuits using high-speed logic have a capacitor mounted next to every single active component. Typical computer motherboards can have hundreds of them. When you look at the schematic for such a circuit it may look redundant to have dozens of identical capacitors all connected in parallel between ground and VCC in different places, but by having each smoothing capacitor physically located next to an active component on the board they each help to decouple the associated component from supply fluctuations. This approach provides an overall capacitance value equivalent to a large capacitor, while maintaining the frequency-response benefits of a small capacitor.

As a general rule of thumb a 100nF capacitor is a good value to use in a typical digital circuit, and you'll find that many experienced engineers and experimenters buy 100nF monolithic capacitors by the hundred so they always have plenty on hand to use in just about everything they build.

The second design decision is one that might seem a bit backward at first: connecting the indicator LEDs between Arduino outputs and +5V. What this means is that to turn on one of the LEDs the associated output must be set low; to turn it off, the output must be set high. This seems to be the opposite of what you might expect, particularly if you come from a software background and years of experience have drilled into your head that TRUE, 1, HIGH, and ON are conceptually similar and mean "yes," while FALSE, 0, LOW, and OFF are conceptually similar and mean "no." Sending an output high to turn it off and low to turn it on just feels intuitively wrong.

You'll come across this "inverted" logic in many circuits, and there are good electrical reasons for it. In this particular project it would work just as well with the LEDs connected through to ground so that the outputs could be driven high to turn them on, but we want to get you into good habits as early as possible even if it does feel a little uncomfortable at first. And this gives us a good excuse to explain why many engineers prefer to do it this way!

The output pins on a chip such as an ATMega CPU are rated to source (supply) or sink (accept) up to a certain limited amount of current. Sourcing current means supplying current to pass out through the pin of the chip and then through the load (a resistor and an LED in this case) to ground. Sinking current means having current come from the +5V supply and then through the resistor and LED, then into the pin, and from there straight to ground inside the IC (see Figure 13-6).

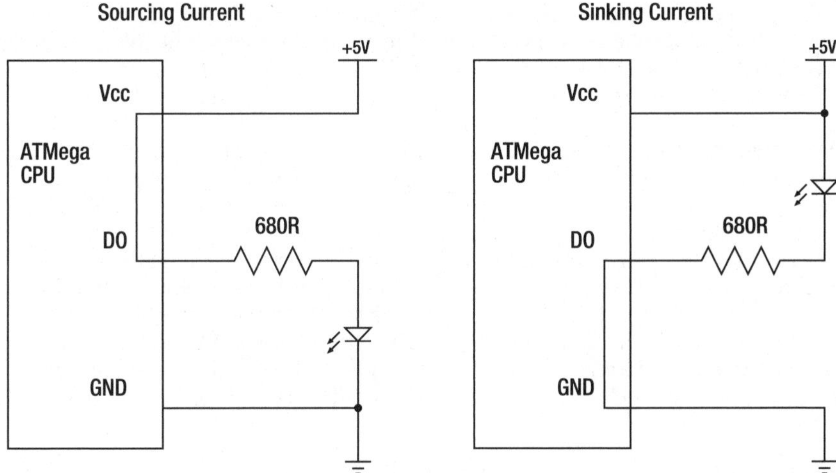

Figure 13-6. Sourcing versus sinking current

In many chips the sink current rating is considerably higher than the source rating because inside the chip itself there is a relatively large transistor that switches the pin directly to ground, and sinking current to ground, therefore, puts very little load on the IC itself. When switched low, the pin basically becomes simply a short-circuit to ground and quite high currents can pass through it without affecting the rest of the chip. Many chips can, therefore, sink much more current than they can source.

In the case of an ATMega we don't get this particular benefit because it's limited to 40mA per pin plus a combined limit of a total of 200mA across all the I/O pins, and the sink and source current ratings are identical.

Most of the time you would never even notice or care if loads you control cause micro variations in the internal voltage of the CPU, but sometimes it can come back to bite you when you least expect it. For example, when measuring the level of an analog input the IC uses a carefully calibrated internal reference voltage for its ADC (Analog-to-Digital Converter) circuitry, but if you're also switching an LED or other load at the same time, the supply rail could experience enough jitter that the readings on the analog input will degrade. Not having a consistent reference voltage can seriously impact analog inputs because, for the CPU, it's like trying to measure something with a ruler made of rubber: if everything is holding still you can use it just fine, but if the ruler is being alternately stretched and contracted very rapidly by even a small amount it's very hard to get a good reading.

So having external loads connected to their own supply rails (possibly even with independent smoothing capacitors) and just using the CPU to switch them to ground is generally a good habit to get into, even when you're dealing with relatively low-current loads such as LEDs.

The third design choice that might seem strange is the value of the current-limiting resistors on the debug LEDs. Most LEDs are designed to operate at a current of around 15 to 20mA and drop about 1.8V. For a 5V supply, a typical value for a current-limiting resistor in many circuits would be somewhere in the region of 220 to 330R.

However, we've specified 680R resistors, which will result in a current limit of just 5mA. The reason once again is to limit the load on the CPU by drawing no more current than we absolutely must. Because those LEDs are purely for debug purposes and not for general day-to-day use of the device, there's no need to make them full brightness. A typical LED will still glow quite strongly on just 5mA of current. If you are using LEDs as part of a user interface you would normally tune them up to full brightness using resistors around 330R, but for our purposes that's just not necessary. Instead, we elected to save a little bit of load at the expense of LEDs that aren't as bright as normal. The mantra to keep in your head is that you shouldn't use power if you don't really need it. Use just the minimal amount to get the job done and not a milliwatt more. The result will generally be a more stable overall system with less voltage fluctuations, and decreased chance of interference or other unwanted interaction between different parts of the circuit.

The fourth puzzling design choice is the inclusion of the 1K resistor to connect the data pin of the receiver module to the input pin of the Arduino. Once again, this is something that is entirely optional, but it falls into the "good design principle" category: the 1K resistor is low enough in value that it won't impede the flow of data, but it provides a bit of extra safety by acting as a current-limiter between the two different parts of the system. With the 1K resistor in place, the current flowing between the receiver and the CPU can never be more than a few milliamps, even if one or the other has a major malfunction. The circuit will work perfectly fine with a direct jumper in place instead of the resistor, but for an extra few cents it's a tiny bit of extra insurance that's worth putting in. It's definitely a good habit to get into with your own designs. If you can decouple parts of a circuit simply by including an extra resistor here and there without decreasing the performance of the system, then you might as well do it.

Assemble the Receiver Shield

Fit the RXB1 433MHz receiver module to the prototyping shield and connect one of the ground pins (2, 3, or 17) to GND on the shield. Note that even though the module only has a total of 8 pins, the manufacturer numbers them as if the board was fully populated from end to end as a SIP (Single Inline Package) device, so the first four pins from the left are numbered 1 through 4, and the four pins on the right are numbered 14 through 17. Pins 5 through 13 simply don't exist on the package (see Figure 13-7).

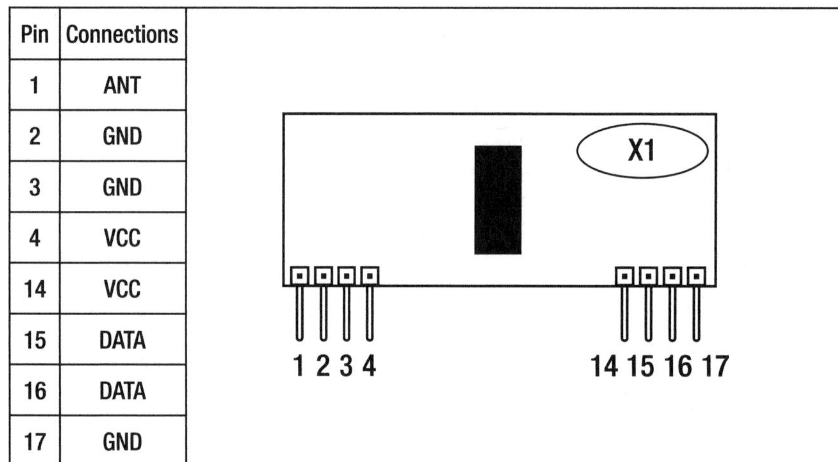

Pin	Connections
1	ANT
2	GND
3	GND
4	VCC
14	VCC
15	DATA
16	DATA
17	GND

Figure 13-7. *RXB1 pinout*

On the SparkFun prototyping shield we used for this project, the RXB1 gave us a bit of a problem because it is the equivalent of 17 pins long while the pad area on the shield is only 16 pins long. However, this problem was easily solved by bending pin 17, the ground pin on the extreme right end, up out of the way. Because the ground connection is replicated on pins 2, 3, and 17, we can just use one of the other ground pins instead and leave pin 17 unconnected. Keep in mind, though, that sometimes there is a good reason for radio-frequency devices to provide several ground connections such as to squelch internal ground loops. Leaving the extra ground pin unconnected could marginally decrease the sensitivity of the receiver, but in our testing it worked just fine with only one ground connection.

The RXB1 receiver is a 5V module and pulls a tiny 3mA in operation, so connect either of the VCC pins (4 or 14) directly to the +5V connection on the shield. On our prototype we used pin 4. Also install the 100nF monolithic capacitor between the adjacent GND and VCC pins (3 and 4, respectively) as a decoupling capacitor to help keep the supply rail clean as discussed previously. In Figure 13-8 the smoothing capacitor looks like a tiny yellow egg on the left.

Figure 13-8. *RXB1 receiver mounted on shield*

To keep things neat, we also installed a PCB-mount header for the antenna connection, visible at the extreme left in Figure 13-8. You don't actually need to do this, and you could choose to solder the antenna directly to the board if you prefer.

Next install the debugging LEDs and their dropper resistors. The green LED connects to Arduino digital I/O pin 6, and the red LED connects to I/O pin 7. Install the two LEDs on the shield and connect the anode (longer) leads to +5V. The other side of the LEDs needs to be connected to Arduino pins 6 and 7 via 680R resistors to limit the current through them, so solder a 680R resistor between each of the cathode (shorter) LED leads and the respective I/O pads on the shield.

Note that it doesn't actually matter whether you have the dropper resistor on the +5V side of the LED or on the ground side: on our prototype board we connected the LEDs directly to +5V and then used the resistors to connect the other side of the LED to the Arduino pin, simply because it made mechanical sense when laying out the board. However, you could just as easily have them installed in the other order (see Figure 13-9).

Data received by the RXB1 module is made available on both pins 15 and 16. Given the orientation of the receiver module it would seem to make sense to connect one of those DATA pins to an Arduino digital I/O pin somewhere down that end of the shield, perhaps pin 2 or pin 3. For many projects using the RXB1 module you can do that and it will work perfectly well, but this project is a little different because the software in the Arduino will be detecting transition edges in the received signal and measuring the timing to convert the raw signal into data. Unfortunately, that means we can't just open a serial connection and read values from the data line. Instead we have to connect it to pin 8, which has special functionality because it's connected to pin PB0 on the ATMega CPU. This pin is also designated ICP1, for Input Capture Pin. The ATMega supports extremely accurate timing of signal transitions on ICP1, down to the region of only a couple of clock cycles—perhaps a microsecond or so. We'll make use of that capability in the program to decode the data stream.

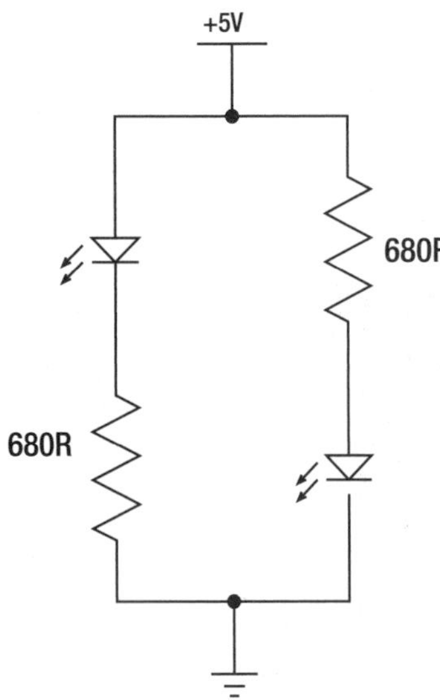

Figure 13-9. The LED on the left and the LED on the right are functionally equivalent circuits

Install a 1K resistor with one end connected to receiver pin 15 or 16 and the other end running across to Arduino digital pin 8 (see Figure 13-10).

Figure 13-10. LEDs, dropper resistors, data connection resistor, and power connections in place

To increase the sensitivity of the receiver, it needs an external antenna. Radio antennas need to be "tuned" to the correct wavelength for the frequency you are listening for, and the wavelength of a 433MHz signal is approximately 69cm or 27in. A good tuned length to go for in this case is 1/2 wavelength, which is 34.5cm or 13.5in.

We need to allow a little distance for the length of the pin and track, so we'll create an antenna just slightly shorter than half-wave. Cut a piece of lightweight hookup wire about 33cm (13in) long and strip back a few millimeters from one end, then tin it with solder so it's ready to connect to the board. On the prototype we soldered the end of the antenna to a female header so it could be easily removed from the board.

Having a 33cm piece of wire hanging loose might not be very convenient, so to keep things neat you can wrap it around a nonconductive former so that it forms a widely spaced coil. Our prototype antenna is wrapped around a piece cut from the body of a ballpoint pen and held in place with tape, but if you wanted to make it look a bit neater you could slip a length of heat-shrink tubing over the top to hold everything in place (see Figure 13-11).

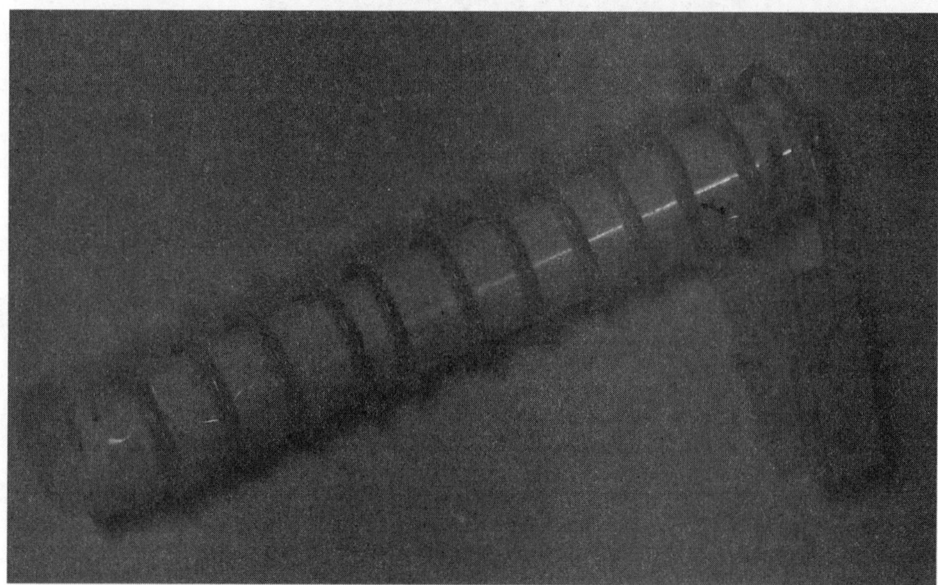

Figure 13-11. *Antenna wrapped around body of ballpoint pen*

You should now have a fully assembled receiver shield ready to go, so plug it into your Arduino and connect it to your computer via USB (see Figure 13-12).

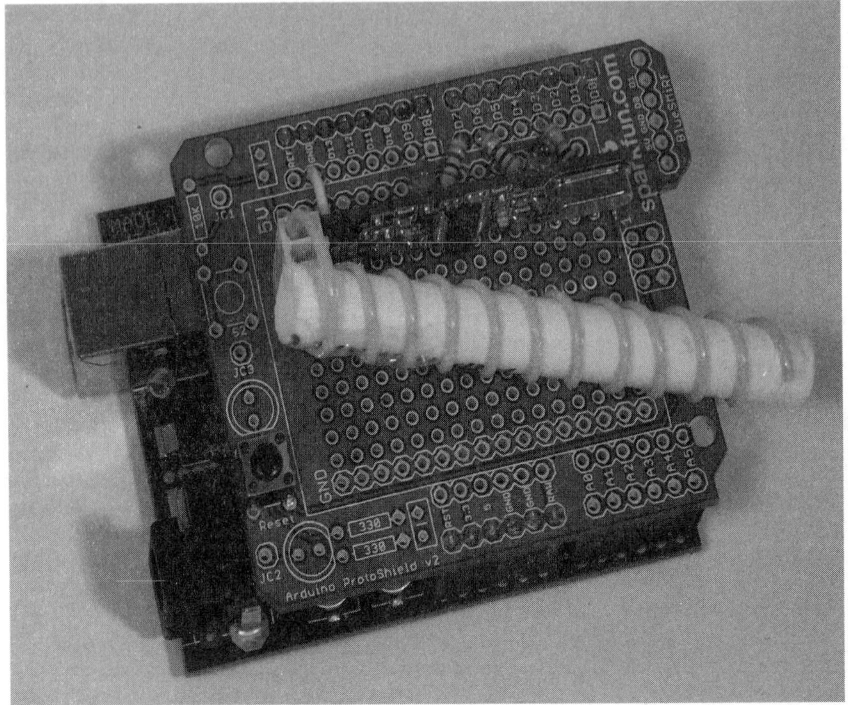

Figure 13-12. Arduino, receiver, and antenna assembled and ready for use

Weather Station Receiver Program

The program for this project is one of the more complex ones in the book and uses a number of things you might not have seen in Arduino sketches before. It's fairly long, so you definitely shouldn't bother trying to type it all in: just download it from the project page on the *Practical Arduino* web site at `www.practicalarduino.com/projects/weather-station-receiver`.

Unlike many Arduino programs it's not all contained within a single .pde file, but is instead split into two files: WeatherStationReceiver.pde for the main program and WeatherStationReceiver.h for some general declarations. Splitting code across multiple files is standard practice in larger software projects and provides a number of major benefits, including easier navigation in a code editor, conceptual encapsulation of sections of the project, easier change tracking in source code management systems, and less problems when multiple people work on the codebase simultaneously.

Many larger software projects have their code split up across dozens, hundreds, or even thousands of files. A tiny microcontroller such as an Arduino simply doesn't have the memory to run very large programs, but even for projects with just a few thousand lines of code you might find it helpful to use multiple files. The Vehicle Telemetry Platform project in Chapter 15 uses this approach to encapsulate different sections of functionality into different files, and goes one step further by using compile-time flags to skip over parts of the code that don't need to be built if that feature is not required by the user.

We'll start by looking at the WeatherStationReceiver.h file.

The file starts by checking for an "include guard" variable to make sure it hasn't already been invoked, then sets the variable. This is the same technique as explained in more detail in Writing An Arduino Library in Chapter 16.

```
#ifndef WSR_H_
#define WSR_H_
```

It then defines some human-readable tokens for use in the main program using a compiler directive called a "define."Lines starting with #define are not technically part of the sketch itself, but are commands to the compiler that tell it to process the source files in a certain way. A #define sets up a convenient token that can be used elsewhere in the sketch as an alias for an actual value.

The easiest way to understand how #define works is to think of it as a predefined rule for a global find/replace through the code, and that rule is run for you automatically just before the sketch is compiled. By defining a token and then using it in your code, it's as if you wrote out the value directly.

The first couple of #define entries are a trivial example, setting up aliases for variable types "unsigned int" and "signed int" so they can be referred to in the sketch as simply "uint" and "sint." This is purely a personal preference by the programmer and not necessary for the sketch to function: variable declarations in the program could have used the original, longer version of the variable type instead, but doing this makes the sketch a little easier to read if you're accustomed to the uint/sint convention.

```
typedef unsigned int        uint;
typedef signed int          sint;
```

Next, it defines three constants starting with ASCIINUMBASE, which as its name suggests is a token representing the ASCII number base (i.e., the position of the number 0 in the ASCII code table) and is given a hex value of 0x30.

Note that a define is not at all the same thing as a variable because it can't be changed after the program has been compiled. In this case, the ASCIINUMBASE token is removed from anywhere it appears in the program code and replaced with the literal value 0x30, so doing things this way results in exactly the same program as if ASCIINUMBASE had never been defined and everywhere it occurred we had simply typed 0x30 instead.

The carriage return and linefeed characters are also defined in the same way.

```
#define  ASCIINUMBASE        0x30
#define  CHAR_CR             0x0D
#define  CHAR_LF             0x0A
```

So far it probably sounds like a waste of time setting up all these #define entries. Often the token is longer than the value it represents, so rather than saving typing in the sketch it actually makes it longer. So why bother? The two major reasons are consistency and readability of the main program code.

By defining ASCIINUMBASE once like this, and then using that token throughout the program, it's easy to change its value in one place if necessary. For example, if you discovered that ASCIINUMBASE should really have been 0x31 instead of 0x30, how would you change all the references to it in your code? You can't just do a global find/replace in your text editor, because you don't know that every single instance of 0x30 in the code is actually there because that part of the code was referring to the ASCII number base. Perhaps 0x30 is also used to represent something totally different in another part of the code, and blindly replacing every instance of 0x30 with 0x31 to fix an incorrect ASCII number base value would break a totally unrelated part of the code where the value 0x30 was used for a different reason.

By referring to values like this using a human-readable name such as ASCIINUMBASE you can look through the code and understand the reason that value was used in that particular context, and you don't need to remember what the specific value is. Looking at a calculation involving the hard-coded value 0x30 doesn't help you understand what that number represents, but a calculation involving ASCIINUMBASE is much more self-explanatory.

The file then goes on to define many more entries that you'll see used elsewhere in the program.

```
#define WSR_TIMER_PERIOD_US          4
#define WSR_PERIOD_FILTER_MIN        ( 300/WSR_TIMER_PERIOD_US)
#define WSR_PERIOD_FILTER_MAX        (1800/WSR_TIMER_PERIOD_US)
#define WSR_SHORT_PERIOD_MIN         WSR_PERIOD_FILTER_MIN
#define WSR_SHORT_PERIOD_MAX         ( 600/WSR_TIMER_PERIOD_US)
#define WSR_LONG_PERIOD_MIN          (1200/WSR_TIMER_PERIOD_US)
#define WSR_LONG_PERIOD_MAX          WSR_PERIOD_FILTER_MAX
#define WSR_STATE_IDLE               0
#define WSR_STATE_LOADING_BITSTREAM 1
#define WSR_BIT_NONE                 0
#define WSR_BIT_ZERO                 1
#define WSR_BIT_ONE                  2
#define WSR_PACKETARRAYSIZE          8
#define WSR_TIMESTAMP_BIT_OFFSET     (4*8)
#define WSR_RFPACKETBITSIZE          52
#define WSR_RESET()                  { bICP_WSR_State = WSR_STATE_IDLE;
bICP_WSR_PacketInputBitPointer = WSR_TIMESTAMP_BIT_OFFSET; }
```

You'll notice that defines can reference each other. For example, the WSR_TIMER_PERIOD_US entry is substituted into several other entries immediately following it.

Next comes the macro section. A macro is substituted into the main code just like the #define values, but rather than being a simple value it is more like a mini function that performs an operation. Once again the end result is exactly the same as if you had typed these out in full in the code rather than using their more convenient label.

For example, the main program code could have included `((PORTD & (1<<PORTD6)) != 0)` but reading and understanding what that does takes longer than if the code simply contains a much more self-explanatory entry, such as the following:

```
GREEN_TESTLED_IS_OFF()
```

The macros defined are as follows:

```
#define INPUT_CAPTURE_IS_RISING_EDGE()    ((TCCR1B & _BV(ICES1)) != 0)
#define INPUT_CAPTURE_IS_FALLING_EDGE()   ((TCCR1B & _BV(ICES1)) == 0)
#define SET_INPUT_CAPTURE_RISING_EDGE()   (TCCR1B |=  _BV(ICES1))
#define SET_INPUT_CAPTURE_FALLING_EDGE() (TCCR1B &= ~_BV(ICES1))

#define GREEN_TESTLED_IS_ON()     ((PORTD & (1<<PORTD6)) == 0)
#define GREEN_TESTLED_IS_OFF()    ((PORTD & (1<<PORTD6)) != 0)
#define GREEN_TESTLED_ON()        ((PORTD &= ~(1<<PORTD6)))
#define GREEN_TESTLED_OFF()       ((PORTD |=  (1<<PORTD6)))
#define GREEN_TESTLED_TOGGLE()
if(GREEN_TESTLED_IS_ON()){GREEN_TESTLED_OFF();}else{GREEN_TESTLED_ON();}

#define RED_TESTLED_IS_ON()       ((PORTD & (1<<PORTD7)) == 0)
#define RED_TESTLED_IS_OFF()      ((PORTD & (1<<PORTD7)) != 0)
#define RED_TESTLED_ON()          ((PORTD &= ~(1<<PORTD7)))
```

```
#define RED_TESTLED_OFF()        ((PORTD |=  (1<<PORTD7)))
#define RED_TESTLED_TOGGLE()
if(RED_TESTLED_IS_ON()){RED_TESTLED_OFF();}else{RED_TESTLED_ON();}
```

Finally, the WeatherStationReceiver.h file ends by closing the "if" check on the include guard.

```
#endif
```

Next we get to the main program file itself, WeatherStationReceiver.pde. Even with all the previous defines simplifying things, this is still a big chunk of code so we'll go through it in little steps. Before getting into the details, though, it's worth looking at the overall structure of the program and understanding what it is trying to do.

To save battery power the weather station transmitter only powers up when it needs to send an update. This can cause problems for the inexpensive 433MHz receiver used in this project because it isn't "squelched," which means it just listens continuously to whatever is floating around at that frequency and don't disable its output if the input-level signal received is below a certain power level. If you've heard a CB radio receiver with the squelch control turned right down or an AM/FM radio mistuned and playing nothing but static, that's exactly what the receiver blasts at the Arduino whenever the transmitter isn't sending a message. The trick that this program performs is listening to that continuous blast of random noise and figuring out the difference between meaningful bit values and meaningless static.

The receiver's output is fed to a special pin designated as an Input Capture Pin (ICP) that the CPU can process in a different way to other I/O pins. The ICP provides very accurate timing and edge detection so that the CPU can examine the shape of the waveform being presented to it, and analyze it for specific characteristics that represent meaningful data. In the case of La Crosse weather stations the data is sent as a pulse-width and transition-encoded bitstream, so it's not enough to simply treat it as a simple stream of binary data like a serial port.

First, the program includes the header file we examined earlier so that all the #define entries will be available.

```
#include "WeatherStationReceiver.h"
```

Next, it defines some variables that will be used later in the program. You'll notice that, in this case, the variables have been named using a convention that prepends each one with the type of the variable so that later in the program it will be easy to see what type of data each one can contain. For example, all the "byte" type variable names start with "b," the "signed int" types with "si," the "unsigned int" types with "ui," and so on. Once again this is just a matter of programmer preference and doesn't change the meaning of any of the variables.

```
uint uiICP_PreviousCapturedPeriod;
byte bICP_CapturedPeriodWasHigh;
byte bICP_PreviousCapturedPeriodWasHigh;
unsigned long ulICP_Timestamp_262_144mS;
byte bICP_WSR_State;
byte bICP_WSR_PacketData[WSR_PACKETARRAYSIZE][4+8];
byte bICP_WSR_PacketInputPointer;
byte bICP_WSR_PacketOutputPointer;
byte bICP_WSR_PacketInputBitPointer;
uint uiICP_WSR_ReceivedPacketCount;
unsigned long ulWSR_LastTimestamp_262_144mS;
byte bWSR_StationTransmitterID;
```

```
sint siWSR_CurrentTemperature;
byte bWSR_CurrentHumidity;
byte bWSR_CurrentWindDirection;
uint uiWSR_CurrentWindSpeed_m_per_sec;
uint uiWSR_RainfallCount;
unsigned long ulWSR_Rainfall_mm_x10;
```

The last variable item defined next is a multidimensional array, or an array of arrays. It has 16 elements, each of which holds a subarray containing four elements. It's also prepended with the "const" (constant) keyword to tell the compiler that this variable can never be modified within the program, and can only be referenced. In Arduino sketches declaring const causes the value to be placed into flash memory along with the program itself, a great way to save RAM space and store large blocks of text, lookup tables, and other large unchanging data.

In this case, the 16-element array of four character text strings are used to hold the wind direction labels reported out the serial port in readable text.

Note that there is always a hidden NULL (0x00) byte at the end of a string so that any print or string handling function knows that a string ends when it sees the NULL, which is why the three-character strings such as "NNE" are declared as four bytes each.

```
const char strWindDirection[16][4] =
{
  "N  ", "NNE", "NE ", "ENE",
  "E  ", "ESE", "SE ", "SSE",
  "S  ", "SSW", "SW ", "WSW",
  "W  ", "WNW", "NW ", "NNW"
};
```

To help with figuring out the communications protocol and to see more detail about what the program is doing, you can define DEBUG at the start of the program to change how it behaves. With this line commented out as shown next the program will run as normal, but if you remove the double slash and recompile the program it will run in debug mode and output additional information.

```
//#define DEBUG
```

The setup routine appears very simple because it hands off most of the work to a pair of initialization functions that we'll examine in a moment. It also opens a serial connection back to a host computer at 38400bps and says hello.

```
void setup(void)
{
  Serial.begin( 38400 );
  Serial.println( "Weather Station Receiver has powered up" );

  Init_Ports();
  Init_RF_Interpreters();
  interrupts();
}
```

The main program loop looks even simpler because it just calls the same function over and over again as fast as possible. Most of the bitstream processing is invoked by interrupts so it doesn't need to be explicitly done here.

```
void loop(void)
{
  Packet_Converter_WS2355();
}
```

The next function sets DDRB to a specific value. DDRB is the Data Direction Register for port B, so it sets the input/output mode of digital pins 8 through 13. Explicitly setting DDRB to a specific value is simply a shorthand and very efficient equivalent to making a whole series of calls similar to "pinMode(8, INPUT)". Setting the registers directly like this is very common in microcontroller projects, but it's not generally considered to be "the Arduino way" because it's more opaque and harder to debug than a series of individual calls. Looking at the following code, you can't tell which pins are affected unless you happen to know that port B is connected to Arduino digital I/O pins 8 through 13, and even if you did know that it's not obvious which way around the byte is applied. Is pin 8 the first bit and being set to an output, or is it the last bit and being set to an input? You can't tell just by looking at it.

In this example, pin 8 is represented by the least significant bit at the end of the byte and pin 13 is represented by the most significant bit at the start of the byte. This is much more confusing than a simple call to pinMode, but this technique can be very useful in some situations so it's worth keeping in mind for future reference.

```
void Init_Ports()
{
  DDRB = 0x2F;    // B00101111
}
```

The main loop calls the packet converter function repeatedly. It doesn't take any arguments because it operates on global variables that are set elsewhere in the program.

Each time through it checks whether there is a fresh message packet waiting to be processed by comparing the packet input pointer and the packet output pointer.

```
void Packet_Converter_WS2355(void)
{
  byte b;
  byte c;
  sint si;

  if( bICP_WSR_PacketInputPointer != bICP_WSR_PacketOutputPointer )
  {
```

While in debug mode, the program outputs a spacer line if it has been more than about two seconds (actually, 8 × 144 milliseconds), so that individual packets are visually separated in the serial monitor.

```
    #ifdef DEBUG
    if( (ulICP_Timestamp_262_144mS - ulWSR_LastTimestamp_262_144mS) > 8 )
    {
      Serial.println();
    }
    #endif
```

While trying to figure out the communications protocol it can be very handy to output the raw message packet so you can see what is being sent. We only want that to happen if the DEBUG flag has been set, though, so first we check if it has been defined. Then the binary form of the message is sent to the host via the serial port by walking through it one bit at a time.

```
    #ifdef DEBUG
    Serial.print("BINARY=");
    for( b = WSR_TIMESTAMP_BIT_OFFSET; b < (WSR_RFPACKETBITSIZE+WSR_TIMESTAMP_BIT_OFFSET); b++
)
    {
      if( (bICP_WSR_PacketData[bICP_WSR_PacketOutputPointer][b >> 3] & (0x80 >> (b&0x07))) !=
0 )
      {
        Serial.print( '1', BYTE );
      } else {
        Serial.print( '0', BYTE );
      }
      if( b == 31 )
        Serial.print( ' ', BYTE );
    }
    Serial.println();
```

The value is also printed out in hexadecimal form in the same way, working through it one nibble (half-byte) at a time. On each pass through the loop it prints out the top nibble of the byte followed by the bottom nibble, but on the last pass through it doesn't print the bottom nibble because it's not part of the 52 incoming bits that form the message.

```
    Serial.print("HEX=");
    for( b = 0; b < ((WSR_RFPACKETBITSIZE+WSR_TIMESTAMP_BIT_OFFSET)/4); b += 2 )
    {
```

Printing the top nibble is as follows:

```
      c = bICP_WSR_PacketData[bICP_WSR_PacketOutputPointer][b >> 1];
      Serial.print( (c & 0xF0) >> 4, HEX );
```

Then printing the bottom nibble, but only before the last byte, is as shown here:

```
     if( b < (((WSR_RFPACKETBITSIZE+WSR_TIMESTAMP_BIT_OFFSET)/4)-1) )
      Serial.print( (c & 0x0F), HEX );
```

After the sixth byte a space is printed to separate out the timestamp from the rest of the message.

```
      if( b == 6 )
        Serial.print( ' ', BYTE );
    }
    Serial.println();
    #endif
```

A little later in the program we define a function to calculate the checksum of the message that has been received and return either true or false depending on whether it passes or fails. Now that the message has been loaded into a global variable, the checksum calculation is called and the rest of the function is only executed if it returns true.

```
if( PacketAndChecksum_OK_WS2355 )
{
```

Each weather station transmits a pseudo-unique station identifier that is generated each time it powers up. The station identifier is printed out in case you need to differentiate between multiple weather stations in the same area.

```
b  = (bICP_WSR_PacketData[bICP_WSR_PacketOutputPointer][5] << 4);
b += (bICP_WSR_PacketData[bICP_WSR_PacketOutputPointer][6] >> 4);
bWSR_StationTransmitterID = b;
Serial.print( "STATIONID=" );
Serial.println( bWSR_StationTransmitterID, DEC )
```

Rather than sending one data packet containing readings from all the sensors at once, the La Crosse transmitter acts as a gateway and passes on values from the various sensors individually as they become available. Each message packet therefore contains the data for just one sensor, and after working through the first part of the header containing the timestamp and the station ID the next part of the header contains a sensor ID in bits 4 and 5. Obviously with only two bits to store the sensor ID there are only four possible IDs: b00 (decimal 0), b01 (decimal 1), b10 (decimal 2), and b11 (decimal 3). Those four IDs correspond to temperature, humidity, rainfall, and wind sensors, respectively.

To extract the sensor ID we grab the appropriate byte from the message packet, then apply a shift-right operator and apply a logical AND to mask out the rest of the byte that we don't care about.

```
b = bICP_WSR_PacketData[bICP_WSR_PacketOutputPointer][5];
b = (b >> 4) & 0x03;
```

Then it's a simple matter of checking the value of the sensor ID and processing the rest of the message to suit the requirements of that particular sensor.

Sensor ID 0 is the temperature sensor which puts the first temperature digit in the lower nibble of byte 7. We extract that and multiply it by 100 because it's in the hundreds column, then put the value into the si variable. We then move on to processing the additional temperature digits in the upper and lower nibbles of byte 8, multiplying the tens digit by 10 and simply adding the ones digit as is.

```
switch( b )
{
  case 0:
  {
    si  = ((bICP_WSR_PacketData[bICP_WSR_PacketOutputPointer][7] & 0x0F) * 100);
    si += ((bICP_WSR_PacketData[bICP_WSR_PacketOutputPointer][8] >> 4) * 10);
    si +=  (bICP_WSR_PacketData[bICP_WSR_PacketOutputPointer][8] & 0x0F);
```

At this point we're very close to having the value we need, but because the value that is sent through is an unsigned number it can't represent negative values and it also doesn't have a decimal point. Not much good if the temperature drops below 0. The number sent through is, therefore, multiplied by 10 to remove the decimal place and then offset by 300 above the actual value, so to determine the real value we subtract 300 from whatever value the sensor reported and then divide by 10.

```
    siWSR_CurrentTemperature = (si - 300);
```

The value is then printed to the host via the serial port, but even this requires a little trick because after we've divided the number by 10 it will become a decimal value and can't be passed directly to

Serial.print. Therefore we print the divided value which will print just the part before the decimal point, then manually send a period, then send the modulus of the temperature to get just the decimal part.

```
    Serial.print("TEMPERATURE=");
    Serial.print( (siWSR_CurrentTemperature/10), DEC );
    Serial.print( '.', BYTE );
    if( siWSR_CurrentTemperature < 0 ) {
      Serial.println( ((0-siWSR_CurrentTemperature)%10), DEC );
    } else {
      Serial.println( (siWSR_CurrentTemperature%10), DEC );
    }
    break;
  }
```

Sensor ID 1 is the humidity sensor, which is treated in almost the same way as temperature. It's actually a little simpler, though, because we don't need the 300 offset (humidity can never be negative!), and it's always a whole number so there's no need to mess around with printing a decimal value to the host.

```
  case 1:
  {
    c  = ((bICP_WSR_PacketData[bICP_WSR_PacketOutputPointer][7] & 0x0F) * 10);
    c +=  (bICP_WSR_PacketData[bICP_WSR_PacketOutputPointer][8] >> 4);
    bWSR_CurrentHumidity = c;

    // Print to serial port
    Serial.print("HUMIDITY=");
    Serial.println( bWSR_CurrentHumidity, DEC );
    break;
  }
```

Sensor ID 2 is the rainfall sensor. After dealing with the last two sensors the routine should be familiar by now: grab the appropriate bytes out of the packet, add them together, and apply a transformation to convert it to the correct units which in this case is millimeters of rain.

```
  case 2:
  {
    si  = (sint)(bICP_WSR_PacketData[bICP_WSR_PacketOutputPointer][7] & 0x0F) << 8;
    si +=        bICP_WSR_PacketData[bICP_WSR_PacketOutputPointer][8];
    uiWSR_RainfallCount = (uint)si;
    ulWSR_Rainfall_mm_x10 = (((unsigned long)uiWSR_RainfallCount * 518) / 100);

    Serial.print("RAINFALL=");
    Serial.print( (ulWSR_Rainfall_mm_x10/10), DEC );
    Serial.print( '.', BYTE );
    Serial.println( (ulWSR_Rainfall_mm_x10%10), DEC );
    break;
  }
```

The final sensor ID is 3 and, though it's similar to the others, it does have a slight twist to it: this particular packet contains two values within the same message. Wind speed and direction are bundled together, with the speed taking up the first byte-and-a-half of data and the final nibble providing the direction.

Therefore we start by doing a logical AND to mask off half the second byte and process it to get the wind direction, then perform similar tricks to extract the wind speed.

We don't just print out the wind direction directly, though, because it's a number that won't mean much. Instead, we use that number to reference a specific element in the wind direction array we defined way back at the start of the program and extract the string found there to display a human-readable value such as "NNW."

```
        case 3:
        {
          bWSR_CurrentWindDirection = (bICP_WSR_PacketData[bICP_WSR_PacketOutputPointer][8] &
0x0F);

          //wind speed, decimal value is metres per second * 10 (1 fixed deciml place)
          si  = (sint)(bICP_WSR_PacketData[bICP_WSR_PacketOutputPointer][7] & 0x10) << 4;
          si +=      ((bICP_WSR_PacketData[bICP_WSR_PacketOutputPointer][7] & 0x0F) << 4);
          si +=       (bICP_WSR_PacketData[bICP_WSR_PacketOutputPointer][8] >> 4);
          uiWSR_CurrentWindSpeed_m_per_sec = (uint)si;

          Serial.print("WINDDIRECTION=");
          Serial.println( strWindDirection[bWSR_CurrentWindDirection] );

          Serial.print("WINDSPEED=");
          Serial.print( (uiWSR_CurrentWindSpeed_m_per_sec/10), DEC );
          Serial.print( '.', BYTE );
          Serial.println( (uiWSR_CurrentWindSpeed_m_per_sec%10), DEC );
          break;
        }
```

The code should never get to the default section of the case statement because sensor IDs should only ever be from 0 to 3. Then we wrap up the alternative to the if condition on the checksum test so that if the checksum failed we print a message saying so.

```
        default:
        {
          break;
        }
      }
    } else {
      Serial.print( "   Bad checksum or packet header" );
    }
```

The timestamp variable needs to be updated so that next time through it can be checked to see if a blank line needs to be inserted between packets.

```
    ulWSR_LastTimestamp_262_144mS = ulICP_Timestamp_262_144mS;
```

Now that we're done with this message packet the output pointer can be moved along.

```
    bICP_WSR_PacketOutputPointer = ((bICP_WSR_PacketOutputPointer+1)&(WSR_PACKETARRAYSIZE-1));
```

```
  }
}
```

Because there is a high probability that data sent by the transmitter will be corrupt or only partially received, it's important to have some way to check the validity of the message. The La Crosse transmitter includes a checksum in the message so the receiver can make sure it arrived correctly.

The checksum calculation function doesn't take any arguments because when invoked it operates on global variables that have already been set, and all it needs to return is a pass/fail response value. Internally, the function uses the variable dataPos to indicate the position within the data array that it will examine, and it accumulates the result of examining each byte into the checksum variable

```
byte PacketAndChecksum_OK_WS2355(void)
{
  byte dataPos;
  byte checksum;
```

It skips across the first four bytes, though, because they're the timestamp and aren't included in the checksum calculation, which only applies to the first 48 bites (12 nibbles) of the message payload.

```
  checksum = 0;
  for( dataPos = 4; dataPos < 10; dataPos++ )
  {
    checksum += (bICP_WSR_PacketData[bICP_WSR_PacketOutputPointer][dataPos] >> 4);
    checksum += (bICP_WSR_PacketData[bICP_WSR_PacketOutputPointer][dataPos] & 0x0F);
  }
```

The accumulated value then has a bitwise AND operator applied against the value 0x0F.

```
checksum &= 0x0F;
```

The result is then compared to the checksum value sent in the transmission and the function immediately exits with a false value if it fails the test.

```
  if( checksum != (bICP_WSR_PacketData[bICP_WSR_PacketOutputPointer][10] >> 4) )
  {
    return( false );
  }
```

The next thing that is checked is the first non-timestamp byte of the message payload, which must always be 0x09, or binary 00001001. This appears to be a general identifier for this type of weather station and might be different for other models, but for our purposes we can simply do a direct comparison and ignore messages that don't have this byte set correctly.

```
  if( bICP_WSR_PacketData[bICP_WSR_PacketOutputPointer][4] != 0x09 )
  {
    return( false );
  }
```

If those checks all passed then the message is probably okay, so the function returns true and bails out.

```
  return( true );
}
```

The Init_RF_Interpreters function is called once during setup() to make sure everything is ready to go, and makes extensive use of macros that were defined in the header file. This approach can dramatically improve the readability of your code at a high, abstract level because you can read a line such as WSR_RESET() and know that it resets the weather station receiver state machine. On the other hand it can make the details of your code more opaque, because seeing a call to WSR_RESET() doesn't help you understand how that macro works. Use of macros to simplify your code is a balancing act between conciseness and opacity.

In this project, WSR_RESET() simply resets the state machine value and the packet bit position pointer.

```
void Init_RF_Interpreters(void)
{
  WSR_RESET();
```

The next cryptic-looking steps are critical to the entire operation of the sketch. First, it sets the Input Capture Pin into a floating input by setting the appropriate bit in DDRB (Data Direction Register, port B) and then writing to the same bit in PORTB to ensure the pull-up resistor is also disabled.

```
  DDRB  &= ~(1<<DDB0);

  PORTB &= ~(1<<PORTB0);
```

The green and red test LEDs are then set up.

```
  DDRD  |=  B11000000;
  GREEN_TESTLED_OFF();
  RED_TESTLED_ON();
```

Next, the input capture is set up with the necessary settings for noise cancelling and prescaling, and another macro is called to set it to trigger on a rising edge.

```
  TCCR1A = B00000000;
  TCCR1B = ( _BV(ICNC1) | _BV(CS11) | _BV(CS10) );
  SET_INPUT_CAPTURE_RISING_EDGE();
```

Then Timer1's mask is set to enable Input Capture Interrupt Enable (ICIE1) and Timer Overflow Interrupt Enable (TOIE1).

```
  TIMSK1 = ( _BV(ICIE1) | _BV(TOIE1) );
}
```

Because the weather station receiver is likely to be left running indefinitely, we need to add a little workaround for a design problem in the core Arduino system. In most projects it's enough to use the millis() function to return the number of milliseconds since the Arduino started up, but unfortunately the value is stored internally in an unsigned long integer meaning that it can only store a maximum value of up to 2^32. In milliseconds that works out to about 49 days and 17 hours, after which any timing in the program can go drastically wrong.

To get around this problem we define an interrupt service routine (ISR) to be executed whenever the ATMega's internal Timer1 overflows. Timer1 increments on every CPU cycle so it overflows very fast—about every 262.144ms for a CPU running at 16Mhz. The last line shown previously set the Timer Overflow Interrupt Enable, which then causes this next function to be automatically executed every time an overflow occurs.

Then on every call to this ISR we increment an unsigned long integer, giving us a counter that steps up in increments of 262.144ms. It can still only count to 2^32, like millis(), but because it's updating only 1/262 as fast it will last 262 times as long (i.e., about 35 years) before it will overflow.

Even when it does overflow, though, it won't be a problem for this particular program because the value is only ever used to calculate a delta against the previous timestamp. As long as the delta calculation is performed using the same 32-bit unsigned data types, the delta will still read correctly even when an overflow has happened between one timestamp and the next.

```
ISR( TIMER1_OVF_vect )
{
  ulICP_Timestamp_262_144mS++;
}
```

The next function is also an ISR and it was also enabled by the Init_RF_Interpreters function shown previously. Rather than being invoked on timer overflow, this one is invoked when the conditions set for the ICP cause it to be tripped. Using this approach it doesn't matter when the receiver sends data through to the Arduino because it will be processed on demand by the ISR.

Elsewhere in the book we go out of our way to stress that ISRs should be kept as short and fast as possible: just get in, update a global variable, and get right out again without wasting CPU cycles. This particular ISR breaks that rule by putting most of the processing required by the program inside the ISR or in other functions that the ISR invokes (something else you almost never see!), but in this case it's justified because the whole program is written around analyzing events that trigger this particular interrupt.

First, the ISR grabs the current capture time and stores it in a variable, then turns on the green LED so that we can see it flicker for visual feedback as a datastream arrives.

```
ISR( TIMER1_CAPT_vect )
{
  uiICP_CapturedTime = ICR1;
  GREEN_TESTLED_ON();
```

Then it uses macros to grab the current capture polarity and reverse it to catch all the subsequent high and low periods arriving so they can be analyzed by the RF interpreter to follow. First, though, it makes a record of whether the period that was just captured was high or low.

```
  if( INPUT_CAPTURE_IS_RISING_EDGE() )
  {
    SET_INPUT_CAPTURE_FALLING_EDGE();
    bICP_CapturedPeriodWasHigh = false;
  } else {
    SET_INPUT_CAPTURE_RISING_EDGE();
    bICP_CapturedPeriodWasHigh = true;
  }
```

Then, it calculates the period that was just measured.

```
  uiICP_CapturedPeriod = (uiICP_CapturedTime - uiICP_PreviousCapturedTime);
```

At this point the program knows both the polarity of the pulse (high or low) and its duration, so it calls the RF interpreter function to process them. There's no need to pass arguments to the function because the values are stored in global variables.

```
  RF_Interpreter_WS2355();
```

After the interpreter finishes the capture data from this set is stored so that it can be used again next time around to perform the period calculation.

```
  uiICP_PreviousCapturedTime            = uiICP_CapturedTime;
  uiICP_PreviousCapturedPeriod          = uiICP_CapturedPeriod;
  bICP_PreviousCapturedPeriodWasHigh    = bICP_CapturedPeriodWasHigh;
```

Finally the green test LED is turned off. This whole function will have been executed within the space of a few milliseconds, so it will just look like the LED is flickering as a bitstream is received.

```
  GREEN_TESTLED_OFF();
}
```

After the event timing has been stored by the previous function the RF interpreter examines each event to find out what type of bit the incoming period is. La Crosse weather stations transmit 52 bits per message packet, and they represent a logic 0 by sending a long high period followed by a long low period, and a logic 1 by sending a short high period followed by a long low period.

The important thing to remember about the next section is that RF_Interpreter_WS2355() is called a single time on each rising or falling edge transition of the ICP interrupt service routine.

As long as 52 consecutive valid bit periods come in, it will convert and load all of them into the incoming bICP_WSR_PacketData[] array, timestamp it, and set it as a good received packet for the main loop to deal with.

```
void RF_Interpreter_WS2355()
{
  volatile byte b;
  byte bValidBit = false;
```

If the captured period is outside the expected range it's probably noise, so the rest of the processing is only performed if the range is acceptable.

```
  if( (uiICP_CapturedPeriod >= WSR_PERIOD_FILTER_MIN) && (uiICP_CapturedPeriod <=
WSR_PERIOD_FILTER_MAX) )
  {
```

It then checks if this is a valid 0 (long high) or 1 (short high) bit, or an invalid period in between.

```
    if( bICP_CapturedPeriodWasHigh )
    {
      if( (uiICP_CapturedPeriod >= WSR_SHORT_PERIOD_MIN) && (uiICP_CapturedPeriod <=
WSR_SHORT_PERIOD_MAX) )
      {
        bValidBit = WSR_BIT_ONE;
```

```
      } else if( (uiICP_CapturedPeriod >= WSR_LONG_PERIOD_MIN) && (uiICP_CapturedPeriod <=
WSR_LONG_PERIOD_MAX) ) {
        bValidBit = WSR_BIT_ZERO;
      } else {
```

If the code got to this point, it must be an invalid period in the dead zone between short and long bit period lengths, so the program assumes it's just seeing noise and calls the reset macro to set everything back to a default state and start waiting for the next bit transition to arrive.

```
        WSR_RESET();
      }
    }
```

The program then enters a little state machine to load and prepare the incoming bits into a potentially complete packet, performing different actions depending on the current state.

```
    if( bValidBit != false )
    {
      switch( bICP_WSR_State )
      {
        case WSR_STATE_IDLE:
        {
          if( bValidBit == WSR_BIT_ZERO )
          {
```

A good La Crosse bitstream packet always starts with a 0 bit, so if the sketch receives a 0 while the state machine is "idle" and still waiting for a good packet start, it loads the bit into the packet data buffer, increments the input bit pointer, and moves on to the next state to continue loading the rest of the potentially good packet.

```
            bICP_WSR_PacketData[bICP_WSR_PacketInputPointer][bICP_WSR_PacketInputBitPointer >>
3]
                &= ~(0x01 << (bICP_WSR_PacketInputBitPointer&0x07));
            bICP_WSR_PacketInputBitPointer++;
            bICP_WSR_State = WSR_STATE_LOADING_BITSTREAM;
          } else {
            WSR_RESET();
          }
          break;
        }
        case WSR_STATE_LOADING_BITSTREAM:
        {
```

At this point a potentially valid packet bitstream is on its way in, so the program keeps loading it up.

```
          if( bValidBit == WSR_BIT_ZERO )
          {
            bICP_WSR_PacketData[bICP_WSR_PacketInputPointer][bICP_WSR_PacketInputBitPointer >>
3]
                &= ~(0x80 >> (bICP_WSR_PacketInputBitPointer&0x07));
          } else {
```

```
            bICP_WSR_PacketData[bICP_WSR_PacketInputPointer][bICP_WSR_PacketInputBitPointer >>
3]
              |=  (0x80 >> (bICP_WSR_PacketInputBitPointer&0x07));
          }
```

At a fixed location of the incoming bitstream a further check is made to see if the first five bits are the expected 00001, and a test for an occasionally missed first 0 bit is made and corrected for.

The sketch checks the location of the incoming bitstream to see if it is valid, and throws it away if not.

```
          if( bICP_WSR_PacketInputBitPointer == (WSR_TIMESTAMP_BIT_OFFSET + 4) )
          {
            b = bICP_WSR_PacketData[bICP_WSR_PacketInputPointer][4];
            b &= B11111000;
```

An acceptable start to the packet is 00001, but sometimes the sketch will see 00010 if the receiver module missed the first 0. First, it checks for a "missed bit" condition by looking for a packet start of 00010, and if it's a match, the sketch realigns the byte and continues up one position past the inserted missing bit.

```
            if( b == B00010000 )
            {
bICP_WSR_PacketData[bICP_WSR_PacketInputPointer][4/*bICP_WSR_PacketInputBitPointer >> 3*/] =
B00001000;
              bICP_WSR_PacketInputBitPointer++;
```

The only other acceptable alternative is a clean start to the packet of 00001, so if the header didn't match either case it must be invalid and the sketch resets the state machine for another try.

```
            } else if( b != B00001000 ) {
              WSR_RESET();
            }
          }
```

As a final check the sketch tests whether the last packet bit (52 bits in total) has arrived. If it has a complete set of 52 sequential bits, it marks this packet as done and moves the major packet input pointer along.

```
          if( bICP_WSR_PacketInputBitPointer == (WSR_TIMESTAMP_BIT_OFFSET +
(WSR_RFPACKETBITSIZE-1)) )
            {
```

Since it received a full valid packet, the sketch timestamps it for the main loop.

```
            bICP_WSR_PacketData[bICP_WSR_PacketInputPointer][0] =
byte(ulICP_Timestamp_262_144mS >> 24);
            bICP_WSR_PacketData[bICP_WSR_PacketInputPointer][1] =
byte(ulICP_Timestamp_262_144mS >> 16);
            bICP_WSR_PacketData[bICP_WSR_PacketInputPointer][2] =
byte(ulICP_Timestamp_262_144mS >>  8);
```

```
            bICP_WSR_PacketData[bICP_WSR_PacketInputPointer][3] =
byte(ulICP_Timestamp_262_144mS);
```

It then sets the pointer and packet count. The received packet count will overflow and wrap, but that doesn't really matter. It's only set for display purposes so you can see it increment while debugging.

```
            bICP_WSR_PacketInputPointer =
((bICP_WSR_PacketInputPointer+1)&(WSR_PACKETARRAYSIZE-1));
            uiICP_WSR_ReceivedPacketCount++;
            WSR_RESET();
          }
```

The pointer is then incremented to the next new bit location.

```
          bICP_WSR_PacketInputBitPointer++;
          break;
        }
      }
    }
  } else {
```

Way back at the start of the function it checked whether the period was out of bounds. If it failed that match, the state machine is reset to throw away any out of range periods and clean up to try again on the next message.

```
    WSR_RESET();
  }
}
```

With the sketch loaded on your Arduino, open the serial monitor and make sure it's set to 38400bps. Apply power to your weather station receiver and you should see a series of readings reported back via the serial port (see Figure 13-13).

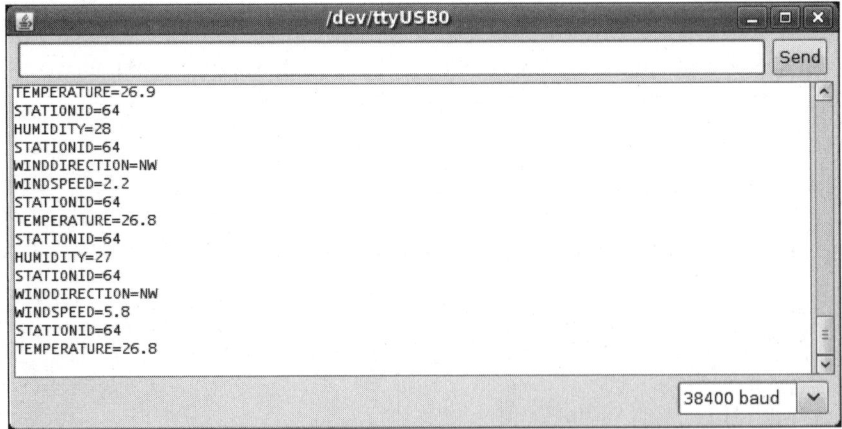

Figure 13-13. *Weather Station Receiver values reported via the serial console*

The weather station seems to transmit some values several times, and different parameters come through at different times rather than all at once in a batch. It's up to you or the software you write to parse the data to keep track of the last reading for each parameter.

Twitter Weather Updates

There are many different things you could do with the data received by the Arduino, but just as a simple example we'll send the temperature values as Twitter updates. This can be done by fitting an Ethernet shield or WiShield to the Arduino and having the Arduino program connect directly to the Twitter API via your network. If you want to investigate this option you'll find lots of handy information at www.arduino.cc/playground/Code/TwitterLibrary.

If you want to use a WiShield to connect via your WiFi network, have a look at the instructions in the Water Tank Depth Sensor project in Chapter 12 for information on using the WiShield. The WiShield comes with a Twitter client example that makes it fairly easy to submit Twitter updates automatically.

However, rather than use an Ethernet shield or WiShield for this project, we're going to demonstrate how to link your Arduino to a program running on your computer via the USB connection. There are many situations where you may want to use a program running on a host computer to control or process data coming from an Arduino, so even though this is a trivial example you may find it useful as the basis for a much more complex project.

The first step is to make the data sent by the Arduino to your serial port available to the program that will run on your computer. Most scripting languages have very poor support for serial communications, so rather than trying to open the serial port directly, we'll cheat by using a program that runs as a daemon and opens the port for us then makes it available as a network socket. Scripting languages are champions at dealing with network sockets, so this approach can dramatically simplify things.

The serial-to-network gateway you need to use will depend on the operating system you are running. The Arduino site has a handy guide to available network proxies at www.arduino.cc/playground/Interfacing/SerialNet.For Mac OS and Windows the most popular seems to be "serproxy," which comes with step-by-step instructions for configuration. Download the appropriate archive for your operating system using the link provided on the page mentioned in the previous paragraph, extract it, and have a look at the README file for more details.

On Linux there is a serial-to-network gateway called "ser2net," which is available prepackaged on most major distributions. To configure it, open the ser2net config file, usually located at /etc/ser2net.conf, and look right at the end. You need to make sure it has a line similar to the following:

```
5331:telnet:600:/dev/ttyUSB0:38400 8DATABITS NONE 1STOPBIT banner
```

That line will open TCP port 5331 using a telnet text interface and expose the device /dev/ttyUSB0 (change to suit your requirements) at 38400bps. Restart ser2net to force it to reload its configuration.

With the appropriate gateway installed and configured, you should be able to connect to the output of your Arduino by closing the serial monitor window in your IDE and opening a telnet connection to port 5331 on localhost.

Now you need a script that will make that connection for you and send the values to Twitter. We used PHP because it's commonly available for pretty much any popular operating system and has a C-derived syntax that should look fairly familiar if you're used to Arduino. PHP scripts don't have to be executed in a web server: they can be executed directly on the command line just like scripts written in other programming languages.

Enter the following code (included as twitter-weather.php in the download for this project) into a text file, configure it with your Twitter username and password, make sure it is marked as executable using a command (such as "chmod +x twitterupdate.php" on Linux), and then run it.

The script will open a socket connection and listen for updates from your Arduino, and temperature and humidity values will be posted to your Twitter account automatically. If you've got this far with Arduino, it should be fairly self-explanatory even if it's not a language you've ever used before!

The only catches to watch out for are that you need to have the CLI (command-line interface) version of PHP installed, and you also need to have CURL installed. Other than that, it should be all smooth sailing.

```
#!/usr/bin/php
<?php
// Set Twitter credentials
$twitter_username = "abc123";  // Replace with your Twitter username
$twitter_password = "abc123";  // Replace with your Twitter password
// Configure the serial-to-socket proxy connection to the Arduino
$arduino_host = "localhost";
$arduino_port = "5331";
$update_interval = 600; // Minimum number of seconds between updates (10 mins)
$last_update_temp = 0;
$last_update_relh = 0;
// Connect to the Arduino
$fp = fsockopen( "tcp://".$arduino_host, $arduino_port, $errno, $errstr, 30 );
stream_set_timeout( $fp, 3000 );
// Watch for changes
while (!feof($fp)) {
  $rawdata = fgets($fp, 200);
  //echo "raw: $rawdata\n";   // Uncomment to watch the raw data stream
  $sample = explode( "=", $rawdata );
  $dataParam = trim( $sample[0] );
  $dataValue = trim( $sample[1] );
  if( strlen( $dataValue ) > 0 )
  {
    switch( $dataParam )
    {
      case "TEMPERATURE":
        if( date("U") - $last_update_temp > $update_interval )
        {
          $message = "The temperature outside is {$dataValue}C";
          $command = "curl -u $twitter_username:$twitter_password -d status=\"$message\"
http://twitter.com/statuses/update.xml";
          shell_exec( $command );
          $last_update_temp = date("U");
        }
      break;
      case "HUMIDITY":
        if( date("U") - $last_update_relh > $update_interval )
        {
          $message = "The relative humidity outside is {$dataValue}%";
          $command = "curl -u $twitter_username:$twitter_password -d status=\"$message\"
http://twitter.com/statuses/update.xml";
          shell_exec( $command );
          $last_update_relh = date("U");
        }
      break;
```

```
      }
    }
  }
  fclose($fp);
  ?>
```

To see the result of this script in action, you can check the weather conditions outside the author's office by following @ivttemp on Twitter at `twitter.com/ivttemp`.

Variations

Private Online Weather Station

Just outside Melbourne, Australia, a group of hang glider pilots is currently investigating installing one of these systems near a favorite but remote launch location that unfortunately has no local weather service. By installing their own weather station nearby and feeding the data to a web service such as Pachube (www.pachube.com), Watch My Thing (www.watchmything.com), or even just to Twitter, they can easily access historical and real-time weather data at the launch location before they leave home, potentially saving them a three-hour drive only to discover that conditions aren't suitable and then driving another three hours home again. Setting up the project as a cooperative venture and splitting the cost between a number of pilots means the cost to each individual is very low. Just one wasted trip would cost more in fuel than contributing to a share in their own personal weather station.

CHAPTER 14

■ ■ ■

RFID Access Control System

RFID technology (pronounced "Arr-Eff-Eye-Dee" or "Arr-Fid") is used for a wide variety of applications including access control, package identification, warehouse stock control, point-of-sale scanning, retail antitheft systems, toll-road passes, surgical instrument inventory, and even for identifying individual sheets of paper placed on a desk. RFID tags are embedded in name badges, shipping labels, library books, product tags and boxes; installed in aircraft; hidden inside car keys; and implanted under the skin of animals or even people. RFID systems work on a wide range of frequencies, have a variety of modulation and encoding schemes, and vary from low-power passive devices with range of only a few millimeters to active systems that work for hundreds of kilometers.

With such a vast range of applications and related technologies it's no wonder that most people are confused about what RFID actually is!

Part of the problem is that the term "RFID" is a generic label for any technology that uses radio communication to check the identity of an object. All sorts of radically different systems fall under the broad banner of RFID.

However, all RFID systems have the same basic two-part architecture: a reader and a transponder. The reader is an active device that sends out a signal and listens for responses, and the transponder (the part generally called the "tag") detects the signal from a reader and automatically sends back a response containing its identity code (see Figure 14-1).

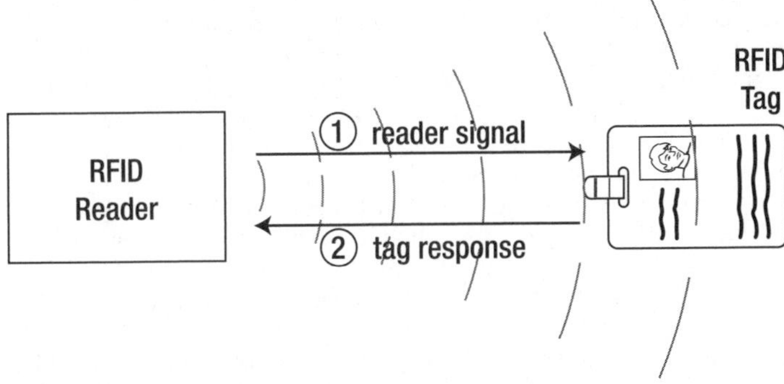

Figure 14-1. Reader challenge and tag response

One of the earliest RFID systems was developed in England in 1939 to solve the problem of Allied aircraft being targeted by friendly antiaircraft guns as they returned to base. Unfortunately, friendly aircraft returning home look pretty much the same as enemy aircraft approaching to attack, so radio transponders called IFF systems (Identification Friend or Foe) were installed that would allow aircraft to automatically send out a coded "I'm a friend— don't shoot me!" signal in response to challenges from defensive emplacements.

Despite the age of the technology, it's really only since the 1990s and the proliferation of inexpensive passive tags that RFID has gone from exotic to ubiquitous. Right now there are probably a dozen or more RFID tags within a few meters of you, and you might not even be aware of most of them.

Different types of RFID tags fall into one of three broad categories: active, passive, and battery-assisted passive.

Active tags are physically large because they require their own power supply such as a battery. They can also have a very long range because the availability of local power allows them to send high-powered responses that can travel from tens of meters to hundreds of kilometres. An active tag is essentially a combination of a radio receiver to detect the challenge, some logic to formulate a response, and a radio transmitter to send back the response. They can even have the challenge and response signals operate on totally different frequencies. The downsides are the size of the tag, a high manufacturing cost due to the number of parts required, and the reliance on a battery that will go flat eventually.

Passive tags can be much smaller and cheaper than active tags because they don't require a local power supply and have much simpler circuitry. Instead of supplying their own power, they leach all the power they need from the signal sent by the reader. Early passive tags operated on the "Wiegand effect," which uses a specially formed wire to convert received electromagnetic energy into radio-wave pulses. Some early passive RFID tags actually consisted of nothing more than a number of very carefully formed wires made from a combination of cobalt, iron, and vanadium, with no other parts at all.

Modern passive tags use a clever technique that uses current induced in their antenna coil to power the electronics required to generate the response. The response is then sent by modulating the reader's own field, and the reader detects the modulation as a tiny fluctuation in the voltage across the transmitter coil. The result is that passive tags can be incredibly small and extremely inexpensive: the antenna can be a simple piece of metal foil, and the microchips are produced in such large quantities that a complete RFID-enabled product label could cost only a few cents and be no thicker than a normal paper label. Passive tags can theoretically last indefinitely because they don't contain a battery to go flat, but their disadvantage is a very short operational range due to the requirement to leach power from the reader's signal, and lack of an actively powered transmitter to send back the response.

Passive tags typically operate over a range of a few millimeters up to a few meters.

A more recent variation that combines active and passive technologies is BAP, or battery-assisted passive. BAP tags are designed to overcome the short life limitation of a normal battery-powered active tag. A BAP tag sits in an idle passive state most of the time and receives challenge signals in the same way as a normal passive tag, but then uses the tiny amount of power leached from the signal to charge a tiny capacitor and wake up the system enough to then activate a local power source, such as a battery, to transmit a very strong response signal before going back to idle mode. A BAP tag could sit passively for years using no power at all and emitting no signal, only drawing on its battery reserves when woken up by a challenge and sending a response. Although BAP tags have the long life advantage of a passive tag (limited only by the shelf-life of the battery), they still have many of the disadvantages of active tags, including high price and physically large size. BAP tags are still very rare and you're unlikely to come across them at a hobbyist level.

Common passive tags that you're likely to find are generally classified as either low-frequency (LF) or high-frequency (HF) tags. LF tags commonly operate at either 125kHz or 134.2kHz, which is close enough that it's sometimes possible to have a reader designed for one frequency communicate with a tag designed for the other, but that's the exception rather than the rule. If you are buying LF tags, it's always wise to check the actual frequency they are designed to operate at and make sure your tags and reader match. 125kHz tags are currently the most common in the U.S., but that frequency is now slowly being phased out in favor of tags that match the 134.2kHz international standard used pretty much everywhere else in the world.

Tags can also have a variety of different modulation schemes, including AM, PSK, and ASK, and different encoding systems. With so many incompatible variations, it's sometimes hard to know if specific tags and readers are compatible. Generally speaking, each type of tag will only function on one specific frequency, modulation scheme, and communications protocol. Readers, on the other hand, are far more flexible and will often support a range of modulation schemes and comms protocols, but are usually still limited to just one frequency due to the tuning requirements of the coil.

Apart from the specific requirements for communicating with them, tags can also have a number of different features. The most common passive tags simply contain a hard-coded unique serial number and when interrogated by a reader they automatically respond with their ID code. Most tags are read-only so you can't change the value they return, but some types of tags are read/write and contain a tiny amount of rewritable storage so you can insert data into them using a reader and retrieve it later. However, most uses of RFID don't rely on any storage within the tag, and merely use the ID code of the tag as a reference number to look up information about it in an external database or other system.

RFID tags are produced in a wide variety of physical form factors to suit different deployment requirements. The most commonly seen form factor is a flat plastic card the same size as a credit card, often used as an access control pass to gain access to office buildings or other secure areas. The most common form by sheer number produced, even though you might not notice them, is RFID-enabled stickers that are commonly placed on boxes, packages, and products. Key fob tags are also quite common, designed to be attached to a keyring so they're always handy for operating access control systems. Some of these are shown in Figure 14-2.

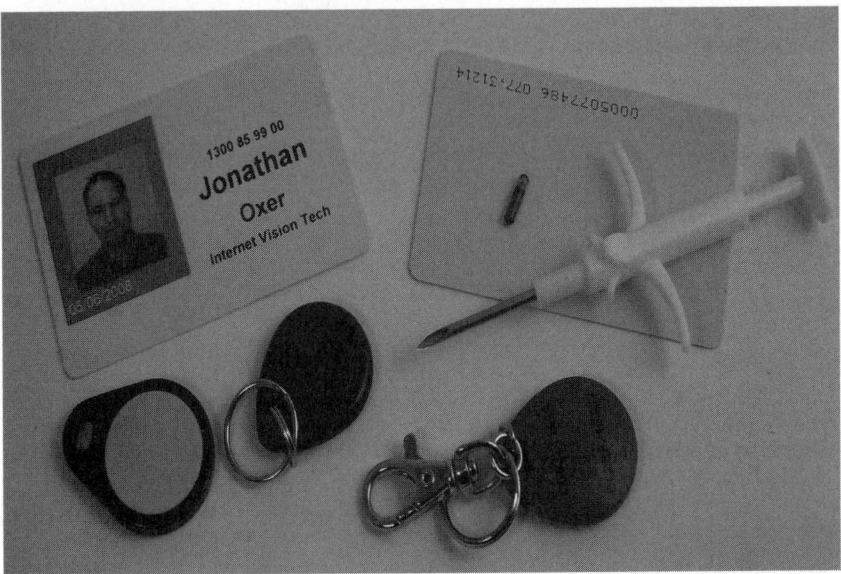

***Figure 14-2.** RFID tags in a variety of form factors including access cards, key fobs, and a surgically implantable pellet*

Another common form factor is surgically implantable tags encased in a special biologically inert glass called "soda glass" and shaped to be approximately the size of a large grain of rice. Implantable tags are often coated with a special sleeve that is slightly porous to allow protein strands to grow into it and prevent it migrating under the skin after implantation. They are commonly used to tag domestic animals such as cats and dogs so they can be identified by a vet or pet shelter using a special RFID reader if they are lost. Some people, including one of the authors of this book, have even implanted RFID tags in themselves so they can operate access control systems without having to carry anything!Tags also come in more exotic form factors such as inside special nails that can be hammered into objects that need to be tagged. They are also available as a ceramic bolus designed to be swallowed by cattle so it will sit in their stomach indefinitely for external scanning, and in tags attached to the ears of livestock.

Several companies are also experimenting with producing paper that has a passive RFID tag embedded inside every individual sheet: by building an RFID reader into a pad that sits on a desk or on shelving, it's possible for your computer to track the location of every single page individually. No more problems with a misplaced sheet in a big pile of paper.This project uses a prebuilt RFID reader module to interrogate commonly available passive tags, looks up the tag ID in an internal database, and releases a lock using an electric strike plate if the tag is authorized.

You can also combine this project with the Speech Synthesizer project in Chapter 9 for audible feedback, or fit it into a handheld case and add an LCD to create a portable RFID reader. By combining it with flash memory for datalogging and a GPS module to log the location at which each scan was performed, you could build a reader with more features than just about any commercial device on the market today, but at a lower cost than even the most basic commercial readers.

The required parts are pictured in Figure 14-3 and the complete schematic in Figure 14-4.

Parts Required

1 x Arduino Duemilanove, Arduino Pro, or equivalent

1 x Prototyping shield

1 x 4-pin PCB-mount header with 90 degree bend

1 x 4-pin line header socket

2 x 2-pin PCB-mount screw terminals

1 x 12V electric strike plate

1 x LM7805 voltage regulator

2 x 100nF capacitors

1 x 22uF electrolytic capacitor

2 x 1N4001 or equivalent power diodes

1 x 4K7 resistor

1 x 100K resistor

1 x BC547, BC548, 2N2222, or equivalent NPN transistor

1 x Red LED

1 x Green LED

2 x 680R resistors

1 x 12V 1A power supply or plugpack

20cm Ribbon cable

1 x 125kHz RFID tag

1 x Small PVC box

1 x ID-12 RFID reader module (www.id-solutions.com)

1 x ID-12 breakout board or custom PCB, as explained in the text

or

1 x RDM630 125kHz RFID module (UART version) from Seeed Studio

For optional manual-release exit button:

1 x Single-pole, single-throw (SPST) momentary pushbutton

1 x 2-pin PCB-mount screw terminal

Lightweight two-core cable, such as figure-8 speaker cable

Source code available from
`www.practicalarduino.com/projects/rfid-access-control-system`

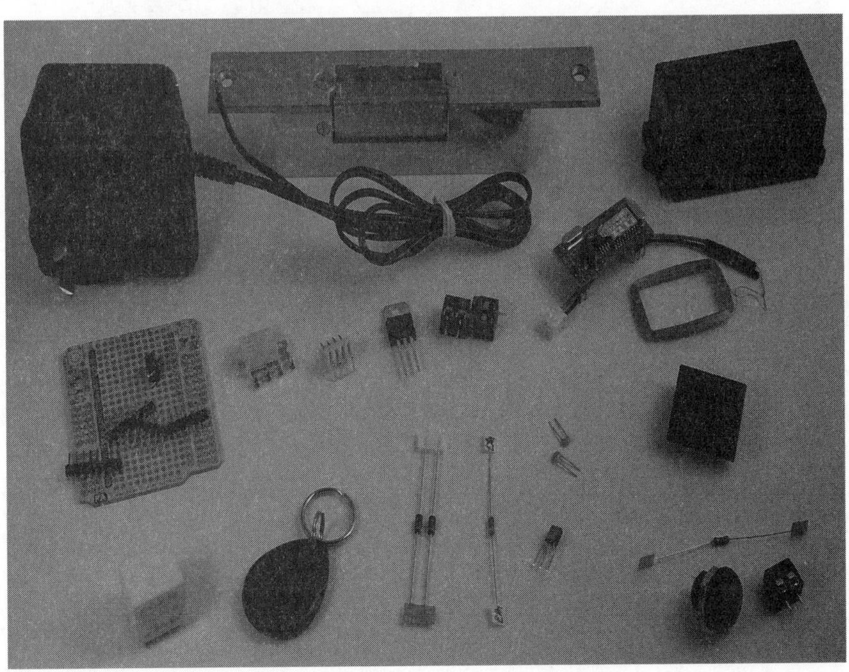

Figure 14-3. *Parts required for RFID Access Control System*

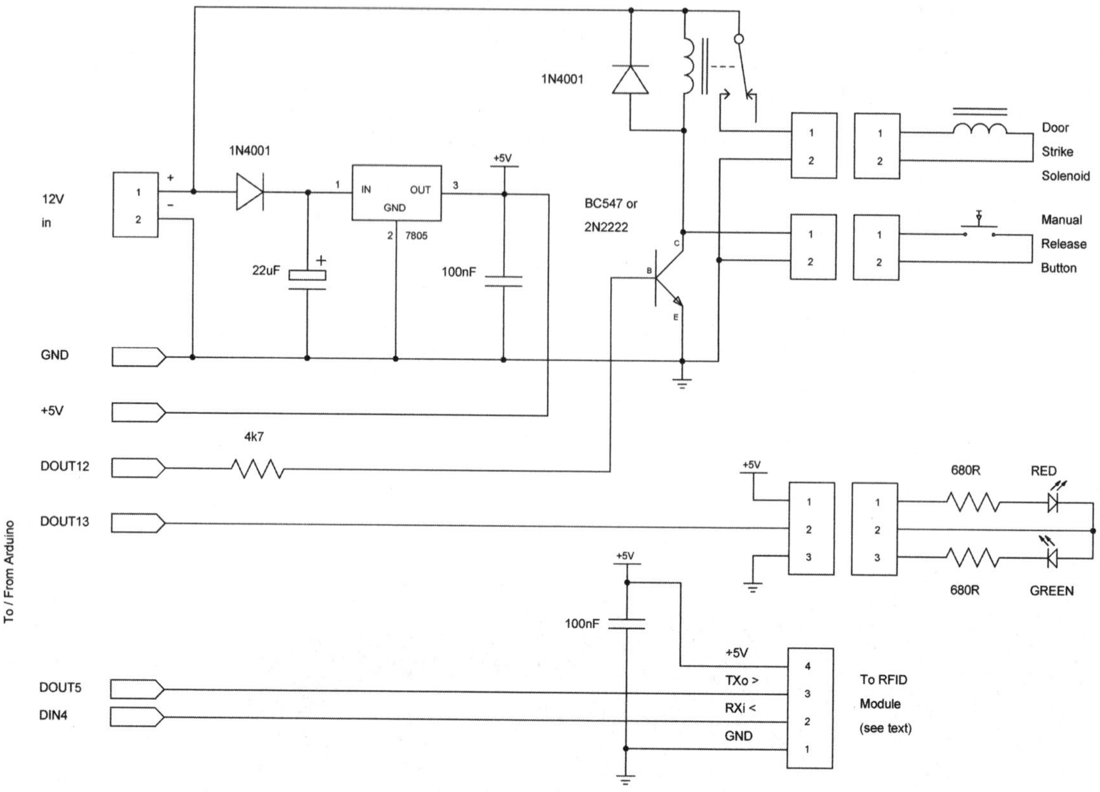

Figure 14-4. Schematic of common section of RFID Access Control System. Schematics for specific RFID modules included later

Instructions

For this project you have several options for compatible RFID reader modules, all of which communicate using a serial interface with RS-232–style comms at a 5V logic level— perfect for interfacing with an Arduino. The two we have listed are the ID-12 module from ID Innovations (available from online retailers, including SparkFun) and the RDM630 module (available from online retailers, including Seeed Studio), which both read a variety of 125kHz low-frequency tags. You can also substitute other modules if your requirements are different. For example, to read 13.56MHz MiFare-type tags you could use an RDM880 module, also available from Seeed Studio, which uses the exact same host interface.

Whatever module you go for, look for one with a "UART" interface rather than a "Wiegand" interface. The UART interface is designed for serial communications with a host such as an Arduino, so you can just treat the module as another serial device. The Wiegand interface requires a little more work to process from the host side. It's not difficult to do and you can use a Wiegand module and modify the code to suit if that's all you have available, but the example code we present here assumes you are using a UART RFID module.

So, which to use—ID-12 or RDM630?

Both modules have pros and cons. The ID-12 is neatly packaged in a robust plastic container filled with resin to make it very strong, but has the downsides that the package uses nonstandard 2mm pin spacing so you can't fit it to a standard prototyping board, and it's more expensive. The RDM630 is cheaper and has a larger coil that's separate to the module so the read range might be slightly better, but the module itself is physically larger than the ID-12, and because it's an exposed PCB you have to be a bit more careful about mounting it. In the parts shown in Figure 14-3, you can see both an ID-12 module (the black square on the right) and an RDM630 (the PCB and separate coil just above the ID-12). You can choose for yourself based on your mounting requirements.

Whichever module you use, the prototyping shield needs to be assembled in exactly the same way.

Assemble the Prototyping Shield

Because this project runs the Arduino as a stand-alone system independent of a host computer, it needs a regulated power supply to keep it running. The Arduino itself contains a built-in voltage regulator but it tends to run very hot if it's given more than about 9V. Because the electric strike plate requires a large jolt of 12V power to unlock it, we've included a simple 5V power supply circuit on the shield so both the Arduino and the strike plate can run from the same 12V supply. That same supply is also switched through to a pair of output terminals for connection to the electric strike plate, so everything is as self-contained as possible with minimal cabling.

One optional step before going on with the rest of the assembly is to install a 100K resistor between Arduino digital pin 0 (RX) and ground on the shield. You might not need it depending on your Arduino, but without it you might find the Arduino doesn't boot properly when USB is disconnected. The resistor biases the RX pin to 0V while still allowing it to be pulled to +5V if required, rather than floating randomly between 0V and +5V. With a USB cable in place, the RX pin is asserted either high or low all the time and everything is fine, but if you power your Arduino from an external power supply and don't have USB connected, the RX line could see random data and prevent the Arduino from booting. Biasing it to ground prevents this happening and makes sure it will start up reliably when it's mounted in some inaccessible place such as under the floor or inside the ceiling while still allowing a USB connection to function normally.

Power Supply

The 5V power supply on the shield consists of an LM7805 linear voltage regulator, a 1N4001 or equivalent power diode, and a 22uF electrolytic capacitor (see Figure 14-5).

Start by fitting the 2-pin screw terminal that will be used to connect the 12V plugpack, with one terminal connected directly to the ground rail on the shield. Use a felt-tip pen to clearly mark that terminal "–" and the other terminal "+" so you know which is which when it comes time to connect the external power supply.

Then fit the LM7805 regulator so that the OUT pin is connected directly to the +5V rail on the shield. The 1N4001 diode can then be fitted between the "+" connection on the screw terminal and the "IN" connection on the LM7805. The diode is not strictly necessary and the + input could be connected directly to the voltage regulator's IN pin, but including the diode is a good safety precaution just in case the power is ever connected up backward. Current will only flow through the diode in a forward direction so it acts as a one-way valve to prevent things from being damaged if the power supply is reversed by mistake.

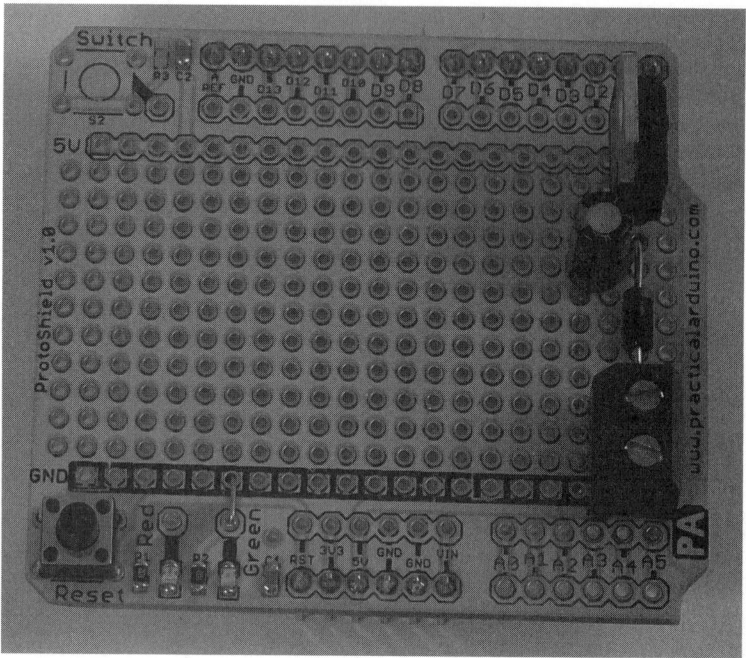

Figure 14-5. *5V power supply assembled on shield*

Insert the 22uF electrolytic capacitor so that the positive lead connects to the joint between the regulator and the diode. Electrolytics normally have a long lead for positive and a short lead for negative, and the negative lead will also be marked on the body with a line and a minus symbol so you can tell which is which even after the leads have been cut to the same length. With the positive lead connected, bend the negative lead all the way down to the ground bus on the shield and solder it in place. If the lead isn't long enough, use a short length of hookup wire or a component lead off-cut.

The purpose of the capacitor is to provide smoothing of the input voltage since typical cheap plugpacks contain a tiny transformer that generates a rectified sine-wave output that varies between 0V and the maximum output voltage. Putting a capacitor across the input has the effect of holding the voltage high during the downswings of the sine wave, and provides a cleaner supply to the voltage regulator. The 22uF value isn't anything special and was simply picked because it was high enough to provide a decent amount of filtering, while being low enough for the capacitor package to by physically small. If you have a different value handy that's fine— you could use a 1uF or a 470uF capacitor, or anything in between.

The final step in assembling the power supply is to connect the COMMON (center) pin of the voltage regulator to ground. Depending on the layout of your shield, you can probably connect it to the negative lead of the smoothing capacitor using a short length of component lead.

Before doing anything else it's a good idea to test the power supply section of the project to make sure you're providing the correct voltage to the shield. Without connecting the shield to an Arduino, connect up a 12V plugpack to the input terminals and put a volt meter (such as a multimeter in voltage mode) across the ground and +5V rails of the shield. You should see a voltage between 4.95V and 5.05V, which means the voltage regulator is working as expected.

Doing an isolated test of the power supply circuit before continuing with construction is a good habit to get into with all your projects because if you made a mistake, you won't damage anything else on the board. For example, an easy mistake to make is to forget to link the COMMON pin of the voltage regulator to ground. The result is that the voltage regulator runs in an unregulated state with no 0V reference voltage and, therefore, provides the full input voltage on the output—very dangerous to your Arduino! Testing the power supply in isolation helps you discover problems like this before any damage is done.

You can see in Figure 14-5 that the prototyping shield we used for this project includes a couple of general-purpose LEDs that are connected to +5V through current-limiting resistors. We therefore put in a link from one of the LEDs to the adjacent ground bus so that it would provide a handy power-on indicator.

RFID Serial Connection

To make it easy to connect different RFID modules we used a 4-pin PCB-mount male header. If you're doing the same, fit the header so that one end is connected to the +5V bus on the shield and then link the pin on the other end to ground. There's no real standard for serial interface connections, but just out of habit the authors have commonly used headers that connect as shown in Figure 14-6.

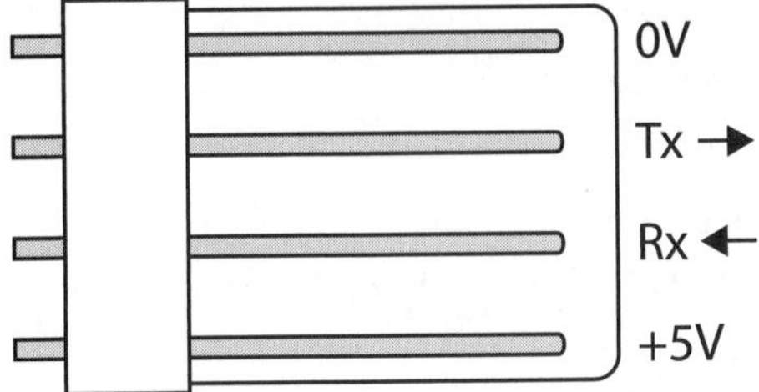

Figure 14-6. *Serial connection pin assignments on an oriented 4-pin male header*

Both of the RFID modules recommended for this project use serial communications at 9600bps, so our example program uses the SoftwareSerial library to run a serial connection on digital I/O lines 4 and 5. We used line 4 as RX and line 5 as TX from the Arduino (see Figure 14-7).

If all you want to do is power the device from an external power supply and read RFID tags then that's all you need to do on the shield itself, but we're going to use a relay to control an electric strike plate so we also need to connect a transistor-switched output.

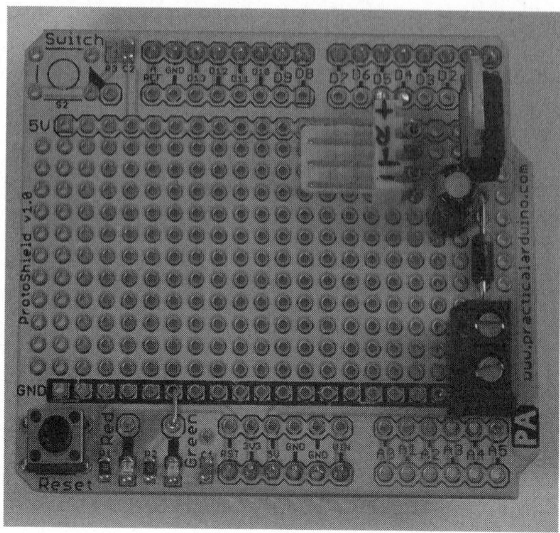

Figure 14-7. Serial connection mounted shield for RFID module

Relay Output

The outputs of an Arduino are only rated to 40mA of current each, with a total limit of 200mA across all outputs combined. A relay big enough to activate an electric strike plate is likely to exceed the limit, so we use a digital output to control a transistor which in turn controls the relay (see Figure 14-8).

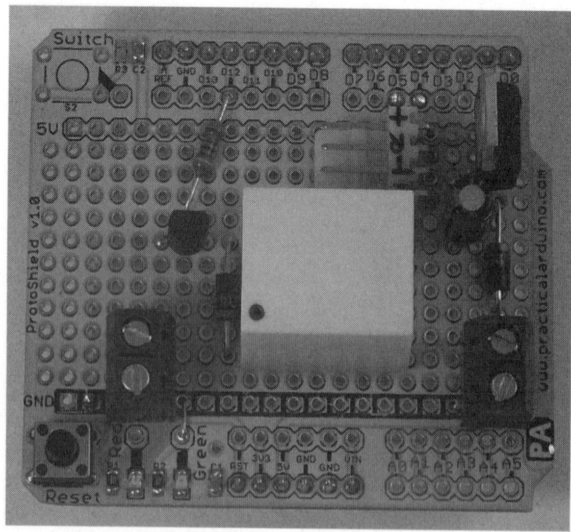

Figure 14-8. Transistor output driving a relay

But before installing the rest of the parts the relay itself needs to be fitted, and that can be more tricky than it sounds because many relays don't fit neatly on a 0.1-inch grid. We used a SPST (single-pole, single-throw) relay. The four outer pins could have been bent enough to fit through normal holes on the prototyping shield, but the center (common) pin for the outputs fell directly between four holes. We had to drill a new hole through the prototyping shield, keeping in mind that something to be very careful of is that many prototyping shields have a ground plane that covers the entire shield surface between all the pins. If you drill a small hole through the shield just big enough for the pin to fit through, you'll probably find that the pin will short-circuit to ground when you solder it in place. We had to drill a large hole that cleared the pin by a good margin and then solder a jumper wire to the pin while keeping the joint clear of the edges of the hole.

A short length of heat-shrink tubing is a good idea to prevent short-circuits if the wire is bumped (see Figure 14-9).

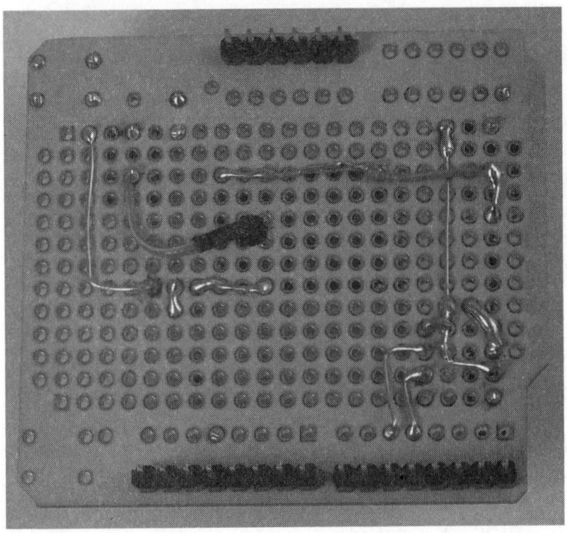

Figure 14-9. *Connection to "common" connection on relay through a hole drilled in the shield*

Once the relay is in place, use a short length of hookup wire to join one of the coil connections to the "NO" (normally open) connection and then to the +12V terminal on the power connection. Then fit the second 1N4001 power diode across the coil connections so that the end with the band (the cathode) is joined to the coil connection that is linked to +12V.

The purpose of the diode is to short out any reverse-voltage charge that is induced across the relay coil when it turns off. Without this protection diode in place a high-voltage reverse spike could damage other parts in the circuit. Even if you don't see a failure immediately, it can still cause degradation of parts over time.

Insert the transistor so that the collector pin connects to the relay coil connection at the nonbanded (anode) end of the diode. Use a short length of hookup wire to join the emitter pin of the transistor to the ground bus on the shield (see Figure 14-10). The actual selection of diode isn't particularly critical because it's just being used as a simple electronic switch in this application. As long as it's a small NPN transistor you should be fine, so it could be a 2N2222, a BC547, a BC548, or any other common NPN low-power switching transistor.

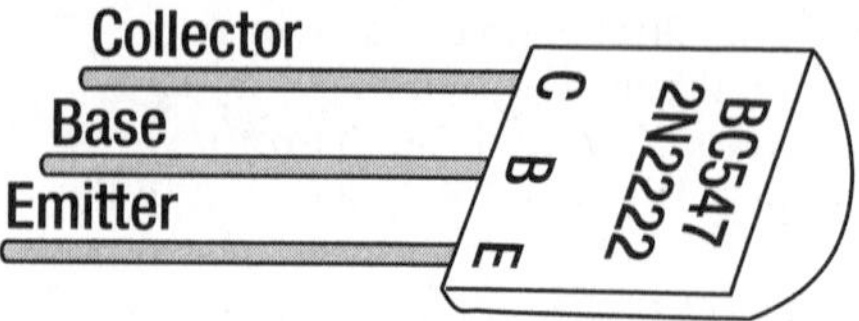

Figure 14-10. *Pinout of BC547 and 2N2222 transistors*

Next, insert the 4K7 resistor so that it connects to Arduino digital I/O pin 12 at one end and the transistor's base lead at the other. The resistor limits current flowing through the output pin but allows it to bias the transistor either on or off to match the state of the output. Don't connect the base of the resistor directly to the I/O pin, or the ATMega CPU will see it as a short-circuit to ground and deliver maximum current flow into it unnecessarily.

As you can see in the schematic in Figure 14-4, the relay coil has one end connected to +12V while the other end connects to the transistor's collector. The transistor emitter connects to ground, so if the transistor is turned on hard the collector will also be pulled to ground and the relay coil will see 12V difference across the connections and be turned on. If the transistor is turned off, the collector voltage will float high thanks to conductivity through the coil which will see 0V across it and be turned off.

Fit the second 2-pin PCB-mount screw terminal with one terminal pin connected to the ground bus on the shield. Then connect the other terminal pin to the relay common connection using a short length of jumper wire passing through the hole in the shield to connect directly to the pin.

Indicator LEDs

Fitting indicator LEDs is optional but it can be handy when testing and also help provide feedback once it has been installed near a door. On the prototype, we fitted two LEDs, with a red LED to indicate "locked" and a green LED to indicate "unlocked." However, because the two LEDs are used in such a way that only one is on at a time, we used a little trick to control them both from a single output pin. Because there are so few pins used in this project, that's not really necessary, but it can be a handy thing to know for other projects and simplifies the software a little.

As you can see in the schematic one of the LEDs is connected via a 680R current-limiting resistor to +5V, while the other is connected via a similar resistor to ground. By joining them both to the same output, we can turn on one or the other depending on whether the output is high or low. In normal operation the output will be low so the red LED will be illuminated, but when a tag has been successfully read and the output goes high, the red LED turns off and the green LED turns on. Of course when the output is in a high-impedance "floating" state both LEDs will be dimly illuminated, so when power is first applied they will both glow until the sketch sets the state of the output.

The LEDs could even have been connected to the same digital output as the transistor so that when the transistor (and hence the strike plate) is off the red LED will be illuminated, and when the transistor turns on the green LED will illuminate. However, that limits your ability to use them to indicate other events, such as a bad read, without triggering the strike plate.

If you are going to mount the Arduino some distance from the RFID reader, you will need to use long enough leads to reach from the reader location to the Arduino. A typical application might see the Arduino, shield, and power supply all mounted either under the floor of your house or inside a ceiling, with wires running through the wall to the RFID reader mounted beside the door and the strike plate mounted in the door frame. For convenience, you may want to do what we did and fit a 3-pin male header to the shield so you can easily connect or disconnect the LED indicator assembly.

We fitted a 3-pin header with the pin on one end connected to +5V, the pin on the other end connected to ground, and the center pin connected to Arduino digital output line 13 using a short jumper wire (see Figure 14-11).

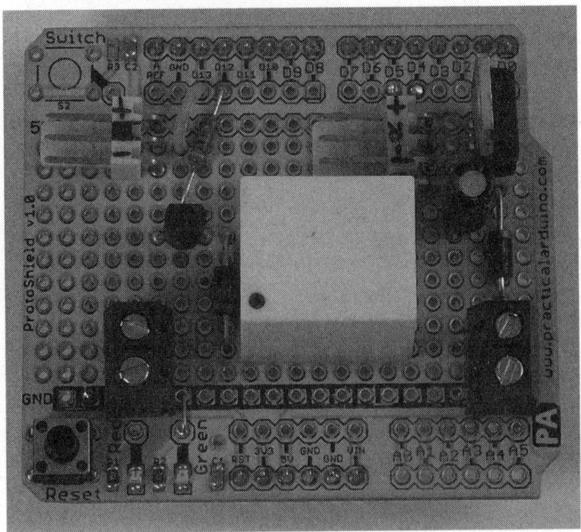

***Figure 14-11.** Header and jumper in place for connection to indicator LED assembly*

If you are mounting your reader module inside a box or behind a blank electrical wall plate like the one we used in our prototype, start by drilling holes to fit the red and green LEDs and clip or glue them into position. When mounting them, remember that you will be linking the anode (long) lead of the green LED and the cathode (short) lead of the red LED together with resistors, so orient them appropriately.

Once the LEDs are in place, solder the two 680R resistors in series and bridge them from one LED to the other as shown in Figure 14-12. The central joint of the two resistors will be connected to the Arduino's digital output.

Cut off a length of three-core cable, such as a strip of ribbon cable, long enough to reach from the mounting location of the Arduino to the mounting point for the reader. Connect a 3-pin female header to one end and solder the other end to the LEDs and the center point of the resistors. The +5V lead connects to the cathode (short) lead of the green LED, while the ground lead connects to the anode (long) lead of the red LED. The pin 13 connection goes to the center of the two resistors.

The leads also need physical support because it's never a good idea to rely on a solder joint to provide mechanical strength as well as electrical connectivity. We used two-part epoxy resin to hold the whole LED assembly in place, including the resistors and the cable, taking the strain off the solder joints.

The shield is now complete and ready to go, so next you need to assemble an RFID reader module to connect to the 4-pin serial port added to the shield.

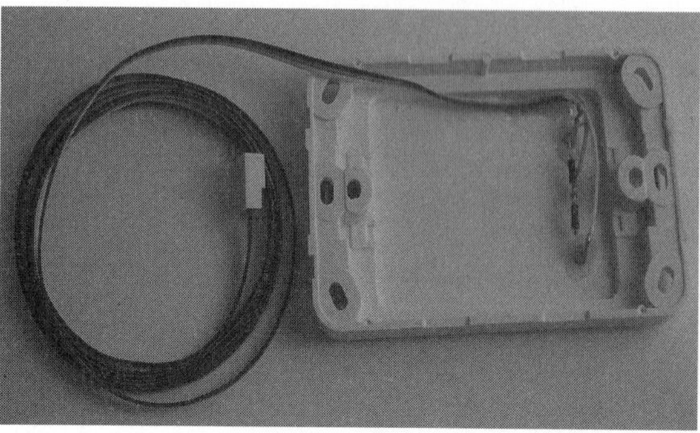

Figure 14-12. Status indicator LEDs mounted in a blank electrical wall plate

Manual Release Button

It may be handy to have a pushbutton mounted inside a protected door so people need to swipe their RFID card on the way in, but anyone can exit simply by pushing a button even if they don't have a card. The schematic and parts list show a momentary-action button that can be wired between the transistor's collector and ground. Whenever the button is pressed it pulls the collector pin to 0V and allows the relay to activate, triggering the strike plate.

This method is a very simple way to provide a bypass for the lock because it will function even if the Arduino has failed for some reason. It's not dependent on any of the rest of the circuit being operational for it to function. However, it will only operate for as long as the button is pushed, so an alternative approach would be to connect the button to a digital input on the Arduino and have it trigger an interrupt that in turn fires the transistor output and holds it on for a predetermined interval. This way, a quick push of the "exit" button could cause the lock to disengage for several seconds, giving time to pull the door open after releasing the button.

Assemble the ID-12 Reader Module

Unfortunately, the ID series RFID modules all have one major annoying idiosyncrasy: instead of having their pins spaced on a 0.1in imperial grid like the vast majority of electronic parts, they're spaced on a 2mm metric grid. Since 0.1in is about 2.54mm, that means it's impossible to simply plug an ID-12 module into a breadboard or fit it on a prototyping shield unless you either do surgery on the shield to drill additional holes or mount the ID-12 on a breakout board that converts it to a standard 0.1in grid.

For this project we wanted to mount the module behind a blank wall plate separated from the Arduino and shield so the problem isn't quite as frustrating as it could have been, but it still makes things awkward. If all else fails you could solder wires directly to the appropriate pins on your ID-12, but that won't provide much mechanical support. An alternative is to buy a generic prototyping board with a nonstandard 2mm grid, but that tends to be very expensive and not commonly available. Or you could etch a tiny custom circuit board that provides the correct pin spacing for the ID-12 module plus mounting pads, or buy one ready-made from a supplier such as SparkFun. Because this is such a simple PCB, you can easily fabricate it yourself at home using either a resist pen to draw it out by hand or photographic exposure techniques.

If you are using a PCB, start by inserting your ID-12 module into the board and soldering the pins in place. Then fit the end of a length of four-core cable, such as a length stripped from a ribbon cable, to the +5V (pin 11), Gnd (pin 1), TX (pin 9), and RX (pin 8) connections. Connecting the reader on a PCB produces a mechanically strong subassembly that can be mounted separately and then easily connected or disconnected as required. It also means you can create a longer cable and mount the reader totally separately: you may want to have the reader mounted near a conveyor belt to track items passing along it, or on the end of a pole so you can reach up high to read tags attached to boxes on shelving in a storage facility. Or, as you'll see at the end of this project, on a pole so it can be inserted into a penguin burrow to read RFID tags surgically implanted in a colony of Little Penguins!

To put the ID-12 module into the correct mode it's also necessary to make a few additional connections between different pins on the module.

Pin 2 is the reset pin, which is active-low, so link it to pin 11 (+5V) to prevent the unit from resetting.

Pin 7 is the format (mode) pin. When held high, it puts the module into "Wiegand26" mode to emulate an older Wiegand-format reader. If connected to pin 10, the module goes into a "magnet emulation" mode in which it pretends to be a magnetic card reader. If held low the module goes into ASCII mode, which happens to be exactly what we want. Link pin 7 to pin 1 (ground) for operation with an Arduino (see Figure 14-13).

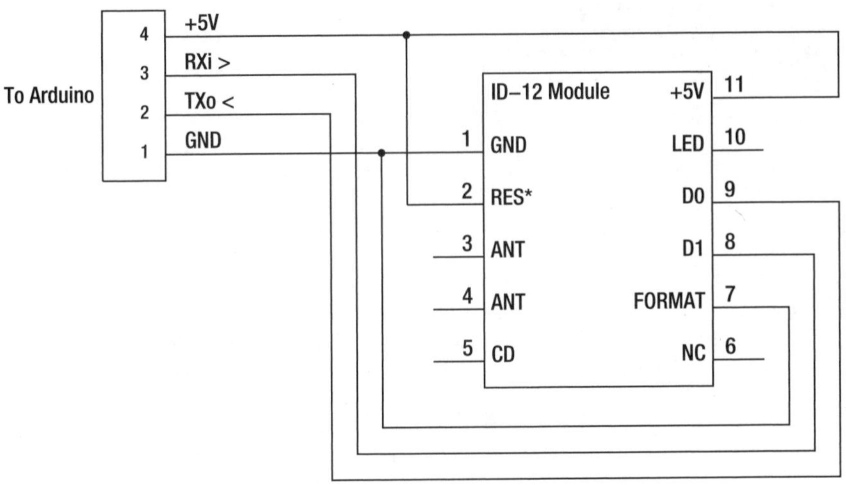

Figure 14-13. Schematic of ID-12 module connection to Arduino serial interface

Fit a 4-pin–oriented female header to the other end of the cable to match the connections on the shield, keeping in mind that you need to reverse TX/RX on the RFID module compared to the Arduino. The TX pin on the module (pin 9) needs to go to RX (pin 4) on the Arduino. We don't use it with the ID-12 module, but for completeness you can also connect the RX pin on the module (pin 8) to the Arduino's TX on pin 5.

Mount the ID-12 module itself inside your case or front panel, keeping it flat against the case. The read range can be quite limited and nearby metal could alter the tuning, so the closer you can get it to the location of the tag the more reliable it will be. For our prototype we mounted the ID-12 inside a blank wall plate along with the indicator LEDs (see Figure 14-14).

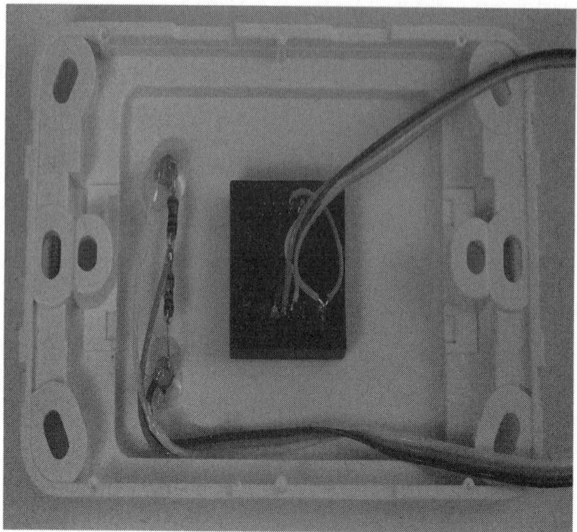

Figure 14-14. ID-12 module mounted behind a blank electrical wall plate

A link to the ID-12 datasheet is provided on the project page on the *Practical Arduino* web site.

Assemble the RDM630 Reader

The RDM630 is supplied with a separate reader coil and module, with a very short lead to connect the coil to the module. Unlike the ID-12 it doesn't need any special connections to be made to set it into a mode that works well with an Arduino, so wiring it up is extremely simple (see Figure 14-15).

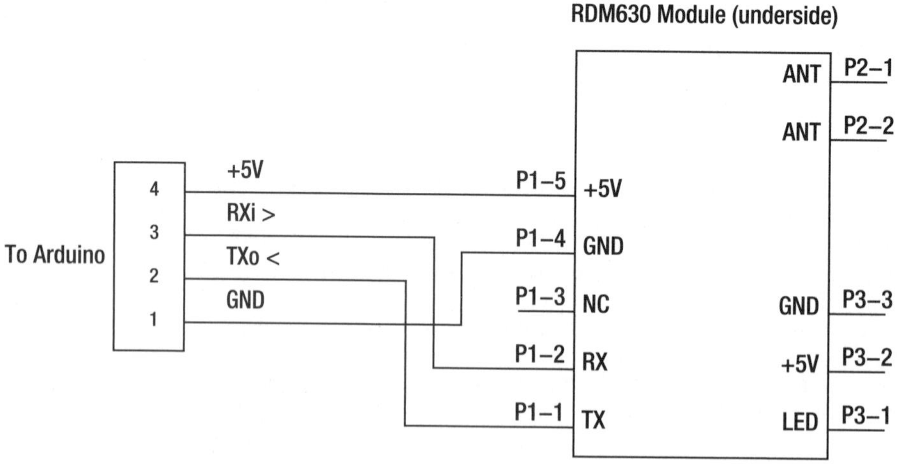

RDM630 Module (underside)
ANT P2–1
ANT P2–2
To Arduino
4 +5V P1–5 +5V
3 RXi > P1–4 GND
2 TXo < P1–3 NC
1 GND
GND P3–3
P1–2 RX
+5V P3–2
P1–1 TX
LED P3–1

Figure 14-15. Schematic of RDM630 module connection to Arduino serial interface

The reader coil comes with a 2-pin female header prefitted and ready to plug into a 2-pin male header on the module. Because our prototype needed to fit inside a very thin wall panel, the header on the module protruded too far so we bent it sideways after popping off the little black plastic spacer.

Next connect a length of four-core cable, such as a strip of ribbon cable, to the +5V, ground, RX, and TX pins. Once again the pins wouldn't fit inside our wall plate, so we bent them sideways and then soldered the wires in place. We also had to pop off the spacers on the P3 connector and bend its pins down to gain some clearance.

Then fit a 4-pin female header to the other end of the cable to connect to the shield, remembering that RX/TX on the RFID module need to be the opposite of RX/TX on the Arduino. Connect the RFID module TX (P1 pin 1) to the Arduino RX (pin 4), and the module's RX (P1 pin 2) to the Arduino RX (pin 5). Of course, we're not actually using the module RX pin in this project but some RFID modules, including the 134.2kHz variant of the RDM630, allow you to write values to the tag, so wiring it up allows you to swap the module out in future if you want full read/write capability.

Mount the antenna inside your project box or wall plate, keeping it as close to where tags will be presented as possible and away from metal. Mount the RDM630 module beside it and fix it in place. Options include double-sided tape or, if you want to make it more permanent and don't mind not being able to remove the module later, something like two-part epoxy resin. In either case, make sure the cable is well anchored so no strain is placed on the solder joints.

Figure 14-16 shows our prototype with the coil held in place temporarily with tape and the module ready to be glued down.

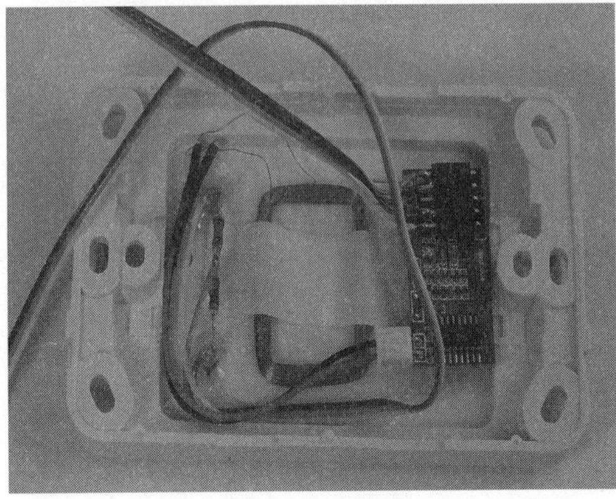

Figure 14-16. *RDM630 module mounted behind a blank electrical wall plate*

A link to the RDM630 datasheet is provided on the project page on the *Practical Arduino* web site.

Simple Stand-Alone Sketch

RFID has so many possible applications that you can use the basic hardware in this project in a huge number of ways. The RFID Access Control Standalone sketch implements a stand-alone RFID access-control system that can operate independently of a host computer or any other device. It scans continuously for RFID tags, and when a recognized tag is identified it toggles the relay output for a configurable duration, typically 2 seconds, to trip an electric strike plate to release a door lock.

Because this sketch is intended to provide a minimal working system it does not have any provision for updates to the tag database to be managed externally from a host, so updates to the accepted cards must be made by changing the values in the code, recompiling the sketch, and reuploading it to the Arduino. It does, however, report card readings (both successful and unsuccessful) via the serial connection so you can monitor the system using a connected computer if you want to for datalogging purposes.

The first thing the sketch does is set up the serial connection to the RFID reader module. The module's TX pin is connected to RX (pin 4) on the Arduino as per the hardware assembly instructions. The module's RX pin doesn't need to be connected to anything since we won't be sending any commands to it, but the SoftwareSerial library requires us to define a pin for TX so we set it to pin 5 and then ignore it. Then we create a software serial object for the connection to the RFID module and call it simply "rfid."

```
#include <SoftwareSerial.h>
#define rxPin 4
#define txPin 5
SoftwareSerial rfid = SoftwareSerial( rxPin, txPin );
```

The system has two outputs: one to drive a relay that applies power to an electric strike plate, and one that controls two status LEDs to show when the system is "locked" (red) or "unlocked" (green). The strike plate relay is driven by digital I/O pin 12, while the status LEDs are connected to digital pin 13.

```
#define strikePlate 12
#define statusPin 13
```

The length of time the lock will be held open can be configured by changing the value of the unlockSeconds variable. This value is multiplied by 1,000 to convert it to milliseconds later in the sketch. The value needs to be long enough to allow a cardholder to swipe their card and then pull the door open, but not so long that they have time to open the door and then close it again before the lock re-engages.

```
#define unlockSeconds 2
```

The tag database consists of two parts. The first part is an array of tag values, with each tag code stored as a separate element in the array. It can be a good idea to add comments after each tag so you know which is which. This list can be extended simply by adding more rows to it.

```
char* allowedTags[] = {
  "0104F5B522",         // Tag 1
  "04146E8BDE",         // Tag 2
  "0413BBBF22",         // Tag 3
};
```

The second part of the tag database is a list of names to associate with each tag. This array must have the same number of elements as the allowedTags array, so if you add a tag code to allowedTags you also need to add an entry to the tagName array. Once again, add comments so you know which name matches which tag; otherwise it can be pretty confusing if you have more than a few tags.

```
char* tagName[] = {
  "Jonathan Oxer",      // Tag 1
  "Hugh Blemings",      // Tag 2
  "Dexter D Dog",       // Tag 3
};
```

The sketch needs to know how many tags have been defined so that later, when it is looping through the allowedTags array, it knows when to stop. We do this with a little trick that doesn't look like it should work until you realize that C arrays don't actually hold data directly: they just provide pointers to the values stored elsewhere in memory. The result is a seemingly trivial little line that can be a bit brain-bending if you try to figure out how it works.

If you simply call sizeof on the allowedTags array you won't get a value that is the total of all the characters. Instead, you get a value equal to the number of bytes used for each pointer multiplied by the number of elements, which is almost certainly not what you want! The solution is to divide the result by the size of one of the pointers. This gives you the number of pointers and, therefore, the number of elements in the array. Because each pointer in the array will be the exact same size regardless of the length of the value it points to, it doesn't even matter whether we divide by allowedTags[0], or allowedTags[3], or even a nonexistent index, such as allowedTags[0xFFFF]. The sizeof function never bothers to dereference (follow) the pointer—it only looks at the size of it! To keep things neat, though, we just use allowedTags[0] so the size of the pointer in the first element is measured.

```
int numberOfTags = sizeof(allowedTags)/sizeof(allowedTags[0]);
```

Then we define a single-byte variable to hold incoming data as we read it from the serial port.

```
byte incomingByte = 0;
```

The setup function is very simple. It sets the two output pins (statusPin and strikePlate) as outputs, sets up communications with a host at 38400bps, sets up the SoftwareSerial object to communicate with the RFID reader module at 9600bps, and then prints a welcome message to the host. Both the ID-12 and RDM630 RFID modules operate by default at 9600bps.

```
void setup() {
  pinMode(statusPin, OUTPUT);
  digitalWrite(statusPin, LOW);
  pinMode(strikePlate, OUTPUT);
  digitalWrite(strikePlate, LOW);
  Serial.begin(38400);
  rfid.begin(9600);
  Serial.println("RFID reader starting up");
}
```

The main program loop is quite long and fairly complex, so we'll step through it a bit at a time. It starts off simply enough by defining some variables that are used in the loop. Most of these will be explained later in the loop or are self-explanatory, but the two to pay close attention to here are tagBytes[6] and tagValue[10].

The ID-12 reader module works with "Unique" tags that output a 5-byte identification code, so normally we would only need tagBytes to be a five-element array. However, we've defined it as having six elements because after reading the tag the sketch calculates the checksum value to make sure there were no read errors, and the checksum is then added to the end as a sixth element.

The tagValue array is an array of characters, and it needs to be 10 elements long because once the 5-byte tag value is converted to an ASCII string it expands to 10 characters. As you can see by looking at the list of tags in allowedTags ealier in the program, each one of them is 10 characters long.

```
void loop() {
  byte i         = 0;
  byte val       = 0;
```

```
byte checksum  = 0;
byte bytesRead = 0;
byte tempByte  = 0;
byte tagBytes[6];
char tagValue[11];
```

Reading from the RFID module is done with the SoftwareSerial library, which unfortunately doesn't have an equivalent to the Serial.available() function. This means the sketch can't loop indefinitely and check for characters available from the serial port each time it loops through: instead it blocks on waiting for the next character from the port every time it calls rfid.read(). That's the reason this simple version of the system can't accept commands from the host via the serial console. If you sent a command to it, the sketch wouldn't see it until after the next tag read when it loops through and accesses the serial port buffer.

First, the sketch reads a byte from the rfid virtual serial device and checks whether it's a header value.

```
if((val = rfid.read()) == 2) {
```

It then resets the bytesRead counter to 0, and then enters a loop so it will continue accepting values from the RFID reader until it has seen a total of 12 characters: the 10-character tag code itself plus a two-character checksum value.

```
bytesRead = 0;
while (bytesRead < 12) {
  val = rfid.read();
```

In case the system ever gets into a confused state, such as when the ID-12 has sent part of a sequence of tag values while the program was busy elsewhere, it checks each value to see whether it's a header or stop byte. If a header or stop byte is seen while the program is still in this loop, it assumes something has gone wrong and calls break to jump out of the loop and start again. This should help the program recover from bad situations such as partially received values.

```
if((val == 0x0D)||(val == 0x0A)||(val == 0x03)||(val == 0x02)) {
  break;
}
```

We store the tag ID in two different formats for convenience later in the program. The first format is as a series of raw values stored in a character array, with only the actual tag ID itself stored. We don't want to include the checksum, so the program only appends the first 10 characters into elements 0 through 9 in the tagValue array.

```
if (bytesRead < 10)
{
  tagValue[bytesRead] = val;
}
```

The second format requires some processing and then stores each value as a separate element in an array of bytes, so the program does some ASCII/Hex conversion to each value.

```
if ((val >= '0') && (val <= '9')) {
  val = val - '0';
```

```
  }
  else if ((val >= 'A') && (val <= 'F')) {
    val = 10 + val - 'A';
  }
```

A byte is a total of 8 bits and can hold a value from 0 to decimal 255, while a hexadecimal digit is a 4-bit value (half a byte) from 0 to F. We can, therefore, store two hex digits in each byte as a pair of 4-bit values. The structure of the code here seems a bit backward because the first part of the code is for dealing with the second of a pair of hex digits, while the second part of the code is for dealing with the first.

The code first checks if it's dealing with the second hex digit of a pair. If it is, the following comparison will be true:

```
  if (bytesRead & 1 == 1) {
```

This part of the code then deals with the second of a pair of hex digits. It makes space for this digit in the current byte using a bitwise operator to shift the existing 4 bits in that byte by 4 bits to the left, leaving space for the second 4 bites to be set using the value in bytesRead.

```
    tagBytes[bytesRead >> 1] = (val | (tempByte << 4));
```

It then checks if it has reached the checksum byte, and if so it calculates the checksum using an XOR operation.

```
    if (bytesRead >> 1 != 5) {
      checksum ^= tagBytes[bytesRead >> 1];
    };
```

This part of the code then deals with the first of a pair of hex digits by simply putting the value directly into a variable. This value will then be shifted 4 bits to the left on the next loop through by the code above.

```
  } else {
    tempByte = val;
  };
```

The sketch then increments the counter that tracks how many bytes have been read and reaches the end of the loop, going back to the start to check if it has finished reading all the digits yet.

```
  bytesRead++;
}
```

The sketch checks if 12 bytes have been read, indicating that it has a complete read and can move on to comparing the acquired value with its list of authorized tags.

```
if (bytesRead == 12) {
```

The tagValue array of characters now contains a sequence of 10 characters in elements 0 through 9, but we need to make sure it's null-terminated so that the sketch can treat it as a string and know where the string ends. We therefore populate the eleventh element (element 10) with the null character.

```
tagValue[10] = '\0';
```

To provide feedback for testing or long-term data logging, the sketch then uses the serial connection to send status information back to the host so you can use the serial monitor in the Arduino IDE to watch what happens when known and unknown tags are read.

```
Serial.print("Tag value: ");
Serial.println(tagValue);
```

It also prints out the checksum that was calculated for this tag, and compares it to the value supplied by the tag reader to see if they match. The result is also sent to the host.

```
Serial.print("Checksum: ");
Serial.print(tagBytes[5], HEX);
Serial.println(tagBytes[5] == checksum ? " -- passed." : " -- error.");
```

If all you wanted to do was read tags and display their values the loop could end right here, but instead the sketch goes on to search its internal tag database for this particular tag to see if it can be identified. Searching the tag database is done using the findTag function that will be explained in a moment. At this point, all you need to know is that findTag will return an integer value greater than 1 if the tag was found, or 0 if it wasn't found.

```
int tagId = findTag( tagValue );
```

We only want the door to unlock if the scanned tag was found in the database, so the sketch checks whether the previous function returned a value greater than 0. If so, it sends some status information to the host so you know it's opening the lock along with the ID number of that tag in its internal database.

```
if( tagId > 0 )
{
  Serial.print("Authorized tag ID ");
  Serial.print(tagId);
  Serial.print(": unlocking for ");
```

Because we want it to not just list the numeric ID of the tag but also give the name of the person that tag was assigned to, it then does a lookup in the tagName array defined at the top of the sketch to find the name that matches this ID. Because the tagName array elements are numbered from 0 up, rather than from 1 up, we need to subtract 1 from the tagId value to find the matching element in the array.

```
  Serial.println(tagName[tagId - 1]);
```

Finally, the sketch makes a call to the unlock function which takes care of firing the actual strike plate.

```
  unlock();
```

If the tag wasn't found in the internal database the tag ID will be 0, so the sketch then sends a status line to the host to say the tag was not authorized.

```
} else {
  Serial.println("Tag not authorized");
```

```
      }
```

The sketch then outputs a blank separator line so you can see each reading as a separate block in the serial monitor, then sets the number of bytes read back to 0 before looping all the way back to the start to wait for another tag to be scanned.

```
      Serial.println();
    }
    bytesRead = 0;
  }
}
```

The unlock() function is very simple. When called, it fires the relay to activate the strike plate for the configured number of seconds by multiplying the value by 1,000 to convert it to a milliseconds value for delay(). It also drives the LED indicator line low, which has the effect of turning off the red LED and turning on the green one for the duration of the lock being released.

```
void unlock() {
  digitalWrite(statusPin, HIGH);
  digitalWrite(strikePlate, HIGH);
  delay(unlockSeconds * 1000);
  digitalWrite(strikePlate, LOW);
  digitalWrite(statusPin, LOW);
}
```

The last function in the sketch searches for a specific tag in the database. It takes a single argument, which is the value of the tag to find, then enters a loop that steps methodically through the allowedTags array and checks the supplied tag against that entry in the array.

The actual comparison is performed using the strcmp (or "string compare") function, which takes two strings as arguments and returns a value based on how alike they are. If the strings are identical it returns 0, so that's the value we check for. Other possible output values are a positive number if the first string is greater than the second string, or a negative value if the first string is less than the second string.

Strcmp requires that both strings be terminated with a null character. When the allowedTags array is defined each element has a null character appended automatically, but the tag value had a null character appended manually before being passed to the findTag function.

If a match is found the function returns the ID of the tag, which is simply the number of the row in the allowedTags array in which the match was discovered with 1 added to it. The reason for this is that array elements are numbered from 0 but we want the first entry to be called 1, the second to be 2, and so on, and for the value 0 to represent no match found.

```
int findTag( char tagValue[10] ) {
  for (int thisCard = 0; thisCard < numberOfTags; thisCard++) {
    if(strcmp(tagValue, allowedTags[thisCard]) == 0)
    {
      return(thisCard + 1);
    }
  }
  return(0);
}
```

Open the sketch in the Arduino IDE. Of course, when you first use the reader you won't know what the values need to be set to in the allowedTags array, so just compile it as-is and upload it to your Arduino. Open up the serial monitor with the baud rate set to 38400bps and place a tag near the reader to see the details displayed in the serial monitor. Take note of the value reported for your tag, update one of the allowedTags entries to match, recompile the program, and upload it again. Open the serial monitor once again, and this time when you bring the tag near the reader it should be scanned and reported as accepted. Do the same for each tag you want to add to the system and it's ready to go.

Once you've tested and configured the reader you need to install it near a door and connect it to an electric strike plate.

Install the Strike Plate

Door locks typically consist of two parts: the lock mechanism that fits into the door, and the strike plate mounted in the frame. In almost all locks the strike plate is nothing more than a piece of folded metal screwed into place with a hole in the middle to allow the lock plunger to engage it. With a standard strike plate, the only way for the lock to be released is if the lock mechanism withdraws the plunger from the strike plate.

An electric strike plate simply replaces the existing static strike plate, mounting into a slot cut into the door frame and providing a similar profile to the original plate with a hole into which the lock plunger can latch. With no power applied an electric strike plate holds its position and the door can only be opened if the mechanical lock is released as usual.

The difference is that electric strike plates contain a solenoid, typically designed to operate at 12V, that causes part of the plate to be released. The door lock can then open even if the lock mechanism is in the "locked" position, because the plunger will deflect the strike plate and swing open.

Adding an electric strike plate does not change the existing behavior of the mechanical lock in any way: it will still lock or unlock with a key as usual so you don't lose any existing functionality. What it does give you, however, is an additional way to release the lock by applying 12V to the strike plate.

Start by marking the position of the existing strike plate on the frame of the door, in particular showing the height of the top and bottom of the plunger hole and the position of the front and back faces of the hole. When you fit the electric strike plate, you need to get the position to match up as closely as possible so the door will close easily without being too loose and rattling in the wind.

Using a combination of a drill, chisel, and/or a router, cut a slot large enough to allow the electric strike plate to set neatly recessed into the frame. Screw it into place and check that the door opens and closes normally with the mechanical lock.

Remove the strike plate again and drill a hole through behind its mounting location to allow a length of figure-8 electrical wire (commonly used as speaker cable) to pass through into the wall cavity. Wall construction techniques vary dramatically so we can't give you any specific instructions, but the end result should be cable running from the back of the strike plate through the wall and terminating where you mount your Arduino, which could be under the floor or inside the ceiling. You might find it handy to tape one end of the cable to a length of plastic stripping, a straightened clothes hanger, or a thin stick to allow you to poke it through to where it needs to go. Once the cable is threaded through, strip the ends of the cable back and screw it onto the terminals on the strike plate before mounting it back in position in the door frame.

Install the Reader

The reader needs to be accessible from outside the protected door, so mount it inside a small plastic case or blank wall plate as described previously and screw it into place beside the door. Use the same technique as used with the strike plate to thread the cable through to the vicinity of where you will mount the Arduino (see Figure 14-17).

Something that might be a good idea is making the reader somewhat tamperproof by putting two-part epoxy glue over the screw heads to make it very hard to remove. Don't do this until you're convinced that everything is working as expected, though!

You also need to make sure that the reader is weatherproof because it contains the reader module and LEDs. If the wall is exposed directly to the weather, you may want to put a small cover above the reader or use silicone sealant around the edges to prevent any water from getting in.

Figure 14-17. *Reader mounted inside a wall plate fitted beside a door*

Install the Arduino

Fit the Arduino and shield inside a weatherproof plastic case and mount it somewhere convenient such as under the floor or inside the ceiling, with the cable running to the mounting location for the reader itself and also to the electric strike plate.

You'll also need to run the 12V power supply to the Arduino. In the unlikely event that you have a power socket near the location of the Arduino you're all set; otherwise, you might need to use some figure-8 speaker cable or similar to extend the plugpack output to the Arduino.

Once it's physically mounted in position connect up the cables from the reader including the reader serial line and the indicator LED cable, and also connect the two wires coming from the strike plate to the output screw terminals. The strike plate will then be energized (unlocked) when the reader scans a recognized tag.

Variations

Extensible Read Head

Phillip Island in Victoria on Australia's south coast is famous for a colony of Little Penguins (sometimes known as "Fairy Penguins") that nest in the dunes behind the beach. The colony is in the Phillip Island Nature Park and attracts over half-a-million tourists each year who come to watch the nightly "penguin parade" as the penguins walk across the beach.

A team of staff and volunteers protect and maintain the colony, tracking the population and logging details of births, deaths, and other events. Many of the penguins have a tiny RFID chip implanted just under the skin so they can be identified in the same way as a lost domestic cat or dog, and as they walk into the dunes they pass through a narrow chute that scans and weighs them automatically. The details are then logged for future reference.

Using a hand scanner to read a tag implanted in a penguin can be tricky because they quickly hide at the back of their burrow, and when approached by an RFID reader they often attack it quite aggressively. Carers at the Phillip Island colony normally use commercial handheld readers and simply reach into the burrow as far as they can, but often have trouble getting a reading on penguins that don't want to cooperate.

One solution is to mount an RFID reader module on the end of an extension pole to allow them to reach much further into a burrow, along with fitting an IR-sensitive security camera and an IR illuminator to the pole and feeding the signal back out to an LCD mounted near the handle so they can see exactly what is going on as they attempt to take readings deep down inside a burrow. Logging the data along with a GPS reference then gives an accurate record of exactly when and where any particular penguin was scanned.

Speech Synthesizer Feedback

The speech synthesizer project in Chapter 9 can be stacked with the basic RFID shield to create an RFID reader that speaks when it performs a reading. As the speech synthesizer project explains, text to be spoken needs to be stored as a series of sounds called "phonemes." The simplest approach to adding speech support to the simple example sketch in this chapter would be to add a third array to the tag database with one element for each tag. Inside that array would be a series of comma-separated allophones which could be passed to the speech synthesizer. For example, you could create an array such as the following:

```
char* tagSpeech[] = {
  "165,136,136,004,141",  // Tag 1, "Jon"
  "184,007,160",          // Tag 2, "Hugh"
};
```

Of course you then need to separate the allophones and send them to the speech synthesizer one at a time, which can be done by stepping through the string and splitting it on the comma with code such as this:

```
char *speechValue = tagSpeech[tagId];
char *allophone;
while ((allophone = strtok_r(speechValue, ",", &speechValue)) != NULL)
{
```

```
  say(allophone);
}
```

The rest of the changes are left as an exercise for the reader—although, if you're lucky, we might make a speech-enabled version of the program available for download from the *Practical Arduino* web site!

Intelligent Desk Pad

Rather than mounting the reader outside a door, you could also put it inside a pad that sits on your desk or embed it inside the desk surface itself. Attaching RFID tags to various objects could allow you to use them as tokens that trigger different behavior in your computer or other systems. For example, you could attach a tag to your mobile phone so that when you put it down on your desk your office phone calls come through to your extension, but when you take the mobile phone away your extension is automatically set to divert. Mounting multiple readers under different parts of the pad or desk would let you create hot zones with different meanings depending on what item you put down and where you put it.

Resources

For more information about RFID there's a good introductory article on Wikipedia at en.wikipedia.org/wiki/Rfid.

Arduino developer Tom Igoe has an excellent tutorial on his site showing how to interface with RFID readers that use an I2C interface:

```
www.tigoe.net/pcomp/code/category/PHP/347
```

CHAPTER 15

Vehicle Telemetry Platform

Have you ever wondered what really goes on under the hood of your car? Do you wish you could peek inside the engine-management system and read values from it? Are you annoyed that your dashboard displays a cryptic "check engine" light but gives absolutely no explanation what the problem might be?

You don't need a $10,000 specialist diagnostic console or even a laptop computer to get access to useful data from your car. This project shows you how to connect an Arduino to the engine-management system in your car and log data to a CSV file on a USB memory stick in real time as you drive around. By reading and storing vehicle data and combining it with GPS values, you can create your very own "black box" flight data recorder for your car to record a complete snapshot of all engine-management parameters at the moment a fault occurs, and even generate graphs of vehicle performance.

Because this project stores everything in a standard CSV file on a memory stick formatted with a normal FAT filesystem, it's really easy to access the data on your computer and manipulate it in any way you like. When you get home from a trip, you can pull out the memory stick, plug it into a computer, and open it in a spreadsheet or convert it into other formats.

Included in this project is a simple script that converts the raw data into KML, the Google Earth data format, allowing you to create an interactive 3D "fly-around" view of a trip. The screenshot in Figure 15-1 was generated using Google Earth and shows the vehicle speed plotted as the height of the line. You can clearly see the speed of the car varying as it goes around corners and through intersections.

Figure 15-1. *Vehicle speed and location plotted in Google Earth*

You can also process the data to generate graphs like the one in Figure 15-2 that shows the coolant temperature gradually rising, the car accelerating and decelerating during the trip ,and finally coming to a halt at its destination. The engine RPM at each part of the trip is also plotted and you can see how it interacts with vehicle speed.

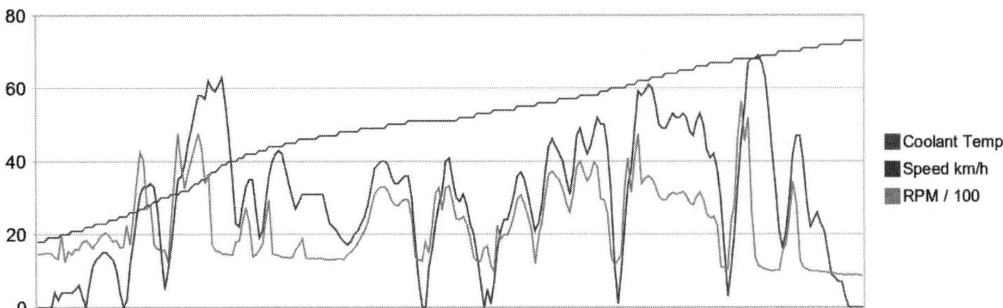

Figure 15-2. *Coolant temperature, vehicle speed, and engine RPM data recorded using an Arduino*

Extracting data from a vehicle's engine-management system while you drive along might seem like magic, but in recent years it has become much easier thanks to a standard called OBD-II, or On-Board Diagnostics version 2. All cars and light trucks sold in the U.S. since 1996 have been required by law to provide an OBD-II interface that provides access to a variety of real-time and historical operational data about the vehicle. Europe followed in 2001 for petrol vehicles and in 2003/2004 for diesels with the EOBD (European OBD) standard, which is basically just OBD-II with a different name. Other parts of the world also have related legislation, such as ADR79/01 in Australia, which is derived from the OBD-II and EOBD standards.

Because car manufacturers try to standardize their production lines, OBD-II vehicles also found their way into many markets outside the U.S. in 1996. Most Japanese car manufacturers in particular deployed OBD-II in other markets very rapidly, even when not legally required to do so. The result is that when you take your car to an auto mechanic, the first thing they usually do is plug in either a dedicated diagnostic console or a laptop using a special adapter, then run software that interrogates the engine-management system to retrieve stored data, such as a list of faults it has detected since the last service.

In this project, we combine an Arduino Mega with an OBD-II adapter, a GPS module, a USB mass-storage module, an LCD module, and control buttons to create a flexible platform for extracting, logging, and reporting data from your car. You won't get Formula One–level telemetry with thousands of data points per second, but you'll certainly get more information than an annoyingly vague "check engine" light!

If you don't want to build such an ambitious system, you might find that much of the project is still useful because it's broken down into a number of subsystems as shown in Figure 15-5 that can be used in your own designs. Even if you don't have an OBD-II–compatible car, you can combine elements, such as the GPS module and memory stick driver, with mechanisms to retrieve data via other means.

Building this project the way we designed it requires an Arduino Mega because we need the extra hardware serial ports provided by the four hardware USART (Universal Synchronous/Asynchronous Receiver/Transmitter) channels in the ATMega1280 CPU. Serial communications can either be implemented in software using careful timing (often called "bit-banging") to send and receive the data stream at the correct rate, or it can be implemented in hardware using a device that takes care of the low-level data transmission on your behalf. A USART is a hardware device specifically designed to do that job.

Figure 15-3. *Arduino-based Vehicle Telemetry Platform*

The advantage of software-based serial communications is that it can be implemented on any digital I/O pins you like, giving you flexibility in how you connect your external devices. The big problem, though, is that data can arrive at the serial port at any time and if the CPU doesn't check the state of the pin often enough it will miss bits of data, leading to communication errors. Using software-based serial communications forces you to write the rest of your program very carefully so that it doesn't use up too much time doing other things and always cycles back to reading the serial data fast enough that nothing is missed. There is an Arduino library called SoftwareSerial that takes care of most of the hard work for you, but it's still very hard to achieve reliable serial comms out of a purely software-based approach. To make it even harder, this project is a worst-case scenario because not only is it using relatively high-speed communications but it drives several serial ports simultaneously.

The advantage of a hardware USART is that it acts as a buffer and manages all the timing of the low-level bitstream on behalf of the main CPU. When using a USART, you can ignore a serial port for a while and the USART will accumulate data internally, reading in each bit sequentially at the configured serial port rate and storing characters in a small buffer. Then when your program is ready to access the data, it simply pulls it from the USART's buffer at high speed. Likewise, the USART takes care of sending data: your CPU can send a number of bytes of data to a USART within a few microseconds, and the USART itself then drip-feeds that data out to the serial device one bit at a time at the correct baud rate while your CPU gets on with running the rest of your program.

The Arduino Mega has an ATMega1280 CPU with a total of four hardware USARTs within the CPU itself, and all four ports are available on the Mega's headers. We take full advantage of them in this project to communicate with GPS, OBD-II, the memory stick, and a host computer simultaneously.

The code in this project is based on OBDuino and MPGuino, associated projects that are developed collaboratively on the EcoModder web site at www.ecomodder.com. Both OBDuino and MPGuino can run on a regular Arduino with a single USART because they don't have GPS support or data-logging to a USB memory stick. MPGuino even works on older cars without OBD-II support because it measures fuel injector pulses directly. They are both supported by an active team of developers and are great alternatives to this project if you want to try something a bit simpler.

The required parts are shown in Figure 15-4. Figure 15-5 shows how all of the pieces fit together.

Parts Required

General Parts:

1 x Arduino Mega

1 x Arduino Mega prototyping shield

1 x Plastic project box to suit mounting requirements (155mm × 95mm × 45mm was used in our prototype)

Power:

1 x LM2940CT-5 voltage regulator

1 x 3A slow-blow fuse and in-line fuse holder

1 x 4700uF electrolytic capacitor (63V rating or higher if possible)

1 x 47uF electrolytic capacitor (16V rating or lower, preferably “low ESR” type)

2 x 100uF capacitors

1 x 47K resistor (1% accuracy or better)

1 x 100K resistor (1% accuracy or better)

1 x 5.6V Zener diode

1 x 1N4001 power diode or equivalent

1 x 2-pin PCB-mount oriented male header

1 x 2-pin oriented female header

Display and Control:

1 x 16x2 or 20x4 HD44780-compatible LCD, VFD, or OLED module

1 x BC557, 2N2907, 2N3906, or equivalent PNP transistor

1 x 220R resistor

1 x 10K trimpot (variable resistor)

3 x Momentary SPST pushbuttons

10cm ribbon cable

Storage:

1 x VDIP1 USB interface module (see www.vinculum.com for suppliers)

1 x USB memory stick with FAT filesystem (default on most memory sticks)

1 x Momentary SPST pushbutton with LED indicator

1 x Red LED

1 x Green LED

1 x Yellow LED

4 x 680R resistors

2 x 10K resistors

3 x 1K resistors

4 x 12-pin female PCB headers (optional)

2 x 12-pin male PCB headers (optional)

10cm ribbon cable (optional)

OBD-II:

1 x ELM327-based OBD2-to-USB (or OBD2-to-RS232) interface adapter

1 x 4-pin PCB-mount oriented male header

1 x 4-pin oriented female header

1 x 8-pin oriented female header

10cm ribbon cable

1 x DB9 panel mount socket (female)

1 x DB9 line plug (male)

1 to 2 meters 8-core flexible cable

GPS:

1 x Locosys LS20031 GPS module (GPS-08975 from SparkFun)

1 x 4-pin PCB-mount oriented male header

1 x 4-pin oriented female header

10cm ribbon cable

1 3.3V FTDI adapter and matching cable (only required during setup of GPS)

Source code available from
`www.practicalarduino.com/projects/vehicle-telemetry-platform`

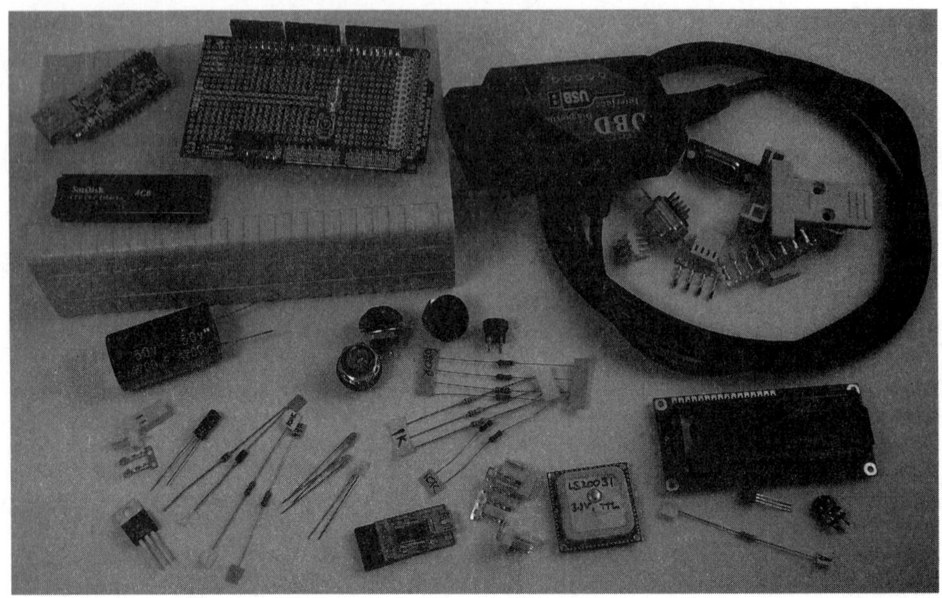

Figure 15-4. Parts required for vehicle telemetry platform

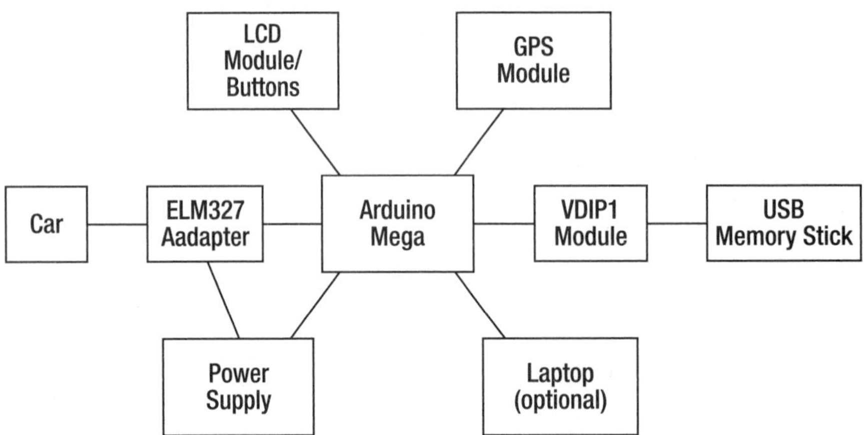

Figure 15-5. Modular structure of vehicle telemetry platform. Schematics of individual modules are included later in the project.

Instructions

Check the Vehicle Interface

Important: Before you order any of the parts, it's best to make sure your car actually has an OBD-II–compatible interface. The OBD-II standard specifies that the connector must be located within three feet of the driver and must not require any tools to access it, so the most common locations are just under the dash near the steering column, behind the ashtray or glovebox, or behind a clip-open panel in the center console. What you're looking for is a connector like the one shown in Figure 15-6.

Figure 15-6. *Location of OBD-II socket under the dash of a Mazda RX-8*

If your car has that physical connector in place you're probably safe, but it's still not an absolute guarantee that it supports OBD-II, and it doesn't tell you which of the several OBD-II communications protocols it uses. Your vehicle's owner manual might tell you (unlikely) or your local mechanic might be able to help, but it's most likely that you'll have to figure it out for yourself.

One of the really annoying things about OBD-II is that it encompasses several different communications protocols, and different cars can use any one of them. The historical reason is that at the time OBD-II was being designed each of the major car manufacturers already had their own systems for communicating with their engine-management systems and they couldn't agree on switching to a single common standard. The result was that for political expediency, the OBD-II standard simply incorporated all of them onto different pins of a single connector and let the individual manufacturers decide which one they wanted to use.

So, different vehicles might all have the same OBD-II connector under the dash, but that doesn't mean they all speak the same language. Ford vehicles generally communicate using a PWM (pulse-width modulation) version of the SAE J1850 standard, while GM vehicles typically use a VPW (variable pulse width) version of the same standard. Many non-U.S. manufacturers use an ISO protocol called 9141-2, which itself can be implemented in several different ways. To make it even worse, there's yet another standard called ISO 14230 KWP2000, which uses the same physical communications layer as 9141-2 and shares the same pins but uses a different message format.

The result is that if you look at the pinout of an OBD-II connecter, you'll see pairs of pins for CAN, J1850, and ISO9141-2/ISO14230. To add to the confusion, because OBD-II doesn't use all the pins in the standard connector, some car manufacturers have used other pins in that same connector for their own proprietary interfaces, so it might be physically installed in your car even if it doesn't actually support any of the OBD-II variants. In a stunningly short-sighted move, some manufacturers even installed OBD-II in all cars on the production line, but then deliberately disabled it in cars sold in countries that didn't require it by law. Infuriating!

Thankfully, sanity has prevailed and by about 2004 most manufacturers had started switching to a common standard they could all agree on called CAN, or Controller-Area Network. CAN has now been mandated for all future vehicles and since 2008 all cars sold in the U.S. have been required to use CAN for their OBD-II interface.

If you can't figure out whether your car supports OBD-II, you can get more information from a number of places online:

`www.geekmyride.org`
`www.mp3car.com` (check in "Forums" under "Engine management"or "OBD-II," etc.)
`en.wikipedia.org/wiki/On-Board_Diagnostics`

Generic OBD-II adapters, therefore, have to support not just one protocol but a whole bunch of them at once. Luckily, they do that remarkably well, presenting the OBD-II connection to you in a generic way (usually as a USB serial device) and hiding the details of the various communications protocols. In the vast majority of cases, you can plug a generic OBD-II adapter into a car and it will simply work, no matter what model of car you have. Behind the scenes, the adapter checks all the pins on the OBD-II port and negotiates with the car to establish a connection, then uses whatever protocol is most appropriate for that model.

While poking around and looking for the OBD-II connector in your car, it's an ideal time to think ahead and consider how you'll mount the Vehicle Telemetry System, taking into consideration the route for the connecting cable.

Obtain a USB/OBD-II or RS-232 Adapter

If you know exactly what communications protocol your car uses, it's possible to build a hardware interface to suit just that specific protocol and ignore all the others. The OBDuino project page includes details for building interfaces specifically for several of the common systems in use, and if you know exactly what your car uses, you can save a bit of money by building just that interface. More information is available online at code.google.com/p/opengauge/wiki/OBDuino.

However, for this project we took the easy way out and used a readily available generic USB/OBD-II adapter that should work with pretty much any car from 1996 onward. Taking this approach means the device should be able to plug in to just about any modern car and simply work, no matter what type of car it is.

Most commercial USB/OBD-II adapters are based on a chip called the ELM327 from ELM Electronics. One solution to connecting an Arduino to your car is to buy one of the chips and fit it to a prototyping shield along with the required supporting components. The ELM327 chip is available directly from www.elmelectronics.com in single quantities for around $31. The OBDuino project has documentation showing how to connect it, if you want to go that way.

It's often possible to buy a complete USB/OBD-II adapter containing the ELM327 chip and all the supporting components on eBay for less than the single-unit price of the chip alone. Considering that you would also need to buy one of the special OBD-II plugs if you wanted to build an interface yourself from scratch, the prebuilt adapters are an absolute bargain because they come with just about everything you could possibly need to connect an Arduino to your car's engine-management system.

USB/OBD-II adaptors are commonly listed on auction sites with a title such as "Car Scanner AUTO Scan Tool CAN BUS OBD2 OBD USB V1.3."

What you're specifically looking for is a so-called "scan tool" using the ELM327 chip. Even if the ad doesn't list what chip is used in the adapter, you can probably guess just by looking at the packaging. If the case looks like the one in the parts picture shown in Figure 15-4 (most likely with a different sticker), or has "v1.3" in the product title then it's almost certainly based on an ELM327. The v1.3 designation refers to the current firmware version in the ELM327. Some older interfaces might be labeled v1.2a if they use a previous generation of the chip. However, v1.2a was missing a feature to easily read multivalue parameters as well as a few other minor differences. Get a v1.3 interface if possible, but a v1.2a interface will do the job if that's all you have available.

One thing to be wary of, though, is cheap cables listed as "RS232 OBD adapter cable" or similar, because they might look tempting but they're probably just a plain cable with an OBD connector on one end and a DB-9 connector on the other. They don't include the vital ELM327 chip that provides the actual intelligence to convert the raw OBD-II interface into something we can communicate with.

Another thing to be careful of is cheap adapters built using a ripped-off clone of an early version of the ELM327 firmware. Some of these units offered for sale on auction sites are based on copies of the v1.0 firmware that were cloned from genuine ELM327 adapters and don't use official ELM chips themselves. There have been a lot of improvements to the firmware since v1.0, so try to avoid the nongenuine clones if you can.

Test the USB/OBD-II Adapter

Most USB/OBD-II adapters ship with a mini-CD containing Windows-compatible diagnostics software that displays a range of engine parameters, so before doing anything else, it's a good idea to load it on a laptop, plug the adapter into your car, and make sure it works as advertised. If your adapter didn't come with software, or you want to try out some alternatives, you can check out the resources listed on www.geekmyride.org.

If you don't have access to a Windows laptop, you can test the adapter using a serial console program on any operating system. The ELM327 provides a very simple serial interface, so all you need to do is plug the adapter into your car, plug the USB cable into your laptop, launch a serial console such as GTKTerm or Minicom (Linux), Cornflake (Mac OS X), or HyperTerm (Windows), and set the serial port to 38400bps 8N1 (8-bit data, no stop bit, 1 parity bit). You can then communicate with the OBD-II adapter by typing commands into the console and seeing the response.

In addition to all the normal OBD-II parameters that we'll explain in the moment, the ELM327 supports a number of additional AT-style commands that it responds to directly. These aren't part of the OBD-II standard itself but are implemented internally by the ELM327. For example, if you type "ATRV" (short for "ATtention: Read Voltage") and hit return, the adapter will echo back the car's current battery voltage whether the car is running or not. If you type "010C" (that's a hexadecimal value, so it's "Zero-One-Zero-Cee," which is the OBD-II parameter for engine RPM), it will query the engine-management system on your behalf and return the current RPM as an unscaled hex value if the engine is currently running. The value won't mean anything to you just yet because most response values need to be processed in order to convert them to something meaningful, but at least it proves the adapter is working.

Understanding OBD-II Modes and Parameters

The full specifications relating to OBD-II are quite long and can be purchased from the SAE standards body. However, automotive hackers have collected extensive information about how it works and you can find lots of the gory details documented on sites such as www.geekmyride.org. For our simple case, we only care about a subset of the parameters accessible through the interface. The ELM327 chip does most of the hard work for us, so all we really need to understand are "modes" and "parameters."

OBD-II modes are really just ways to group together the types of information that the vehicle can report. Some modes are mandatory while others are optional, and any one vehicle model will only support a subset of them.

OBD-II modes are broken up into a number of "basic" and "additional" modes. There are nine basic modes of operation described in the OBD-II standard SAE J1979, as follows:

1. Show current data.
2. Show freeze-frame data.
3. Show stored Diagnostic Trouble Codes (DTCs).
4. Clear Diagnostic Trouble Codes and stored values.
5. Test results, oxygen sensor monitoring.
6. Test results, other component/system monitoring (e.g., Catalyst, EVAP).
7. Show pending Diagnostic Trouble Codes detected during current or last driving cycle.
8. Control operation of on-board component/system.
9. Request vehicle information.

Manufacturers may also define extra modes, called "additional" modes, for their own custom parameters. For example, mode 21 is an additional mode used by Toyota, and mode 22 is defined by SAE J2190 for Ford/GM use.

Each mode contains a number of parameters that are generally referred to as "PIDs" (Parameter IDs) or sometimes "p-codes." Manufacturers are not required to support all PIDs even if they support the mode that contains that PID. A typical car provides access to most parameters in a few of the basic modes plus one or more additional modes for manufacturer extensions.

Because the value returned by the car can only be an unsigned hexadecimal value, the PIDs often don't return the literal reading value. Many PIDs require a formula to be applied to convert the raw value returned by the car into something that makes sense. For example, PID 0x0105 (mode 01, parameter 05, which is engine coolant temperature) needs to be able to represent a negative value, so it has a +40 offset applied before being sent. The value returned is, therefore, always 40 degrees Celsius higher than the actual value, so to determine the real reading you have to convert from hexadecimal to decimal and then subtract 40.

There are hundreds of PIDs, but we'll focus on the ones listed in Table 15-1.

The formula listed against some PIDs includes references to "A," "B," "C," or "D." These variables represent the bytes returned by the interface, so in the case of the first PID (0x0100) the return value will be 4 bytes of data and those 4 bytes are referred to as A, B, C, and D. Another good example is PID 0x0104, the calculated engine load value. It only returns a single byte (A), so the formula A * 100 / 255 means the system needs to take the byte returned and convert it to a percentage of 255.

The most common formula is (A * 256) + B, which is simply a two-byte value that can range from 0 to 65535. Many PIDs are even simpler, using the raw A value to represent a reading from 0 to 255.

Note that modes and PIDs are always referred to as hex values, and parameter values are always given in SI (metric) units. If you want Imperial units for parameters, such as 0105 (engine coolant temperature), you'll need to take the value returned by the listed formula and then apply your own conversion to switch it from degrees C to degrees F.

Some PIDs are bitmaps representing flags that show multiple boolean results combined into a single byte. For these PIDs, the individual bits are specified after the letter, so, for example, "A7" is the most-significant bit of the first byte, while "D0" is the least significant bit of the last byte.

Table 15-1. *Commonly supported parameter IDs*

Mode	PID	Bytes	Description	Min	Max	Units	Formula
01	00	4	PIDs supported.				Bit encoded [A7..D0] == [PID 0x01..PID 0x20]
01	01	4	Monitor status since DTCs (Diagnostic Trouble Codes) cleared. Includes malfunction indicator lamp (MIL) status and number of DTCs.				Bit encoded. http://www.geekmyride.org/wiki/index.php/OBD-II_PIDs - Bitwise_encoded_PIDs
01	02	8	Freeze DTC.				
01	03	2	Fuel system status.				Bit encoded. http://www.geekmyride.org/wiki/index.php/OBD-II_PIDs - Bitwise_encoded_PIDs
01	04	1	Calculated engine load value.	0	100	%	A * 100 / 255
01	05	1	Engine coolant temperature.	–40	215	°C	A – 40
01	0A	1	Fuel pressure.	0	765	kPa (gauge)	A * 3
01	0B	1	Intake manifold pressure.	0	255	kPa (absolute)	A
01	0C	2	Engine RPM.	0	16,383.75	rpm	((A * 256) + B) / 4

01	0D	1	Vehicle speed.	0	255	km/h	A
01	0E	1	Timing advance.	–64	63.5	° relative to #1 cylinde r	A / 2 – 64
01	0F	1	Intake air temperature.	–40	215	°C	A – 40
01	10	2	MAF air flow rate.	0	655.3 5	g/s	((256 * A) + B) / 100
01	11	1	Throttle position.	0	100	%	A * 100 / 255
01	12	1	Commanded secondary air status.				Bit encoded. http://www.geekmyride.org/wiki/index.php/OBD-II_PIDs - Bitwise_encoded_PIDs
01	13	1	Oxygen sensors present.				[A0..A3] == Bank 1, Sensors 1–4. [A4..A7] == Bank 2...
01	14	2	Bank 1, Sensor 1: Oxygen sensor voltage, short-term fuel trim.	0 0	1.275 99.2	volts %	A * 0.005 (B – 128) * 100 / 128 (if B==0xFF, sensor is not used in trim calc)
01	1F	2	Run time since engine start.	0	65,53 5	second s	(A * 256) + B
01	20	4	PIDs supported 21–40.				Bit encoded [A7..D0] == [PID 0x21..PID 0x40]
01	21	2	Distance traveled with malfunction indicator lamp (MIL) on.	0	65,53 5	km	(A * 256) + B
01	22	2	Fuel rail pressure (relative to manifold vacuum).	0	5177. 265	kPa	((A * 256) + B) * 0.079
01	23	2	Fuel rail pressure (diesel).	0	65535 0	kPa (gauge)	((A * 256) + B) * 10

01	2F	1	Fuel level input.	0	100	%	100 * A / 255
01	30	1	Number of warm-ups since codes cleared.	0	255	N/A	A
01	31	2	Distance traveled since codes cleared.	0	65,535	km	(A * 256) + B
01	32	2	Evap. system vapor pressure.	–8,192	8,192	Pa	((A * 256) + B) / 4 – 8,192
01	33	1	Barometric pressure.	0	255	kPa (absolute)	A
01	3C	2	Catalyst temperature Bank 1, Sensor 1.	–40	6,513.5	°C	((A * 256) + B) / 10 – 40
01	40	4	PIDs supported 41–60.				Bit encoded [A7..D0] == [PID 0x41..PID 0x60]
01	42	2	Control module voltage.	0	65.535	V	((A * 256) + B) / 1000
01	43	2	Absolute load value.	0	25,700	%	((A * 256) + B) * 100 / 255
01	44	2	Command equivalence ratio.	0	2	N/A	((A * 256) + B) * 0.0000305
01	45	1	Relative throttle position.	0	100	%	A * 100 / 255
01	46	1	Ambient air temperature.	–40	215	°C	A – 40
01	4D	2	Time run with MIL on.	0	65,535	minutes	(A * 256) + B
01	4E	2	Time since trouble codes cleared.	0	65,535	minutes	(A * 256) + B

01	51	1	Fuel type.				From fuel type table. http://www.geekmyride.org/wiki/index.php/OBD-II_PIDs - Fuel_Type_Coding
01	52	1	Ethanol fuel percentage.	0	100	%	A * 100 / 255
03	N/A	n*6	Request trouble codes.				Three codes per message frame, BCD encoded. http://www.geekmyride.org/wiki/index.php/OBD-II_PIDs - Bitwise_encoded_PIDs
04	N/A	0	Clear trouble codes/malfunction indicator lamp (MIL)/check engine light.				Clears all stored trouble codes and turns the MIL off.
09	02	5x5	Vehicle identification number (VIN).				Returns five lines, A is line ordering flag, B–E are ASCII-coded VIN digits.

Have a look at parameters 0121, 014D, and 014E. Yes, if you take your car to a mechanic after the trouble light has been on for a while, they can tell exactly how long you've been ignoring it. Don't bother trying to give them the old "it just came on yesterday" routine because they'll know if you're being economical with the truth!

You'll notice that some of the parameters simply read "bit encoded" as the formula. These parameters are special cases that pack as much information as possible into only a few bytes of return value, and special conversion rules need to be applied to interpret the values and turn them into meaningful information. Software that reads these PIDs has to know that it should treat each of these results as a special case and have internal look-up tables that map the individual bits to specific flags.

Note also the entries near the end of the table for modes 03 and 04. These are special modes that don't contain any parameters at all, and they need to be treated quite differently than any of the other entries listed. Mode 04, in particular, you need to be very careful of. Simply by requesting that mode, your engine-management system will immediately clear the CEL (check engine light) if it's on, and also any stored information about faults that might have occurred. It won't even ask for confirmation: if you send "04" to the OBD-II adapter, it will simply execute it, no questions asked. It's generally a bad idea to do this yourself because it means that if your car has developed a fault, any information stored about it will be deleted and your mechanic could have a more difficult time tracking down what went wrong. This mode is normally only executed by mechanics after they've extracted all the diagnostic data from your car and repaired any faults they find.

Prepare the USB/OBD-II Adapter

Once you're happy that your USB/OBD-II adapter is working as the manufacturer intended, it's time to open it up and locate the major components inside it.

The first thing you'll notice is that the ELM327 chip is actually a PIC microcontroller rather than a custom IC. This is an increasingly common approach to circuit design: rather than design and fabricate a whole new IC just for one purpose, it's often simpler and easier to use a general-purpose microcontroller running some custom code to implement the required functionality. This brings the cost of special-purpose chips like the ELM327 way down and has the added bonus of allowing the supplier to revise the chip design when required simply by changing the firmware. No more expensive retooling of a chip fabrication plant just because there's a tiny bug in the design!

Other interesting items in your USB/OBD-II adapter are the LM317 and 7805 voltage regulators and the FTDI chip that provides the USB interface (see Figure 15-7).

Figure 15-7. *Inside a typical USB/OBD-II adapter*

The ELM327 provides a serial interface on pins 15 through 18 at 5V, so all the USB/OBD-II adapter does is connect the FTDI chip in front of that interface to convert it to USB. We don't want to use USB, though, so what we'll do is bypass the FTDI chip and talk directly to the communications port on the ELM327.

In the USB/OBD-II adapter we used in our prototype, the ELM327 is based on a PIC18F2480 in a 28-pin SOIC package with serial connections on the following pins:

pin 15: RTS (Ready To Send, active low)

pin 16: Busy

pin 17: RS232Tx (TTL level 0–5V, not full RS-232 voltage)

pin 18: RS232Rx (TTL level 0–5V, not full RS-232 voltage)

pin 8 and 19: Ground

In the photo shown in Figure 15-7, the chip is oriented with pin 1 in the bottom left corner near a tiny dimple, and the rest are numbered counterclockwise from there. This puts pin 15 on the top right corner nearest the silver 4Mhz crystal, pin 16 just left of that, and so on.

Different ELM327 adapters use different casing styles, so you may need to improvise if your adapter is different than ours.

Remove the PCB from the plastic case by gently prying up the edges of the board so that it pops off the four plastic legs that double as screw mounts for the top of the case. In one of the adapters we used for our prototypes the PCB came out easily, but in the other one the plastic legs had been cracked and expanded by the screws holding the case together and the PCB was jammed in tight. We had to use wire cutters to clip each leg off flush with the top of the PCB before we could get it out. If you have to do this, be very careful not to damage any of the nearby surface-mount components.

Next, start slimming down the circuit board by unplugging the ribbon cable that goes to the OBD-II connector, making note of which way around it goes, as the PCB header fits either way. Then remove the USB connection: if your adapter is fitted with a USB "B" connector, you don't need to do anything, but our adapter had a USB cable soldered onto the PCB so we unsoldered them to remove the lead entirely. We wanted to retain the ability to connect the adapter to a laptop, so we soldered a 4-pin male header into place on the PCB where the USB cable previously fitted, and added a 4-pin female socket to the original USB cable so it could be plugged back in if necessary. Alternatively, you could connect a USB "B" socket to the PCB with short lengths of hookup wire so that the adapter can be connected to your laptop using a regular USB printer cable.

Now for the tricky part: tapping into the serial connection between the ELM327 and the FTDI chip. The ELM327 uses four pins for the serial interface, but you won't be using RTS and Busy, so you only need to get access to pins 17 (TX) and 18 (RX).

In both of our adapters, there was a row of LEDs blocking access to the pins along the top of the ELM327, and because the LED leads were covered with plastic sleeves, they couldn't be bent down out of the way. On one adapter, we used wire cutters to carefully clip away a small triangle from the bottom of the sleeves without damaging the LED leads or the PCB, so the LEDs could then be bent over (see Figure 15-8).

Figure 15-8. *Gaining access to TX and RX pins by bending LEDs*

On the other adapter, we removed the original LEDs entirely and soldered tiny surface-mount LEDs in "0805" (2mm × 1.25mm) packages directly to the pads on the PCB. The result is a very slick, low-profile board. If you don't have access to surface-mount LEDs, you could simply resolder the existing 3mm LEDs flush down on the board without the plastic spacers.

Because the FTDI chip provides a high-impedance connection to the ELM327, you might not need to disconnect it. On one of our adapters, we left the connections in place and soldered jumper wires directly to pins 17 and 18 of the ELM327, and it worked fine. Leaving the connection in place allows you to reconnect the USB cable and use the adapter with your laptop again as described previously.

Breaking the TX and RX connections between the ELM327 and the FTDI chip will prevent you from using the adapter again via USB, but might be necessary depending on the model of adapter. If you need to disconnect pins 17 and 18, you can use a sharp scriber to lever up each pin while simultaneously melting the solder with a very fine soldering iron tip, as shown in Figure 15-9.

Figure 15-9. *Separating the TX and RX pins from the PCB*

Because the ELM327 leads are so small, you might need to use a magnifying glass to inspect the pads and make sure there are no solder bridges or slivers getting into places you don't want them. The end result should be two pins sticking out from the side of the chip with no connection to each other or the PCB. It's a good idea to use a multimeter set to high-ohms range to perform a continuity check between pins 17 and 18, and also to adjacent pins.

Whether or not you separate pins 17 and 18 from the PCB, the next step is to connect a serial cable to link the ELM327 to your Arduino.

We used 4-pin oriented headers with matching female connectors and short lengths of ribbon cable. Several projects in this book use serial connections to devices, so we settled on an informal standard that was used throughout the book, with the Arduino connections exposed on a PCB-mount oriented male header, as shown in Figure 15-10.

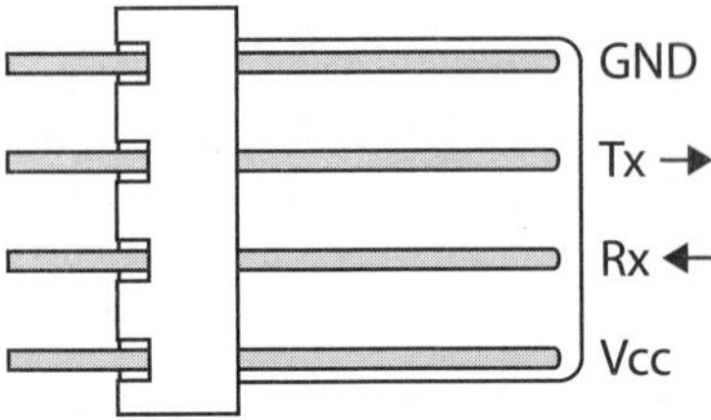

Figure 15-10. Pin assignments for serial connection to oriented male header

Note that the TX/RX labeling is from the perspective of the Arduino, not the device connected to it. Putting just a "TX" or "RX" label on a connector can be ambiguous because it's often hard to determine if the meaning is "This is TX on this device, so connect it to RX on the other device" or "This needs to be connected to TX on the other device, but it's actually RX." Many people put a directional arrow on as well, or append an "I" for "in" or "O" for "out," to make it clear which way the data needs to flow. If you see a marking on a device that reads "TXO," it means it's the transmit line from the device and data flows out of the port, while "RXI" means it's the receive line on the device and data flows into the port.

Cut off a short length of ribbon cable and solder one end to an oriented 4-pin female header. At the other end you need to connect it to ground using either pin 8 or pin 19 on the ELM327, and also connect TX (pin 17) and RX (pin 18) on the ELM327 to the Arduino with the Arduino TX connected to ELM327 RX and vice versa as shown in Figure 15-11. Don't connect the VCC lead to the ELM327, though, because the adapter has its own internal power supply that runs from vehicle power. It might, therefore, seem that a 4-pin connector is a waste and a 3-pin connector should have been used instead, but we chose to use the same 4-pin connector as used elsewhere in the book for other serial connections purely for the sake of consistency. By having the same connector everywhere, it's much easier to swap devices around between different projects.

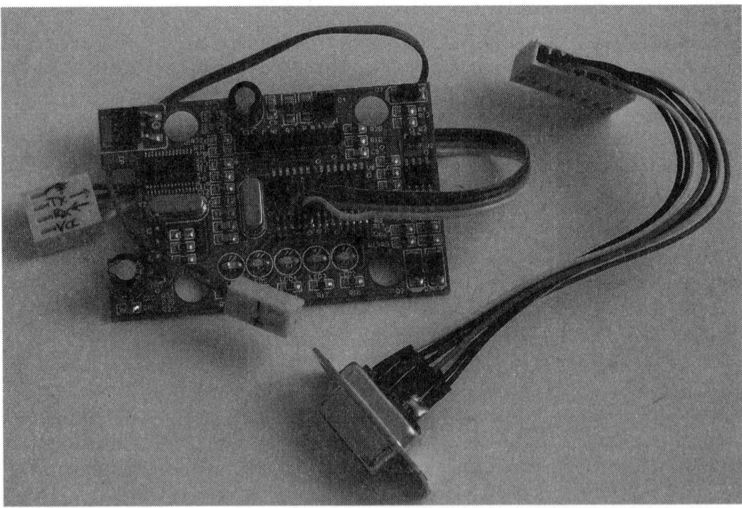

Figure 15-11. USB/OBD-II PCB modified with surface-mount LEDs and with power and serial connections in place

Figure 15-11 shows an ELM327-based adapter that has had the original LEDs replaced with surface-mount LEDs, and the serial cable connected to ground, TX, and RX, with the VCC lead left unconnected at the ELM end. The VCC lead is connected in the socket, but is cut short and left unconnected at the other end. You can also see the 4-pin male header fitted to the USB lead pads on the bottom left corner of the board so a USB cable can be reconnected to use the adapter as it was originally designed.

Power from the car to the Arduino is going to be taken from the OBD-II connection as well, so fit a short length of hookup wire to an oriented 2-pin female header and connect the other end to the GND and +12V pads on the PCB back of the OBD-II header. You can't see it in the photo in Figure 15-11, but the pair of wires connect to the back of the 8-way header, with 0V on the left end and +12V on the right. Unless your OBD-II adapter happens to be exactly the same as ours, you'll need to check out the connections with a multimeter to figure out which is which, but it should also be fairly easy to determine by following through the pin assignments from the OBD-II plug back through to the adapter.

Also shown in Figure 15-11 is an 8-way female header connected to a DB9 panel-mount socket for connecting to the OBD-II cable. If your OBD-II adapter has a different type of connection, you might have to alter the design accordingly.

Assemble the OBD-II Cable

With the ELM327 adapter removed from its case and the connector unplugged, there's no way to plug it back into the car, so we need to assemble a cable that will reach from the OBD-II port to the mounting location for the OBDuinoMega (see Figure 15-12).

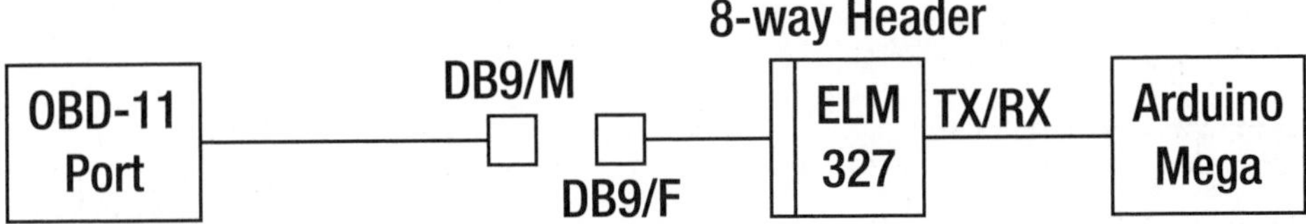

Figure 15-12. Connection from the vehicle's OBD-II port through a connecting cable to the 8-way header on the adapter and finally through to the Arduino

The simplest approach is to take the original OBD-II connector that you removed from the adapter and extend the short leads that run to the 8-pin header so it can be plugged back in. However, because we wanted to mount our prototype in a case with a removable cable, we used an 8-pin header and short lengths of hookup wire to connect it to a DB9 panel-mount socket.

Then we used a DB9 plug and two lengths of four-core cable in parallel to connect to the OBD-II connector. OBD-II to DB9 cables are fairly commonly available at online auction sites, so if you prefer not to wire it up yourself, you could always just buy one. We used the same pinouts as commercial cables we've seen available, so they should be directly compatible with the connections shown in Table 15-2.

Table 15-2. Pinout for DB9 to OBD-II cable

DB9 Pin	OBD-II Pin	Description
1	5	Signal ground
2	4	Chassis ground
3	6	CAN high
4	7	ISO K line
5	14	CAN low
6	10	J1850 bus-
7	2	J1850 bus+
8	15	ISO L line
9	16	Battery +12V

Because OBD-II to USB adapters come with an OBD-II connector, the cheapest approach is to just reuse it, fitting a longer cable and terminating the other end on a DB9 male connector using the pinout shown in Figures 15-12 and 15-13.

It's a good idea to use a fuse in series with the +12V lead on any equipment connected inside a car because car batteries can provide tremendous amounts of energy very quickly, and a short-circuit inside the system could make wires melt and catch on fire. We certainly don't want any of our readers to burn their cars to the ground trying this project, so fitting an in-line fuse holder in series with the +12V line and installing a fuse of about 2A or so is a very good idea.

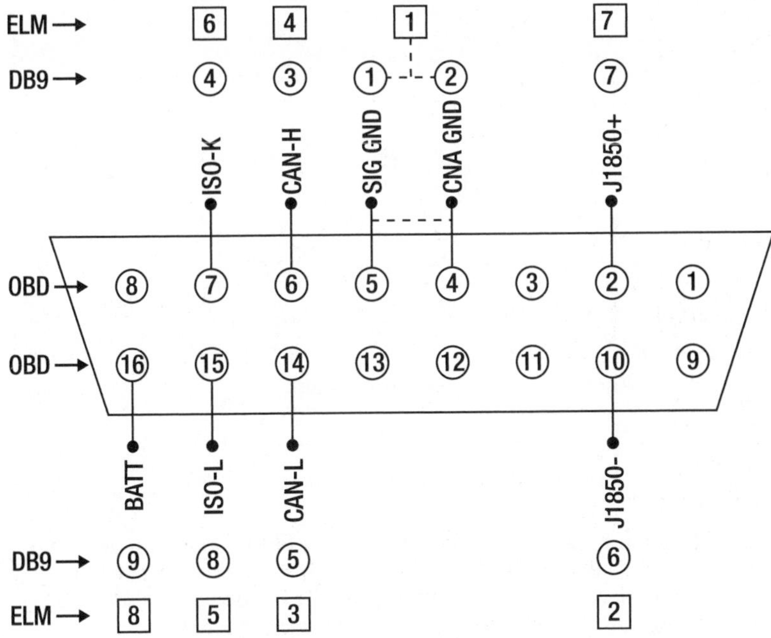

Figure 15-13. Pin assignment for OBD-II connector with equivalent DB9 and ELM header pins

Prepare the GPS Module

The GPS module we chose for this project is a Locosys LS20031, a nice little unit that's available from a variety of online parts retailers such as SparkFun. It's small, has an integrated antenna, runs on a 3.3V supply but has 5V-compatible I/O lines, has configurable baud rate and output formats, and has a decent 5Hz update rate.

The update rate is a measure of how fast it can obtain and report a new locational fix, so with a 5Hz update it obtains a new fix five times per second. The majority of GPS modules only update at about 1Hz and many are even slower, while some models coming onto the market now can update at up to 10Hz or even faster. For our purposes, 5Hz is just fine.

The LS20031 module has a series of five solder pads on the bottom edge of the board, numbered 1 to 5 from left to right when looking at the PCB from the back with the pads aligned at the bottom. These are described in Table 15-3.

Table 15-3. Locosys LS20031 pinout

Pin	Name	Description
1	VCC	Power input (3.3V)
2	RX	Data input (TTL level)
3	TX	Data output (TTL level)
4	GND	Ground
5	GND	Ground

You can see the pads in the photograph in Figure 15-14, on the right side of the board aligned vertically from pin 1 at the bottom to pin 5 on the top, wired to a short length of ribbon cable with an oriented 4-pin female header on the other end. Note that the markings on the header show the connections from the Arduino's point of view, so the line marked "TX" on the connector is actually Arduino TX and needs to connect to GPS RX at the other end. Likewise, the Arduino RX line needs to connect to GPS TX. You can see in the photo that the ribbon cable has the center two wires (TX and RX) swapped just before they join the pads on the GPS module.

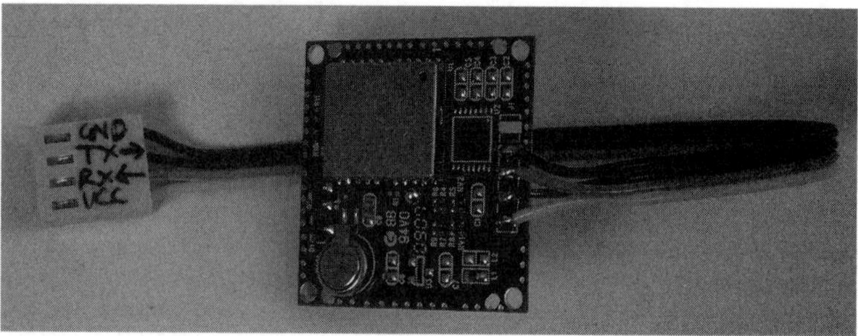

Figure 15-14. *Serial and power connections to LS20031 GPS module*

The GPS module will work with the Arduino just as it is, but there are some settings in the module you can tweak to really improve performance. Unfortunately, the simplest method we've found to do it involves running a Windows program while connected to the GPS module using an FTDI adapter cable. If you don't have a Windows computer handy, the program will run under WINE on Linux too.

If you need to use WINE, run the basic WINE installation and then create a link to the serial device.

```
ln -s /dev/ttyUSB0 ~/.wine/dosdevices/com1
```

Then launch the program using WINE.

```
wine MiniGPS_1.32
```

Even though the LS20031 has TTL level (5V) compatible I/O lines, the module itself needs to run from 3.3V, so you'll need an FTDI adapter cable or board with a 3.3V supply rail. We used an FTDI Basic Breakout 3.3V from SparkFun, but there are a number of options from other suppliers as well. Or if you have an Arduino with a removable CPU handy, such as a Duemilanove, you could pop out the CPU, connect the Arduino's GND header to ground on the GPS module, connect the 3.3V header to GPS power, and connect digital pins 0 and 1 to the GPS module's TX and RX inputs: matching Arduino TX to GPS RX and vice versa. The Arduino can then be used just like a regular FTDI adapter cable.

If you are using a proper FTDI adapter, use four short lengths of hookup wire (breadboard jumpers are perfect) to connect the ground, VCC, TX, and RX pins on the GPS module lead to the equivalent pins on the adapter. Note that if you follow the same format as the serial cable we described previously, the "TX" and "RX" markings shown are already swapped relative to the GPS module and correspond directly to the connections on the FTDI adapter, so connect the cable RX to FTDI RX and cable TX to FTDI TX (see Figure 15-15).

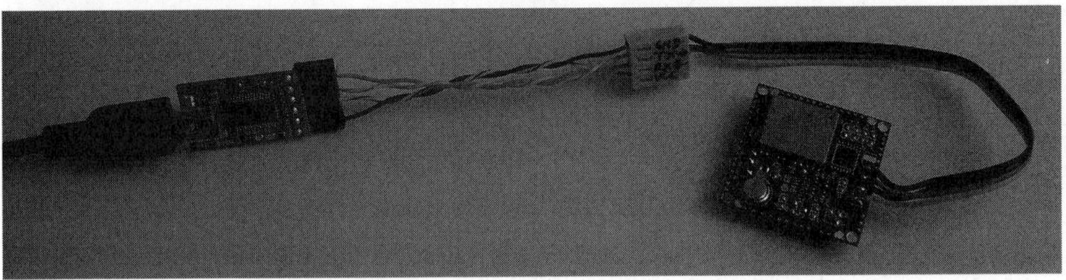

Figure 15-15. *The LS20031 GPS module connected to a host computer using an FTDI adapter*

Next, plug the FTDI adapter into a Windows computer using an appropriate cable. If Windows doesn't yet have the FTDI driver installed (it should if you've been using it for Arduino development because they're bundled with the Arduino IDE), a dialog will pop up telling you that the driver is being set up.

Now download and install a program called "Mini GPS." It's currently available from the SparkFun site at the following URL:

```
www.sparkfun.com/datasheets/GPS/MiniGPS_1.32
```

Once Mini GPS is up and running, you can select the serial port for connection to your GPS module. It will then display status information including the satellites it can currently see, the location fix, and various settings such as baud rate, update rate, and supported formats.

Note, however, that when GPS modules first start up from cold it can take them quite some time to obtain a fix. If Mini GPS connects to your GPS module but it doesn't show your location, just wait for 30 to 60 seconds to give it time to work. GPS modules generally behave quite differently depending on whether they are doing a "cold" or "warm" start: a cold start can take 30 to 60 seconds, while a warm start often takes less than one second. In some situations, such as if their internally stored ephemeral data (including the satellite position almanac) is extremely outdated, it can take up to five minutes to start up. If your GPS is brand new and you've never powered it up before, you could find that you need to leave it running for at least five minutes with a clear view of the sky before it will spring to life.

Of course, you also need to make sure the receiver is seeing an adequate signal, so if you are inside a building with thick roof insulation or metal sheeting, you might never get a fix no matter how long you wait. Try placing the receiver near a window if possible.

Once you have Mini GPS running and connected to your GPS module, select the update rate setting and change it from 1Hz to 5Hz. Also change the baud rate to 38400bps if it's not already set to that (many GPS modules default to the NMEA standard of 4800bps) and then have a look at the list of sentence formats that are supported in the "NMEA Output Settings" section. In Mini GPS, it's presented as a list of acronyms with a drop-down number list beside each one. By default, some are set to 0 and some are set to 1 (see Figure 15-16).

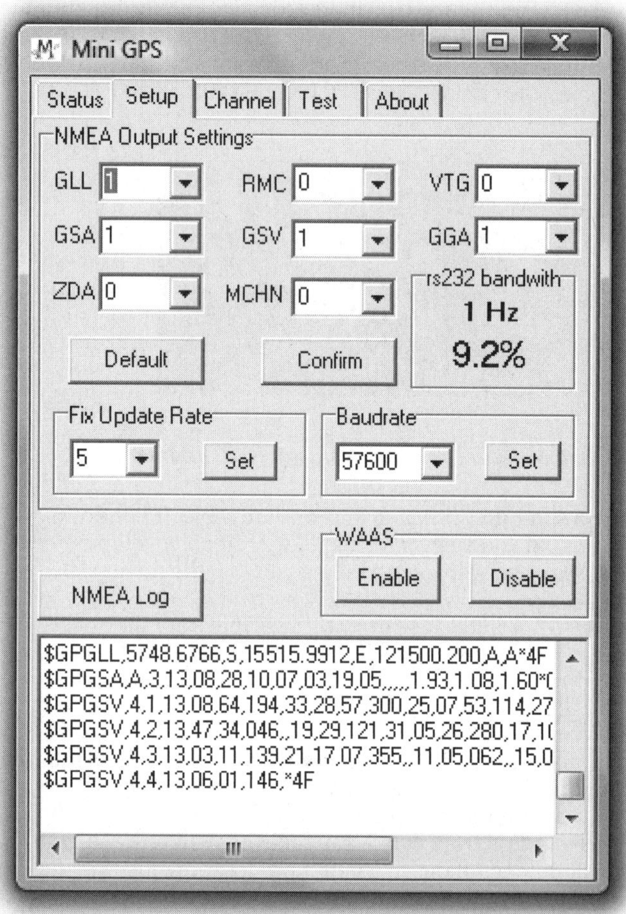

Figure 15-16. *GPS configuration options in MiniGPS*

GPS modules report data as "NMEA 0183 sentences," a format that starts with a preamble to specify the sentence type followed by a series of comma-separated parameter values. Because GPS is used for a variety of different purposes, there are quite a few different NMEA sentence formats, each containing a subset of the fields that can be reported by the GPS module. Most GPS modules will send multiple sentences for each position update, but if you don't care about the fields in some of the sentences, you can turn them off to reduce the traffic through the serial connection.

In our case, the important format is called "GGA," so you can set all mode values except GGA to 0 and set GGA to 1. It's not a problem leaving the other modes on because unused sentences returned by the GPS module are simply ignored, and in our prototype, we decided to leave several other formats turned on in case we wanted to use that data later.

You might be wondering why there is a pull-down menu of numbers next to each sentence type rather than simple checkboxes. The reason is that it's possible to specify different reporting frequencies on a per-sentence basis, but the number is not a direct representation of the sample rate in Hz. It's the number of position fixes that need to be obtained for each output of that particular sentence.

For example, if we switch the LS20031 to an update rate of 5Hz, it has an update period of 200ms (1/5 of a second) for each position fix. If you set a sentence to 0, it is disabled and will never be output. If you set it to 1, it will be output on every location fix, so in this case it would be every 200ms. If you set it to 3, it will be output on every third location fix, which would therefore be every 600ms. If you really want to squeeze the most out of a GPS module and pump the greatest amount of data through the serial connection, you can set some sentences to update very rapidly and others to update more slowly. For this project, though, it's enough to make sure GGA is set to 1 and turn off any others you don't care about.

Once you've set the options in the LS20031, they will be stored by the built-in battery for up to one week if the module loses power. Unfortunately, that means you may need to reset the options if the GPS module is left powered down for more than about one week—very annoying. The module also has the option of writing values to nonvolatile flash memory, but be careful: the manufacturer specifies that the flash settings can only be written about seven times, so you can't keep changing them and writing them to flash. It's best to experiment first and make sure it's behaving as you want it to before committing them to flash.

For reference, the format of a GGA sentence is as follows:

```
$GPGGA,m1,m2,c1,m3,c2,d1,d2,f1,f2,M,f3,M,f4,d3*cc
```

Each field has a specifically defined meaning in the NMEA 0183 standard, as described in Table 15-4.

Table 15-4. *GGA Sentence Format*

Field	Meaning
m1	Current UTC time of position fix in hours, minutes, and seconds (hhmmss.ss).
m2	Latitude component of position in degrees and decimal minutes (ddmm.mmmmmm).
c1	Direction of latitude: N = North, S = South (a).
m3	Longitudinal component of position in degrees and decimal minutes (dddmm.mmmmmm).
c2	Direction of longitude: E = East, W = West (a).

d1	Position type: 0 = Invalid or not available, 1 = Autonomous position, 2 = RTCM or SBAS differentially corrected (n).
d2	Number of satellites used in position computation (nn).
f1	Horizontal dilution position: HDOP (nn.nnn).
f2	Altitude in meters above the reference ellipsoid. For 2-D position computation, this item contains the user-entered altitude used to compute the position computation.
M	Altitude units: M = meters (a).
f3	Geoidal separation in meters (+/–ddd.dd).
M	Geoidal separation units: M = meters (a).
d3	Age of differential corrections in seconds (nnn).
d4:	Base station ID for RTCM use only (nnnn).
cc	Checksum.

Most developers think of NMEA 0183 only as a way to talk to GPS receivers, but it's actually a much more general communications protocol that is used in marine environments for a whole range of devices including echo sounders, autopilots, and weather sensors. Wikipedia has more information about the NMEA 0183 standard at en.wikipedia.org/wiki/NMEA_0183.

Assemble the Power Supply on the Shield

Normally, the power supply circuit is the most boring part of a project, but this one has a few tricks that are worth paying close attention to. See the schematic in Figure 15-17.

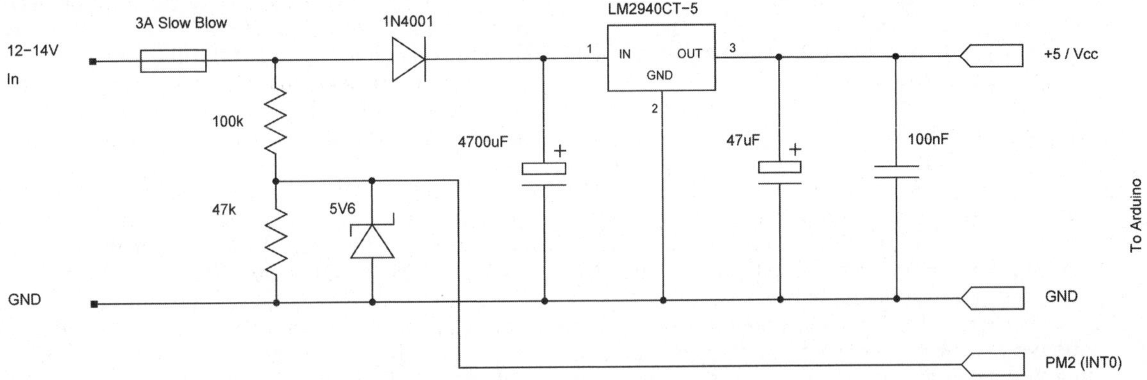

Figure 15-17. Schematic of Vehicle Telemetry Platform power supply

Because this system will run directly from the car's power, we need to regulate it down from the 12–14V range provided through the OBD-II connection to a nice, consistent 5V.

However, keep in mind for other automotive projects that although the vast majority of cars operate on a 12V negative-ground system, there are exceptions: many trucks operate at 24V, motorcycles at 6V, and some modern cars use an internal 42V power bus.

Because we're using the OBD-II connector as the power source, and the OBD-II standard stipulates that it supply 12V, we're fairly safe. But if you try connecting directly to a vehicle power supply, there may be cases where you see something other than 12V. To regulate the 12V supply down to 5V, we're using an LM2940CT-5 linear voltage regulator, which is the automotive-rated version of the ever popular LM7805 voltage regulator. If you've used an LM7805 in another project, then an LM2940CT-5 will seem perfectly familiar: it's in the same physical package, it has the same pinout, and you can drop it directly into a circuit where you would normally use an LM7805 and it will simply work. Reference schematics for the LM7805 abound online, so it's easy to figure out how to hook them up.

You might be wondering why we didn't simply use an LM7805 and went instead for a much more expensive and sometimes hard-to-find, but otherwise apparently equivalent, part.

The answer is found in the electrical environment of a typical car, which runs most commonly at a nominal 12 to 14 volts but can vary wildly outside that range. While powering the starter motor, the battery has to supply an enormous current for several seconds, during which time the voltage across the battery terminals can often drop to as little as 6V. The LM2940CT-5 is designed to allow for that and is an "LDO" or "low drop-out" regulator that can maintain its output voltage at a stable level when the input falls to just 0.5V above the required output. A traditional LM7805, by comparison, needs its input to be at least 2V higher than the desired output. This means an LM7805 can't maintain a 5V output unless you feed it at least 7V on the input. Dropping the input to 6V on an LM7805 could cause your Arduino to spontaneously reset, but an LM2940CT-5 will handle it with ease.

Other than handling under-voltage situations better, the LM2940CT-5 also handles over-voltage spikes and even reverse-voltage inputs far better than an LM7805. Car electrical systems can sometimes experience a phenomenon known as "load dump," when the alternator pushes voltage spikes of 60V or more onto the wiring loom momentarily. This can happen when a battery connection is a little bit loose and the load being driven by the alternator suddenly decreases, causing it to dump the excess power onto the wiring loom in the form of increased voltage before the alternator's built in output monitoring circuit has time to react. Jump-starting a car can have similar nasty effects as the batteries and alternators of both cars interact with each other as the second car starts up and also as the jumper leads are unplugged.

The result of all this is that you can use an LM7805 voltage regulator in an automotive project if you really want to, and it will probably work fine for a while, but it's quite likely that it will eventually find the noisy electrical environment of a car too much to handle and stop working. It's better to save yourself the grief and use a proper automotive-rated voltage regulator right from the start. Automotive-rated parts were designed for a reason, after all!

If you were sharp-eyed, you probably noticed that the ELM327 adapter shown back in Figure 15-7 has a regular LM7805 in it because it's not intended to be left connected permanently and the manufacturer wanted to save a couple of dollars in their manufacturing costs. If you were feeling paranoid, you could clip the LM7805 out and replace it with an LM2904CT-5, but that's probably not worth the effort unless it happens to fail.

The other thing that is a little bit unusual about our power supply circuit is that we've deviated from the typical reference design by fitting an enormous capacitor across the voltage regulator input and feeding the input through a power diode. We've also included a voltage divider in front of the power diode and a Zener diode to act as a voltage clamp on the bottom of the divider.

The reason for doing this is to give the Arduino the ability to elegantly handle power failure. Having a very large capacitor on the input of the voltage regulator provides enough reserve power to keep the voltage regulator running at its rated voltage for a few extra milliseconds after power is disconnected from the input. By having the CPU detect input failure through the voltage divider, it can use that time to quickly put its house in order before the power drops out entirely. Tasks it might need to do in that time include closing any files that are open on the USB memory stick, because if the power fails while a file is open it probably won't be written properly and could end up corrupted or even entirely empty with all your logged data gone forever.

Fit the LM2940CT-5 to the prototyping shield, with the common (center) pin connected to ground on the shield and the output (right) pin connected to +5V. The Mega prototyping shield from NKC Electronics we used in our prototypes has handy ground and 5V rails beside each other down the center of the board, so the voltage regulator can be fitted straight across them with two of the pins on the two supply rails. The input (left) pin will eventually be connected to the car's +12V supply line via the OBD adapter.

If the pins of the voltage regulator are just a little too big to fit comfortably through the holes in the prototyping shield, you can cut them off to about half length and very carefully trim a fraction off the thickness of each leg with wire cutters or a small file. You could alternatively drill out the holes in the PCB with a slightly larger drill bit, but if you do that you'll also remove the through-hole plating inside the holes, so make sure you solder the pins into place on both the top and bottom of the PCB. You also need to be careful not to short out the ground plane if there is one on the particular shield you use.

Also connect the 47uF electrolytic capacitor between the output pin and ground. This capacitor provides high-frequency damping of the output of the regulator and helps the voltage regulator maintain a constant voltage. The specifications for the LM2940CT-5 state that it needs a capacitor of at least 22uF connected to the output stage for stable operation, but we increased this value to 47uF to provide a bit of extra decoupling.

You'll note that the parts list specifies that the 47uF capacitor should be rated to no more than 16V, which at first sounds like a very odd requirement. Normally it's fine to use parts that are rated for a higher voltage than required, but in this case it can actually cause problems. In a perfect world, capacitors would only ever exhibit capacitance and have zero resistance or inductance, but the reality of the manufacturing techniques and materials used in the physical construction of capacitors means they tend to exhibit a small amount of resistance as well. This is referred to as ESR, or equivalent series resistance, and tends to be higher for capacitors rated to higher voltages. The ESR limits the ability of a capacitor to charge or discharge rapidly, preventing it from following high-frequency voltage transients.

To minimize ESR, it's a good idea to use a 10V- or at most a 16V-rated electrolytic in this case, and ideally one specifically rated as "Low ESR" if available. If all else fails, another solution is to put a second, smaller value capacitor (perhaps 100nF or so) in parallel.

The smaller capacitor will help follow high-frequency transients while the larger one will store a larger amount of energy, and between them they will keep the regulator stable. When connecting the 47uF electrolytic, make careful note of the polarity—electrolytics have a nasty habit of going BANG and making a smelly, smoky mess if they are connected backward! Electrolytic capacitors usually have the negative lead marked on the case, and also have their leads cut to different lengths with the positive lead longer than the negative lead. The negative lead goes to ground, while the positive lead goes to the output of the regulator.

Also install the 4700uF electrolytic capacitor between the input pin and ground, once again noting the polarity. The negative (short) lead goes to ground, while the positive (long) lead goes to the input of the regulator. For this capacitor, we specified a 63V or greater rating because it could potentially be exposed to 60V spikes if the alternator ever load-dumps into the loom. The only part we could find locally was a 50V-rated version, but if you can find a 63V or higher rating, that's preferable. A large value capacitor in a high-voltage rating is likely to be physically very large, and you can see that the one we used is about the size of a C-cell battery. There was no way to mount it neatly on the shield, so we had to fit it elsewhere in the case and use short lengths of hookup wire to connect it to the circuit.

Next, fit a 1N4001 or equivalent power diode so that the cathode (banded) end connects to the input pin of the LM2940CT-5, which is also where the positive lead of the 4700uF capacitor is connected. The +12V supply from the car will need to connect to the anode (nonbanded) end, so you can either solder a piece of wire directly in place for the +12V connection or do what we did and fit an oriented 2-pin captive terminal with the other terminal pin connected to ground on the shield. This way, you can make up a handy cable to link to +12V and ground connections from the OBD-II adapter, which has direct access to vehicle ground and power through the OBD-II connector.

In order to detect power loss, the Arduino needs an input from the unregulated (+12V) side of the power-supply circuit. The input needs to change state fast enough for it to be detected and necessary action taken before the large capacitor on the input has time to discharge below the voltage regulator's minimum stable input voltage of about 5.5V. Because the electrical system of a car can be very "noisy" with spikes and transient voltages, it's a good idea to keep the Arduino on the regulated side of the circuit as decoupled from the input side of the power supply as possible. To achieve power-supply sensing, we used a pair of resistors as a voltage divider and a Zener diode as a voltage clamp with the output connected to a digital input on the Arduino.

The voltage divider connects directly in front of the power diode so that it samples the voltage being supplied to it. If the input voltage falls, the voltage divider will see the drop immediately, even though the large capacitor on the voltage regulator input will remain high for a while. The diode prevents the capacitor from discharging back through the voltage divider and vehicle wiring loom and fooling the Arduino into thinking the input voltage is still normal until it's too late.

The voltage divider consists of a 100K upper half and a 47K lower half. The result is that the output of the voltage divider will be the input voltage times a factor of

```
47 / (100 + 47) = 0.32
```

So with a 12V input to the top of the divider, the output will be

```
12 x 0.32 = 3.84V
```

With a 14V input, the output will be

```
14 x 0.32 = 4.48V
```

We can also work back the other way to figure out the threshold at which the input voltage causes the output to fall low enough for the Arduino to detect a "logic low" level and begin its emergency shutdown procedure. The upper threshold for an input low voltage on ATMega CPUs is 0.3 × supply voltage. So for a CPU running at 5V, the trigger point for an input to see a logic low is any voltage below 1.5V.

The minimum voltage that needs to be applied to the top of the voltage divider to cause the input to see 1.5V or more can be calculated as follows:

```
1.5 / 0.32 = 4.7V
```

Simply dividing the voltage down isn't quite enough protection for the Arduino input, though. Imagine what would happen in the case of a load-dump when the alternator pumps 60V into the system—the voltage divider output would rise to 19.2V!

The 5.6V Zener diode across the 47K resistor provides that extra protection. A Zener diode has the unusual property that when exposed to a reverse-biased voltage below a specific "Zener voltage" it acts as an open circuit and you would hardly know it's there, but if the voltage rises above that point the Zener diode begins to conduct almost like a short-circuit. The result is that it can act as an over-voltage protection clamp that prevents the Arduino input from seeing a voltage beyond its rated level. Combined with the high-impedance input presented by the voltage divider, it provides pretty much bulletproof protection against anything a car electrical system can throw at it.

Note that although Zener diodes have a specific rated voltage, their conductivity isn't quite as binary as being totally off below that voltage and totally on above it. They begin to conduct gradually a little below the rated voltage, which is why we chose a 5.6V Zener to protect a 5V input. If we'd chosen something like a 5.1V Zener instead, it would actually start clamping the input prematurely once it rose above about 4.7V or 4.8V. The 5.6V part we selected is just right for protecting a 5V input.

Fit the pair of resistors for the voltage divider, with one end of the 100K resistor joined to the +12V input, the other end joined to the 47K resistor, and the far end of the 47K resistor joined to ground as shown in the power supply schematic in Figure 15-17. Connect the Zener diode in parallel to the 47K resistor with the banded (cathode) end to the joint between the resistors, and the nonbanded (anode) end connected to ground. Then fit a jumper wire that connects the center of the voltage divider to the Mega's digital I/O pin 2. This input is used specifically because it can have an interrupt attached to it in the ATMega1280 CPU, allowing the software to detect changes to it at any time without having to continuously poll the input to see if it has changed. In the software, we will attach a "falling edge" interrupt to pin 2 so that if the voltage transitions from a high state to a low state the program will enter an emergency shutdown mode to protect the data on the USB memory stick.

As a general principle, it's a good idea to always test a newly constructed power supply in isolation from the rest of the circuit. With the shield separate from the Arduino and nothing else fitted on it, connect a +12V power supply to the ground and voltage regulator input connections, and use a multimeter to measure the voltage between the ground and +5V rails on the shield. It should be in the range 4.95V to 5.05V if everything is connected properly. Also measure the voltage on the center of the voltage divider where it connects to Arduino digital I/O pin 2, and make sure it's at the level you expect based on your actual power-supply input voltage and the calculations shown previously.

Fit the Serial Connections on the Shield

Because both the GPS module and the OBD-II adapter use serial interfaces, we need to fit two oriented 4-pin male headers to the prototyping shield for the serial connections. To keep the wiring simple, we fitted them at the end of the board near the Arduino's serial I/O pins.

RX and TX (the first serial port on the Arduino) aren't used by any peripherals, so they remain free for a host to connect to the data logger.

Link the OBD-II serial connection ground pin to ground on the shield, and run short jumper wires to link the RX pin to the Mega's RX1, and the TX pin to the Mega's TX1. These two connections are for the second serial port on the Mega, named "Serial1" because port numbering starts from 0. Technically, the first serial port is Serial0 even though the name is abbreviated to simply "Serial." You don't need to connect the VCC pin on the serial connector to anything because, as mentioned previously, we don't use it to power the OBD-II module. Only ground, TX, and RX need to be connected.

Likewise, link the GPS serial connection ground pin to ground on the shield and run short jumper wires to link the RX pin to the Mega's RX2, and the TX pin to the Mega's TX2. These serial connections are for the third serial port on the Mega, named "Serial2." Yes, the naming can be a bit confusing sometimes!

Because the GPS module needs to be powered from the Arduino, we do need to connect up the VCC pin, but because we're using an LS20031 that runs at 3.3V we can't simply link the serial VCC line to +5V on the shield. Instead it needs to be connected to the 3.3V header on the shield using a short piece of hookup wire.

The two serial ports are wired up in almost exactly the same way, and as far as software is concerned they are interchangeable, but because of the different connections for power it's important to keep track of which one is which. Make a note or put a mark on the board to show which is the OBD-II socket (Serial1, no power) and which is GPS (Serial2, 3.3V).

Prepare the VDIP1 Module

A recurring question on Arduino mailing lists, forums, and blogs is how to connect it to some form of mass-storage device to keep a record of data collected from sensors and inputs. The Arduino's ATMega CPU contains nonvolatile storage called EEPROM (Electrically Erasable Programmable Read-Only Memory), but it has very small capacity: 512bytes in the ATMega168, 1KB in the 328P, and 4KB in the 1280. We use it in this project to store configuration values entered via menus on the LCD, but for storing a larger amount of data we have to look elsewhere. More information about the internal EEPROM is available on the Arduino site at www.arduino.cc/en/Reference/EEPROM.

The next step up in capacity is direct connection to flash memory chips that are fairly commonly available in the region of 1Mbit (128KB) to 4Mbit (512KB) capacity. With an external flash memory chip, the Arduino can certainly store more data, but it's still trapped within your project and can't be easily accessed externally. If you want to access the data later, you will need to have a routine in the Arduino that can read it back out and send it to a host via the serial port or a network connection, and then have a program at the other end capable of reading and storing the stream of data. It's also just a big flat chunk of memory, so you have to keep track of what data you have stored and where it's located within the memory space, because it has no concept of a filesystem. Flash memory chips are typically connected using SPI (Serial Peripheral Interface) or I2C, both of which are very well supported by Arduino. See www.arduino.cc/playground/Code/Dataflash or www.arduino.cc/playground/Code/I2CEEPROM for more information.

Beyond directly connected flash memory chips is the use of things such as MicroSD flash memory cards, commonly used in digital cameras. They're inexpensive, small, and have large capacities: not just megabytes of data, but gigabytes. Something not many people realize is that MicroSD memory cards support a standard SPI connection just like flash memory chips, so they're quite easy to communicate with. One approach that a number of people have taken is to solder wires directly to the metal tabs on a MicroSD card and talk to it directly from an Arduino. Once again, the filesystem itself is the stumbling block, though, because attempting to implement support for even a limited subset of something like a VFAT filesystem on a microcontroller such as an Arduino would use up all its resources and render it pretty much useless for anything else. If you want to go down that path, it's worth looking at a library called SDuFAT (SD micro FAT) that implements a very minimal subset of the FAT filesystem. It works by relying on a host computer to prepare the filesystem and create a single large empty file in advance, which it then fills with whatever data you want to write into it. See www.arduino.cc/playground/Learning/SDMMC for more information.

For this project, though, we've gone another step further again, using a standard USB memory stick formatted with a full FAT16 or FAT32 filesystem. This is the Holy Grail of Arduino mass storage: large, cheap, fast, removable, and the data written to the memory stick is then accessible using standard software such as a text editor or a spreadsheet on a regular PC. We can create files and directories, delete them, and read and write them all using simple routines in an Arduino program. Perfect for a data-logging application like this.

All this is made possible by a chip called a Vinculum VNC1L made by FTDI, the same folks who created the USB interface adapter used in many Arduino models including the Duemilanove and the Mega. The VNC1L builds on their experience creating USB-to-serial interface chips and implements an entire dual-channel USB host/slave device in a single chip.

This sounds great in theory, but the VNC1L comes in an LQFP-48 format—fine if you have your own reflow soldering oven and SMT production line at home, but not so useful if you want to solder it by hand. Luckily, FTDI also supplies the VNC1L preloaded on a handy prototyping module that's available in both single-port (VDIP1) and dual-port (VDIP2) formats at a very reasonable price. The VDIP1 (see Figure 15-18) is perfect for this application and is available for purchase online directly from FTDI's online store at www.vinculum.com, and also from regional distributors such as Dontronics in Australia. It's a really neat solution that should become very popular as a way to add mass storage to Arduino projects.

Figure 15-18. *The VinculumVDP1 single-port USB module*

Both the VDIP1 and VDIP2 modules contain the same VNC1L chip, and in fact the only difference between them is that one has a single USB socket fitted to it and the other has a pair of sockets. Other than that, they are identical and can run the same firmware, and in fact all the connections for the second USB port are included on the single-port VDIP1 so you can even wire up a second connector to it yourself.

The VNC1L can be loaded with a variety of different firmware variations so that the two channels can be any combination of USB client and USB host. The first step is to select the firmware that's most appropriate to our particular application and flash the chip.

One of the neat features of the VNC1L is that it can perform its own firmware updates directly from a memory stick. Just download the required firmware from www.vinculum.com, put it onto a memory stick, and rename it "ftrfb.ftd." Then plug the memory stick into the VDIP1 module and power it up. The VNC1L chip searches memory sticks connected to it for a replacement firmware file that is a different version than the one already installed, and if it finds one it loads the new firmware into its internal nonvolatile memory and then automatically reboots. The whole process is totally painless and changing firmware versions couldn't be easier.

For this project, we use what FTDI refers to as "VDAP" (Vinculum Disk And Peripheral) firmware, which allows it to act as a USB host to other USB slave devices, such as memory sticks and other peripherals, and includes FAT support. If your VDIP1 module was supplied with a different firmware preinstalled, you'll need to download the VDAP firmware from www.vinculum.com and install it using the process just discussed.

The VNC1L supports three communication modes: serial UART, SPI, and parallel FIFO. For this project, we used a serial connection with the VDIP1 in UART mode. The communication mode is set using the jumpers on the pair of 3-pin headers at one end of the board, and putting both jumpers into either pull-down (left) or pull-up (right) positions will select UART mode. The supported jumper modes are shown in Figure 15-9.

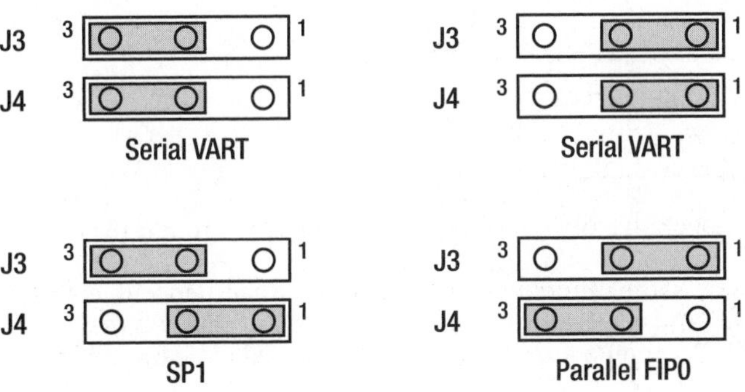

Figure 15-19. *Mode jumpers for VDIP1 and VDIP2 modules*

The data pins on the VDIP1 have different meanings depending on the communications mode. The VDIP1 datasheet includes pinout tables for all modes including SPI and parallel FIFO, but we're using serial UART mode so we'll use the UART pin assignment shown in Table 15-5.

Table 15-5. *VDIP1 pinout in UART mode*

Pin	Name	Type	Description
6	TXD	Output	Tx data output
8	RXD	Input	Rx data input

9	RTS#	Output	Request To Send (active low)
10	CTS#	Input	Clear To Send (active low)
11	DTR#	Output	Data Terminal Ready output (active low)
12	DSR#	Input	Data Set Ready input (active low)
13	DCD#	Input	Data Carrier Detect input (active low)
14	RI#	Input	Ring Indicator input (active low)
15	TXDEN#	Input	Enable Tx for RS485 (active low)

We use only TXD, RXD, RTS, and CTS connections for OBDuinoMega, so pins 11 through 15 can be ignored.

Other than the specific communications pins, the other ones we need to be concerned with are VCC (+5V), GND, PG (program), and RS (reset). VCC and GND connect directly to +5V and GND on the Arduino via the prototyping shield, while both PG and RS are active-low so they need to be biased high to +5V via 10K resistors to disable them.

Being able to apply a hardware reset to the VDIP1 under software control can be very handy during development, so also connect the RS pin to Arduino digital I/O pin 12 via a 1K resistor. By setting pin 12 HIGH in normal operation, it's then possible to force the VDIP1 to reset by pulsing it LOW.The schematic in Figure 15-20 shows the connections required from the Arduino to the VDIP1 module.

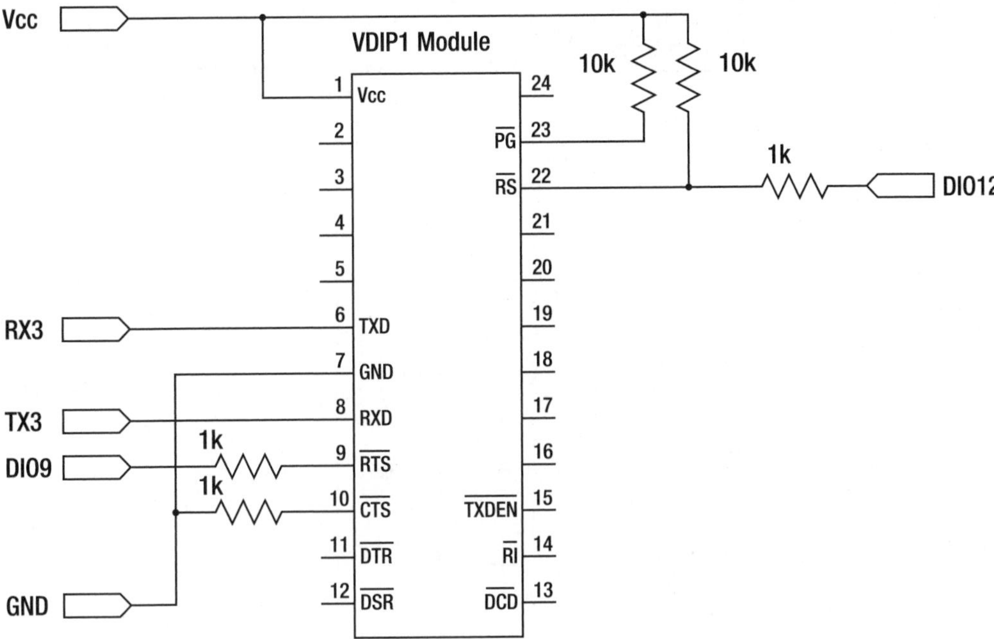

Figure 15-20. Schematic for connections to VDIP1 module

The VDIP1 module could be mounted directly on the prototyping shield, but for ease of access we decided to mount ours on a subassembly glued in place near the front of the case. We first fitted a pair of 12-pin female headers to the prototyping shield to suit the VDIP1 pinout and mounted the associated pull-up and communications resistors on the shield so that the module could be plugged straight in for early testing. Later we used a pair of 12-pin breakaway male headers and some ribbon cable to make mini "extension leads" that connect the subassembly in the front of the case to the headers on the prototyping shield

The LCD Module

Most OBDuino and MPGuino units are fitted with a 16x2 LCD module with a Hitachi HD44780-compatible parallel interface similar to the unit used in the Water Flow Gauge project in Chapter 10. The code has been written to support displays of varying widths and either two or four rows, so by changing a few configuration values you should be able to connect any HD44780-compatible module. We used the schematic shown in Figure 15-21 with both 16x2 and 20x4 versions when building our prototypes.

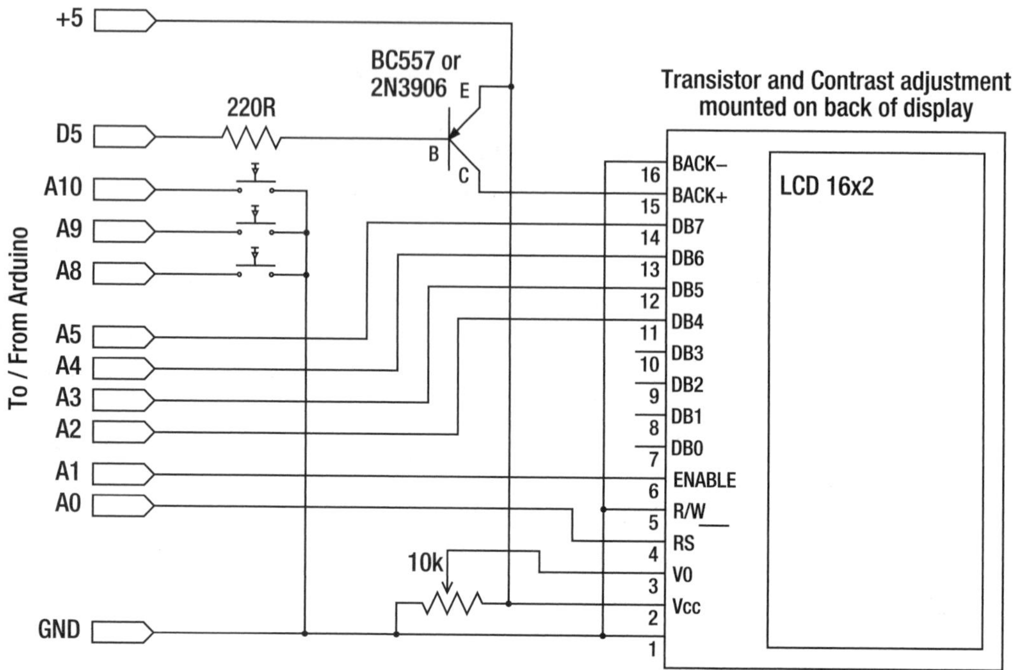

Figure 15-21. Schematic for connecting the HD44780-compatible display module to Arduino

If you are intending to mount the device in your car so that you can see the LCD while driving, it's important to select a display that has a high level of contrast and readability. Some displays, including one of the white-on-blue 20x4 units we used, might look cool but have pathetically poor contrast and are very hard to read unless you're at exactly the right angle. The early black-on-yellow/green LCD design might look a bit dated, but it generally gives the best contrast out of all the color combinations.

An alternative is to go for a more exotic display type. Vacuum-Flourescent Display (VFD) and Organic LED (OLED) modules with HD44780-compatible interfaces are available from some suppliers. They are much harder to find and generally more expensive than regular LCD modules, but they give a far brighter and more legible display, so it may be worth tracking one down if display clarity is critical to you.

The Water Flow Gauge in Chapter 10 has a description of how HD44780 displays work and includes an example of driving a display in 4-bit mode using the LiquidCrystal library. This project deviates from the normal approach, though, because MPGuino/OBDuino don't use the LiquidCrystal library. Instead they implement their own LCD driver functions that are optimized to be as small as possible and only provide the specific features required by the project, all to reduce memory usage. This is a classic situation where a prewritten library might make things simpler from a development point of view, but in the end it just takes up too much space and needs to be replaced by minimal custom-written functions.

Just as in the Water Flow Gauge project, we're going to drive the LCD in 4-bit mode to save on wiring and I/O pins, but the MPGuino/OBDuino codebase on which we based this project also includes a couple of extra features that are quite handy: backlight control and contrast control.

If you are going to leave your car engine datalogger permanently connected, it's important to minimize the power it drains from your car battery while the engine isn't running, and an LCD backlight can use a significant amount of power. MPGuino/OBDuino includes a display-blanking feature that uses a transistor to turn on the display backlight only when it's needed, and then blank it when the engine isn't running. It also uses PWM (pulse-width modulation) from an Arduino digital pin to vary the brightness, giving you more than simple on/off backlight control.

The LCD needs to be wired up in almost the same way as the display in the Water Flow Gauge project, using a strip of ribbon cable to connect ground, +5V, RS, Enable, and D4 through D7. Unlike the Water Flow Gauge project, though, we will also control the backlight from the Arduino rather than hard-wire it to a fixed level using a resistor. The pin assignments are given in Table 15-6.

Table 15-6. *Connections from Arduino to HD44780 LCD module*

Arduino Pin	LCD Pin	Label	Name	Description
GND	1	GND	Ground	Display ground connection
+5V	2	VCC	Power	Display +5V connection
Digital OUT 6	3	Vo	Contrast	Contrast adjustment voltage
Analog IN 0	4	RS	Register Select	Data (HIGH)/Control (LOW)
GND	5	R/W	Read/Write	Read (HIGH)/Write (LOW)
Analog IN 1	6	E	Enable	Enable byte/nibble transfer
	7	D0	Data0	Data bit 0
	8	D1	Data1	Data bit 1
	9	D2	Data2	Data bit 2
	10	D3	Data3	Data bit 3
Analog IN 2	11	D4	Data4	Data bit 4
Analog IN 3	12	D5	Data5	Data bit 5
Analog IN 4	13	D6	Data6	Data bit 6
Analog IN 5	14	D7	Data7	Data bit 7

(Transistor)	15	VB1	Backlight power	Backlight +5V connection
GND	16	VB0	Backlight ground	Backlight ground connection

With the LCD laid out next to the prototyping shield, the pin assignments shown in Table 15-6 should have the LCD connections lined up nicely with the shield connections as in the schematic, allowing you to use a flat piece of ribbon cable to connect one to the other. Almost all the connections to the Arduino will be in a row on one edge of the shield, so for convenience we connected the ribbon cable to a length of male breakaway header strip so it can be easily removed. It might look strange connecting the data lines to analog inputs, but in the software those inputs are switched to digital output mode and used as regular digital pins.

To keep things neat, we cut off a 20-pin length of header strip so that it would run all the way from the +5V connector and adjacent GND pin, across the gap to the A0–A7 connector, and then across the next gap to the A8–A15 connector. The pins in the gaps between the connectors are unused, of course, so they can be pulled out of the plastic strip with a pair of pliers. Pins A8, A9, and A10 are used for the menu buttons, as described in a moment. Figure 15-22 shows that the wire for those buttons has already been connected.

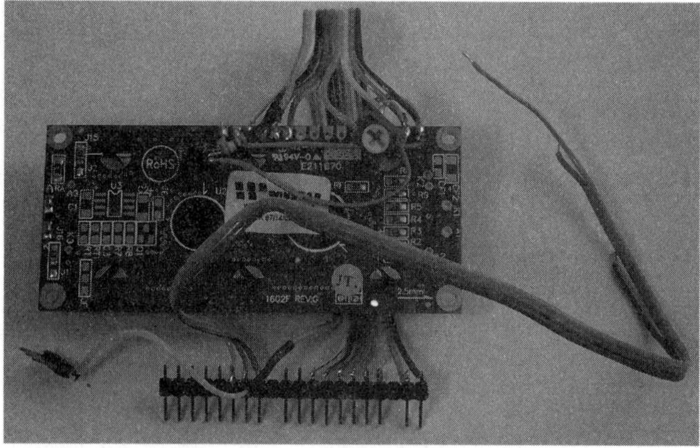

Figure 15-22. *The LCD module connected to the male break-away header strip*

That takes care of most of the connections, with the exceptions of pin 3 (contrast) and pin 15 (backlight power) on the LCD.

We connected LCD pin 3, the contrast control pin, to the center connection of a 10K variable resistor with the other two legs of the resistor connected to GND and +5V so that we could manually vary the contrast.

An alternative is to connect LCD pin 3 instead to Arduino digital I/O line 6, which can operate as a PWM output. The software can then control the LCD contrast by adjusting the PWM ratio, with an output level of 0 (low) giving highest contrast, and an output level of 255 (high) giving minimum contrast. Or if your LCD supports it, you can hard-wire this pin to GND for maximum contrast, as we did in the Water Flow Gauge project.

LCD pin 15, the backlight + supply, connects to a transistor that, in turn, is controlled by the Arduino. Arduino outputs can't supply enough current to drive the backlight directly, so the transistor allows a PWM output to control the backlight supply without danger to the CPU.

Just about any small PNP switching transistor should work as long as it can handle the current required by your LCD module. If your LCD draws less than 100mA, you can use something like the extremely common BC557 or 2N2907. Some backlights can draw more than 200mA, which means you'll need to use a slightly higher rated transistor such as a 2N3906.

We mounted the transistor and resistor directly on the back of the LCD, with the lead from the resistor to Arduino digital pin 5 running to a male breakaway header. We soldered a short length of female header to the top of the prototyping shield to allow the connection to be easily removed.

Logging Control Button and Status LEDs

We wanted a simple way to turn logging on and off, and a pushbutton works very nicely when combined with an interrupt input. By using a button with a center LED, it's possible to have it display the current logging status, so we chose a button with a blue LED mounted in it. You could, of course, simply use a separate LED and a regular button, but having them integrated into a single unit makes the result look a bit nicer and makes it more obvious that the logging state and the button are associated.

The button connects between ground and Arduino digital I/O line 3 using a 1K resistor. I/O line 3 is also connected to +5V via a 20K pull-up resistor inside the ATMega CPU itself. The internal pull-up resistor is activated in the software by setting the pin to INPUT mode and then performing a digitalWrite() to set it to a HIGH state, so when the switch is open (off) the input will be biased high. When the switch is closed (on) the input is pulled low through the button via the 1K resistor.

Because it's only a momentary-action button that is on while pressed, sensing the mode is not quite as simple as checking the state of the input on each pass through the main program loop. Instead, the button is connected to digital I/O line 3 so that we can attach an interrupt to it in the sketch, and when the input transitions from a high (unpressed) state to a low (pressed) state, an ISR (interrupt service routine) is called. The ISR simply sets the output driving the status LED appropriately to either high or low, turning the LED on or off. It also includes some debounce logic that checks the time that has passed since the button was last pressed so that as the mechanical switch contacts settle, the CPU doesn't interpret them as multiple button presses.

Rather than set a logging status flag in a variable, we used a little trick that allows us to use the status of an output pin as a flag: even though the logging status LED is connected to an I/O line in "output" mode, we can still use digitalRead to read whether the output is high or low. The status LED itself, therefore, acts as a sort of hardware status flag for the software!

One other advantage of using a momentary button to toggle the logging state and an LED to indicate the current state is that it's possible to turn logging on or off in the sketch and have it accurately reflected by the LED. With a simple on/off switch, you can end up with a situation where the switch is in an "on" position but logging has been turned off by some software event, while a pushbutton that toggles the state on each press by inverting a flag will always do the right thing.

The system has a total of four status LEDs including the one mounted in the center of the "Log" button. They aren't strictly necessary, but when the system is running in your car and you don't have a laptop plugged in, it can be handy to be able to see what state the system is in just by glancing at the LEDs. You could, of course, display the same information on the LCD module if you prefer, but using LEDs keeps the LCD free to display current vehicle data. The connections are all shown in Figure 15-23. Remember that the 20K resistor shown in the schematic doesn't need to be fitted to the shield because it's contained within the CPU and is activated by the sketch.

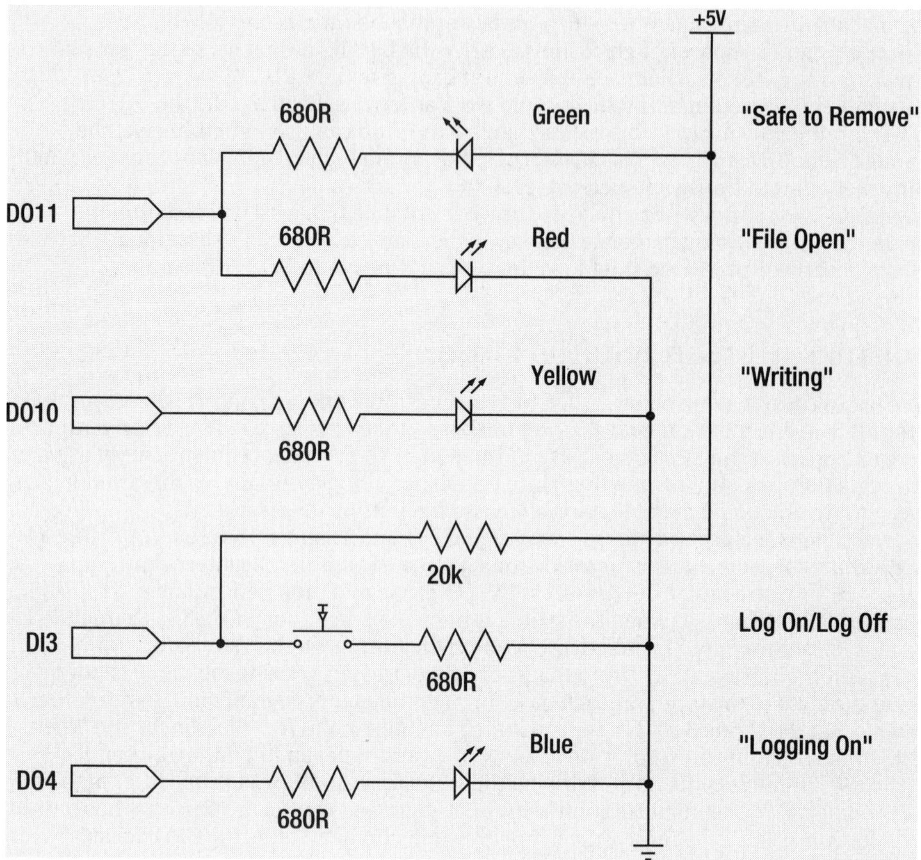

Figure 15-23. *Schematic of logging control button and status LED connections to the Arduino*

You will need to assemble the status LEDs and logging button to suit your particular case. We glued ours in place on the front panel of the project box as described next.

Mount in Sub-Assemblies in the Case

How you mount everything will depend on whether you're aiming for a permanent installation or something you can connect temporarily in any car, and whether you're intending to use the Vehicle Telemetry Platform to provide real-time feedback on driving style or mainly to log data for future analysis.

To provide visibility of the display directly within the driver's line of sight, some people on the EcoModder forums have even experimented with making head-up displays that reflect information in the windshield by laying the display horizontally on top of the dashboard and mirroring the image vertically. Don't try to bite off more than you can chew in one go, though. Work at getting the basic system operational first, then extend it with more exotic modifications. And remember that for initial testing at least, it's probably safest to keep the whole unit totally out of sight of the driver so you're not tempted to play with it while trying to drive. It's best to bring along a passenger or have someone else drive on your first trip with the system so one person can drive while the other checks that it's working as expected.

For our prototype, our emphasis was on an easily removable device so we fitted everything inside a PVC project case that makes it fairly bulky but quite durable. An alternative would be to fit the Vehicle Telemetry System permanently into your dash, with the display and control buttons fitted into the dash surface or into a blank plate designed to fit a radio mounting location. Remember, though, that a unit sitting on a seat or in the passenger's lap will be fairly well protected from vibration while a permanently fixed system will need to have all nuts held in place with lock-washers or thread-locking glue.

We wanted to use it mainly to store data and analyze it later, so visibility of the display while driving wasn't particularly important. We fitted the LCD module into the top of the case, which is fine if it's sitting on a seat beside you and you only look at it occasionally while stationary. If you want to view the display while driving, it would work better mounted in the end of the case so it could be placed up near the driver's line of sight. Remember to always keep safety in mind when using a device like this and don't try driving around only half watching the road because you're distracted by an awkwardly mounted display that's sliding around on the seat beside you.

For our prototype, we mounted the ELM327 interface adapter's PCB vertically in the back corner of the case with 6mm spacers holding it clear of the side, and M3 nuts and bolts keeping it secure. Because the existing holes in the PCB were very large, we used plastic washers to provide a large enough contact area to overlap the holes on both sides of the PCB (see Figure 15-24).

Figure 15-24. *The ELM327 OBD-II adapter mounted in the case*

The DB9 socket was also mounted in the rear panel with the female header fitted to the 8-pin male header on the PCB (see Figure 15-25).

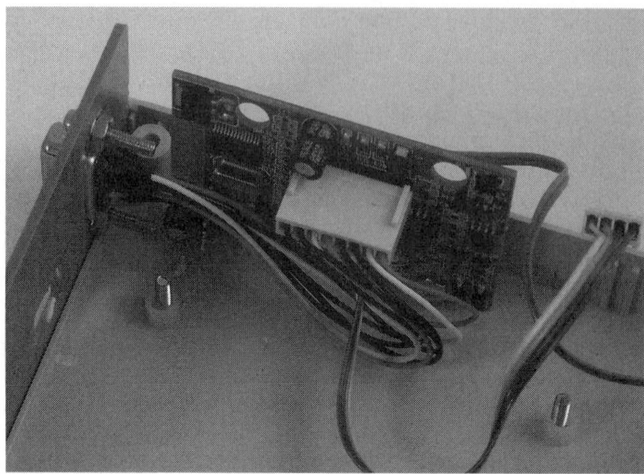

Figure 15-25. The DB9 socket for OBD-II cable mounted in the case

For our prototype, we fitted the Arduino Mega into the bottom of the case using 6mm plastic spacers and 15mm M3 nuts and bolts, with plastic washers on top of the Arduino to prevent short-circuits caused by the nuts. A hole was cut into the back panel to allow the USB socket to protrude, making it easy to reprogram the unit with everything mounted in the case or to connect a laptop for monitoring data via the USB connection while driving (see Figure 15-26).

Figure 15-26. The Arduino Mega mounted on plastic spacers with the USB socket protruding through the back panel

The simplest approach to mounting the VDIP1 would be to put it directly on the prototyping shield with the USB connector protruding through the back of the case, but we wanted the connector on the front so we chose to separate it from the prototyping shield and mount it on a sub-board. We used a bit of scrap veroboard and soldered some female PCB-mount headers to it, soldered short lengths of ribbon cable to the pins that need connections, and used two-part epoxy to glue it into the case so that the module sits with the front of the USB socket just protruding through the front panel (see Figure 15-27).

Remember that the USB socket will take all the mechanical load of the USB memory stick plugged into it including weight, shocks, and vibration. Make sure it's firmly mounted and use a memory stick that's as small and light as possible—definitely don't hang your keychain from the memory stick while it's plugged into the system!

Figure 15-27. *The VDIP1 module mounted on a sub-board with the USB socket protruding through the front panel*

Next, we mounted the LCD assembly prepared earlier into the top of the case. Cutting out the rectangular hole for the LCD was quite tricky, but a panel nibbling tool intended for cutting odd shapes in thin metal helped keep things straight. The edges were cleaned up with a craft knife and the end result was about as neat as can be expected when working with hand tools. Holes were drilled for the three menu buttons (referred to as left, middle, and right in the sketch) and for mounting bolts for the LCD, which was held in place with 6mm plastic spacers to keep the face recessed just behind the case surface (see Figure 15-28).

The position of the LCD and buttons were carefully selected to allow enough clearance inside the case for the VDIP1 module and the prototyping shield.

The menu buttons couldn't be wired up to the LCD assembly and header until it was fitted in the case, so next we connected one side of each button to the ground connection on the LCD and then used ribbon cable to link the other side of the left, middle, and right buttons to analog inputs 8, 9, and 10, respectively.

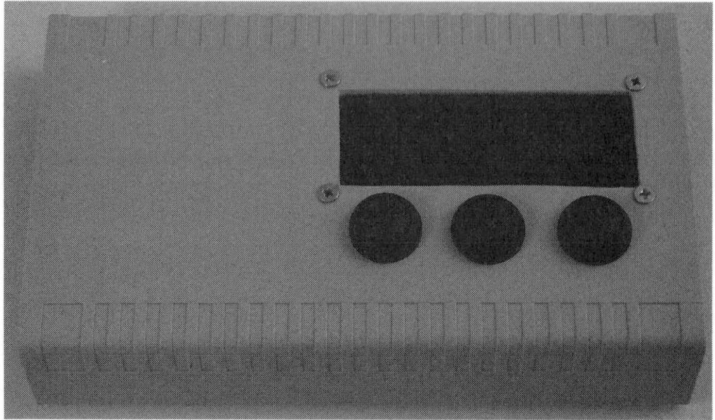

Figure 15-28. The LCD and menu buttons mounted in the case

The result is a self-contained assembly that can be plugged into the prototyping shield or removed with no soldering required, which is very handy when working on the Vehicle Telemetry System because it means you can put the cover aside without it being awkwardly linked to the rest of the unit with short wires (see Figure 15-29).

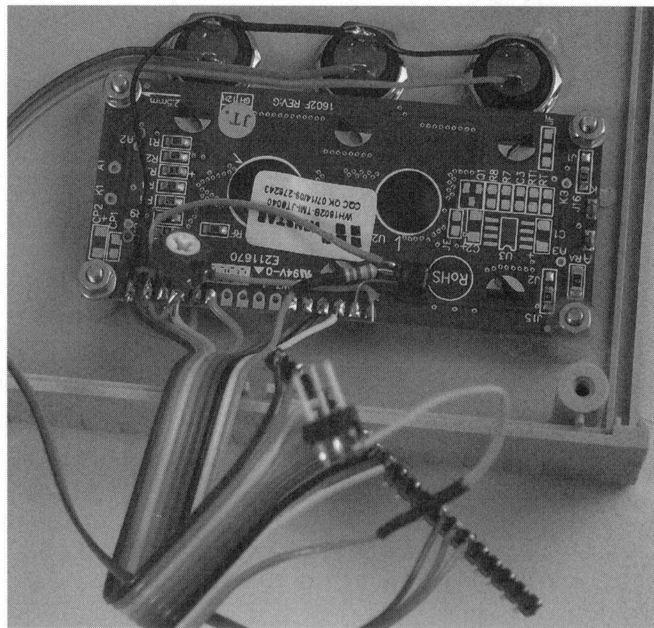

Figure 15-29. Connections to the LCD module and menu buttons

The prototyping shield can then be fitted, containing the power supply and connections for the LCD, buttons, and VDIP1 module. The huge 4700uF capacitor attached to the power supply also needs to be mounted. We used foam tape in our prototype, which seemed reasonably secure, but you could also use a dab of epoxy glue or similar to make sure it definitely won't move even with a lot of shock or vibration.

The GPS module slipped in neatly on one side and attached sturdily to the side of the case with more foam tape (see Figure 15-30). Keep in mind that for optimum performance the GPS antenna (the ceramic square on the LS20031) needs to be pointed at the sky and not be blocked by metal, so think about how the case will be mounted and try to put the GPS on top if possible.

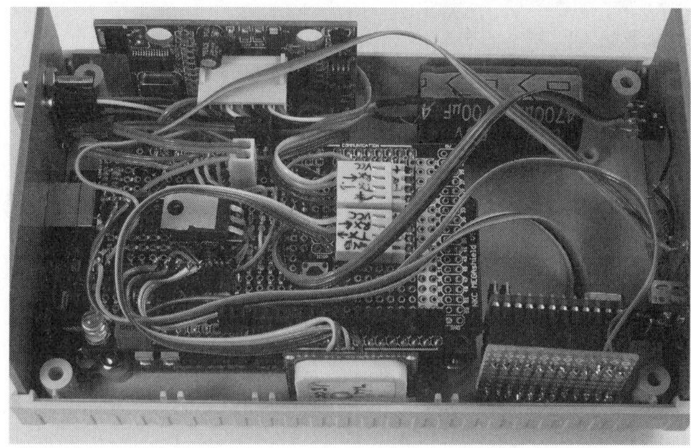

Figure 15-30. *The prototyping shield mounted on Arduino, the 4700uF capacitor taped to the case, and the GPS module attached with foam tape*

The "logging on/off" pushbutton with center-mounted LED was hard-wired to the prototyping shield with short lengths of ribbon cable. As you can see in Figure 15-31, we glued the button in place, being very careful not to get glue on the moving part and only on the case.

We also glued the LEDs in place after rubbing the end of each one flat using fine sandpaper on a flat surface. Doing this squares off the end of the LED and gives it a frosted surface that diffuses the light nicely, and the flat face then sits flush with the surface of the front panel. You could alternatively use mounting bezels if you prefer.

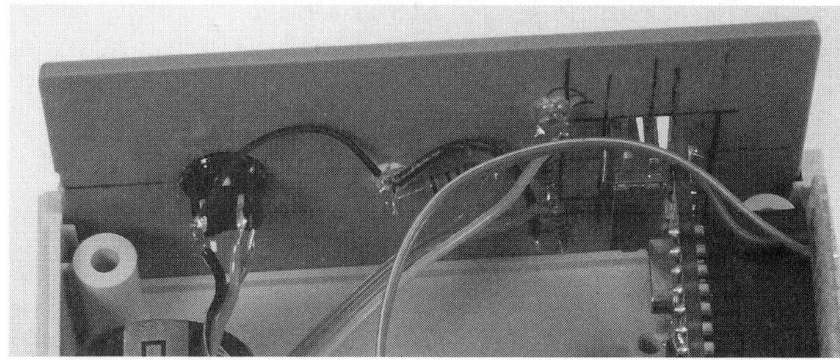

Figure 15-31. *The Logging button and status LEDs glued into the front panel*

That's it! The hardware is now complete and you can plug in the LCD, fit the lid, and screw it together. Our complete prototype is shown in Figure 15-32.

Figure 15-32. *The complete system assembled in a case with USB memory stick attached*

You have a number of options for mounting the system in your car. Self-adhesive velcro is a good option, allowing you to attach the box to a handy flat surface such as the center console or on top of the dash. Just remember that cars can become extremely hot when left parked in the sun, so don't leave it on top of the dash when the car is parked on a hot day.

OBDuino Mega Sketch

The Vehicle Telemetry Platform uses a complex sketch called OBDuinoMega that's still undergoing rapid development, as are the MPGuino and OBDuino32k codebases from which it is derived. It's quite likely that by the time of going to press, the code will have developed well beyond what is presented here. The fundamentals should still be the same, though, so rather than provide line by line commentary on all 4500+ lines of code, we'll skip through most of it and just discuss the interesting sections. The full source code is available for download from the project page on the *Practical Arduino* web site.

The sketch itself is split into a number of different source files. If you download the project directory, copy it into your sketchbook directory, and open it in the Arduino IDE, you'll see that there are a number of tabs across the top instead of just a single tab as you see in most projects. Each tab is a separate file. There are several reasons for splitting up the code this way, but probably the most important is to provide conceptual encapsulation of the different sections of the code. Large software projects almost always divide their code between multiple files because it makes it easier to find the particular functions you're looking for, simplifies the main code, and therefore makes it easier to understand the overall flow of the program. In addition, when multiple programmers are working on the project at the same time and using a source code management system, it minimizes the risk of getting in each other's way.

Another motivation for structuring it this way is that the original OBDuino32k codebase is designed to fit within the 32KB of memory (less bootloader) of an ATMega328 CPU, like the ones used in a Duemilanove. Just about all available memory is used and the project only barely fits, so the intention is that OBDuinoMega should be able to be built in two forms: one with the original functionality and still able to fit into an ATMega328, and one with extended functionality that requires the ATMega1280 CPU found in an Arduino Mega. The use of compile-time switches allows the same codebase to be built for both targets with additional functionality included or excluded, depending on settings in the main file.

Depending on the options you use, there are two libraries you might need to install, both written by Mikal Hart.

TinyGPS is a minimal NMEA parser that takes a raw stream from a GPS module and extracts various useful parameters from it. It's designed to be lightweight by avoiding floating-point math where possible and ignoring many of the NMEA fields that aren't likely to be interesting. TinyGPS makes interfacing with serial GPS modules, such as the Locosys LS20031, amazingly easy. TinyGPS is available for download from the Mikal's Arduiniana web site (arduiniana.org/libraries/tinygps/), so grab it and extract it into the libraries directory inside your sketchbook directory.

PString is a very small class that extends the Print class already included in Arduino and allows you to print data into a buffer . It's extremely handy because you can use regular syntax that you're already familiar with from functions, such as Serial.print(), and use it to format and store data for later access. It's used in OBDuinoMega to manage a buffer containing data collated from multiple sources prior to being written to the USB memory stick all at once. It's available at arduiniana.org/libraries/PString/.

OBDuinoMega.pde

The main program file starts with a whole series of compilation modifiers. These change the way the project is built, allowing you to include or exclude different features to suit your requirements as discussed previously. This also helps keep the resulting hex file as small as possible, but remember that some features are dependent on others.

The first option is DEBUG, which causes the OBDuinoMega sketch to skip the initialization of the OBD interface and move right along as if it was attached to a car, even if it isn't. It also causes calls made to retrieve OBD values to return hard-coded values so the system will look like it's working, but in fact it's just faking it. It's much easier to work on the project while sitting inside in a comfortable chair with the datalogger sitting on a bench, so this is a handy option for when you want to test things without sitting in your car for hours.

With the option commented out, OBDuinoMega does a normal build; uncommented it does a debug build.

```
//#define DEBUG
```

The MEGA option causes a number of things to switch around within the code to suit the different architecture of a Mega compared to a Duemilanove or equivalent. We definitely need this option for the Vehicle Telemetry Platform.

```
#define MEGA
```

Building with either the ENABLE_GPS or ENABLE_VDIP options set requires that the MEGA option be set as well. Power-fail detection is currently only useful if ENABLE_VDIP is enabled, and it causes the OBDuinoMega sketch to attach an ISR that ends logging and closes currently open files if the voltage on the input side of the power supply drops.

```
#define ENABLE_GPS
#define ENABLE_VDIP
#define ENABLE_PWRFAILDETECT
```

The next few build options relate to the way the sketch connects to the OBD interface in your car. The hardware we've described here uses an ELM327 chip to do all the hard work, but the OBDuino documentation includes alternative interface hardware that can be used if you know what specific interface protocol your car uses and you want to avoid the expense of an ELM327.

For our version, we set the ELM flag, which means the following few options all need to be turned off. If you prefer to use an MC33290 ISO K line chip as described in the OBDuino project online, you should comment this out.

```
#define ELM
```

Newer cars that follow the ISO 9141 standard only use the K line, while older cars use both the K line and the L line. If you have an older car and have the K and L line wiring in place instead of an ELM327 you need to uncomment this.

```
//#define useL_Line
```

If you aren't using an ELM327, you need to specify which init sequence to use depending on your car's interface. Only one of the options should be enabled, and you don't need any of them if you have an ELM327 like we do in the Vehicle Telemetry Platform.

```
//#define ISO_9141
//#define ISO_14230_fast
//#define ISO_14230_slow
```

The system can use ECU polling to see if the car is on or off. If you want it to just try PIDs without needing to find the ECU first, you can comment this option out.

```
#define useECUState
```

Normally, the ISO 9141 interface does not need to reinitialize after a period of no ECU communication, but in some cars it might be necessary. Uncommenting this option enables forced reinitialization. If this is turned on, you also have to turn on the useECUState option so that the sketch knows whether comms are working or not.

```
//#define do_ISO_Reinit
```

Enabling the carAlarmScreen option causes the sketch to display a fake "car alarm" screen with a scanning asterisk on the LCD whenever the car is not running.

```
//#define carAlarmScreen
```

The sketch then includes a few miscellaneous header files that we won't bother showing here, and then sets up memorable tokens representing serial connections. Rather than referring to serial ports directly throughout the rest of the sketch, such as using Serial.print(), a number of defines are set up so there's no confusion about which serial port is connected to which peripheral.

The baud rates are also set here so they can be reconfigured in one handy location rather than digging around inside the main program code, and the port used for the OBD connection varies depending on whether we're building for a Mega or a normal Arduino. Some OBD-II adapters ship configured to run at 9600bps, while some are configured to run at 38400bps. Check that the setting here matches your adapter.

The logActive flag is also only defined if we're running on a Mega.

```
#ifdef MEGA
#define HOST Serial
#define HOST_BAUD_RATE 38400
#define OBD2 Serial1
#define OBD2_BAUD_RATE 38400
#define GPS  Serial2
#define GPS_BAUD_RATE 57600
#define VDIP Serial3
#define VDIP_BAUD_RATE 9600
byte logActive = 0;
#else
#define OBD2 Serial
#define OBD2_BAUD_RATE 38400
#endif
```

Likewise, the LCD pin assignments vary depending on whether we're building for a Mega or a regular Arduino.

```
#ifdef MEGA
#define DIPin 54 // register select RS
#define DB4Pin 56
#define DB5Pin 57
#define DB6Pin 58
#define DB7Pin 59
#define ContrastPin 6
#define EnablePin 55
#define BrightnessPin 5
#else  // LCD Pins same as mpguino for a Duemilanove or equivalent
#define DIPin 4 // register select RS
#define DB4Pin 7
#define DB5Pin 8
#define DB6Pin 12
#define DB7Pin 13
#define ContrastPin 6
#define EnablePin 5
#define BrightnessPin 9
#endif
```

The sketch then declares prototypes for a number of functions defined later, then sets values related to keypress handling (not shown here) before setting up the pins used for the three menu buttons.

The OBDuinoMega sketch uses analog pins as digital inputs for the menu buttons, and one of the more interesting aspects of this sketch is that it sets up a port-level interrupt on an entire analog port (8 pins) and then uses a bitmask to determine which button has been pressed when the interrupt has been triggered.

This is different than the way interrupts are normally done in Arduino projects and it's quite clever because it allows you to use a large number of pins to trigger interrupts rather than limiting you to just the defined interrupt pins. Normally, you would connect an interrupt pin, such as digital I/O pin 2, to a button, and then attach an interrupt service routine to interrupt0 because that's the one bound to pin 2. If the ISR is entered, you then know that pin 2 was asserted.

Port-level interrupts aren't quite so simple because when an interrupt is triggered you only know that a line on that port has been asserted, not which line it is. The ISR therefore has to do a bit more work to figure out which line caused the interrupt to fire, and that's why the following code defines a bit value for each button in addition to a pin. The bit value represents the line in the port so that the sketch can check whether that bit (and, therefore, line) has been asserted using macros that are defined next.

```
#ifdef MEGA  // Button pins for Arduino Mega
#define lbuttonPin 62 // Left Button, on analog 8
#define mbuttonPin 63 // Middle Button, on analog 9
#define rbuttonPin 64 // Right Button, on analog 10
#define lbuttonBit 1 //  pin62 is a bitmask 1 on port K
#define mbuttonBit 2  // pin63 is a bitmask 2 on port K
#define rbuttonBit 4  // pin64 is a bitmask 4 on port K
#else   // Button pins for Duemilanove or equivalent
#define lbuttonPin 17 // Left Button, on analog 3
#define mbuttonPin 18 // Middle Button, on analog 4
#define rbuttonPin 19 // Right Button, on analog 5
#define lbuttonBit 8 //  pin17 is a bitmask 8 on port C
#define mbuttonBit 16 // pin18 is a bitmask 16 on port C
#define rbuttonBit 32 // pin19 is a bitmask 32 on port C
#endif
#define buttonsUp 0 // start with the buttons in the 'not pressed' state
byte buttonState = buttonsUp;
```

Macros are then defined for the three buttons, each applying a logical AND between the buttonState variable and the bit that represents the particular button being checked.

The buttonState value represents the port (totaling 8 pins equivalent to 8 bits) to which the buttons are connected. In the case of a Mega build, the buttons are attached to the first three pins on the second analog port, or port K in AVR terms. For example, if the middle button (attached to analog pin 9) is pressed, the port will have a binary state of B00000010. That has a decimal value of 2, which happens to be the value defined above for mbuttonBit.

Applying a logical AND between the current state and the button bit will, therefore, return true if the button is currently pressed, and false if it's not. All that is wrapped up in three little macros.

```
#define LEFT_BUTTON_PRESSED (buttonState&lbuttonBit)
#define MIDDLE_BUTTON_PRESSED (buttonState&mbuttonBit)
#define RIGHT_BUTTON_PRESSED (buttonState&rbuttonBit)
```

The software brightness control divides the brightness range into a series of stages from full-on to full-off, and the next section of code allows you to control how many steps it uses. You also need to tell it how many rows and columns it has available on the LCD. The smallest display it can handle is 16x2, but it also works well with larger displays. The center point of the display is then calculated along with the number of PIDs that can be displayed in total with two per row.

```
#define brightnessLength 7 //array size
const byte brightness[brightnessLength]={
   0xFF,
   0xFF/brightnessLength*(brightnessLength-1),
   0xFF/brightnessLength*(brightnessLength-2),
   0xFF/brightnessLength*(brightnessLength-3),
   0xFF/brightnessLength*(brightnessLength-4),
   0xFF/brightnessLength*(brightnessLength-5),
   0x00};
byte brightnessIdx=2;
```

```
#define LCD_ROWS 4
const byte LCD_width = 20;
const byte LCD_split = LCD_width / 2;
const byte LCD_PID_count = LCD_ROWS * 2;
```

The OBDuinoMega sketch uses the TinyGPS library to parse GPS data rather than attempt to deconstruct the NMEA format itself. The library is only included if GPS has been enabled as a build option, though. The file containing the floatToString() helper function is also included because it's used to send GPS values back to the host.

```
#include <TinyGPS.h>
TinyGPS gps;
float gpsFLat, gpsFLon;
unsigned long gpsAge, gpsDate, gpsTime, gpsChars;
int gpsYear;
byte gpsMonth, gpsDay, gpsHour, gpsMinute, gpsSecond, gpsHundredths;
#include "floatToString.h"
```

The sketch then sets up a series of #define entries for all the supported PIDs to make the OBD sections of the sketch easier to read. Seeing an entry for FUEL_PRESSURE later in the code is a lot more self-explanatory than 0x0A, and this is a perfect example of why it's often better to use human-readable identifiers rather than cryptic literal values.

The list of supported PIDs goes on for over one hundred lines, so you can check out the full list in the original source.

```
#define PID_SUPPORT00 0x00
#define MIL_CODE      0x01
#define FREEZE_DTC    0x02
#define FUEL_STATUS   0x03
#define LOAD_VALUE    0x04
#define COOLANT_TEMP  0x05
... etc
```

There are also a number of "fake" PIDs defined to represent values that might need to be displayed or logged, but that aren't present in regular OBD-II data. This is a clever way to do it, because the code that handles menus, display, and logging doesn't need to care about which PIDs are real OBD-II data and which are internally generated because they're all treated the same way at a high level. Only the low-level function that retrieves the data for a given PID has to care about where it comes from. A call to fetch PID values will work in exactly the same way whether the PID is real or not, but hidden away behind the scenes it can treat some PIDs differently and return values from other sources that could include calculations, stored values, or even GPS values, just as if they'd come from the car engine-management system.

For example, one of the fake PIDs is TRIP_COST, which is the result of a calculation that multiplies fuel used so far in the current trip by the price of fuel. A very handy piece of information to display, but certainly not something you'd get out of the engine-management system.

```
#define OUTING_WASTE  0xE9    // fuel wasted since car started
#define TRIP_WASTE    0xEA    // fuel wasted during trip
#define TANK_WASTE    0xEB    // fuel wasted for this tank
#define OUTING_COST   0xEC    // the money spent since car started
```

```
#define TRIP_COST     0xED    // money spent since on trip
... etc
```

Each PID also needs a short, human-readable label that can be used on the LCD to show what the value represents. These are defined in a big array that is then stored in program memory using the PROGMEM keyword so they don't fill up the limited available RAM in the ATMega CPU.

```
prog_char *PID_Desc[] PROGMEM=
{
"PID00-21", // 0x00  PIDs supported
"Stat DTC", // 0x01  Monitor status since DTCs cleared.
"Frz DTC",  // 0x02  Freeze DTC
"Fuel SS",  // 0x03  Fuel system status
"Eng Load", // 0x04  Calculated engine load value
"CoolantT", // 0x05  Engine coolant temperature
... etc
```

In the PID table discussed previously, we saw that each PID has a certain number of bytes of data that it should return. When a PID is requested from the car, the OBDuinoMega sketch needs to know how many bytes to listen for in the response. It therefore defines an array that lists the number of response bytes for each of the supported PIDs, and once again stores it in program memory to save on RAM, because these values won't change.

```
prog_uchar pid_reslen[] PROGMEM=
{
  // pid 0x00 to 0x1F
  4,4,2,2,1,1,1,1,1,1,1,1,2,1,1,1,
  2,1,1,1,2,2,2,2,2,2,2,2,1,1,1,4,

  // pid 0x20 to 0x3F
  4,2,2,2,4,4,4,4,4,4,4,4,1,1,1,1,
  1,2,2,1,4,4,4,4,4,4,4,4,2,2,2,2,

  // pid 0x40 to 0x4E
  4,8,2,2,2,1,1,1,1,1,1,1,1,2,2
};
```

The virtual "screens" of values to be displayed on the LCD are then set up, along with the menu items used to navigate around them.

Parameters relating to fuel cost calculation are also set up, including a struct (structure) to store information about trips. Each trip contains distance traveled, fuel used, and fuel wasted. Rather than store them separately, they are grouped together in a struct called trip_t containing those three elements.

A structure is a compound datatype made up of other structures and primitive datatypes. It's a convenient way to store a group of related variables all in one place, a little like database records that contain a number of different columns that collectively define the record. In this example, the struct is a simple one containing three long ints.

```
typedef struct
{
  unsigned long dist;
```

```
  unsigned long fuel;
  unsigned long waste;
}
trip_t;
```

A similar process is used to define a struct called params_t for configuration values that are stored in EEPROM, including the engine displacement, whether to use metric (SI) units, and the size of the fuel tank. These could also have been handled as individual variables but combining them into a struct makes them easier to manage as a group.

After params_t is defined, it's loaded with default values so the sketch will have a reasonable starting point that can then be adjusted to suit the specific vehicle.

A series of #define entries then set up easily memorable labels for OBD-II communications tokens.

```
#define NUL     '\0'
#define CR      '\r'  // carriage return = 0x0d = 13
#define PROMPT  '>'
... etc
```

The Vehicle Telemetry Platform connects to the VDIP1 module using a serial connection, but also uses a number of digital pins for control and status display. The VDIP1 hardware reset line can be asserted using the pin defined as VDIP_RESET; the status of the module is displayed using LEDs connected to pins defined by VDIP_STATUS_LED, VDIP_WRITE_LED, and LOG_LED; serial flow control is managed using the pin connected to VDIP_RTS_PIN; and a button connected to LOG_BUTTON activates and deactivates logging.

```
#ifdef ENABLE_VDIP
// Vinculum setup
#define VDIP_RESET      12
#define VDIP_STATUS_LED 11
#define VDIP_WRITE_LED  10
#define VDIP_RTS_PIN     9
#define LOG_LED 4
#define LOG_BUTTON 3
#define LOG_BUTTON_INT 1
```

The PID values written to the logfile on the memory stick are determined by the logPid byte array immediately after the GPS data. The number of elements in the array is also determined and stored in logPidCount.

```
byte logPid[] = {
  LOAD_VALUE,
  COOLANT_TEMP,
  ENGINE_RPM,
  VEHICLE_SPEED,
  TIMING_ADV,
  INT_AIR_TEMP,
  MAF_AIR_FLOW,
  THROTTLE_POS,
  FUEL_RAIL_P,
  FUEL_LEVEL,
  BARO_PRESSURE,
```

```
    AMBIENT_TEMP,
    FUEL_CONS,
    BATT_VOLTAGE
    };
byte logPidCount = sizeof(logPid) / sizeof(logPid[0]);
```

In the current version of the sketch, this list is hard-coded and can't be overridden by the configuration menu, and because the logfile doesn't contain any headers it's necessary to know specifically what each column represents.

Most of the setup() function is pretty straightforward, just lots of boring calls out to initialization routines where the real work is done setting up the various subsystems.

Where it does get interesting, though, is setting up the port-level interrupt for the menu buttons.

As discussed previously, the three menu buttons are connected to a port (the second analog port in the case of a Mega build, otherwise the first analog port) that sets an interrupt if any of the pins in that port change state. There's no particular reason that an analog-capable port was used for this purpose other than the physical location of the pins, and this technique could have been done with other ports too.

First, the three relevant pins are set up as inputs, then their internal pull-up resistors are activated by writing a HIGH state to them while they are in input mode.

```
  pinMode(lbuttonPin, INPUT);
  pinMode(mbuttonPin, INPUT);
  pinMode(rbuttonPin, INPUT);
  digitalWrite(lbuttonPin, HIGH);
  digitalWrite(mbuttonPin, HIGH);
  digitalWrite(rbuttonPin, HIGH);
```

An #ifdef check then determines which port to use based on whether this build is for a Mega, and port-level interrupts are also enabled for the appropriate pins. This is a handy technique that could be useful in your own projects.

Each port has a "pin change mask," or PCMSK, numbered according to the port. For a regular Arduino based on an ATMega328P, the assignments are shown in the Table 15-7.

Table 15-7. *Pin-change interrupts for Arduino Duemilanove*

Pins	Port	PC Interrupt No.	PC Interrupt Enable	PC Mask
D0-D7	PD	PCINT 16-23	PCIE2	PCMSK2
D8-D13	PB	PCINT 0-5	PCIE0	PCMSK0
A0-A5	PC	PCINT 8-13	PCIE1	PCMSK1

The Arduino Mega obviously has far more I/O pins but it still only has three ports that can be used with pin change interrupts, and because there's a more complicated mapping of Arduino pins to ATMega ports, the assignments are also a little more complex. These are shown in Table 15-8.

Table 15-8. Pin-change interrupts for Arduino Mega

Pins	Port	PC Interrupt No.	PC Interrupt Enable	PC Mask
A8-A15	PK	PCINT 16-23	PCIE2	PCMSK2
D0-D3,D5	PE	PCINT 8	PCIE1	PCMSK1
D10-D13,D50-D53	PB	PCINT 4-7, 3-0	PCIE0	PCMSK0
D14,D15	PJ	PCINT 10,9	PCIE1	PCMSK1

To make use of port-level interrupts, use the following steps:

1. Select the pin that you want to watch.
2. Find which Pin Change Interrupt number (PCINT) is associated with it.
3. Find which Pin Change Mask (PCMSK) is associated with it.
4. Logically OR the Pin Change Mask with the Pin Change Interrupt.
5. Logically OR the Pin Change Interrupt Control Register (PCICR) with the Pin Change Interrupt Enable for that port.

This sounds like quite a convoluted process, but when you see a specific example you'll realize it's not too complicated.

For the Mega version, we have the menu buttons connected to analog pins A8, A9, and A10. Looking at Table 15-8, you can see these correspond to PCINT16, PCINT17, and PCINT18. You can also see that they all correspond to interrupt enable PCIE2, and to port change mask PCMSK2. That's all the information we need to set up the interrupt.

First, the PCMSK2 is set to a logical OR with PCINT16, 17, and 18.

```
#ifdef MEGA
PCMSK2 |= (1 << PCINT16) | (1 << PCINT17) | (1 << PCINT18);
```

Then the Pin Change Interrupt Register is set to a logical OR with Port Change Interrupt Enable 2.

```
PCICR  |= (1 << PCIE2);
```

And that's it! All done in just two lines. The alternative version for non-Mega builds does the same thing but with different port change interrupt numbers, mask, and enable register to suit analog pins A3, A4, and A5 on a regular Arduino, such as a Duemilanove.

```
#else
PCMSK1 |= (1 << PCINT11) | (1 << PCINT12) | (1 << PCINT13);
PCICR  |= (1 << PCIE1);
#endif
```

Something to remember, though, is that pin change interrupts aren't quite the same as a regular interrupt. For one thing, they're called "change" interrupts for a reason: they trigger on both rising and falling edges, so you have to figure out which change happened inside your ISR. They also call the same ISR for all pins associated with a port, so your ISR has to do some work to figure out which pin caused it to be invoked.

You'll see more detail about this in a moment when we look at the ISR.

The parameters are then loaded from EEPROM (using default values if necessary) and LCD pins are then set up. The startup message is displayed and the engine-management system is checked to see which PIDs it supports using the check_supported_pids() function that we'll see a bit later.

Two regular hardware interrupts are then set up. The first is attached to the log on/off button so that it will be handled as soon as it's pressed. The input is biased high but pulled low by the button, so the interrupt is attached to a falling edge. The powerfail detection interrupt is then attached in the same way.

```
attachInterrupt(1, modeButton, FALLING);
attachInterrupt(0, powerFail, FALLING);
```

The main loop manages to farm off most functionality to separate functions, so it doesn't contain too much logic itself. Even so, it's quite long simply because there's so much to do on each pass through.

It starts by calling out to functions to process the serial buffers for connections to the host and the VDIP module.

```
processHostCommands();
processVdipBuffer();
```

Writing to the CSV file on the memory stick requires a sequence of bytes of a known length, as we'll see a little later in the sketch. Because the log entry to be written needs to accumulate values from various parts of the program, we need some kind of buffer that we can build up progressively.

OBDuinoMega uses the PString library to manage the buffer because it has some cool convenience functions that make buffer manipulation trivially easy.

Creating a buffer with PString requires us to define a char array to be used as the raw buffer, and then create a new PString object with the array and its length passed in as arguments. The buffer is currently set to 160 characters, which is plenty for the values being logged, but you might need to adjust the length if you make changes to the selected values.

```
char vdipBuffer[160];
```

A new PString object called logEntry is then created.

```
PString logEntry( vdipBuffer, sizeof( vdipBuffer ) );
```

The interesting thing about PString is that we can now access the original array directly, but we also gain a whole lot of new functions by accessing it through the logEntry object. PString is derived from Print, so it uses much of the same familiar syntax as Serial and LiquidCrystal, allowing you to do things such as

```
logEntry.print("Add this to the buffer");
```

to append text to the existing buffer. You can also do simple appends using a "+=" syntax, and get the number of characters currently in the buffer and the length of the buffer using simple methods.

```
int length = logEntry.length();
int capacity = logEntry.capacity();
```

It's also safer to append entries this way rather than using your own loop writing directly into an array because PString won't let you accidentally overfill the allocated buffer size and write into unprotected memory. The worst that can happen is that your buffer will be truncated. An operation such as the following might look dangerous, but in fact it will give a harmless result.

```
char buf[10];
PString str(buf, 10, "Hello, ");
str += "world";
```

At the end of this example, the buffer str will simply contain "Hello, wo" with a terminating null character to make up the buffer capacity of 10 characters. The extra characters will simply be dropped rather than causing a dangerous overflow into unallocated memory.

Before moving on, the main loop then makes a call to processGpsBuffer(), a function that pulls any pending data out of the serial buffer for the GPS connection and passes it to the global GPS object. This function can safely be called at any time and needs to be executed regularly to prevent the GPS serial buffer from being filled and characters dropped.

```
  processGpsBuffer();
```

In the current version of the sketch, GPS data is only processed if the Vehicle Telemetry Platform is actively logging, but in the future this could change. In a future version, the GPS data will probably be mapped to fake PIDs so that it will be possible to display Lat and Lon values on the LCD.

The GPS object created using the TinyGPS library has methods to retrieve specific values from the NMEA fields. Accessing them is a simple matter of referencing variables for the object to update. Fetching the current latitude and longitude as floating-point values and the age of the fix in milliseconds as an int is very easy.

```
    gps.f_get_position( &gpsFLat, &gpsFLon, &gpsAge );
```

Likewise, the sketch makes calls to other methods to retrieve values and convert them to strings, then appends them to the log buffer.

```
    floatToString(valBuffer, gps.f_altitude(), 0);
...
    floatToString(valBuffer, gps.f_speed_kmph(), 0);
```

The main loop then performs a series of checks, such as whether the engine-management system thinks the car is running, and displays values and updates the timestamp.

Next it checks whether the engine has just been turned off, in which case the values from this trip need to be saved to EEPROM for future reference.

```
  if(has_rpm==0 && param_saved==0 && engine_started!=0)
```

It then makes a call to params_save(), sets the param_saved value to 1 so this can only happen once each time the engine stops, displays a message on the LCD to say the trips have been saved, waits two seconds to give enough time for the message to be read, turns off the LCD backlight to save power, and (if configured) activates the car alarm screen.

Once each time through the loop, the OBDuinoMega sketch calls out to the test_buttons() function to check whether the user has pressed any of the three menu buttons and then take appropriate action. The details of this function will be shown in just a moment.

```
test_buttons();
```

By this point, the main loop has just about finished everything it needs to do including displaying current values for the PIDs configured for the display. The last thing to do is fetch the PIDs that we want to store on the memory stick and append them to the log buffer and then write the buffer to disk.

The sketch only needs to do this if logging is currently active, though, so it checks the logActive flag, then loops over the logPid array that contains the list of PIDs to store. For each one, it makes a call to getPid() to fetch the value, then appends it to the buffer after inserting a comma separator. The comma is always added even if the PID fails to be retrieved so that each subsequent parameter still ends up in the correct column.

```
if( logActive == 1 )
{
  for(byte i=0; i < logPidCount; i++) {
    logEntry += ",";
    if (get pid( logPid[i], str, &tempLong))
      logEntry += tempLong;
  }
}
```

The routine to write the buffer to disk is worth a close look. Even though it's quite simple, you might find it handy to use something similar in other projects, and it's a good illustration of how easy it is to work with the Vinculum chip.

Logging is only performed if the logActive flag is set and it's been more than LOG_INTERVAL milliseconds since the log was last written.

```
if( logActive == 1 )
{
  if(millis() - lastLogWrite > LOG_INTERVAL)
  {
```

The blue LED indicating that a sample is being written is illuminated, and the position counter for the log buffer is reset.

```
    digitalWrite(VDIP WRITE_LED, HIGH);
    byte position = 0;
```

The log entry length and the entry itself are sent to the host for debugging purposes.

```
    HOST.print(logEntry.length());
    HOST.print(": ");
    HOST.println(logEntry);
```

Now for the interesting bit. A WRF (WRite File) command is sent to the VDIP1 with a single argument that tells it the number of bytes of data to follow in the actual message. Because each log entry will have a newline character appended, we have to take the current logEntry length and add 1 to it to get the actual message length.

Note that before doing this, the VDIP1 needs to be initialized, and that process is taken care of by a function that we'll see in just a moment.

```
VDIP.print("WRF ");
VDIP.print(logEntry.length() + 1);
VDIP.print(13, BYTE);
```

The position counter is used to walk through the log buffer array one character at a time to send it to the VDIP1. However, the RTS (ready to send) pin on the VDIP1 is checked prior to transmission of each character to make sure the VDIP1 input buffer still has free space. If RTS is low (inactive) it's clear to send the character and increment the position counter. Otherwise it shouts loudly to the host to notify you that the VDIP1 buffer was full. In production, you probably wouldn't want the error message being sent to the host, but it can be handy when doing development.

```
while(position < logEntry.length())
{
  if(digitalRead(VDIP_RTS_PIN) == LOW)
  {
    VDIP.print(vdipBuffer[position]);
    position++;
  } else {
    HOST.println("BUFFER FULL");
  }
}
```

After sending a WRF command to the VDIP1, it will keep accepting data until it has received exactly the number of bytes specified in the WRF argument. The number passed in was one greater than the number of bytes in the buffer, so if nothing else was sent, the Vinculum chip on the VDIP1 would sit patiently waiting for the next character. If a mistake is made calculating the number of bytes to be sent, it's easy to end up in a situation where you send one byte too few and the Vinculum doesn't finish reading. Then, your program continues on around the loop and comes back to send more data to the VDIP1 on the next pass through. It then starts sending the WRF command, but because the Vinculum never exited write mode last time around, it sees the "W" character as the final character of the last write, then interprets "RF" is the start of another command. RF is meaningless to it so it will then output an error and you'll end up with the original entry written to the file with a trailing W and nothing written for the second pass at all.

So the moral of the story is to always, always, always check your message length very carefully when preparing data to send to the Vinculum chip. If you send fewer characters than it is expecting, it will remain in write mode waiting for more data; if you send too many characters, it will treat the excess as separate commands. If you're really unlucky, those excess characters could constitute a command to perform a dangerous action such as deleting a file!

Something that could be done to minimize the risk is to send the characters one at a time and implement a check to look for the prompt response that the Vinculum will send when it finishes writing to the file. If the prompt comes back unexpectedly, it's better to skip sending the rest of the buffer rather than to keep sending data. If the prompt doesn't come back after all the characters have been sent, the message could be padded by sending spaces until the prompt returns.

In this case, though, we're just carefully counting characters including the trailing newline, so the program then sends the newline character and turns off the LED that indicates a write is in progress. It then sets the lastLogWrite variable to the number of milliseconds since startup so next time through the loop it can check whether it's due to record another log entry.

```
      VDIP.print(13, BYTE);
      digitalWrite(VDIP_WRITE_LED, LOW);
      lastLogWrite = millis();
    }
  }
```

Way back in setup(), we looked at pin change interrupts and the way changes to the menu button states cause an ISR to be invoked. This is the definition of that ISR, and you can see that it uses an #ifdef check to substitute a different version of the function, depending on whether this is a Mega or non-Mega build.

The Mega version is attached to PCINT2, and the first thing it does is check whether it has been more than 20 milliseconds since it was last invoked. If not, it's probably a problem with the physical switch bouncing open and closed rapidly as it settles, so it's ignored. If it is greater than 20 milliseconds, the buttonState global variable is updated with the value of the PINK register, which reads the value of all the pins in port K. Analog inputs 7 through 13 on a Mega are all part of port K.

```
#ifdef MEGA
ISR(PCINT2_vect)
{
  static unsigned long last_millis = 0;
  unsigned long m = millis();

  if (m - last_millis > 20)
  {
    buttonState |= ~PINK;
  }

  last_millis = m;
}
```

The non-Mega version does the same thing but with PCINT1, and reads from the port C register using PINC.

```
#else
ISR(PCINT1_vect)
{
  static unsigned long last_millis = 0;
  unsigned long m = millis();

  if (m - last_millis > 20)
  {
    buttonState |= ~PINC;
  }

  last_millis = m;
}
#endif
```

Reading from the ELM327 is pretty much the core function of the OBDuinoMega sketch. Everything else in the sketch is really just life support for a dozen or so lines of code in a function called elm_read()

that simply listens to the serial connection until it sees an "\r" character followed by a prompt, indicating that the ELM327 has finished sending its message.

The function requires two arguments: a pointer to a character array for the response to be stored in, and a byte indicating how many elements it's allowed to put in that array.

It then defines variables to hold response values and the number of characters read so far.

```
byte elm_read(char *str, byte size)
{
  int b;
  byte i=0;
```

It loops reading from the serial port until it either sees a prompt character (in which case it knows it got a complete response) or runs out of space in the array. It inserts each character into the array and increments the position counter only if the character is a space character or greater, which is hex value 0x20 in the ASCII table. This excludes any control characters that could be sent through.

```
  while((b=OBD2.read())!=PROMPT && i<size)
  {
    if(b>=' ')
      str[i++]=b;
  }
```

The two possible outcomes at this point are that the number of characters received is less than the array length and therefore the program got a prompt, or that the number of characters reached the array length and therefore the response was probably meaningless.

If the counter "i" is not equal to the array size, everything is probably okay, so the last character entered into the array pointer (most likely a carriage return) needs to be replaced with a null character to indicate the end of the string. The function then returns the prompt character to indicate success.

Otherwise, the program assumes the response was meaningless and returns the value 1, signified by the DATA placeholder defined at the start of the sketch, to indicate that there is raw data in the buffer.

```
  if(i!=size)
  {
    str[i]=NUL;
    return PROMPT;
  }
  else
    return DATA;
}
```

The response that comes back from the ELM327 is an ASCII string that represents a hexadecimal number. It may look like hex but don't be deceived—it's not!

For example, if the ELM327 sends a response of 1AF8 to mean a decimal value of 6904, what we actually receive from the serial port is the ASCII values that represent those individual characters: 0x31 to represent 1, 0x41 to represent A, 0x46 to represent F, and 0x38 to represent 8. This is not at all what we wanted, and if you process the bytes literally, you'll get an incorrect answer.

To make sense of the response value, the sketch really needs it as an actual numeric type rather than a string, so the elm_compact_response() function accepts a raw ELM327 response and turns it into a real hex value stored in a byte array.

Because the response from the ELM327 starts with an echo of the mode plus 0x40 and then the PID, the sketch has to skip the first few bytes. For example, if the request 010C was sent, the response would be something like "41 0C 1A F8," so the first byte we would actually care about would be the seventh character. The end result that we want is the numeric value 0x1AF8 ready to send back to the calling function.

Note that the call to strtoul (string to unsigned long) passes in a third argument of 16, the base required for the response. Base 16 is hexadecimal.

The return value from the function is simply the number of bytes in the converted value.

```
byte elm_compact_response(byte *buf, char *str)
{
  byte i=0;
  str+=6;
  while(*str!=NUL)
    buf[i++]=strtoul(str, &str, 16);

  return i;
}
```

Initializing the serial connection to the ELM327 is quite straightforward. First, the serial port itself is opened at the rate configured at the start of the sketch, then the serial buffer is flushed to ensure there's no stray data sitting in it.

```
void elm_init()
{
  char str[STRLEN];
  OBD2.begin(OBD2_BAUD_RATE);
  OBD2.flush();
```

Just in case the ELM327 had already been powered up and had settings changed, it's then sent a soft-reset command.

```
  elm_command(str, PSTR("ATWS\r"));
```

A message is then displayed on the LCD to show progress. If the first character back is an "A," the program assumes that it's echoing the command and skips ahead to read the response from the fifth character (position 4) onward. Otherwise, it simply displays the message as is.

```
  lcd_gotoXY(0,1);
  if(str[0]=='A')
    lcd_print(str+4);
  else
    lcd_print(str);
  lcd_print_P(PSTR(" Init"));
```

To get responses back from the ELM327 a little faster it's a good idea to turn off command echo, otherwise every response will be bloated with several bytes taken up just repeating the command we sent to it. The ATE0 command suppresses command echo.

```
  elm_command(str, PSTR("ATE0\r"));
```

The sketch then goes into a do-while loop trying to verify that the ELM327 is alive and communicating by sending a request for PID 0X0100 (PIDs supported) repeatedly until it gets a response. If you start up the system without putting it into debug mode or connecting it to an ELM327, and it ends up sitting on a screen that reads "Init" forever; this is the loop it's trapped in.

```
do
{
  elm_command(str, PSTR("0100\r"));
  delay(1000);
}
while(elm_check_response("0100", str)!=0);
```

When using the OBD-II interface to communicate with a vehicle's internal communications bus, there are typically multiple ECUs (electronic control units) sharing that bus. The primary ECU that responds with OBD-II values is identified as ECU #1, and the ELM327 can either direct its requests generally to all devices on the bus or it can direct them to a specific ECU.

By default, the ELM327 shouts its requests to the world, but by modifying the communications header that it sends to the car, it's possible to make it specifically ask for the primary ECU.

This is done by setting a custom header that the ELM327 uses for messages sent to the car, but the format of the header depends on what communications protocol it's using. Because the ELM327 takes care of all the protocol conversion behind the scenes, the sketch doesn't generally need to know the details of what's going on, but to determine the car's protocol it can send an ATDPN (ATtention: Describe Protocol by Number) command to have the ELM327 report which protocol it has autonegotiated with the car.

```
elm_command(str, PSTR("ATDPN\r"));
```

The OBDuinoMega sketch can then set a custom header specifying that all requests should go to ECU #1 using the appropriate format for that particular protocol.

```
  if(str[1]=='1')  // PWM
    elm_command(str, PSTR("ATSHE410F1\r"));
  else if(str[1]=='2')  // VPW
    elm_command(str, PSTR("ATSHA810F1\r"));
  else if(str[1]=='3')  // ISO 9141
    elm_command(str, PSTR("ATSH6810F1\r"));
  else if(str[1]=='6')  // CAN 11 bits
    elm_command(str, PSTR("ATSH7E0\r"));
  else if(str[1]=='7')  // CAN 29 bits
    elm_command(str, PSTR("ATSHDA10F1\r"));
}
```

All done. The ELM327 should now be running in a reasonably well optimized state, with no command echo and all requests specifically directed to ECU #1.

The get_pid() function is called by the display() function to fetch values to display on the LCD, and also in the main loop by the logging code to fetch values to write to the CSV file on the memory stick. The majority of the code in this very long function is a massive switch statement that checks which PID is being requested and then sources the result and processes it appropriately, putting the numeric value in a long pointer and a version formatted for string output into a buffer. The return value of the function indicates whether retrieval of the PID was successful or not, so a simple call to this function and then a check of the response will give access to just about any information accessible by the Vehicle Telemetry Platform.

The start of the function takes the requested PID and sets up some variables.

```
boolean get_pid(byte pid, char *retbuf, long *ret)
{
#ifdef ELM
  char cmd_str[6];   // to send to ELM
  char str[STRLEN];   // to receive from ELM
#else
  byte cmd[2];    // to send the command
#endif
  byte i;
  byte buf[10];   // to receive the result
  byte reslen;
  char decs[16];
  unsigned long time_now, delta_time;
  static byte nbpid=0;
```

It then checks if the PID is supported by calling out to another function. If it is not supported, it puts an error message in the return buffer and returns a FALSE value.

```
  if(!is_pid_supported(pid, 0))
  {
    sprintf_P(retbuf, PSTR("%02X N/A"), pid);
    return false;
  }
```

Way back at the start of the sketch, each PID was defined along with the number of bytes to expect in response to each one. The sketch then reads the receive length value out of EEPROM by referencing the memory position for that PID.

```
  reslen=pgm_read_byte_near(pid_reslen+pid);
```

The request is then sent to the vehicle using one of two methods, depending on whether the system was built using an ELM327 as in our prototype, or uses interface hardware specific to the particular car.

The ELM version formats the request by appending the PID to the mode then adding a carriage return at the end, then sends it to the ELM327, and then waits for the response. The response value is checked to make sure there's no error value. If there is, "ERROR" is put in the return buffer and the function bails out with a FALSE return value.

Assuming the response was good and the function didn't bail out, it then proceeds by sending the value off to be converted from an ASCII string to an actual numeric value using the elm_compact_response() function previously defined.

```
#ifdef ELM
  sprintf_P(cmd_str, PSTR("01%02X\r"), pid);
  elm_write(cmd_str);
  elm_read(str, STRLEN);
  if(elm_check_response(cmd_str, str)!=0)
  {
    sprintf_P(retbuf, PSTR("ERROR"));
    return false;
  }
  elm_compact_response(buf, str);
```

The non-ELM version follows almost exactly the same process, but rather than use calls to ELM functions, it uses equivalent ISO functions.

```
#else
  cmd[0]=0x01;    // ISO cmd 1, get PID
  cmd[1]=pid;
  iso_write_data(cmd, 2);
  if (!iso_read_data(buf, reslen))
  {
      sprintf_P(retbuf, PSTR("ERROR"));
      return false;
  }
#endif
```

By this point, the sketch has the raw result as a numeric value, but as explained previously most PIDs require a formula to be applied to convert the raw bytes into meaningful values.

Because many PIDs use the formula (A * 256) + B, the sketch then calculates the result of that formula no matter what the PID is. The result may be overwritten later if this particular PID is an exception, but determining a default value first, even if it's thrown away later, saves 40 bytes over conditionally calculating it based on the PID. With the original MPGuino/OBDuino codebases designed to squeeze into smaller ATMega CPUs, every byte counts.

```
  *ret=buf[0]*256U+buf[1];
```

The rest of the function is a huge switch statement that applies the correct formula for the particular PID being requested. We won't show the whole statement here, but you'll get the idea by looking at a few examples.

The first check is whether the requested PID was the engine RPM. In debug mode it returns a hard-coded value of 1726RPM, and otherwise it takes the return value and divides it by 4. The full formula for the engine RPM is ((A * 256) + B) / 4, but because the return value was already calculated, the first part of the formula has already been applied and it just needs the division portion.

```
  switch(pid)
  {
  case ENGINE_RPM:
#ifdef DEBUG
    *ret=1726;
#else
    *ret=*ret/4U;
#endif
    sprintf_P(retbuf, PSTR("%ld RPM"), *ret);
    break;
```

The Mass Air Flow parameter is similar: return a hard-coded value in debug mode, or take the precalculated value and divide it by 100 as per the required formula.

```
  case MAF_AIR_FLOW:
#ifdef DEBUG
    *ret=2048;
#endif
    long_to_dec_str(*ret, decs, 2);
```

```
    sprintf_P(retbuf, PSTR("%s g/s"), decs);
    break;
```

Vehicle speed is a trivial parameter, and then it gets to the fuel status parameter. Fuel status is a bitmap value, so each bit in the response value is checked in turn by comparing it to a simple binary progression (compared in the code using the hex equivalent value) and the matching label is then returned. In the case of this particular parameter, it's not really the numeric value that is useful, but the label associated with it.

```
  case FUEL_STATUS:
#ifdef DEBUG
    *ret=0x0200;
#endif
    if(buf[0]==0x01)
      sprintf_P(retbuf, PSTR("OPENLOWT"));  // Open due to insufficient engine temperature
    else if(buf[0]==0x02)
      sprintf_P(retbuf, PSTR("CLSEOXYS"));  // Closed loop, using oxygen sensor feedback to
determine fuel mix. Should be almost always this
    else if(buf[0]==0x04)
      sprintf_P(retbuf, PSTR("OPENLOAD"));  // Open loop due to engine load, can trigger DFCO
    else if(buf[0]==0x08)
      sprintf_P(retbuf, PSTR("OPENFAIL"));  // Open loop due to system failure
    else if(buf[0]==0x10)
      sprintf_P(retbuf, PSTR("CLSEBADF"));  // Closed loop, using at least one oxygen sensor
but there is a fault in the feedback system
    else
      sprintf_P(retbuf, PSTR("%04lX"), *ret);
    break;
```

A number of parameters require an identical formula of (A * 100) / 255, so they're all applied in a group.

```
  case LOAD_VALUE:
  case THROTTLE_POS:
  case REL_THR_POS:
  case EGR:
  case EGR_ERROR:
  case FUEL_LEVEL:
  case ABS_THR_POS_B:
  case CMD_THR_ACTU:
#ifdef DEBUG
    *ret=17;
#else
    *ret=(buf[0]*100U)/255U;
#endif
    sprintf_P(retbuf, PSTR("%ld %%"), *ret);
    break;
```

The function continues in a similar way for the rest of the PIDs. If you want to see the details of how a particular PID is processed, it's best to look in the OBDuinoMega source code.

Other functions in the main file then provide features such as calculation of current (instant) fuel consumption and the distance that could be traveled, using the fuel remaining in the tank.

Once on every pass through the main loop, a call is placed to the accu_trip() function to accumulate data for the current trip by adding current values to trip values. Among other things, it increments the duration of the trip in milliseconds; the distance traveled in centimeters (allowing a trip of up to 42,949km or 26,671mi because the distance is stored in an unsigned long); fuel consumed; and mass air flow.

One particularly interesting value it accumulates is "fuel wasted," which is the amount of fuel that has been consumed while the engine was idling.

The display() function takes care of fetching the value associated with a specific PID and displaying it at a nominated location on the LCD. Because the PIDs defined at the start of the sketch can be either real (provided by the engine-management system) or fake (generated by the sketch internally or from some other data source), this function explicitly checks for a number of PIDs that require data to be returned by a specific function.

```
void display(byte location, byte pid)
  char str[STRLEN];
  if(pid==NO_DISPLAY)
    return;
  else if(pid==OUTING_COST)
    get_cost(str, OUTING);
  else if(pid==TRIP_COST)
    get_cost(str, TRIP);
  else if(pid==TANK_COST)
    get_cost(str, TANK);
```

It goes on in a similar way for dozens of PIDs that it knows about specifically until it falls through to the default behavior, which is to pass the request on to the get_pid() function we just saw.

```
  else
    get_pid(pid, str, &tempLong);
```

The function then sets a null string terminator into the result string at the LCD_split position, which was calculated back at the start of the sketch as half the width of the LCD. This effectively truncates the result at half the display width so that it can't overwrite an adjacent value.

```
  str[LCD_split] = '\0';
```

It then does some manipulation of the "location" argument that was passed in to determine which row it goes on given that there are two locations per line, then checks if it's an even number and should therefore go on the left, and finally calculates the start and end character positions for that location.

```
  byte row = location / 2;  // Two PIDs per line
  boolean isLeft = location % 2 == 0; // First PID per line is always left
  byte textPos    = isLeft ? 0 : LCD_width - strlen(str);
  byte clearStart = isLeft ? strlen(str) : LCD_split;
  byte clearEnd   = isLeft ? LCD_split : textPos;
```

It's then just a matter of going to that location and printing the string to the LCD.

```
  lcd_gotoXY(textPos,row);
  lcd_print(str);
```

The last thing the function needs to do is get rid of any leading or trailing characters that might still be visible on the LCD after the value was written. This can happen if the previously displayed value used more characters than the current value, and because characters are only replaced if they are explicitly written to, it's necessary to write spaces into characters we don't care about.

```
  lcd_gotoXY(clearStart,row);
  for (byte cleanup = clearStart; cleanup < clearEnd; cleanup++)
  {
    lcd_dataWrite(' ');
  }
}
```

For maintenance purposes, one of the most important pieces of information available via OBD-II is the response to mode 0x03, "Show diagnostic trouble codes." It's also one of the most complex because of the variations in the type of data that it needs to return.

Mode 0x03 doesn't contain any PIDs, so there's no need to request anything but the mode itself, and it always returns four bytes of data. A typical response could be as follows:

```
43 17 71 00 00 00 00
```

The "43" header is because it's a response to a mode 0x03 request, and response headers always start with the mode plus 0x40.

The rest of the message is three pairs of bytes, so this example would be read as 1771, 0000, and 0000. The zero value pairs are empty but are always returned anyway so that the response length is consistent.

In this example, the only stored trouble code is 0x1771, so let's look at how to convert it into something meaningful and figure out what might have gone wrong with the car.

The first byte is 0x17 (or binary 00010111), which consists of two digits, 1 and 7. If we split that binary value into two halves (nibbles) we end up with 0001 representing the first digit, 1, and 0111 representing the second digit, 7.

The first digit represents the DTC prefix that tells us what type of trouble code it is and whether its meaning is standards-defined or manufacturer-defined. To complicate things a little more, the first digit is in turn divided into two sets of bits, so we can't just take it at face value.

In our example, the first digit is 1, or binary 0001. That needs to be split into a pair of two-bit numbers, so in our case it will be 00 and 01. Each pair can have four possible values, with the first pair representing the section of the car in which the problem occurred, and the second pair specifying whether that DTC is defined by the SAE standards body or the manufacturer.

The four possible values for the first pair of bits are shown in Table 15-9.

***Table 15-9.** DTC location codes*

Binary	Hex	Code	Meaning
00	0	P	Powertrain code
01	1	C	Chassis code

10	2	B	Body code
11	3	U	Network code

There are also four possible values for the second pair of bits, but unfortunately their meaning can vary depending on the value of the first pair. These are given in Table 15-10.

***Table 15-10.** DTC definition source*

Binary	Hex	Defined By
00	0	SAE
01	1	Manufacturer
10	2	SAE in P, manufacturer in C, B, and U
11	3	Jointly defined in P, reserved in C, B, and U

Because the meaning of the second value can vary based on the first value, the easiest way to approach it is so create a big look-up table that maps all 16 possible values of the first four bits (the first character in the response) to its specific meaning. These are given in Table 15-11.

***Table 15-11.** DTC location and definitions combined*

Binary	Hex	Prefix	Meaning
0000	0	P0	Powertrain, SAE-defined
0001	1	P1	Powertrain, manufacturer-defined
0010	2	P2	Powertrain, SAE-defined
0011	3	P3	Powertrain, jointly defined
0100	4	C0	Chassis, SAE-defined
0101	5	C1	Chassis, manufacturer-defined

0110	6	C2	Chassis, manufacturer-defined
0111	7	C3	Chassis, reserved for future use
1000	8	B0	Body, SAE-defined
1001	9	B1	Body, manufacturer-defined
1010	A	B2	Body, manufacturer-defined
1011	B	B3	Body, reserved for future use
1100	C	U0	Network, SAE-defined
1101	D	U1	Network, manufacturer-defined
1110	E	U2	Network, manufacturer-defined
1111	F	U3	Network, reserved for future use

Going right back to the start of this example, our DTC value was 0x1771. If we now take the first digit of that code, look it up in the Hex column of Table 15-11, and replace it with the matching value in the Prefix column, you end up with the final trouble code string P1771.

So now we know what the trouble code is—a powertrain problem—and that this particular code is manufacturer-defined rather than part of the standard.

The code alone doesn't really help, though, so next you need to look it up and find out what problem 771 in a powertrain is, keeping in mind that because it's manufacturer-defined the exact same code could mean totally different things depending on what make and model of car you have. Because many manufacturers can be secretive about their trouble codes, this can be quite tricky to determine.

There are a number of really handy online resources for decoding DTCs, including a web site called OBD-Codes at www.obd-codes.com. The OBD-Codes site includes references for different DTCs and forums where people can discuss what different codes mean and what could be causing them. Another handy site is Engine Light Help at www.engine-light-help.com, which has DTCs and their meanings listed by manufacturer.

Assuming our hypothetical car was a Mazda, these sites tell us that DTC P1771 indicates "TPS circuit open to transmission control module." This could be extremely helpful if you know what a TPS is (a Throttle Position Sensor, in case you were wondering) and why it might be open-circuit, or it could be no help at all if you've never heard of a TPS. At this point, the car has told you as much as it can and it's up to you to know what to do with the information!

The process of retrieving DTCs is handled by a function in the OBDuinoMega sketch called check_mil_code(), so named because "Diagnostic Trouble Codes" are sometimes also referred to as "Malfunction Indicator Lamp codes." The first thing check_mil_code() does is submit a request for PID 0x0101, which returns a compound result consisting of (1) the current status of the "check engine" light

(CEL) in bit 7 of the first byte, (2) the number of trouble codes that have been logged in bits 0 through 6 of the first byte, and (3) whether certain on-board tests have been completed using bytes 2, 3, and 4 as bitmaps. The OBD-II standard specifies that up to six DTCs can be stored.

The call to get_pid() for the MIL_CODE value (0x0101) sets the value into str and tempLong and returns either true or false to show success or failure. If a false value is returned, the check_mil_code() bails immediately.

```
void check_mil_code(void)
{
  unsigned long n;
  char str[STRLEN];
  byte nb;
#ifndef ELM
  byte cmd[2];
  byte buf[6];
  byte i, j, k;
#endif

  if (!get_pid(MIL_CODE, str, &tempLong))
    return;
```

Bit 7 of the first byte is then checked using a bitwise operator to determine if the CEL is currently illuminated.

```
  n = (unsigned long) tempLong;
  if(1L<<31 & n)
  {
```

If it is, a notice is sent to the LCD showing how many DTCs have been stored after extracting the number from the first byte, excluding the bit used to indicate CEL status.

```
    nb=(n>>24) & 0x7F;
    lcd_cls_print_P(PSTR("CHECK ENGINE ON"));
    lcd_gotoXY(0,1);
    sprintf_P(str, PSTR("%d CODE(S) IN ECU"), nb);
    lcd_print(str);
    delay(2000);
    lcd_cls();
```

What happens next depends on whether the Vehicle Telemetry Platform is connected via an ELM327 or using a protocol-specific circuit.

The code for handling an ELM327 hasn't yet been fully developed, so at present it simply requests 0x03 and checks that the response header begins with "43." If not, it immediately returns. Eventually this section of the code will need to be expanded to support decoding of the response value and displaying meaningful messages on screen, but for now it just prints the raw result to the LCD and pauses for five seconds.

```
#ifdef ELM
    elm_command(str, PSTR("03\r"));
    if(str[0]!='4' && str[1]!='3')
      return;
```

```
    lcd_print(str+3);
    delay(5000);
```

The non-ELM327 version of the code is much more feature-complete, reading the stored DTCs and converting them from a raw value to include the P (powertrain), C (chassis), B (body), or U (network) header depending on the status of the first two bits in the first byte and displaying them on the LCD. Like the ELM327 version, it sends a 0x03 command to retrieve the codes.

```
#else
    cmd[0]=0x03;
    iso_write_data(cmd, 1);
```

Each received packet contains three codes.

```
    for(i=0;i<nb/3;i++)
    {
      iso_read_data(buf, 6);

      k=0;
      for(j=0;j<3;j++)
      {
        switch(buf[j*2] & 0xC0)
        {
        case 0x00:
          str[k]='P';
          break;
        case 0x40:
          str[k]='C';
          break;
        case 0x80:
          str[k]='B';
          break;
        case 0xC0:
          str[k]='U';
          break;
        }
        k++;
```

The first digit can only be between 0 and 3 because we need to ignore the pair of bits that specify the code type as well as the other half of the byte that represent the second digit, so it's masked with 0x30 and bit-shifted four spots to the right to get a valid result consisting of just the third and fourth bits moved into positions seven and eight. All other bits set to 0.

```
        str[k++]='0' + (buf[j*2] & 0x30)>>4;
```

The second digit simply needs to be masked with 0x0F to ignore the first byte.

```
        str[k++]='0' + (buf[j*2] & 0x0F);
```

The next byte is also processed twice, once for the first nibble with a mask and a shift, and then for the second nibble with just a mask.

```
        str[k++]='0' + (buf[j*2 +1] & 0xF0)>>4;
        str[k++]='0' + (buf[j*2 +1] & 0x0F);
      }
```

Finally, the string needs to be null-terminated so it can be sent to the LCD, then the LCD moves to the second line and the process is repeated for the second set of three DTCs.

```
      str[k]='\0';
      lcd_print(str);
      lcd_gotoXY(0, 1);
    }
#endif
  }
}
```

Each pass through the main loop makes a call to the test_buttons() function to check whether any of the buttons have been pressed and take appropriate action based not just on individual buttons but on combinations of buttons.

```
void test_buttons(void)
{
```

Pressing the middle and left buttons together triggers a tank reset.

```
  if(MIDDLE_BUTTON_PRESSED && LEFT_BUTTON_PRESSED)
  {
    needBacklight(true);
    trip_reset(TANK, true);
  }
```

Pressing the middle and right buttons together invokes the trip reset screen, and then also gives an option to reset the outing as well. The different trip types are used for tracking fuel consumption and economy for different durations.

```
  else if(MIDDLE_BUTTON_PRESSED && RIGHT_BUTTON_PRESSED)
  {
    needBacklight(true);
    trip_reset(TRIP, true);
    trip_reset(OUTING, true);
  }
```

Pressing the left and right buttons together causes the text labels for the currently displayed PIDs to be shown. There isn't enough room on the LCD to show PID names and values at the same time, and after a while you'll remember what each value represents anyway, but being able to press left and right together and have the names displayed momentarily can be very handy if you forget what they are.

```
  else if(LEFT_BUTTON_PRESSED && RIGHT_BUTTON_PRESSED)
  {
    display_PID_names();
  }
```

OBDuinoMega defines three "screens" of values, and pressing the left button alone cycles through them.

```
else if(LEFT_BUTTON_PRESSED)
{
  active_screen = (active_screen+1) % NBSCREEN;
  display_PID_names();
}
```

The right button, if pressed on its own, cycles through brightness settings for the LCD.

```
else if(RIGHT_BUTTON_PRESSED)
{
  char str[STRLEN] = {0};

  brightnessIdx = (brightnessIdx + 1) % brightnessLength;
  analogWrite(BrightnessPin, brightness[brightnessIdx]);

  lcd_cls_print_P(PSTR(" LCD backlight"));
  lcd_gotoXY(6,1);
  sprintf_P(str,PSTR("%d / %d"),brightnessIdx + 1,brightnessLength);
  lcd_print(str);
  delay(500);
}
```

The middle button is the menu button, and pressing it sends the sketch into the config_menu() function that we'll discuss in a moment.

```
else if(MIDDLE_BUTTON_PRESSED)
{
  needBacklight(true);
  config_menu();
}
```

After processing the state of the buttons, it needs to be reset so that it is ready to be updated again by the next button interrupt.

```
  if(buttonState!=buttonsUp)
  {
    delay_reset_button();
    needBacklight(false);
  }
}
```

The on-screen configuration menu invoked by the button handler is handled by the aptly named config_menu() function, and it's a monster: over 400 lines of nested "if" statements. There's nothing especially surprising in it from a coding point of view, and you can see the whole thing in the project source code, so we won't plod through it all here.

One thing worth noting, though, is that changes to configuration values using the on-screen menu cause a call to the params_save() function.

Rather than force people to reconfigure their system by changing values in the source and recompiling, the sketch uses the nonvolatile EEPROM inside the ATMega CPU to store config parameters. This means it's possible to reconfigure it using on-screen menus, pull out the power, plug it back in, and all your settings will still be in place.

Even the ATMega168 has 512 bytes of EEPROM, which is plenty for this project. The ATMega328P has 1KB and the ATMega1280 has 4KB, so they have more than enough.

Because the config parameters are kept in a global variable during operation, it's quite straightforward to copy them into EEPROM. The params_save() function doesn't even need any arguments passed to it.

The function declares a variable to hold the CRC (cyclic redundancy check) value that is used to verify that the data has not been corrupted, then calculates the CRC value by looping through the params variable and adding each byte.

It then calls eeprom_write_block() and passes it the parameters to be stored, telling it to start at address 0 (the start of the EEPROM) and giving it the number of bytes that need to be stored.

It then calls eeprom_write_word() and tells it to begin at the address after the end of the params block and write the CRC value.

```
void params_save(void)
{
  uint16_t crc;
  byte *p;

  crc=0;
  p=(byte*)&params;
  for(byte i=0; i<sizeof(params_t); i++)
    crc+=p[i];

  eeprom_write_block((const void*)&params, (void*)0, sizeof(params_t));
  eeprom_write_word((uint16_t*)sizeof(params_t), crc);
}
```

Pulling the config parameters out of EEPROM at startup is really just the same process run in reverse. The params_load() function defines some variables, then calls eeprom_read_block() starting at address 0 to fetch the params stored in EEPROM. It then reads the stored CRC value using eeprom_read_word(), and then, just as before, it walks through the params to calculate the actual CRC.

Finally, the stored CRC is compared to the calculated CRC, and if they are equal the program knows everything is good and overwrites the existing params global variable with the values loaded from EEPROM.

This version of the function doesn't handle a CRC mismatch and just fails silently in that situation, but it could be extended to return TRUE or FALSE depending on the result so that the calling function knows if it succeeded or not.

```
void params_load(void)
{
  hostPrint(" * Loading default parameters   ");
  params_t params_tmp;
  uint16_t crc, crc_calc;
  byte *p;

  eeprom_read_block((void*)&params_tmp, (void*)0, sizeof(params_t));
  crc=eeprom_read_word((const uint16_t*)sizeof(params_t));
```

```
  crc_calc=0;
  p=(byte*)&params_tmp;
  for(byte i=0; i<sizeof(params_t); i++)
    crc_calc+=p[i];

  if(crc==crc_calc)
    params=params_tmp;

  hostPrintLn("[OK]");
}
```

If you're used to working with larger systems with (relatively!) vast quantities of memory and a kernel that largely takes care of memory allocation for you, it can be easy to forget about the serious memory limitations in a microcontroller like the Arduino. The ATMega8 CPU has just 1KB of RAM available, the ATMega168 has 2KB, and the ATMega1280 has 8KB. This tiny amount of memory has to contain all the static variables defined in the program, the stack, and the heap (see Figure 15-33).

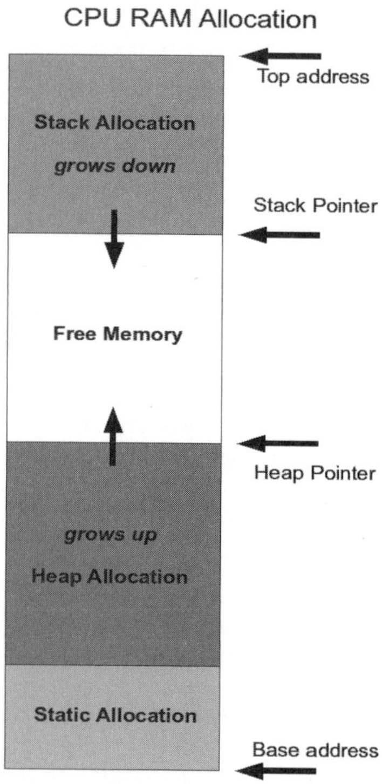

Figure 15-33. *CPU RAM allocation*

Static variables are placed into the bottom of the memory address space because their size is predictable at compile-time. The heap (used for dynamically allocated memory and things such as global variables and objects) starts just above the static region, and the position of the top of the heap is tracked using the "heap pointer." The stack (used for variables allocated within functions and arguments in function calls) grows down from the top of the available RAM, and the position of the bottom of the stack is tracked using the "stack pointer."

If the heap growing up and the stack growing down ever meet in the middle, it means your program has run out of memory. In an unprotected system such as a microcontroller, very bad things can happen, such as variables changing value for no apparent reason and functions failing to return. At the very least, the program will behave strangely and you can waste a lot of time trying to figure out where you made a mistake in your code, when technically the code itself is correct and the problem is just that it ran out of memory.

Every time one function calls another, the CPU has to push a number of items onto the stack so that it can reinstate the original calling function after the child exits. As functions return to their caller, the stack shrinks again.

When working on a complex sketch that has lots of functions calling each other, it can therefore be very handy to be able to keep track of how much space is left in free memory, so you know how close to danger you are.

The OBDuinoMega sketch includes a small function called memoryTest() that returns the number of bytes currently free in RAMI. If you work on large projects or are pushing the limits of the CPU by storing large amounts of data or making recursive function calls, it might be a good idea to use a similar function yourself.

The function looks quite simple, but is worth close inspection to understand how it works. Look through it carefully and then see the following explanation.

```
extern int  __bss_end;
extern int  *__brkval;
int memoryTest(void)
{
  int free_memory;
  if((int)__brkval == 0)
    free_memory = ((int)&free_memory) - ((int)&__bss_end);
  else
    free_memory = ((int)&free_memory) - ((int)__brkval);
  return free_memory;
}
```

The extern (external) variable declarations just before the function are explicit references to globals. Using the extern flag forces the compiler not to allocate local memory for them and shows unambiguously that they are not local scope.

The variable __bss_end is a pointer to the top of the statically allocated memory range, and the variable __brkval is the current address of the top of the heap. If there have been no calls to malloc (the dynamic memory allocator) since the program started, the bottom of free memory will be __bss_end, and __brkval will have a zero value. However, if malloc has started putting things in the heap, the bottom of free memory will be __brkval.

The free_memory variable is used in two different ways inside the function. Its obvious use is to store the result of the calculation of the size of free memory, but it's also used within the calculation itself. That's because it was just declared as a local variable a few lines before and will be the last thing that is pushed onto the stack. By using the address given by the pointer to that variable, we can tell the current value of the stack pointer! Very clever.

The difference between the stack pointer and either __bss_end or __brkval (as appropriate) will, therefore, tell us how much space is left in memory between the heap and the stack.

For more background information about this issue and a more fully featured memory-checking routine wrapped up as a simple library, have a look at the posts in the following interesting thread on the Arduino forums:

```
www.arduino.cc/cgi-bin/yabb2/YaBB.pl?num=1213583720/20
```

LCD.pde

The LiquidCrystal library is very handy for driving parallel LCD modules with minimal effort, and is used elsewhere in this book, such as the Water Flow Gauge project in Chapter 10. However, if you're really tight for memory space and only need a few of the functions of a library, it's sometimes worth implementing those functions yourself or copying just the parts of the library you need directly into your sketch. Sketch size isn't a problem for us compiling for an Arduino Mega, but the original MPGuino and OBDuino codebases were designed to squeeze into the more limited memory footprints of the ATMega168 and 328P CPUs found on a typical Arduino. Rather than suck in the entire LiquidCrystal library unnecessarily, the developers decided to write minimal functions to do just what they needed to do and no more.

For the OBDuinoMega sketch, we moved the LCD functions out of the main program file and into a separate supporting file called LCD.pde to keep everything neat and tidy, but the functions themselves are otherwise identical to those found in OBDuino.

Moving the cursor to a specific location prior to writing characters to the screen is a basic requirement taken care of by the lcd_gotoXY() function, but it's far from self-explanatory. In keeping with the minimal-space theme, it's written in a way that's designed to use the least amount of memory possible, which makes it rather inscrutable unless you know how the HD44780 interface works.

The arguments are simply the column (the X position starting at the left and moving right) and row (the Y position starting at the top and moving down) at which to place the cursor. However, character positions in an HD44780 display aren't referenced internally as rows and columns: they're referenced as unique memory positions in a section of the display controller's RAM that is referred to as the Display Register.

The thing to keep in mind is that even though we mere humans think about the layout of the LCD in terms of rows and columns, inside the controller the Display Register is just a single long row of memory addresses. Different sections of that memory space map to different rows on the display, so to set the desired location on the display, we need to figure out the offset in the Display Register corresponding to that location.

The base memory address of the Display Register is 0x80, corresponding to the very first character position on the very first row. Other positions on the display are all offset from this base address.

To position the cursor we, therefore, need to send a command to the LCD telling it to select Display Register address 0x80 plus the necessary offset, so we need to process the requested X/Y position to determine what that offset needs to be.

The actual memory addresses for the first character position in each of the four rows on a four-row display are as follows, starting from the top and including the 0x80 base memory address for the Display Register:

```
0x80 + 0x00 (row 0)
0x80 + 0x40 (row 1)
0x80 + 0x14 (row 2)
0x80 + 0x54 (row 3)
```

The simplest scenario is to jump to a character position on the first row, in which case the address offset is simply the number of positions along that we want to move the cursor. We can totally ignore the Y value because the row offset is 0, simply adding the 0x80 Display Register base address to the X value to get the memory address.

So the function starts by simply adding the base address and the X position into the variable dr to calculate the initial required Display Register address. This stage is the same no matter which row is required, so this calculation is always performed.

```
void lcd_gotoXY(byte x, byte y)
{
  byte dr = 0x80 + x;
```

If the Y value is 0 and the required position is, therefore, on the first row, that's it! Job done. The dr variable will now hold the correct Display Register address.

However, if Y is greater than zero it means we need to add an extra offset depending on the required row. This can be done using a couple of simple bitwise operators applied to the requested Y value. It might look cryptic, but it'll all make sense in a moment.

```
  if (y&1) dr+= 0x40;
  if (y&2) dr+= 0x14;
```

Think about the binary representation of the requested Y value for a moment. If it was row 0, that's B00. If it row was 1, that's B01. If it was row 2, that's B10. If it was row 3, that's B11.

Now look at the logical AND operator in those previous two lines of code. If row 1 was requested, the first comparison will match and 0x40 will be added to the Display Register address. If row 2 was requested, the second comparison will match and 0x14 will be added to dr. If row 3 was requested, both bitwise comparisons will match and 0x54 will be added.

And with that, the correct row offset has been applied and a row/column coordinate pair converted into a single Display Register memory address in just three lines of code. This is extremely efficient in both memory use and speed, but it does have the limitation that it won't work with displays of more than 20 columns.

The final calculated value is then sent to the LCD.

```
  lcd_commandWrite( dr );
}
```

A number of simple functions are also defined for printing values to the display and clearing it, but they are far more self-explanatory than the cursor-position function.

Initializing the LCD takes a bit of work, partly because the OBDuinoMega sketch defines some custom characters to display special symbols. Rather than waste four whole characters on the cramped LCD just to display "km/h," the program defines a pair of custom characters that pack the same information into just two display positions.

Before we get to that, though, the lcd_init() function needs to perform some voodoo to set the LCD module into the correct mode, beginning with a delay of at least 15 milliseconds to allow it time to boot up.

```
void lcd_init()
{
  delay(16);
```

Setting the LCD to 4-bit mode requires the nibble (half-byte) B0011 to be sent to LCD data lines 7 through 4 a total of four times with a timed sequence applied to other control lines. That's all taken care of by the lcd_commandWriteSet() function, which in turn calls lcd_tickleEnable(). There's a lot going on here behind the scenes. The sequence being repeated four times is as follows:

1. Write 0011 to data lines 7 through 4.
2. Drive Enable pin low.
3. Wait 1 microsecond.
4. Drive R/W pin low.
5. Drive Enable pin high.
6. Wait 1 microsecond.
7. Drive Enable pin low.
8. Wait 1 microsecond.
9. Wait at least 4.1 milliseconds (the code delays for 5).

All that is handled by the following innocuous looking piece of code:

```
for(byte i=0; i<3; i++)
{
  lcd pushNibble(B00110000);
  lcd commandWriteSet();
  delay(5);
}
```

Then, just when you think it's all done, the previous sequence is executed one final time but with the value B0010.

```
lcd pushNibble(B00100000);
lcd commandWriteSet();
delay(1);
```

After that, the LCD will be initialized and it's possible to write commands to it much less laboriously. The function lcd_commandWrite() can now be used to send subsequent commands, so first it's set to 4-bit mode with a 5 × 8 font, as follows:

```
lcd_commandWrite(B00101000);
```

Then display control is turned on with a hidden cursor and no blink, as follows:

```
lcd_commandWrite(B00001100);
```

Entry mode is set for automatic position increment with no display shift, as follows:

```
lcd_commandWrite(B00000110);
```

The LCD is now ready to go but the function still needs to define those custom characters. The controller can store up to eight user-defined characters, so the OBDuinoMega sketch uses them for the following:

- Character 0: not used
- Characters 1 and 2: L/100

- Characters 3and 4: km/h
- Character 5: ° (degree)
- Characters 6 and 7: mi/g

Because the program needs to define a total of only seven custom characters, it doesn't use the first character position in memory, so it defines NB_CHAR and then calls lcd_commandWrite() to set the character-generator memory address to 0x08 (B1001000) to skip the first eight rows.

```
#define NB_CHAR  7
  lcd_commandWrite(B01001000);
```

The characters are defined using a simple bitmap, which means that if the data is formatted in the correct way and you squint your eyes just right, you can pretend you're in *The Matrix* and actually see the characters in the binary data just by looking at the array.

To make it really easy for you to see, we've made the "high" bits bold.

```
  static prog_uchar chars[] PROGMEM ={
    B10000,B00000,B10000,B00010,B00111,B11111,B00010,
    B10000,B00000,B10100,B00100,B00101,B10101,B00100,
    B11001,B00000,B11000,B01000,B00111,B10101,B01000,
    B00010,B00000,B10100,B10000,B00000,B00000,B10000,
    B00100,B00000,B00000,B00100,B00000,B00100,B00111,
    B01001,B11011,B11111,B00100,B00000,B00000,B00100,
    B00001,B11011,B10101,B00111,B00000,B00100,B00101,
    B00001,B11011,B10101,B00101,B00000,B00100,B00111,
  };
```

If you look at the first character on the left, you'll make out the "L" in the top left corner, then the forward slash "/," and then the "1" in the bottom right corner. You can then see the pair of "0" characters (actually just rectangles because they're so tiny) in the bottom half of the second character.

As you can see, it's relatively simple to define your own characters. If you want to create your own, you can start with a 5 × 8 grid or a piece of graph paper and fill in the squares (pixels) you want to make active on the LCD. Then just create an array using the format shown with 1 for every active pixel and 0 for every inactive pixel.

Now that the raw character data has been defined in an array, it just needs to be clocked into the LCD controller's character-generator RAM. The following nested loops read through each character position in turn (the outer loop), and then through chunks of eight bytes in the inner loop.

```
  for(byte x=0;x<NB_CHAR;x++)
    for(byte y=0;y<8;y++)
      lcd_dataWrite(pgm_read_byte(&chars[y*NB_CHAR+x]));
```

The initialization sequence is now done, so it sends a "clear screen" command (define elsewhere in the sketch) and then sets the RAM address to 0.

```
  lcd_cls();
  lcd_commandWrite(B10000000);
}
```

The sketch then defines a series of other helper functions that are largely self-explanatory, most of which are called by the initialization routine we just saw.

GPS.pde

Most of the hard work of communicating with the GPS module is taken care of by the TinyGPS library, so the GPS.pde file doesn't need to do a whole lot. The entire file is wrapped in an "#ifdef ENABLE_GPS" block so that, unless GPS is included in the build options, none of the file will be compiled at all.

The initGps() function is trivially simple, just sending acknowledgment to a connected host that the serial connection to the GPS module is being set up and then setting it to the appropriate baud rate.

```
void initGps()
{
  hostPrint(" * Initialising GPS              ");
  GPS.begin(GPS_BAUD_RATE);
  hostPrintLn("[OK]");
}
```

One of the most important parts of this file is the processGpsBuffer() function. It's fairly trivial code, but it performs the vital role of pulling data from the serial buffer connected to the GPS and feeding it into the GPS object instantiated from the TinyGPS library. It's important that this function be called frequently so that the serial buffer doesn't overflow and drop characters being sent by the GPS, so calls to processGpsBuffer() are interspersed throughout the main program loop and in other places that could take a while to complete.

```
bool processGpsBuffer()
{
  while (GPS.available())
  {
    if (gps.encode(GPS.read()))
      return true;
  }
  return false;
}
```

The GPS.pde file also contains a monster function called gpsdump() that mostly comes from the example code included with TinyGPS. In normal operation, this function isn't called at all, but while working on the GPS code it can be useful to place a call to this function somewhere in the main loop so that you can see all the possible data you can get from it. It uses the GPS library to extract every possible parameter from the datastream being returned by the GPS module and prints it to the host via the serial port.

VDIP.pde

One of the most interesting parts of the Vehicle Telemetry Platform project is the USB mass storage made possible by the Vinculum chip on VDIP1 and VDIP2 modules. This entire file is wrapped in an "#ifdef ENABLE_VDIP" check so that it's skipped for builds without VDIP enabled.

It includes the initialization function for the VDIP module, called during startup of the datalogger. Most of the function is totally boring, just twiddling the I/O lines used to control the VDIP status LEDs, providing the RTS (ready to send) handshaking, and applying hardware reset to the module under software control of the Arduino. The part to pay attention to, though, is where it asserts the pin connected to the VDIP reset line for 100ms to ensure it comes up in a clean state, then opens a serial connection to it at the configured baud rate set in the main file.

Next, it sends the string "IPA," which is a command string to tell the VDIP to enter ASCII communications mode. The Vinculum chip has two modes: ASCII and binary. The binary mode is more terse and efficient, but for ease of debugging we're running it in ASCII mode so we can read messages sent to and received from the module and understand what's happening.

There is an equivalent command string of "IPH," which switches the Vinculum into binary mode, and there are also binary equivalents of both the IPA and IPH commands. The module is smart enough to be able to recognize both the ASCII and binary forms of both commands in both modes, so we can issue the ASCII command form of IPA and it will always switch the module to ASCII mode irrespective of whether it was in ASCII or binary mode to begin with.

```
void initVdip()
{
  hostPrint(" * Initialising VDIP            ");
  pinMode(VDIP_STATUS_LED, OUTPUT);
  digitalWrite(VDIP_STATUS_LED, HIGH);
  pinMode(VDIP_WRITE_LED, OUTPUT);
  digitalWrite(VDIP_WRITE_LED, LOW);
  pinMode(VDIP_RTS_PIN, INPUT);
  pinMode(VDIP_RESET, OUTPUT);
  digitalWrite(VDIP_RESET, LOW);
  digitalWrite(VDIP_STATUS_LED, HIGH);
  digitalWrite(VDIP_WRITE_LED, HIGH);
  delay( 100 );
  digitalWrite(VDIP_RESET, HIGH);
  delay( 100 );
  VDIP.begin(VDIP_BAUD_RATE);  // Port for connection to Vinculum module
  VDIP.print("IPA\r");     // Sets the VDIP to ASCII mode
  VDIP.print(13, BYTE);
  digitalWrite(VDIP_WRITE_LED, LOW);
  hostPrintLn("[OK]");
}
```

The processVdipBuffer() function simply pulls any characters stored in the serial buffer from the VDIP module and passes them on to the host. By periodically calling this function in the main loop, it's possible for you to see the responses that the module sends to commands.

```
void processVdipBuffer()
{
  byte incomingByte;

  while( VDIP.available() > 0 )
  {
    incomingByte = VDIP.read();
    if( incomingByte == 13 ) {
      HOST.println();
    }
    HOST.print( incomingByte, BYTE );
```

```
  }
}
```

The final function in the VDIP.pde file is modeButton(), an interrupt service routine that is attached to interrupt 1 on digital I/O pin 3 on the Mega using a falling-edge trigger. That pin is held high by the CPU's internal pull-up resistor, and is connected to 0V via the "log on/off" button on the front panel. Pressing the button causes the level to fall and the ISR is invoked, which then checks the time since the last time the interrupt fired to provide a debounce mechanism, and then toggles the state of the logging LED. That LED is used in the main loop as a flag and checked on each pass through to determine whether to execute the logging portion of the code, so simply toggling the state of the LED is sufficient to indirectly activate or deactivate logging on the next pass while allowing the current logging cycle to complete.

```
void modeButton()
{
  if((millis() - logButtonTimestamp) > 300)  // debounce
  {
    logButtonTimestamp = millis();
    digitalWrite(LOG_LED, !digitalRead(LOG_LED));
  }
}
```

Host.pde

Rather than just reporting events to a connected host such as a laptop computer, the OBDuinoMega sketch has a simple command handler that allows you to control it from the host as well. The first function in Host.pde is processHostCommands(), called regularly by the main loop to check the incoming serial buffer for the host connection and act on any commands that have been received.

Prior to checking for commands via the serial port, however, it checks for state changes in the logging status LED. As we just saw in VDIP.pde, one of the front panel buttons invokes an ISR that toggles the state of the logging LED. That LED is checked at this point to see if there is a discrepancy between the state of the logActive flag and the state of the LED. If logging is on but the LED has been deactivated, the VDIP status LED is set to inactive, the VDIP module is sent a command telling it to close the currently open OBDUINO.CSV file, and a message is sent to the host saying logging has stopped. Conversely, a mismatch in the other direction causes the VDIP status LED to be set to active, the VDIP is instructed to open the logfile, and the host is informed that logging has started.

```
void processHostCommands()
{
  // Check for state change from the front panel button
  if(logActive && !digitalRead(LOG_LED))
  {
    logActive = 0;
    digitalWrite(VDIP_STATUS_LED, LOW);
    VDIP.print("CLF OBDUINO.CSV\r");
    HOST.println("Stop logging");
  }
  else if( !logActive && digitalRead(LOG_LED))
  {
    logActive = 1;
```

```
    digitalWrite(VDIP_STATUS_LED, HIGH);
    VDIP.print("OPW OBDUINO.CSV\r");
    HOST.println("Start logging");
  }
```

Next, it checks the serial port buffer for commands from the host. Commands are currently limited to single characters, using numbers to control common tasks. This makes it really easy to control the Vehicle Telemetry Platform using the numeric keypad on a connected host.

```
  if( HOST.available() > 0)
  {
    char readChar = HOST.read();
```

The command "1" tells the sketch to open the CSV logfile on a connected USB memory stick and start logging to it. The status LED for the VDIP module is also switched from green to red to indicate that a file is open, showing that it's not safe to remove the memory stick.

If the file doesn't currently exist, the Vinculum chip will create an empty file and open it.

```
    if(readChar == '1')
    {
      HOST.println("Start logging");
      logActive = 1;
      digitalWrite(VDIP_STATUS_LED, HIGH);
      digitalWrite(LOG_LED, HIGH);
      VDIP.print("OPW OBDUINO.CSV\r");
      HOST.print("> ");
```

Likewise, command "2" deactivates logging by setting the appropriate states on the indicator LEDs and sending a "close file" command to the VDIP. This version also includes some test code to indicate whether the VDIP has failed to assert its active-low Ready To Send pin, meaning that the Vinculum's internal buffer is full and it can't accept more commands right now. In this version, the sketch just sits and spins until the Vinculum indicates that it's ready to receive more data, which could potentially lead to the sketch blocking at this point. Ultimately, the VDIP code will need to be extended with more robust buffer checks and communications timeouts to prevent it from blocking the main loop.

```
    } else if( readChar == '2') {
      HOST.println("Stop logging");
      while(digitalRead(VDIP_RTS_PIN) == HIGH)
      {
        HOST.println("VDIP BUFFER FULL");
      }
      logActive = 0;
      digitalWrite(VDIP_STATUS_LED, LOW);
      digitalWrite(LOG_LED, LOW);
      VDIP.print("CLF OBDUINO.CSV\r");
      HOST.print("> ");
```

Command "3" appears to be quite simple but it has a bit of a trap for the unwary. It sends a command to the VDIP telling it to read out the contents of the logfile. Immedately after receiving this command, the VDIP will start sending the contents of the file to the Arduino's serial connection as fast as it can. In the VDIP.pde file discussed previously, we saw a function called processVdipBuffer() that is called once per main loop, but because of all the other time-consuming things that happen in the sketch, it's quite likely that by the time it starts processing the buffer, the VDIP will have already overflowed it. The result is that for very small logfiles of only a few lines, this command works just fine, but once the logfile grows a little bigger, this command fails to complete properly.

As an ugly workaround to this problem, the processVdipBuffer() function is called immediately after requesting a file read. Just be warned that if you execute this command with a big logfile, you'll have to sit there and wait for the entire file to be printed before the sketch can proceed!

```
} else if (readChar == '3'){
  HOST.println("Reading file");
  VDIP.print("RD OBDUINO.CSV\r");
  processVdipBuffer();
  HOST.print("> ");
```

File deletion, command "4," is quite simple. Because this command could be issued at any time, even when a file is open and being written to, it first performs the same actions as if a request had been made to stop logging (which will fail harmlessly if there was no log open), and then sends a "delete file" command to the VDIP.

```
} else if (readChar == '4'){
  logActive = 0;
  digitalWrite(VDIP_STATUS_LED, LOW);
  digitalWrite(LOG_LED, LOW);
  VDIP.print("CLF OBDUINO.CSV");
  HOST.println("Deleting file");
  VDIP.print("DLF OBDUINO.CSV\r");
  HOST.print("> ");
```

Command "5," directory listing, is a convenience function that can be handy during testing just to make sure that a file is actually being created, without having to continually remove the memory stick and put it in another computer.

```
} else if (readChar == '5'){
  HOST.println("Directory listing");
  VDIP.print("DIR\r");
  HOST.print("> ");
```

Command "6," reset, can be extremely handy when messing around with commands to the VDIP module. When sending data to the module, it's necessary to know in advance exactly how many bytes will be sent, including any terminating characters. If you make a miscalculation, the module can end up in a state where it sits waiting for more characters to arrive and never finishes. After having that happen once too many times while experimenting with data formats and then having to power-cycle the whole Vehicle Telemetry Platform, we connected the reset pin on the VDIP to a digital pin on the Arduino so we could reset it under software control and have everything continue on. The reset command performs almost the same actions as the initVdip() function, but assumes that the digital I/O lines have already been set to their correct modes and jumps straight in to asserting the hardware reset and then forcing ASCII mode using the IPA command.

```
} else if (readChar == '6'){
  HOST.print(" * Initializing flash storage   ");
  pinMode(VDIP_RESET, OUTPUT);
```

```
      digitalWrite(VDIP_RESET, LOW);
      delay( 100 );
      digitalWrite(VDIP_RESET, HIGH);
      delay( 100 );
      VDIP.print("IPA");
      VDIP.print(13, BYTE);
      HOST.println("[OK]");
      HOST.print("> ");
```

Finally, if a character is received that the host command processor doesn't recognize, it displays a help message to explain what commands are available.

```
    } else {
      HOST.print("Unrecognized command '");
      HOST.print(readChar);
      HOST.println("'");
      HOST.println("1 - Start logging");
      HOST.println("2 - Stop logging");
      HOST.println("3 - Display logfile");
      HOST.println("4 - Delete logfile");
      HOST.println("5 - Directory listing");
      HOST.println("6 - Reset VDIP module");
      HOST.print("> ");
    }
  }
}
```

The final two functions at the end of this file are really just wrappers for Serial.print() and Serial.println(), which might sound like a waste of time but it helps to simplify code elsewhere in the sketch. Because the OBDuinoMega sketch is designed to support being built without support for a serial connection to the host, these functions allow us to place calls that send messages to the host throughout the sketch without worrying about whether a host serial connection even exists. The functions themselves wrap their internal functionality inside "#ifdef MEGA" checks so that if the sketch is not built specifically for a Mega target, they will simply accept whatever is passed to them and immediately exit without doing anything. However, if the sketch was built for a Mega target, these functions invoke print() and println() to the appropriate serial port.

```
void hostPrint( char* message )
{
  #ifdef MEGA
  HOST.print(message);
  #endif
}

void hostPrintLn( char* message )
{
  #ifdef MEGA
  HOST.println(message);
  #endif
}
```

PowerFail.pde

The setup() function attaches the powerFail() interrupt service routine to a falling-edge on interrupt 0, which is on digital pin 2 and, therefore, connected to the voltage divider on the input of the power supply.

If the voltage being provided to the power supply falls, this ISR is invoked. It then turns off the logging LED as a flag to the main loop that it needs to close the logfile on the USB memory stick on the next pass through, and also turns off the LCD backlight to save power.

Ultimately, this function should probably be extended to shut down the GPS module as well to save even more power and make the power-supply capacitor last a few milliseconds longer, but this is not as easy as it might sound. Because the ISR could be called at any time, it could be invoked while the GPS is being read, resulting in the main loop blocking on a read that will never complete after the ISR turns off the GPS and exits. Using an ISR can have unexpected side effects and you always need to consider the result of it being executed at different points within the main program loop.

```
void powerFail()
{
  digitalWrite(LOG_LED, LOW);
  analogWrite(BrightnessPin, brightness[0]);
}
```

Using the OBDuinoMega Sketch

Menu Buttons

The three buttons perform different roles depending on whether the system is displaying real-time data or is in menu mode.

Real-time mode uses the following buttons:

- Left: Rotate to next virtual screen.
- Middle: Enter menu mode.
- Right: Cycle through LCD brightness settings.
- Left + Middle: Tank reset. Use this after filling up.
- Middle + Right: Trip and outing reset.
- Left + Right: Display PID information for current screen.

Menu mode uses the following buttons:

- Left: Decrease.
- Middle: Select.
- Right: Increase.

Options you can set in the menu include the following:

- LCD Contrast (0–100 in steps of 10). In our prototype, we used a variable resistor rather than controlling the display contrast from the sketch, but the menus allow for it in case you connect up contrast to a PWM output.
- Use Metric units (NO/YES). NO gives miles and gallons; YES gives kilometers and liters.
- Use Comma format (NO/YES). NO uses a period as the decimal place; YES uses a comma.
- Fuel/hour speed (0–255). Below this speed, the display can show L/100KM or MPG; above it, the display switches to L/h or GPH.
- Tank size (xx.y). Size of your tank in liters or gallons.
- Fuel price (xx.y). Price of fuel per liter or gallon.
- Fuel Adjust (0–255%). Fuel consumption calibration factor. This can be tweaked after you've gone through a few tanks of fuel and manually checked how much is put in each time.
- Speed Adjust (0–255%). Speedometer calibration factor. If your car speed sensor isn't accurate, you can compensate using this value.
- Engine Displacement (0.0L–10.0L). Only used with a MAP sensor. Newer cars use a MAF (mass air flow) sensor, but some cars use a MAP (manifold absolute pressure) sensor, in which case the MAF output has to be simulated using the MAF value and the engine displacement. Most cars shouldn't need this value to be set.
- Outing stopover (0–2550 minutes). Increments in periods of 10 minutes. If the car is turned off for more than this period of time, the outing will be automatically reset. Any stop shorter than this will be considered part of the same outing. For example, if you stop briefly at a shop and start the car again it will still be considered part of the same outing. Setting the value to 0 minutes will cause the outing to be reset every time the car is restarted.
- Trip stopover (1–255 hours). Like the outing stopover value, but for longer periods such as a trip. This allows you to have a long journey with multiple stops, such as a road trip with hotel stays, all treated as a single trip, even if it consists of multiple "outings."
- Configure PIDs (NO/YES). Select YES to set the PIDs you want to display on each of the three virtual screens. You will then be asked to select the PID for each position. Selecting the current value with the middle button leaves it as is, while the left and right buttons decrement and increment the selection. Other than the regular OBD-II PIDs, there are also a number of additional nonstandard PIDs provided by the system itself. These are given in Table 15-12.

Table 15-12. *Additional non-standard J("fake") PIDs provided by the OBDuinoMega sketch*

PID	Label	Description
0xE9	OutWaste	Fuel wasted idling for this outing
0xEA	TrpWaste	Fuel wasted idling for this trip
0xEB	TnkWaste	Fuel wasted iding for this tank
0xEC	Out Cost	Cost of fuel used for this outing
0xED	Trp Cost	Cost of fuel used for this trip
0xEE	Tnk Cost	Cost of fuel used for this tank
0xEF	Out Time	Time the car has been running
0xF0	No Disp	No display, blank corner
0xF1	InstCons	Instant fuel consumption rate
0xF2	Tnk Cons	Average fuel consumption for the tank
0xF3	Tnk Fuel	Fuel used for the current tank
0xF4	Tnk Dist	Distance done on the current tank
0xF5	Dist2MT	Remaining distance possible on the current tank
0xF6	Trp Cons	Average fuel consumption for the trip
0xF7	Trp Fuel	Fuel used for the current trip
0xF8	Trp Dist	Distance of the current trip
0xF9	Batt Vlt	Car battery voltage

0xFA	Out Cons	Average fuel consumption for the outing
0xFB	Out Fuel	Fuel used for the current outing
0xFC	Out Dist	Distance of the current outing
0xFD	Can Stat	CAN status including TX/RX errors
0xFE	PID_SEC	Number of PIDs retrieved per second
0xFF	Eco Vis	Visual display of economy (free memory in debug mode)

Running Logging

In normal operation, the green "safe to remove" LED will be illuminated, meaning that the VDIP1 is not trying to access the memory stick and it can be insert or removed.

To start logging, insert the memory stick and wait a few seconds to give the VDIP1 time to recognize it. If you have a computer connected to the USB port on the system and run the serial monitor in the Arduino IDE, you'll see a message reported back when the VDIP1 probes the memory stick, so if things don't seem to be working try running it with a computer connected so you can see if it generates any errors.

Press the "logging on/off" button briefly and you'll see the green "safe to remove" LED extinguish and the red "file open" LED illuminate. You'll also see a flicker about once per second on the yellow "log activity" LED as it writes another line to the CSV file.

Pressing the button again will turn logging off. When the green "safe to remove" LED comes back on, you can take out the memory stick, insert it into a computer, and process the logfile. The logfile generated by the system is a regular CSV file using the fields specified in Table 15-13, so you can open it with a text editor or spreadsheet program.

Table 15-13. *Fields stored in CSV logfile*

Column	Field	Description
1	GPS_LAT	GPS latitude
2	GPS_LON	GPS longitude
3	GPS_ALT	GPS altitude in meters above sea level

4	GPS_SPEED	GPS speed in km/h
5	LOAD_VALUE	Engine load in %
6	COOLANT_TEMP	ECU coolant temperature in C
7	ENGINE_RPM	Engine RPM
8	VEHICLE_SPEED	Vehicle speed in selected units
9	TIMING_ADV	Timing advance in degrees
10	INT_AIR_TEMP	Intake air temperature
11	MAF_AIR_FLOW	Mass air flow
12	THROTTLE_POS	Throttle position in %
13	FUEL_RAIL_P	Fuel rail pressure in kPa
14	FUEL_LEVEL	Fuel level in %
15	BARO_PRESSURE	Barometric pressure
16	AMBIENT_TEMP	Ambient temperature
17	FUEL_CONS	Fuel consumption rate
18	BATT_VOLTAGE	Battery voltage

Generate Google Earth Track

Included with the project source code is a directory called OBDtoKML that contains a simple PHP script called obd-to-kml.php. This script takes a logfile and extracts the latitude, longitude, and vehicle speed, and then uses them to generate a KML file that can be opened in Google Earth. Note, though, that it's not intended to run on a web server: even though it's written in PHP it's designed to be executed directly like a shell script. You need to have the CLI (command-line interface) version of PHP installed and also set execute permissions on the script. Then you can launch it just like any other script.

The script takes a single argument, which is simply the name of the logfile to convert, and then creates a new file in the same location but with a .kml extension tacked on the end. For example, on a Linux or Mac OS machine with a logfile sitting on the desktop, you could open a terminal and execute.

```
./OBDtoKML/obd-to-kml.php ~/Desktop/OBDUINO.CSV
```

You'll then end up with a file at ~/Desktop/OBDUINO.CSV.kml that you can open in Google Earth.

For Linux users, we've also included an obd-to-kml.desktop file that allows you to drag and drop your logfile onto the icon and have it converted in one easy action. If Google Earth is associated with the .kml extension and everything is set up correctly, generating a track of a logged trip is as simple as the following steps:

1. Insert the memory stick into the computer. It should open automatically.
2. Drag the logfile onto the obd-to-kml icon.
3. Double-click the resulting .kml file to launch Google Earth and open the track.

Inside the script, you can see it extracts the values for all the data fields even if it doesn't use them, so changing it to plot a different parameter, such as RPM against location, is trivial. Just change the parameter near the end of the script where the output line is generated and run it again.

If the resulting .kml file doesn't seem to work, it's quite likely that the original data included invalid lines such as GPS coordinates returned as "0.000". If you open the generated .kml file in a text editor and scroll through it, you may see obviously bogus lines. Simply delete them, save the file, and reload it in Google Earth.

Generate Charts of Parameters

To plot parameters, start by opening the logfile in a spreadsheet program, and delete the columns you don't care about. Most spreadsheet software includes charting tools that let you select data ranges and generate various charts from them. If you don't have a spreadsheet program installed on your computer, you can also use free online services such as Google Docs, importing the logfile into an online spreadsheet and then generating a chart from there.

Variations

Keep in mind that modifying a car is potentially hazardous to yourself and also to other drivers, passengers, and pedestrians, and some of the suggestions here may not even be legal in some parts of the world. Please use your own common sense and obey any relevant local regulations.

Mobile Internet Connection

Mobile broadband modems that use 3G networks to provide high-speed Internet access while mobile are now commonly available, and some providers such as Three in Australia also have available a mobile broadband router that uses a 3G modem to provide wired Ethernet connectivity. By adding an Ethernet shield to the Vehicle Telemetry Platform, you could have your car connected to the Internet and potentially accessible from anywhere in the world. One trap to be careful of, though, is to use a provider who doesn't use private, nonroutable IP addresses or you won't be able to connect to your car.

Vehicle Control

In this project we used the Arduino to collect and report on data from the car, but you could also extend it to control the car itself. The Mega has plenty of spare I/O lines, so by adding some relays and modifying the wiring loom of your car, you could set it up so the Arduino can lock, unlock, start, and stop the car. One of the authors has even combined this with a constant mobile Internet connection via 3G broadband so that his car can be started, stopped, and tracked, and the engine-management data interrogated live from anywhere in the world using nothing more than a web browser. You can learn more about it at www.geekmyride.org/wiki/index.php/Jon's_RX-8.

Speech Synthesizer Output

Ever since Kitt appeared in "Knight Rider" in the early 1980s, every teenage boy has wanted a car that can talk. Extending the Vehicle Telemetry Platform to include a speech synthesizer would be relatively simple using the design of the speech synthesizer shield described in Chapter 9. The output of the synthesizer could be fed into the vehicle sound system to have voice prompts played through it.

3D Accelerometer

By integrating the speed data from the OBD-II interface, you can calculate linear acceleration, and by doing the same to the positional data returned by the GPS, you can generate acceleration in other axes as well, but at fairly low accuracy. Using an I2C connection, you could add a Wii Nunchuck controller and read X, Y, and Z axis accelerometer values to be stored along with the other data.

Digital Compass

The GPS module can approximate heading based on successive position fixes, but you could add a simple magnetic compass module with an I2C interface to allow the system to display an accurate heading value.

"Knight Rider"–Style Alarm Status

If the carAlarmScreen option was enabled at build time, the displayAlarmScreen() function is invoked when the engine isn't running. It simply displays a scanning asterisk on the LCD, but because the Mega has plenty of spare I/O pins, it would be easy to connect up a row of LEDs and have this function drive a "Knight Rider"–style scanner as well, if you wanted something a bit more attention-grabbing.

Battery Condition Check

The ELM327 provides a battery voltage reading even when the car isn't running because it's permanently connected to an unswitched battery line. Periodically reading the battery voltage when the car isn't running could allow the Vehicle Telemetry System to turn off other devices in the car if necessary—or even turn itself off!

Resources

This project is very heavily based on the OBDuino project at www.ecomodder.com. Make sure you check out the EcoModder site for lots more information about OBDuino, MPGuino, and ways to improve the fuel economy of your car.

The VDIP1 module and all its commands are very well documented on the Vinculum site at `www.vinculum.com`.

CHAPTER 16

■ ■ ■

Resources

In the project chapters of *Practical Arduino* we covered a range of electronics topics using real-world examples. In this chapter, we provide a little grab bag of additional electronics techniques and topics that you might find useful. On the *Practical Arduino* web site, you'll find a complementary set of hints and tips on the software side of Arduino development. We elected to split things in this manner, as the software side of Arduino is moving relatively faster than the electronics topics we wanted to cover.

Simple Voltage Regulators

Often your project will need regulated power beyond what can be tapped from the Arduino board itself. One of the simplest ways to achieve this is through the use of a three-terminal regulator. The most common of these are the 78xx series parts where *xx* is the output voltage—05, 06, 08, 12, 15 for 5V, 6V, 8V, 12V and 15V outputs, respectively.

Figure 16-1 shows a simple 5V supply based on a 7805. Most of the components other than the regulator and 0.1µF capacitor are optional. We include them because it represents good design practice. The capacitors all serve to help the circuit deal with transient demands from the connected circuitry. The 0.1µF part helps the regulator remain stable, so it's good practice to install it and have it as close as reasonably possible to the regulator itself. The diode back across the regulator limits how much current will flow back into the regulator from the capacitors on the output side when the input power is removed.

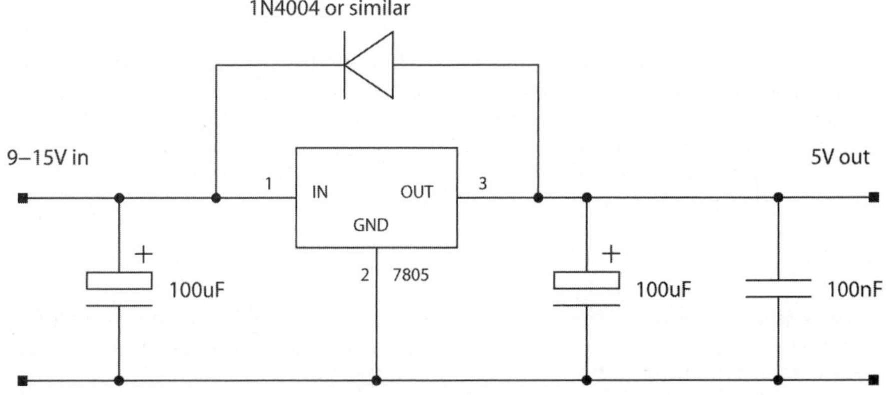

***Figure 16-1.** Simple 5V regulator circuit*

The attraction of the 78xx series regulators is that they are pretty much built-in and they come preset to the voltage required and can cope with an input voltage of 10V or 20V above the output voltage. However, there are a few catches to be aware of, chief among them being power dissipation and dropout voltage.

Power Dissipation

In a so-called "linear regulator" circuit such as this, the voltage regulator device itself is effectively acting like a resistor in which the value changes as required to maintain the desired output voltage. Thus, if the input of the regulator is at 12V and the output at 5V, the regulator circuitry acts like a resistor of the value required for the 7V difference to be absorbed by the regulator. Therefore, the power that "disappears" in the regulator is converted into heat. The more current that is flowing through the regulator, the more power (heat) that 7V will amount to. The regulator must dissipate this heat safely; otherwise it will shut down or, in extreme cases, be damaged. For example, at a 100mA current draw the regulator must dissipate 0.7W into the environment.

For the most common package type 7805, a TO-220 pack that has a metal tab at the rear of the device and dissipation up to about 0.5W without a heatsink is usually fine. Anything beyond this and the tab should be attached to a heatsink or a metal chassis. It's important to note that the tab is connected to ground, so it's usually desirable to electrically insulate the regulator from the heatsink or chassis. Thermally conductive washers that do this are readily available.

Dropout Voltage

The second characteristic to consider is dropout voltage—the difference between input and output voltage, below which the regulator isn't guaranteed to operate correctly. For 7805 parts, this voltage is 2V, so ideally you should ensure that the input voltage is always above 7—tricky if you're using a 6V battery pack.

Low dropout (LDO) regulators exist that minimize this value down to 0.5V or less. Parts to investigate include the LH117, LM2940, and LM3940 series. Being readily available, there's a good argument to standardize on these instead of the 78xx parts.

Efficiency

Linear regulators are quite inefficient, as by design they convert all the excess power into heat. In many applications this is outweighed by their design simplicity, but for battery-powered applications, as well as the growing focus on energy efficiency, this might not be an acceptable trade-off. In these circumstances, we suggest you investigate switch-mode regulators, which while more complex to design with, have far greater flexibility and efficiency. We leave this as an exercise to the reader, however!

Driving LEDs

LEDs have been used in a number of projects in *Practical Arduino* to provide a simple indication of status. These previous examples have used LEDs in quite straightforward applications. In this section, we discuss LEDs in more detail and introduce a few ways of driving them.

LEDs are diodes that emit light. Like diodes, they have a forward voltage drop (V_f) as well as maximum and peak forward current ratings (I_{max} and I_{peak}, respectively). These values vary among LEDs and can be found on the datasheet for the specific LED you have chosen. In the absence of a datasheet, some rules of thumb are as follows:

- Modern red LEDs have a forward voltage drop (V_f) of 1.5–2.2V.
- Green LEDs have a V_f of 2–3V.
- Blue LEDs have a V_f in of 2.5–3.5V or more.
- Yellow LEDs have a V_f of 1.5–2.5V.
- White LEDs have a V_f of 3.5–4V.

LEDs have a fairly sharp cutoff voltage below which they don't produce any light at all. Typically, this is a few tenths of a volt below V_f.

Maximum continuous forward current for 5mm LEDs will be in the range 15–70mA, and exceeding this will likely damage the LED over time. Peak currents are usually of the order of three to five times the continuous rating for 5mm LEDs, but can be considerably higher for larger LEDs—amps in some instances.

Like most devices, LEDs are susceptible to damage when they overheat, which will occur if the average power dissipation is too high. This damage can be subtle, such as a reduction in lifetime and slowly decreasing output, or more rapid if you operate far outside the ratings. Higher power LEDs (in the 1–3W plus range) are normally designed to have some sort of heatsink attached.

If you're using an LED as a simple status indicator as we have in many of the *Practical Arduino* projects, put a 200–300Ω in series with it and move on. The exact figures previously given aren't going to come in to play!

However, if you're dimming LEDs using PWM or are multiplexing/charlieplexing them, a little more nuance is required in your design.

Multiplexing

Multiplexing is a very common way of driving LEDs, particularly when they are assembled as either a dot matrix display or a number of seven-segment/numeric displays. Multiplexing relies on the fact that if a light source is switched on and off fast enough, the human eye perceives it as being continuously lit even though it is in fact only on for a brief period.

Figure 16-2 shows a two-digit seven-segment display connected to an Arduino. Note that the seven segments are connected directly to the Arduino output pins and the "common cathode" of the display (all the LED cathodes) are connected through a transistor to ground. These bases of the transistors are, in turn, connected to an output pin on the Arduino.

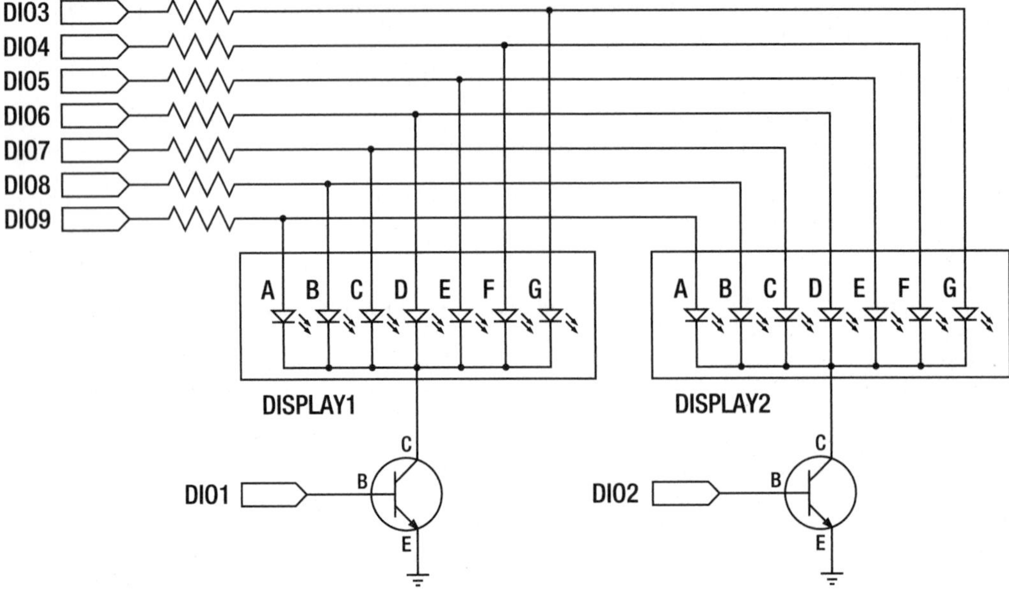

Figure 16-2. Schematic for a two-digit seven-segment multiplexed display

In order to display two different numbers on each display, we use a procedure much like the following:

```
repeat {
        Set Outputs 3 to 9 as required for first digit;
        Turn Output 1 On;
        Delay;
        Turn Output 1 Off;

        Set Outputs 3 to 9 as required for second digit;
        Turn Output 2 On;
        Delay;
        Turn Output 2 Off;
}
```

If we repeat this rapidly enough, our eye will perceive both displays as being continually lit showing the digits we want. The general idea can, of course, be expanded to more digits—four or six for a clock, for example, and this is precisely how most LED clocks work.

Multiplexing doesn't come entirely free. Because the LEDs aren't on all the time, they appear dimmer. In our example, the duty cycle (ratio of "on" time to "off" time) for each display is 50%. For a four-digit display, it would be 25%, and so on.

To get around this, we can increase the current being sent to each display, this being where the peak current rating of the display becomes important. For a typical seven-segment display, it's likely to be acceptable to increase the current to 50mA per segment. Higher than that, start checking datasheets and doing some calculations to ensure you don't overstress the devices. By driving the LEDs with a higher peak current, they output more LED for the time they are on so they appear brighter. They also have time to cool during the off time, hence avoiding damage.

There is a caveat with driving LEDs at their peak, rather than constant, current rating: it's very important that your software doesn't inadvertently leave them on too long, or the device can be damaged. This can be problematic during development/debugging if your code crashes with the LEDs in an on state. It is prudent to do initial coding with the LED or display run with resistors chosen to keep it at its constant current rating.

The next issue with multiplexing is that, of course, the ATMega must update the state of the LED or display at regular intervals. This reduces the amount of processor time available for other tasks. With careful design, the impact of this can be minimized, but should be taken into account. Consider using a periodic interrupt to do the display updates.

Charlieplexing

Charlieplexing is a technique that can be used to maximize the number of LEDs or switches that a microcontroller can address with a limited number of pins. It makes use of the fact that a modern microcontroller (ATMega/Arduino obviously included) can actually set its pins to one of three states: High, Low, or Input ("Hi-Z" as it is sometimes called). We'll confine our remarks here to driving LEDs. The *Practical Arduino* web site has links for references on this topic, if you wish to read up on more exotic setups, as well as links to the original articles on the topic.

Figure 16-3 shows two LEDs connected between a pair of Arduino output pins through a dropping resistor. Note that the LEDs are connected with opposite polarity. Two pins to drive two LEDs is hardly remarkable, but bear with us a moment and we'll illustrate the basic principle.

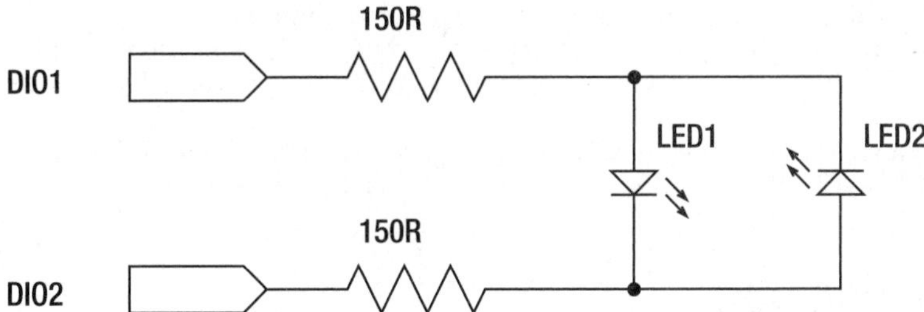

Figure 16-3. *A two-pin charlieplexed LED display*

To turn LED1 on, we would make Output1 High, and Output2 Low. For LED2 we'd do the opposite: Output1 Low and Output2 High. To turn the LEDs off, we can either set the pins to be inputs or the outputs to be the same state (both Low or both High)

Figure 16-4 shows a more interesting arrangement. Here we drive six LEDs from just three pins by making use of the Arduino's ability to set a pin to be an input or an output in a high or low state.

Referring to the diagram, to turn LED1 on, we'd set DIO1 to be an output and to be high, DIO2 to be an output and low, and DIO3 to be an input. LED2 would be turned on by DIO1 being an output and set low, DIO2 being an output and set high, DIO3 still being an input. Jumping around, LED4 you'd set DIO1 to be an input, DIO2 to be low, and DIO3 to be high. LED6 would call for DIO1 to be low, DIO2 to be an input, and DIO3 to be high, and so on. A bit of thought and careful programming will allow you to create a general-case piece of code that can turn on any LED required.

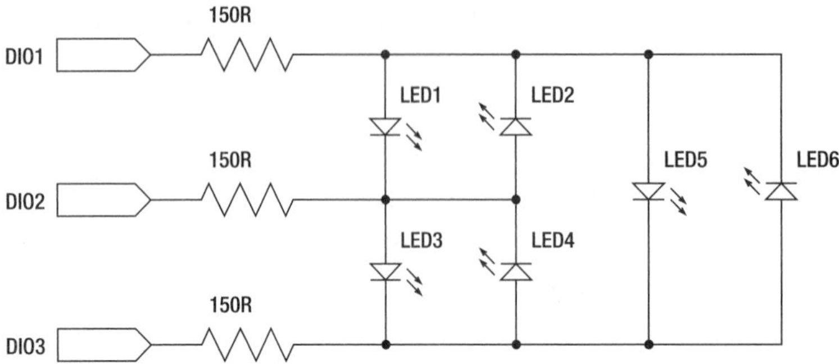

Figure 16-4. *A three-pin six-LED charlieplexed display*

You'd be correct to wonder why when LED6 is on, LED1 and LED3 aren't. They're connected between the same pins, after all, and with the correct polarity. The answer here is the forward voltage drop—there isn't a high enough voltage across the two LEDs when connected in series to allow them to light because it's below the threshold or V_f level.

If, as is often the case, you want to have more than one LED on at a time, you can use a multiplexing arrangement, switching to each LED in turn in rapid succession. Avoid the temptation to simply skip an LED that is off. If you do so, then the brightness of any LED that is on will change depending on how many LEDs are on at any one time. Of course, if the number of LEDs that are on is constant—as would be the case for hands on a clock, say—that would be acceptable. LEDs that are off can be skipped completely in such a case. As noted in the previously, you'll need to consider running the LEDs at higher currents to keep the brightness up, and the same caveats about duty cycle come into play.

Finally, note that the current-limiting resistors are half the value you'd normally expect to use. This because the LED being driven is always being powered by the Arduino through two pins and, hence, two dropping resistors.

If you're curious, the general case for the number of LEDs that you can drive from n pins is $n^2 - n$. For example, eight DIOs yield 56 LEDs; 12 DIOs yield 132 LEDs; and so on. That's a lotta LEDs!

Output Circuitry and Isolation

The ATMega168, like all microcontrollers, is limited in its ability to provide current to external devices. When the internal drive capabilities are insufficient, it is necessary to employ additional circuitry to correctly and safely switch the load in question.

Before considering the type of device that best suits your application, you need to consider four parameters: current, voltage, switching frequency, and isolation. The first three are, in a sense, hard numbers; the final is more of an engineering decision.

Current and voltage are interrelated (as we discussed in Chapter 1), so switching high currents at low voltages is a different engineering problem than low currents at very high voltages, for example. For the purposes of this discussion, we can consider high voltages to be anything over 24V, and high currents as anything over a few hundred mA. Switching frequency will vary enormously with application.

Isolation, as the name suggests, is the practice of having electrical and/or physical separation between two parts of a circuit, typically the "low" and "high" power sections. Isolation is necessary for safety reasons when high voltages are involved and/or mains switching is the task at hand. It can also be prudent for high-current applications, even at lower voltages, simply to avoid the risk of damaging the relatively sensitive circuitry in the Arduino and/or connected devices.

Semiconductor and Mechanical Switches

For practical applications, there are two broad types of switching devices available: semiconductor and mechanical. Semiconductor devices include a few different types of transistors, optocouplers, and solid state relays (SSRs); mechanical devices come down to different types of relays.

Solid state devices are often physically smaller, consume less power, and are able to switch more rapidly than mechanical devices because there are no moving parts. The lack of moving parts nominally makes semiconductors more reliable, but well-designed relay circuits will often last just as long. Only certain classes of semiconductor devices provide electrical isolation between input and output. Some solid state devices are a little trickier to use and less forgiving if used incorrectly.

Mechanical switching devices have the advantages of providing electrical isolation, being pretty bulletproof to design with, and are easily understood. On the downside, they tend to need higher drive currents and so can themselves need additional circuitry to be driven from the Arduino. They are also limited in switching frequency. This latter limitation can manifest as either being unable to switch fast enough to support higher frequencies or wearing out too quickly—limited number of cycles. As a rule of thumb, switching frequencies of 1Hz or faster for any continually operated circuit with a mechanical relay is marginal at best.

Having discussed some of the general issues in selecting output circuits, we now look at some practical examples.

Reed Relays

Reed relays consist of a switching element (the "reed") within a coil of wire. When current flows through the energized coil, the resulting magnetic field closes or, in some cases, opens the contacts. If the switch is open when the coil is off, the relay is said to be "Normally Open" or "NO." If the switch is closed then the device is "Normally Closed" or "NC." Some reed relays have both NC and NO contacts.

The construction of the relay provides a high degree of electrical isolation, but because the contacts within the reed are quite small, the contacts have limited current- and voltage-handling capability. However, the small size of the contacts has an upside: only quite small currents (typically under 15mA) are needed to keep the coil energized and the contacts closed.

Reed relays commonly have coil voltages designed to be compatible with 5V digital circuitry, and so in many cases can be driven directly by the Arduino. Figure 16-5 is a schematic of a reed relay connected in this manner.

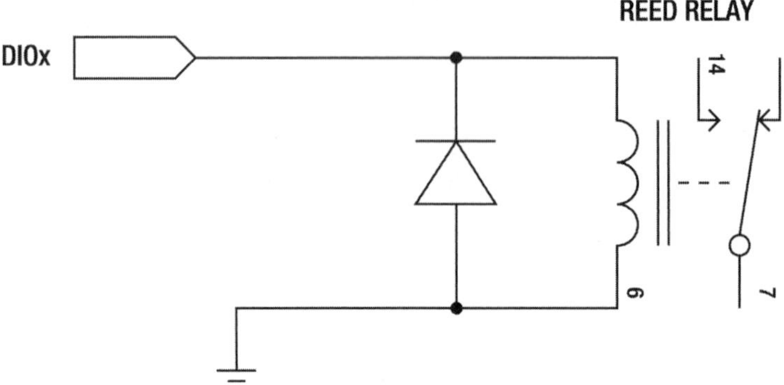

Figure 16-5. Reed relay driven by an Arduino output pin

■ **Note** When driving devices that have a coil or filament, such as a relay or incandescent light bulb, bear in mind that such devices have both a peak and steady state current requirement. Peak current is drawn while the magnetic field is stabilizing or the filament heating up before it falls to the steady state value. Your chosen drive circuit (or lack thereof if directly connected to the Arduino) must be able to cope with this current transient.

When current is removed from devices with a coil, the magnetic field collapses and a reverse or "Back-EMF" voltage is generated. Depending on the type of device and circuit configuration, this voltage can be several tens of volts and will have the opposite sign of the supply circuit. It is possible for this voltage transient to damage the drive circuit if it is not suitably protected. Notice in Figure 16-5 that there is a diode connected across the coil of the reed relay. This diode soaks up or "quenches" this reverse transient.

Relays

Relays are a variation on the reed relay previously described and differ primarily in their mechanical construction. Typically, the coil of wire, or solenoid, causes a lever to move that opens and/or closes the relay contacts. Relays typically have higher voltage and current ratings at the expense of slightly slower switching speed and higher coil current. In the advantages column, these higher voltage and current ratings are joined by greater flexibility in contact configurations—multiple poles (separate switches) and changeover (NC + NO) is commonplace.

The somewhat higher current demands of a conventional coil relay generally precludes driving them directly from the Arduino. If only one or two relays are being used, then a simple bipolar transistor, as discussed in the next section, will do the job nicely. If four or more relays are being used, it is worth considering a specialized transistor array or driver chip, which we touch on later in the Transistor Arrays section.

Figure 16-6 shows a relay being driven from the Arduino using a conventional bipolar transistor to provide additional current-handling capability. Note that like the reed relay circuit in Figure 16-5, a back-EMF diode is used. We describe this circuit further in the next section.

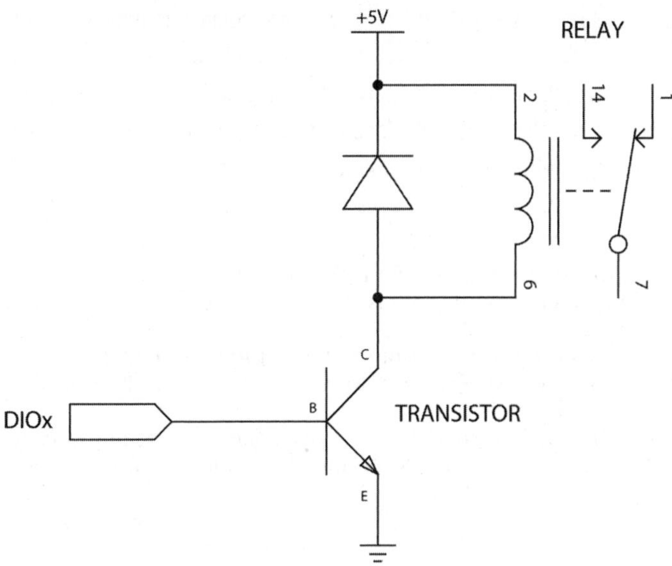

Figure 16-6. *Bipolar transistor used to drive a relay*

■ **Note** Mechanical contacts like those used in reed relays, conventional relays, and switches have a minor design quirk that you should be aware of if you're designing for high-reliability applications. With the exception of exotic "wetted" contacts, it's desirable to ensure at least 10mA or so flows through the contacts when on in order to ensure they stay free of oxidization and corrosion. If you're just tinkering, it's pretty safe to ignore this, though!

Bipolar Transistors

The first semiconductor output device we consider is the humble bipolar transistor. Bipolar transistors come in two basic types: NPN and PNP. The N and P refer to the semiconductor material used to construct the device; in practice it denotes how the device needs to be used.

In digital applications, bipolar transistors can be considered an electronic switch allowing something like a low-power microcontroller to control higher currents. A small current flowing through the base (B in Figure 16-6) controls the larger current flowing collector to emitter (C and E, respectively, in Figure 16-6). If the current flowing into the base is sufficiently high, the transistor is said to "saturate," or turn completely on, and so has very little resistance or power dissipation.

■ **Note** Transistors are also commonly used in analog circuits outside their saturation region where the collector to emitter current varies proportionally with the base current. This is the basis of virtually all analog circuitry such as amplifiers, oscillators, and so forth. When the transistor is operating in this manner, it will dissipate power (in the form of heat) in proportion to its (now higher) on resistance. Well designed analog circuitry, of course, accounts for this by using heatsinks. We don't dig into this topic further in *Practical Arduino*, however.

Looking back out our relay drive circuit, we are making use of an NPN transistor in a common emitter or low-side switch configuration. Note that the emitter pin is connected to ground and the collector to the "low" side of the relay coil or load.

Common bipolar transistors are capable of switching a few hundred milliamperes up to amps, depending on the type chosen. Switching frequencies can easily run to several megahertz and well beyond this if appropriate devices and circuit configurations are used.

For practical applications, bipolar transistors make a good and simple choice for switching currents up to an amp or two. For currents higher than this, it is worth considering FETs which we discuss in a moment.

Transistor Arrays

Transistor arrays, as the name suggests, are devices that have many transistors in the same package. The principle advantage is packaging density and convenience—a single 18-pin DIP device can provide seven or eight transistors configured as high- or low-side switches.

The ULN2003 is perhaps the best known part and provides eight transistors that can switch around 500mA each in a low-side (or common emitter) configuration. Slightly less common is the UDN2981, which provides eight high-side switches that can source around 500mA per output. For both devices, consult the datasheet to check that you are operating them within their limits, particularly if you are getting close to maximum per-pin current as it is possible to exceed overall device limits.

FETs

FETs, or field effect transistors are, like bipolar transistors, an electronic switch. Their internal construction differs in the way the semiconductor materials are laid out, most notably in the gate, the pin that is functionally similar to the base of a bipolar transistor. The other two pins of a FET, the drain and source pins, roughly correspond to the collector and emitter, respectively, of a bipolar transistor. Metal-oxide–semiconductor field-effect transistors (MOSFETS) are the most common form of FET. At the risk of offending purists, we will use the terms interchangeably hereafter.

The internal construction of the MOSFET is such that the gate terminal exhibits a very high resistance (or impedance) relative to the source and drain pins—it is effectively a capacitor. In practice, this means that the device requires very little current to switch on fully. When switched completely on, MOSFETs have a very low on resistance, less than that of a bipolar transistor, making them an excellent choice for high-current applications. The main design considerations with a FET is that it be switched on (or off) very quickly because its ability to cope with being in the intermediate region is limited, and that adequate gate voltage is applied relative to the supply voltage.

Optocouplers

In practical applications, optocouplers slot into a similar niche as reed relays in being suited to switching relatively low currents in situations where electrical isolation is required. As such, they are useful in situations where a low-power system needs to control a high-power system. If you need to turn on/off a 250V motor, you really don't want to run the risk of that 250V getting back into your 5V Arduino. Optocouplers allow an Arduino to control scary devices, and limit the risk of blowing out the ICs on the ATMega. Optocouplers are used when good engineering practices dictate isolating a potentially harmful system.

Internally, optocouplers have an LED on the "input" side that is optically coupled to a switching device, often an FET or bipolar transistor on the "load" side. This absence of moving parts yields higher switching speeds (typically a few milliseconds or even microseconds for some devices) and higher reliability.

Typical optocouplers can switch around 150mA at 40V, so they are really most useful as an isolation device. However, they have a big cousin in the form of solid state relays.

Solid State Relays

Solid state relays (SSRs) combine the isolation and current-handling capabilities of conventional relays with the lack-of-moving parts benefits of optocouplers. Hence, they can switch high currents and voltages at high speeds (milliseconds) reliably for many on/off cycles and have low drive currents so can be driven directly from the Arduino.

There are various different package styles: PCB-mount units handling up to 5A at 240VAC, and larger units designed to bolt to a chassis coping with even greater currents. Most units designed for AC use provide "zero crossing switching," meaning the output is switched on when the AC supply is at the zero point. This makes for a more gentle on transition, reducing wear on the load and electrical noise.

There are a few gotchas when using SSRs. Some devices have a minimum load current below which they might not switch reliably. The leakage current when a device is off can be relatively high—a few milliamperes, which can result in unnecessary power usage for infrequently used devices. Finally, if an SSR fails, they often do so in the "on" state, meaning the load will remain energized in the failure state, which might not be desirable depending on your application.

Digital Input/Output Expansion

The Arduino has 20 general-purpose I/O pins, which is more than enough for most projects. However, there are situations where more inputs or outputs are required. By making use of the Arduino's SPI support, we can use a simple logic element—a shift register—to provide virtually unlimited digital input or output capabilities.

Shift Registers as Outputs

When using a shift register to provide outputs, we must provide three signals from the Arduino: clock (CLK), data (D), and latch (Q). We might also want to provide an output enable (OE) signal so that the outputs remain off until we initialize them properly.

■ **Note** The small number of signals required to provide additional outputs can also be helpful if the driven devices are located a short distance from the Arduino itself. Thus instead of running, say, eight wires plus power and ground, you can run three or four and power/ground.

Taking the example in Figure 16-7, we have a single eight-output serial in parallel out shift register/latch connected to the Arduino. To set Output 3 high and all other outputs low, we would set D low, transition CLK Low-High four times, set D high, transition CLK Low-High once, set D low again, then transition CLK a further three times. Thus, we "shift" in the sequence 00001000 into the register. Finally, we transition the Q (latch) signal Low-High-Low to move this new pattern to the output pins themselves.

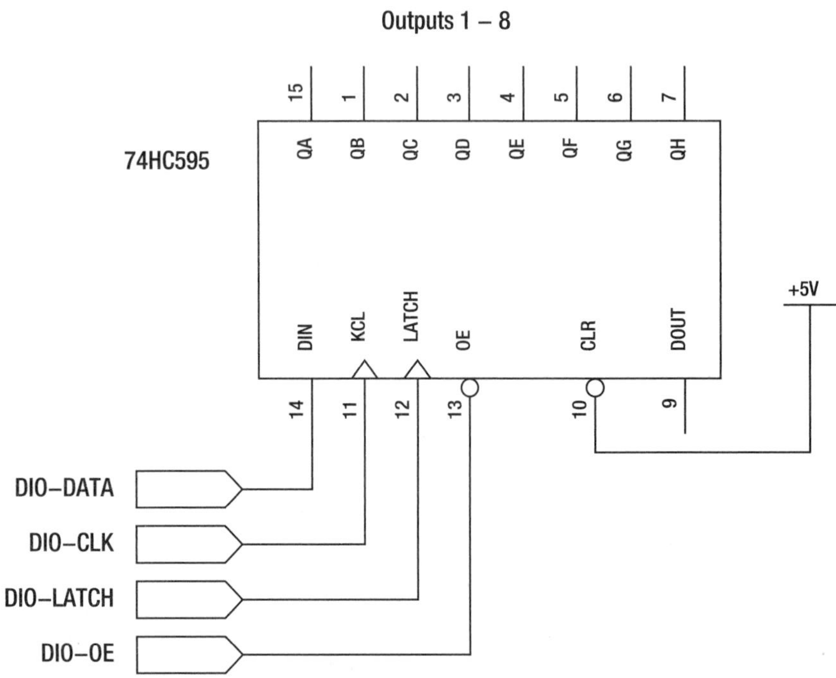

Figure 16-7. Adding output pins with single eight-output shift register

Compare now with Figure 16-8 where we have two eight-output latches connected. The number of pins used on the Arduino stays the same. We simply daisy chain the Data Out from the first latch to the Data In on the second. We now must shift 16 bits to fully define the state of the outputs. This basic arrangement can be repeated many times over. The main limitation is the number of CLK and Q signals that can be driven from the Arduino—anything over 16 could be marginal.

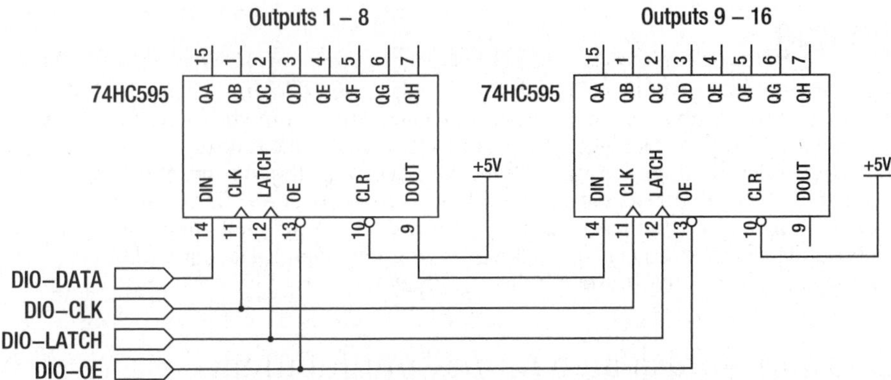

Figure 16-8. Cascading multiple shift registers for more output pins

This approach to outputs doesn't come entirely free. As you'll probably have guessed, each update to the output pins will take a few dozen instructions being executed by the CPU to clock the data out rather than a single write to the relevant port. However, if the Arduino's internal UART is used in SPI mode, this overhead can be reduced.

For practical applications, there are at least a few devices to consider. The 74HC595 is a basic logic level serial in/parallel out shift register. It's good for about 20mA per pin tops, and is inexpensive and easy to find. A little more expensive, but more versatile, is the TPIC6595, which is essentially a 74HC595 and ULN2003 combined. It's a serial in/parallel out shift register with high current drivers—about 200mA per pin.

■ **Note** PWM with shift-register based outputs is still possible, it just requires software to generate the relevant output signals. Look at using a timer to generate an interrupt to run a routine to do the calculations and shift out the new data at regular intervals. Alternatively, if you merely want to do PWM on all outputs the same (such as for dimming an LED display at night), you could use a hardware PWM pin to drive the OE signal of the latches. A caveat to this approach: if the display itself is multiplexed, you could get odd issues with flickering, depending on the phase relationship of the two.

Shift Registers as Inputs

As you might guess, there is a complementary device to those previously mentioned for output expansion: the parallel-load shift register. An example would be the 74HC165, this being a commonly available part.

The principle of operation is very similar to that used for the output circuit. The Arduino provides a clock (CLK) and load (LD) signal using a pair of output pins, and senses the state of the data (D) line back from the shift register using an input pin.

The state of the inputs is loaded (or "latched") into the shift register by transitioning the LD pin High-Low-High. For each of the 16 bits, we transition the CLK pin Low-High-Low, reading the state of the D pin, which the yields the state of each input in turn.

Input Conditioning

In the previous section, we discussed various techniques for driving external loads that required higher currents and/or operating voltages than those that the Arduino can provide directly. In the same way that the Arduino, or more specifically the ATMega168, can only provide limited output currents/voltages, it can only tolerate limited input voltages, too. Typically, the maximum voltage applied to an input pin should be the same as the supply voltage —5V in most Arduino boards.

If it is necessary to deal with inputs that use higher voltages than the supply rail, there are a few techniques at your disposal. The choice largely comes down to whether isolation is required (for example, if mains is involved) or if the environment is electrically noisy.

Voltage Dividers and Nonisolated Input Conditioning

Figure 16-9 shows two resistors connected in series in what is called a "voltage divider." The voltage applied to the top of the divider is 15V and, intuitively, we know that all the resultant current must disappear within the divider circuit (ignoring what we tap through the output connection). It follows, then, that the voltage across each resistor must be some fraction of the input voltage—the fraction being dependent on the resistor value.

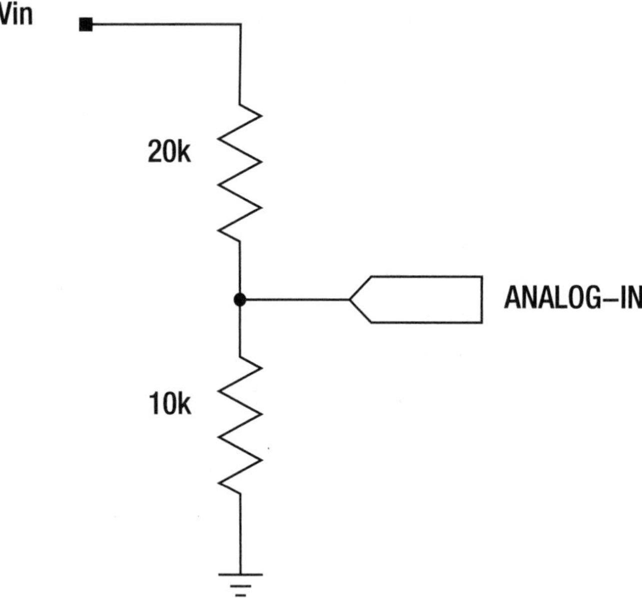

Figure 16-9. A simple voltage divider

The values chosen of 20k and 10k mean that for a 15V input, we will get 5V out; for 3V in, 1V out; and so on. We now have a simple way of monitoring voltages or inputs that are greater than the 5V or 3V3 limit on Arduino input pins. This same circuit can be used for digital and analog inputs.

While the simple divider shown will work fine in benign environments, in noisier or less controlled situations, such as monitoring a battery or the state of the headlights of your car, it's prudent to add some additional circuitry. This can be as simple as adding a Zener diode, as shown in Figure 16-10. Zener diodes in this configuration act as a voltage-sensitive switch of sorts. While below their operating voltage, their resistance is very high—essentially they're "off." Once the operating voltage is reached, the resistance drops dramatically. In the case of our circuit, this effectively ensures that the voltage is clamped at 5.1V. A word of caution here: Zener diodes used in this manner aren't perfect and might not catch very fast transients or spikes. Further, if they are used to protect an analogu input, their tendency to start conducting below their rated voltage can have the effect of introducing nonlinearity into the circuit near the maximum input.

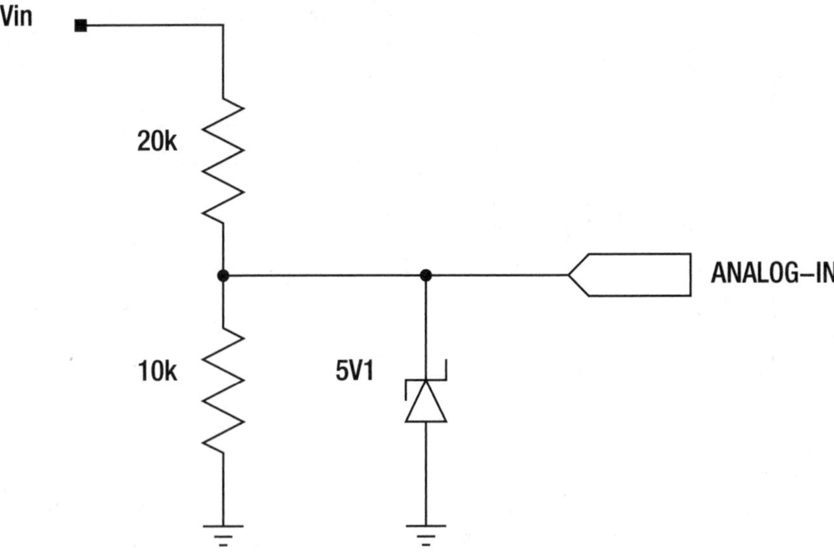

Figure 16-10. Zener-protected input conditioning circuit

Oh, and please don't even think about using a voltage divider to reduce mains voltage down into an Arduino pin without proper isolation!

■ **Note** A variable resistor, or "pot," forms a voltage divider if wired in a similar manner to that in Figure 16-9. One end of the pot goes to 5V, the other end to ground, and the wiper (typically the center pin) to the Arduino input. This can provide an inexpensive way of adding a knob to a project to set some value.

Isolated Input Conditioning

Earlier in this section we discussed output circuits that electrically isolated the switched device from the Arduino. Often, it's desirable to go the other direction and isolate a signal we're monitoring from the Arduino. Once again, optocouplers come to the rescue.

The circuit in Figure 16-11 shows a simple isolated digital input. The input side can be virtually any voltage, provided the resistor value is selected so that no more than 10mA flows through the LED side of the optocoupler. We provide a few suggested values in the diagram for various input voltages.

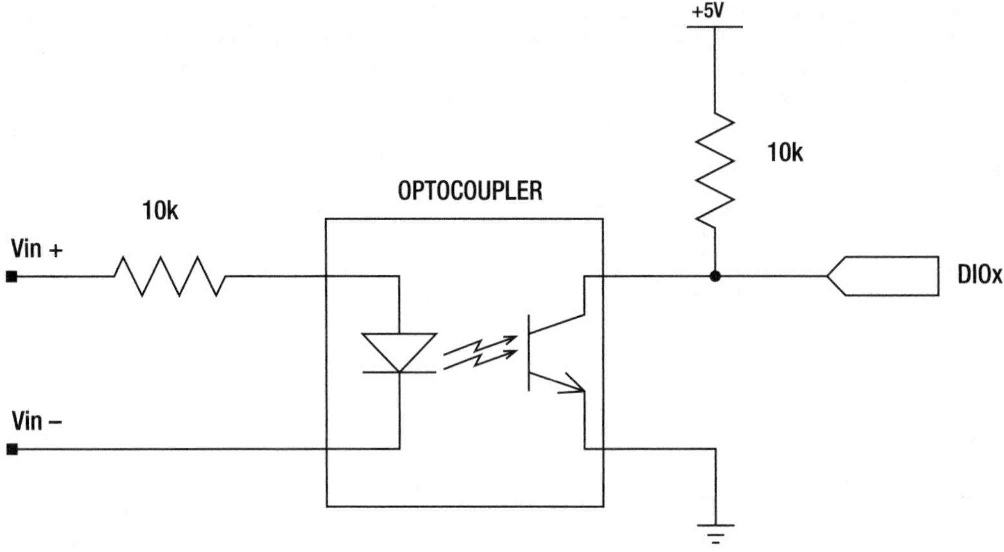

Figure 16-11. *An optically isolated digital input*

It's also possible to isolate analog signals, but this is a more complex topic. As a starting point, if you're looking to isolate an AC signal consider a small transformer and some filtering circuitry. To deal with an AC or DC signal, dig into purpose-built analog isolation using devices like Isolation Amplifiers—Burr Brown ISO100 being the start of a long line of these specialist devices.

■ **Note** We can apply the principle of this optocoupler-based isolation circuit to provide a mains synchronised 50Hz/60Hz reference signal. Figure 16-12 shows the general approach: 12 VAC is provided from a plugpack/wall wart to power the LED in the optocoupler. The external diode means that the optocoupler only sees voltage for one half of the mains cycle and so the transistor will be turned on at 50 or 60Hz depending on the local mains frequency. The external diode is preferred to relying on the LEDs own diode action because it ensures the reverse voltage on the optocoupler isn't exceeded. The plugpack can, of course, be used to power the rest of the circuitry through a suitable bridge rectifier, filter, and regulator.

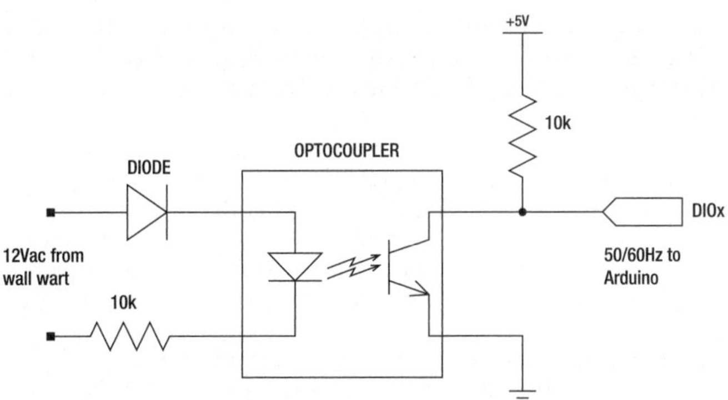

***Figure 16-12.** Using mains to provide accurate 50/60Hz reference*

Inexpensive DIY Prototyping Shields

One of the most annoying idiosyncrasies of the physical design of standard Arduino boards is that the header connections for plugging in a shield don't sit neatly on a standard 0.1in grid: the top two headers are spaced 160mil (0.16in) apart, which makes it impossible to create a shield using a cheap piece of standard stripboard or perfboard with male breakaway headers soldered on.

To get around this problem, there are some really neat prototyping shields available from a number of suppliers including Adafruit Industries, Seeed Studio, SparkFun, and many others. Figure 16-13 shows a popular protoshield from SparkFun. Commercial prototyping shields vary in features. Some include stackable headers, or an extra reset button so it's easily accessible with the shield mounted on an Arduino, or status LEDs, or mounting pads for surface-mount chips. For most projects, a commercial prototyping shield will do just what you need.

***Figure 16-13.** A simple prototyping shield*

But it would have been nice if the Arduino design had the shield headers on a consistent 0.1in grid so that if you just wanted to grab a piece of inexpensive stripboard and put some male breakaway headers on it, you could plug it straight in. All is not lost, though: Luke Weston has come up with a simple way to modify an Arduino so that you can do exactly that.

Start by finding an 8-pin female PCB header either from an electronics parts supplier or included in a commercial prototyping shield kit, then hold it beside the regular digital I/O pin 8–13 header on your Arduino so that the pins protrude down beside the Arduino PCB. Then slide it along slightly toward pin 13, so that the horizontal spacing between the first pin (next to pin 8) on the new header and the existing pin 7 on the old header is exactly 0.2 inches; i.e., twice the distance between two header pins. A tiny drop of superglue (alpha-cyanoacrylate) can then be used to glue the new header firmly to the old header and keep it in place.

The safest way to perform this positioning step is to make yourself a DIY prototyping shield by soldering some male breakaway headers onto a piece of stripboard and plugging it in to the Arduino, with the new female header held in place by the shield. This way, when you glue the header in place, you know the spacing will be correct. You can see the DIY shield in Figure 16-14.

Figure 16-14. *Creating a protoshield with stripboard and male breakaway headers*

Now that the header is physically glued in the correct position, turn your Arduino over and bend over all the header pins so they come out at a slight angle and align with the solder joints for the existing header. Finally, solder each one of them in place and you're all set to create your own prototype shields for only a few dollars each using inexpensive stripboard and some breakaway headers! You can see the Arduino in place on the shield in Figure 16-15, and the extra female header attached to the Arduino in Figure 16-16.

The neat thing about this hack is that it only costs a few cents for the extra female header and it doesn't restrict the normal operation of the Arduino. After adding the new header, you'll be able to plug either regular or DIY shields into your Arduino interchangeably.

Figure 16-15. Arduino with additional female header on the protoshield

Figure 16-16. Arduino with additional female header in place

Writing an Arduino Library

The Arduino development environment comes with a range of handy libraries and there are many more available online, but often it can be useful to create your own custom library to simplify your sketches and allow other people to make use of your functionality in their projects. The good news is that it's not particularly difficult: if you know how to write an Arduino sketch, you already know just about everything required to create a library.

While writing this book, we created several new Arduino libraries, including a driver for 4-wire resistive touch screens like the ones used in the Nintendo DS, as well as many aftermarket touch screen kits for netbooks. The TouchScreen library is quite simple, but serves as a good illustration of how to go about turning your existing sketch into a self-contained library, so we'll work through the process step by step to see how it was done.

Develop Functionality as a Sketch

The initial version of the functionality was implemented directly as an Arduino sketch, which is always a good way to get started. Developing your functionality in the IDE where you can recompile and upload to an Arduino for rapid testing is easier than trying to develop that functionality in the context of a library. Then, when you're done with the functionality and happy that it works as intended, you can convert it to a library for the convenience it provides.

The first version of the touch screen driver was written as a simple Arduino sketch that looked something like this:

```
int xVal = 0;
int yVal = 0;

void setup()
{
  Serial.begin(38400);
}

void loop()
{
  // Set up the analog pins in preparation for reading the X value
  pinMode( 15, INPUT );      // Analog pin 1
  pinMode( 17, INPUT );      // Analog pin 3
  pinMode( 14, OUTPUT );     // Analog pin 0
  digitalWrite( 14, LOW );   // Use analog pin 0 as a GND connection
  pinMode( 16, OUTPUT );     // Analog pin 2
  digitalWrite( 16, HIGH );  // Use analog pin 2 as a +5V connection
  xVal = analogRead( 1 );    // Read the X value

  // Set up the analog pins in preparation for reading the Y value
  pinMode( 14, INPUT );      // Analog pin 0
  pinMode( 16, INPUT );      // Analog pin 2
  pinMode( 15, OUTPUT );     // Analog pin 1
  digitalWrite( 15, LOW );   // Use analog pin 1 as a GND connection
  pinMode( 17, OUTPUT );     // Analog pin 3
  digitalWrite( 17, HIGH );  // Use analog pin 3 as a +5V connection
  yVal = analogRead( 0 );    // Read the Y value

  // Report the values back to the host
  Serial.print(xVal);
  Serial.print(",");
  Serial.println(yVal);

  delay(100); // Wait 100 milliseconds before repeating
}
```

It's a short program that interfaces with a resistive touch screen using analog pins 0 through 3, which can also be referenced in an Arduino sketch as digital pins 14 through 17. If you're interested in how resistive touch screens work and how this program reads from them, it's all explained in detail in the Touch Control Panel project in Chapter 8.

As programs go it's fairly short, but keeping track of which analog pin is connected to which touch screen electrode can be a bit brain-bending, and the repetitive code to twiddle the I/O lines is fairly ugly, so abstracting it away as a library would make the program much easier to read. Even more important, though, we want to make the code more flexible and reusable so that other people can incorporate touch screen support into their projects without having to learn the details of how to drive them.

Create the Library Header File

The first step to creating a new library is making a new directory for it inside the directory called hardware/libraries in your Arduino installation. The directory needs to be named to match your library, so in this case we created a directory called TouchScreen. The Arduino project's naming convention is for libraries to have their names in CamelCase and be kept short and clear. Of course it's important for libraries to have unique names, so make sure you aren't using a name that someone else has already used. Take a look at www.arduino.cc/en/Reference/Libraries and www.arduino.cc/playground/Main/InterfacingWithHardware to see what's already been created.

Inside the directory you just created, you then need to create a header file that defines the things your library will contain, such as constants, global variables, and data structure definitions. Once again, it should be named after the library but with a .h (header) extension, so create a text file called TouchScreen.h.

Because libraries are included in other programs, there is the danger that a library could be inadvertently included twice, causing the compiler to abort and output an error. To avoid this problem, we'll start by putting a preprocessor macro wrapper into TouchScreen.h that checks if it has previously been defined, and skips the rest of the library code if that happens. This is called an "include guard," and looks like this:

```
#ifndef TouchScreen_h
#define TouchScreen_h
#endif
```

The next thing we need to do is include WProgram.h, which is a file that gives our library access to the constants and variable types that are defined as part of the Arduino environment. When you compile an Arduino sketch, this file is automatically included for you, which is why you don't see it referenced in normal projects, but Arduino libraries aren't preprocessed in the same way, so you have to manually specify it instead. The previous header file then becomes this:

```
#ifndef TouchScreen_h
#define TouchScreen_h

#include "WProgram.h"

#endif
```

Most of the time when you are writing Arduino sketches, you can ignore its C++ origins if you prefer and rely on the simplified Arduino environment to hide it from you. However, all Arduino libraries need to be invoked as C++ objects so that they can appear as a self-contained box of functionality to the rest of the program.

If you've never worked on object-oriented code before, this might sound scarier than it is. Conceptually, defining an object is just a matter of taking a bunch of functionality, sticking it all into a big box so nobody can see the details of how it works, and then specifying the methods other programs can use to access the functionality inside that box.

This is a process called "encapsulation," and it's all about grouping related functionality together and then hiding it behind a consistent interface so other people can make use of that functionality without necessarily understanding how it works. The methods they use to access the functionality constitute the Application Programming Interface, or API, and that is all anyone should need to care about if they want to use the functionality of that library in their program. A well designed API will allow programmers to treat the object as a black box and have it simply work intuitively when they access methods defined in the API.

To wrap up the library into an easy-to-use object, we need to start by specifying the name of the class that we will use to define it. A class is simply a blueprint for an object. It says how it will behave and how it can be used by other programs. We'll give our class the same name as the library because that's what it is defining.

After adding the class declaration to TouchScreen.h, it looks like this:

```
#ifndef TouchScreen_h
#define TouchScreen_h

#include "WProgram.h"
class TouchScreen
{
};

#endif
```

At this point, the TouchScreen class declaration is like an empty box with a label stuck on the outside. It's ready for us to start defining functionality to go inside it, but right now it's just a shell.

It's important to understand that what we're doing when defining a class is creating an abstract definition or plan for how the object will behave. Rather than creating a unique, one-of-a-kind object like a craftsman would, it's like first drawing up a set of plans for the object so that it is ready to be mass produced: on their own the plans are just a lifeless set of diagrams and instructions, but you can follow those instructions to construct an object that matches them. And in fact, you can follow those same plans over and over again to create many different objects that all have the same characteristics because they were constructed from the same plans.

Taking the class definition (the plans) and using them to build an actual object based on it is the job of a special method, appropriately called a "constructor," that is stored right inside the class itself. When a program instantiates the class, the constructor is executed automatically, causing the abstract plans to spring to life as a new object with a name and all the attributes and characteristics defined in the class.

So the first thing we need to put inside the box is the constructor, which once again is named the same as the class and, hence, the library. It also includes the parameters that will need to be passed in when setting up the object.

```
#ifndef TouchScreen_h
#define TouchScreen_h

#include "WProgram.h"

class TouchScreen
{
```

```
  public:
    TouchScreen(byte pinX1, byte pinX2, byte pinY1, byte pinY2);
};

#endif
```

You'll notice that we've put the constructor inside a section of the class called "public." That's because methods in objects can be specified to be either externally accessible by the program that uses it and therefore part of the API, or kept private and only accessible internally.

To flesh out the class, we also need to declare any other public and private methods and variables. From the point of view of a library developer, this means thinking about how we want programs to interact with our particular library. What methods do we want them to be able to call in the API, and what variables will pass in or out of the library?

Other than the constructor, the TouchScreen library will only have one externally accessible method, the read() method, so we'll declare that as public right under the constructor. There are also some global variables we want to use inside the library so we'll declare those as well, but make them private so they are hidden from the outside world and can only be seen by methods inside the class.

After doing that, our TouchScreen.h file has now grown to look like this:

```
#ifndef TouchScreen_h
#define TouchScreen_h

#include "WProgram.h"

class TouchScreen
{
  public:
    TouchScreen(byte pinX1, byte pinX2, byte pinY1, byte pinY2);
    void read(int *coordinates);
  private:
    byte _pinX1;  // Analog pin connected to screen line X1
    byte _pinX2;  // Analog pin connected to screen line X2
    byte _pinY1;  // Analog pin connected to screen line Y1
    byte _pinY2;  // Analog pin connected to screen line Y2
    int _xVal;    // Current X coordinate
    int _yVal;    // Current Y coordinate
};

#endif
```

Notice that the private variables we declared have a leading underscore. That's not technically required, but it's a convention commonly used as a visual indicator to the programmer that those are private variables that exist only inside the object. The use of these variables will become clear in just a moment.

That's it for the header file, so let's move on to the main C++ class file itself.

Create the Library Class File

Next we create a text file called TouchScreen.cpp to contain the main C++ library code. The first thing to do is include the header file we just defined above, as follows:

```
#include "TouchScreen.h"
```

We need to flesh out the public methods we declared previously in the header file, so we'll start by defining the constructor. The :: syntax might look a little strange, but it's just a way of specifying that this method is part of a specific class. Because both the class and the constructor have the same name, the method definition ends up looking like this:

```
TouchScreen::TouchScreen(byte pinX1, byte pinX2, byte pinY1, byte pinY2)
{
  _pinX1 = pinX1;
  _pinX2 = pinX2;
  _pinY1 = pinY1;
  _pinY2 = pinY2;
}
```

In our case, the constructor doesn't do very much. It simply takes the arguments passed in by the program and stores their values inside equivalent private variables that we declared previously in the header. This allows programs using this library to specify the pin connections to the touch screen rather than have them hard-coded within the library itself.

The only other item in this particular class is the public read() method, which is where we finally get to the guts of the library. We want programs using this library to be able to call the read() method to obtain the X and Y coordinates currently being touched on the touch screen, so most of the code in this method is a direct copy of the code from the test program we started with in the first place.

However, because our test program had hard-coded values for the pins that are used to connect the touch screen, we've removed those hard-coded values and instead used the values passed in to the constructor. This way our library can be used on touch screens with different pin connections without changing any of the code internally.

One little complication in this example is that the code refers to pins by both their analog and digital identifiers, so sometimes we need to refer to a pin as the variable value and sometimes we need to add 14 to it just like in the original sketch that we're converting. To make the code read a little more clearly, we'll add a line just before the constructor that reads as follows:

```
#define DIGITAL_OFFSET 14
```

The complete read() method then ends up looking like this:

```
void TouchScreen::read(int *coordinates)
{
  pinMode( _pinX2 + DIGITAL_OFFSET, INPUT );
  pinMode( _pinX1 + DIGITAL_OFFSET, INPUT );
  pinMode( _pinY1 + DIGITAL_OFFSET, OUTPUT );
  digitalWrite( _pinY1 + DIGITAL_OFFSET, LOW );
  pinMode( _pinY2 + DIGITAL_OFFSET, OUTPUT );
  digitalWrite( _pinY2 + DIGITAL_OFFSET, HIGH );
  _xVal = analogRead( _pinX2 );

  pinMode( _pinY1 + DIGITAL_OFFSET, INPUT );
  pinMode( _pinY2 + DIGITAL_OFFSET, INPUT );
  pinMode( _pinX2 + DIGITAL_OFFSET, OUTPUT );
  digitalWrite( _pinX2 + DIGITAL_OFFSET, LOW );
  pinMode( _pinX1 + DIGITAL_OFFSET, OUTPUT );
  digitalWrite( _pinX1 + DIGITAL_OFFSET, HIGH );
```

```
  _yVal = analogRead( _pinY1 );

  coordinates[0] = _xVal;
  coordinates[1] = _yVal;
}
```

Because it's a part of the TouchScreen class, it starts with TouchScreen:: just like the constructor.

If we only wanted to return a single coordinate, such as the X or Y value alone, we could simply make this function return a variable at the end. However, we want to return both X and Y values together, so we have a bit of a problem. C++ methods can't return arrays, so instead we require the sketch that uses this library to first create a two-element array and then pass in a reference to it so we can modify it within the read() method. The "int *coordinates" argument to the method is the pointer to an array of integers that the program wants us to put the results into.

After obtaining the X and Y values, we need to give the calling program access to the results, so the very last thing the method does is use the pointer provided and place the values into the first two cells in the array.

That's it! Looking at the TouchScreen.cpp file all together so we can see it complete, it now looks like this:

```
#include "TouchScreen.h"
#define DIGITAL_OFFSET 14

TouchScreen::TouchScreen(int pinX1, int pinX2, int pinY1, int pinY2)
{
  _pinX1 = pinX1;
  _pinX2 = pinX2;
  _pinY1 = pinY1;
  _pinY2 = pinY2;
}

void TouchScreen::read(int *coordinates)
{
  pinMode( _pinX2 + DIGITAL_OFFSET, INPUT );
  pinMode( _pinX1 + DIGITAL_OFFSET, INPUT );
  pinMode( _pinY1 + DIGITAL_OFFSET, OUTPUT );
  digitalWrite( _pinY1 + DIGITAL_OFFSET, LOW );
  pinMode( _pinY2 + DIGITAL_OFFSET, OUTPUT );
  digitalWrite( _pinY2 + DIGITAL_OFFSET, HIGH );
  _xVal = analogRead( _pinX2 );

  pinMode( _pinY1 + DIGITAL_OFFSET, INPUT );
  pinMode( _pinY2 + DIGITAL_OFFSET, INPUT );
  pinMode( _pinX2 + DIGITAL_OFFSET, OUTPUT );
  digitalWrite( _pinX2 + DIGITAL_OFFSET, LOW );
  pinMode( _pinX1 + DIGITAL_OFFSET, OUTPUT );
  digitalWrite( _pinX1 + DIGITAL_OFFSET, HIGH );
  _yVal = analogRead( _pinY1 );

  coordinates[0] = _xVal;
```

```
  coordinates[1] = _yVal;
}
```

Create the Example Sketch

The library is now complete and ready to be used, so let's create a very simple sketch that provides the exact same functionality as our original test code, but does it using our shiny new library instead of doing all the hard work itself.

Create an Arduino sketch called ReadTouchscreen and put in the following:

```
#include <TouchScreen.h>

TouchScreen ts(3, 1, 0, 2);

void setup()
{
  Serial.begin(38400);
}

void loop()
{
  int coords[2];
  ts.read(coords);
  Serial.print(coords[0]);
  Serial.print(",");
  Serial.println(coords[1]);
  delay (1000);
}
```

This is now much simpler than the original code.

By including the TouchScreen.h file at the top the sketch, we specify that we want to use the TouchScreen library. We then create a new object that we name ts as an instance of the TouchScreen class, and pass in the analog pins to use for the x1, x2, y1, and y2 electrodes, respectively. This is the point at which the constructor we defined earlier is automatically executed, and it uses the values passed in to populate the internal variables for _pinX1, _pinX2, _pinY1, and _pinY2.

The setup() function simply opens a serial connection to the host computer so the coordinates can be reported back. The main program loop then declares a variable called cords, which is a two-element array of integers. That is the array we want the TouchScreen library to use to store the values it reads. Next we use the ts object created earlier and call the read() function, passing in a pointer to the coords[] array we just defined.

At this point, the code in the library springs into action and does its stuff. The read() function will be executed as discussed previously, using the analog pins specified in the constructor to read the X and Y values from the connected touch screen and put the results into the array that was given to it.

After ts.read() finishes, we should have the values nicely stored inside the coords[] array with X in the first element and Y in the second, so we can send them to the serial port to report them to the host computer just as before.

It's always nice to provide example code with libraries so that other people can see how to use them, and since we've just created a small test program to verify that the library works, let's include it with the library as an example.

Inside the TouchScreen library directory create another directory called examples. The Arduino IDE looks inside libraries for an examples directory and includes anything it finds inside that directory in the sketchbook menu as a read-only entry grouped under the list of libraries, so copy the entire ReadTouchscreen directory (including the contents, such as ReadTouchscreen.pde) into hardware/libraries/TouchScreen/examples inside your Arduino installation to bundle it with the library.

You can then bundle up your whole library and examples as a single ZIP archive or tarball, so it can be published online for other people to download and install in the hardware/libraries directory of their Arduino IDE.

Create Supporting Files

Something else you might like to add is a README file containing some information about the library, a copyright notice, and any licensing information you may want to apply. A well documented library is far more useful than an undocumented one, so it's worth putting a little effort into making it easy for other people to pick it up and use it in their projects.

One final bit of polish you can give to your library is a hint file for the syntax highlighting used in the Arduino IDE. Because we defined a new class along with its methods, the IDE doesn't know anything about them, so it won't know how to highlight them correctly and they will just appear as regular black text in the code editing window.

Add a file called keywords.txt to your library directory and list the class and functions in it. After each one, add a single tab (not spaces) and specify whether it is a class (KEYWORD1) or method (KEYWORD2). In our case, we have just one class and one public method, so the end result looks like this:

```
TouchScreen	KEYWORD1
Read	KEYWORD2
```

If our class happened to have more methods in, it they would also be labeled with KEYWORD2. The IDE will then highlight anything labeled KEYWORD1 in orange and anything labeled KEYWORD2 in brown.

Restart your IDE, open the example ReadTouchscreen program again, and you should see that the syntax highlighting is now correct.

The complete TouchScreen library is available for download from GitHub, so if you want to see the end result and how it all fits together you can grab it from github.com/practicalarduino/TouchScreen.

Platform-Specific Variations

Most of the time you can write a library that will run perfectly well on just about any Arduino, from a Mini to a Mega, with no changes required. Sometimes, though, there are differences between the various Arduino models that can cause problems, and the TouchScreen library we used in this example is one of them. The code as described here will work perfectly well on almost all Arduino models, but will break on a Mega because it has a different system for numbering its analog and digital pins. On most Arduino models analog pins 0 through 5 can also be referenced as digital pins 14 through 19, and we do that in the library by simply adding 14 to the analog pin number to derive the digital pin number.

But the Mega has far more I/O pins, so rather than starting the analog pins at number 14, it starts them at number 54. The result is that the code we've created here will appear to compile cleanly on a Mega, but will totally fail to work because it will be referencing the wrong pins.

Luckily, this problem is made very easy to solve because we used a #define to specify the value for DIGITAL_OFFSET, and we can use special values set in the build environment to make decisions about how the library should be compiled and then build it differently in different circumstances. Doing an explicit check for the ATMega1280 CPU used in the Arduino Mega, we can change the original single #define entry so that it instead defines one value for the Mega and a different value for anything else.

```
#if defined(__AVR_ATmega1280__)
  #define DIGITAL_OFFSET 54
#else
  #define DIGITAL_OFFSET 14
#endif
```

The library will then work interchangeably on normal Arduino models and also on the Mega.

Index

Symbols and Numerics

A

■F

■G

■H

■I, J

K

L

M

N

■ O

■ P

■Q

■R

■ S

■T

■U

■V

W, X, Y

■Z